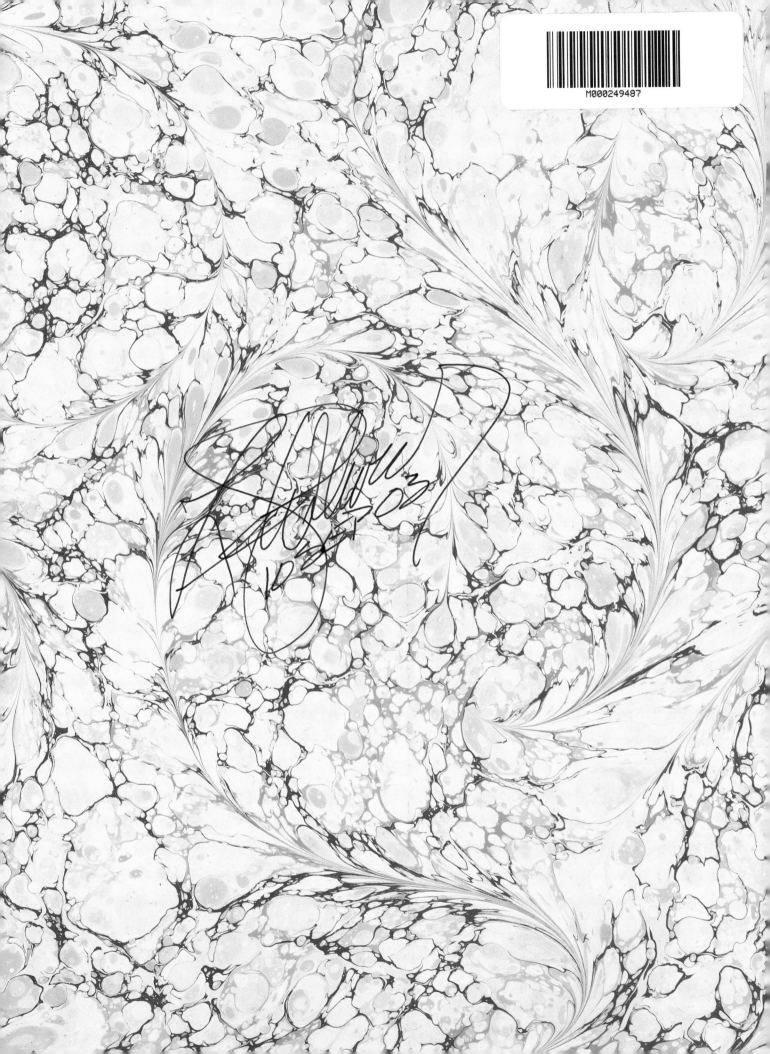

LAST VICTORY IN RUSSIA

LAST VICTORY IN RUSSIA
The SS-Panzerkorps and Manstein's Kharkov Counteroffensive
February-March 1943

George M. Nipe, Jr.

Schiffer Military History
Atglen, PA

Dedication
This book is dedicated to my wife Linda, who has fought a battle against breast cancer with as much bravery as the battlefield courage demonstrated by the soldiers mentioned in the following pages. She has refused to allow the anxieties and fears that accompany this terrible and sinister disease to control her life and happiness. Linda remains a positive and caring person, giving compassion and comfort to friends and strangers alike who are experiencing the terrors of this disease for the first time or who are facing their last days after months or even years of painful struggle.

Book design by Robert Biondi.

Copyright © 2000 by George M. Nipe, Jr.
Library of Congress Catalog Number: 00-101168.

Printed in China.
ISBN: 0-7643-1186-7

We are always looking for people to write books on new and related subjects. If you have an idea for a book, please contact us at the address below.

Published by Schiffer Publishing Ltd.
4880 Lower Valley Road
Atglen, PA 19310
Phone: (610) 593-1777
FAX: (610) 593-2002
E-mail: Schifferbk@aol.com.
Visit our web site at: www.schifferbooks.com
Please write for a free catalog.
This book may be purchased from the publisher.
Please include $3.95 postage.
Try your bookstore first.

In Europe, Schiffer books are distributed by:
Bushwood Books
6 Marksbury Ave.
Kew Gardens
Surrey TW9 4JF
England
Phone: 44 (0)208 392-8585
FAX: 44 (0)208 392-9876
E-mail: Bushwd@aol.com.
Free postage in the UK. Europe: air mail at cost.
Try your bookstore first.

CONTENTS

PREFACE

In early 1943 the German Army in southern Russia was on the verge of a complete collapse. Beginning in November, 1942 the Russians launched a series of successful offensives that drove the Germans back for hundreds of kilometers and cost them hundreds of thousands of casualties. The first of these offensives encircled more than 200,000 German and Axis troops of the German 6. Armee at Stalingrad. Successive Russian offensives destroyed the Italian 8th Army and Hungarian 2nd Army and severely damaged the German 2. Armee. The momentum of war was entirely on the side of the Russians. German reserves were nearly nonexistent and the armies of Hitler's Axis allies had been essentially knocked out of the war. Huge gaps had been torn in the line and there were no reserves available to plug them. Stalin and many of his key commanders believed that the Germans could be finished off with one more great effort.

Accordingly, during the last days of January, 1943 the Soviets rapidly planned two major offensives which were code named "Gallop" and "Star." These operations were intended to recapture the industrial city of Kharkov and destroy the remaining German and Axis troops in the southern Ukraine, which consisted of 4. Panzerarmee, 1. Panzerarmee, Armeeabteilung Hollidt and Armeeabteilung Fretter-Pico. Coming on the heels of the final death throes of 6. Armee at Stalingrad and the destruction of the Axis armies, the loss of these four German armies would probably have resulted in a decisive German defeat on the Eastern Front. Stalin and his generals believed that victory over Germany was within their grasp in early 1943 and decided to launch the two offensives even before the surrender of the Stalingrad garrison.

The weight of "Gallop" and "Star" fell primarily upon Heeresgruppe Don, a newly established army group that had relatively few resources given the demands placed upon it. It was commanded by Erich von Manstein, who is considered by many to have been Germany's finest military commander of World War II.

During this period, Manstein struggled not only with the sledgehammer blows of the Soviet offensives and abundant Soviet reserves, but also with the interference and stubbornness of Adolf Hitler. When three armies of the Soviet Voronezh Front quickly threatened to recapture Kharkov, Hitler's obsession with holding the city nearly resulted in the destruction of two SS Panzergrenadier divisions and the elite Army Panzergrenadier Division "Grossdeutschland." These divisions were of critical importance because Manstein intended to use them in a dramatic counter stroke that would reverse the course of the war in Russia. Literally at the last moment, the commander of the SS-Panzerkorps, Paul Hausser, disobeyed Hitler's order to fight to the last man and ordered a withdrawal from Kharkov that saved the two SS divisions. Shortly thereafter, the third SS division of the SS-Panzerkorps arrived and gave Manstein the divisions he needed to carry out his counteroffensive. The subsequent battles for possession of Kharkov marked the first time the three oldest divisions of the Waffen-SS, "Leibstandarte," "Das Reich" and "Totenkopf," fought together under a unified SS corps command.

In the first phase of the operation, SS divisions "Das Reich" and "Totenkopf" drove 100 kilometers south of Kharkov and blocked the Soviet 6th Army's attempt to capture the Dnepr River bridges, while "Leibstandarte" successfully defended the corps base of supply at Krasnograd. Sepp Dietrich's division turned back determined attacks by the major part of the Soviet 3rd Tank Army during the last weeks of February, 1943. After securing the Dnepr bridges, "Das Reich" and "Totenkopf" turned north and regained control of the vital railroad network south of Kharkov. The 3rd Tank Army was forced to abandon its attack upon Krasnograd and regroup south of Kharkov in order to protect the city from Hausser's divisions. At that point "Leibstandarte" joined its two sister divisions in operations that destroyed the 3rd Tank Army, clearing the path for the recapture of Kharkov. Almost exactly a month after the city was abandoned to the Russians, it was back in German hands.

Strangely enough, there are no comprehensive accounts of the Kharkov fighting from the German standpoint in the English language. The coverage found in the general works on the Eastern Front tend to be incomplete at best. The notable exception is the detailed description of Operations "Gallop" and "Star" found in *From the Don to the Dnepr* by Colonel Glantz.

It is hard to understand why the remarkable and fascinating operations of the SS-Panzerkorps and 4. Panzerarmee have been neglected considering their importance. The events that took place in the southern Ukraine in early 1943 were tremendously dramatic. In mid-February, 1943 Germany teetered on the brink of an early defeat in World War II, until Manstein's Kharkov counteroffensive reversed the course of the war in southern Russia. By the third week in March, four Soviet armies had been destroyed or badly battered and the southern Ukraine was firmly in control of Manstein's army group. There were two fascinating episodes during this campaign which involved Paul Hausser, the senior officer of the Waffen-SS and commander of the SS-Panzerkorps. The first of these occurred on February 14, 1943 when Hausser went against the specific orders of Adolf Hitler and withdrew from Kharkov. Hausser's decision was undoubtedly militarily correct and prevented the destruction of the only full strength mobile divisions available to Manstein. Interestingly enough, Manstein himself opened the door for Hausser to make his choice to abandon the city.

The second episode happened when the SS-Panzerkorps was poised to recapture Kharkov on March 10, 1943 and three attack columns of "Leibstandarte" plunged into the center of the city. Hausser has been accused of disobeying his orders and directly assaulting the city, thereby incurring heavy casualties in order to make up for the transgression of losing the city. In fact, Manstein issued a directive that mentioned this course of action to Hausser. In addition Hitler clearly told Sepp Dietrich, the commander of "Leibstandarte," that he wanted Dietrich's division to assault the

city and take it from the Russians. Hitler's words carried a great deal of weight with Sepp Dietrich because for many years Dietrich considered himself and "Leibstandarte" to be solely responsible to Adolf Hitler. However, regardless of the circumstances of the recapture of the city, a large percentage of the casualties suffered by the SS divisions occurred during the earlier defensive fighting.

In January 1943, "Leibstandarte," "Das Reich" and "Totenkopf" were at the high point of their power. They had been upgraded to Panzergrenadier divisions during the latter half of 1942 and were equipped with two battalions of tanks. The highly motivated volunteers of the three divisions were superbly conditioned and their officers were hardened by years spent in the inferno of combat. The SS regimental, battalion and company commanders were products of modern training principles and were taught to be bold and daring. They were schooled in the basic German command philosophy of leading from the front and mission oriented command, which placed a premium on initiative and aggressive leadership from non-commissioned officers and field grade officers. They were audacious, aggressive and brazenly confident of their own abilities and the capabilities of their men and weapons.

The three SS divisions were at their peak in terms of the caliber of their personnel and the quality of their leadership, particularly at regimental level and below. Hausser's SS divisions provided the main offensive striking power of 4. Panzerarmee and were the key to the success of Manstein's counteroffensive. The Panzergrenadier divisions of the SS won a critical victory at a point when Germany was on the brink of defeat in Russia and the Soviet high command believed that an early end to the war was in their grasp. However, the victory was won at a high cost in SS casualties, a large percentage of which were lost during the bitter defensive fighting that took place in the first weeks of February, 1943. Total SS-Panzerkorps losses from 1 January to 20 March 1943 totaled nearly 12,000 killed, wounded or missing. The three divisions were never of the same quality. After the blood bath, the Germans were forced to replace their losses with thousands of Luftwaffe transfers and even conscripts. However, the blood sacrifice of the SS divisions temporarily reversed the course of the war in Europe and provided Germany with its last major victory of World War II.

FOREWORD

The reader interest in the Second World War has continued unabated for the more than half century since the conflict concluded. It is certain that no other event has had more influence on the world as we know it than the conflagration that consumed the world and resulted in possibly fifty million civilian and military deaths. With the passage of time and resulting declassification of archival material, the detailed amount of available information has constantly increased and the number of specific facets of this war still to be examined seems almost endless.

Among the most enthusiastically studied topics is the Waffen-SS, a revolutionary armed force that influenced modern warfare perhaps more than any other group in this century. The influence of the Waffen-SS can be seen in the armed forces of today and its mystique, initially due to legend as well as a paucity of accurate published material, has only increased with the passage of time.

As primarily a biographical researcher, I have had the often unique opportunity to meet and correspond with many Waffen-SS veterans who were direct participants in the battles of the Second World War. These have ranged from privates and platoon leaders to divisional commanders, many of whom won Germany's highest decorations for bravery and leadership during their military service. As an apolitical researcher with a simple interest to learn, I was astonished to find that I was the first and often only historian some of these former soldiers spoke with regarding their careers. My own interest, while covering all Waffen-SS units, leans heavily towards the three initial formations that became "Leibstandarte," "Das Reich" and "Totenkopf."

Apart from the personal facts and recollections of an individual, of important interest to me was their opinions. Foremost was inquiring what person influenced them as military men and the combats that stood out most vividly during the war. By far the most influential, admired and respected leader in the Waffen-SS, as well as its senior commander, was Paul Hausser. Commanding first a division and subsequently corps, army and finally army group, his effect on the Waffen-SS began in the prewar years when he organized the SS officer school training system.

Most of the persons I have known saw service from the start of the war through its conclusion. Almost to a man, those who fought in the 1943 battles for Kharkov recalled those months as the most intense combat of their military service. The ferocity of the fighting and the unyielding nature of the opponents was evident in the faces of those I have met. Little of significance in English has been published giving an overall view as well as first person detail of that series of battles, until now.

As he did with his previous work, "Decision in the Ukraine" my close colleague George Nipe has delved into the mass of records at all levels to relate a detailed and accurate account of a pivotal battle on the Eastern Front. I am especially pleased, having persuaded him initially to undertake the study that resulted in this work, the enormity of which should be appreciated. His significant contribution will finally show in great detail a story that must be related for historical preservation as well as a full understanding of the period. As the foremost tactical researcher I know, it is my most fervent wish he continues with further studies on the battle history of the Waffen-SS.

Mark C. Yerger

ACKNOWLEDGMENTS

Few writers are able to complete a book of this nature without a great deal of help from others. First of all, I want to thank my good friend, Mark Yerger, although a simple thanks is not sufficient to acknowledge his many contributions to the research, collection of pictures, text corrections and general motivation. In fact, he suggested that I write about the Kharkov campaign in the first place. His powerful argument was that there are no complete accounts in English about the German side of this complex series of battles. At the time, I was researching another project, but Mark persuaded me to do the book and it was a good decision. Later in the writing process, when I was having doubts about the timing of the project, he gave me some much needed encouragement and got the writing back on track.

Mark was always available to answer my e-mailed questions, identify people from grainy pictures or provide photos and information that he has collected over the years from his personal relationships with many veterans of the Waffen-SS. Whenever I needed to know a date, could not find the rank of a Waffen-SS junior officer or needed an answer to a hundred other questions, he could always dig it up from his enormous archives consisting of unpublished German records, original documents or his extensive library of reference books. In many cases he knew the answer off the top of his head because he has an encyclopedic memory for historical detail.

In addition, Mark generously allowed me to borrow many of the pictures of German officers and men that are in the book. He also provided information from privately held unit reports, in particular the war records of Regiment "Deutschland's" 16./Kompanie (Pioniere). Using his archival materials and documents, he furnished biographical information on many of the German Army and Waffen-SS commanders mentioned in the book, which saved me a great deal of time and effort. Mark is an accomplished historian who has written extensively about the men and organizations of the Waffen-SS. He is a repository of knowledge gleaned from his personal friendships with many Waffen-SS veterans, extensive writing and many years of research. In a sense, this has been his project too and the readers and I owe him a significant and heart felt thanks.

I also wish to thank the staff at the National Archives II in College Park, Maryland for their patient help. Neils Kordes, Jim Kellen and the other members of the staff of the Microfilm Room helped me find information, shared their extensive knowledge of the captured German records on microfilm, kept the copy machines running and were unfailingly courteous and helpful.

Bob Ruman, owner of Articles of War, helped me find a number of rare books, with a degree of personal service far above that exhibited by the average dealer in military texts.

I also want to thank my parents, Dr. and Mrs. George M. Nipe, for their genuine interest and encouragement in my projects and for furnishing a home environment filled with books and reading.

Lastly, I wish to thank my wife Linda and son George for their toleration of the demands in time, work and travel that go into writing a book of this type.

NOTES ON SOURCES
AND TERMINOLOGY

A great deal of the primary source research was done at the National Archives II in College Park, Maryland where most of the captured German records brought to this country after World War II are on microfilm. Fortunately, nearly all of the records of the German corps and armies which were involved in the fighting were available for the period that I chose to study. In addition to the SS-Panzerkorps records, these include the daily records of 4. Panzerarmee, Armeeabteilung Lanz/Kempf, Korps Raus and XXXXVIII. Panzerkorps. The records of Armeeabteilung Fretter-Pico, 1. Panzerarmee and XXXX. Panzerkorps furnished valuable supplementary information as well.

Record Group T-354, the Waffen-SS records, provided invaluable information on the conduct of the battle and communication between the SS-Panzerkorps and higher command formations. These records also contain a very useful series of maps, many of which are reproduced in this text and furnish an invaluable account of the battle, as well as information on tank strength, casualties and orders. The use of this archival material is absolutely essential for anyone who writes about the German Army and Waffen-SS during World War II. Those authors who do not use this primary material are destined to depend upon the opinions of others, with all the potential dangers inherent in that course of action. Failure to use available primary documents results in the continued fostering of pseudo-history. Anyone who desires to write seriously about the war from the German standpoint without studying this material is making a grave mistake. You will find that the staff at the Archives is enormously helpful and extremely knowledgeable.

It has proven useful to utilize a number of SS division combat histories in order to provide personal accounts of the soldiers and commanders who actually took part in the fighting. It is wise to double check the information contained in these volumes, because the memories of veterans are sometimes clouded by time and personal relationships. One can spend many hours trying to resolve contradictions between these accounts and information based on the primary sources. Only through studying all available information can one hope to provide a reasonably accurate account of a battle, which is by nature an event that is chaotic and complex.

Mark C. Yerger's *Knight's of Steel*, volumes I and II, is an organizational and biographical source of detailed information regarding the 2. SS-Panzergrenadier-Division "Das Reich" that is not available in any other study. In addition, his two volumes on Waffen-SS Commanders furnished important biographical information on the key commanders of the SS during the Kharkov campaign. Mark's works should be required reading for the serious student of the Waffen-SS.

Wolfgang Vopersal's *Soldaten, Kämpfer, Kameraden – Marsch und Kämpfe der SS-Totenkopf-Division*, is a monumental, eight volume work of impressive scope and is the most comprehensive division history that I am aware of. It is however, available only in German and is out of print. The translations of Rudolf Lehmann's history of the "1. SS-Panzer-Division-Leibstandarte SS Adolf Hitler" are also important resources, as is Kurt Meyer's Grenadiere. Former Waffen-SS officer Otto Weidinger wrote an excellent divisional history about "Das Reich" that provides a great deal of detailed information on that division's part in the Kharkov fighting. Several volumes of this series have been published in English.

Two other books provided absolutely essential information on the Kharkov battles. The first is Colonel David Glantz's *From the Don to the Dnepr: Soviet Offensive Operations from December, 1942 to August, 1943*. This volume is the only detailed English language study covering the Soviet conduct of the second and third battles for Kharkov. It is priceless for its depth of information and insights into Soviet command decisions. The maps are of great interest and document the progress of the battle day by day.

Befehl des Gewissens: Charkow Winter 1943 is another valuable source of information. This book consists of the photocopied pages of the war diary of Armeeabteilung Lanz/Kempf. The records reproduced in this book are available at the National Archives but it is simpler to use the book. It also contains transcripts of some SS-Panzerkorps records and a number of very useful maps reproduced in color.

Some brief comments about terminology, particularly in regard to the method of designating German armies and divisions, will be helpful to the reader, particularly those have not read extensively about the German Army in World War II. I have chosen to utilize German unit designations, in part to easily differentiate German formations from Soviet formations. For instance, Russian units will be described in basic English designations such as the Soviet 1st Guards Army or the 5th Guards Tank Corps. An example of a German army designation as described above is 4. Panzerarmee, which in English would be the 4th Panzer Army.

German regiment designations can be potentially confusing when discussing the named Waffen-SS regiments. Some of the complete names of these regiments are lengthy and somewhat unwieldy. For clarity and brevity I have chosen to describe certain SS regiments in a simpler and abbreviated fashion, which was used by the Germans also. Some examples are listed below, with the complete name on the left and the shortened version on the right.

A. SS-Panzergrenadier-Regiment 3 "Deutschland" = Regiment "Deutschland"

B. SS- "Totenkopf"-Panzergrenadier-Regiment 3 = SS-"Totenkopf"-Pz.Gren. Rgt. 3 until February 26, 1943, thereafter as Regiment "Eicke."

C. SS-"Totenkopf" Panzergrenadier-Regiment 1 = Regiment "Totenkopf"

D. SS-Panzergrenadier-Regiment 1 "Leibstandarte-SS-Adolf Hitler" = SS-Pz.Gren.- Rgt.1 "LAH"

E. SS-Panzergrenadier-Regiment 2 "Leibstandarte-SS-Adolf Hitler" = SS-Pz.Gren.-Rgt. 2 "LAH"

F. SS-Panzergrenadier-Regiment 4 "Der Führer = Regiment "Der Führer"

I have also chosen to describe battalions using the simple German method. The Germans assigned battalions of a regiment a Roman numeral, thus the 1st Battalion of SS-Panzergrenadier-Regiment 3 "Deutschland" is identified as I./Regiment "Deutschland." Similarly, the Third Battalion of SS-Panzergrenadier-Regiment 2 "Leibstandarte-SS-Adolf Hitler" is described as III./SS-Pz.Gren.-Rgt. 2 "LAH."

One German regiment that is noted above changed its official designation during the battles for Kharkov. This regiment was a unit of the "Totenkopf" division and was named SS-"Totenkopf"-Panzergrenadier-Regiment 3 as of January, 1943. After the death of "Totenkopf's" division commander, Theodor Eicke, the name of the regiment was officially changed to honor the fallen commander and became SS-Panzergrenadier-Regiment 3 "Theodore Eicke." In the text I describe the regiment after February 26,1943 as simply Regiment "Eicke."

There is one last question of terminology that I would like to address, although it does not refer to military terms. After my first book was published, which was entitled "Decision in the Ukraine," a number of people informed me that it was improper to refer to the independent state presently known as Ukraine as 'the Ukraine.' However, it needs to be remembered that in the year 1943, this region was one of the republics of the Soviet Union. It is perfectly correct to use the term "the Ukraine" in that context because it was not an independent state in 1943. The Ukraine, as I have used the term, is a geographical description of a region of the former Soviet Union during World War II.

WAFFEN-SS RANKS AND U.S. ARMY EQUIVALENT RANKS

Waffen-SS rank	U.S. Army rank
Enlisted men	
SS-Grenadier	Private
SS-Oberschütze	Private First Class
SS-Sturmmann	no precise equivalent
SS-Rottenführer	Corporal
NCOs	
SS-Unterscharführer	Sergeant
SS-Scharführer	Staff Sergeant
SS-Oberscharführer	Technical Sergeant
SS-Hauptscharführer	Master Sergeant
SS-Stabsscharführer	First Sergeant
SS-Sturmscharführer	Sergeant Major
Junior and Field Grade Officers	
SS-Untersturmführer	Second Lieutenant
SS-Obersturmführer	First Lieutenant
SS-Hauptsturmführer	Captain
SS-Sturmbannführer	Major
SS-Obersturmbannführer	Lieutenant Colonel
SS-Standartenführer	Colonel
SS-Oberführer	no equivalent U.S. rank
Generals	
SS-Brigadeführer und Generalmajor der Waffen-SS	Brigadier General
SS-Gruppenführer und Generalleutnant der Waffen-SS	Major General
SS-Obergruppenführer und General der Waffen-SS	Lieutenant General
SS-Oberstgruppenführer und Generaloberst der Waffen-SS	General

LAST VICTORY IN RUSSIA

1

CRISIS IN SOUTHERN RUSSIA

Stalingrad

On 19 November 1942, the Soviet Southwestern and Stalingrad Fronts began final preparations before launching Operation "Uranus," the offensive intended to destroy the German 6. Armee, commanded by General der Panzertruppen Friedrich Paulus. The 6. Armee was fighting for the possession of Stalingrad, an important industrial city on the Don River and was the strongest German army in Russia. Due to a lack of sufficient numbers of German divisions, the German Army was compelled to use Rumanian and Hungarian forces to protect the flanks of Paulus' army. However, Germany's Axis allies were greatly inferior to their German counterparts, primarily due to lack of competent leadership at all levels, ineffective training and poor equipment. The Soviets had targeted the Rumanian troops as the weak links on both of the flanks of Paulus' army.

The newly created Southwestern Front had been formed from parts of the combined forces of the former Southeastern/Stalingrad Fronts and was commanded by Lieutenant General N.F. Vatutin. The remainder of the old Southeastern Front, reinforced and under command of Lieutenant General Konstantine Rokossovsky, was renamed the Stalingrad Front in September of 1942. The Southwestern Front occupied the east bank of the Don River, north of Stalingrad. Near the town of Serafimovich, Vatutin had established a bridgehead over the Don and positioned a newly arrived armored force, the 5th Tank Army, in the bridgehead. Vatutin's main effort was to be made by the 5th Tank Army, supported by the 21st Army and the 65th Army. The objective of the front was to attack out of the bridgehead to the south and drive to the area west of Stalingrad, forming the northern pincers of a classic envelopment attack. The main blow of Vatutin's offensive fell on the Rumanian 3rd Army, which, in fact, had been identified as an area of concern by Hitler himself in early November. However, German intelligence did not detect any significant warning signs in the area until it was too late to do much about it.

South of Stalingrad, across from a sector defended by a mixed Axis and German formation, designated 4. Panzerarmee, the Stalingrad Front planned a drive north. The attack was made by the 57th Army under command of Lieutenant General F.I. Tolbukhin and the 51st Army led by Lieutenant General N.I. Trufanov. The Soviets had targeted the Rumanian 6th Army Corps, defending the center of the army, as the weak link of 4. Panzerarmee. The two Soviet armies were to push to the north, join hands with forces of the Southwestern Front to the west of Stalingrad, near the town of Kalach, thus encircling Paulus' 6. Armee.

The Stalingrad Front began its offensive on the morning of 20 November. The 57th and 51st Army attacked the 6th Rumanian Army Corps, defending the center of 4. Panzerarmee. The commander of the army, Colonel General Hermann Hoth, reported that the Rumanians had succumbed to 'an indescribable tank panic.' He further stated that the Rumanian 6th Corps disintegrated so quickly that measures designed to restore the situation failed because the entire first line of defense had completely ceased to exist. Most of the Rumanian infantry fled, throwing down their weapons and abandoning trenches. The Rumanian withdrawal was described by Hoth as being 'a fantastic picture of fleeing remnants.' The collapse of the center split Hoth's army into two parts by dawn on 21 November. The German IV. Armeekorps, along with 29. Panzergrenadier-Division, was forced into the Stalingrad perimeter, while the Rumanian 6th and 7th Corps were broken by the Soviet assault and pushed west and south.

The Southwestern Front's 5th Tank Army assaulted the 3rd Rumanian Army in an early morning assault, supported by shells from 3500 mortars and guns. Under this pounding, morale quickly faltered in the Rumanian trenches. When the barrage lifted and Soviet infantry charged forward, resistance was not strong in many sectors of the front. Those Rumanians who did fight were overwhelmed or forced to withdraw when flanking positions were quickly overrun. The front line was penetrated at many points and was completely shattered within hours. The front collapsed so abruptly that by 1300 hours, the 26th and 1st Tank Corps of the Soviet 5th Tank Army were committed and reached their first objectives easily. By late afternoon, the two tank corps penetrated to a depth of fifteen to twenty kilometers. Rumanian infantry abandoned their positions in droves, having become panic stricken when Russian tanks rolled across the snow covered steppe toward them. The only Rumanian troops who fought back with determination were those under the command of General Mihail Lascar.

On the left or eastern flank of the 5th Tank Army, the 21st Army, under command of Major General I.M. Chistyakov, also broke through the Rumanian front lines without difficulty. The 4th Tank Corps and 3rd Guards Cavalry Corps were committed and the stricken 3rd Rumanian Army collapsed under the weight of Russian armor.[1] Only in the sector of the Southwestern Front's 65th Army, commanded by Lieutenant General P.I. Batov, did the Russians meet any determined resistance. In this area, the Soviet infantry ran up against German infantry divisions and Batov's attack made little progress on the first day of the attack.

On 22 November, elements of the Soviet 26th Tank Corps captured a bridge over the Don River near Kalach. German troops in the town held out for another day, but on 23 November, Stalingrad Front's 4th Mechanized Corps linked up with the 4th Tank Corps of the Southwestern Front. On that date, Stalingrad was encircled. At this point, with the southern sector seemingly ready to collapse, Hitler called upon a man whom he hoped would be able to restore the situation on the Eastern Front. The man Hitler chose for this command was Erich von Manstein, an officer that many historians consider to be the finest German commander of the war.

Manstein had held several different posts during World War I, including regimental adjutant with the 2nd Guards Reserve Regiment and served in a number of staff positions before the end of the war. Manstein remained in the Army after the establishment of the Reichswehr and was promoted to Generalmajor in 1936 when he took the position of Quartermaster General of the Army. Just before the invasion of Poland, Manstein was appointed chief of staff of General Gerd von Rundstedt's Heeresgruppe Süd. After the war broke out, the obviously talented officer received a series of rapid

Friedrich Paulus, the commander of the German 6. Armee which was encircled and destroyed by the Soviet Army at Stalingrad. Paulus was promoted to Generalfeldmarschall shortly before the fall of the city. Hitler intended that Paulus would choose to commit suicide instead surrendering to the Russians. However, Paulus chose to go into captivity with the 91,000 ragged survivors of his army. Only five thousand survived Soviet captivity and returned to Germany, years after the end of World War II. (Credit National Archives)

promotions, beginning with his appointment to the command of XXXVIII. Armeekorps, which he led with distinction during the campaign in France. His successful command of 11. Armee in the Crimean fighting led Hitler to give him command of a newly created army group, Heeresgruppe Don, in order to halt the advance of the Russians in the south.

Manstein reached the newly organized Heeregruppe Don Headquarters on 27 November. The task which had been given to him must have seemed nearly impossible, considering the difficult situation existing in the Stalingrad area by the end of the month. The Soviet forces arrayed against Manstein's army group were formidable. Vatutin's Southwestern Front had eighteen rifle divisions and three tank corps, with a total of 894 tanks. It was reinforced by two

---

[1] Earl F. Ziemke and Magda Bauer, *Moscow to Stalingrad: Decision in the East*. U.S. Army Center of Military History. (New York, 1988) pg. 472.

cavalry corps, tank and motorized brigades and eighteen artillery regiments.

In contrast, Manstein's weak army group consisted of the nearly useless remnants of the 3rd and 4th Rumanian Armies, some Hungarian troops and the shattered 4. Panzerarmee. Hoth's shadow of an army had been redesignated as Armeegruppe Hoth, reflecting its lowered combat capabilities. In fact, Hoth told Heeresgruppe Don that if the Russians made any significant effort in his area, they could not help but have the "greatest success."[2] Fortunately for 4. Panzerarmee, it was allowed some time to recover in the days after the first, crushing Soviet attacks and Manstein began to organize a relief mission with the intention of restoring mobility to Paulus' surrounded army. Manstein had emphatically told Hitler that to expect anything more from the army group was impossible because of the limited forces he had at hand. Hitler, having been assured by Reichsmarschall Hermann Göring that the Luftwaffe could supply

the Stalingrad pocket, ordered Paulus' 6. Armee to shorten its front and prepare to hold the pocket until rescued. Göring insisted that he could deliver 600 tons of supplies a day to Stalingrad, a statement that many officers received with incredulity. Those who doubted the Luftwaffe's ability to transport that much tonnage, included General der Infanterie Kurt Zeitzler, Hitler's Chief of the General Staff, Paulus and the corps commanders of 6. Armee as well.

By 28 November the Soviet grip on Stalingrad had solidified and an inner ring of Russian divisions was pressing in on the pocket from all directions. The majority of the divisions of the Southwest, Don and Stalingrad Fronts became involved in the reduction of the pocket which contained many more Axis troops than the Soviets realized. Early Soviet estimates of the number of German soldiers in the pocket were in the 85,000 to 95,000 range. In fact, at least 250,000 Axis soldiers were trapped and the Russians slowly began to appreciate this fact. By the end of the month, ninety-four divisions of the three Soviet fronts were committed to the battle for

---

[2] Ibid, pg. 478.

A Sturmgeschütz III leads an assault group of German Pioniere (combat engineers) into battle during the Stalingrad fighting. The entire city, along with its civilian population, was devastated during the months of fighting. (Credit National Archives)

Stalingrad, while forty-nine divisions were assigned to block Hoth's 4. Panzerarmee from conducting a rescue mission.

During the last days of November, 4. Panzerarmee prepared to conduct an operation designed to open a supply corridor to Stalingrad, which was code named "Wintergewitter" (winter storm). The LVII. Panzer-Korps, which had been detached from 17. Armee in the Caucasus, arrived and assumed command of three divisions. The strongest of these was 6. Panzer-Division, commanded by General der Panzertruppen Erhard Raus, which was on the way from France, where it had been resting and refitting. The 1. Panzerarmee gave LVII. Panzer-Korps the 23. Panzer-Division, which had sixty-nine tanks. The division was a veteran unit and experienced in the rigors of combat on the Eastern Front. Also attached to the corps was 15. Luftwaffefelddivision, which had little combat value, although its complement of 8.8 cm dual purpose guns and both 2cm and 3.7cm Flak guns were very valuable in support of both offensive and defensive operations.

Hoth was also given XXXXVIII. Panzer-Korps, which had only one panzer division, the excellent 11. Panzer-Division, led by one of the outstanding armor commanders of the war, Generalmajor Hermann Balck. Also attached to the corps was 336. Infanterie-Division, which was a good quality, though below strength infantry division. The third division of the corps was another Luftwaffe unit, 7. Luftwaffefelddivision, which was never more than a third rate formation. Balck's Panzer division was rested and sufficiently well equipped for a division that had been in heavy combat for many months in Russia. It had been in reserve since early October and had repaired most of its damaged Panzers. However, the real strength

Two infantrymen of 6. Armee man a machine gun position. They have dug a foxhole next to a knocked out T-34 tank, which furnished excellent protection from mortar and artillery fire. (Credit National Archives)

of the division lay in its experienced personnel and its excellent command leadership. The regimental and battalion commanders were experienced and skillful. In Balck's own words:

We were fortunate that after the hard fighting in the previous campaigns, all commanders whose nerves could not stand the test, had been replaced by proven men. There was no commander left who was not absolutely reliable.[3]

---

[3] Sadarananda, Dana V. *Beyond Stalingrad: Manstein and the Operations of Army Group Don.* (New York and London: 1990) pg. 21.

A German machine gun team moves up during the fighting for Stalingrad. The man running in the background carries extra ammunition boxes. Assistant gunners carried ammunition and at least one extra barrel for the MG-34 and MG-42 machine guns. The barrels overheated with extended use, but could be changed very quickly. Note the Russian PPSH-41 machine pistol used by the man on the far left. (Credit National Archives)

On 2 December, the Soviet 5th Tank Army, commanded by General P.L. Romanenko, began an attack against the Chir River area in the Nizhne-Chirskaja sector. Heeresgruppe Don believed that the Soviet objective was the destruction of the Rumanian forces, in order to further isolate the Stalingrad pocket. Actually, Romanenko had been ordered to destroy XXXXVIII. Panzer-Korps and eliminate German forces in the Nizhne-Chirskaja bridgehead on the Chir River. The 5th Tank Army numbered about 70,000 men and consisted of six rifle divisions, the 1st Tank Corps and 216th Tank Brigade, with a total of about 180 tanks and eight artillery regiments. The army was also reinforced by two cavalry divisions and additional infantry strength from the Soviet 21st Army.[4]

The XXXXVIII. Panzer-Korps' 336. Infanterie-Division was moved up to the Chir River, occupying defensive positions along the river. The Russians attacked the German infantry division in costly frontal attacks. Romanenko sustained such heavy initial losses that he pulled back to regroup. He brought up additional artillery and prepared another assault upon 336. Infanterie-Division. Five days later, the 5th Tank Army again attacked German positions along the river and this time made substantial gains, which the Soviets quickly reinforced with armor, infantry and artillery troops. The German infantry could not seal off the many penetrations in its front and Balck's 11. Panzer-Division was called upon to clean up the situation. In a series of well executed counterattacks, the division eliminated two dangerous Soviet bridgeheads, temporarily blocking the Soviet advance and destroyed a great deal of Romanenko's armor. After a week of continuous action, Balck succeeded in actually regaining some lost ground, but the division was exhausted and went over to defensive operations.[5]

Disappointed by the failure of the 5th Tank Army to destroy XXXXVIII. Panzer-Korps, the Stavka reinforced Romanenko with a reserve army and attacked once again in the Chir area. It was extremely vital for the Germans to retain the Chir bridgeheads in order to utilize the crossings as assembly and jump off points for the relief attempt operation. Additionally, a Soviet breakout from the threatened sector could have turned south and endangered the Tatsinskaya and Morozovsk airfields, from which the Luftwaffe supplied the Stalingrad pocket. Although the 5th Tank Army was not able to achieve any great success, it forced the Germans to keep XXXXVIII. Panzer-Korps on the Chir River front, where it remained completely involved in defensive operations. As a result, it was unable to support the relief operations of LVII. Panzer-Korps, which

Rumanian General Mikhail Lascar, who won the German Knight's Cross while commander of the Rumanian 1st Mountain Brigade on January 18, 1942. He was the first foreign commander to be awarded the Oakleaves to the Knight's Cross, receiving the decoration on November 22, 1942 for gallantry while commanding the Rumanian 6th Infantry Division. (Credit National Archives)

seriously weakened the forces available for Operation "Wintergewitter."

At this point in time, however, events in the sector defended by the Italian 8th Army forced the Germans to abandon the relief attempt completely. Intelligence information had warned the German command that the Soviets were building up for an offensive in the 8th Army area, but the exact direction of attack remained unknown. The Soviet General Staff or Stavka, had assigned General A.M. Vasilevsky to supervise the planning and execution of this operation. The new Soviet offensive, which had been planned by the Southwestern Front, was originally code named "Operation Saturn."

The initial objective of Operation "Saturn" was the destruction of the Italian 8th Army, in position opposite the Don and Chir Rivers and Armeeabteilung Hollidt which was arrayed on the Chir River. Three tank corps and six rifle divisions of the 1st Guards Army were to attack the 8th Army front on the boundary of the 2nd and 35th Corps and advance southward toward the town of Millerovo which lay on the important railroad line running from Kamensk, on the Northern Donets, northward to Kantemirovka and then Rossosh. This route of attack would pass through the communications zone of the southern two thirds of the Italian army and enter the rear areas of Armeeabteilung Hollidt. Simultaneously, the 3rd Guards Army was to launch a frontal attack upon Armeeabteilung Hollidt from across the Chir River. The army was made up of five rifle divisions and a mechanized corps. The first objective of the 3rd Guards Army attack was also Millerovo. Once the two armies linked up at Millerovo, the second and most important phase of the opera-

---

[4] Glantz, Col. David M. *From the Don to the Dnepr: Soviet Offensive Operations - December 1942 - August 1943*. (London: 1991) pg. 14-15.

[5] Manstein, Erich von, *Lost Victories* (Chicago: 1958) pg. 325-326 and Sadarananda, pg. 25-30.

tion would begin. After having secured the Rossoch-Kantemirovka-Millerovo railroad line, thus obtaining a supply lifeline, the four mobile corps were to thrust southward. Their objective was the key city of Rostov. The capture of Rostov would cut off all German troops east of the city and in the Caucasus.[6]

Before the Soviet could launch Operation "Saturn" 4. Panzerarmee began Operation "Wintergewitter," which forced the Soviet command to react by shifting additional forces to meet this new threat. Vasilevsky decided to use the 2nd Guards Army to reinforce the defensive effort against LVII. Panzer-Korps. The 2nd Guards Army had been allotted to the Southwestern Front, and its removal from the available formations represented a significant loss of manpower. Due to this change the operation's objectives were adjusted to conform to the reconfiguration of forces available to the Southwest Front. Vasilevsky realized that he did not have the necessary strength to drive all the way to Rostov and accordingly proposed to adjust the attack direction and objectives of the offensive. This new plan, more modest in scope, was known as Operation "Little Saturn."

The 1st Guards Army was to attack the Italian army from the same assembly areas as had been assigned to it for "Saturn," but change its direction of attack to the southeast, toward the key airfields at Tatsinskaya and Morozovsk. The 24th and 25th Tank Corps objective was to capture the airfields, while the 17th and 18th Tank Corps were to advance west of this thrust, parallel to the Rossoch-Kantemirovka-Millerovo railroad. These two tank corps intended to clear Axis forces from this important lateral rail line and push southwards until reaching the Northern Donets River between Voroshilovgrad and Kamensk. A successful advance to the river would position its columns east of and in the rear of Armeeabteilung Hollidt, threatening its lines of supply.

The 3rd Guards Army was directed to make a frontal assault upon Armeeabteilung Hollidt and drive the German/Axis army out of its positions behind the Chir River. The operational mobile group of the 3rd Guards Army was the reinforced 1st Mechanized Corps. After the infantry divisions of the army created a sufficiently deep penetration, the army intended to use the mechanized corps to penetrate Armeeabteilung Hollidt's front at a point about sixty kilometers east of Millerovo and then drive towards Morozovsk. The army was expected to reach the airfield by the fourth day of the offensive.

The 5th Tank Army was to assault Axis divisions holding the lower Chir River east of Morozovsk, penetrate Armeeabteilung Hollidt's southern flank and support the attack upon the airfield.

---

[6] Glantz, pg. 13-14.

Romanenko's rifle divisions were supported by the 5th Mechanized Corps and the 8th Cavalry Corps.

On 16 December, 1942, the first phase of Operation "Little Saturn" was launched against the Italian 8th Army. The northernmost corps of the army was the elite Alpine Corps, consisting of three divisions. To its south was the 2nd Italian Corps, with two infantry divisions, reinforced with the very weak 27. Panzer-Division and elements of the German 285. Infanterie-Division. Holding the corps sector adjacent to the 2nd Corps, was the Italian 35th Army Corps, with the Italian Pasubio Division and the German 298.Infanterie-Division. On the extreme right flank of the army, XXIX. Armeekorps held the sector that bordered the northern flank of Armeeabteilung Hollidt.

The 1st Guards, 6th Army and 3rd Guards Army began their attacks in the morning hours, after a largely ineffective artillery preparation. Fog and bad weather limited the effectiveness of both Russian artillery and the planned air support. None of the three armies were able to penetrate into the depth of either the Italian 8th Army or Armeeabteilung Hollidt. German troops had reinforced both of the armies at several points and these troops inflicted heavy casualties on the Soviet infantry. At the end of the first day, the Soviet attacks had gained very little ground. However the weather was better on the next day and Soviet artillery and air support was much improved.

Early in the morning of 17 December, the Southwestern Front renewed its attacks upon the Italian 8th Army and Armeeabteilung Hollidt. Tanks were detached from the three Soviet tank corps and assigned to the rifle divisions, in order to expedite the breakthrough phase of the operation. The main bodies of the 17th, 18th and 25th Tank Corps remained in position to exploit the creation of gaps in the main attack zone, which was located in the 1st Guards Army sector between Novaja Kalitva and Boguchar. The 24th Tank Corps remained in close reserve with its 159 tanks. Soviet forward artillery observation was much improved, providing more organized support for the offensive and this aiding the speed of the advance.

Late in the day, the central section of the Italian 8th Army began to collapse under the pressure of Soviet infantry and armor, which was aided by essentially unopposed operations of the Russian air force. By evening, a gap had been opened in the Axis lines between the towns of Boguchar and Novaja Kalitva which was of sufficient depth to allow the army to commit its tank corps.

The 17th, 18th and 25th Tank Corps entered the penetration area and pushed to the south and southwest. Their advance continued during the night, with the 17th Tank Corps reaching the Boguchar River and the 25th Tank Corps actually crossing the river at a point west of the town of Boguchar. The 18th Tank Corps,

Generalfeldmarschall Erich von Manstein, appointed by Hitler to command Heeresgruppe Don during the Stalingrad relief operation. He commanded 11. Armee in 1941 and conducted a brilliant campaign in the Crimea, after which Hitler promoted him to the rank of Field Marshall. Heeresgruppe Don (later Heeresgruppe Süd) initially consisted of Paulus' 6. Armee, 4. Panzerarmee and the Rumanian 4th Army. (Credit National Archives)

commanded by Major General B.S. Bakharov, was faced with more steadfast opposition by the German 298. Infanterie-Division and slowly pushed toward Boguchar from the north. Behind the two leading armored formations, the 24th Tank Corps, commanded by Major General V.M. Badanov, followed in echelon.

The Southwestern Front unleashed its tank corps after it was clear that a breakthrough of the main defense zone was accomplished. The leading tank corps began the exploitation phase of the offensive and the Soviet armor met little resistance. The deep penetration made by the tank corps cut the Italian 8th Army in two. The 298. Infanterie-Division maintained its hold on the town of Boguchar, on the eastern flank of the gap and this slowed the advance of the 18th Tank Corps. Meanwhile the 17th and 25th Tank Corps, followed by the 24th Tank Corps, plunged southward, crossed the Boguchar River and pushed further south toward the Millerovo area.

By nightfall on 18 December, the 25th Tank Corps, commanded by Major General P.P. Pavlov, was only twenty-five kilometers northeast of Millerovo. The forward elements of the tank corps approached the northern edge of the communications zone of Armeeabteilung Hollidt, at a point about thirty kilometers to the rear of Hollidt's positions on the Chir River. This advance threatened not only to sever the lines of communications of Armeeabteilung Hollidt, but presented a potential threat to the airfields at Tatsinskaya and Morozovsk, the loss of which meant disaster for 6. Armee in Stalingrad. The 294. Infanterie-Division began to bend its defensive front back to the west, in order to block the advance of the 25th Tank Corps.

On 19 December, the Italian 8th Army dissolved, opening a gap from Kantemirovka on the north, to the boundary with Armeeabteilung Hollidt in the south. Taking advantage of the situation, Vatutin personally took over the coordination of the advance at this juncture, directing the 24th and 25th Tank Corps to expedite their exploitation to the south, toward the airfields. Poluboyarov's 17th Tank Corps was to proceed to Millerovo as quickly as possible. Meanwhile, the 18th Tank Corps had broken through the German defenses at Boguchar on 17 December. By the morning of 19 December, the forward elements of the corps approached the town of Meschkov, which was about fifty kilometers north of Millerovo. A small detachment of newly arrived SS and Police troops, under command of SS-Standartenführer Hinrich Schuldt, was driven back into the town on 19 December. When the Russians threatened to encircle Meschkov, Schuldt pulled back but not quite in time to escape. The Kampfgruppe was cut in two by a column of Russian tanks, forcing the two groups of the fragmented column to withdraw in different directions. The main group, under Schuldt,

moved away from the Soviet armor, moving to the east, in the direction of the Bystraja River.[7]

By 19 December the forward detachments of the 25th Tank Corps, leading the advance of the Soviet armor, had already reached a point twenty kilometers due east of Millerovo. Pavlov's tanks continued driving southeast, toward the Bystraja River and on 20 December reached Pervomaiskoje, on the northern bank of the river, above Morozovsk. Badanov's 24th Tank Corps, on the following day, passed through the town of Degtevo, which was fifteen kilometers northeast of Millerovo. Both tank corps continued their advance to the southeast, toward Tatsinskaya and Morozovsk, while the 17th and 18th Tank Corps converged on Millerovo.

In the Armeeabteilung Hollidt sector, the 3rd Guards Army was able to enlarge a number of its penetrations during 19 December and the Army's Rumanian infantry divisions began to fold up. On the northern flank of the army, adjacent to the southern flank of the Italian 8th Army, the resistance of the 1st Rumanian Corps diminished rapidly. The resulting gap, after the collapse of the division, left German 62. Infanterie-Division and the neighboring XVII. Armee-Korps struggling to try to limit the width of the resulting gap and to protect their suddenly exposed flanks. The northern 1/3 of Armeeabteilung Hollidt, the 1st Rumanian Corps, abruptly fell apart as well.

The 62. Infanterie-Division, isolated on both sides by the collapse of the Rumanian divisions on both its flanks, pulled back west of the Chir River and attempted to establish a stable defensive front. However, with the 24th and 25th Tank Corps having already disrupted their communications zone, Armeeabteilung Hollidt's 294. Infanterie-Division and 22. Panzer-Division withdrew southward toward the Bystraja River, in order to block the Soviet advance on the key air fields.

The Creation of Armeeabteilung Fretter-Pico

In order to plug the gap which resulted from the destruction of the 8th Italian Army, Heeregruppe B was given the HQ of XXX. Armeekorps, under General der Artillerie Maximilian Fretter-Pico. The former corps was designated Armeeabteilung Fretter-Pico, although it was not given the support troops normally attached to an army. It initially consisted of the remnants of the headquarters detachments of XXIX. Armeekorps, Gruppe Kreysing (elements of 3. Gebirgs-Division) in Millerovo and Schuldt's Kampfgruppe of SS and Police troops. Additional troops included the 304. Infanterie-Division which was just arriving and large numbers of Italian troops,

[7] Lehmann, Rudolf. *The Leibstandarte III* (Winnipeg: 1990) pg. 12.

although many of the Italians had thrown away their weapons and were useless. The one first class unit available to Fretter-Pico was Generalmajor Kreysing's reinforced regimental Kampfgruppe in Millerovo. Fretter-Pico also took command of various small detachments of Police, SS and rear area troops scattered throughout the sector north of Voroshilovgrad. Most of these were in Schuldt's ad hoc Kampfgruppe although some of the Police troops had been forced into Millerovo, when the Russian tanks tore through Schuldt's column south of Meschkov. Hinrich Schuldt was a competent infantry commander with extensive combat experience in Russia, having won the Knight's Cross while commanding 4.SS-"Totenkopf" Infanterie-Regiment in April of 1942. However, the makeshift Kampfgruppe he commanded at that point suffered from lack of training and had not worked together extensively before it was thrown into battle.

The fact that such an impoverished, under strength Armeeabteilung was given the responsibility of holding such an important sector of the Northern Donets region between Voroshilovgrad and Kamensk, tells us much about the condition of the German army in Russia in late 1942. The enormous casualties that Hitler's armies had sustained during the first two years of the war in Russia had resulted in a disastrous shortage of combat soldiers, particularly infantrymen, on the Eastern Front. By late 1942, the Germans had suffered nearly 1,000,000 permanent losses, most of them on the Eastern Front.[8] To be sure, hundreds of thousands of Rumanian, Hungarian and Italian troops fought in Russia along side their German comrades, but most were never more than 3rd rate fighting forces in most instances. Finnish troops and a division of Spanish soldiers gave a much better account of themselves and were respected by the Germans and Russians alike.

With this motley assortment of troops, Armeeabteilung Fretter-Pico prepared to hold the vital sector of the Donets River between the cities of Voroshilovgrad and Kamensk. The only armor available to Fretter-Pico's makeshift army detachment was a dozen or so tanks designated as Panzer-Abteilung 138. On 19 December, Armeeabteilung Fretter-Pico reported by radio to Heeresgruppe B Headquarters for the first time and received orders to assemble in Starobelsk. Preparations to establish a permanent radio communications network were begun and Fretter-Pico received a report on the situation north of the Northern Donets above Voroshilovgrad and Kamensk. He could not have been enthusiastic about the presence of three Soviet tank corps in the area he was to defend. Already the 24th and 25th Tank Corps were approaching the impor-

A Rumanian machine gun position in the field. The Rumanian troops were generally poorly led by an inept, uncaring officer corps and showed little enthusiasm for the war in Russia. The Rumanians were hampered by an inadequate logistical system and lack of effective anti-tank guns. When attacked by Russian tanks Rumanian infantry often succumbed to what Hermann Hoth, the commander of the German 4. Panzerarmee, characterized as an 'indescribable' tank panic. (Credit National Archives)

tant airfields south of the Bystraja River. The Soviet tank columns had flowed around several station/depots along the Rossoch-Kantemirovka-Millerovo railroad, encircling Axis troops at Gartmaschevka and Chertkovo.

The mission of the newly formed Armeeabteilung was to block the gap between the southern flank of Heeresgruppe B and the shambles of the northern wing of Armeeabteilung Hollidt, which had been created out of the wreckage of the 8th Italian Army. The staff of the former XXX. Armeekorps, upgraded to Armeeabteilung status in name only, arrived at Dnepropetrovsk on 20 December, 1942. Its first task was to find transport to Voroshilovgrad, on the Northern Donets. Almost immediately there were difficulties, primarily due to the inexperience of some of the troops assigned to the army. The only full strength division in the Armeeabteilung order of battle was the newly arrived, but unproven 304. Infanterie-Division.[9]

Heeresgruppe B ordered Fretter-Pico to use 304. Infanterie-Division to close the gap between Armeeabteilung Hollidt and his own southeastern flank, in order to protect the crossings of the Northern Donets at Voroshilovgrad and Kamensk. German air reconnaissance spotted a large number of Russian tanks and armored vehicles in the area west of Millerovo and suspected, quite correctly, that at least a Soviet tank corps was in the sector. This was Major General Poluboyarov's 17th Tank Corps, which had reached

[8] Ziemke, Earl F. *From Stalingrad to Berlin: The German Defeat in the East.* U.S. Army Center of Military History, 1968, pg. 213. A permanent loss is defined as those killed, missing or completely disabled and unable to return to active service in any capacity.

[9] NA/T-312, roll 1613, 1a KTB Armeeabteilung Fretter-Pico, Darstellung der Ereignisse, frame 005-0012.

the town of Voloshino on 22 December. Unknown to Fretter-Pico, a second Soviet tank corps, Major General Bakharov's 18th Tank Corps, was also approaching east of Millerovo. The 24th and 25th Tank Corps had already passed through the sector and were east of Kamensk, approaching the airfields at Tatsinskaya and the area north of Morozovsk.

Temperatures of minus 25 degrees Centigrade froze all roads solid on the morning of 26 December. Armeeabteilung Fretter-Pico began its defense of the Northern Donets in earnest soon after dawn. Troops of 304. Infanterie-Division occupied positions north of the river, between Voroshilovgrad and Kamensk, skirmishing with Soviet troops at several points. East of Kamensk, in the distance, artillery fire could be heard, signaling that the 5th Tank Army was in combat against the northern wing of Armeeabteilung Hollidt. The Soviets made slow progress against Hollidt and slowly pushed westward, toward the Northern Donets River east of Kamensk. Soviet artillery shelled the Millerovo perimeter, while east of the town, XXIX. Armeekorps Headquarters and Gruppe Schuldt were encircled at the town of Krassnojarovka by a tank column of the 24th Tank Corps on its way toward Tatsinskaya.

Hoping to build a solid front north of the Northern Donets River, Hollidt ordered 298. Infanterie-Division to fight its way to the sector northwest of Millerovo and build up a defensive front. However, the division had been cut into pieces by the attacks of the Soviet tank corps. It was no longer a coherent formation capable of any concerted offensive action. The dispersed fragments of the division stumbled westward, dodging Russian tank columns and harassed by Soviet aircraft. The men were often without supplies or food and were primarily driven by the desire to reach safety. Some reached Millerovo, Chertkovo or Gartmashevka, only to be trapped when the Russians encircled each of these towns. Those less fortunate were cornered and gunned down by the advancing Russians or taken prisoner and sent marching eastward. Small groups of determined survivors continued to trek westward, through snow and ice for days afterward, eventually reaching safety if they successfully evaded the Russians.

One column of the division reached the town of Chertkovo and these men were trapped when the Soviet 41st Rifle Division encircled the town. There were large numbers of Italians and Rumanians in the town, but they were generally of little combat worth. Many did not even have weapons. Help was on the way however, as 19. Panzer-Division had been ordered to assemble west of Chertkovo, cross the Derkul river and break the siege of Chertkovo. Another assortment of Axis troops remained trapped at Gartmaschevka, a large railroad station north of Chertkovo, on the Kamensk-Millerovo-Kantemirovka rail line.

During the period of 25-30 December, fighting intensified in the Northern Donets area between Voroshilovgrad and Kamensk and remained very heavy in the Tatsinskaja-Morozovsk sector. The XXIX. Armeekorps HQ group and Gruppe Schuldt withdrew from Krassnojarovka, in the direction of Skassyrskaja, on the Bystraja River. Elements of Armeeabteilung Hollidt's 306. Infanterie-Division, reinforced by a Luftwaffe division, moved up to the southern bank of the river and attempted to prevent the 24th and 25th Tank Corps from crossing the Bystraja River. However, on the night of 24-25 December, the 24th Tank Corps, minus its 24th Motorized Rifle Brigade, which was bringing up the rear, crossed the Bystraja west of Skassyrskaja and pushed to the south, toward Tatsinskaya. Arriving north of the airfield before dawn, Badanov split his force into separate columns and surprised the small German detachments guarding the airfield and town.[10]

After opening the attack on the German positions with a barrage of rocket fire, Badanov launched concentric attacks on the German positions and quickly captured the town and its airfield. Unfortunately for the Soviets, they had nearly expended their supply of fuel which limited the mobility of Badanov's tanks and hampered all of his further operations at Tatsinskaya. Although some attempts were made by the Russians to deliver fuel and ammunition by airdrop, these were inadequate and Badanov had little choice but to dig in and await reinforcements. A portion of the 24th Motorized Infantry Brigade fought its way into the town on 26 December, but brought little additional fuel or ammunition.

By 27 December, elements of 306. Infanterie-Division and 6. Panzer-Division began to close in on Badanov's now encircled corps, blocking the roads leading to the airfield and Tatsinskaya itself. With a ring of German forces closing in on his stranded tank corps, Badanov radioed for assistance. Not wanting to lose Badanov's corps, Vatutin ordered the 25th Tank Corps and the 1st Guards Mechanized Corps to fight their way to Tatsinskaya and rescue Badanov's beleaguered tank corps.[11]

The two Soviet corps reached the northern bank of the Bystraja and advanced toward Morozovsk, but by 27-28 December, units of 11. Panzer-Division had joined the battle north of Morozovsk, strengthening the German forces seeking to block the 3rd Guards Army from reaching Badanov. Additional German armor followed soon after, with 48 tanks of 6. Panzer-Division's Panzer-Regiment 11, reaching assembly positions east of Tatsinskaya on the following day. Gruppe Unrein, consisting of Panzergrenadier-Regiment 4, reinforced by a battalion of assault guns and artillery, had al-

[10] Glantz, pg. 65.
[11] Ibid. pg. 67-69.

ready reached the Tatsinskaja area and had blocked the road leading in the town from Skassyrskaja. A second group of the division, Gruppe Hünersdorff, named for the commander of the panzer regiment, remained in positions north of Morozovsk.

On 26 December, 6. Panzer-Division assaulted Badanov's positions, reinforced by infantry of 306. Infanterie-Division, but the hard fighting Russian tankers inflicted heavy losses on the Germans and stubbornly maintained their hold on the airfield and town. By the end of the fighting on 27 December, Badanov's ammunition was nearly exhausted and it was not certain if he would be resupplied. The fighting continued on the next day, with the Germans finally pushing Badanov's tankers out of the town, after suffering heavy losses to the Panzergrenadier companies. One battalion of Panzergrenadier-Regiment 4 had only eighty men still in action by nightfall of 29 December. The remnants of Badanov's corps fought its way out of Tatsinskaya and joined the main body of the 24th Motorized Rifle Brigade, although much of the heavy equipment and armor had to be left behind. The records of 6. Panzer-Division state that thirty-four Russian tanks were destroyed or captured. Badanov was not able to fight his way back across the river and occupied a defensive position in a wooded area north of Tatsinskaya.[12]

Meanwhile, the 14th Guards Rifle Corps of the 3rd Guards Army, tried to force its way across the Bystraja River northwest of Morozovsk and join forces with the 25th Tank Corps and 1st Guards Mechanized Corps. Assault groups of the Soviet 203rd and 266th Rifle Divisions succeeded in reaching the southern bank of the river near Skassyrskaja and established a series of shallow bridgeheads. However, the Soviet rifle regiments had endured substantial losses during the hard fighting of the last weeks and were running short of ammunition and food as well. Gruppe Hünersdorff, reinforced by Panzergrenadiers of 23. Panzer-Division, assembled during the night of 27-28 December and launched an attack on the Soviet bridgeheads at dawn on 28 December.

Hünersdorff himself directed the battle from a command tank, leading ten tanks of Panzer-Regiment 11 in a violent assault which destroyed four Soviet tanks, captured twenty prisoners and counted a total of 250 Russian dead. Throughout the day 6. and 11. Panzer-Divisions conducted mop up operations, which continued through New Years Eve, 1942. During the next several days, several Russian attacks were launched from the Uryupin area, in futile attempts to reach the airfields. The two Panzer divisions and the infantry of 306. Infanterie-Division, counter-attacked the remaining Soviet forces between the Bystraja and Morozovsk. The Soviets withdrew

Hinrich Schuldt, shown here as an SS-Standartenführer, won the Knight's Cross while commanding 4.SS-"Totenkopf" Infanterie-Regiment in April of 1942. Schuldt served in the German Navy for six years before he volunteered for "Leibstandarte-SS-Adolf Hitler," in 1933. He took command of an assortment of SS and Police troops subordinated to Armeeabteilung Fretter-Pico and led this formation during the defense of the Northern Donets in the Millerovo-Voroshilovgrad sector. (The author's collection)

from the town along roads leading to the north, trying to reach and cross the Bystraja River. Uryupin was to be occupied by troops of 8. Luftwaffefelddivision. However, through a misunderstanding regarding its mission, the Luftwaffe troops did not hold the town as ordered and the Russians promptly moved back into Uryupin.[13]

By 1 January, the last remaining tanks of the 24th Tank Corps ran out of fuel and were immobile. In addition, the tankers were

---

[12] Paul, Wolfgang, *Brennpunkte-Die Geschichte der 6. Panzer-Division* (Osnabrück: 1993) pg. 280-281.

[13] Ibid, pg. 282-283.

down to their last rounds of ammunition. Badanov's men abandoned their tanks and heavy weapons and attempted to make their way north by foot, trying to reach the Soviet lines north of Morozovsk. The 25th Tank Corps and 1st Guards Mechanized Corps, which had less than fifty tanks between them on 29 December, were burnt out during the battles to reach Badanov and Morozovsk. The declining strength of the two corps and the heavy losses of the decimated rifle divisions doomed any breakthrough operations to failure after German armor arrived in the Bystraja River sector. In the meantime, the fighting at Millerovo grew in intensity after the 17th and 18th Tank Corps assembled north and east of the town.[14]

The Battle for Millerovo

The first Soviet assaults on Millerovo began on 26 December. During this period, Kreysing's men benefited from support by the Luftwaffe, which remained active in the Northern Donets area. Unfortunately for the Germans, the Soviet air force was in operation also. A Russian bomber dropped a stick of bombs inside the perimeter and scored a direct hit on a large ammunition bunker, which detonated with a deafening blast heard many miles away.

Soviet attacks against Millerovo escalated during the last days of December, but the defenders held their perimeter, while inflicting heavy casualties upon the Russians. The OKH, in response to the situations then developing at Tatsinskaya and Uryupin, ordered Fretter-Pico to cut the supply lines of the 24th and 25th Tank Corps, which passed through the Kalitva River Valley, with an attack by 304. Infanterie-Division. The division slowly got its regiments on line south and southeast of Millerovo and began its advance toward the Kalitva. However initial reports were suspiciously vague and confusing as to the progress of the attack and the exact location of the attack groups. Subsequent aerial reconnaissance revealed that the division had not reached any of its objectives and at some points was halted after contacting very weak Russian defenses. When counterattacked, the inexperienced German troops had immediately stopped their advance and gone over to the defensive. Later investigations revealed that a number of officers completely lost control of their units and some of the troops, lacking strong leadership, had panicked in their first action.

The next day, the division again tried to occupy and block the Kalitva but Soviet counterattacks drove back one regiment and completely halted the advance of another. One battalion of 575. Grenadier-Regiment managed to hold its positions on a hill near the town of Jekaterinovka. There were other setbacks as well. While Fretter-

Pico was engaged in attacking east of Millerovo, a strong Russian assault on Donskoj nearly crushed the German garrison and captured the town. Only by mounting a desperate, last ditch counterattack were the defenders able to turn back the Soviet attack. Unfortunately for the small force, its commander, Oberst von der Lancken, was killed in the action.

The 304. Infanterie-Division continued to experience difficulties during the fighting on the next day. A Soviet counterattack broke through a regimental perimeter and a small attack group approached the division's artillery positions around the town of Antonovka. The regimental commander became distraught and requested that he be allowed to withdraw his men.

It became clear to Armeeabteilung Fretter-Pico that due to its command deficiencies and lack of experience, the division was unable to clear up the penetration at Antonovka with the forces on hand. Gruppe Schuldt, which had been reinforced with additional Flak batteries and infantry guns, as well as a Police mortar detachment, was ordered to provide armored support to the division.

On 30 December, the division seemed at first to be getting over its jitters and was reported that it was able to retake some ground southeast of Millerovo. Other elements of the division established contact with reconnaissance troops of Armeeabteilung Hollidt farther to the southeast. However, subsequent reports regarding the position of its regiments were once again vague and later in the day, communications ceased altogether. Only reports from German air reconnaissance provided the vital information about the true progress of the division's attack.

The left regiment of the division had gained no ground at all and in the center, the attack remained stalled near the town of Golovo Kalitwenskoje, which had been reached on the previous day. One battalion of Grenadier-Regiment 574 was attacked by a Soviet battalion and driven off a hilltop defensive position, although another of its battalions was able to hold its ground. Fretter-Pico decided to send a Panzer company from Panzer-Abteilung 138 in order to provide armor support to the inexperienced infantry. However, the order was countermanded at 1045 hours by a new order which directed the company to rejoin the battalion, in order to attack Soviet tanks and motorized infantry which had surrounded the German garrison of Grekovo-Petrovsky, a small town on the railroad line south of Millerovo. Fretter-Pico ordered a battalion of 304. Infanterie-Division to furnish infantry support to Panzer-Abteilung 138 for the attack.

The town of Grekovo-Petrovsky itself and its small German garrison remained surrounded and isolated, but the attack drove the main body of the Soviet force away from a section of the vital railroad south of Millerovo. The German troops in Grekovo-Petrovsky

---

[14] Glantz, pg. 72-73.

remained encircled until the night of 1-2 January. Under cover of darkness, the garrison, carrying their wounded, broke through the Russian lines and reached safety.[15]

On 31 December, 19. Panzer-Division had reached the town of Streltskovo on the Kamyschnaja River, which was about twenty kilometers northwest of Millerovo. The division planned to strike eastward from Streltskovo and reach the area just west of Millerovo, cutting the lines of communication of the 17th Tank Corps forces at Voloshino. Gruppe von der Lancken, which had been placed under command of a new officer since von der Lancken's death, was to conduct an attack supporting the division. The new commander assigned to the Kampfgruppe at Donskoj, Oberst Nagel, was in Kamensk and could not join his new command immediately. In his absence, the Armeeabteilung sent orders to the garrison, directing it to support the attack of 19. Panzer-Division on 1 January, 1943.

Panzer-Abteilung 138 assembled in the town of Tarasovka, which was located on the Millerovo-Kamensk railroad, south of Millerovo and ordered to clear up the dangerous situation along the railroad. It was to be supported by a battalion of infantry from 304. Infanterie-Division, which had been provided with a number of trucks to give it adequate mobility. The morning of 1 January, 1943 brought renewed fighting throughout the Armeeabteilung sector. Panzer-Abteilung 138 reached Tarasovka and launched its attack on the Russian forces in the Grekovo-Petrovsky area. Supported by II./Grenadier-Regiment 573, the Panzer battalion was able to drive Russian troops off two hills east of Tarasovka and retake a small village nearby. One Russian tank was knocked out and two anti-tank guns were captured. The attack made good progress and approached a main road, which left Millerovo's eastern edge and entered the Kalitva River valley.[16]

During the next several days Armeeabteilung Fretter-Pico remained concerned with other situations along its tenuously held front. The 304. Infanterie-Division's poor performance also continued to be worrisome. Throughout the next several days, the Russians tried to cut the last supply routes entering Millerovo from the south with strong attacks made by the 197th Rifle Division against elements of Grenadier-Regiment 575, which held positions along the Millerovo-Kamensk railroad. German radio intercepts revealed that the 197th Rifle Division was in radio contact with a newly arrived Soviet tank corps which was identified as the 23rd Tank Corps. By 5 January, Armeeabteilung Fretter-Pico speculated that the east flank of the Armeeabteilung, held by 304. Infanterie-Division would probably be attacked in conjunction with attacks upon

An SdKfz 10 light half track with a 2cm Flak gun mounted behind the driver. Mobile Flak guns, in addition to Sturmgeschütz IIIs, were utilized by the garrison encircled in Millerovo. SS and Police troops separated from Hinrich Schuldt's Kampfgruppe were combined with the Flak gun vehicles and a battery of Sturmgeschütze to form Kreysing's mobile reserve during the fighting for Millerovo. (Credit National Archives)

Millerovo. It was decided that Gruppe Schuldt would be reinforced with the motorized battalion from 304. Infanterie-Division, Panzer-Abteilung 138 and additional Flak and mortar detachments, in order to counterattack the expected Soviet attack or to conduct mobile reconnaissance missions as needed. On 6 January, 7. Panzer-Division arrived south of the gap between Armeeabteilung Hollidt and Armeeabteilung Fretter-Pico. This positive note was countered when German intelligence confirmed the arrival of the entire Soviet 23rd Tank Corps, with at least 70 tanks. The information was interpreted by Armeeabteilung Fretter-Pico as a sign that the expected Russian attacks would not be long in coming.

This suspicion proved correct, for on 9 January, the northeast flank of the Armeeabteilung was attacked along the entire front of 304. Infanterie-Division. The Russians also thrust at the Millerovo-Kamensk railroad, attacking the rail line at the rail station at Staraja Staniza, which was just south of Millerovo's southern edge. Surprisingly, the division held its defensive positions in the center of the line, near the towns of Chorssijevo and Ssidoro. In the morning the Millerovo perimeter had been assaulted by company strength attacks at isolated points, but by the afternoon the attacks had grown to battalion strength at numerous points along the perimeter. Armeeabteilung Fretter-Pico responded with its only mobile reserve, Schuldt's collection of SS and Police infantry and Luftwaffe Flak detachments.[17]

Gruppe Schuldt, supported by one company of tanks, carried out its first real combined forces attack from near the town of Staraja

---

[15] NA/T-312, roll 1613, 1a KTB, Darstellung der Ereignisse, Armeeabteilung Fretter-Pico. Frame 00067
[16] Ibid. frame 00082.

[17] NA/T-312, roll 1613, Darstellung der Ereignisse, Armeeabteilung Fretter-Pico. frame 000129-000133.

Staniza. German ground attack planes and Stukas supported the attack, strafing and bombing in support of the attack, although adequate artillery support was lacking. In spite of command and organizational difficulties, Kampfgruppe Schuldt cleared Russian troops out of several villages along the railroad and made good progress. The cannon fire from the German tanks and Flak guns quickly disheartened the Russian infantry who uncharacteristically abandoned their defensive positions and fell back quickly before the advance of the Kampfgruppe. However, German infantry casualties were heavy, probably due as much to the lack of artillery as the level of combat training of Schuldt's troops.

After the day's fighting, Schuldt reported to Armeeabteilung Fretter-Pico that his mobile force had many deficiencies, in particular mentioning the Police troops who suffered from insufficient tactical training and lack of combat experience. He requested that an SS company encircled in Millerovo be pulled out and assigned to his Kampfgruppe. Schuldt stated that a further attack was not justified, given the problems and losses encountered during the morning's operation. Fretter-Pico agreed, despite the difficult circumstances of the Armeeabteilung and proposed that Schuldt be allowed to have four to five days of additional training time. He also decided to pull out the SS company that remained in Millerovo and reunite the company with it's parent unit. This did not occur however, as Kreysing refused to give up the SS detachment, which was his only mobile reserve.

At the end of five days, Gruppe Schuldt was to be ready for further commitment, which the Armeeabteilung stated would probably be a reconnaissance thrust conducted on the right or eastern flank of the front, in the Scharapajevka sector. On 10 January fighting remained heavy in the sector of 304. Infanterie-Division, particularly near Scharpajevka and in the center, in the Jeketerinovka-Antonovka-Gorny area. A Soviet attack column consisting of six tanks and thirty other vehicles broke through the center of the division's front north of the exposed battalion in Gorny and advanced in the direction of the village of Kurno Lipovka. A second large Soviet breakthrough occurred on the right flank of the division and it appeared that the Russians were trying to envelop the center of the front held by 304. Infanterie-Division and destroy the battalion in Gorny. Gruppe Schuldt, in spite of the difficulties of the previous day, was instructed to prepare to conduct a reconnaissance in force towards Kurno Lipovka.

The Soviet attacks against the Millerovo perimeter remained heavy and a local breakthrough was achieved by Russian infantry on the northeast section of the perimeter. The penetration was sealed off and eliminated by counterattacks by the SS company and a handful of assault guns. All other attacks were turned back by artillery barrages and machine gun fire. As Kreysing was under continuous attack and heavy pressure, Fretter-Pico allowed the detached company of SS men to remain in Millerovo. During the course of the day, the main effort of the Soviets was determined to be in the Kurno Lipovka-Antonovka area.

That night, Schuldt's Kampfgruppe assembled east of Tarasovka, in the village of Rossosh. At dawn it began its attack, driving eastward toward the neighboring village of Matvejevka, which was occupied by Soviet troops. The battalion of Army Grenadiers and the SS infantry advanced behind a handful of German tanks, while 2cm and 3.7cm Flak guns shelled Russian defensive positions. The determined attack drove the Soviet troops out of the village and forced them to withdraw several kilometers to the east. After mopping up the last remnants of Soviet resistance, Schuldt's battle group assaulted and captured a hill a short distance east of the village, where Russian infantry had taken up hasty positions after being forced out of Matvejevka. However, after the assault and capture of the hill, the attack ran out of steam.

The Kampfgruppe's successes were won at a heavy cost, again attributable to the inadequate level of training of the Police troops and poor performance by II./Gren. Rgt. 575. Schuldt reported that the Army battalion lost half of its men in the assault. Several tanks of Panzer-Abteilung 138 were knocked out as well, losses that the Germans could not afford. Disturbed by the casualties and tank losses, Fretter-Pico realized that to commit Schuldt's Kampfgruppe to continuous counterattacks would result in the destruction of the only mobile force he had at hand. Since he expected the most dangerous situation likely to occur on the eastern flank of the Armeeabteilung front, Fretter-Pico decided to send Gruppe Schuldt to where it could maneuver against a Soviet breakthrough on that vulnerable flank. It was hoped that the Kampfgruppe could recover and conduct additional training, while remaining available to cover the gap between the right flank of Armeeabteilung Fretter-Pico and Armeeabteilung Hollidt's northern flank.[18]

On 12 January, thirty to forty Soviet tanks were reported approaching the gap on Armeeabteilung Fretter-Pico's southern flank, near the town of Djadin. Gruppe Schuldt was ordered to block the advance of any Soviet mobile group that broke through the gap. By the afternoon of that day Schuldt's Kampfgruppe arrived in the area of Novy Jerochin, which was about ten kilometers east of Kamensk, on the Kalitvenez River. Fortunately for the Germans, the Russians were largely inactive in this sector for a time and for the most part, the realignment proceeded according to plan and without serious

---

[18] NA/T-312, roll 1613- 1a KTB, Darstellung der Ereignisse Armeeabteilung Fretter-Pico. Frame 000143-000144.

interruption. However, this short period of quiet proved only to be the calm before the storm when the Russians burst out of the gap south of Armeeabteilung Fretter-Pico's right (southeastern) flank, driving toward Kamensk and the Donets crossings. In the path of the Soviet armor was Gruppe Schuldt at Novy Jerochin and a hastily organized detachment of German troops near Kamensk.

Early on the morning of 14 January, a Soviet armored force of approximately forty tanks advanced toward Novy Jerochin, while a total of fifty other tanks were reported at the nearby town of Orechkova. These tanks belonged to the 26th and 99th Tank Brigades of the 2nd Tank Corps, which had come out of Stavka reserve in late December and joined the 3rd Guards Army in early January. Gruppe Schuldt was quickly overwhelmed by the Soviet tank attacks. Within a short time, the German defenses folded up and the Russian tank column continued west, without suffering significant losses. Most of the surviving members of Gruppe Schuldt made their way out of the battle area and headed south toward Kamensk.

Led by the armor of the 26th Brigade, the 2nd Tank Corps completely broke through the weak German defenses and continued on a westward course roughly parallel to the Donets. In a short time the rampaging Soviet tank columns reached a point approximately fifteen kilometers north of Kamensk, completely severing the southern flank of 304. Infanterie-Division from contact with German forces in Kamensk. At the same time, attacks began in the Donskoj area, which were quickly recognized as an attempt to encircle the strong point. Apprised of these developments, Heeresgruppe B ordered each of the strong points to be held, strictly forbidding any withdrawals.[19]

The main body of the 2nd Tank Corps continued west, cutting the Millerovo-Kamensk railroad line. A smaller Soviet detachment, consisting of about a dozen tanks with infantry riding on the tank decks, lunged south toward Kamensk. This lightning quick thrust arrived at the northern edge of the town and took the Germans by surprise. Before the defenders could react, the T-34s raced into the center of the town. The Soviets were attempting to reach the main bridge over the Donets, which was defended by heavy Flak batteries, a few anti-tank guns and German Pioniere troops. However, the German troops at the bridge had been alerted by the time the T-34s careened into sight and the gun crews were at their weapons and ready for action. Eight T-34s were hit by 88s or German anti-tank guns and were put out of action, forcing the Soviet infantry to scramble off the tanks and try to rush the bridge. Heavy fire from the 2cm Flak guns and MG-42s pinned down the surviving Russian

infantry. Immediately the Germans launched counterattacks on the remaining Russian troops, which forced them to withdraw.[20]

By the later hours of the morning, German air reconnaissance discovered that the 26th Tank Brigade, after reaching the Millerovo-Kamensk railroad, had also turned south, towards Kamensk and the Donets. In the wake of the tank brigade followed a 200 vehicle column of motorized infantry, towed guns and truck mounted rocket artillery. This force assembled along the railroad north of Kamensk during the course of the day, after the failure to seize the bridge by surprise attack. It was obvious that a strong attack upon Kamensk could be expected within a short time and Fretter-Pico informed Heeresgruppe B that he had no counterattack force available. The armor and main body of 7. Panzer-Division, en route from Heeresgruppe Don's Armeeabteilung Hollidt, was still twenty kilometers southeast of Kamensk and not immediately available to provide the mobility and firepower to oppose the Russian advance. Fretter-Pico transmitted a message to Heeresgruppe Don also, requesting Panzergrenadier troops, anti-tank guns and assault gun detachments. In response, the army group notified Fretter-Pico that 7. Panzer-Division would be placed at the disposal of the Armeeabteilung and would take up positions south of the river and west of Kamensk. The 302. Infanterie-Division was also assigned to the army, but its main elements were still in transit and only part of a Pioniere company of the division had actually arrived in Kamensk.

Gruppe Kreysing and 304. Infanterie-Division found themselves in danger of being entirely cut off when their supply lines leading to the Northern Donets were severed by the Soviet attack. Due to the swiftness of the advance and the overwhelming strength of the Soviet force, Fretter-Pico issued orders for Kreysing to abandon Millerovo and conduct a fighting withdrawal to the west. German and Italian garrisons at Chertkovo and Gartmaschevka were also instructed to break out and attempt to make their escape.[21]

The 304. Infanterie-Division was ordered to swing its right flank back and link up with Kreysing, in order to attack the remaining Soviet forces in the Glubokij area, all the while conducting a phased withdrawal. This was a complicated maneuver for even an experienced combat division, much less a mediocre unit encumbered with wounded and accompanied by its rear area and supply troops. Later

---

[19] NA/T-312, roll 1613- 1a KTB, Darstellung der Ereignisse Armeeabteilung Fretter-Pico. Frame 000185.

[20] Ibid. Frame 000185-186.

[21] Led by a handful of tanks and assault guns, German troops, supported by a few still combat capable Italian Blackshirt troops, broke out of their encirclements on 15-16 January. Stukas and other German ground attack planes conducted repeated attacks on Soviet strong points blocking the advance of the attacks. The desperate columns were able to punch through Russian lines and the survivors of both garrisons eventually reached safety, after incredible suffering and unimaginable hardships. A grim account of the escape from Chertkovo, and the breakout from Gartmaschevka, is available in the book *Few Returned*, an account written by an Italian officer who took part in the breakout.

Two defensive positions on the perimeter of the town of Millerovo. The only first class troops belonging to Armeeabteilung Fretter-Pico was the battle group of 3. Gebirgs-Division, commanded by Generalmajor Hans Kreysing. In December of 1942, the tough mountain troops defended the key town of Millerovo against two Russian tanks corps. Kreysing only abandoned the devastated town when it was encircled and cut off from contact with the rest of Armeeabteilung Fretter-Pico. (Credit National Archives)

in the day, the division was ordered to pull back to the river. Gruppe Kreysing was directed to fight its way to freedom, carrying its wounded and whatever heavy weapons could be moved. After breaking out of Millerovo, Kreysing intended to fight his way to Donskoj and link up with the troops there. The Donskoj garrison still had a handful of operational assault guns and tanks, which were invaluable for spearheading the withdrawal to the Donets.

Gruppe Schuldt remained out of radio contact with the Armeeabteilung for most of the day, while its remnants struggled into Kamensk throughout the night and following morning. It was ordered to reinforce Gruppe Baer, the Kampfgruppe defending Kamensk and both of these detachments were subordinated to XXXXVIII. Panzer-Korps on the following day. Armeeabteilung Fretter-Pico itself became part of Manstein's Heeresgruppe Don on 16 January, 1943. Fretter-Pico promptly reported his most serious immediate shortage, which was a lack of anti-tank capability. Heeresgruppe Don provided immediate help, assigning 7. Panzer-Division a major portion of the right flank of the Armeeabteilung. The XXXXVIII. Panzer-Korps took over defense of the Kamensk sector and was reinforced with newly arrived elements of 302. Infanterie-Division.

Over the next several days, Gruppe Kreysing and the Donskoj garrison conducted a grueling retreat to the southwest, toward the Derkul River, which it was ordered to hold. About ten kilometers due north of Voroshilovgrad, the Northern Donets formed a roughly triangular shaped bend approximately twelve kilometers in breadth at its base. Voroshilovgrad lay approximately ten kilometers south of the point of the triangle. The Derkul River intersected with the

Donets River about fifteen kilometers east of this bend, flowing into the larger river from the north. Gruppe Kreysing was under attacks on both flanks and was burdened with a growing number of casualties. The wounded endured sub-zero temperatures during harsh nights spent in the open steppe and suffered from frostbite.

The fighting and constant retreat took its toll and Kreysing made it clear that his exhausted men could not hold a line on the Derkul River for long if attacked in strength. He stated that a continuation of the retreat to the Derkul, over open ground, in the dead of winter, would only result in additional casualties and further erode the fighting strength of the unit. The river "line" itself had no prepared positions and under these circumstances, the Armeeabteilung subsequently realized that the exhausted troops of Gruppe Kreysing would be unlikely to be able to hold the Derkul River line for any length of time. Kreysing was therefore ordered to turn south, cross the Donets and occupy a sector of the triangular river bend north of Voroshilovgrad. On the following day, after an uneventful crossing, Kreysing's rear guard reached the southern bank the Donets River without any contact with Russian troops. A few artillery shells struck along the march route but the previous active and close pursuit was abandoned by the Soviet tank corps.

The 304. Infanterie-Division suffered to a lesser extent, because the Russians did not maintain close contact with the division during much of the retreat. The main Soviet forces turned south towards Kamensk or drove further west, advancing upon Voroshilovgrad. When the division withdrew southward, its route of withdrawal was west of the attacks on Kamensk and passed south of the main Soviet columns driving to the west. The only contacts were made by Russian reconnaissance detachments, which harassed the division as it made its way slowly toward the river. By 18 January, the bulk of 304. Infanterie-Division crossed the Donets, only lightly pressured by the Russians.

Armeeabteilung Fretter-Pico attempted to pull its scattered elements together and build up a defensive line along the Donets. Gruppe Schuldt, along with weak detachments of 7. Panzer-Division, assembled east of Voroshilovgrad, at the town of Novo Sswetlovka. It was soon to be reinforced by a high quality SS battalion. In light of the seriousness of the situation, earlier in January, the OKH had ordered the SS-Generalkommando to send other SS troops to Armeeabteilung Fretter-Pico, in order to reinforce Gruppe Schuldt.

Accordingly, the SS command dispatched I./Regiment "Der Führer," reinforced with a platoon of Pioniere troops of 16. /"Der Führer," two batteries of 10cm howitzers and a Flak battery. This welcome reinforcement arrived in Voroshilovgrad on 22 January. By the next day, the reinforced battalion occupied defensive position west of the city, between the villages of Alexandrovka and Sabovka. The commander of the battalion was SS-Hauptsturmführer Hans Opificius. Due to the industrious efforts of the SS officers, the battalion grew to nearly regimental strength during the next few days, incorporating various volunteers and small units. On 28 January, 1943 Schuldt took over command of the entire odd assortment of troops, which included the remnants of his SS and Police troops and Panzer-Abteilung 138. His combat group occupied a section of the perimeter around the town of Voroshilovgrad.[22]

The Soviet 6th Guards Rifle Corps, made up of the 44th, 38th and 58th Guards Rifle Divisions, advanced upon Voroshilovgrad. A group of Soviet armor, consisting of forty to fifty tanks was detected by a German pilot south of the Donets. The Russian armor was near the villages of Makarov Jar and Krushilovka, which were just east of Voroshilovgrad. That area of the front was held by the Italian Division "Ravenna," and Fretter-Pico knew that a Soviet tank attack on that hapless division could be expected to succeed very quickly. By evening, however, the Soviet tanks spotted by the German aircraft had somehow disappeared and their exact location was unknown. It was expected however, that the armor would support the attack of the 6th Guards Rifle Corps upon Voroshilovgrad, probably attacking from the east.[23]

On 24 January, Armeeabteilung Fretter-Pico was ordered by Heeresgruppe Don to occupy a defense line along the undefended

[22] Weidinger, Otto. Division *Das Reich-1943*: vol. IV, (Osnabück: 1979) page 463.

[23] NA/T-312, roll1613, Darstellung der Ereignisse, Armeeabteilung Fretter-Pico. Frame 000233-235.

Marshal Ion Antonescu, the Rumanian military leader and head of state, reviews Rumanian army troops in southern Russia in late 1942. Manstein stands on the left of this picture. Antonescu was deposed in August of 1944, when the Rumanians grew tired of the war and it was clear that Germany was going to lose the war. (Credit National Archives)

Aidar River, in order to close the gap which existed between the Northern Donets and Heeresgruppe Mitte's 2. Armee. The river's course extended north, from a point just northwest of the triangular bend. The river ran from the Northern Donets into the town of Starobelsk. The 19. Panzer-Division and the very weak remnants of 27. Panzer-Division were located in the Starobelsk area and were fighting for possession of the town against elements of the Soviet 6th Army. The two divisions were assigned to the Armeeabteilung by Heeresgruppe Mittle. Although somewhat strengthened by the much weakened Panzer divisions, the Armeeabteilung felt its forces remained inadequate to defend the Donets, much less the Aidar as well. There still existed the possibility that strong Soviet forces north of the Donets might lunge west, cross the Aidar in strength and advance on Izyum, a key city on the Northern Donets, where the river swung to the north after passing west of Voroshilovgrad. Beyond Izyum was Kharkov, the largest and most important industrial city in the southern Ukraine.

Additional help was on the way, in the form of a new infantry division, the 335. Infanterie-Division, although its units arrived slowly and had to be committed piece meal. Elements of 7. Panzer-Division continued to arrive by land march and rail and took over defense of a stretch of the Donets west of Voroshilovgrad, although other formations of the division were still passing through Kamensk on that date. The Soviets had crossed the Donets at many points by that time, establishing a number of small bridgeheads to the north and east of Voroshilovgrad. On 25 January, Kampfgruppe Schuldt counterattacked Soviet troops occupying the town of Sheltoje, which was on the southern bank of the Donets, at a point a few kilometers to the northwest of Voroshilovgrad. The SS troops recaptured the small town and drove the Russians back across the still frozen river. Gruppe Kreysing wiped out several other small Soviet bridgeheads northwest of the city, his weary troops suffering serious casualties in the fighting.

On the southeastern flank of the Armeeabteilung, the forces of the 5th Tank Army continued to assemble east and north of Kamensk during the last days of the month while the Soviet 6th Army battled 19. Panzer-Division for the possession of Starobelsk. The available units of 7. Panzer-Division remained ready for action west of Voroshilovgrad, awaiting the attack of the Soviet tank corps. Soviet reconnaissance attacks probed the front of 304. Infanterie-Division constantly, seeking to find gaps or weak spots. At a number of locations, the German records state that the Russians had thrown ice bridges (Eisbrücken) across the Donets, although exactly how this was done is not mentioned.[24]

On 28 January, 335. Infanterie-Division took over defense of a large sector of the river west of Voroshilovgrad. Armeeabteilung Fretter-Pico, based on the level of Russian reconnaissance activity, decided that it could expect attacks designed to destroy Axis forces in Voroshilovgrad. It was assumed that two attacking forces would attempt to link up west of Voroshilovgrad and encircle the city, or possibly attack the perimeter from two directions at once.

Soviet activity gradually grew in intensity throughout the next day, particularly on both flanks of the Armeeabteilung. Air reconnaissance reported large Soviet forces massed north and east of the river and by 30 January the German command recognized that a new, full scale Soviet offensive had commenced. This was the beginning of the operation known as "Gallop," which was launched at the same time as a second major offensive to the north, code named "Star." The drama of the battles for Kharkov and Manstein's counterattack, the last major German victory in Russia, was about to begin.

The Defensive Battles of Armeeabteilung Fretter-Pico

After Operation "Little Saturn" lurched to a halt south of the Bystraja River and along the Northern Donets River, Soviet offensive operations gradually ceased due to combat exhaustion and logistical deficiencies which doomed any sustained penetration operations. The Russians had accomplished the destruction of the Italian 8th Army and had severely pummeled Armeeabteilung Hollidt, however the offensive had fallen behind schedule almost immediately. The Axis troops holding the key towns along the Rossosh-Kantemirovka-Millerovo-Voroshilovgrad were to have been wiped

Manstein in a staff car trying to make his way through a column of Rumanian and German soldiers and vehicles. The road is in poor shape and a vehicle has become stuck in the mud in front of Manstein's car. The picture was dated November of 1942 and apparently was taken shortly after Manstein took command of Heeresgruppe Don. (Credit National Archives)

Hitler on one of his rare visits to the Eastern Front in early 1942. After he assumed complete command of the German military Hitler and Manstein disagreed frequently over the conduct of the war in Russia. Manstein was a gifted strategist and probably Germany's finest commander. He understood mobile warfare and could visualize long term concepts. Hitler often hampered Manstein's conduct of the war after he gave him command of Armeegruppe Don. The dictator flew to the army group headquarters in early 1943, possibly planning to sack Manstein for the loss of Kharkov. (Credit National Archives)

---

[24] Ibid. frame 000265.

out by the third day of the offensive and the airfields at Morozovsk and Tatsinskaya taken by the end of operations on the fourth day. None of these goals were accomplished, primarily due to the defensive fighting by German troops at various points in the sector which slowed the Soviet rate of advance by stubbornly holding on to key towns and stations along the railroads. The attrition suffered by Russian infantry and tank troops during the fighting weakened the Soviet offensive from the start. The offensive was not able to create major Soviet penetrations across the Northern Donets or Bystraja Rivers and did not establish strong bridgeheads across either river.

By the end of the first week of January, encircled Axis troops at Millerovo, Gartmaschevka and Chertkovo tied down major elements of the 1st Guards Army during a critical phase of the offensive. The fighting to capture these stubbornly held towns consumed vital Russian infantry and armor strength, as well as artillery and fuel supplies that could have been of vital importance farther south. By the time the armies approached the Northern Donets River, Soviet rifle divisions were reduced from a strength of 3500 to 5000 men, to less than 1000 effectives in some cases. Ammunition, fuel and artillery were in short supply and the 17th and 18th Tank Corps spearheads were bogged down in the fighting for Millerovo, Donskoj and possession of the railroad south of Millerovo. Additional Soviet forces were occupied by the attacks of 19. Panzer-Division at Streltskovo. The weakening of the Soviet rifle divisions, insufficient logistical capabilities and losses of armor left them too weak to sustain operations south of the Bystraja River and the 24th Tank Corps was eventually forced to give up the airfield at Tatsinskaya.

The dogged resistance of Armeeabteilung Fretter-Pico in the Voroshilovgrad area would prove to be of great significance when the events of January-February 1943 unfolded to the west and north of this area. When Kuznetsov's 1st Guards Army was unable to drive Kreysing's division from Millerovo with the forces initially at hand, it was forced to concentrate three rifle divisions around the town and begin concentric assaults on the Millerovo defensive perimeter. Armor from the mobile groups of the army had to be used to support infantry attacks on the town. This tied up dwindling Soviet tank, infantry and artillery strength when these resources were needed to force a crossing of the Northern Donets and capture the key airfields. The 18th and 17th Tank Corps, which had reached the Millerovo area by 23-25 December, 1942, were still there in mid January of 1943. Without control of Millerovo and the Kantemirovka-Millerovo-Kamensk railroad, the poor road net in the surrounding area was not adequate to maintain Soviet offensive momentum.

The Chertkovo garrison was encircled on 22 December and began a protracted defense of the town that lasted until 16 January.

German and Italian troops, after being encircled by Soviet mobile groups, fought on at the towns of Gartmashevka and near Arbuzovka. At both towns, stubborn defensive efforts forced the Russians to conduct costly and time consuming operations to eliminate the defenders. This robbed the Russian mobile groups of infantry support, critically hampering them and contributed to the failure of the Russians to achieve decisive offensive gains further to the south. The encircled Axis forces, in defensive actions of primarily German troops, by effective, though doomed resistance, limited Soviet gains south of the Donets to small bridgeheads south of the river. These bridgeheads were established late in the month, after attrition had eroded the ability of the Soviets to exploit these river crossings.

It is interesting to consider Hitler's orders demanding that his divisions stand and fight to the last man, in the light of the "Little Saturn" offensive. Although clearly not the desirable course of action, this tactic was not entirely without merit, particularly considering the constantly diminishing mobility of the German infantry divisions, which were not nearly as mobile as is commonly believed. By the second year of the war in Russia, stocks of motor vehicles remained inadequate to fully supply even the German mobile divisions. Most of the German infantry divisions still depended on horses to move their artillery and other heavy weapons.

In any event, the stubborn resistance of the Axis forces encircled at a number of locations, forced the Stavka to conduct multiple missions by the 1st Guards Army and the 3rd Guards Army. Simultaneously with the continuing deep operational phases, each was forced to mount difficult and costly siege operations at Millerovo, Chertkovo and Gartashevka as well as at several other smaller encirclements. This eroded the tank strength of the Soviet tank corps and fatally delayed their exploitation operations.

All of these factors robbed the Soviet armies of offensive strength before the critical attacks of the 24th and 25th Tank Corps upon Tatsinskaya and Morozovsk and the 17th and 18th Tank Corps advance toward the Northern Donets. After the Soviet tank corps were halted by Armeeabteilung Hollidt south of the Bystraja and drained of their strength around Millerovo, the offensive ran out of steam. Although fighting continued north of the Donets throughout the remainder of January, the offensive never regained its momentum primarily due to the grinding, costly defensive fighting against Armeeabteilungen Fretter-Pico and Hollidt.

Soviet force structure shortcomings, logistical deficiencies and attrition had threatened to undermine the likelihood of a complete success from the start. Casualties in many Soviet rifle divisions were heavy even before the offensive began and tank corps had suffered 30 to 50 per cent tank losses by the end of December. Even in this weakened condition, the Russian attack overwhelmed and destroyed the Italian 8th Army and fragmented German divisions attached to the army. The offensive also doomed any possibility of the Germans conducting a successful relief operation to reach Stalingrad. However, the dogged resistance of surrounded, desperate German troops at bleak towns like Millerovo prevented the Russians from crossing the Northern Donets in early December. Worn out German Panzer troops and emaciated infantry divisions encircled and destroyed the 24th Tank Corps around Tatsinskaya and inflicted heavy losses on the 25th Tank Corps and 1st Mechanized near Morozovsk.

It is unlikely that Armeeabteilung Fretter-Pico could have prevented the 1st Guards Army tank corps from crossing the Donets in strength if the Soviets had not been delayed at Millerovo and other towns. Had the 17th and 18th Tank Corps been able to reach the Northern Donets on 23-24 December, there would have been little the Germans could have done to prevent the Russians from crossing the frozen river and exploiting further to the south. What affect this would have had regarding the operations of Armeeabteilung Hollidt forces fighting the 24th and 25th Tank Corps at Tatsinskaya and north of Morozovsk, cannot be known. It would have forced the Germans to commit scarce armor strength against the 17th and 18th Tank Corps to block a potential Soviet advance southward from the Northern Donets. The influence of such an offensive drive on decisions made by Hitler or Manstein can only be speculated upon.

Remarkably, Fretter-Pico's inadequate collection of disparate troops sufficiently delayed the Soviets and prevented them from crossing the Northern Donets until 1. Panzerarmee arrived and took over defense of the river at the end of January. Once the subsequent Soviet offensives, known as Operations "Gallop" and "Star" began, 1. Panzerarmee, holding a line from Voroshilovgrad to Slavyansk, gradually deflected the Soviet attack to the west. The Soviet swing westward, due in part to stalwart defense of the river by 1. Panzerarmee, contributed to conditions that were ultimately fatal to "Gallop" and "Star," In February, as the Russian attempts to create a decisive penetration south of the Northern Donets were frustrated and blocked time and again, the Stavka swung the tank corps of the Southwestern Front west of the stubbornly held bas-

tion at Slavyansk. This stretched the already faltering Soviet supply organization past its limits. At the same time, Russian overconfidence contributed to a faulty analysis of intelligence information and a mistaken estimation of German capabilities and intentions. As a result of this miscalculation, the tank reserves of the front were committed to a drive to capture the Dnepr crossings and the rail line between Dnepropetrovsk and Kharkov. This effort diluted the strength of the Soviet effort in the decisive direction, which was due south of the Donets, towards the coast of the Sea of Azov.

This relocation of Soviet forces to the west handed the Germans an opportunity to launch a counteroffensive against the overextended Russian spearheads pushing westward toward the Dnepr and the railroad lines between Dnepropetrovsk and Kharkov. This counteroffensive was planned and orchestrated by Manstein and directed by Hermann Hoth, the commander of 4. Panzerarmee. It was led by the only German Panzer divisions in the East that were capable of conducting the counteroffensive, the reorganized SS Panzer divisions. The Army Panzer divisions were not able to lead the attack, as they were too weak from months of hard fighting. Most of the Army divisions had less than twenty operational tanks, their Panzergrenadier regiments were reduced to the size of weak battalions and most artillery regiments possessed less than a dozen guns. The nearly exhausted divisions were still able to conduct supporting operations, but could not carry the main weight of the attack.

Manstein turned to the only available Panzer divisions that had the strength and the aggressive confidence to lead the counteroffensive. These were the three SS Panzergrenadier divisions of the SS-Panzer-Korps, commanded by the senior combat commander of the Waffen-SS, Paul Hausser. Two of these divisions were almost lost to Manstein, due to decisions made by Adolf Hitler, who committed them to the defense of the city of Kharkov, where they were nearly encircled and destroyed. Only through the courage of Hausser, who defied a direct order by Hitler, were they saved from ruin before Manstein needed them. Although "Das Reich" and "Leibstandarte" were weakened by weeks of hard fighting, which cost them many casualties and serious losses of tanks, they combined with "Totenkopf" to form the primary attack group of Manstein's Kharkov counteroffensive.

2

THE CREATION OF THE SS-PANZERKORPS

Before the outbreak of World War II, Hitler allowed the creation of SS combat formations because he believed the military elite of the party should pay a price in blood during the war so that they could be respected in the post war years.[1] This concept was held by some of the higher leaders of the SS as illustrated by SS-Obergruppenführer Erich von dem Bach-Zelewski's opinion that it was important that the 'most senior leadership cadres of the Schutzstaffel will have made a blood sacrifice in this life or death struggle of the people.'[2] The SS combat divisions served under various Army corps commands, while Reichsführer-SS Heinrich Himmler established more and more Waffen-SS divisions. He intended to create SS corps and then armies, building a substantial body of troops more or less under his control, although most remained under Army command. These ambitious plans caused some discomfort among Army officers, who found that 'the limitless SS plans of expansion . . . were disquieting.'

The endlessly scheming Himmler had given thought to the organization of a corps of SS field troops even before the beginning of the war. In 1938, he speculated about removing all those Allgemeine SS personnel who were serving in the Army, in order to provide experienced men and officers to lead his expanding private army. Requests submitted to the Reich Finance Minister in 1941-42, provide an unmistakable indication that Himmler intended to establish Waffen-SS corps long before 1943. These funding requests included appropriation of funds for six SS-Obergruppenführer positions, a rank equivalent to Army corps commander. The successful military performance of the Waffen-SS divisions during the first years of the war lent support to Himmler's ambitions.

The wartime performance of officers and men of his personal bodyguard troop, "Leibstandarte-SS-Adolf Hitler" influenced Hitler greatly and he probably needed little encouragement to agree with Himmler when the Reichsführer proposed to establish the first SS-Panzer-Korps. In addition, the senior officer of the SS military divisions, SS-Obergruppenführer Paul Hausser, had pressed Himmler and Hitler about the need for a full complement of tanks for the three SS divisions, insisting that the armor would increase their effectiveness. The Führer agreed, in spite of the misgivings of the Army and many of its officers. Although they did not complain about the hard fighting Waffen-SS divisions when they were placed under their command during the war, some Army officers looked with wariness and apprehension upon the expansion of the SS before and during the war. However, Hitler decided to allow Himmler to establish the SS-Generalkommando on 13 May, 1942. Two months later, the corps was formally established by a 9 July, 1942 order and began forming in France under Hausser.[3]

Hitler believed that the SS divisions were imbued with sufficient 'will' and fighting spirit to provide him victories in the East, even under the most trying conditions. The SS-Panzer-Korps, made up of the three oldest and most experienced divisions of the Waffen-SS, was given an opportunity to justify his confidence in their abilities in Manstein's Kharkov counteroffensive.[4]

The "Leibstandarte-SS-Adolf Hitler," 2.SS-Division "Das Reich" and 3.SS-"Totenkopf"-Division were withdrawn from the Russian front at various times during 1942. They were subsequently sent to France in order to rest, reorganize and recover from months of heavy fighting on the Eastern Front. Each of the divisions was to

[1] Koehl, Robert L. *The Black Corps: The Structure and Power Struggles of the Nazi SS*. (Madison: 1983) pg. 198.
[2] Wegner, Bernd. *The Waffen SS: Organization, Ideology and Function* (Oxford: 1990) pg. 292.

[3] Wegner. pg. 342.
[4] Bender, Roger J. and Taylor, Hugh Page. *Uniforms, Organization and History of the Waffen SS*. (San Jose: 1971) vol. 2, pg. 32.

Reichsführer-SS Heinrich Himmler on a visit to the Eastern Front in 1943. Himmler had unlimited plans for the growth of the Waffen-SS and had prepared for the creation of SS corps in 1942. He encouraged Hitler to create more and more SS divisions and enthusiastically agreed with Paul Hausser, the senior military officer of the Waffen-SS, who proposed that the SS divisions needed tanks and armored vehicles to maximize their effectiveness. The ground work for creating additional SS divisions and corps was begun by Himmler in mid-1942 and was not a consequence of the recapture of Kharkov, as is commonly believed. (Credit National Archives)

be converted into a Panzergrenadier division by the addition of a tank battalion and the required support units. In fact, the divisions all received a complete Panzer regiment of two battalions of tanks and were Panzer divisions in every way but name. One Panzergrenadier battalion of each division received a full complement of lightly armored half tracks. The other battalions of the Panzergrenadier regiments were motorized and were equipped with trucks, heavy cars and various vehicle types. These included companies equipped with motorcycles, armored cars and amphibious Volkswagens, the versatile and valuable Schwimmwagen.

The history of each of the first three SS divisions is closely interwoven with the life of their first divisional commanders. These men organized, trained and shaped the personality and military performance of their divisions to an extraordinary degree. Each had a strong, distinctive personality, which greatly influenced the character of the divisions which they commanded. They were extremely dissimilar men, shaped by very different cultural and military backgrounds. They had little in common except duty in the Waffen-SS and service in the German Army during World War I. One was a rough, battle scarred former Bavarian artillery and tank service NCO, named Josef (Sepp) Dietrich, who organized and led the SS guard units that eventually became 1.SS-Panzergrenadier-Division "Leibstandarte-SS-Adolf Hitler." The second was Paul Hausser who organized and trained the SS regiments that evolved into 2.SS-Panzergrenadier-Division "Das Reich." Hausser was a former German Army Generalleutnant, a lean, acerbic Prussian with General Staff training who was also the founder of the SS Officer school organization. The third man, the first commander of 3. SS-"Totenkopf"-Division, was Theodore Eicke, who was a virulent National Socialist and former commander of Dachau concentration camp. Like many other German veterans, Eicke had found no place for himself in the Germany of the post war years, until he joined the SS and discovered his life's calling. The three men could hardly have been more different, but each left his own strong imprint on their divisions, as well as the combat history of the Waffen-SS itself.

SS-Obergruppenführer Sepp Dietrich and 1.SS-Panzer-Grenadier-Division "Leibstandarte-SS-Adolf Hitler"

Sepp Dietrich played a key role in or witnessed many of the seminal events of the Nazi Party and of the Waffen-SS. Dietrich was born in the Bavarian province of Swabia in 1892, the oldest of six children and was the only son of three that survived the war. Dietrich served with the 4. Bayerische-Feldartillerie-Regiment until he was injured shortly before the beginning of World War I and had to leave the army. With the outbreak of war, he again enlisted, serving in 7. Bayerische-Feldartillerie-Regiment. He was wounded twice before being transferred to Infanterie-Artillerie-Abteilung 10.

The battalion furnished artillery support for the elite assault troops of the German Army, the Stösstruppen. The gun crews wheeled their short barreled infantry howitzers into position to fire at close range, in direct fire support of Stösstruppen assaults. The crews had to be special men, as they were required to man handle their stubby barreled guns over trenches and the debris of no man's land. This obviously called for a good measure of physical strength, as well as ample courage. Dietrich won an Iron Cross, 2nd class sometime during 1917 and may have won the Iron Cross, 1st class also. In 1918 he was transferred to an A7V tank detachment, which put him on the scene of a historic development in the German Army, the first deployment of German armor. While serving with the Bavarian tank detachment, he was again decorated, winning the Bavarian Military Service Cross, 3rd Class.

Dietrich was discharged from the Army in 1918, although he would have rather have remained in the service. After he left the Army he entered the civil unrest, economic disaster and rebellion that was post-war Germany. He became a member of the Freikorps Oberland and fought in Silesia in 1919, opposing Polish irregular forces who attempted to seize the territory after a plebiscite resulted in a vote by the majority of the population to remain part of Germany. He never lost the pragmatic, rough and ready, freewheeling mentality typical of the Freikorps units. His command style reflected a roughshod man experienced in hardship, bloodshed and the harsh realities of war.

Dietrich was familiar with the relaxed form of relationship between men and officers in the Waffen-SS because of his wartime service with the Stösstruppen units. These elite combat troops called their officers by first names, used the familiar du' when speaking

Paul Hausser, the senior Waffen-SS commander during World War II. Hausser was a former Generalleutnant of the German Army who had extensive command experience during World War I. After his retirement from the Army Heinrich Himmler persuaded Hausser to join the SS and gave him the task of bringing competence and professionalism to the SS officer corps. Hausser organized a number of SS military training schools, known as Junkerschulen, and developed a standardized program of military education. He instituted modern training principles that emphasized realistic training methods, less emphasis on parade drill and a high standard of physical fitness. He was also the first commander of the SS-Verfügungsdivision, later redesignated as 2.SS-Panzergrenadier-Division "Das Reich." Hausser survived the war despite several serious wounds and died at the age of 92. He was widely respected and his funeral was attended by thousands of former members of the Waffen-SS. (Credit National Archives)

with them and were a highly trained, elite assault force. The Stösstruppen developed tactics which emphasized mobility, combined arms fire power and penetration of defensive lines using infiltration methods. Very different from the more traditional Army relationships between officers and men, the Waffen-SS developed a style of discipline during the prewar years that was designed to create a closer comradeship which was based on mutual respect and performance.

The front line experience of trench warfare and the post war service with the embittered, nihilistic Freikorps veterans produced men who were described by fellow veteran and writer Ernst Junger as:

> 'Princes of the trenches, with their hard set faces, brave to madness, tough and agile, with keen blood-thirsty nerves'

The Freikorps veterans were interestingly described by none other than Herman Göring, as men who 'could not be de-brutalized.' Seeking to lead and be led, despising both the new government and a society in which he had found little satisfaction, Dietrich found a home in the comradeship of the SS.

Dietrich probably saw Adolf Hitler for the first time when he heard Hitler speak before a group of military troops. At this time Dietrich was a policeman, a member of the Bavarian Landpolizei although he maintained ties with the "Oberland" Freikorps. Two years later he was in Munich with other men of the "Oberland" Freikorps when Hitler attempted to launch a National Socialist revolution in the ill-fated Beer Hall Putsch. In 1928 he joined the SS and was appointed commander of the Munich SS-Standarte 1. Dietrich was one of the small group of rough brawlers who served as bodyguards and drivers for Hitler. They were absolutely loyal to Hitler and defended him with all the brutal expertise learned from their years in the trenches.

Sepp Dietrich, the commander of 1. SS-Panzergrenadier-Division "Leibstandarte-SS-Adolf Hitler." He was also a veteran of World War 1 and served in a Bavarian field artillery unit attached to elite Stösstruppen units. Toward the end of the war, he was a gunner in one of the first tanks used by the Germans and took part in some of the earliest tank versus tank combat. Dietrich organized and led the SS guard detachments responsible for Hitler's personal safety in the early years of the Nazi party. The original 120 man guard unit gradually expanded to regiment size and its mission changed from parade and guard tasks to preparation for full combat duty. Dietrich led the division until spring 1943 when he took command of I. SS-Panzer-Korps. He later commanded 6. Panzerarmee in the winter of 1944, during the German counteroffensive in the Ardennes known as the Battle of the Bulge. (Credit National Archives)

The 1a, or chief of staff, of "Leibstandarte" was Rudolf Lehmann, pictured here as an SS-Obersturmbannführer. Lehmann joined the SS in 1933, volunteering for service in "Leibstandarte." In 1935 he was sent to the Junkerschule at Bad Tolz and finished his officer training in 1936, completing the course of instruction with the rank of SS-Untersturmführer. He was posted to "Leibstandarte" in 1942 and proved to be an exceptionally intelligent and valuable addition to Dietrich's staff. Dietrich had no formal military training and depended heavily upon his chief of staff's training and ability. Lehmann commanded "Das Reich" at the end of the war. He won the Knight's Cross and Oakleaves as well as both grades of the Iron Cross and the German Cross in Gold. (Courtesy of Mark C. Yerger)

In time however, a more organized security detachment became necessary to adequately protect Hitler and other Nazi leaders. On March 17, 1933, Dietrich was ordered to organize the Berlin "Stabswache" (headquarters guard detachment) which was charged with the protection of the Führer. At its establishment the "Stabswache" was placed under the administrative authority of a Prussian police unit known as Police Detachment "Wecke," named after its commander. The Stabswache was in effect a police auxiliary unit, whose budget was paid out of the federal budget. Although it was an SS formation and technically a Police unit, it was not under the direct control of Himmler or the Police. Dietrich and his men were essentially responsible only to Hitler himself.

In the summer of 1934 Dietrich and the "Leibstandarte" were chosen by Hitler to be among the SS units that carried out the arrest and executions of members of Ernst Roehm's SA leadership during the "Night of the Long Knives." The emasculation of the SA solidified support for Hitler by the German Army when it eliminated the threat to the Army posed by the SA. The Army showed its gratitude through public praise for Hitler and an increased level of cooperation with SS commanders with regard to training. Obviously relieved at the demise of the SA, it was evident that the Army did not feel threatened at the time by the SS due to its small size.

Dietrich's relationships with higher SS authorities, including even Himmler himself, often demonstrated that he considered Adolf Hitler as the only authority that he had to answer to. As a result, he proved to be a source of irritation to Himmler on more than one occasion. In 1938 Himmler wrote a stern note to Dietrich after he was offended by statements Dietrich made to the German press regarding publicity concerning the fifth anniversary of the establishment of "Leibstandarte."

'Your officers are good enough to recognize me personally, but otherwise the "Leibstandarte-SS-Adolf Hitler" is an undertaking for itself and does what it wants without bothering about orders from above and which thinks about the SS leadership only when some debt or other, which one of its gentlemen has incurred, has to be paid or when someone has fallen into the mud and has to be pulled out of the mess . . .'[5]

Dietrich further angered Himmler by maintaining close ties with certain individuals and units of the Army, including General Werner von Fritsch, the commander of the Wehrkreis that included Berlin. A particularly close relationship was formed with men and

The first commander of "Leibstandarte's" Panzer regiment was SS-Obersturmbann-führer Georg Schönberger (foreground of picture) shown as several tanks of his regiment division pass behind him. He led the regiment through the Kharkov fighting in early 1943 and the German summer offensive of 1943 known as Operation "Citadel." Schönberger won the German Cross in Gold on December 26, 1941. He was killed in action in December of 1943 and posthumously awarded the Knight's Cross. (Courtesy of Mark C. Yerger)

officers of Infanterie-Regiment 9, which furnished training and facilities for the men of the Stabswache. Dietrich also came into conflict with Paul Hausser.

During the years before the war, Hausser and Dietrich had a number of purely jurisdictional disputes over matters related to a disagreement in regard to the mission of the "Leibstandarte" units. Dietrich had a disagreement with Hausser in May of 1938 after Dietrich refused to provide "Leibstandarte" personnel to be used for the formation of an SS Standarte (regiment) to be raised in Austria. Hausser wrote Himmler, complaining about Dietrich's stubborness in this situation and offered his resignation. At that point Himmler intervened personally to avoid losing Hausser and found a way to salvage the situation. There seems to have been no later significant problems between the two men and after the war Hausser corrected the belief that he and Dietrich had a lingering personal animosity toward each other. Hausser attributed this impression to incorrect reporting of their relationship by post war authors. It is understandable that Dietrich resisted any change that he viewed as a threat to the independent status of "Leibstandarte" and its prewar mission, which was to serve as guard and ceremonial troops of the SS.

However, when it was clear that war was approaching and the "Leibstandarte" detachments were included in the Verfügungstruppen, Dietrich realized that his troops not completely prepared for military service at that time. While Hausser had built the Verfügungstruppen into units fit for deployment in the field, the initial task given to Dietrich's "Leibstandarte" had been to fulfill

---

[5] Höhne, Heinz, *The Order of the Death's Head: The Story of Hitler's SS.* (London and Edinburgh: 1980) pg. 443.

duties as a guard and ceremonial unit. Felix Steiner commented on this difference in mission directives, stating that he and Hausser were tasked to 'develop an army on a par with the old Reichwehr' while Dietrich 'viewed his main task to be the creation of a well-behaved and representative elite guard.'

Late in 1938 most of the unit was moved to an Army training area in order to participate in war game exercises with the Army's 1. Panzer-Division. This was further evidence of a clear shift in roles for "Leibstandarte." In addition, Heinz Guderian, one of the guiding lights of the development of the early German Panzer force, informed Dietrich that "Leibstandarte" would be under his command when the war began. It appears that Guderian and Dietrich had a good relationship and it can be assumed that Dietrich's close relationship with Hitler was not lost on Guderian.

How much influence Dietrich had with Hitler on matters regarding the Army is unknown. However, his influence on the officers and men of "Leibstandarte" is clear and unquestioned. He infused them with the reckless spirit of the Stösstruppen, the boldness of the experienced soldier and the love of combat of the Freikorps. This was a man who in the last days of the First World War had gone back into his disabled, burning A7V tank, through heavy enemy fire in order to "rescue" a bottle of Schnapps. It was an incident that won him lasting fame in the folklore of his battalion. He was a charismatic leader and romantic figure to the young soldiers of the SS. Dietrich could not have failed to impress these young men because he was a decorated combat veteran and a physically tough individual, who loved outdoor sports and exuded a rough charm.

The influence of Dietrich on the development of the officers and men who served under his command at the regimental and divisional level may have been his most important legacy in regard to the Waffen-SS. Many of the officers who served in the early "Leibstandarte" went on to become legendary Waffen-SS leaders. It was not his military knowledge that most affected them as he was lacking in formal command training but rather his charismatic leadership and his stalwart manner of a man among men. Many postwar accounts incorrectly describe Dietrich as little more than a brute. In fact he was a unique individual, possessing exceptional inspirational abilities. Guderian described him after the war as '. . . a rough soldier . . . with a lot of heart for his soldiers. An extremely good comrade who stood up as much as he could for his subordinates, irrespective of the consequences for himself.'

Rudolf Lehmann, a former Waffen-SS officer and post war historian of the Waffen-SS, served as "Leibstandarte" 1a (Chief of Staff) under Dietrich and remembered him as a dynamic leader who had an extraordinary charisma. While Dietrich depended heavily

The commander of "Leibstandarte's" SS-Panzergrenadier-Regiment 1 was SS-Standartenführer Fritz Witt, here pictured as an SS-Obersturmbannführer. Witt was one of the original company of SS men picked for the first Stabswache company that was organized to guard Hitler. He later became a company commander in SS-Regiment "Deutschland" and won the Knight's Cross in September of 1940 after the French campaign. Shortly thereafter Witt returned to "Leibstandarte" and took command of the regiment which he led through most of 1943. For the accomplishments of his men and his own leadership he was awarded the Oakleaves to the Knight's Cross by Hitler on March 1, 1943. He later commanded 12. SS-Panzer-Division "Hitlerjugend" until he was killed by naval artillery fire shortly after the Allied invasion at Normandy. (Credit National Archives)

on well trained subordinate officers for technical and organizational know-how, he built a division which established an exceptional record of achievements during the war. Many of the junior officers of the division who served under Dietrich went on to become divisional commanders during the war. These include Lehmann, Theodor Wisch, Hugo Kraas, Kurt Meyer and Wilhelm Mohnke. "Leibstandarte" veterans set high standards for aggressive bravery and audacity in battle. Men such as Max Wünsche, Jochen Peiper, Rudolf von Ribbentrop, Michael Wittman, Gerd Bremer and Max

Hansen, as well as many others can be included in this group. All exemplified the concept of "harte," the term for reckless leadership, toughness and disregard for danger, personified by their first commander, the alte Kämpfer of the Freikorps and the Waffen-SS, Sepp Dietrich.

Service in the East

In June 1941, Dietrich led "Leibstandarte," then a motorized, reinforced brigade, into the Soviet Union. After months of hard fighting, the remnants of "Leibstandarte" began boarding trains bound for the West on 11 July, 1942. The division was billeted west of Paris, where it immediately began training exercises. The first "Leibstandarte" tank battalion, initially designated Panzerabteilung "Leibstandarte-SS-Adolf Hitler," was ordered formed on 30 January. It trained at the Army training area at Wildflecken, under command of SS-Obersturmbannführer Georg Schönberger. By Octo-

ber, a second tank battalion was added, creating a full strength Panzer regiment. SS-Sturmbannführer Max Wünsche and SS-Sturmbannführer Martin Gross commanded the two tank battalions. A heavy tank company (equipped with "Tigers") was established and completed training at the Army training grounds at Fallingbostel. The battalion received its instruction and training at the same time as heavy companies of the elite "Grossdeutschland" Division and "Das Reich."[6]

The motorized infantry regiments were reorganized and equipped as Panzergrenadier regiments, each with three battalions. SS-Standartenführer Fritz Witt commanded SS-Panzergrenadier-Regiment 1 "Leibstandarte-SS-Adolf Hitler," while SS-Panzergrenadier-Regiment 2 "Leibstandarte SS Adolf Hitler" was led by SS-Standartenführer Theodor Wisch. Witt was one of the original 119 men of the Stabswache and won the German Cross in Gold, the

---

[6] Lehmann, Rudolf, *The Leibstandarte III.* (Winnipeg: 1990) pg. 223-225.

SS-Standartenführer Theodore Wisch, the commander of SS-Panzergrenadier-Regiment 2 "LAH" is pictured on the left. He is standing with Jochen Peiper, the commander of Wisch's half track battalion. Wisch was another of the first volunteers who joined Hitler's guard detachment in 1933. He won the Knight's Cross as a battalion commander and took command of the division in 1944 until he was severely wounded and was permanently disabled. (Courtesy of Mark C. Yerger)

Knight's Cross and the Oak leaves before his death in 1944. Wisch was one of the early volunteers of the fledgling SS, joining "Leibstandarte" in the spring of 1933. He also won the Knight's Cross and led the regiment until he was permanently crippled by wounds in 1944.

One battalion of the Panzergrenadier regiments was equipped differently from the motorized battalions. The III./SS-Panzergrenadier-Regiment 2 "LSSAH" was organized as an armored battalion, which meant that it received a full complement of half tracks, known as Schützenpanzerwagen or SPWs. The battalion was commanded by SS-Sturmbannführer Joachim (Jochen) Peiper a graduate of SS Junkerschule Braunschweig. Peiper is best known for his military exploits in Russia and as the commander of the Kampfgruppe that spearheaded the attack of "Leibstandarte" during the battle of the Bulge in 1944.

The artillery of the division was restructured extensively during the reorganization in France. The SS-Panzer-Artillerie-Regiment "Leibstandarte-SS-Adolf Hitler" had 4 battalions of artillery and was commanded by SS-Standartenführer Walter Staudinger. Three of the battalions were fully motorized, while II./SS-Artillerie-Regiment "LSSAH" was outfitted with self-propelled 10cm guns, known as "Wespe." Later the regiment also received a complement of 15cm self-propelled guns, built on a Panzer IV chassis which was known as the "Hummel." The I./SS-Artillerie-Regiment "LSSAH" was equipped with 10cm light field howitzers, while III./SS-Artillerie-Regiment "LSSAH" was the heavy battalion of the regiment and had three batteries of 15cm or 17cm howitzers. The IV./Artillerie-Regiment "LSSAH" was a mixed unit, with a battery of Nebelwerfer (rocket launchers), a second battery of heavy field howitzers and a 10cm howitzer battery.

The Panzerjägerabteilung (anti-tank detachment) was first organized in early March of 1942 from cadre of the original Panzerjäger Kompanie. The battalion was equipped with new 7.5cm Pak 40 anti-tank guns, mounted on a lightly armored superstructure built on Czech Panzer 38 chassis. This vehicle was known as the Sdkfz. 138 or more commonly "Marder." The battalion was commanded by SS-Sturmbannführer Jakob Hanreich. The Sturmgeschützeabteilung (assault gun) battalion was organized from cadre of Sturmgeschützkompanie "Schönberger," formerly commanded by Georg Schönberger. It had three batteries, each supplied with 7 Sturmgeschütze III assault guns, equipped with 7.5cm guns. The detachment was led by SS-Sturmbannführer Heinz von Westernhagen. The divisional reconnaissance battalion, SS-Aufklärungsabteilung 1, was equipped with armored cars, SPWs and a company of heavy weapons. It was led by one of the most aggressive and audacious soldiers of the division, SS-Sturmbann-

Walter Staudinger, pictured here as an SS-Oberführer, was the artillery regiment commander of "Leibstandarte." He won the Knight's Cross late in 1944 while serving as the artillery commander of 5. Panzerarmee. (Courtesy of Mark C. Yerger)

On the right is SS-Sturmbannführer Heinz Westernhagen, the commander of SS-Sturmgeschützabteilung 1, the assault gun battalion of "Leibstandarte." On the left is Peiper. (Courtesy of Mark C. Yerger)

führer Kurt Meyer, know as "Panzermeyer." Meyer had been awarded the Knight's Cross for outstanding leadership during the Greek campaign. Before the end of the war, he had won the Oak leaves and Swords and later commanded 12.SS-Panzer-Division "Hitler Jugend."[7]

The division remained in France until the end of December of 1942. On 30 December, the division received new orders and winter clothing. In the first days of January, 1943 1.SS-Panzergrenadier-Division "Leibstandarte-SS-Adolf Hitler," prepared to return to the Eastern Front.

2.SS-Panzergrenadier-Division "Das Reich" and Paul Hausser

Although Paul Hausser was the commander of the SS-Panzer-Korps in January of 1943 and did not command "Das Reich" during the Kharkov counteroffensive, he left an indelible mark upon the division. In fact, he greatly influenced the military development of the Waffen-SS as a whole. When Heinrich Himmler established the Inspectorate for the Militarized Formations of the SS (Inspektion der SS-Verfugungstruppe) on 1 October 1936, one of his primary goals was to bring standardization of training and military proficiency to what became the Waffen-SS. The man Himmler chose to bring military professionalism to the SS and who became the first Chief of the Inspectorate was Hausser, a former Army Generalleutnant who had previously retired from the Army. Hausser served throughout World War I, holding a number of positions, including command of Füsilier-Regiment 38 and as a corps chief of staff. After the end of World War I, he joined the Stahlhelm, a paramilitary organization and was briefly a member of the SA before transferring to the SS to take control of the Inspectorate. He supported the pre-war policies of National Socialism, for reasons he described after the war.

SS-Obergruppenführer Georg Keppler, the commander of "Das Reich" when the division returned to Russia in January, 1943. Keppler served in the German Army during World War 1, was wounded several times and ended the war with the rank of Oberleutnant. He was awarded the Wound Badge in Silver and both classes of the Iron Cross while serving in the Army. During his service with the Waffen-SS, Keppler won the Knight's Cross in August of 1940. He commanded the division twice, the first time in 1942, until he had to be evacuated due to illness on 10 February, 1943. He returned to the division later in the year before assuming command of I.SS-Panzer-Korps in 1944. When the war ended Keppler was in command of XVIII. SS-Korps on the Upper Rhine. (Credit National Archives)

Not only myself, but a considerable part of the Reichswehr officers, especially the younger men, as well as the NCO's were attracted to National Socialism before 1933 because of:

a. its struggles against Versailles in the name of military sovereignty and national defense;

b. its social attitudes respecting the 'national community' and its commitment to peaceful labor re-relations and its rejection of the class struggle.

c. its attempt to take a fundamental position against Bolshevism and Communism . . .'

Hausser implemented a uniform and in some ways revolutionary officer training program for the SS, in order to provide leadership for the SS combat divisions. He saw this as his only goal and did not concern himself with political matters, as these were, in his words, 'none of my business but rather that of the political leadership.' In a post war article in the SS historical journal, *Der Freiwillige*, he described his sense of the situation in 1936.

---

[7] The term Abteilung was used by the Germans to refer to various types of units, ranging from Armeeabteilung or army sized formations, to battalion sized or smaller detachments. A divisional Panzerjägerabteilung, Aufklärungsabteilung or Sturmgeschützabteilung was essentially a battalion sized formation at normal strength.

'What was actually to become of it no one told me, and I asked no one about it. I said to myself, "Let's put the shop in order" and then build up the three regiments properly.'

It was evident to Hausser, as a former General Staff officer that training standards needed to be developed and energetically implemented. Prior to 1936, SS officers evidenced significant differences in amount of training, competency to lead and military experience. Some were former police officers who had received only paramilitary training and there were ex-Army NCOs with no formal officer training. Of course, there were also a number of experienced, ex-Army or Luftwaffe officers of various ranks who had seen combat during World War I. However, as late as the summer of 1936, a number of SS training exercises were canceled due to the lack of sufficiently trained officers. The head of the SS Central Bureau, SS-Gruppenführer August Heissmeyer, stated that these men had 'not yet gained the self-confidence to set written tactical assignments for their officers.'

Very quickly, Hausser moved to remedy this unsatisfactory situation. He established the SS officer schools, known as Junkerschulen and found qualified men to teach the instructional courses. The Junkerschulen graduates brought a much needed infusion of command skill, training and organizational ability. Classroom training was adapted from Army methods, although modified substantially under SS guidelines.

Combat training was developed according to an SS military philosophy designed to develop a modern, elite fighting organization. Tactical combat training was of a comprehensive, practical nature and reflected the experiences of the Stösstruppen during World War I. A number of influential SS officers were veterans of these elite assault units, including Sepp Dietrich and Felix Steiner. Hausser would have been familiar with these revolutionary tactics also, given his command positions during the war. The Stösstruppen assault principles of World War I were refined and developed into the assault tactics of the Waffen-SS.

In choosing Stösstruppen officers a premium was placed on personal initiative, innovative action and rapid decision making by leaders from regimental commanders down to small units NCOs, which required leaders to be in superb mental and physical condition. Command and leadership training in the SS evolved accordingly because the SS assault team tactics required commanders who could make swift tactical decisions, in order to direct the fire and maneuver of his men. These tactics also influenced the combat structure of small units at all levels. Companies, platoons and even squads could utilize a maneuver element, supported by a fire element equipped with automatic weapons and high angle fire weapons (mortars or rifle grenades). Each squad was equipped with at least one light machine gun and the squad leader was often equipped with a machine pistol. Regiments of the higher quality Waffen-SS divisions, in addition to their complement of Panzergrenadier companies, contained companies of Pioniere (combat engineers), heavy companies equipped with mortars, anti-tank guns and infantry howitzers and even motorcycle companies. In effect, each regiment was a combined arms formation, possessing great fire power and mobility.

Attacks proceeded along the path of least resistance, with maximum use of terrain and were not limited to a specific zone of attack. Unfavorable terrain or formidable enemy positions could be bypassed, reducing the opponent's ability to quickly discern the main area of attack. This minimized casualties, allowed the maximum tactical freedom of action and increased the depth and speed of penetrations. The Waffen-SS pioneered other innovations as well. It was the first military organization to utilize camouflage uniforms in order to facilitate the use of such tactics.[8]

The Waffen-SS method of training was characterized by battle focused training exercises and practical class room learning, while parade drill was considered to be of lesser importance. This system combined realistic, live fire battle training with a high level of physical conditioning to create a superb body of troops. A remarkable demonstration of the physical condition attained by men of Regiment "Deutschland," took place during the 1938 SS Road March Championships. A battalion of the regiment covered the twenty-five kilometer course in full battle gear, including a 45lb pack, in the phenomenal time of 3 hours, 35 minutes and 55 seconds. Upon reaching the review stand, the battalion broke into the strenuous parade march (goose step), crossing the finish line in immaculate order.

There is evidence that the SS training, besides the physical fitness component, had benefits of practical use on the battlefield. In May 1939, Regiment "Deutschland" conducted a combat exercise at the Munsterlagen Training Area before an audience that included Hitler, Himmler and a number of Army officers. The exercise plan called for a battalion assault on a prepared enemy position behind outposts and barbed wire, accompanied by live artillery fire. Hitler observed the attack from a vantage point near the artillery impact area. So skillfully did the camouflage uniformed SS assault troops use cover to advance during the assault, that Hitler did not realize that the attack had begun. When he somewhat testily asked

---

[8] Foreign Military Studies - Historical Division, Headquarters United States Army, Europe. MS # D-155. Kurt Gropp, Comparison between the infantry battalion and the assault battalion developed by the Waffen-SS during the course of the war. pg. 6-7.

regiment commander Felix Steiner when the infantry were to attack, he was informed that the troops had begun their assault some minutes ago. Only under closer scrutiny was Hitler able to observe the SS troopers advancing on the position. The Führer was so impressed that he refused to take cover in a concrete bunker, preferring to observe the attack from in front of the bunker, even after the live artillery fire began to impact less than 300 meters in front of the observation point.

Hausser's major prewar achievement was that he enabled the SS to become a competent military organization by providing a core of well trained officers to lead Himmler's SS units and provided a basis for standardized training. The Junkerschulen turned out aggressive, well trained and supremely confident young officers. Approximately 15,000 men passed through the officer schools of the Waffen-SS from 1934 until 1945, a truly remarkable number considering that Hausser had only a short time to work with the school system before the beginning of the war necessitated his devotion to other tasks. The training methods and tactical innovations pioneered by the SS were militarily ahead of their time in many ways, although they may not have always embodied the political ideal that Heinrich Himmler envisioned, a fact that irked the SS leader. Himmler complained to Hausser on more than one occasion when reports reached his ears regarding criticism of his policies originating from the younger officers of the division. He stated that the junior officers saw fit to question everything "from military regulations" to "political measures." Regardless of this criticism by Himmler, he appointed Hausser to be the first divisional commander of the SS. Regiments "Deutschland," "Der Führer" and "Germania" were combined to form the division which later became SS-Division "Das Reich."

Officers who began service in the Waffen-SS with "Das Reich" carried advanced methods of training and the modern, combined arms fire team tactics with them to each new command. A number of officers of the division who graduated from the Junkerschulen or served as small unit commanders under Hausser later commanded SS divisions. This list includes Werner Ostendorff, Otto Kumm, Felix Steiner, Sylvester Stadler and Heinz Harmel.

Kumm served as commander of Regiment "Der Führer" and later led both 7.SS-Freiwilligen-Gebirgs-Division "Prinz Eugen" and "Leibstandarte." Steiner first commanded 5.SS-Panzer-Division "Wiking" and subsequently III. Germanische-Panzer-Korps. Sylvester Stadler commanded 9.SS-Panzer-Division "Hohenstaufen" and former Regiment "Deutschland" commander Heinz Harmel was given command of 10.SS-Panzer-Division "Frundsberg" in 1944. Ostendorff was an intelligent and outstanding officer who was the first 1a of SS-Generalkommando, which became

The first commander of "Das Reich's" Panzer Regiment was Herbert Vahl. Vahl had extensive combat experience gained through his service in the German Army during World War 1. He remained in the Army after the end of the war and held the rank of Oberstleutnant at the start of World War II. Vahl first led Panzer troops when he took command of II./Panzer-Regiment 4 in 1936. He was transferred to the Waffen-SS in early 1943 when an SS regimental commander with the necessary experience was not available to lead "Das Reich's" new Panzer Regiment. After Georg Keppler left Russia due to sickness, Vahl assumed command of the division until he was wounded on March 18. He won both the German Cross in Gold and the Knight's Cross before he was killed in an automobile accident, soon after taking command of 4. SS-Polizei-Grenadier-Division. (Courtesy of Mark C. Yerger)

the SS-Panzer-Korps. He later assumed command of 17.SS-Panzer-Grenadier-Division in January of 1944 and subsequently led "Das Reich" before his death from wounds in early 1945.

After suffering 11,000 casualties in Russia during the first 6 months of the war in the East, SS Division "Reich" was withdrawn from combat in March of 1942 and sent to France for rest and extensive reorganization. By late fall of 1942, the division completed its transformation into a Panzergrenadier division although it was a full strength Panzer division in every way but name. Hausser was no longer commander of the division, which was renamed 2.SS-Panzergrenadier-Division "Das Reich," when it returned to duty from the East. He had been severely wounded in Russia and was recovering during the first part of 1942 and after his return to duty, Hausser took command of the first SS corps, the SS-Panzer-Korps. He skillfully led it during the difficult battles for Kharkov and during the battle of Kursk in the summer of 1943. On 28 June, 1944, he became the first SS officer to lead an army, when he was appointed to command of 7. Armee. He commanded the army during the bitter fighting in France after the Allies landed in Normandy. Hausser was wounded again during the breakout of 7. Armee from the Falaise Pocket and spent the remainder of the year in recovery. After his return to duty in early 1945, Hausser took command of Heeresgruppe G and held this post until April of 1945. This was his last combat command and at the end of the war, he was serving on the staff of Oberkommando West.[9]

SS-Gruppenführer Georg Keppler took command of the division in April, 1942. Keppler was also a World War I veteran. After the war, he spent time in various police units and became a Major der Polizei of the Schutzpolizei by 1933. In 1935, Keppler left the Police and joined the SS, taking command of I./SS-Standarte-"Deutschland" in October, 1935. In the spring of 1938, he was given command of the newly formed, primarily Austrian SS regiment, "Der Führer." Keppler oversaw the transition of the division to full fledged Panzergrenadier division status.[10] The most significant addition to the division was of course the Panzer Regiment.

The first battalion of SS-Panzer-Regiment 2 was formed by order of the SS-Führungshauptamt dated 11 February, 1942. A second battalion was formed from cadre of a battalion of Regiment

---

[9] Yerger, Mark C. *Knights of Steel: The Structure, Development and Personalities of the 2.SS- Panzer- Division.* vol. 2 (Lancaster: 1994) pgs 26-27.
[10] Ibid. pgs.39-41.

SS-Standartenführer Heinz Harmel (standing in the command car) gestures while talking with Otto Kumm (left). During the Kharkov fighting of 1943, Harmel was the commander of "Das Reich's" Regiment "Deutschland." His first military service was in the German Army in 1926 but he had to leave the army when he suffered an eye injury. He joined the SS in October of 1935 and reached the rank of SS-Obersturmführer by January, 1938. Harmel took command of Regiment "Deutschland" in December of 1941 and held that post until he was wounded on October 2, 1943. He later commanded 10.SS-Panzer-Division "Frundsberg" and led that unit until the end of the war. He is still alive at this writing. (Courtesy of Mark C. Yerger)

"Langemarck," a motorcycle regiment which had been attached to the division in mid-1942. The Panzer regiment's first commander was SS-Standartenführer Herbert Vahl, who was transferred from the Army, due to the lack of a SS regimental commander with sufficient combat experience in leading Panzer troops. SS-Obersturmbannführer Hans-Albin von Reitzenstein was the first commander of I./SS-Panzer-Regiment 2. In October of 1942, a second battalion was organized and its commander was SS-Sturmbannführer Christian Tychsen.

Like "Leibstandarte," the division had two Panzergrenadier regiments, each with three battalions. Regiment "Deutschland" was commanded by SS-Standartenführer Heinz Harmel who began his Waffen-SS career as a junior officer in Regiment "Der Führer." He took command of Regiment "Deutschland" in 1942, commanding the regiment during the difficult winter and summer battles of 1943. Harmel was awarded the Knight's Cross in March, 1943, later winning the Oak Leaves and Swords. The second Panzergrenadier regiment was SS-Panzergrenadier-Regiment "Der Führer," which had originally been raised in Austria and was led by an outstanding soldier of the division, SS-Obersturmbannführer Otto Kumm. Kumm won the Knight's Cross in February, 1942 and subsequently was awarded the Oak Leaves and Swords to the Knight's Cross during later years of the war. He was awarded the German Cross in Gold and was the first solder of "Das Reich" to win the Oakleaves to the Knight's Cross.

The artillery regiment, SS-Artillerie-Regiment 2, was commanded by SS-Oberführer Kurt Brasack, who had been an artillery battalion commander in "Totenkopf" until March, 1941. On that date he was transferred to 5.SS-Panzergrenadier-Division "Wiking" and commanded I./SS-Artillerie-Regiment 5 until January of 1942, when he replaced SS-Oberführer Dr. Gunther Merk as commander of the artillery regiment of "Das Reich." The Aufklärungsabteilung and Sturmgeschützabteilung (assault gun detachment) were established and furnished with new men, vehicles and equipment. The Aufklärungsabteilung was commanded by SS-Hauptsturmführer Hans Weiss, while SS-Hauptsturmführer Walter Kniep led the Sturmgeschütze Bataillon. The assault guns of the Sturmgeschütz-abteilung were to play important roles in the fighting around Kharkov during the period of February and March of 1943, as did the Kradschützen-Bataillon, commanded by SS-Sturmbannführer Jakob Fick.

During 1942, the Kradschützen-Bataillon (motorcycle battalion) underwent several structural and command changes. For a time the battalion was part of a third regiment of the division, Regiment "Langemarck," which had a second mobile battalion under command of Christian Tychsen. Regiment "Langemarck" was com-

Otto Kumm, pictured here with the rank of SS-Obersturmbannführer, was the commander of Regiment "Der Führer" in February of 1943. He was a former member of the SA, who transferred to the SS in 1931 and reached the rank of SS-Untersturmführer in 1934. After the regiment was formed in 1938 Kumm took command of III./"Der Führer" and held that post until July 11, 1941 when he took command of the regiment. In January of 1941, the regiment was engaged in extremely heavy fighting in the Rzhev area and by the end of February was reduced to a total of thirty-five men. Kumm was recommended for the Knight's Cross for his leadership during that period. He later commanded 7. SS-Freiwillige-Gebirgs-Division "Prinz Eugen" and was the last commander of "Leibstandarte." Otto Kumm is still alive at the time of this writing. (Credit National Archives)

manded by Hinrich Schuldt, before he took command of the collection of SS and Police troops assigned to Armeeabteilung Fretter-Pico that was designated as Kampfgruppe Schuldt. In October of 1942, Tychsen's battalion was transferred out of "Langemarck" and assigned to the Panzer regiment as cadre for a battalion of SS-Panzer-Regiment 2. The Kradschützen-Bataillon remained intact and was commanded by SS-Sturmbannführer Jakob Fick. The battalion was a versatile, fast moving detachment with 4 companies of Grenadiers mounted on motorcycles and a motorized heavy company. The schwere (heavy) 5./Kompanie consisted of a platoon of anti-tank guns, a platoon of infantry howitzers and a Pioniere (combat engineer) platoon.[11]

SS-Sturmgeschütz-Abteilung 2 was formed in October of 1942 and equipped with the new, high velocity L40 gun of 7.5cm, which replaced the stubby barreled 7.5 infantry howitzer that was standard for the early models of the assault guns. The battalion had three batteries of seven guns and an additional Sturmgeschütze command vehicle. An April 1942 order from the SS-Führungshauptamt, stated that if available, three additional assault guns, outfitted with 10.5cm howitzers, were to be added to each battery. It is not known if these vehicles were assigned to the battalion while it was training in France, although Ernst August Krag, a former commander of 2./SS-Sturmgeschützabteilung 2, informed Mark Yerger, the American historian, that the battalion had twenty-eight vehicles when it returned to Russia. Krag had previously served in the artillery regiment and as a company commander in the Aufklärungsabteilung, before taking over command of his assault gun battery.[12]

3.SS-Panzergrenadier-Division "Totenkopf" and Theodor Eicke

Theodor Eicke was born in October 1892 and joined the Army in 1909. He served as a paymaster in two different Bavarian infantry regiments, winning the Iron Cross, 2nd Class. After the war Eicke found employment as a Police officer but had difficulty finding steady employment, due primarily to his anti-government activities, which cost him jobs in both the security police and criminal police. In 1923 he secured employment as a security officer for I. G. Farben in Ludwigshafen, a job which lasted until 1932. By that time Eicke was already a member of the Nazi Party, having joined in 1928. He was a member of the SA until August 20, 1930, when he transferred to the SS.

After recognizing his considerable organizational abilities, Himmler appointed him commander of the concentration camp at Dachau in 1933. While at this post Eicke developed a harsh and brutal codified system of conduct for the men of the camp guards, known as the SS-"Totenkopfverbände." The men of the "Totenkopfverbände" guarded the camp's inmates, who were mostly political detainees of one type or another at that time. Eicke's system was considered by Himmler to be so successful that on July 4, 1934, the Reichsführer appointed him as Inspector of Konzentrationlager and SS "Totenkopfverbande," placing him in command of the entire camp guard organization.

Theodore Eicke, the first commander of 3. SS-Panzergrenadier-Division "Totenkopf." He served in the German Army during World War 1, winning the Iron Cross 2nd Class and several Bavarian Army awards. Before the war Eicke served in a number of Police detachments but was dismissed because of his radical political views. He joined the SS in 1930 and found his life's calling, reaching the rank of SS-Standartenführer in 1931. In 1934 Eicke was given command of the SS concentration camps and camp guard units, a position which ideally suited him. Beginning in 1939, he organized and trained a division created from the Totenkopfverbände (camp guard units) which became 3.SS-Division "Totenkopf." (Credit National Archives)

Each of four main camps was garrisoned by an SS guard regiment or SS-Totenkopf-Standarte. By September 1938 there were four SS-Totenkopf-Standarten, which included "Oberbayern" at Dachau, "Brandenburg" at Sachsenhausen, "Thuringen" at Buchenwald and SS-Totenkopf-Standarte IV at Linz. There were also 50,000 men in reserve Totenkopfverbande or in various auxiliary units.

The prewar guard units were instructed according to Eicke's blend of political instruction, mental conditioning and paramilitary training. Just as Dietrich did not initially consider his troops to be under command of Hausser's SS Verfügungstruppen, Eicke emphasized to his men that they were a unit apart from the other armed

---

[11] Yerger, Mark C. *Knights of Steel.* pgs. 25-28.
[12] Ibid. pgs. 95-98.

formations of Germany, even the other SS formations. He stated that 'We belong neither to the army nor to the police nor to the Verfügungstruppen; our cohesion is based upon the comradeship inherent in our National Socialist ideology.'

Just before the outbreak of war, the status of the Totenkopfverbande changed radically, as had the mission originally assigned to "Leibstandarte." An August 17, 1938 decree by Hitler expressly delineated the wartime duties and status of the militarized formations of the SS. This directive stated that the SS Verfügungstruppen included, in addition to Hausser's three regiments, "Leibstandarte," the Junkerschulen and Eicke's Totenkopfverbande, including the reserve Totenkopf-Standarten. It was inconspicuously specified that the reserve Totenkopfverbande regiments were to provide replacements for the armed SS units in the event of war. This statement, little noted at the time, provided Himmler with the means to covertly expand the prewar Waffen-SS by actively recruiting men into the SS reserve Standarten. Since there were no manpower limits placed on the reserve regiments, the SS was allowed to recruit as many men as it could sign up.

Hitler gave military legitimacy to the Waffen-SS when he explicitly stated that the armed SS would go to war under command of the Army. This arrangement was accepted by the Army in a September 17, 1938 regulation that also stated that the members of the 'SS militarized formations . . . had the same rights and duties as soldiers of the Wehrmacht for the duration of their incorporation.' Although the Army had previously balked at bestowing these rights upon Eicke's camp guards, this decree technically legitimized their status as military units.

In October 1939, three SS "Totenkopf" Standarten were used to form the core of the SS-"Totenkopf"-Division, which was a completely motorized unit under the command of Eicke. A divisional staff was chosen, administrative units established and support units such as anti-tank, reconnaissance, supply and artillery were organized and trained. For the first time, there was a substantial influx of personnel from the other military units of the Waffen-SS, including transfers from the Verfügungstruppen and the reserve SS Standarten. When war began, Eicke's division was not ready to participate in the Polish invasion as a combat unit, primarily due to the lack of sufficient training time and organizational difficulties.

After the defeat of Poland, Eicke pushed his men and officers mercilessly through an intensive schedule of training designed to develop military proficiency and command competence. Eicke's determined efforts began to bear fruit on 2 April, 1940, when Generaloberst Maximilian von Weichs, commander of 2. Armee, visited a divisional training exercise. Up to that time, Von Weichs held a low opinion of Eicke's men, considering them little more

SS-Standartenführer Hellmuth Becker, the commander of SS-"Totenkopf" Panzergrenadier-Regiment 3, which later became known as Regiment "Eicke" after the death of division commander Theodore Eicke. Becker joined the German Army in 1920 and was an NCO in several units before leaving the Army in 1932. In February, 1933 Becker joined the SS after brief service in the SA. Between 1935 and 1939 he commanded a variety of Totenkopf formations until taking command of I./ SS-"Totenkopf" Infanterie-Regiment 1 in November of 1939. In March, 1942 after promotion to SS-Obersturmbannführer he took command of SS-"Totenkopf" Infanterie-Regiment 3. He became division commander in 1944, serving in that position until the end of the war, surrendering to the American Army. He went into Soviet captivity after the United States Army turned the men of the division over to the Russians. Becker was executed in February of 1952, while serving with a reconstruction unit made up of German prisoners. (Credit National Archives)

than a semi-trained formation of camp thugs. However, he was visibly impressed when he discovered that the division was fully motorized and lavishly equipped. As the day went on, von Weichs realized that the division, soon to be under his command, was a modern, well equipped unit and he was impressed with the obvious superb physical condition of the men. He noted their aggressive spirit during combat exercises.[13]

[13] Sydnor, Charles W. *Soldiers of Destruction: The SS Death's Head Division-1933-1945.* (Princeton: 1977) pg. 82-84.

The attitude of the Army officers gradually began to change from "cold and hostile" (Eicke's description) to a more enthusiastic acceptance. It is interesting to note that von Weichs had difficulty in spotting the movements of camouflaged SS troops carrying out a assault training exercise. This was similar to Hitler's experience during his earlier observation of the Verfügungstruppen. After these visits, Von Weichs was personally instrumental in obtaining guns for a heavy artillery battery, as well as seeing to it that gunnery training was provided for Eicke's artillery units at Army artillery schools.

War experience gained during the fighting in France greatly benefited the division. Officers and men who were not suited for combat, due to physical, mental or emotional weakness were weeded out. Eicke had no patience with those who did not exhibit sufficient fighting spirit or did not possess the trait that he valued over all others, which was instant obedience to orders.

As a result of the combat experience gained in France, a much improved combat division entered Russia in June of 1941. By the end of the year, the division was in the Demyansk area, where it was encircled along with most of II. Armeekorps. It remained trapped in the pocket from January to October of 1942 and Eicke and his division played a major role in the successful defense of the perimeter. After Eicke was evacuated with severe foot wounds and lower leg nerve damage, the division was placed under command of regimental commander Max Simon. In spite of repeated demands that he be allowed to resume command of his division, Himmler refused to allow Eicke to return to Russia. Simon, in constant communication with Eicke during his absence, believed that the division would be completely destroyed by the losses it sustained during the remainder of 1942.

In October of 1942, the division was finally pulled out of the pocket and evacuated through a narrow corridor punched through the encircling Russian troops. When "Totenkopf" was withdrawn from the Demyansk salient, the division had nearly been destroyed, numbering only about 6500 men, from a peak strength of 20,000 men in June of 1941. This was in spite of the fact that the division received thousands of replacements during the long months of fighting. Many of the men who were evacuated from the pocket were in such poor shape that 30% were not fit for further active military service. Those who were able to recover required many weeks of recuperation after the physical and mental stresses of the bitter fighting.[14]

The division still had shortages of trained officers, non-commissioned officers and men in December of 1942. Some units of the division had actually ceased to exist during the Demyansk battles and had to be reconstituted completely. "Totenkopf" assembled in nine training camps near Angouleme, France, under temporary command of 1. Armee, commanded by Generaloberst Blaskowitz. Hitler had personally ordered Eicke to have his division ready for combat on 10 January, 1943. This provided considerably less time for training than the other two SS divisions had been given but Eicke had great talents for organization and administration. Under his harsh and watchful eye, the division staff immediately began the transformation into a full fledged Panzergrenadier Division.

Some of the process of rebuilding began in France before the remnants of the division were pulled out of Russia. A former 1a of the division, SS-Obersturmbannführer Heinz Lammerding, was assigned to direct the training and organization of the new units. Thousands of new recruits, a number of specialty troops and new weapons and vehicles arrived from training and replacement depots all over Germany and Europe. The division received 6000 recruits to replace the losses of 1942. Many of these were 17 and 18 year old volunteers and conscripts, who evidently were not very impressive in their physical or mental make up. The first group of 1500 arrived after undergoing five to eight weeks of basic training with either SS-Totenkopf-Infanterie-Ersatz-Bataillon I in Warsaw or SS-Totenkopf-Infanterie-Ersatz-Bataillon III in Kuhberg. Eicke complained to Hitler and Himmler that most of them were of mediocre quality and lacked sufficient training. He also remained disturbed by weapon and equipment shortages and bombarded Himmler's office with a constant barrage of complaints and requests for tanks, equipment and better human material.[15]

The division structure was similar to the organization of the other two SS divisions, with one exception. In addition to its two Panzergrenadier regiments, the division was assigned a third, motorized infantry regiment. An existing SS formation, the motorized SS-Infanterie-Regiment 9, was combined with the remnants of SS-Totenkopf-Kradschützen-Bataillon in order to create a unique regiment. The new regiment was named SS-Schützen-Regiment "Thule" and was a mobile, combined arms formation with impressive amounts of heavy weapons. Its infantry companies were equipped with trucks, heavy cars or the new Volkswagen Schwimmwagen and had mortar and heavy machine gun platoons. Each of the two battalions of the regiment had a heavy company, which was equipped with 7.5cm infantry howitzers, anti-tank guns and a Pioniere platoon. Two companies of the regiment, 3. and 7. Kompanie, were supplied with SPWs (armored cars and half tracks). The regiment also had additional anti-tank guns and other heavy weapons, such

[14] Ibid. pg. 230.

[15] Sydnor, pg. 260-263.

Hermann Priess, the artillery regiment commander of "Totenkopf." Priess joined the German Army in 1919, left to serve in Freikorps "von Brandis" for several months and then re-enlisted, remaining in the Army until 1931. He joined the SS in 1933 and the following year was transferred to the SS-Verfügungstruppen. He took artillery training courses during 1939, later becoming a battalion commander in the artillery regiment of the SS-Verfügungsdivision. In 1940 he became the artillery regiment commander in Eicke's "Totenkopf" division, a post he held until taking temporary command of the division in April of 1943. In October, 1943 he took full command of "Totenkopf" and commanded both XIII.SS-Armeekorps and I.SS-Panzer-Korps before the end of the war. (Credit National Archives)

Heinz Lammerding, pictured after his promotion to SS-Brigadeführer, was the commander of SS-Schützen-Regiment "Thule" during the Kharkov campaign. The regiment was detached from the rest of the division for most of the fighting. In the prewar years he earned a degree in engineering from the Brunswick Technical School and was employed as an engineer until 1931. In April, 1935 Lammerding joined the SS, after which he was appointed to the formation staff of the Pioniere battalion of the SS-Verfügungsdivision. He taught combat engineering at Junkerschule Braunschweig until leaving to become the first commander of "Totenkopf's" Pioniere Bataillon. After promotion to SS-Obersturmbannführer he took command of Regiment "Thule" until July, 1943. He commanded "Das Reich" in 1944 and later served as 1a of Heeresgruppe Weichsel. He survived the war and died from cancer in 1971. (Courtesy of Mark C. Yerger)

SS-Standartenführer Max Simon was the commander of SS-"Totenkopf"-Panzergrenadier-Regiment 1 and was a trusted subordinate of Theodor Eicke. He was also a veteran of World War 1 and won the Iron Cross 2nd Class. After leaving the Army in 1929 with the rank of Wachtmeister, Simon joined the SS in 1933. He was commissioned as an SS-Untersturmführer in November 1934, subsequently assuming command of the guard detachment at Sachsenburg concentration camp. When Eicke established the division, he named Simon to command "Totenkopf" Infanterie-Regiment 1. He took command of the division at Eicke's death and later commanded 16. SS-Panzergrenadier-Division-"Reichsführer-SS," finishing the war at the head of XIII. SS-Armeekorps. He died of heart failure in 1961. (The author's collection)

as motorized Flak guns in various configurations, making it a formation possessing a great deal of firepower and mobility.[16]

By the end of the summer, the first 1130 new SS recruits began to arrive for training. Also on hand were training battalions of artillery under SS-Sturmbannführer Josef Swientek, a Flak Abteilung commanded by SS-Hauptsturmführer Otto Kron and a Panzerjäger-Kompanie under SS-Sturmbannführer Georg Bochmann, in addition to companies of infantry gun and Pioniere troops. While the new regiment was trained and organized, the original regiments and battalions of Eicke's battered division received new weapons. Most of the regimental, battalion and company commanders were veterans of the Demyansk ordeal and were trusted by Eicke.

SS-"Totenkopf"-Panzergrenadier-Regiment 1, consisting of three battalions, was commanded by SS-Standartenführer Hellmuth Becker. The half track battalion of the regiment was commanded by one of the outstanding soldiers of the division, SS-Sturmbannführer Otto Baum. Baum had been awarded the Knight's Cross on 8 May, 1942, for valor during the fighting in the Demyansk salient. He later won the Oak Leaves and Swords and by the end of the war served as a divisional commander. The second Panzergrenadier regiment was SS-Totenkopf-Panzergrenadier Regiment 3, which was commanded by SS-Standartenführer Max Simon. The regiment had three battalions, which were supplied with trucks and heavy cars. One company of each battalion was a heavy company, equipped with heavy machine guns, mortars and infantry guns. Both regiments had attached support troops and additional heavy weapons, including motorized Flak guns and anti-tank guns.

[16] Vopersal, Wolfgang, *Soldaten - Kämpfer - Kameraden, Marsch and Kämpfe der SS-Totenkopf- Division.* (Osnabrück: 1987) pg. 29.

The SS-Artillerie-Regiment 3, consisting of 4 battalions, was commanded by SS-Standartenführer Hermann Priess, who later took over the division command and led "Totenkopf" during the battle of Kursk, in the summer of 1943. The reconnaissance battalion, SS-Aufklärüngsabteilung 3, was commanded by SS-Sturmbann-führer Walter Bestmann and SS-Sturmgeschütz-Abteilung 3 (assault gun battalion) was led by SS-Hauptsturmführer Werner Korff. SS-Sturmbannführer Max Seela commanded SS-Pioniere-Abteilung 3, while SS-Hauptsturmführer Armin Grunert led SS-Panzerjäger-Abteilung 3, the anti-tank battalion.

The first commander of SS-Panzer-Regiment 3 was SS-Sturmbannführer Karl Leiner, who was trusted by Eicke but had no previous experience commanding tanks. Training began in June, 1942, at the Panzer training area located at Weimar-Buchenwald. Key personnel were trained at various Army Panzer schools and in October, the orders were issued to establish a second Panzer battalion. Tanks for the regiment were initially in short supply and the first battalion received only six tanks by June, 1942. It was October before the men and officers, as well as the necessary technical specialists for both battalions assembled. SS-Hauptsturmführer Erwin Meierdress commanded I./SS-Panzer-Regiment 3 and SS-Hauptsturmführer Eugen Kunstmann took command of II./SS-Panzer-Regiment 3.

Most of the first tanks that were supplied to Eicke's division were Panzer IIIs, although it possessed a few of the more modern Panzer IVs. The heavy company of the Panzer regiment, which was to be equipped with "Tigers," was not established until November. Its personnel were assisted in their training by Army troops of Schwere Panzer-Abteilung 502, an independent "Tiger" tank battalion. However, the SS company initially had no "Tigers" of its own and most of the training was conducted using Panzer IIIs. This was an unsatisfactory arrangement because the capabilities, technical needs, handling characteristics and operational tactics associated with the "Tiger" tank were completely different from the Panzer III. Not until January of 1943 did the company actually receive its full complement of "Tigers," which left little time for the tank crews to master the use of the technically more complex heavy tanks. The lack of training time for the Panzer Regiment was evident in some of the first operations of the regiment.[17]

The preparation and training of the division was further disrupted on 8 November, 1942, by the American landings in North Africa, which forced Hitler to occupy Vichy France in order to secure the Mediterranean coastline in southern France. Late in December the detached elements of the division were finally replaced

SS-Sturmbannführer Karl Leiner, here pictured in civilian dress, was the commander of the newly established SS-Panzer-Regiment 3, when "Totenkopf" returned to Russia in early 1943. In 1939, Leiner was an SS-Obersturmführer in the SS Regiment "Heimwehr Danzig." He commanded the Panzerjägerabteilung of "Totenkopf" in 1940, and attended a short Staff officer training course for battalion commanders at an Army Panzertruppen Schule. In March of 1941 Leiner took command of "Das Reich's" Panzerjägerabteilung until he was wounded in action on July 22, 1941. Leiner did not show great aptitude for handling Panzer troops and although he had been trusted by Eicke, was replaced by SS-Sturmbannführer Eugen Kunstmann when Hermann Priess took command of the division in April of 1943. (Courtesy of Mark C. Yerger)

by a security division and began the return to their former training camps. However, the time lost could not be made up and the schedule of training was severely disrupted. Eicke sent a message to Himmler complaining that his division could not possibly be ready to return to Russia on the date expected. Eicke explained that half of his vehicles were not in serviceable condition and the Panzer regiment had received less than half of its tanks. In addition, the communications units were critically short of radios and trained personnel and 60 per cent of the drivers had received less than adequate instruction. Eicke estimated that nearly three quarters of the new recruits were not adequately familiar with their weapons.

---

[17] Vopersal, pg. 41-43 and 78.

On 3 January, 1943, Himmler met with Hitler to explain the situation and Himmler was told he could have an additional four weeks of training time for Eicke. However, the emergency situation on the Eastern Front was worsening with every day that passed and it was clear that there would be no further delays. The division had to be ready to return to Russia in early February, whether training was concluded or not.

Preparation resumed at a feverish pace, as Eicke implemented a crash training program and drove every member of the division through a grueling schedule of training and weapons familiarization. Field exercises continued nearly around the clock, winter clothing and boots began to arrive and the division's vehicles were painted with winter white camouflage. On 19 January, an order arrived at Eicke's Headquarters, stating that the division would entrain for Russia beginning on 31 January. Shortages of various kinds continued to plague Eicke, up until the last minute before departure. Some of the division's units did not receive their full complement of vehicles and new weapons until the third week of January, only days before the first trains were to arrive.

The trains returning the division to the east began to pull into nearby railroad stations late in the month, and loading began on 31 January, 1943. The I./Regiment "Thule," commanded by SS-Hauptsturmführer Ernst Häussler, left France on the first train leaving the Angouleme training camps. With the departure of this unit of "Totenkopf" troops, the last division of the newly established SS-Panzer-Korps was on its way to Russia. Other units of the division continued their training schedule literally until the last hour before they were to begin to load on the trains leaving for Russia. While Eicke's men worked to prepare for the coming fighting, the other two divisions of the SS-Panzer-Korps were already in Russia.

"Das Reich" and "Leibstandarte" – The Return to the Eastern Front

On 31 December, 1942, Manstein received a communiqué from OKH which stated that Hitler had decided to send the SS divisions to Manstein's Heeresgruppe Süd. Hitler's intention was to assemble the SS-Panzer-Korps near Kharkov and conduct a relief operation for Stalingrad using the newly equipped SS Panzergrenadier divisions. In January, SS-Panzer-Korps was ordered transferred to Russia, although adequate transportation was not available at that time and "Totenkopf" had not had sufficient time to complete all of its reorganization and rebuilding. "Das Reich" and "Leibstandarte" were ready for combat, but the lack of sufficient numbers of trains to transport the divisions prevented their immediate return to Russia.

After weeks of delays in organizing transportation to the east, the operation to use the SS divisions to rescue the defenders of Stalingrad became unnecessary after the deterioration of the situation there. Hitler then decided to use the SS divisions to defend the city of Kharkov. At 1200 hours, 29 January, 1943, "Das Reich" and "Leibstandarte" were officially subordinated to the Generalkommando-SS-Panzer-Korps, under Hausser. The SS divisions were ordered to proceed to Kharkov, where a provisional Armeeabteilung was organizing and preparing to defend the Oskul River, some 90 kilometers east of the city. Armeeabteilung Lanz, named for its commander, General der Gebirgstruppen Hubert Lanz, was faced with a critical situation, as Operation "Star" was already in full swing. The divisions of three armies of the Voronezh Front were approaching the city from the east, with over 300 tanks and 200,000 men.

The SS divisions were arriving just as a Soviet storm was descending upon Kharkov. The fighting for the city would threaten to destroy both "Leibstandarte" and "Das Reich" before "Totenkopf" could even arrive in Russia. Adolf Hitler, with his passion for holding territory to the last man, nearly destroyed the divisions before Manstein was able to use them to launch a counterattack. Only through the courageous action of Paul Hausser, the senior soldier of the armed SS formations, were the two divisions, along with "Grossdeutschland," spared from destruction. Hausser risked his career and even possibly his life, when he decided to defy a direct order from Adolf Hitler that would have probably resulted in the annihilation of "Das Reich" and "Leibstandarte." Hausser's action came at a time when the Germans could not afford to lose the two SS divisions to satisfy Hitler's desire to hold the city. The two SS Panzergrenadier divisions, along with "Totenkopf," were the only German Panzer divisions in southern Russia that would be even close to full strength in early 1943. Without them, the counterattack of 4. Panzerarmee, which began in February of 1943, would not have been possible and the course of the war in Russia could have been altered dramatically.

3

OPERATIONS "GALLOP" AND "STAR"

Preliminary Soviet Operations - January 1942

Throughout late December and early January, Heeresgruppe Don uneasily watched the unfolding developments along the entire Armeeabteilung Fretter-Pico front. The initiative was entirely in the hands of the Russians, because they had adequate reserves to launch a series of offensives which shattered the southern flank of Heeresgruppe B and opened a huge gap in the German lines when the 8th Italian Army fell apart. During the last weeks of January, while Armeeabteilung Fretter-Pico struggled to hold the northern Donets with its assortment of troops, Manstein's Armeeabteilung Hollidt was just beginning a tortuous withdrawal from the Don River to the Donets River southeast of Kamensk. The 4. Panzerarmee was trying to withdraw from the Caucasus before it was trapped by a Soviet thrust aimed at the city of Rostov.

While the Germans struggled to accomplish even modest operations, the Russians planned and executed one offensive after the other. Of great importance to the Soviets was regaining the use of the lateral railway lines opposite Heeresgruppe B positions, particularly the Liski-Kantemirovka-Millerovo-Kamensk line. According to Shtemenko, the Soviet High Command was 'convinced that no fresh large-scale offensive operations could be carried out without possession of this railway.' It is assumed that Shtemenko was referring to the Soviet intention of thrusting across the Northern Donets River in the Voroshilovgrad-Kamensk area and advancing to the Sea of Azov.[1]

The Stavka viewed securing this line as critical for maintenance of proper lines of supply for subsequent offensives. Some Russian forces had advanced more than 250 kilometers from the

nearest rail lines and the Soviet logistical system was not able to supply the amounts of fuel, weapons and men necessary to sustain operations further to the west. This was primarily due to the lack of sufficient numbers of supply trucks, personnel carriers and prime movers for artillery. Poor road systems and bad weather were added factors that increased the difficulties of providing supplies to the formations conducting deep operations. Supplies were slow to arrive and often inadequate to keep Soviet mobile spearheads moving and properly supplied.

Stalin was undoubtedly informed that during Operation "Little Saturn," Soviet tank and mechanized corps, while engaged in exploiting breakthroughs, had seen their fighting power gradually dissipate in the course of sustained operations. This was largely due to inadequate force structure and poor logistical organization. There were instances where tanks and other equipment was lost due to lack of fuel or ammunition while in combat against adequately supplied German mobile units. However, in spite of the recognition of these deficiencies, the Russian high command made no significant corrections in its force structure and ordered new offensives for late January.

On 21 December, 1942, Stalin issued a directive calling for an attack by General F.I. Golikov's Voronezh Front, in order to regain the Liski-Kantemirovka-Millerovo-Kamensk railroad line and further reduce German and Axis strength in the area. This attack was known as the Ostrogozhsk-Rossosh Operation and was carried out by Golikov's Front. The goal of the operation was to eliminate the Hungarian 2nd Army, which held the center of the Heeresgruppe B sector. The main blow was struck by the 3rd Tank Army and fell upon the Hungarian/German forces north of the Kantemirovka area, which the Russian command believed was the weakest point of the Axis defenses. The 3rd Tank Army consisted of the 12th and 15th

---

[1] Shtemenko, S.M., *The Soviet General Staff at War: 1941-1945.* (Moscow: 1970) pg. 97.

Tank Corps, four rifle divisions and some additional artillery. At the last minute, Golikov's Front received additional infantry, ski troops and a tank brigade, which he assigned to the 3rd Tank Army.[2]

The 3rd Tank Army was commanded by Major General P.S. Rybalko, one of the rising stars of Soviet armored operations in 1942. Rybalko was Ukrainian, born near Kharkov and served as an ordinary soldier in the infantry during World War I. He was a member of the Red Guards during the Civil War and began to show his command ability during this period. Toward the end of the Civil War he commanded the 61st Cavalry Regiment. Rybalko subsequently attended the Frunze Military Academy and after completing his course of instruction, later commanded the 7th Cavalry Regiment. He took an additional three year program of command studies at Frunze and shortly before the invasion of Russia taught at the Kazan Tank School. At the direction of Stalin, Rybalko was given command of the 3rd Tank Army in 1942 and he led the army throughout the entire war.[3]

The execution of the Front's operation benefited from the presence of both Marshal Georgi Zhukov, appointed by Stalin as his Deputy Supreme Commander in 1942 and the chief of the Soviet General Staff, General A.M. Vasilevsky. After 3 January, Zhukov and Vasilevsky took over the planning for the attack. The preparations were characterized by Zhukov's typical thoroughness and attention to detail, as well as insistence on the codified methods of secrecy, deception and tight security known as "maskirovka."[4] Maskirovka was the Soviet term for established principles of military concealment, disinformation and deception that were used to hide Soviet intentions from the enemy and to conceal force movements and concentrations.

The concentration of Soviet forces opposite the Hungarians went largely undetected, contributing greatly to the element of surprise once the operation began. Although the Soviets did not always display great skill in the area of deception before Stalingrad, they learned many valuable lessons during that campaign regarding the value of surprise concentration of forces and the clouding, if not outright concealment of their intentions. By mid-war the Russians were often able to build up enormous troop concentrations and supply dumps while the exact size and purpose of Soviet forces remained unclear because the amount of information collected by German intelligence was insufficient to correctly predict Russian intentions. This was of great value to the Russians because it served to induce the factor of uncertainty into the German reaction to the information that was available.

Italian infantry of the Alpini Corps in Russia and a light infantry gun in 1942. Like the Rumanians and Hungarians, the Italian troops serving on the Eastern Front had little motivation to fight well and were often poorly led by their officers. The Italian artillery was adequate, particularly in the elite divisions, but the infantry suffered from the lack of an effective anti-tank gun. (Credit National Archives)

The Germans normally realized that something was in the air before Russian attacks began and they often knew the general area in which operations were likely to occur, but frequently they could not predict anything else with confidence. The intention of Soviet maneuver elements was suspected, but their exact location generally remained undetected. In some cases, Soviet forces literally seemed to disappear before the Germans eyes. On one occasion, the location of the armor of the 18th Tank Corps remained hidden while it regrouped just before the launching of Operation "Gallop." Although they intercepted radio communications the Germans mistakenly thought that the corps was northeast of Voroshilovgrad, when in reality it was in assembly areas northwest of the town, preparing for the launching of "Gallop."

The Soviets did not have enough time to plan extensive, Front level "maskirovka" preparations before the start of "Gallop" or "Star," due to the fact that the armies of both Voronezh Front and Southwestern Front were actively engaged in combat operations. However, it is apparent that routine implementation of "maskirovka" principles occurred at the tactical level, as evidenced by the examples cited above.

The Ostrogozhsk-Rossosh Operation was planned to begin on 12 January, but delays due to assembly and supply difficulties caused the assault to be postponed until 14 January. Preliminary reconnaissance attacks in battalion strength began on the night of 12-13 January and resulted in some unexpected successes. A 40th Army rifle battalion, probing in the direction of the army's main attack, broke through the Axis lines unexpectedly and was able to capture a section of the first trench line. Moskalenko quickly seized this

[2] Erickson, John. *The Road to Berlin*. (Boulder: 1983) pg. 33.
[3] Glantz, David, Jukes Geoffrey, Erickson, John et al. *Stalin's Generals* (New York: 1993) pg. 209-214.
[4] Erickson, pg. 33.

opportunity and committed additional troops, quickly building up a formidable bridgehead from which the main attack could jump off. Other probes along the front of the army were able to gain footholds in various sectors and were similarly reinforced. These activities succeeded in unnerving the Axis divisions before the main attack even began and contributed to their rapid collapse once the operation commenced.

The Hungarian 7th Infantry Division was routed during the opening operations of the offensive on the following day, abandoning its section of the line in panic. The Soviets realized what was happening very quickly and skillfully exploited the fluid situation. Golikov committed the tank corps of Rybalko's 3rd Tank Army on 14 January, enabling his attack to gain 7 kilometers of ground by the end of the day. Rybalko's tank columns quickly smashed through the center of the Hungarian positions and pushed forward nearly twenty kilometers before evening of the second day. The huge gap in the center of the army's front could not be closed and subsequent Soviet successes broke the back of the Hungarian 2nd Army. Soviet mechanized troops and cavalry routed the Italian 5th Infantry Division several days later and the defenses of the entire army quickly began to disintegrate. The army had no operational mobile reserves available with any hope of restoring the situation. By the third day of the Soviet offensive, there was little remaining organized resistance and the army was reduced to fleeing mobs of soldiers who were concerned only with escape from the Russians. The Soviet attacks obliterated the Hungarian army, completely destroying its combat effectiveness, although German detachments retained their unit cohesion and fought back tenaciously.

After the collapse of the Hungarians, Heeregruppe B could do little to restore the front on its southern flank. A gap of more than 100 miles in width was created by the disintegration of the 2nd Army, a situation which presented another opportunity to the Soviet command. Realizing the desperate situation that Heeresgruppe B found itself in after the Hungarian rout, Vasilevsky proposed that the Voronezh Front launch a subsequent attack, literally from the march. This attack, known as the Voronezh-Kastornoye Operation, was directed at Heeresgruppe B's German 2. Armee, commanded by Feldmarchal Maximilian von Weichs, which held the southern sector of the Heeresgruppe Front.

The German 2. Armee defended the area west of Voronezh and found itself in a dangerous situation after the collapse of the Hungarians to the north and the Italians to its south. Vasilevsky proposed to attack 2. Armee with Major General N.P. Pushkov's 13th Army and three armies of Golikov's Front. The plan for the Voronezh-Kastornoe operation proposed to attack von Weich's twelve divisions on both flanks of the salient which had been formed by the earlier Soviet operations.

The Soviet Voronezh-Kastornoye Operation was launched after a heavy artillery preparation and immediately met with success, in spite of terrible weather conditions. A heavy falling snow and a dense fog limited visibility in the early hours of the morning, which caused the Soviet artillery preparation to be delayed until late in the morning. In the 3rd Tank Army sector, the artillery fire on the forward enemy positions lasted a half hour. When it lifted and shifted to rear areas, the Russian rifle divisions began their attacks, which met with early success. After the Soviet infantry overran the positions of the defending Axis troops, the Soviet armor rolled forward. The 12th and 15th Tank Corps were ordered to begin their attacks and promptly penetrated the Axis front.

By the following day, the 15th Tank Corps cut the Rossosh-Rovenki road and the 12th Tank Corps reached the town of Rossosh itself. The Italian infantry regiment defending Rossosh fell apart,

General der Infanterie Karl Hollidt was the commander of Armeeabteilung Hollidt in late 1942. His command was made up of various Axis and German troops which fell back to the west after the fall of Stalingrad. By February of 1943 Armeeabteilung Hollidt established itself in defensive positions on the west bank of the Mius River, where it remained until August of 1943 when a Soviet offensive launched after the battle of Kursk dislodged the army, which had been renamed 6. Armee by that date. (Credit National Archives)

with many of its men surrendering to the Russians as soon as Russian tanks made their first appearance. The Italian regimental commander was captured, along with his entire staff. The Italian Alpine Corps was cut off in the Podgornoye area by the advance of the Soviet armor but insufficient Russian infantry was assigned to reduce the pocket and the Italians broke out of their encirclement. As they withdrew west, the Italians caused some confusion along the communications lines of the 12th Tank Corps, but did not seriously disrupt the advance of the Russian tank corps.[5]

Deep snow and icy roads made supply very difficult and the Russians armored columns began to run short of fuel and ammunition on the third day of the attack. This situation was remedied by emergency resupply by air. Soviet planes located the tanks by signal fires and landed on makeshift airfields with tins of fuel or flew at extremely low altitudes and made emergency drops of supplies. The 13th Army drove towards Kastornoye and within days 2. Armee's two southern corps were encircled by the Soviets. The remaining northern corps gave ground slowly northward and was hard pressed to avoid major breakthroughs along its front. On 28 January, the Soviet 13th Army closed in on Kastornoye from the north while Voronezh Front elements approached the town from the east and south.

On the following day, the Russians drove the remaining Germans out of the town, crushing the last significant resistance in the pocket. The destruction of the southern flank of 2. Armee created a large gap which extended for 100 kilometers to the south of Kastornoye, its southern boundary reaching the Kupyansk area. As a result of its losses, Heeresgruppe B was unable to provide forces of any consequence to Armeeabteilung Fretter-Pico during its critical defense of the Donets in early January. This aggravated an already potentially serious situation on the northern flank of Heeresgruppe Don. If the Soviet succeeded in crossing the Northern Donets, the northern flank of the army group, held by Armeeabteilung Hollidt and the communications zone of Heeresgruppe Don was vulnerable.[6]

Armeeabteilung Hollidt, which was a great deal stronger than Fretter-Pico's ad hoc army detachment, had two corps of seven infantry divisions and also possessed a moderate amount of armor. The army was commanded by tough, competent General der Infanterie Karl Hollidt. Hollidt began his service in the Bavarian

[5] Armstrong, Richard N. *Red Army Tank Commanders - The Armored Guards*. (Atglen: 1994) pg.168.

[6] Armstrong, pg. 166.

German tanks in a Russian village west of the Mius River in late 1942. The Panzer IIIs probably belong to either 7. Panzer-Division or 23. Panzer-Division, both of which were attached to Hollidt's army in the latter part of 1942. The 23. Panzer-Division was still in the order of battle of the army when it was attacked on the Mius River in the summer of 1943. (Credit National Archives)

Army in 1908 as an officer cadet assigned to 3. Kompanie, Infanterie-Regiment 117. In 1910 he was promoted to the rank of Leutnant and he saw combat as an infantry officer during World War I. He commanded an infantry company and later a battalion, surviving the battles of Verdun, the Aisne and Somme. Hollidt was wounded in action, won both classes of the Iron Cross during the war and was a Captain by the time the Armistice was signed. He was a member of the Hessische Freikorps and served in the Reichswehr, first as Regimentsadjutant of Infanterie-Regiment 15 and later in several staff positions. By January 1935, Hollidt was promoted to Oberst i.G. and was appointed Chef des Generalstabes of I. Armeekorps, under General von Brauchitsch. He was promoted to Generalmajor in 1938 and led 50. Infanterie-Division into Russia, winning the Knight's Cross on 8 September, 1941. In January, 1942 Hollidt took command of XVII. Armeekorps, which he led for nine months until receiving command of what became known as Armeeabteilung Hollidt, which later was designated the second 6. Armee.

Hollidt had just less than a hundred tanks, belonging to two mobile divisions, 5. and 22. Panzer-Division. Most of the division's tanks were Panzer IIIs armed with the 5cm gun or Panzer IVs still equipped with the short barreled 7.5cm howitzer. However, they were not badly under strength for German Panzer divisions at this period of the war in Russia. Hollidt had conducted a fighting retreat westward toward the Donets River, covering forty miles by 6 January. Communication was established with Armeeabteilung Fretter-Pico's southern flank by the middle of the month, when Armeeabteilung Hollidt reconnaissance troops made contact with 304. Infanterie-Division troops northeast of Kamensk. Fretter-Pico immediately requested help from Hollidt, as his Armeeabteilung was very short of mobile troops. Hollidt sent help, in the form of the newly arrived 7. Panzer-Division, even though his own army had more than enough troubles of its own, as the Armeeabteilung was charged with protecting the northern flank of 4. Panzerarmee. The 4. Panzerarmee was at that time conducting a difficult withdrawal, under heavy pressure from the Russians. Elements of the 7. Panzer-Division slowly assembled in the Voroshilovgrad area, although not arriving in time to block the Soviet breakout that resulted in the evacuation of Millerovo, Chertkovo and Gartmaschevka.

The operations of Heeresgruppe Don were repeatedly affected by orders from Hitler that delayed decisions that needed to be made on the spot or countermanded Manstein, forcing the Field Marshall to argue for days in support of his conduct of the battle. Manstein, in *Lost Victories*, commented on the decisions of the Führer regarding the defense of the southern wing of the front, and the results of the orders emanating from Berlin. Manstein understood the possible long term consequences of the strategy that demanded the unconditional holding of all territory regardless of the military situation and he was very critical of Hitler in his descriptions of this period of the war. However, contrary to commonly held opinions, Hitler's orders were not always entirely without merit, primarily due to deficiencies of both the German and Russian armies. Manstein's post war accounts do not take into account the lack of mobility of the German army, particularly the infantry divisions, who depended primarily upon horses to move their heavy equipment. Only in rare cases were the average infantry divisions even equipped with adequate numbers of assault guns and seldom, if ever with sufficient trucks and vehicles to enable them to conduct mobile defensive operations. Although Manstein criticized Hitler for not understanding a war of movement, at least in some instances, Hitler probably was correct at insisting that infantry divisions hold their ground at all costs. Given their lack of mobility, the alternative course for the divisions may have been to conduct a withdrawal into the open steppe, unable to bring all of its artillery or ammunition stores with it. As difficult and costly as these defensive operations were, they may have been preferable to conducting a retreat on foot, at the height of the Russian winter, carrying wounded and towing heavy weapons with steadily diminishing numbers of horses.

Hitler remained guided by his own vision of how the war should be conducted and his decisions often seemed to beyond what the depleted German divisions could be expected to accomplish. However, it is likely that more often than most military historians would generally admit, Hitler's hold at all cost strategy resulted in some benefits to the Germans. During the first winter of the war, when massive Soviet counteroffensives threw his armies back from Moscow, Hitler's iron willed orders, which riveted the German divisions in place, saved the Germans from an ugly rout and an even more disastrous setback.

In addition, there were characteristics of the Russian Army which gave Hitler's tactics at least somewhat of a logical basis. The lack of an efficient logistical system meant that Russian offensives, after a time, were nearly always hamstrung by poor supply flow, lack of adequate vehicle maintenance and flaws of force structure. Eventually, due to these deficiencies, at least in the first years of the war in Russia, Soviet offensives often shot their bolt within a matter of weeks and momentum was lost. Given that belief, Hitler became convinced that if the encircled German units could tie up enough Russian strength fighting in the rear areas, it would reduce the forces available at the point of the main attack that much sooner. In fact, the hold at all costs principle often did tie up a large part of the Russian strength, but it was only effective in the tactical sense.

For this type of strategy to have been completely successful, the Germans would have required numerous strong, available armored and mobile reserves with which to restore the front before the encircled troops were annihilated or starved into surrender. However the Germans did not possess the necessary amount of reserves and as an effective plan of defense on the strategic level, the Führer's defensive stratagem failed in the long run. At the time however, due to the deficiencies of the German infantry divisions and the lack of fresh Panzer troops, the Germans often had little other choice but to stand and fight, until increasingly exhausted Panzer divisions arrived to try and restore the situation. The superior Soviet strategic reserves seldom allowed the Germans to completely recover and as a result, the initiative often lay in Soviet hands after December of 1942.

Manstein clearly saw the larger picture of the strategic situation and spoke of the danger faced by the Germans in southern Russian in late 1942 and early 1943. He correctly identified the underlying problem which was a strategic error committed during the previous year.

> The issue was no longer the fate of a single army, but of the entire southern wing of the front and ultimately of all the German armies in the east . . . Indeed, thanks to the errors of leadership in the summer and autumn campaigns of 1942, the principal aim-at least to begin with-could only be, in the words of Schlieffen, "bring defeat underfoot."[7]

The Russians were under no delusions as to the opportunities offered to them in late 1942 and the first days of 1943. By the middle of January, 1943 Soviet armies west of the Don River were closer to the main Dnepr crossings at Zaporozsche and Dnepropetrovsk than were Heeresgruppe A, 4. Panzerarmee, 1. Panzerarmee and Armeeabteilung Hollidt. These German forces were perched precariously at the end of long and easily threatened railroad lines extending east from the Dnepr for hundreds of miles. Armeeabteilung Hollidt, weakened by lengthy fighting and heavy casualties, stretched its divisions along a projecting shoulder that extended westward for 60 miles. The shoulder was at right angles to the main front line defenses that had withdrawn under pressure of the 5th Shock Army and 2nd Guards Army. The only force available to protect the northern flank of Hollidt's army was Fretter-Pico's worn out German infantry, SS and Police detachments and meager armored reserves.

---

[7] Manstein, pg. 367.

The Soviet command eagerly seized upon what they clearly saw as a golden opportunity to deal a fatal blow to the entire German southern flank in Russia. The Stavka had begun considering a number of operations during the last months of 1942. In these operations, the ultimate goal was to first weaken the German forces in the Ukraine and Caucasus, and secondly, encircle and destroy them. After the events of mid January, when the 2nd Italian and German 2.Armee were essentially destroyed, the confidence of the Russian command reached new highs and the Stavka dared hope that the Germans could be dealt a fatal blow.

Operation "Gallop"

N.F. Vatutin, commander of the Southwestern Front, offered an ambitious operational plan to the Soviet Stavka on 19 January. He proposed to create a mobile group that would penetrate Heeresgruppe Don's porous front, drive deep into the rear of the army group and then swing south toward the shores of the Gulf of Taganrog. By reaching a point on the coastline approximately 100 miles west of Rostov, Vatutin hoped to sever the rail and road network extending east from the Dnepr River and thereby cut off 1. Panzerarmee, 4. Panzerarmee and Armeeabteilungen Fretter-Pico and Hollidt. This ambitious plan was code named Operation "Gallop" and its daring scope was typical of Vatutin, whose operational ambitions were characterized by aggressive optimism throughout his career.

Vatutin was born in 1901, in the Voronezh province, in modest circumstances and received his early education at a trade school. In 1920 he joined the 3rd Reserve Rifle Regiment and later served in the 113th Reserve Rifle Battalion and fought partisans in the Ukraine. In 1921, after he attended a command course at the Soviet army infantry school in Poltava, he embarked upon a rapid rise through the army. After compiling an outstanding record of service in a number of positions, Vatutin was selected to attend additional officer training courses. He proved to be an outstanding student and qualified for entrance to the Frunze Military Academy.

The young officer showed a talent for evaluating military situations correctly and understood technological changes and their likely impact on the military. In 1940 he was appointed Chief of Staff of the Southern Front and was promoted to Lieutenant General before his appointment as First Deputy Chief of the General Staff (Stavka). He played a key role in the defense of Leningrad and in 1941 was made Chief of Staff of the Northwestern Front during its defense of Moscow. Vatutin's service during the first year of the war was characterized by frank appraisals of military situations and aggressive offensive operations, notably a daring airborne

LEFT: A forward artillery observers position in the Armeeabteilung Hollidt area in December of 1942. There was little high ground in this part of the Ukraine, although generally the western banks of larger rivers were higher than the more swampy eastern banks. (Credit National Archives) RIGHT: A heavy German field gun, probably a K 18 or a sFH 18 howitzer which fired a 15cm shell. The German artillery regiments were equipped with excellent weapons, served by highly trained officers and men, and were often the backbone of the infantry divisions in Russia. When the manpower shortage became critical after 1941, it was often only the artillery which enabled German infantry divisions to hold defensive fronts that were much too broad for their reduced strength. (Credit National Archives)

assault on German positions in the Demyansk salient. In October, 1942 Vatutin assumed command of the Southwestern Front and led it until February, 1944 when he and an advance command group were ambushed by Ukrainian partisans. Vatutin suffered severe leg wounds, from which he eventually died on 15 April 1944. It is ironic that Vatutin was killed by Ukrainians, the very people that he had fought to free from Nazi domination.

Vatutin was well aware of the weakness of the German forces defending the Northern Donets line of defense in the Voroshilovgrad-Kamensk area. During the last weeks of January, divisions of the 1st Guards Army had pushed across the Derkul and Aidar Rivers, north of Voroshilovgrad and slowly advanced westward toward the Krassnaja River. However, due to the fatigue of his own tired rifle divisions and weakened tank formations, the army was not able to decisively thrust south of the river. In addition, Axis forces in his rear occupied men and weapons that could have been utilized during the battles against Armeeabteilung Fretter-Pico forces north of the Donets.

After the remnants of the Italian and German garrisons of Millerovo, Gartmaschevka and Chertkovo broke through the Soviet troops encircling each town and escaped, the 1st Guards Army was free to attack to the west, without the distraction of enemy troops in their rear. Soviet columns overwhelmed the two weakened panzer divisions trying to hold the Aidar, and drove west, pushing 19. Panzer-Division battle groups to the eastern banks of the Krasnaya River, north of Lisichansk. Disorganized and generally hapless mobs of Italian and Rumanian troops fled before the Russian advance, while fragmented groups of 298. Infanterie-Division fought their way west, often straggling along behind the Soviet advance or between columns of Russian tanks and infantry.

The northern wing of Heeresgruppe Don remained open after Golikov's Voronezh-Kastornoje Operation destroyed Axis forces on the southern or right wing of Heeresgruppe B and created a large gap between the southern flank of the army group and the northern flank of Manstein's army group. The German's predicament east of Kharkov and along the Northern Donets between Voroshilovgrad and Kamensk led Vatutin to believe that the Axis armies were on the verge of irrevocable collapse. While this was undoubtedly true in the case of the Italians, Hungarians and Rumanians, Vatutin did not reckon on the ability of the Germans to improvise and recover.

The Stavka, optimistically believing that the war in southern Russia could be ended quickly, accepted Vatutin's proposal on 20 January, even though the advance of the 3rd Guards Army and the 5th Tank Army had slowed due to the stubborn resistance of Armeeabteilung Fretter-Pico and the general weakness of the armies of the Southwestern Front. Planning for Vatutin's proposed offensive began immediately, as the operation was to be launched without pause to regroup the front's tiring formations. This proved to be a significant, although perhaps understandable mistake, as Soviet forces were already weakened during the long weeks of fighting in December and January. Shortly after adopting Vatutin's plan, the Soviet high command decided to launch another key offensive simultaneously, this one aimed at the Kharkov sector. This operation was code named "Star," and was to be conducted by Golikov's Voronezh Front.

Golikov was born in 1900, the son of a doctor and proved to be an industrious, hard working student. During the turmoil of the Civil War, he served with a rifle regiment known as the "Red Eagles" and showed an aptitude for political studies which resulted in being posted to the 3rd Army as a political officer. Having impeccable political credentials, Golikov apparently played a role in the officer purges of the Soviet Army ordered by Stalin in the 1930's. Golikov was well connected politically and in 1941was appointed to be the head of the GRU or Soviet Military Intelligence. His first command was of the 10th Reserve Army, which he competently organized and led during the Soviet counterattack after stopping the Germans at Moscow, in the winter of 1941. Golikov took command of the Voronezh Front in the spring of 1942.[8]

After the completion of the Voronezh-Kastornoe operation, Golikov was to begin Operation "Star" on 2 February, just days after the start of "Gallop." The staggered launching of these twin hammer blows, following the disasters inflicted on Axis forces during December and early January, were designed to destroy the remaining strength of Heeresgruppe B and encircle Heeresgruppe Don. The new offensives, if successful, would destroy Armeeabteilungen Fretter-Pico and Hollidt, capture the key cities of Kharkov and Kursk and isolate 17. Armee and 1. Panzer Armee as well. The destruction of these forces, coming on the heels of the loss of 250,000 German soldiers at Stalingrad, would have meant the loss of the war in Russia for Germany, for the Eastern front would have collapsed into the huge void existing in southern Russia.

Vatutin's Southwestern Front consisted of the 1st Guards, 3rd Guards, 5th Tank and the 6th Armies, plus a mobile group commanded by Lieutenant General M.M. Popov, consisting of the depleted 3rd, 4th, 10th and 18th Tank Corps with a total of 212 tanks. The Southwestern Front reserve possessed two additional tank corps, the 1st Guards and 25th Tank Corps, with 300 tanks. The armies of the Southwestern Front had approximately 325,000 men. They were opposed by about 40,000 men and less than fifty tanks of 1. Panzerarmee and Armeeabteilung Hollidt's 100,000 men and eighty to ninety tanks.

The first phase of Operation "Gallop" was the penetration of the German and Axis defenses along the Krassnaja River and Northern Donets west of Voroshilovgrad, in order to create gaps for the commitment of Mobile Group Popov. Situated on the Front's northern flank, Lieutenant General F.M. Kharitonov's 6th Army consisted of 4 rifle divisions, reinforced by a weak tank brigade and tank regiment. The two tank formations had only forty tanks between them. There were additional support troops assigned to the rifle divisions, most important of which were three artillery regiments. The mission assigned to the 6th Army was to attack and destroy the German 298. Infanterie-Division and 320. Infanterie-Division defending the northern section of the Krassnaja River. Kharitonov's main effort was on the right flank, where three rifle

divisions were to attack 298. Infanterie-Division and penetrate its front. The primary objective of the army's advance was to protect the northern flank of the Front's offensive, through its advance to Kupyansk, located on the Oskol River.

The 1st Guards Army, commanded by General V.I. Kuznetsov, was somewhat stronger than Kharitonov's army, having been assigned seven rifle divisions, although it had no little or no inherent armor and the rifle divisions were probably all significantly below normal strength. On the right or northern flank of Kuznetsov's army, the 4th Guards Rifle Corps, was to force the Krassnaja River and attack German defenses along the river north of Lisichansk. The 19. Panzer-Division held the sector, which was too broad for the division to effectively defend. It occupied a screen of defensive positions blocking crossing sites on the river, however, large gaps existed between the strong points. On the left or southern flank of the army, the 6th Guards Rifle Corps was to assault and cross the Northern Donets and capture the town of Lisichansk. The approaches to the town were held by elements of 19. Panzer-Division and the remnants of the much weakened 27. Panzer-Division. The main effort of the army was in the 4th Guards Rifle Corps sector, where Mobile Group Popov was to be introduced.

The primary goal of the 4th Guards Rifle Corps was to create a gap of sufficient width and depth to allow General M.M. Popov's Mobile Group to begin its attack toward the south and break out of the penetration zone. After assisting in the breakthrough operations against German front line defenses, the 4th Guards Rifle Corps was to turn south and advance on the town of Slavyansk. The tank corps of Mobile Group Popov were to proceed through the 4th Guards Rifle Corps and begin the exploitation phase of the Front's offensive.[9]

Mobile Group Popov had the most important role in Vatutin's offensive. It consisted of four understrength tanks corps, each of which had an average of just over fifty tanks. The objective of Popov's group was to cross the Northern Donets west of Lisichansk and drive south to the Stalino area. From there, leading elements of the mobile group were to thrust to Mariupol, on the coast of the Sea of Azov, thus severing all lines of communication of the German armies east of Stalino. Popov's mobile headquarters group was to coordinate the advance of the tank corps, some of which were assigned additional rifle brigades, in order to provided much needed infantry support.[10]

South of the 1st Guards Army sector was the 3rd Guards Army, which consisted of nine rifle divisions under command of two corps headquarters. The army had three tank corps with a total of only a

---

[8] *Stalin's Generals*, pg. 77-80.

[9] Glantz, pg. 92-93.
[10] Op cit.

hundred tanks, in addition to one mechanized corps and a cavalry corps. The 3rd Guards Army was commanded by Lieutenant General D.D. Lelyushenko, who was a former cavalry commander and another veteran of the Russian Civil War. Lelyushenko first saw combat as an enlisted infantryman and later served in the Russian cavalry. During the prewar years, he completed a number of advanced officer training courses, eventually attending the Frunze Military Academy. By September of 1939, he commanded the 39th Independent Light Tank Brigade and led it through a series of valuable, though non-combat operations.

Lelyushenko first led his brigade into combat in the Finnish war and participated in the successful attack against the Mannerheim Line by the Soviet 13th Army. He was promoted to Lieutenant General and given command of the 21st Mechanized Corps in 1941. Later in the year, he was appointed commander of the newly organized 1st Guards Rifle Corps, a dubious honor because the corps did not actually have any combat formations. Proving to be resourceful, Lelyushenko collected a motorcycle regiment and various army training school personnel and gathered together what forces he could find. Adept at improvisation, Lelyushenko found ways to commit his 'corps' to battle.[11]

In order to utilize the guns of the Tula Army Artillery School, he commandeered a fleet of buses to haul the guns to the front. He placed an NKVD Regiment under his command and later received the 4th Tank Brigade, the 6th Guards Rifle Division and tough paratroopers of the 201st Airborne Brigade. With this hastily organized force defending the approaches to Mtensk, Lelyushenko successfully delayed Panzer Gruppe Guderian for nine days, allowing the Bryansk Front time to reorganize farther to the east. His command skills were recognized and he was given command of the 30th Army. In 1942, Lelyushenko took command of the 3rd Guards Army, which had seen a great deal of combat during the last months of the year and his rifle divisions were significantly weakened due to combat losses.[12]

The 3rd Guards Army attack, with the main effort on the right flank, was to advance on a wide front and cross the Northern Donets in the Voroshilovgrad-Kamensk area. The army was to capture Voroshilovgrad and Kamensk, and then continue to drive southwest to the Stalino area. At that point, Lelyushenko's army would have penetrated into the rear areas of Armeeabteilung Hollidt and introduced a broad wedge severing German main lines of communication running through the Stalino sector. It was to assist Mobile Group Popov in the penetration to the Mariupol area.

---

[11] Armstrong, pg. 265.
[12] Ibid. pg. 266.

Vatutin's 5th Tank Army, commanded by Lieutenant General I.T. Shelmin, was the weakest of the Southwestern Front's armies and actually possessed no armor at the time. Its three rifle divisions were to cooperate with the 3rd Guards Army in the capture of Kamensk and after the offensive passed south of the Northern Donets, was to attack Armeeabteilung Fretter-Pico and the portion of Armeeabteilung Hollidt forces which were holding the Kamensk sector. After taking Kamensk, the army was to drive west, passing parallel to the course of the Donets between Voroshilovgrad and Kamensk.

The missions assigned to the armies of the Southwestern Front were very ambitious for a number of reasons. First of all, the offensive was launched essentially without pause, in order to prevent the Germans from recovering from the consecutive shocks they had been dealt since Stalingrad. This meant that the tank corps were at less than full strength and the tanks that were available often needed mechanical attention. The Soviet logistical problems remained unsolved and placed serious limitations on the ability of the tank corps to keep moving and sustain deep penetrations. However, the major problem concerning the Soviet command during the planning stage of Operation "Gallop," was the condition of the Soviet rifle divisions. As they were all worn down from constant fighting, it remained to be seen if they would be able to quickly punch through the German lines without requiring support by the tank corps. Because the rifle divisions were so weakened by casualties and heavy equipment losses, the offensives planned by the Stavka were very risky. If Soviet armor had to be committed to breakthrough operations, any significant attrition jeopardized both offensives from the very first. There were some in the Soviet High Command who were concerned about these issues, but the rising tide of optimism drowned out their reservations, which were probably not strongly voiced.

The Soviet Gamble

When the Russians decided to launch two major offensives from the march, they took a substantial risk. If substantial portions of Popov's tanks were required to assist the rifle corps in creating gaps for the introduction of the exploitation forces, the resulting delays would throw the Soviet operational time table behind schedule. This would then allow the Germans time to bring up additional mobile reserves. In addition, length and costly breakthrough operations would further weaken already understrength rifle divisions. It would also consume artillery shells, supplies and fuel reserves before the exploitation phase was begun. Truck shortages made resupply of artillery shells and relocation of artillery units a slow and difficult process, which was exacerbated by the miserable weather conditions.

Soviet infantry strength inadequacies foreshadowed potential problems for the four armies of the Front and Mobile Group Popov during the exploitation phase of its attack. Popov could not afford to have his armor consumed in order to achieve the initial objectives of the rifle divisions. The Soviets made some attempts to address the force structure deficiencies identified during Operation "Little Saturn" and each of the tank corps was given additional motorized infantry support for the exploitation phase of the attack. It had been seen in the Tatsinskaya and Morozovsk attacks that the tank corps did not have enough integral infantry strength to allow them to sustain deep operations or conduct successful defensive operations after German reserves entered the battle. When the inevitable German counterattacks were launched upon the flanks of forward elements, Soviet armored attacks typically failed or were fatally delayed.[13]

Once having made penetrations the Soviet tank corps commanders were forced to decide whether to secure their lines of communications with already scarce infantry or to leave their supply lines vulnerable. Most decided to put as much strength as possible in their attack groups, in order to sustain the momentum of the operation. Often this allowed the Germans to bring up reserves and successfully conduct attacks on inadequately secured Soviet lines of communication. Even with weak combat groups, the Germans regularly disrupted the flow of supplies, replacement tanks and reserves to Soviet forward elements. An example of such a situation was during the Tatsinskaja attack conducted by Badanov's 24th Tank Corps. When small German combat groups blocked the roads leading into Tatsinskaja from the north, Badanov could do little to affect the situation. By that time, he had so few infantrymen left that he was forced to use tank crews who had lost their tanks as supplements to his infantry detachments.

Operation "Gallop" was an ambitious plan, and the Stavka recognized that there would be risks involved in such an operation. The relocation of artillery and the coordination of the batteries once they had been moved was a substantial problem for the Soviets at that stage of the war. The inability to relocate artillery support adversely affected the ability of the Soviets to sustain deep penetration operations of the forward mobile groups. Once the Germans began to conduct counterattacks, Soviet mobile spearheads were forced to conduct defensive operations against German counterattacks and suffered from a lack of artillery. Some attempts were made to offset the situation by including truck mounted rocket launchers

in the order of battle of the tank corps or adding heavy mortar detachments. These were stopgap measures however, and it was not until late 1943 or 1944 that many of the Soviet tank corps were equipped with integral artillery regiments.

These deficiencies caused justifiable concern to the Soviet command as they were well aware of this problem due to frank study and diagnosis of past failures of deep operations. The Soviet Army of late 1942 was still a force very much in transition. The Russians had begun to correct their force and command structure based on analysis of the problems identified from previous operational shortcomings. However, logistical deficiencies lingered, in part because the Russians devoted much of their vast industrial capacity to producing weapons rather than trucks. As a result, in spite of receiving tens of thousands of American trucks and jeeps, the Soviets struggled with supply and maintenance deficiencies throughout the remainder of 1943 and even later in the war. Tanks, planes and artillery pieces remained a higher priority than supply vehicles, as the Soviet army could make do without trucks, but could not fight without tanks.

In the glow of overconfidence that followed a long string of defeats inflicted on the Germans since late 1942, the Soviet High Command decided to proceed with Operation "Gallop," believing that the possible rewards justified the risk. The Stavka believed that the combined assault of the Voronezh and Southwestern Front, coupled with the simultaneous attacks of the Southern Front, would overwhelm the Germans. Most of the Soviet command believed that Hitler's armies were on the verge of irreversible collapse. Certainly Stalin was convinced that this was true and his opinion was of course, the final word. The deficiencies in the supply structure and the continuation of a major offensive without pause to rest and refit, were acceptable risks to the Stavka. In fact, the Russians even decided to launch another major operation, simultaneously with Operation "Gallop."

Stalin and the Stavka, after receiving a report on the front situation from Zhukov on 23 January, decided to attack the Kharkov-Kursk sector as well. This operation, code named "Star," was assigned to Golikov's Voronezh Front and its first phase was the capture of the crossings of the Northern Donets River east of Kharkov. The primary objective was the capture of Kharkov and Kursk.[14]

Operation "Star"

Golikov's Voronezh Front was also given a short time to ready his front for the new operation and his staff had little more than a week

---

[13] Glantz, pg. 87 and 93.

[14] Shtemenko, pg. 99-101.

to plan and gather supplies for the offensive. The conduct of the offensive was affected adversely by the simultaneous involvement of elements of the Front in mopping up actions in the Kastornoye area, which occupied forces of the Front even after the offensive began.

The basic plan for Operation "Star" was presented to Golikov on 23 January. He was initially to begin the attack on 1 February, but was forced to delay the launching until a day later because the armies had not finished regrouping in time. This delay was at least partially due to the inadequate road network and extremely bad weather. All of the primary roads were dirt tracks, covered with ice and packed snow. Any sudden, momentary thaw converted them into deep, paralyzing mud tracks, that froze into formidable ruts when the sun went down. As the Russians had to travel at night as much as possible, in order to prevent German air reconnaissance from discovering these movements, the tanks and other vehicles experienced extremely poor road conditions. There were inevitable breakdowns of vehicles that were already in poor shape mechanically.

To make the situation worse for the Russian armies, Stalin felt confident enough to add to the proposed list of objectives for Operation "Star." At the last minute, on 26 January, the attack objectives were expanded to include the city of Kursk.[15] This was at the urging of Zhukov and also as a result of optimistic reports from other Soviet Front commanders, who believed that the initiative had been irrevocably taken from the Germans. Some of these reports undoubtedly came from the always optimistic Vatutin, who believed that the Germans intended to withdraw behind the Dnepr as quickly as possible. Soviet Intelligence estimates indicated that the Germans did not have sufficient reserves to enable them to recover and establish a stable defensive line east of the Dnepr. Stalin ordered General Rokossovsky to establish a new army group, known as the Central Front, using two armies from the strategic reserve and other forces brought up from the Stalingrad area. The Central Front was to be inserted north of the Voronezh Front and was charged with attacking the southern flank of Heeresgruppe Mitte while Golikov endeavored to destroy capture Kharkov and Kursk.[16]

Three armies of Golikov's Voronezh Front were arrayed along a broad front, approximately 120 kilometers from Kharkov. The army's front bent south at a point along the northern reaches of the Oskol River and extended southward along the western bank of the river to a point directly east of Kharkov. North of the city, Lieutenant General K.S. Moskalenko's 40th Army was approaching the

A German infantry squad preparing to go on patrol in the winter of 1942-43. Most of the men wear the standard issue heavy wool blend winter overcoat and a variety of head gear. (Credit National Archives)

city on the northern flank of the Voronezh Front. In the center was the 69th Army and on the southern flank, the 3rd Tank Army. The 3rd Tank Army and the 69th Army had crossed the Oskol River and were advancing westward, on a broad front, towards the weak German defensive positions east of Kharkov.

The 3rd Tank Army, commanded by Lieutenant General P.S. Rybalko, was the strongest formation of the front in terms of tank strength. The army possessed the armor of the 12th and 15th Tank Corps and the 6th Guards Cavalry Corps. Additional armor, in the form of a tank brigade and tank regiment, were assigned to support the rifle divisions of the army. Rybalko's army was to cross the Northern Donets southeast of Kharkov, drive past the city's southern edge and then link up with Moskalenko's 40th Army west of Kharkov, encircling the German forces defending the city.

Lieutenant General K.S. Moskalenko's 40th Army had eight rifle divisions and the 4th Tank Corps, plus additional supporting armor. However, three of the army's rifle divisions and the 4th Tank Corps were not able to take part in the first phase of the offensive, because they were still fighting groups of encircled German troops in the Kastornoye area.

Moskalenko had been born in the Donbas region, in 1902, at the town of Grishino. He joined the Red Army during the Civil War, seeing combat with the 1st Cavalry Army. His early military education took place at various artillery schools in the Kharkov area and he served as a battery commander in the 6th Cavalry Division. During the 1930s he attended various training courses for mechanized troops and staff command duties. He was posted to the 6th Army as its Deputy Commander in 1942 and first led an army when he took command of the 38th Army. He took part in the disastrous Operation "Mars" in the spring of 1942 and subsequently com-

[15] Glantz, pg. 85.
[16] Seaton, Albert, *The Russo-German War: 1941-1945*. (London: 1971) pg. 179.

manded the 1st Guards Army during the Stalingrad operation. Late in 1942, he was given command of the 40th Army, just before the beginning of Operation "Star."[17]

Moskalenko's army was to first attack and take Belgorod, which was approximately 70 kilometers north of Kharkov. Once past Belgorod, a number of avenues of approach led to the approaches to Kharkov's west and northwest edge. To the west of Kharkov was the town of Ljubotin and the vital communications net which ran through the area of Poltava-Valki-Merefa, southwest of the city. After securing Belgorod, the 40th Army was to advance to the southwest, move past Kharkov's northwest corner and link up with Rybalko's 3rd Tank Army at Ljubotin.

Between the 3rd Tank Army and Moskalenko's 40th Army, Lieutenant General M.I. Kazakov's 69th Army was to attack Kharkov from the northeast. The army had only four rifle divisions and possessed just fifty tanks, which were doled out among the rifle divisions for close support during the attack.

Armeeabteilung Lanz defends the Northern Donets and Kharkov

As the Russians prepared to launch Operations "Gallop" and "Star," the Germans were trying to recover from the hammer blows that had been dealt them, seemingly without pause, since November of 1942. The front in the south had gained some semblance of coherence during the first weeks of January, although a crisis seemingly existed at nearly every point. Only a brief regrouping by the Soviet armies preparing to launch the two offensives provided the Germans with any breathing room. A large gap remained between Heeregruppe Don's northern flank and Heeresgruppe B's southern flank and it could not be closed with the troops available.

At the end of January, Armeeabteilung Fretter-Pico, with the newly arrived 335. Infanterie Division added to its order of battle, once again became XXX. Armeekorps, under the command of 1. Panzerarmee. The 1. Panzerarmee, after moving several of its divisions out of the Caucasus, took over the defense of the Voroshilovgrad-Kamensk sector, while Armeeabteilung Hollidt manned the line east and southeast of the Kamensk area, where it was opposed by the 5th Tank Army.

The 304. Infanterie-Division was assigned to XVII. Armeekorps of Armeeabteilung Hollidt but proved handicapped by inexperience and was not dependable in combat. Hollidt's army detachment possessed 6 German infantry divisions, including 306. Infanterie-Division and 294. Infanterie-Division, which were good quality units,

[17] *Stalin's Generals*, pg. 137-142.

The vast open terrain in much of southern Russia stretched the resources of the Germans beyond the breaking point. The German infantry divisions were not able to build a continuous trenchline such as was normal in World War 1 and did not have sufficient manpower to hold it. The divisions were forced to adopt a defensive strategy of establishing widely spaced strongpoints, with gaps between each position covered by artillery fire and machine guns. Here an MG-34 machine gun team mans its weapon with the limitless Russian steppe stretching into the distance before them. (Credit National Archives)

but under strength due to the earlier fighting. Also available was 62. Infanterie-Division, which along with 294. Division had been attached to the 3rd Rumanian Army and had suffered heavy casualties in the retreat that resulted after the disintegration of the Rumanians. The 8. Luftwaffefelddivision was also assigned to Hollidt but its men, untrained in ground warfare, proved a waste of excellent quality manpower. The division, like most of the Luftwaffe divisions, usually suffered heavy losses during combat and many of the Luftwaffe divisions collapsed at the first heavy fighting. However, even given its own shortcomings, Armeeabteilung Hollidt was in a better position than the defenders of Kharkov.

Armeeabteilung Lanz, commanded by General der Gebirgstruppen Hubert Lanz, initially had only two divisions, which were of greatly varying quality. Under command of Korps Cramer, the elite army division, Panzergrenadier-Division "Grossdeutschland" was concentrating in the sector due east of Belgorod, approximately 90 kilometers northeast of Kharkov. The 168. Infanterie-Division was holding an extended front 30 kilometers northeast of the town of Belgorod, which was about 60 kilometers north of Kharkov. "Das Reich" and "Leibstandarte" were deploying their battalions from the march, taking up positions east of Kharkov, marching toward the front as they disembarked from various railheads in the city.

However, with only 168. Infanterie-Division available to screen the northern approaches to Kharkov, Lanz's defense of Kharkov was imperiled by the advance of the Soviet 40th Army toward Belgorod from the very beginning. The German division lacked the strength and mobility to prevent the Soviets from sweeping around its open northwest flank and capturing Belgorod. From that point, the Soviet army could drive southwards, towards the communications center of Ljubotin, which was just a few kilometers west of Kharkov. The 40th Army formed the northern pincers which descended upon the city from the direction of Belgorod, while the southern pincers, the 3rd Tank Army, thrust westward, towards the city from bridgeheads on the west bank of the Oskul River. The 69th Army advanced in the center, it main attacks falling upon Panzergrenadier-Division "Grossdeutschland."

While under heavy pressure by two Soviet armies from the east and northeast, Lanz was soon forced to extend elements of "Grossdeutschland" westward, in vain attempts to shore up 168. Infanterie-Division and protect Belgorod from encirclement by 40th Army spearheads. While the two German Army divisions defended the area north and east of Belgorod, "Das Reich's" Regiment "Deutschland" dug in along a 30 kilometer wide front east of Kharkov, establishing strong points just west of the Oskul River. The regiment's positions were situated between the towns of Olkhovatka and Veillike Burluk. The southern or right flank of the SS regiment was open, because the next German forces between Regiment "Deutschland" and 298. Infanterie-Division was a battalion of Police troops in the village of Dvuretschnaja. South of Dvuretschnaja, 298. Infanterie-Division elements held the town of Kupyansk, while the rest of the division was dispersed south of the town, along a stretch of the Oskul River. The Oskul ran southward and entered the larger Northern Donets near the town of Izyum. East of the 298. Infanterie-Division sector, 320. Infanterie-Division held positions along the middle stretch of the Krassnaja River.

Panzergrenadier-Division "Grossdeutschland" was returning to the fighting after a short rest and recuperation. The first units of the division to arrive in the sector were a battalion of the division's Füsilier-Regiment and I./Grenadier-Regiment "Grossdeutschland," which detrained between 19 and 21 January. Immediately, the battalions were sent east and northeast of Belgorod, in order to defend the area from Soviet forces approaching Belgorod from the east. The other battalions of the two regiments joined their comrades several days later, after unloading at Kupyansk, which was still held at that time by 298. Infanterie-Division. Additional combat formations of the division, including the Aufklärungsabteilung of "Grossdeutschland," reached the front and prepared to deploy. "Grossdeutschland's" front consisted of reinforced battalion strong points situated primarily along major roads, with undefended gaps between each position. This was not as critical in the winter months, as contrasted to the summer dry season when the region's dirt roads were firm. Ice and snow made much of the countryside all but impassable for wheeled motor vehicles during the winter months and

difficult to traverse even for tanks and other tracked combat vehicles. However, even though they were often covered with snow or ice, the main roads seemed to provide the most likely method of movement through the area, particularly those that were built on elevated banks or which ran parallel to railroads. The Germans concentrated on defending the main roads, a tactic which proved to be inadequate. However, due to the extended front defended by "Grossdeutschland," there was no alternative course of action.[18]

The somewhat unsteady 168. Infanterie-Division was in a similar situation further north of Belgorod, but possessed considerably less combat strength and will to fight. Its front consisted of a thin screen of weak defensive positions backed up by small battle groups made up of a company or two of mobile infantry, reinforced with an assault gun or mobile flak detachments. Since 168. Infanterie-Division had no armor and few remaining heavy anti-tank guns, it had no effective counter measures when attacked by strong Soviet armored forces. The division's artillery regiment possessed a dozen 10cm guns and a handful of heavy, 17cm howitzers.

Neither of the German divisions defending the area north and northeast of Kharkov could tie in securely with a friendly unit on either flank. Given that plight, the only possible countermeasure was to vigorously and continuously patrol the gaps and hope that a Russian attack could be detected soon enough to counterattack it effectively. However, only "Grossdeutschland" had sufficient mobile units to implement this strategy with any chance of success. Their opponents, in particular the Russian rifle divisions, were not at full strength either. The Russian rifle divisions were much weakened after long weeks of fighting and probably reduced to about 4000 to 6000 men per division and Voronezh tank corps were below normal establishment strength as well. In spite of the weakness of individual Russian divisions, Golikov's armies enjoyed a significant numerical advantage over the Germans, in both men and tanks. On 28 January, of 1943 Armeeabteilung Lanz had a total of no more than about 30,000 German troops, not counting the SS divisions.[19]

The three Soviet armies of the Voronezh Front had a total of 315 tanks immediately available and 300 in reserve. In contrast, the only armored division available to Lanz, Panzergrenadier-Division "Grossdeutschland," had a total of thirteen combat ready tanks. The division had eighteen other tanks needing short term repairs (under fourteen days of repair time) while two others needed more extensive work. Even if all of the division's tanks had been in

[18] Spaeter, Helmuth, *Die Geschichte der Panzer-Korps "Grossdeutschland."* (Bielefeld: 1958) pg. 13-16.
[19] NA/T-314, roll 489, 1a KTB, Generalkommando z.b.v. Cramer. frame 000554-000565.

operating order, the Germans faced a terrible disadvantage in tank strength, compared to the amount of armor available to the Russians.

In addition to the German troops, there were some Hungarian units which had been driven ahead of the Soviet tide and pushed into the Kharkov area. The 23rd Hungarian Light Division and the remnants of the 1st Hungarian Tank Division were ordered to march toward the Belgorod sector in order to reinforce 168. Infanterie-Division, with relatively fresh troops. The only other divisions available to Lanz were the two SS divisions, which were gradually assembling in the Kharkov area. Operations "Gallop" and "Star" were designed to tear apart the entire German front in southern Russia and deal a fatal blow to the Axis armies in the Soviet Union.[20] On the heels of the disaster at Stalingrad, which removed a quarter of a million Axis soldiers from the order of battle on the Eastern Front, Germany could not withstand the destruction of Heergruppe Süd. If Manstein failed to reverse the Soviet tide Germany faced the collapse of the entire Eastern Front and the loss of the war in early 1943.

---

[20] Glantz, pg. 152.

4

THE BATTLE FOR KHARKOV BEGINS

Operation "Gallop" began on 29 January, when the South western Front's 6th Army attacked German positions along the Oskul River. On that morning, the 350th Rifle Division, of the 6th Army's 15th Rifle Corps, launched full scale attacks on 298. Infanterie-Division positions in and around the town of Kupyansk. The Oskul ran through the middle of Kupyansk, and its marshy banks made crossing difficult unless the river and marshes were frozen solid. The 350th Rifle Division began frontal assaults on German positions east of the town late in the day and by night-fall, various combat groups of Soviet infantry were able to fight their way to the eastern banks of the Oskul. On the following morning, Russian infantry attacks broke through the German defenses on the northeast environs of Kupyansk. A small assault group of Russian infantry fought their way into the town and took up positions in several houses. They were forced to withdraw by quickly mounted German counterattacks, supported by an assault gun and Flak detachments.

East of Izyum, 320. Infanterie-Division detachments came under assault as well. The division reported that its left flank de-fenses were attacked by a strong Russian infantry force, which was preceded by heavy artillery fire. During the course of the next day Soviet breakthroughs forced the division to withdraw west, towards Izyum. Throughout its retreat, 320. Infanterie-Division retained its cohesion and methodically covered its withdrawal by the action of skillful and determined rear guard troops. During the night of 30-31 January, the Russians moved armor into the area and attacked on the next day with renewed vigor.

At 1230 hours, 1 February, the division reported that it had knocked out three Russian tanks and inflicted heavy losses on the Russian infantry, but the battle was still in progress. Continued heavy Russian assaults, supported by tanks, forced the division to with-draw toward Izyum, a key bridge site on the Donets River. Two of its three regiments conducted their retreat toward Izyum in good order, but Grenadier-Regiment 586, the division rear guard, reported that it was surrounded by Russian troops and its path to the river blocked.

Late in the day, German air reconnaissance reported that a large number of Russian troops were seen crossing the river north of Kupyansk in three longs columns, some of which were accompa-nied by tanks. These were formations of Rybalko's 3rd Tank Army, probably the 111th Rifle Division and the lead element of the 6th Guards Cavalry Corps, which was the 201st Tank Brigade. The 62nd Guards Rifle Division, the 161st Rifle Division and the 48th Guards Rifle Division crossed the river north of Kupyansk, between Dvuretschnaja and Olkhovatka, where Regiment "Deutschland" was dug in. The 219th Rifle Division, supported by the 6th Anti-Tank Brigade, began concentrating west of Olkhovatka.[1]

In the area of north of Dvuretschnaja, other elements of Rybalko's army crossed the river and began to prepare for subse-quent operations to the west. The village of Kamenka, north of Dvuretschnaja, which was lightly defended by German security units, was easily captured by the Russians. Detachments of the 201st Tank Brigade approached Dvuretschnaja, but were initially turned back by the German Police garrison defending the town. To the north and south of the town the Soviet onslaught continued to march west, while Soviet infantry assembled east of Dvuretschnaja in or-der to root the Germans out of the town. The 201st Tank Brigade, the forward element of the 6th Guards Cavalry Corps, bypassed Dvuretschnaja and was able to thrust twenty kilometers to the west. This advance on the southern flank of the attack, threatened an im-

---

[1] Glantz, pg. 160-161.

portant lateral railroad in the area, the Kupyansk-Volchansk rail line, on the first day. The 298. Infanterie-Division troops continued to hold Kupyansk and its bridges, even though the town was outflanked to the north and south. Using makeshift bridges, Soviet infantry and armor flooded over the Oskul River in the Kupyansk area. However, farther to the north, in the "Das Reich" and "Grossdeutschland" sectors, the Soviets did not enjoy as much success.

North of Kupyansk, the Oskul flowed through Veillike, which was located on a stretch of the river which bulged to the east for a distance, before flowing into the town of Volokonovka. Veillike was located at the eastern most apex of the bulge, fifty kilometers north of Kupyansk. West of this bulge, Regiment "Deutschland," under command of SS-Standartenführer Heinz Harmel, came under pressure from elements of two Soviet rifle divisions on the first day of Operation "Star." East of the town of Olkhovatka, the regiment deployed two of its battalions forward, defending roads passing through the towns of Borki and Kosinka. The I./"Deutschland," led by SS-Sturmbannführer Fritz Ehrath, was held in reserve near Olkhovatka. Soviet infantry attacks in battalion strength struck at SS defenses at Borki, held by III./"Deutschland" and Kosinka, defended by II./"Deutschland."

At both villages the initial attacks were thrown back, with the advancing Russian infantry suffering substantial losses. During the day, the Russians launched repeated attacks against the two SS battalions. The 6th Guards Cavalry Corps, led by the 201st Tank Brigade, advanced westward from the Oskul sector, accompanied by Soviet ground attack planes. To the north of Regiment "Deutschland" positions in the Olkhovatka area, at Werchnij Lubjanka, the Soviets attempted to outflank the regiment's position, but were blocked by SS-Aufklärungsabteilung 2. The reconnaissance battalion had been deployed on the far northern flank of the division's sector, patrolling the undefended gap to the regiment's north. Its neighbor to the north was "Grossdeutschland" but no contact between the two divisions was established on 1 February. A gap of approximately fifteen kilometers existed between the northern flank of "Das Reich" and the southern flank of "Grossdeutschland."

During the day, "Das Reich" division commander, SS-Gruppenführer Georg Keppler adjusted and reinforced his defenses west of the Oskol River. The 15./Kompanie of Regiment "Deutschland" was dispatched to the aid of the Police garrison at Dvuretschnaja. SS-Sturmbannführer Jakob Fick's motorcycle battalion was ordered to replace SS-Aufklärungsabteilung 2 on the northern flank of Regiment "Deutschland." The I./Regiment "Deutschland" was used to reinforce the defenses at Kosinka. Meanwhile, Regiment "Der Führer" approached the Olkhovatka area, where it was to assemble, along with armor of the division. This

Jacob Fick commanded SS-Kradschützen Bataillon 2 of "Das Reich" during the Kharkov battles. He is pictured here as an SS-Hauptsturmführer. In early February, his battalion was called upon the defend the northern flank of a salient position held by Regiment "Deutschland." (Courtesy of Mark C. Yerger)

Kampfgruppe was formed as a counterattack force, which was to be utilized when the main Soviet thrust against the division was identified.[2]

In the meantime, the 62nd Rifle Division passed through an undefended gap between Dvuretschnaja and Kupyansk and made an eight kilometer advance toward the Burluk River south of Olkhovatka, where the headquarters of Regiment "Deutschland" was located. As the fighting continued into the afternoon, the situation north and south of Dvuretschnaja became more critical as the Soviet 111th Rifle Division followed in the wake of the 201st Tank Brigade and crossed the rail line that ran between Voltschansk and Kupyansk.[3] Regiment "Deutschland" could spare only one com-

---

[2] *Befehl des Gewissens: Charkow - Winter 1943.* pg. 10. This valuable book is a collection of xerox copies of the daily reports of the 1a KTB for Armeeabteilung Lanz/Kempf (later 8. Armee) and contains transcripts of the daily reports compiled by the SS-Panzer-Korps. The book was produced by the Bundesverband der Soldaten der ehemaligen Waffen-SS.

[3] Glantz, pg. 161.

pany to launch a counterattack on the Russian troops that had penetrated the gap between its positions east of Olkhovatka and Dvuretschnaja.

The 15. Kompanie, Regiment "Deutschland," which was a motorcycle company, was ordered to cut the communication lines behind the main forward element of the 201st Tank Brigade and make contact with the Police troops in Dvuretschnaja. At 1630 hours, on 1 February, the company approached the northern edge of the village, where it ran into a column of Russian troops marching to the west. The 15./Kompanie was able to fight its way into Dvuretschnaja, but the major part of the Soviet attack continued without serious interruption.

The SS company remained in contact with Russian infantry north of the town, but at 1930 hours, other Soviet troops were reported to be moving to the north and south of Dvuretschnaja. It appeared that the Soviets were attempting to encircle the village and the SS detachment, although the road leading west remained open. However, the Russian forces marching to the west were apparently not concerned with the small German force defending the town and left the capture of the town to the Soviet infantry assembling east of the town. By that time small detachments of infantry from 298. Infanterie-Division had filtered into the town and were used to strengthen the defenses. The Germans prepared for all round defense of the village.

Other SS units were arriving or being committed to the fighting in the Kupyansk area as well. From Chugujev, where units of "Leibstandarte" were unloading, 2. Kompanie of Aufklärungs-abteilung "LAH" was sent immediately toward Kupyansk. The detachment was ordered to screen the area between Kupyansk and Dvuretschnaja and make contact with 298. Infanterie-Division. The company left at 1700 hours and reached Kupyansk after a five hour long, night time trek over frozen, treacherous roads. SS-Untersturmführer Gerhard Maurer, the commander in charge of the reconnaissance group, reported to the headquarters of 298. Infanterie-Division at Kupyansk and was assigned defensive positions on the northern edge of the town.

The two companies obviously could not defend the 17 kilometer sector between Dvuretschnaja and Kupyansk and Maurer decided to mount a continuous patrol of the road between the two towns in order to detect a Soviet advance through the area. He led the first patrol, leaving Kupyansk in the morning and traveling to Dvuretschnaja, receiving only harassing fire from Soviet troops east of the road. Mortar fire occasionally impacted between houses or along the eastern perimeter and machine gun fire could be heard from time to time.[4]

Helmut Schreiber, pictured here as an SS-Hauptsturmführer, commanded 10./ Kompanie Regiment "Deutschland" during the battles in the Belyi Kolodes salient. The salient was located west of the Oskol River and north of Kupyansk. Schreiber won the Knight's Cross in the summer of 1943. (The author's collection)

On Maurer's trip back to Kupyansk he intercepted a solitary German vehicle heading toward Dvuretschnaja and when he spoke to the passengers, he was startled to find that occupying the back seat was none other than Paul Hausser, the commander of the SS-Panzer-Korps. After warning Hausser about possible Soviet mortar and gun fire on the road, Maurer offered to escort his commander to the town. However, Hausser told the young SS officer that he was not needed and continued toward Dvuretschnaja. Maurer, concerned about any possible threat to the vehicle, followed behind at a distance, carefully remaining out of sight until Hausser returned to Kupyansk.[5]

It became obvious that the garrison in Dvuretschnaja was not delaying the Soviet advance and to continue to hold the town would

[4] Lehmann, pg. 41.
[5] Ibid. pg. 43.

result in the complete encirclement and loss of the troops holding it. Since 298. Infanterie-Division could not establish a solid front north and maintain contact with the garrison, the defending troops were ordered to withdraw from the town and pull back to the west. At 1420 hours, the town was abandoned.

Everywhere along the front, reports of heavy fighting and overwhelming Soviet strength were received by Armeeabteilung Lanz. Hausser, eager for a fight, even though his corps was not yet completely assembled, radioed Armeeabteilung Lanz and proposed to attack the Russian advance in the Kupyansk area. Hausser wanted to strike the Russian spearheads in the Olkhovatka area with "Das Reich's" Panzer regiment and III./"Der Führer," the armored Panzergrenadier battalion of the division.

When this was reported to Heeresgruppe B, the army group reminded Lanz of an order from Hitler, which stated that he did not want the SS-Panzer-Korps split up and wasted in piece meal fashion. However, in light of the rapidly deteriorating situation, the army group approved the use of Regiment "Deutschland" and the Aufklärungsabteilung for use in counterattack operations. The rest of the SS-Panzer-Korps remained under command of OKH and were not supposed to be used without its permission. Due to the rapidly unfolding series of crisis situations, although it was contrary to the orders of the OKH, parts of the SS divisions were dispersed to different areas of combat as soon as they arrived.[6]

Meanwhile, north of the sector held by "Das Reich," Division "Grossdeutschland" put together Gruppe "Kassnitz," which consisted of the Füsilier Regiment "Grossdeutschland," reinforced with mobile heavy weapons and a few assault guns. Its mission was to counterattack the Soviet forces north of the "Das Reich" sector and clear up a penetration between the two divisions, in order to allow the building of a new defensive line west of the Oskul. The attack began well and Kassnitz reported that his men had captured a Soviet occupied village at 1600 hours. Then the Kampfgruppe ran up against stronger Soviet defensive positions, and made little further progress. The strength of the Russian forces driving west became slowly apparent to the Germans late in the day. "Grossdeutschland," having given up its intentions of driving the Russians back over the Oskul by counterattack, was ordered to cover the north flank of Korps Raus. This was undoubtedly because the Russians were overrunning the positions of 168. Infanterie-Division east and north of Belgorod, collapsing the north flank of the corps.

Late in the day, new orders were issued to the German formations in combat east of Kharkov. Armeeabteilung Lanz realized that the sustained attacks across the Oskul were more than reconnaissance operations after German intelligence reported that a reinforced

Russian rifle division faced 298. Infanterie-Division and elements of two Soviet rifle divisions were attacking Regiment "Deutschland." It was not always easy to decide when the Russians launched major attacks as it was common for them to aggressively conduct battalion strength reconnaissance attacks along a broad front during fluid situations. There had been a general lack of heavy, sustained Soviet artillery preparation and this caused further uncertainty in the German command during the day. It was normal for the Russians to mass as much artillery as possible to support their operations. However there were two factors at work that limited the amount of artillery available to initially support the offensive. First of all, the enormous Soviet losses of artillery and vehicles of the first year and a half of the war had not been replaced and much of what was available was tied up in the Stalingrad operations. There had not been time to relocate most of the artillery strength from that sector of the front. Secondly, the artillery that was available could not be moved in time to support the new offensive, which had been begun without a sufficient organizational pause that could have allowed the Russians to bring up their guns and ammunition supplies. However, when Russian armor was reported at many points along the front and many large Soviet tank and infantry columns were spotted by air reconnaissance, the scope of the attack became clear. Early on the morning of 2 February, three Soviet columns, estimated at over 6000 men each, were detected by German pilots after they crossed the Oskul River.

Farther to the east 320. Infanterie-Division partially occupied defensive positions along the Krassnaja River, which ran parallel to the Oskul River. The division was assigned a front that was nearly forty kilometers in length. On the first day of Operation "Gallop" the Southwestern Front's 6th Army struck the forward elements of the division with parts of at least three rifle divisions and a reinforced rifle brigade. Pressure was heaviest on the left flank, where Soviet tanks of the 3rd Tank Corps and infantry of the 267th Rifle Division attacked in the area of the village of Kißlovka. Three Russian tanks were knocked out, but the attacks continued along the entire front held by the division, which did not have all of its regiments on line yet. At nightfall, one regiment was just crossing the Northern Donets at Izyum, a second had taken up positions south of Kupyansk and a third was forming for use as the division reserve.[7]

In Kupyansk itself, the Germans were hard pressed to fight off the Soviet infantry and tank forces assaulting its positions. It was now clear that the relatively weak German forces in the Oskul-Krassnaja sector could not hope to hold a defensive line given the width of the front and the existing gaps. "Das Reich" and

---

[6] *Befehl des Gewissens*, pg. 15-16.

[7] *Befehl des Gewissens*, pg. 17.

An 8.8cm Flak gun in a defensive position during the winter of 1942-43. The "88" was deadly against Soviet tanks and other armored vehicles because its shell could penetrate the frontal armor of any tank then in existence at distances far beyond the effective range of the T-34 or KV series tanks. (Credit National Archives)

"Grossdeutschland" were ordered to disengage strong forces from contact with the Russians and form mobile groups, in order to conduct blocking and delaying operations until SS "Leibstandarte" could assemble and take up defensive positions east of Kharkov. "Grossdeutschland" was ordered to conduct only small, tactical attacks and was reminded that its mission was primarily defensive unless a counterattack was ordered.

During the night and following day, 320. Infanterie-Division was overrun and split into regimental groups after continuous attacks by the Russians shattered its front. Long columns of Soviet troops passed between the regiments in an uninterrupted flow, marching toward the west. Reports from the division were fragmentary, as could be expected in such a fluid situation and the regimental group at Kißlovka remained encircled and largely out of communication with the Armeeabteilung throughout the morning hours. Later, one officer and 50 men of the group were able to slip through the Soviets lines and reach safety, while the main group of the regiment continued to fight its way west. Retreating under intense and constant pressure, the regimental groups were forced to move cross country and their progress was hindered by deep snow and icy slopes. The division's Grenadier-Regiment 587 radioed that it intended to fight its way to the Donets bridge at Izyum, while the men encircled at Kißlovka planned to breakout of the town and

escape to the west. Meanwhile, its neighbor to the south, 298. Infanterie-Division, was also under heavy pressure. The division's front was penetrated at several points and the division commander ordered it Pioniere detachments to begin to make preparations to destroy bridges over the Oskul and ammunition dumps, in preparation for withdrawal to the west bank of the river. The Ia of the division reported from Kupyansk that Russian troops were moving past the town on all sides, pushing toward the west.[8]

German air reconnaissance along the western bank of the Oskul, reported several new columns of Russians crossing the river, each numbering more than a thousand men. Counterattacks by weak company and battalion sized battle groups could not stop the advance of an entire army. The 320. Infanterie-Division found itself in an increasingly dangerous situation by nightfall, as Russian columns split the division into fragments. The remains of the encircled regimental group at Kißlovka were able to fight their way out of the town and reached German lines relatively intact. The division was ordered to withdraw through Izyum, an order which began a bloody, difficult withdrawal which was to severely test the men and officers of the division for many brutal days to come.

---

[8] Ibid. pg. 19.

LEFT: Gustav Knittel, commander of 3./Kompanie of Kurt Meyer's SS-Aufklärungsabteilung 1, which was in the thick of the fighting in the Kharkov area soon after its return to the East in late January, 1943. (Courtesy of Mark C. Yerger) RIGHT: SS-Obersturmführer Heinz Macher, the commander of 16./Kompanie Regiment "Deutschland" which was the Pioniere or combat engineer company of the regiment. The Pioniere detachments were well armed with explosives and flame-throwers, in addition to being fully motorized. They were often utilized as assault troops by the Germans, suffering extensive casualties in this role. By the end of March, 1943 the company was reduced to the strength of only thirty three men. (Courtesy of Mark C. Yerger)

The 298. Infanterie-Division, somewhat optimistically, was expected to hold the Kupyansk-Ssenkovo sector in order to block access to the northern approaches to Izyum. This was to cover the route of retreat by 320. Infanterie-Division's three regimental groups and the assembly of "Leibstandarte" southeast of Kharkov. By the next morning, 3 February, the situation looked grim for Armeeabteilung Lanz and the German forces east of Kharkov. Lanz flew to the headquarters of Korps Cramer in order to confer with Cramer about the unfavorable situation shaping up north of Belgorod. Cramer's two divisions were under heavy attack, particularly at the town of Nikitovka. Lanz realized that the Oskul could no longer be held and ordered the SS-Panzer-Korps to prepare to defend the eastern bank of the Northern Donets along the Kupyansk-Voltschansk road and block the Soviet advance toward Kharkov. Hausser was given the responsibility for organizing the defense of this line by the two SS divisions and whatever flotsam of broken units that could be collected and thrown into battle. The 320. Infanterie-Division, under command of Generalmajor Georg Postel, was to conduct a deliberate withdrawal, delaying the advance of the Soviet forces toward the Northern Donets as long as possible, in order to allow the Armeeabteilung to establish a solid defense of the river.[9]

———————

[9] Postel joined the German Army in 1914 and served as a company commander in Infanterie-Regiment 15. After the war, he remained in the Reichsheer and served as a tactical instructor. Before the beginning of the Polish campaign, Postel was promoted to the rank of Oberstleutnant and served with II./Infanterie-Regiment 109. Early in 1940 he was an infantry battalion commander and by the end of the year, he was chosen to command Infanterie-Regiment 364. During his command of that regiment, Postel won the Knight's Cross and was promoted to Generalmajor on 1 January, 1943, when he took command of 320. Infanterie-Division. Information from Mark C. Yerger's archives.

The Russians pressured the regimental groups of 320. Infanterie-Division continually as they retreated from the Oskul toward the Izyum crossings. After reaching the town, the division continued its stubborn fighting withdrawal toward the bridge over the Northern Donets at Balakleya. Elements of the Soviet 172nd and 6th Rifle Divisions drove a wedge between the division and several retreating columns of 298. Infanterie-Division that were trying to escape to the west. A regimental group of 298. Infanterie-Division still maintained possession of Kupyansk as ordered by Armeeabteilung Lanz, however, at 2300 hours on 2 February, the Armeeabteilung had given the division permission to conduct an orderly withdrawal to the southwest. It was hoped that the division could reach the area south of Kharkov and protect the southern flank of "Leibstandarte." The 298. Infanterie-Division was commanded by Generalleutnant Arnold Szelinski. The division trained in the west during 1942 and arrived on the Eastern Front just before the beginning of Operation "Gallop."[10]

For both 320. and 298. Infanterie-Divisionen, the 3 February were very difficult days, due to extremely heavy Soviet pressure. Units of the Russian 6th Rifle Division, moving faster than the slow moving 320. Infanterie-Division, with its horse drawn artillery and supply wagons, cut off the division's path of retreat to the Northern Donets. By that time, the regiments were carrying significant numbers of wounded with them, treating them as best they could during the retreat. The more seriously wounded suffered terribly while being carried in unheated trucks and horse drawn wagons. Those wounded who could still walk and fight did so. Frostbite began to take its toll among the weaker men during the bitter cold nights, when temperatures plunged to far below freezing after the sun went down. The less seriously wounded actually benefited from the cold because it froze the blood in the wound and stopped bleeding.

Near Balakleya, on the northeastern flank of the division, elements of the Soviet 6th Rifle Division assaulted retreating elements of the division. To the south, infantry of the 267th Rifle Division, attacked Grenadier-Regiment 585, forcing it to turn and defend itself. As a result, the regiment fell behind and lost even tenuous contact with the other regiments. The three regimental columns were then surrounded on all sides, while they moved roughly parallel to the Russian attack. The Russians were not able to encircle and pin down the regiments as Postel and his regimental commanders were able to master every situation and keep moving.

Heinz Werner, commander of 10./Kompanie Regiment "Der Führer" in "Das Reich." He was one of the more highly decorated members of the regiment. Werner won the Knight's Cross in August of 1944 and later that same year was decorated with the Oakleaves, while commanding III./Regiment "Der Führer." (Courtesy of Mark C. Yerger)

From 3-5 February, the situation continued to deteriorate for the Germans at Belgorod and east of Kharkov. The very situation that Hitler and Manstein had feared, the commitment of the units of the SS-Panzer-Korps as they arrived, in piecemeal fashion, was already taking place. Due to the speed and strength of the Soviet attack, particularly the 3rd Tank Army east of Kharkov and Mobile Group Popov, on the northern or left flank of Heeresgruppe Don, the German plan to assemble Hausser's rebuilt and full strength SS divisions was seriously threatened. Manstein realized that if the SS divisions could not be extricated from the battles of attrition east of Kharkov, they would suffer the same fate as other Panzer divisions of Heeresgruppe Don. They would be worn down by continual fight-

---

[10] Szelinski joined the Army in 1910 and served with Infanterie-Regiment 61. Szelinski remained in the Army after the end of World War I and reached the rank of Oberstleutnant in 1935. He began the war as the commander of Infanterie-Regiment 38 and was promoted to Generalmajor on 1 February, 1942, shortly after taking command of 298. Infanterie-Division. He was awarded the Knight's Cross in 1941. Information from Mark C. Yerger's archives.

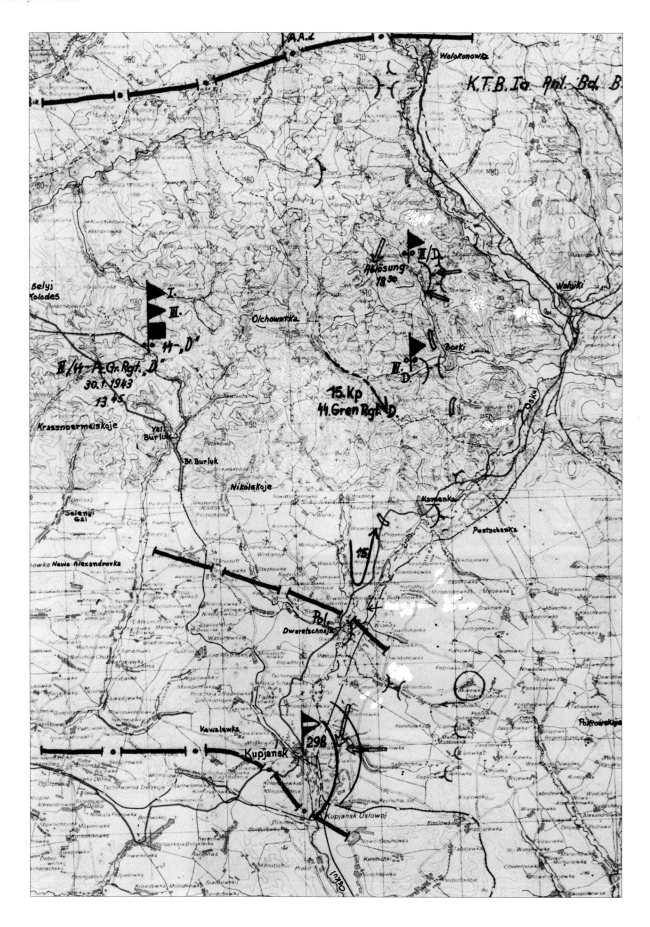

ing at one hot spot after another and never able to recover. However, they had been sent to defend Kharkov by Hitler's express order and by the first days of January, were heavily engaged in battle.

Manstein planned to use the SS-Panzer-Korps to spearhead the counterattack that was restore the situation in the Ukraine. Already, the plans for a counter stroke were forming in Manstein's mind, as he waited to see how the Soviet attacks would develop around Kharkov itself and between Kharkov and the sector of 1. Panzerarmee. There were some indications of the Soviet intent, particularly south of Kharkov, where the Soviet 3rd Tank Army was obviously advancing toward the Northern Donets in order to attack the city from the southeast. The German command was also aware that Mobile Group Popov, with its four tank corps, had crossed the Northern Donets south of Kupyansk, and begun to attack to the south. It was clear, at least to Manstein, that this was the most dangerous Soviet operation, while Hitler seemed fixated on Kharkov.[11]

Mobile Group Popov had advanced through Kuznetsov's 1st Guards Army and begun its attack on the left flank of 1. Panzerarmee on 30 January. The 1st Guards Army attack zone began from west of Voroshilovgrad, extended along the Donets for about 100 kilometers due west, to the vicinity of the town of Lisichansk. In January, the 1st Guards Army had occupied the last towns abandoned by Axis troops north of the Northern Donets in the Millerovo-Chertkovo-Streltskovo sector. This secured the assembly areas for Mobile Group Popov in the area northwest of Voroshilovgrad. In late January, the four Soviet tank corps regrouped hurriedly along the eastern bank of the Krassnaja River and north of the Northern Donets. The Germans never realized that an assembly for a major new offensive was taking place.

What Armeeabteilung Fretter-Pico mistakenly thought to be columns of Soviet armor arriving to attack the Northern Donets area between Kamensk and Voroshilovgrad, were probably elements of Mobile Group Popov's tank corps assembling for Operation "Gallop." This could explain why large mobile columns or tank groups were spotted on the move through or heading into the area and then later "disappeared." The most reasonable explanation for these events is that as the Soviet columns neared their assembly area, they utilized standard "maskirovka" practices. The tank columns would then have moved only at night and during the day light hours, remained hidden in wooded areas or camouflaged assembly areas.

OPPOSITE: The defensive positions of "Das Reich" east of Kharkov on 30 January 1943. The Soviet 69th and 3rd Tank Armies crossed the Oskul River in the sector between the town of Wolokonovka in the north and Kupyansk in the south. The SS division was forced back into the Veliky Burluk-Olkchovatka-Belyi Kolodes salient, which it defended against major portions of the 69th Army. South of the salient, the 298. Infanterie-Division tried to defend Kupyansk but was outflanked by the Soviet advance north and south of the town.

The 1st Guards Army Assaults the Krassnaja River

In preliminary assaults that began on 29 January, the right wing of the 1st Guards Army, consisting of three rifle divisions, led the advance with an attack on the towns of Kaban'ye and Kremennaja, on the Krasnaja River, north of Lisichansk. The Soviet attacks commenced as 19. Panzer-Division was withdrawing over the river and pulling back toward Lisichansk. Kaban'ye was north of Kremenaja and on 29 January had been abandoned by Panzergrenadier-Regiment 73, which was withdrawing southward along the eastern bank of the river. As the regiment attempted to reach the crossing sites at Kremenaja, the first Soviet attacks struck its flanks. Divisional artillery shelled Soviet advance elements and covered the retreat, while the division launched a relief attack from Kremenaja. Led by Lehrregiment 901 (training regiment) and assault guns of 3./Sturmgeschütze-Abteilung 209, the thrust threw back a number of Soviet troops that had already reached the east bank of the river, north of Kremenaja.[12]

The Germans put up a stronger defense at Kremennaja, and brought the advance of the Soviet 195th Rifle Division to an abrupt halt. The Russian infantry fell back before deadly artillery fire and fierce counterattacks. Kuznetsov had to commit Poluboyarov's 4th Guards Tank Corps to support the attack of the 195th Rifle Division, in order to renew the advance. Even after the Russian tanks joined the assault upon the town, Panzergrenadier-Regiment 74 held Kremenaja until the last division troops crossed the river on 30 January. The regiment pulled back under cover of artillery and rear guard detachments and began to take up new positions defending Lisichansk. The division withdrew toward the south and occupied Krassny Liman and screening positions north of the Northern Donets. The 4th Tank Corps struck south, toward the river, while the 35th Guards Rifle Division and 195th Rifle Division approached Krassny Liman. After crossing the Krassnaja River, the two Soviet rifle divisions rapidly pushed to the southwest, toward Krassny Liman, an important railroad center north of the key town of Slavyansk. Rail lines led out of the town to the northwest, crossing the Donets near Izyum. From that point the rail line continued west, passing through the key town of Slavyansk and then on to Barvenkovo. From Barvenkovo, the railroad ran west to the main crossing of the Dnepr River at Dnepropetrovsk. The situation was rapidly deteriorating in this sector, while Soviet divisions were driving toward Kharkov, as Armeeabteilung Fretter-Pico could do little to stop the Russian advance.[13]

[11] *Befehl des Gewissens*, pg. 25.
[12] Hinze, Rolf. *Die 19. Infanterie und Panzer-Division*, (Düsseldorf; 1997) pg. 445-447.
[13] Glantz, pg. 98.

However, by 1 February, the 1. Panzerarmee divisions were deploying along the Donets and began to take over defense of the river from Armeeabteilung Fretter-Pico. The III. Panzer-Korps, consisting of 19. Panzer-Division (reinforced by elements of 27. Panzer-Division) and 7. Panzer-Division, was already involved in fighting in the Krassny Liman sectors by the first day of the month. Later in the day, Armeeabteilung Fretter-Pico, by order of Heeresgruppe Don, was redesignated as XXX. Armee-Korps once again and was absorbed by 1. Panzerarmee. Its mission was to hold the right flank of the army, in the Voroshilovgrad-Kamensk area. The III. Panzer-Korps, which was to be reinforced by 3. Panzer-Division on 4 February, was to block the Soviet advance over the Donets north of Slavyansk. Due to incredibly difficult road conditions and deep snow drifts, 3. Panzer-Division did not arrive according to schedule. The first units of the division did not begin to replace elements of 7. Panzer-Division around Slavyansk until 5 February. After the arrival of XXXX. Panzer-Korps, the second Panzer corps assigned to 1. Panzerarmee, which began to detrain on 4 February, the army was directed to destroy any Soviet forces south of the river.[14]

The Russians had crossed the Donets south and west of Krassny Liman during 1 February and the night of 1-2 February. The 35th Guards Rifle Division, after reaching the west bank of the frozen river, advanced westward on a broad front toward Izyum and Barvenkovo. A regimental group of the division struck out along the railroad line toward the train depot at Barvenkovo. By daylight on 2 February, it was clear the Russians were already across sections of the Donets in strength and 1. Panzerarmee issued orders to III. Panzer-Korps to make every effort to hold on to the center section of the front between Slavyansk and Lisichansk. The mission assigned to the corps by the army was to block the further advance of the Soviets to the south from this sector. This set the stage for a prolonged fight for possession of Slavyansk and the surrounding area, a struggle which increasingly attracted more and more German and Soviet troops and tanks. The resulting series of battles caused delays and subsequent Soviet frustration over the disruption of the offensive timetable. In the long run, these delays resulted in a readjustment of the direction of the offensive to the west, which although dangerous, were not as quickly fatal as a deep penetration to the south could have been.[15]

On 3 February, although moving with difficulty due to deep snow drifts, the 195th Rifle Division deployed to assault Slavyansk,

Gerd Bremer, the commander of 1./Kompanie of Kurt Meyer's SS-Aufklärungsabteilung 1. Bremer shared the aggressive spirit of his battalion commander and won the Knight's Cross early in his military career, soon after the invasion of Russia. Bremer commanded the reconnaissance battalion of 12. SS-Panzer-Division "Hitlerjugend" in France during the bitter fighting after the invasion of Normandy by the Western Allies. (Courtesy of Mark C. Yerger)

with the expected support of the 57th Guards Rifle Division, which was approaching the town from the north. Due to the weather and road conditions, all of the regiments of the 195th Rifle Division were not in position to make their attack in a coordinated manner. The leading elements of one regiment attacked the northern section of the town, while the others were just approaching Slavyansk. At this point, the Russian regiment arriving from the north was attacked by 7. Panzer-Division. The German division, advancing in two battle groups, overran the regiment's columns on the march on roads north of the town and scattered them. Meanwhile, the leading regiment had become involved in fighting for the possession of Slavyansk itself. Confusion reigned due to the unexpected German

[14] NA/T-313, roll 46, 1. Panzerarmee 1a KTB, Darstellung der Ereignisse, frame 727924-727938.

[15] NA/T-313, roll 46, 1. Panzerarmee KTB, Darstellung der Ereignisse, frame 7279425.

attack and the 195th Rifle Division was forced to withdraw its regiment that was fighting in Slavyansk.[16]

Poluboyarov's 4th Guards Tank Corps, after crossing the Donets on 1 February, had passed to the west of Slavyansk and proceeded south, toward Kramatorsk, in order to bypass Slavyansk, leaving the task of taking the town to the following rifle divisions. The road conditions slowed the Soviet tank columns, but did not stop their thrust around the flank of the army. However, the rifle troops assigned to support the 4th Guards Tank Corps, the 38th Guards Rifle Division, were delayed by the unexpected attack of 7. Panzer-Division at Slavyansk. Poluboyarov's tank corps occupied Kramatorsk without difficulty, but his tanks were short of fuel and ammunition and were not able to continue the advance.

Farther to the east, the 6th Guards Rifle Corps continued to concentrate its forces in the Lisichansk sector. The Soviet 41st Guards Rifle Division, supported by the 18th Tank Corps, attacked German defenses around Lisichansk, which was held by units of 19. Panzer-Division. The division had deployed its forces beyond the perimeter of the town. The troops were located in small towns, generally 10 to 15 kilometers from the edge of the city and blocked the main roads leading into Lisichansk. Panzergrenadier-Regiment 73 held the left flank of the division, its defense centered around the town of Jama. Lisichansk itself was held by Panzergrenadier-Regiment 74. The remnants of 27. Panzer-Division reinforced the division and occupied defensive positions between the two Panzergrenadier regiments, while Lehrregiment 901 defended the right flank of the sector, holding positions around the town of Belaja Gora. The 335. Infanterie-Division held the sector east of Lisichansk to Voroshilovgrad.

The 41st Guards Rifle Division had succeeded in making a small penetration into the Lisichansk perimeter on 2 February, but German counterattacks limited any expansion of the gap. During 3 February, the Soviets crossed the Donets and attacked German defensive positions southwest of Lisichansk in several regimental strength assaults. The objective of the Russian attack appeared to be the town of Belaja Gora and the positions held by Lehrregiment 901.[17] Meanwhile, the Soviet 52nd Rifle Division began concentrating in the area and battle groups of the division began to push into the boundary area between 19. Panzer-Division and 7. Panzer-Division east of Slavyansk. Elements of 27. Panzer-Division counterattacked this Soviet advance and halted it, temporarily stabilizing the situation.

However, although this attack was turned back, southeast of Lisichansk two Soviet rifle divisions crossed the Donets and after hard fighting, established a number of small bridgeheads on the southern bank of the river. These penetrations took place near the small town of Borowskoje and could not be sealed off or destroyed. Immediately, the Russians brought up additional troops, in order to expand and reinforce these bridgeheads, which provided jump off points for further Soviet attacks. The concentration of Soviet forces southeast of Lisichansk, potentially threatened the lines of communication leaving the southern edge of the town.

From 4-6 February, the 41st Guards Rifle, 44th Guards Rifle and part of the 78th Rifle Divisions fought to take Lisichansk. Continuous Soviet pressure forced the Germans back from positions along their defensive perimeter, pushing them closer to Lisichansk. From information gained through prisoner interrogation, the Germans learned that three Soviet rifle regiments had assembled at Borowskoje. A thrust by this attack force was expected at any time and on 5 February, the Russian attack materialized from the Borowskoje area. Russian forces crossed the solidly frozen Donets upstream from the town, near Belaja Gora, which was about five kilometers southeast of Lisichansk. The Russians pushed past Lehrregiment 901, creating another crisis and stretching German reserves past the breaking point. This thrust was designed to sever German lines of communication south of Lisichansk and was one pincer of an envelopment attack against the town. The other pincer attack was launched by the 38th Guards Rifle Division, when it attacked the town of Yama, which was west of Lisichansk. The 38th Guards thrust to a point only about ten kilometers from the Soviet bridgehead near Belaja Gora. From north of Lisichansk, strong Soviet attacks pushed the Germans back into the northwestern edge of the town, keeping pressure on the division perimeter. It was clear that the attack from Belaja Gora was meant to link up with the thrust by the 38th Guards Rifle Division and encircle Lisichansk from the west and south.[18]

In spite of heavy Soviet pressure, Lisichansk remained in German hands until 6 February. At that time, the penetrations from the western and southeastern sectors finally forced the German defenders to abandon Lisichansk before the two attack forces linked up and cut off the town. The Germans broke out of the town and attacked through the shrinking corridor leading to safety. The Russians were not able to encircle and destroy the German troops, as 19. Panzer-Division conducted a skillful delaying operation south of the town and frustrated the pursuit by Soviet armored forces. The weather cooperated with the Germans as the fighting was conducted in the midst of a blinding snow storm. Visibility was so

[16] Glantz, pg 98-99 and T-313, roll 46, frame 7279426.
[17] Hinze, pg. 449-450.

[18] T-313, roll 46, 1. Panzerarmee KTB, Darstellung der Ereignisse, frame 7279433-7279434.

reduced that the German troops had to use a compass to ensure that they withdrew in the correct direction.[19]

While the defenders of Lisichansk were squeezed out of the town, Poluboyarov's 4th Guards Tank Corps, now with only thirty-seven tanks, remained entrenched in the town of Kramatorsk. By mounting numerous concentric attacks on the tank corps perimeter, 7. Panzer-Division seized the initiative and forced Poluboyarov to remain on the defensive. In a situation uncomfortably familiar to him, Poluboyarov found that he did not have the adequate artillery or infantry strength necessary to repulse the German counterattacks and still have sufficient strength to continue his attack. Had the 4th Guards Tank Corps broken free and continued its thrust to the south, Poluboyarov would have not been able to leave enough troops behind to completely secure his supply lines. His situation was not clearly understood by the Stavka and Poluboyarov was urged to continue his advance.

However, fuel supplies remained low and Poluboyarov had already lost nearly 25 % of his tanks. The Germans were less than full strength as well and did not have sufficient strength to crush the Soviet tank force. The 1. Panzerarmee remained content to keep the Soviet armor bottled up and unable to continue its advance further south. Poluboyarov's corps had little choice but to remain in defensive positions at Kramatorsk and wait for the 3rd Tank Corps to arrive. However, when the 3rd Tank Corps finally fought past German blocking positions and reached Kramatorsk on 5 February, it had only twenty-three tanks still in action and was short of ammunition and fuel. During its crossing of the Northern Donets and the movement to Kramatorsk, German attack planes harassed the Soviet armor, destroying several tanks and numerous other vehicles.

The fuel supplies available to Poluboyarov were marginally increased by small amounts of fuel brought in by the 3rd Tank Corps. In addition, welcome infantry support arrived in the form of ski troops of the 7th Ski Brigade. Popov also sent the 9th Tank Brigade to join Poluboyarov, although it had only a dozen tanks by the time it fought its way into Kramatorsk. While Popov tried to get his offensive rolling again west of Slavyansk, the 10th Tank Corps had already reached and crossed the Northern Donets, east of the town.

On 5 February, German air reconnaissance spotted several long columns of Soviet troops on the move from the Krassny Liman-Jampol area, which was east of Slavyansk. These columns probably belonged to the 10th Tank Corps, commanded by Major General V.G. Burkov. Burkov's tank corps slowly approached the III. Panzer-Korps defensive sector, accompanied by infantry of the 52nd Rifle Division. A brief local thaw turned the dirt roads into impass-

able quagmires or mud and the Soviet tanks had been forced to travel cross country to reach the Northern Donets. The fact that the Russian tanks could move at all was due to an innovative idea by the Soviet tank troops. Burkov had heavy pieces of steel angle iron welded to the front of some of his tanks, which were utilized as makeshift plow blades. The lead vehicles, employing these crude devices, scraped the snow and the meter deep black mud down to the firm clay base and the rest of the tanks followed behind. Needless to say, these conditions reduced the speed of Burkov's advance to a snail's pace and it can be imagined how hard it was on the running gear of the lead tanks. The delays to the 10th Tank Corps advance, caused by the mud, enabled the Germans to reinforce their defenses between Lisichansk and Slavyansk with 3. Panzer-Division. By the time that Burkov's tanks crossed the river between Slavyansk and Lisichansk, 3. Panzer-Division had incorporated its lead units into the defense of the area, blocking attacks by the 52nd Rifle Division and preventing Burkov's 10th Tank Corps from breaking free once it had crossed the Donets. On 11 February, Burkov's weakening tank corps was still engaged in fighting against 3. Panzer-Division.[20]

This experienced Panzer division, commanded by Generalleutnant Franz Westhoven, had been the last division of 1. Panzerarmee to cross the bridge over the Don River at Rostov on 2 February. It had served as the rear guard, covering the withdrawal of the army and suffered serious vehicle and equipment losses during these actions. The division losses in vehicles and heavy weapons were greater than the destruction of equipment during the retreat from Moscow in 1941-42. After covering the withdrawal of the army, it was assigned a section of the front south of the Northern Donets, in the center of the army. The division's Panzergrenadier-Regiment 3 and the motorcycle battalion were immediately committed to action. Panzergrenadier-Regiment 394 and the command group of Panzer-Regiment 6 arrived at Artemovsk, where Westhoven reported to a former commander of his division, Generalleutnant Breith, who then commanded III. Panzer-Korps.[21]

The arrival of the new Panzer division freed 7. Panzer-Division to disengage some of its forces from the fighting of Slavyansk and concentrate on attacking the Soviet armor at Kramatorsk. While German panzer divisions continued to arrive and take over sectors

---

[19] Glantz, pg. 104.

[20] Glantz, pg. 105 and 1a KTB 1. Panzerarmee, T-313, roll 46, frame 7279434.

[21] Hermann Breith joined the German Army in 1910, at the age of 18 and served as a Leutnant in Infanterie-Regiment 60. He remained in the Reich sheer after the end of World War I and was promoted to Oberstleutnant in 1936. Breith was given command of Panzer-Regiment 36 in 1938 and by the start of the war had reached the rank of Oberst. After leading 5. Panzer-Brigade in the first years of World War II and winning the Knight's Cross, he was promoted to the rank of Generalmajor. Given command of 3. Panzer-Division on 2 October, 1941, he proved to be a daring and skillful leader and won the Oak Leaves to the Knight's Cross while commanding the division. Information from Mark C. Yerger archives.

of 1. Panzerarmee's front, Popov had become very concerned about his Mobile Groups lack of progress. In an attempt to get his faltering attack moving again, Popov ordered Poluboyarov to begin preparations for the continuation of offensive operations. After the arrival of the 3rd Tank Corps in Kramatorsk, Poluboyarov reorganized his tank brigades, distributing the newly arrived tanks between his 14th and 12th Guards Tank Brigades. Popov also shifted the 41st Rifle Division to the west from Lisichansk, reinforcing the tiring 195th Rifle Division and the 57th Rifle Division at Slavyansk. Costly fighting there continued to use up infantry strength and ammunition supplies at a rate the Soviets could scarcely afford. To the east, in front of III. Panzer-Korps' defensive positions, the 10th and 18th Tank Corps remaining bogged down in heavy fighting at Slavyansk and in areas further eastward.

When Popov's tank corps were forced to remain on the defensive at Kramatorsk, the Russians shifted forces from the east to try and force a decision at Slavyansk. At the same time, the Germans brought up what reserves they still possessed and were able to block Soviet progress south of the Northern Donets River. By 5 February, the Soviet attack was seriously behind schedule, having been unable to quickly break through the center of 1. Panzerarmee or thrust past Kramatorsk toward Stalino.

While the 4th Guards and 3rd Tank Corps were unable to advance south of Kramatorsk, the other two tank corps of Mobile Group Popov were forced to participate in costly and time consuming operations assisting rifle division attacks east of Slavyansk. The Soviet rifle divisions attempting to push the Germans out of their defensive positions on the south bank of the Donets in the Slavyansk-Voroshilovgrad area were too weakened by earlier fighting to succeed without tank support. As a result, the Russians had to use tanks from Mobile Group Popov to support the breakthrough operations of the rifle divisions. This was one of the ultimately fatal deficiencies of Popov's tank corps. The Russians had believed that even their weakened rifle divisions could still punch through the German defenses, because they were convinced that the Germans were finished. They had gambled and lost. After the prolonged fighting for Lisichansk and Slavyansk, the chances for a decisive Soviet breakthrough began to disappear.

By 5 February, it was clear that the Soviet tank corps did not have enough tank strength to be able to support infantry attacks and still penetrate the German front. Adding to the difficulties facing Popov's Mobile Group, were the weather and logistical shortcomings of the Soviet Army. Ice, deep snow drifts and periodical brief thaws created supply problems the Russians could not solve. Vehicles moving over difficult roads in the winter broke down at a high rate, thus exacerbating an already existing shortage of supply trucks and other vehicles.

A Panzer III of SS-Panzer-Regiment 2 with several "Das Reich" Panzergrenadiers perched on its decks. When the division occupied defensive positions along the Oskul River in late January, the Panzer Regiment had 66 Panzer IIIs in its two battalions. It is armed with a 5cm cannon which was later upgraded with a longer barreled gun of the same caliber. The improved gun had a much greater shell velocity. (The author's collection)

Doubtless the surprising tenacity of the Germans also surprised Soviet commanders, given the existing estimation of German intentions and resolve before the launching of the offensive. Due to a combination of factors, in the period before 7-8 February, the 1. Panzerarmee defenses in the Slavyansk-Lisichansk area succeeded in critically delaying Popov's southern progress and began to force the Soviets towards a path of less resistance, which lay further to the west. This would ultimately contribute to the creation of an opportunity for a counterattack by Manstein's Panzer divisions. Although the operations of Mobile Group Popov remained a concern, the situation around Kharkov was more serious and greatly disturbed Manstein. The 1. Panzerarmee, although hard pressed, seemed to have the situation under control by 7 February, while at that date, the situation in the Kharkov area seemed to be worsening every day. With absolutely no uncommitted Panzer reserves, Manstein cast a nervous eye toward Kharkov in the first days of February. In *Lost Victories,* he discussed the difficulties facing the German armies during this period.

Above all, the situation in the area of Army Group B – i.e. in the region of Kharkov – was shaping so ominously that all sorts of opportunities were opening up to the enemy. Not only could he drive through to the Dnepr crossings at Dnepropetrovsk and Zaporozsche and cut off Don Army Groups communications there: it was even possible for him to cross the river further up stream and block it from the west. Besides shifting Fourth Panzer Army over to the western wing of the Army Group, therefore it would be necessary to form a new grouping of forces to replace Army Group B's allied armies, which had by now gone almost completely to pieces.[22]

The new forces Manstein referred to were the handful of divisions available to Armeeabteilung Lanz. This army, charged with forming lines of defense east of Kharkov, was in danger of losing Kharkov to the advancing units of the 6th Army and the 3rd Tank Army before it could even fully assemble. North and northeast of the city, 168. and "Grossdeutschland" were pushed back toward the city, while it was only a matter of time before the positions of Regiment "Deutschland" were isolated and overrun. Rybalko's 6th Guards Cavalry Corps was already approaching the Northern Donets southeast of the city. Meanwhile, Rybalko's 12th Tank Corps had crossed the Oskul north of Kupyansk and was on the move through the rear areas of 298. Infanterie-Division, pushing quickly toward Chugujev, which was slightly southeast of Kharkov. The town was located on the west bank of the Northern Donets and was a key railroad, bridge site and road junction.

However, as the Russians approached the river in the Chugujev sector, units of Dietrich's "Leibstandarte" were taking up defensive positions on the eastern bank, at the towns of Martovaja and Chotomlja. Russian reconnaissance attacks probed the SS defenses along the river and forward elements of the 3rd Tank Army were approaching from the east, having reached the town of Petschenegi. This town was only a few kilometers due east of the "Leibstandarte" lines at Chugujev. The division had positioned battle groups of its SS-PzG.-Rgt. 1 "LAH" east of the town. Behind it were stationed meager reserves, consisting of a company of Grenadiers from SS-PzG.-Rgt. 2 "LAH," supported by self-propelled anti-tank guns of the Panzerjäger-abteilung and a battery of assault guns.

The division's Aufklärungsabteilung, under its aggressive young commander, SS-Sturmbannführer Kurt Meyer, received orders to conduct a reconnaissance attack southeast of the "LAH" positions at Petschenegi. Meyer was to reach the bridges at Balabajevka and Wassilenkovo, in order to secure the retreat of a battle group belonging to 298. Infanterie-Division. Meyer was ordered to hold the bridges and allow the retreating German infantry to cross over the Burluk River to safety. However, when Meyer's

SS-Hauptsturmführer Heinrich Springer, commander of 3. Kompanie SS-Panzergrenadier-Regiment 1 "LAH." Springer won the Knight's Cross in January of 1942. (Courtesy of Mark C. Yerger)

forward reconnaissance squads scouted the roads leading to the river, it was discovered that Soviet units were already over the Burluk in strength and moving west of the river in several strong columns.

One of these SS reconnaissance detachments, advancing in the dark toward the village of Wassilenkovo, unexpectedly found themselves in a dangerous situation when it reached a stretch of road leading into a forest and sensed the presence of Soviet forces. The small detachment of reconnaissance troops watched as signs of Russian activity became noticeable along the road and in the forest itself. The commander of the troop, SS-Untersturmführer Maurer, detected signs that made him uneasy about trying to make their way through the woods at night and decided to bypass the forest. Fortunately for the small detachment, Maurer's decision was correct. When the company moved around the woods they were detected and fired upon but were able to escape and continue.[23]

[22] Manstein, pg. 415.

[23] Lehmann, pg. 44-45.

In the meantime, the remaining elements of 298. Infanterie-Division which were still holding Kupyansk were in danger of being totally destroyed and had received orders to abandon the town and fight their way to the west. There were already Russian troops operating in the division's rear, marching through its communications zone, towards the Donets River crossings southeast of Kharkov. Part of Meyer's reconnaissance battalion, under command of SS-Hauptsturmführer Gustav Knittel, provided mobile fire support to the 298. Infanterie-Division battle group, covering its withdrawal from Kupyansk. All around the German column, a broad tide of Soviet troop columns flowed westward, advancing both to the north and south and threatening to cut off Knittel and the Army troops. West of Kupyansk, on the road leading toward Chugujev, Maurer's small detachment joined up with Knittel's group in order to assist in providing rear guard protection for the column.

Somewhat unrealistically, given its condition, the division had been given orders to establish a new defensive position on both sides of Schevtschenkovo during the night of 3-4 February. The small town of Schevtschenkovo was just south of the bridges over the Burluk which were in the hands of Rybalko's 12th Tank Corps and was south of Regiment "Deutschland" positions west of Olkhovatka. It is probable that Armeeabteilung Lanz intended to move the division into a position where it could occupy positions securing the flank of the SS regiment, tying in with Regiment "Deutschland" to the north and "Leibstandarte" to the south.

However, due to their swift progress after crossing over the Oskul north of Kupyansk, the Russians had rendered these orders useless. Once across the river, the only German opposition to the 3rd Tank Army's advance through the gap between Kupyansk and Regiment "Deutschland" positions to the north of the city, were attacks from the Luftwaffe. Stukas had attacked elements of the 15th Tank Corps on 3 February, causing some losses in vehicles and equipment, but not causing any appreciable delays. Given the situation, the order to establish a defensive position on the west bank of the Burluk was obviously no longer possible, even if the division had been capable of carrying out such a mission in the first place. The rapid rate of advance by the 3rd Tank Army gave the Germans a taste of the disruption of Blitzkrieg, as events moved faster than the German command could react. Orders received at the Headquarters of 298. Infanterie-Division were rendered useless by the speed of advance by the Soviet armored spearhead. However, the speed of the breakthrough caused problems for the Russians as well.

The advance of the lead units of the 3rd Army left the main elements of Kharitonov's 6th Army rifle divisions far behind, because they were not motorized. In addition, some of Kharitonov's infantry was delayed by the resistance put up by 320. Infanterie-Division and the various Army, SS and Police detachments in the area. The slow, mostly road bound sled columns of the Soviet rifle divisions laboriously followed in the wake of the wide tracked T-34s and KV tanks. Russian tank formations were able to drive off the road, outflank a defensive position and lose very little time before proceeding again. In doing so, however, they left the slower infantry columns behind.

The Germans also experienced difficulties due to a critical lack of sufficient vehicles. Once any non-motorized German units were forced to abandon their defensive positions, they experienced similar problems in moving quickly if rail transport was not available. Neither the 298. or 320. Infanterie-Division were motorized, although the headquarters detachments probably still possessed a few vehicles. However, most of their artillery and heavy weapons were horse drawn. Within a short time, the poor animals pulling guns and heavy loads of ammunition, lacking proper food and rest, became totally exhausted. As a result, both divisions had difficulties moving their artillery and some of their vital guns eventually had to be destroyed and left behind. Meanwhile, the Soviet tank columns flowed around the division's regiments on all sides, while attacking Russian rifle divisions pursued relentlessly.

There was not much Lanz could do to aid the embattled divisional battle groups fighting their way through icy terrain and deep snow, as he had no reserves to spare. Food and supplies quickly became scarce, because it was not possible to consistently supply the divisions by air, due to the difficulty in locating the moving units and because the Russian could direct heavy anti-aircraft fire on German supply planes attempting to drop supplies and ammunition. Lanz remained in contact by radio with the beleaguered German troops and sent small SS mobile detachments to cover the retreat. The Armeeabteilung was pressed too hard on all fronts east of Kharkov to be able to create a battle group strong enough to have a reasonable chance to fight its way through to the encircled divisions. They were left on their own, to fight through to safety or be destroyed.

Lanz wanted to pull Regiment "Deutschland" back to Volchansk and assemble the entire division in that area, shortening his defensive lines. However, in order to do so, it was necessary for "Grossdeutschland" to take over the defense of the sector northeast of Kharkov, in the Olkhovatka area. Given the pressure exerted upon it by the 69th Army, the Army division could not disengage any of its forces to take over the "Das Reich" sector. It was impossible for the division to pull an entire regiment out of line in order to replace "Deutschland." In any event, Regiment "Deutschland" was also heavily engaged, under constant attack and could not have been easily withdrawn itself.

The SS regiment was forced to give up its positions at Kosinka and Borki in any event and had to withdraw to avoid being cut off. When Soviet penetrations threatened to envelope the regiment's two forward battalions, the SS troops were forced to pull back and II./and III./"Deutschland" conducted a fighting withdrawal to positions west of Olkhovatka. There the two battalions dug in behind I./ "Deutschland," which was already entrenched in forward positions. The regiment built a bulwark around Olkhovatka which slowed the right wing of the 3rd Tank Army considerably during the next several days.

Although the advance of the 3rd Tank Army in the Regiment "Deutschland" area was slowing, Rybalko's army enjoyed more success in the south, where Soviet forces continued to advance rapidly. The 111th Rifle Division pushed further to the west, supported by tanks of the 6th Guards Cavalry Corps. Lead elements of the division's infantry, riding on tanks of the 201st Tank Brigade, pushed to the Northern Donets north of the Petschenegi area. This penetration drove a solid wedge between 298. Infanterie-Division and created a southern border to a salient forming around the positions held by Regiment "Deutschland" It also threatened the approaches to the Northern Donets River crossings at Chugujev and Petschenegi. Frustrated by the failure to dislodge the SS Grenadiers, Rybalko decided to reinforce his one success, which was in the south. He committed the 12th and 15th Tank Corps in an attack on Petschenegi, while the 201st Tank Brigade and 111th Rifle Division were to continue their advance toward Chugujev and capture the town. On the right wing of the army, the 48th Guards Rifle Division and the 160th Rifle Division were to attack Regiment "Deutschland" at Olkhovatka and cross the Plotva River, which flowed from north of Olkhovatka toward the Northern Donets.

While Rybalko's attack continued to gain ground in the 6th Guards Cavalry Corps area, the Soviet 69th and 40th Armies also continued their offensives. Lieutenant General K.S. Moskalenko's 40th Army had four rifle divisions in his first echelon and the support of a tank brigade. On the second day of his attack, Moskalenko unleashed two mobile groups, each built around a tank brigade. One group, consisting of the 116th Tank Brigade and elements of the 183rd Rifle Division, was ordered to break through the German positions north of Belgorod and envelope the city to the west, while the second was to take Gostischchevo, which was a few kilometers due north of the northern edge of Belgorod.

The 116th Tank Brigade found an undefended gap in the German defenses, after passing through the lines of the 309th Rifle Division, proceeded south and reached the western environs of Belgorod on the following day. The second mobile group, made up of the 192nd Tank Brigade and infantry of the 309th Rifle Division,

captured Gostischchevo on 6 February. Other elements of the 40th Army marched further west of the 116th Tank Brigade mobile group and began to effect the complete envelopment of Belgorod. In the meantime, Moskalenko's 4th Tank Corps and accompanying rifle divisions, which had been involved in cleaning up German and Axis troops in the rear areas of the army, finally began to reach the army.[24]

The German situation at Belgorod was critical, as Korps Raus's 168. Infanterie-Division alone could not hold the city against the onslaught of the entire 40th Army. The German command had already sent whatever reinforcements could be spared to reinforce the division, but a few assault guns and a company or two of security troops were not much help. The Hungarian troops were of no use in any real fighting. In order to counter Moskalenko's assault into the rear of Korps Raus, elements of "Grossdeutschland" were sent to the aid of 168. Infanterie-Division. Heeresgruppe B ordered the Aufklärungsabteilung of "Grossdeutschland" to proceed to Belgorod. The weather conditions were bad however, and the frozen roads prevented the battalion from reaching the city until 4 February.

As soon as the battalion arrived, it was ordered to conduct a reconnaissance to the north of the city and block the advance of Russian columns that had penetrated the defenses of 168.Infanterie-Division and were sweeping westward. Armeeabteilung Lanz pivoted II./Grenadier Regiment "Grossdeutschland" and III./Füsilier Regiment "Grossdeutschland" around to defend the sector between Belgorod and Voltschansk. After moving into the area north and east of Belgorod, these units made several sharp counterattacks against Russian troops it contacted. Kampfgruppe Kassnitz, named after the commander of a battle group which consisted of the reinforced Füsilier Regiment "Grossdeutschland" (minus III./Füsilier-Regiment) took over the defense of the sector northeast of Volchansk.

Kampfgruppe Kassnitz arrived on 5 February and took over a defensive sector in the valley of the Neshegol River. In the meantime, the Aufklärungsabteilung "GD" established a blocking position north of Belgorod. However, no sooner had it arrived, than the battalion was ordered to provide rear guard cover for major elements of 168. Infanterie-Division, which were falling back toward Belgorod. The front around Belgorod was penetrated in numerous areas, the Russians pouring through gaps in the disintegrating defensive front of the infantry division. Air reconnaissance reports and intelligence information revealed the location of the most dangerous Russian advances. One was the attack of the two mobile groups, spearheaded by the 116th and 192nd Tank Brigades, and the other was the advance of the Soviet 69th Army.

---

[24] Glantz, pgs. 163-170.

The assault gun battalion of "Das Reich" was commanded by SS-Hauptsturmführer Walter Kniep in the winter of 1942-43. The picture shows a battery of freshly painted Sturmgeschütz IIIs in the street of a Russian village. The man on the right is battery commander SS-Untersturmführer Wolfgang Otto. On the left is SS-Obersturmführer Hartmut Braun. (Courtesy of Mark C. Yerger)

Kazakov's 219th and161st Rifle Divisions attacked towards Belgorod while to the south, two other rifle divisions split the undefended seam between "Grossdeutschland" and "Das Reich." This attack, made by the 270th Rifle Division, captured the village of Barsuk, which had been occupied by Hungarian troops. The Hungarians hurriedly evacuated Barsuk as soon as they were threatened by the Soviet attackers. The Axis troops, their morale destroyed by the rigors of a very difficult retreat, made no pretense of trying to put up a fight.

During the course of the following days, the 69th Army, attacking with four rifle divisions abreast, drove "Grossdeutschland" gradually to the west. On the right or northern flank of the army, the advance of the 219th and 161st Rifle Divisions was temporarily held up by the stubborn defense of elements of the Füsilier Regiment "GD." For two days main elements of the Soviet divisions fought to take the town, while the left flank of the army, the 270th and 180th Rifle Divisions, continued their advance until they were halted at Pankov and Belyi Kolodes. North of the Plotwa River, at Pankov, I./Füsilier Regiment "GD," supported by SS-Kradschützen-Bataillon 2, finally halted the advance of the 270th Rifle Division. The only sector in which the Russian advance continued was in the 40th Army sector and southeast of Kharkov, where the 6th Guards Cavalry Corps remained on the move.

The slowing of the advance of the 69th Army and the failure of the 3rd Tank Army to achieve a significant breakthrough frustrated the Voronezh Front commander. Golikov urged Rybalko to make every effort to quickly get his army moving, as it was imperative to take the Donets River before the Germans could withdraw to the west bank and prepare an organized defense of the river line. Golikov's concern was transmitted to Rybalko and resulted in 3rd Tank Army making its main effort for 3 February on its southern flank.

Rybalko's assault on the Northern Donets was led by two spearheads of tanks and motorized infantry. The 12th Tank Corps and 15th Tank Corps assembled behind the 62nd Guards Rifle Division during the night of 2-3 February and began their attack on the next day. On the southern flank of the attack, the 12th Tank Corps armor advanced in column formation toward Chugujev, along with its 13th Motorized Rifle Brigade. The other corps attack was spearheaded by the 15th Tank Corps, whose objective was Petschenegi, on the Donets just north of Chugujev. The two tank corps found their advance blocked by SS units holding the crossing sites on the river.

At Petschenegi, the 15th Tank Corps, accompanied by infantry of the 160th Rifle Division, made contact with the first defending SS units on 3 February. These were two companies of SS-PzG.-Rgt. 1 "LAH," holding a defensive position about seven kilometers west of the river, at the town of Artemovka. After brief fighting, the two SS companies pulled back to the main defensive positions at Petschenegi, on the Donets itself. The river was frozen solid and infantry of the 160th Rifle Division crossed the ice without difficulty and assaulted the "Leibstandarte" defensive positions in an ill advised frontal attack. Attacking across the frozen river, which provided no cover at all, proved to be a tactical disaster, particularly when the SS troops were equipped with the new MG-42 machine gun with its extremely high rat of fire. The attacks failed to establish a bridgehead and the bodies of hundreds of Russians lay in heaps on the ice of the river. After these assaults were repulsed, the remaining infantry of the forward detachments of the 15th Tank Corps searched for suitable alternate crossing sites, while waiting for reinforcements, in the form of the 13th Motorized Rifle Brigade to arrive. The column, which was strung out far behind the forward detachment, was delayed by the condition of the roads and did not arrive for some time.

While the Russians prepared for another attack at Petschenegi, the 12th Tank Corps and infantry of the 62nd Guards Rifle Division passed south of the 15th Tank Corps columns and approached Chugujev. Soviet troops occupied two small villages five to ten kilometers east of Chugujev on 3 February. Early on the morning of 4 February, Rybalko ordered the 6th Guards Cavalry Corps, in cooperation with infantry of the 6th Army's 350th Rifle Division, to advance to the river south of the town. Cavalry detachments occupied the town of Shevchenkovo, which lay astride the main road over which 298. Infanterie-Division was withdrawing toward the Donets. These were the forces that Meyer's patrols had discovered when conducting reconnaissance operations east of the main "Leibstandarte" positions. The two divisions of the SS-Panzer-Korps were thus faced with the difficult problem of holding the Donets, which meant maintaining mobile groups for counterattacks, while simultaneously keeping the lines of retreat open for both 320. and 298. Infanterie-Division and covering their withdrawal. The primary effort had to be the defense of the Donets and there was little that could be done to provide the two infantry divisions with more than a few platoons of reconnaissance troops, without jeopardizing this mission.

The intentions of the 3rd Tank Army were now clear to Hausser and Armeeabteilung Lanz. The two attack groups, one in the Olkhovatka area and the other (12th and 15th Tank Corps) in the Artemovka-Chuguyev area, were meant to cross the river, cut off the retreating German infantry divisions southeast of Kharkov and subsequently position themselves for the assault on Kharkov. As it was already apparent that the city was threatened in the north by the forces of the Soviet 40th Army, then advancing west of Belgorod,

the main objective of Operation "Star" became clear to the German command. Golikov's attack was meant to capture Kharkov and destroy its defenders.

The consequences of a Russian success in that area were simply disastrous, although not because of the city itself. More than the loss of a prestigious city of the Ukraine, the loss of Kharkov would mean that the SS-Panzer-Korps assembly area would be threatened. This meant that any hope of conducting a counterattack utilizing the rail and road net around Kharkov would be impossible. In addition, if the SS divisions were destroyed defending the city, the last strong Panzer reserves available to Manstein would be lost. With that in mind, Armeeabteilung Lanz ordered Korps Raus and the SS-Panzer-Korps to hold their positions at all costs. Lanz instructed 298. and 320. Infanterie-Divisionen to fight through to the Donets, hoping that they could arrive with at least some of their fighting strength intact. Their delaying actions occupied significant Soviet infantry strength at a time when it was needed elsewhere and at least proved to be an impediment to the Soviet advance east of Kharkov.[25]

At that time, 320. Infanterie-Division was split into three regimental battle groups, increasingly short of heavy weapons and burdened with ever growing numbers of wounded. Similarly, 298. Infanterie-Division painfully battled its way westward, leaving behind it a trail of destroyed equipment and snow covered graves. On 5 February, the two army divisions received new instructions. They were ordered to link up at the town of Andrejevka and then to establish a defensive position to defend that area. Armeeabteilung Lanz hoped to build a firm southern flank below Kharkov with the two divisions, in order to secure "Leibstandarte's" southern flank, but that hope was essentially a pipe dream. The two divisions were exhausted by continuous fighting and exposure to the elements and it was questionable whether either could even reach Andrejevka, much less establish a credible defense of the sector.

In attempts to establish contact with their Army comrades, "Leibstandarte" conducted several reconnaissance operations southeast of the Donets. The 1./Aufklärungsabteilung "LAH," under command of SS-Hauptsturmführer Gerhard Bremer, attacked from Chugujev toward the village of Annovka, which was occupied by mobile troops of the 12th Tank Corps, including at least a few tanks. Bremer's company was supported by artillery of the division and a few 88mm guns of the Flak battalion. Positioned on the western bank of the Donets, which is higher than the flat eastern river plain, the 88s were able to hit Soviet tanks at a distance of several kilometers, using their superior sights, which were designed for anti-air-

---

[25] NA/ T-354, roll 120, 1a KTB SS-Panzer-Korps, frame 3753551-3753553.

craft defense. After destroying Russian forces which were contacted near Annovka, Bremer pulled his battalion back to the river under cover of the artillery and heavy Flak cannons.[26]

SS-Sturmbannführer Hugo Kraas, commander of I./SS-PzG.-Rgt. 2 "LAH," led a small, mobile detachment on a raid southeast of Petschenegi, toward Izyum, hoping to make contact with 320. Infanterie-Division. They did not find the German troops, however and encountered tanks of the 201st Tank Brigade and the 6th Guards Cavalry Corps instead. When Kraas's detachment turned and sped back toward their own lines, elements of Russian cavalry tried to cut them off, and they had to fight their way through quickly, in order to avoid being caught by the main elements of the column. After receiving the report of the presence of Soviet cavalry and armor from Kraas, his battalion was reinforced with anti-tank guns and an additional company of infantry. A third attack was made by 3. Kompanie of Aufklärungsabteilung "LAH," under command of SS-Hauptsturmführer Gustav Knittel, which attempted to attack the Soviet cavalry detachment which had occupied Shevchenkovo. On the way to the town, the SS vehicles became mixed up with a large, strung out column of Italian and German troops. In the midst of this confusion, a number of Soviet tanks took advantage of the situation and launched an attack upon the company. It lost several vehicles and was scattered by the attack, later regrouping and being joined by Maurer's small group.

After spending the night near Shevchenkovo, Knittel decided to try to push through Soviet troops traveling along the road to the town of Malinovka, which was on the east bank of the Donets, southeast of Chugujev. A German pilot had dropped a note informing Knittel that there were Soviet cavalry units blocking the road. At first, the thrust went well and the SS column dispersed a few small groups of Russian horsemen as it pushed down the road. However, as the column neared the town of Koroboschkino, it encountered heavier resistance. A small column of Soviet infantry was scattered by the company, and a number of Germans who had been captured by the Russians, were freed. The SS vehicles sped onward, until swinging around a bend in the road east of Korobotschkino, where they ran head on into a Soviet road block. Russian infantry and anti-tank gun positions held the position and instantly the company was smothered with machine gun fire, grenades and anti-tank gun shells. The SS drivers gunned their motors and raced past the road block, but several vehicles were hit and destroyed. Other SS Grenadiers leapt from their SPWs and assaulted Russian anti-tank gun crews and machine gun positions. Most were killed or wounded, but their sacrifices allowed the rest of the column to fight its way

past the road block and eventually reach Malinovka, where it linked up with Bremer's company.[27]

To the north of the Chugujev area, Regiment "Deutschland" continued to prove a serious obstacle to the advance of Rybalko's army. After being forced to pull back from Olkhovatka, the regiment remained entrenched around the town of Veliky Burluk and awaited the Russians. Attacks began on the afternoon of 4 February, when Soviet infantry, supported by T-34s, assaulted the SS perimeter from the north and east. SS-Panzer-Korps records state that the regiment knocked out ten tanks and inflicted severe casualties upon the attacking Soviet infantry. During prisoner interviews, captured Russian soldiers stated that their losses exceeded 50% and that in many battalions, all the officers had been killed. Regiment "Deutschland" was able to throw back all Russian attacks during the day, once again frustrating Rybalko's attempts to take Veliky Burluk and destroy the SS Grenadiers.[28]

The Veliky Burluk salient, held by Regiment "Deutschland," protruded eastward and remained a concern of the Soviets on 5 February, because the salient provided a bridgehead from which the Germans could launch counterattacks to the north and south. South of Veliky Burluk, the 15th Tank Corps had crossed the Burluk River and penetrated some twenty kilometers to the east of the positions of Regiment "Deutschland" and its northern flank remained vulnerable to thrusts from the salient. While Harmel's regiment fought off the Soviet attacks, Regiment "Der Führer" moved up to assemble at the town of Belyi Koledes. In this manner, Regiment "Der Führer" established strong positions securing the northern flank of the Regiment "Deutschland" salient. After the arrival of the second SS Panzergrenadier regiment, Russian concerns about the SS salient proved to be justified.

At first light on 5 February, a Regiment "Der Führer" Kampfgruppe prepared to conduct an attack from the Belyi Koledes area southeastward, in order to strike the flank of the Soviet infantry concentrated in front of Regiment "Deutschland" at Veliky Burluk. The SS-Panzer-Korps ordered "Leibstandarte" to continue to hold the Chugujev-Petschenegi sector and reconnoiter to the southeast and retain contact with the remnants of the two encircled army divisions. Regiment "Deutschland" was to hold its defensive salient at Veliky Burluk, in spite of the presence of Soviet troops threatening its flanks.

The III./Regiment "Der Führer," commanded by SS-Hauptsturmführer Vincenz Kaiser and I./SS-Panzer-Regiment 2, led by SS-Sturmbannführer Herbert Kuhlmann, began their attack from

---

[26] Lehmann, pg 47.

[27] Lehmann, pg. 42.
[28] NA/T-354, roll 118, 1a KTB, Tagesmeldung SS-Panzer-Korps. frame 3751512.

assembly areas near Belyi Kolodes. In order to strike into the rear of the Soviet troops engaged in combat with Regiment "Deutschland," the columns motored north for a few kilometers until turning east again, after reaching the main road running into Olkhovatka from the north. By moving along this road the Kampfgruppe moved into position to attack southward and hit the northern flank of the Russian rifle division that was attacking the eastern edge of the salient. During the advance, as the Kampfgruppe pushed through the Plotwa River valley, the speeding SS armor left a wake of fleeing Russian troops as the column passed through several lightly defended villages.

The attack was supported by an attack of 16./Rgt. "Deutschland" from the northwest of Veliky Burluk. This attack was made with the objective of attacking Soviet positions south of Veliky Burluk and reaching the rail line just southeast of that village. In this manner, it was hoped to divert Soviet reserves and attention from the main attack carried out by the "Der Führer" Kampfgruppe. The attack was led by the company commander, SS Untersturmführer Heinz Macher.

The 16./Rgt. "Deutschland" (the regimental Pioniere, or combat engineer company) began its attack at 0800 hours. The company was reinforced with a 5cm anti-tank gun, a heavy machine gun squad of 12./Rgt. "Deutschland," and a mortar detachment. Starting from west of Veliky Burluk, 16./Rgt. "Deutschland" reached the old German positions west of the village, and found them free of Russians. The company occupied the entrenchments and awaited further orders, while a platoon reconnoitered to the northwest outskirts of Veliky Burluk, which were clear of any Russian troops.[29]

The "Der Führer" group penetrated about ten kilometers into the flank of the 48th Guards Rifle Division west of Olkhovatka. One group attacked due south, attacking the flank of the Soviet 48th Guards Rifle Division, while a second group, supported by SS Panzers, advanced toward Olkhovatka. The southern SS thrust cut off the rifle division's 146th Rifle Regiment and forced most of the rest of the Soviet troops attacking Veliky Burluk, to recoil to the south. Kaiser's second Kampfgruppe pushed further east, towards Olkhovatka and approached the perimeter of the town by 1400 hours. The Russians threw a rifle battalion, the 179th Tank Brigade and a regiment of anti-tank gun troops at the SS attack, in order to block its advance upon Olkhovatka. Supported by an attack of Stukas, the SS Panzers drove Soviet troops away from Olkhovatka, pursuing them to the north. The SS tanks followed the Soviet force for the rest of the afternoon, delayed time after time by rear guard troops. It appeared that the Russians were on the run and the SS armor

failed to reconnoiter properly as it pursued the Soviet troops. As a result, Kaiser's column blundered into an ambush. The Russians organized a well camouflaged position south of the town of Kupin at nightfall, emplacing a screen of anti-tank guns and dug in tanks across the line of attack of the SS column. Advancing in the darkness, the lead tanks of I./SS-Panzer-Regiment 2 ran into the Russian ambush and suffered heavy losses. Stung by the loss of over a dozen tanks, Kuhlmann pulled back and waited for daylight.[30]

Although the attack had thrown back the infantry forces assaulting Regiment "Deutschland," the Soviet armor advancing further to the south, was not affected. The Armeeabteilung decided that there was little chance of conducting a continuation of the attack to reach Kupyansk, with the limited forces at hand. It contented itself with the clearing of the Plotwa Valley and planned only a subsequent strike into the rear of the Russian forces attacking "Leibstandarte" in the Petschenegi-Chugujev area. The condition of the roads made any operations of mobile units uncertain in any event and by 5 February Kupyansk was already in Soviet hands.

While the "Das Reich" counterattack chopped up the Soviet forces east of the Veliky Burluk-Belyi Koledes salient, "Leibstandarte" was busy repulsing continuous reconnaissance attacks by Rybalko's 3rd Tank Army along the Donets River. Infantry of the 62nd Guards Rifle, 111th Rifle and 160th Rifle Divisions probed the river line during the day, trying to find suitable crossing sites. At the same time, Russian mobile columns could be seen moving across the entire front. SS observers and air reconnaissance reported large columns of Soviet troops heading south, past the southern flank of the SS defenses. These were probably columns of the 12th Tank Corps or the 6th Guards Cavalry Corps, on the march towards crossings of the Donets south of Kharkov.

To the north, Armeeabteilung Lanz could do little but watch as 168. Infanterie-Division continued to give ground back towards Belgorod, while "Grossdeutschland" mobile units fought to delay the advance of the 40th Army north and east of the city. Elements of "Grossdeutschland" battled the 69th and 40th Armies, while "Das Reich" continued to hold up the advance of Rybalko's 3rd Tank Army in the Belyi Koledes-Veliky Burluk sector. Meanwhile, southeast of the city, along the Northern Donets, "Leibstandarte's" Panzergrenadier regiments and the divisional mobile battalions defended the river line. Between the Donets and the Kupyansk-Izyum sector, 320. and 298. Infanterie-Division continued to struggle west, harried by Soviet cavalry and infantry.

On the morning of 6 February, bedraggled groups of soldiers from 298. Infanterie-Division began to reach German lines. Mov-

---

[29] Information from a privately held unit KTB courtesy of Mark C. Yerger.

[30] NA/T-354, roll 120,1a KTB SS-Panzer-Korps, Darstellung der Ereignisse an 5.2.1943. frame 3753555.

ing like the walking dead, half frozen and wrapped in rags for warmth, the exhausted infantrymen stumbled into German lines. After they reached safety, many of the men had to be compelled to take their place in defensive positions. Some began to recover somewhat after receiving warm food and hot tea and a number of the men were used as crews to man ten 7.5cm Pak 40s (anti-tank guns) and several heavy infantry howitzers. Kurt Meyer's reconnaissance battalion had found the guns abandoned on a train in Malinovka and had appropriated them for their own use. The anti-tank guns where dragged into position and placed into positions covering the approaches to the town. At 1100 hours, a group of about 600 men from 298. Infanterie-Division reached "Leibstandarte" positions, and an hour later, a second column of 800 men from the same division limped past the SS lines and entered Malinovka.[31]

Russian infantry and ski troops had made company and battalion strength reconnaissance attacks on the division's forward positions during the entire night of 5-6 February. They tirelessly searched for a weak gap in the SS positions along the river between the Chotomlja-Martowaja-Petschenegi-Malinovka strong points. At several places gaps were discovered and Russian infantry infiltrated between the German units. South of Malinovka, a Russian company crept through the German forward positions completely undetected and occupied the village of Gniliza. Once their presence was discovered, this group of infiltrators was counterattacked promptly by a hastily organized Kampfgruppe, commanded by SS-Obersturmführer Josef Diefenthal. Diefenthal's counterattack was assisted by mobile flak guns of 5./Flakabteilung "Leibstandarte." The Soviet troops in the village were cleared out by the afternoon. Throughout the day, the division conducted a very active defense of their sector.

Kurt Meyer's Aufklärungsabteilung attacked a Soviet battalion marching in column in the afternoon, catching it on open ground as it advanced east of Chugujev. Moving without adequate flank security, the Russians walked into an ambush set up by the enterprising Meyer. After reconnaissance patrols spotted the Russian vehicles and infantry moving along a road near Andrejevka, Meyer positioned anti-tank guns and assault guns in concealed positions located on higher ground. When the Russians entered the killing zone, the trap was sprung and the column was destroyed. For a loss of four German dead and thirteen missing or wounded, the Germans inflicted over 250 casualties on the Russian column and captured an anti-tank gun, several heavy guns and 200 horses. However, the Russians continued to infiltrate the SS lines and great vigilance had to be maintained at all times. The Soviet infantry often

Alfons Stegmaier, assault gun platoon commander in SS-Sturmgeschütz Bataillon 2. Stegmaier won the German Cross in Gold in December of 1943 for actions which included combat operations during the Kharkov fighting. (Courtesy of Mark C. Yerger)

picked the most inhospitable terrain, such as swamps or marshes, knowing that these areas would be less heavily watched. Near Martovaja, a platoon sized force of Russian infantry had penetrated the defenses of I./SS-PzG.-Rgt. 1 "LAH" and entrenched themselves in a small, wooded marsh along the river before they were detected.[32] After their presence became known, the division planned to assault the woods on the following day and clear the Russians out.

---

[31] Ibid. frame 3753559.

[32] NA/T-354, roll 120,1a KTB SS-Panzer-Korps, Darstellung der Ereignisse an 5.2.1943. frame 3753561.

At Skripai, to the south of Malinovka, a larger Russian attack against I./SS-PzG.-Rgt. 2 "LAH," broke through the town defenses and occupied a section of the perimeter. A counterattack was ordered and a Kampfgruppe was quickly organized by the regiment. Within minutes, supported by assault guns and mobile 2cm Flak guns, Grenadiers of the regiment counterattacked the Russians. Advancing behind the assault guns, the SS Grenadiers assaulted the penetration at its base, while 2cm explosive shells, fired from the Flak guns, blasted Russian positions. As the Russians were not allowed time to dig in, they were vulnerable to counterattack and heavy weapons fire. The quick German response sealed off the penetration and forced the Russian infantry to fight their way out of the trap and abandon Skripai.

By the end of the day, Rybalko's infantry attacks still were not able to get across the Northern Donets directly east of Kharkov. After conferring with Golikov and Vasilevsky, he proposed to swing the 6th Cavalry Corps, still led by the 201st Tank Brigade, further to the south in an attempt to outflank "Leibstandarte's" defenses. The corps was to cross the river below the town of Zmiev and thrust towards the town of Ljubotin, passing through an undefended gap south of Kharkov. This was the sector that 298. Infanterie-Division was supposed to have occupied, but that division was not able to defend the gap and a dangerous situation began to develop.

A 6th Cavalry Corps attack across the Donets into the gap at Zmiev, would cut vital rail lines entering Kharkov from the south. The stubborn resistance of Regiment "Deutschland," coupled with the counterattack of the "Der Führer" Kampfgruppe, had prevented Rybalko from crossing the river east of Kharkov and Rybalko hoped that the cavalry could push through the gap created by the attack of the 6th Army south of the Kupyansk area. The only German forces in the gap were the remnants of 298. Infanterie-Division, and these troops proved no hindrance to the Soviet cavalry, as they had not established a solid defensive front. Golikov approved Rybalko's decision and the 6th Guards Cavalry Corps assembled east of Zmiev, in preparation for its enveloping attack around the southeastern edge of Kharkov.[33]

In the evening of 6 February, SS-Panzer-Korps received orders from Armeeabteilung Lanz for the following day. Lanz requested radio reports from 320. Infanterie-Division regarding its progress toward Andrejevka, but received only partial reports. Lanz knew that the main elements of the division remained southeast of the German lines but did not have any detailed information. The 586. Grenadier Regiment remained completely out of contact with the division's headquarters and its exact location was altogether unknown. Elements of the division were ordered to concentrate at the town of Ssawinzy while its rear guard was busy fighting off Russian attacks near Balakleya. The Soviet 172nd Rifle Division pushed the Kampfgruppe holding Balakleya out of the town and continued its pursuit of the Germans. The 6th Rifle Division tried to encircle and crush units of the division northwest of the town, but the desperate German troops broke through the Russian troops and fought steadily to the west and safety. Due to the fluid, uncertain nature of the division's tortuous withdrawal, it was difficult to plan relief or escort operations because the location or intentions of the separate regimental battle groups were often not known.

The Russians were also frustrated by the division's actions, which occupied a significant portion of the 6th Army's strength. Although the stubborn delaying actions of the division had not appreciably slowed the advance of the lead units of the 6th Army, its commander, Lieutenant General Kharitonov had committed elements of three divisions to the task of destroying Postel's division. Major portions of the 350th, 172nd and 6th Guards Rifle Divisions attempted to block its withdrawal and destroy the division before it could fight its way into German lines and reach safety. Kharitonov planned to wipe out the stubborn German infantry battle groups struggling toward the Donets and then cross the river south of the 6th Guards Cavalry Corps. His divisions would then drive westward, with the intention of cutting the Kharkov-Losovaya railroad line, which ran out of Kharkov to the south.

Meanwhile, the Germans preparations for the defense of the city of Kharkov itself proceeded. The staff of the 213. Sicherungs-Division (security division) was transported to the city and began putting together local defense units, in anticipation of the inevitable Russian attack on Kharkov. Several batteries of 88mm Flak guns were emplaced covering likely routes of advance for armor and an emergency tank company was organized and equipped with a half dozen captured T-34 tanks. North and east of Kharkov, the situation continued to grow worse. At Belgorod, 168. Infanterie-Division was falling back at all points and the city was threatened with encirclement by Soviet troops to the west and northwest. Air reconnaissance discovered long columns of the 40th Army advancing toward Kharkov from the north.

The Russian pressure north and west of Regiment "Deutschland" remained a problem, as a breakthrough in that area would threaten the communications lines of the reinforced Regiment "Der Führer." It appeared that it was necessary for "Grossdeutschland" to secure the northern flank of SS-Panzer-Korps above Olkhovatka and protect the SS counterattack, which had been specifically ordered by Hitler himself. He had specified that it should proceed to the southwest, with the right flank units driving in the

---

[33] Glantz, pg. 166.

direction of Artemovka. Artemovka was an elongated village a few kilometers east of the Northern Donets, at a point near Petschenegi, near the center of the front held by "Leibstandarte." An attack that reached Artemovka would have considerably relieved Soviet pressure upon "Leibstandarte" and so Hitler's orders are perfectly understandable.[34]

Manstein describes the complex situation around Kharkov, as it existed in that period, in *Lost Victories*. He had just completed a marathon conference with Hitler regarding the further conduct of the defensive operations in Heeresgruppe Don's sector and the situation in southern Russia in general. Hitler had given his permission to withdraw from the eastern section of the Donets Basin and pull behind the Mius and Donets Rivers. However, accomplishing this task was far from certain, given the realities of the situation. Manstein still had to co-ordinate the realignment of the armies of Heeresgruppe Don, as well as react to the multiple Russian offensives unfolding from north of Kharkov to Stalino. A successful defense of Kharkov remained doubtful given the strength of the Russian offensive and the relative weakness of the forces available to defend the city. The 168. Infanterie-Division was on the verge of collapse at Belgorod, a development that threatened to unhinge Armeeabteilung Lanz' hold upon the entire Kharkov sector. Heeresgruppe Don, in communication with Armeeabteilung Lanz, made it clear that Kharkov was to be the cornerstone of the northern flank of Heeresgruppe Don, and was to be held at all costs. At that point, there were still military justifications for holding on to Kharkov.[35] Loss of Kharkov meant that the Russians might be able to quickly drive past the city to the west and reach the Dnepr crossings, far to the rear of Manstein's armies and cut the lines of communication to Heeresgruppe Don. However, even if the city could be held, his army group was faced with difficult battles and other challenging situations. Before 4. Panzerarmee had completed its move, the 1. Panzerarmee's defense of the Northern Donets was of great importance to the survival of Heeresgruppe Don. Once 4. Panzerarmee completed its move, it was in position to block any Soviet advance upon the Dnepr crossings and the defense of the city of Kharkov was of diminished importance.

Hoth's 4. Panzerarmee had moved from the eastern flank of the army group to the western flank, moving over roads nearly impassable with ice and snowdrifts or on rail lines sabotaged by Russian partisans every night. During the transfer, Armeeabteilung Hollidt had strong Russian mobile forces threatening to penetrate into its rear areas, with the intention of driving south to reach Stalino or Mariupol and thereby cut the lines of communication and supply

to the army. In the first week of February, while Hollidt fell back towards the Mius, his army was farther east than the Soviet armies that were attempting to drive through 1. Panzerarmee and encircle his army. Hollidt was also hard pressed to defend his front from the attacks of the 5th Tank Army and the 5th Shock Army of General R.I. Malinovsky's South Front. If Soviet mobile groups broke through the army's thin shell of defense, the retreat of Armeeabteilung Hollidt threatened to become a race to see who would reach the Mius first. There was also the danger, that even if Hollidt was able to conduct a successful withdrawal to the old German defensive positions on the west bank of the Mius, his army might find that it was cut off by Mobile Group Popov's march to the shore of the Sea of Azov.

The 1. Panzerarmee, commanded by General der Kavallerie Mackensen, had settled into the defense of the middle Donets area, from the Voroshilovgrad area and westwards along the river. Eberhard von Mackensen joined the German Army in 1908, first serving with Hussar Regiment 1 as a Leutnant der Kavallerie. He served in the Army during World War I and the Reichsheer in the post-war period. By 1934 he reached the rank of Oberst (Colonel) and in late 1937 commanded of 1. Kavallarie-Brigade. On 1 January, 1939, Mackensen was promoted to Generalmajor and served as Chief of Staff of 12. Armee until January of 1942, when he took command of III. Panzer-Korps. In November of 1942, Mackensen assumed command of 1. Panzerarmee having been promoted to Generalleutnant while leading III. Panzer-Korps. His 1a was Oberstleutnant Wolf-Rüdiger Hauser, a thirty-six year old Staff officer who previously served as an adjutant to the chief of the General Staff. He came to the army after serving as the 1a of 21. Panzer-Division.[36]

Mackensen's army was only able to bring a single Panzer division, one and a half infantry divisions and two corps headquarters out of the Caucasus. This was due entirely to decisions made by Hitler, and this time he had made the wrong choice. The blame for the isolation of the much needed divisions of the army rested squarely on his shoulders. He had delayed allowing the Panzer army to move through Rostov and using it to reinforce Manstein's Heeresgruppe Süd until the Soviet capture of Rostov closed the gate, trapping the rest of Mackensen's divisions in the Caucasus.

Crisis at Kharkov

When dawn broke on 7 February, Armeeabteilung Lanz was faced with a number of crisis situations. A Soviet storm was descending

[34] *Befehl des Gewissens,* pg. 46.
[35] Ibid. pg. 45.

[36] Information from Mark C. Yerger archives.

upon the entire sector, advancing from the north, east and south. By 0800 hours, German air reconnaissance reported the Soviets were moving to attack in all sectors of the front from north to south. In the north, a column of approximately 1000 men and twenty tanks was spotted north of Belgorod and a second column of unknown strength was observed farther to the east. To the south, lead elements of the Soviet 172nd Rifle Division pursued 320. Infanterie-Division, moving along the rail line towards Zmiev. South of the stretch of the Donets held by "Leibstandarte's" two Panzergrenadier regiments, the 350th Rifle Division had thrown bridgeheads over the Northern Donets River, near Zmiev, while the 201st Tank Brigade, still in the lead of the 6th Guards Cavalry Corps, moved closer to the Donets. All along the front held by "Leibstandarte" Russian rifle and tank troops were assembling for an attack upon the division's entire front along the river. In the center, Regiment "Deutschland" still held its salient, but the regiment's position became more precarious by the hour. This was particularly true when Grenadier-Regiment "Grossdeutschland" was pulled out of the division's sector north of the Veliky Burluk salient and sent to reinforce the faltering 168. Infanterie-Division.

The 168. Infanterie-Division was involved in difficult fighting early in the morning and was pushed back along its entire front, in spite of reinforcements from "Grossdeutschland." The Aufklärungsabteilung "Grossdeutschland," defending the approaches to Belgorod through the Northern Donets River valley, was forced to give ground as well. It was reinforced on 7 February by a Kampfgruppe of the Führer-Begleit-Bataillon, consisting of 5 Panzer IVs, two assault guns and two Pak 40 anti-tank guns, as well as two companies of Grenadiers. Elements of the Grenadier Regiment were arriving, but these troops were too little, too late. Welcome as these troops were, a few tanks, a weakened regiment and several batteries of assault guns could do little more than help to temporarily blunt one of the attacking Soviet columns closing in on Belgorod.

By mid-afternoon, the situation had become so critical, that the Grenadier Regiment "Grossdeutschland," at that time on the march from Kharkov, was given the assignment of blocking the Soviet advance along the roads leading into Kharkov from the north. Lanz anticipated that the Russians would break through the defenses of 168. Infanterie-Division before the regiment could reach its assigned defensive positions. The Füsilier Regiment "Grossdeutschland," defending on "Das Reich's" northern flank, was ordered to fall back westward, conducting delaying actions as it withdrew. This completely exposed the northern flank of the SS regiment. At 1600 hours, Russian troops were reported to be entering the environs of Belgorod from the north and east.

A Fieseler Storch (a light reconnaissance plane that could land on a very short makeshift runway) was dispatched to find the commanding general of 320. Infanterie-Division. The pilot was instructed to attempt to gather information about the division's plans for its breakout to the west and safety. The division's lost regiment, 586. Grenadier Regiment remained out of contact with the remainder of the division and the survival of the regiment remained uncertain. Late in the day, eighty men of the regiment, under command of a captain, fought through Russian forces and reached German lines. The group commander stated that only about 100 other survivors of the regiment could be expected to make their way to safety. This proved to be a pessimistic assessment of the situation, as nearly the entire regiment was able to fight their way out of encirclement by nightfall. Shortly after noon, the commander of the division, Generalmajor Postel, was flown to Chugujev via the Storch which had been provided to him. At Sepp Dietrich's HQ, Postel telephoned Lanz to brief him on the situation. After receiving Postel's reports, preparations went ahead for the arrival of the wounded division and Postel returned to his division.

A makeshift landing runway was constructed to allow Junkers transport planes to evacuate the wounded of the division who survived the ordeal and reached Chugujev alive. Plans were made to assist the retreat of the remainder of 320. Infanterie-Division with close support attacks by Stukas. Ammunition and supplies were dropped by air to the surviving battle groups, some of which were still in the Balakleya area on the Kharkov-Chuguyev-Kupyansk railroad. Halfway between the remaining main elements of the division and the safety of Chugujev, was the town of Andrejevka, which also was located on the rail line. After receiving air dropped provisions and ammunition west of Balakleya, the division was to attempt to break through to Andrejevka, where a mobile Kampfgruppe of "Leibstandarte" was to make contact with Postel and assist in the withdrawal.

A rear guard was to cover the retreat of the forward elements, who were burdened with hundreds of wounded. A Stuka mission was planned for 9 February, in order to provide air support the breakout operation. The division reported that strong Soviet elements were moving beyond its northern flank, toward the west and the Donets. These Soviet troops were likely formations of the 6th Guards Cavalry Corps, which was on the move towards the Donets crossings south of the "Leibstandarte" positions at Chugujev.

The situation was grim for Postel's division, and its escape remained in question, although a second group of 250 men from the lost 586. Grenadier Regiment, under the leadership of its commanding officer, Oberstleutnant Rickmers, reached German lines. The many days of exposure to cold and wind, fighting with little rest and inadequate food and the loss of heavy equipment, steadily reduced the fighting ability of the division. The men and officers who endured the demands of retreat conducted while experiencing the extreme conditions of the Russian winter were becoming exhausted mentally and physically. As in the case of the survivors of the 298. Infanterie-Division's retreat, only a resolute few could be expected to be in any shape to fight once they reached safety. The 298. Infanterie-Division was a division in name only and those members of its formation not temporarily incorporated into the "Leibstandarte" in ad hoc battle groups, were listed as Sturm-Bataillon 298.

The Loss of Belgorod

Moskalenko's 40th Army pushed 168. Infanterie-Division back into the perimeter of Belgorod on the morning of 7 February. The division reported it was under heavy attacks from the north and northeast and was in retreat everywhere. The Führer-Begleit-Bataillon, a combat battalion of Hitler's personal guard detachment, arrived on the north edge of the city and resolutely held a sector of the front, but one more German battalion would not change the situation. The escort battalion was joined by Aufklärungsabteilung "Grossdeutschland" and subordinated to the commander of the Army battalion, Rittmeister Wätjen. The Hungarian 1st Tank Division was utilized to cover the withdrawal toward the city, but was not realistically expected to be very effective. While much of the ground forces were deteriorating, the Luftwaffe, fortunately for the Germans, remained active and effective.

Korps Raus reports indicate that German planes constantly attacked Soviet columns approaching the city, inflicting losses upon Russian tank and infantry troops. In spite of the best efforts of the Luftwaffe, air power alone could not stop the Soviet advance. The 40th Army descended upon Belgorod from the north, Moskalenko's mobile groups enveloping the town to the west. Kazakov's 69th Army, battling fiercely, gained ground in unrelenting and costly frontal assaults on "Grossdeutschland" and Regiment "Deutschland" east of Belgorod. The combined assaults of the 161st, 219th and 270th Rifle Divisions drove the hard pressed German forces westward. Reinforced by the 37th Rifle Brigade and the 73rd Tank Brigade, the Soviet infantry outflanked or enveloped "Grossdeutschland" blocking positions on roads between Belgorod and Voltschansk. Meanwhile, "Das Reich" maintained its hold on the Belyi Kolodes-Veliky Burluk salient, which projected twenty kilometers to the east of Voltschansk. The advance of the Soviet 40th Army threatened to cut off the regiment by cutting its lines of communication west of the salient.[37]

In spite of the threat of a thrust of the Soviet 73rd Tank Brigade, which approached Voltschansk from the northeast on 7 February, the SS division repelled all Soviet attacks against the salient. Regiment "Deutschland" turned back an attack by Russian infantry and tanks south of Veliky Burluk, destroying several Soviet tanks. At 1250 hours, the Russians attacked the regiment at the same place, and were again driven back with heavy infantry losses. In the afternoon, following the first battles, air reconnaissance provided evidence that the Russians were assembling a strong force of armor and additional infantry east and south of Veliky Burluk. Other elements of "Das Reich" were also involved in defensive fighting along an arc east of Voltschansk. The Kradschützen Bataillon fought delaying actions on the northern boundary line between "Das Reich" and "Grossdeutschland."

Late in the day, the 3rd Tank Army and the 69th Army attacked the flanks of the salient held by Regiment "Deutschland." From assembly positions near Veliky Burluk, Rybalko's 184th Rifle Division, supported by T-34s, launched a series of very strong attacks upon the southern boundary of the salient, particularly upon III./Regiment "Deutschland." These attacks prevented the battalion from conducting attacks to support the counterattack of Regiment "Der Führer." At first light, the Russians also attacked the northern flank of the division, defended by SS-Aufklärungsabteilung 2, commanded by SS-Hauptsturmführer Hans Weiss. After shelling by mortars and rocket fire, Russian infantry assaulted the defensive positions of the battalion at the villages of Jefremovka and Tschaikovka. Lines of Soviet infantry emerged from the morning fog and charged toward the German positions, shouting and firing their machine pistols. The SS motorcycle troops were hard pressed to hold their positions, but the new MG-42s, with their high rate of fire, swept the snow covered flat terrain, chopping down the Russians troops as they sprinted forward. The first attack was followed by another, and then a third. The attacks finally began to diminish late in the day, leaving many dead or wounded Russians lying in the snow in front of the German positions. The wounded froze quickly where they lay, unless they survived until nightfall and were able to drag themselves back to their own lines under cover of darkness.[38]

Hausser concluded that the division had to deal with the situation on the southern boundary of the salient first, in order to secure the supply lines of the salient. He decided to strike the Soviet forces attacking from Veliky Burluk, with the "Der Führer" Kampfgruppe,

[37] NA/T-314, roll 489, 1a KTB Korps Raus - Tagesmeldung an Armeeabteilung Lanz vom 7.2.1943, frame 000597.

[38] NA/T 354, roll 120, 1a KTB SS-Panzer-Korps, Darstellung der Ereignisse, 7.2 1943, frame 3753567-3753568.

reinforced with SS-Sturmbannführer Jakob Fick's Kradschützen Bataillon. After Fick's men were pulled out, "Grossdeutschland" had to replace the SS troops, in order to secure the northern boundary of the salient. The SS motorcycle battalion was replaced on the night of 7-8 February by "Grossdeutschland" units. The battalion immediately began its march toward Belyi Koledes, in order to reinforce the attack by the "Der Führer" Kampfgruppe, which was to push southward at the same time that 320. Infanterie-Division made a last breakout attempt toward German lines. However, the attack was postponed until the night of 8-9 February, due to inconsistent communication with the Army division and uncertainty about its exact location and intentions. It was decided to wait one more day, when a Stuka attack could also be organized to support the operation. The commander of Heeresgruppe B, Feldmarschall von Weichs, personally communicated with Hitler and requested that everything possible should be done to rescue the encircled division.

While the preparations for the attack continued, "Das Reich" struck back at the Russian forces assaulting Veliky Burluk. At 1250 hours, I./SS-Panzer-Regiment 2 and three companies of "Der Führer" Panzergrenadiers launched a counterattack upon Veliky Burluk. The attack stopped the Russian advance but the SS tank battalion suffered heavily, when it ran into a wall of Soviet anti-tank gun fire. Eight "Das Reich" tanks were total losses after they were struck by 7.6cm anti-tank gun fire and burned out. A number of other tanks were temporarily knocked out of commission. These losses, coming on the heels of those suffered on the first day of the counterattack, severely reduced the number of operational tanks the division possessed.[39]

When "Das Reich" counterattacked the Russians east of Veliky Burluk, there was defensive fighting along the "Leibstandarte" defensive sector. Southwest of Petschenegi, at 1100 hours, a regiment of Russian infantry entrenched in a small wooded area were wiped out by a battle group of "Leibstandarte" Panzergrenadiers with support of divisional artillery and a few assault guns. After a stunning concentration of artillery fire, the SS infantry moved into the woods behind the assault guns, their treads crunching through the splintered tangle of tree branches and smoking underbrush. The tree bursts from 10cm and 15cm howitzers had wreaked a deadly havoc upon the Russian infantry in their trenches. The SS Grenadiers reported that the Russians left 350 dead behind when the survivors abandoned the woods.

At Skripai, on the southern flank of the "Leibstandarte" sector, the Russians mounted several strong attacks against SS-PzG.-Rgt.

2 "LAH." Skripai was several kilometers east of the course of Northern Donets and was about five kilometers north of the Kharkov-Zmiev-Andrejevka railroad line. The town was a forward outpost, from which the division could support the defense of the town of Andrejevka, which lay on the railroad line itself. The SS-Panzer-Korps ordered "Leibstandarte" to occupy Andrejevka, in order to maintain a line of retreat for 320. Infanterie-Division on the night of 7-8 February. The division did not have many troops to spare, but two companies of "Leibstandarte" Panzergrenadiers occupied the town, supported by assault guns of 3./Sturmgeschützeabteilung "LAH." Later in the day it became apparent to the SS Grenadiers that strong Soviet forces were gathering to attack Andrejevka and that large Russian columns had bypassed the town to the north and south. The commander of the "Leibstandarte" group holding Andrejevka, SS-Obersturmführer Paul Guhl, recognizing his precarious situation, urgently requested reinforcements. All along the front of "Leibstandarte," German observers and reconnaissance information noted the assembly of heavy weapons and armor, in addition to strong infantry elements, which indicated that the Russians were preparing to launch their attack in the near future.

Another dangerous situation was the northern flank of the Regiment "Deutschland" salient, in the gap between the SS positions and the right flank of "Grossdeutschland." The situation east of the Northern Donets began to deteriorate when the gap northwest of the Regiment "Deutschland" positions at Belyi Koledes could not be blocked. "Grossdeutschland" struggled unsuccessfully to fill the gap, but it was stretched beyond the limits of its capabilities by the necessity to help defend Belgorod at the same time. East of Belgorod, its battle groups met repeated Soviet thrusts, delaying the Soviet advance with blocking positions set up in villages or nearby high ground. There was no question of building up a coherent defensive front due to the width of the sector entrusted to the division. This type of fighting, physically exhausting and mentally draining, gradually dissipated the energy and confidence of even the elite "Grossdeutschland" troops.

The Soviet 69th Army's 161st and 270th Rifle Divisions pushed Füsilier Regiment "Grossdeutschland," the division's reconnaissance battalion and its decimated tank regiment relentlessly backwards, flowing into the gap. At that time, the 180th Rifle Division moved to attack Belyi Koledes, assaulting the northern flank of the salient. Although "Das Reich" was able to hold the salient east of Voltschansk, its position was slowly becoming untenable, because its northern flank was increasingly extended and more vulnerable. To the south, the situation was more manageable for the time being, but it was clear that the Russians were preparing to launch a full scale assault on the Northern Donets River. While

---

[39] NA/T 354, roll 118, 1a KTB SS-Panzer-Korps, Fernschreiben an Armeeabteilung Lanz 7.2.43.

"Grossdeutschland," "Das Reich" and "Leibstandarte" held their ground, the other divisions assigned to Armeeabteilung Lanz were either in danger of complete destruction or not capable of fighting any more.

During the night of 7-8 February, the 40th Army brought up all of its available artillery and massed three rifle divisions for a final assault upon Belgorod. At dawn, Russian spearheads broke into the perimeter of 168. Infanterie-Division at several different points. The entire front of the division was pushed back toward the town, delayed by stubborn resistance at some points. The Hungarian 1st Tank Division, brought up to reinforce German troops defending Belgorod, gave a surprisingly good account of itself for a time and turned back battalion strength Soviet attacks. However, when Russians began to flow around their sector to the north and south, the Hungarians tried to pull back. T-34s and Russian artillery caught the unfortunate Axis troops in the open and destroyed most of the remaining Hungarian tanks. The Luftwaffe continued to attack Soviet motorized columns aggressively during the day, but could not halt the Soviet onslaught. Reporting that it expected the city to fall at any moment, 168. Infanterie-Division stated that it had moved its headquarters out of Belgorod.[40]

The situation continued to deteriorate, as the Soviets pushed the division back toward Belgorod. The Führer-Begleit-Bataillon, sent to support the division, disabled 3 Soviet T-34s, while a number of 88s, situated to protect main roads into the city, knocked out a few other tanks. In response, the Soviets either quickly bypassed these positions or infiltrated infantry into their rear and forced them to withdraw. These small units were able to temporarily block some of the main roads, but when Russian infantry appeared behind them, the German detachments holding key positions pulled back, time after time. At 0800 hours the first elements of 168. Infanterie-Division were forced back into the city. The division was cut into several different regimental groups by advancing Russian columns and all efforts to conduct an organized withdrawal collapsed. At 1300 hours, Armeeabteilung Lanz informed Korps Raus that 168. Infanterie-Division was to fight through Belgorod to the south, to prevent the Soviet armor from driving directly through the town and breaking free to the south. However, the division retreated westward, towards the town of Tomarovka. This direction of withdrawal took the division out of the path of the 40th Army's main direction of advance, which was south, toward the prize of Kharkov.[41]

The division had reached the end of its capabilities and was exhausted, with its battle strength only about 2000 men. After the loss of Belgorod and the precipitate withdrawal of 168. Infanterie-

Division, the Führer-Begleit-Bataillon and Aufklärungsabteilung "Grossdeutschland" escaped to the south along the main road exiting the southern edge of the city. Both battalions had suffered grave losses in men and equipment during the fighting. The two weakened battalions pulled back, under pressure by Russian tanks and strafing by Soviet ground attack aircraft, while 168. Infanterie-Division fled west, toward the town of Tomarovka. The remnants of the division, instead of withdrawing to the south as ordered, left the Führer-Begleit-Bataillon and the "Grossdeutschland" troops to fight their way to safety alone. However, the shattered German infantry division still did not escape to safety unscathed, because Russian tanks caught the tail end of the division 10 kilometers east of Tomarovka and attacked it. The T-34s rolled forward, running down many of those who had escaped the barrage of cannon and machine gun fire. The survivors of the rear guard fled over the snow, leaving wounded and dying men and horses in the bloody snow. The Russian tanks rolled over towed guns and trucks, while burning vehicles sent plumes of smoke into the air.[42]

In the meantime, to the south, the 320. Infanterie-Division continued its agonizing withdrawal westward, trudging over the snow covered steppes east of the Northern Donets. No one could say if the division would escape intact or end up like 298. Infanterie-Division, without any heavy weapons and too weak to fight. Although Postel's division had carried out its orders to slowly withdraw and delay the Soviets, columns of Russian troops had slipped around its flanks and approached the Donets south of Kharkov. By the end of the day, Soviet forces had launched attacks all along the front. The 40th Army overwhelmed the German divisions defending Belgorod and threatened to exploit this success and encircle Kharkov. The 3rd Tank Army thrust to the south of the city, aiming to link up with the armor of the 40th Army. The events of 8 February were a grave indication of additional disasters to come, during the following days. In fact, the fall of Kharkov was only a matter of time, because there were no reserves at hand to fill the gaps between the thin German lines. While Armeeabteilung Lanz tried to hold on to Kharkov, its flanks remained open to the north and south, and the Russians soon discovered this German weakness. In the next few days, mobile battle groups swept around the city and threatened to encircle Armeeabteilung Lanz. Two of the divisions of Hausser's SS-Panzer-Korps were thus in danger of being destroyed before the entire corps had even completely assembled. The destruction of the SS divisions meant more than a failed defense of Kharkov, it meant that the only German divisions capable of launching an effective counterattack would be lost.

---

[40] *Befehl des Gewissens*, pg. 54.
[41] Ibid. pg. 61.

[42] *Befehl des Gewissens*, pg. 54-60.

5

COMMAND AND CONTROVERSY: HAUSSER AND THE WITHDRAWAL FROM KHARKOV

By 9 February the 3rd Tank and 69th Armies had broken through the defensive fronts of Korps Raus north and east of Belgorod and pushed the Germans out of the eastern perimeter of the city. The 168. Infanterie-Division had reached Tomarovka, pursued by Soviet tanks and aircraft. The last tanks of the 1st Hungarian Tank Division were knocked out and the Führer-Begleit-Bataillon and "Grossdeutschland" Aufklärungsabteilung were forced to pull back toward Kharkov. The Grenadier-Regiment "Grossdeutschland" did not arrive in time to save the city and would not have been able to do much more than delay the inevitable in any event. The sector west of Belgorod was undefended and as a result the mobile spearheads of the 40th Army were approaching the sector northwest of Kharkov. Finding little resistance in front of them, columns of T-34s rumbled southward, turning the western flank of Armeeabteilung Lanz. However, east of Kharkov the Russians had encountered more stalwart resistance.

The 3rd Tank Army remained slowed by the stubborn delaying actions of Regiment "Deutschland" in the Veliky Burluk salient. The SS regiment continued to hold on to the sector even though its northern flank was even further exposed by the withdrawal of "Grossdeutschland." Dietrich's "Leibstandarte" was under pressure along its entire front along the Northern Donets east of Kharkov and its southern flank remained open south of Zmiev. Armeeabteilung Lanz had hoped that 320. Infanterie-Division or 298. Infanterie-Division would fall back across the river and block this sector but this had not occurred. "Leibstandarte" remained on the defensive due to heavy Soviet pressure along its defensive line on the Northern Donets. As a result, it could not do anything to help secure "Das Reich's" flanks. The division's salient became even more vulnerable, because with the loss of Belgorod the supply lines

of the division were potentially threatened by the advance of the 69th Army.

Units of Theodore Eicke's 3. SS-Panzergrenadier-Division "Totenkopf" had begun to reach rail stations in Poltava beginning on 6 February but the division would arrive too late to significantly influence the fighting at Kharkov. While Eicke's troops slowly assembled east of Kharkov, the situation remained discouraging for Armeeabteilung Lanz. The 168. Infanterie-Division had collapsed under relentless Soviet pressure and although "Grossdeutschland" fought stubbornly at all points, it was forced to give ground before the advance of the 40th and 69th Army. Soviet mobile forces driving from Belgorod were poised to encircle Kharkov and the 6th Guards Cavalry Corps was approaching an undefended gap south of "Leibstandarte's" right flank. However, in spite of this situation Heeresgruppe B and OKH remained insistent that "Das Reich" should continue the "Der Führer" counterattack and drive toward Kupyansk, south of Veliky Burluk. Commanders closer to the realities of the front were aware that the situation was rapidly changing by the hour and that the original objectives for the attack could not be achieved by the forces at hand. The initiative and numerical superiority rested with the Russians and this situation was not likely to change, even with the arrival of one additional German division. The proposed "Das Reich" attack, conducted by a reinforced battalion of Panzergrenadiers and supported only by a decimated battalion of tanks, had a poor chance of accomplishing anything worthwhile.

The 1a of the SS-Panzer-Korps, SS-Standartenführer Werner Ostendorf, during a heated conference with the 1a of Armeeabteilung Lanz, stated that the strength of the Russian forces south of Olkhovatka and on the flank of the proposed direction of the attack promised heavy casualties and little chance of success. "Das Reich's" Panzer regiment had already suffered significant tank losses in one battalion and the operation, in the opinion of SS-Panzer-Korps was not worth the probable cost. Ostendorf suggested that if the attack resulted in a serious reduction of the strength of the division it might not be able to continue to defend the approaches to the Northern Donets east of Kharkov. It was not certain that the salient perimeter could be held with the forces available to Armeeabteilung Lanz in any event. Lanz replied that the order to attack came from Hitler himself and thus remained in effect. However, events beyond the control of Lanz and Hitler dictated a change in the German plans.

One of the 40th Army mobile groups, made up of the 116th Tank Brigade and elements of the 183rd Rifle Division, swung south from Belgorod. By the morning of 8 February it passed through a gap in the German defenses west of the city and struck out for Kharkov. On that day German reconnaissance reports detected a Soviet column consisting of fifteen tanks and a battalion of motorized infantry, which was heading south toward Kharkov. This column was almost surely the 116th Tank Brigade battle group. While the envelopment of the city continued to the west, the 40th Army approached the city from the north encountering stalwart resistance from "Grossdeutschland."

East of the city, the 40th Army's 161st and 219th Rifle Divisions forced "Grossdeutschland" back, in spite of suffering heavy losses. This further uncovered the northern flank of the "Das Reich" defensive positions in the Veliky Burluk salient. Southeast of Kharkov, "Leibstandarte" was ordered to continue to hold the river line in order to have any hope of saving 320.Infanterie-Division. South of Postel's withdrawing division there existed an undefended gap that was nearly 40 kilometers wide. The 6th Guards Cavalry Corps and elements of several Russian rifle divisions were pouring through the gap and driving west. Small groups of men belonging to 298. Infanterie-Division trudged in quiet desperation through the gap, moving ever westward, trying to dodge columns of Russian infantry and tanks. While the situation remained uncertain in the south, discouraging battle reports from the northern and eastern approaches to Kharkov were arriving at the headquarters of Armeeabteilung Lanz.

Attacked by strong infantry forces, which were well supported with tanks and artillery, "Grossdeutschland" could not hold back the advance of the 270th and 161st Rifle Divisions. This pressure threatened to create another dangerous situation, because unchecked the Soviet advance menaced the lines of communication of the SS-Panzer-Korps. With this in mind, Ostendorf radioed Armeeabteilung Lanz at 1100 hours, citing the Soviet threat to "Das Reich's" northern flank and the dangers of a potential advance into the rear areas

German troops manhandling a howitzer off of a flatbed rail road car in the railroad yards at Poltava in early January, 1943. Moving equipment and men belonging to a single division took many trains and increasingly became more difficult due to partisan sabotage. (Credit National Archives)

of the division. Once more he requested that the attack for the following day be canceled due to the changed situation. There was no immediate response from Lanz's headquarters. "Das Reich" reported that it had 24 tanks available for action to support the attack of III./ Regiment "Der Führer." Keppler stated that the difficulties of launching the attack were considerable and would likely result in little success. After conferring with the Chief of Staff of OKH, Kurt Zeitzler, Lanz was told that the attack was to be made although with more modest objectives and contingent on increasing Soviet pressure from the east. This order was transmitted to Hausser's HQ, where it can be assumed it was received with little enthusiasm.[1]

In "Leibstandarte's" sector, the day began with an attack by Russian infantry supported by tanks upon Andrejevka which was defended by Kampfgruppe Guhl, a reinforced platoon. Soon after Guhl's men had reached the town, a German reconnaissance plane dropped a note describing the approach of a small group of German troops. Guhl assumed that this was one of Postel's regimental columns and sent a patrol out to meet the group, only to find a bedraggled, ragged group of survivors from 298. Infanterie-Division.

The SS company returned to Andrejevka, where it fed and provided medical attention to the exhausted Army troops. During the day it became apparent that large numbers of Russian troops were on the move all around the isolated outpost, marching west in long dark columns. Guhl immediately requested reinforcements and issued a warning to German supply columns to be aware of the presence of Soviet troops throughout the area leading back toward Kharkov. Guhl requested that he be reinforced when it became apparent that the Russians would attack Andrejevka after Soviet rifle battalions were observed assembling east of the town. Guhl's fears were justified.

[1] *Befehl des Gewissens*, pgs. 55-57.

On the next day the Russians attacked Andrejevka in force, with infantry and several T-70 light tanks. After sustaining severe casualties and the loss of a tank, the first Russian attack faltered and then collapsed. Shortly before noon, the Soviet 106th Rifle Brigade attacked with great determination, breaking into the town at several points. The hard fighting Russian infantry drove Kampfgruppe Guhl out of the town and forced it to withdraw to the west. The loss of Andrejevka was a serious blow to the chances of 320. Infanterie-Division reaching German lines. The main body of the division, pursued by the Soviet 350th Rifle Division, continued to slowly make its way toward Andrejevka. Postel's rapidly weakening division, increasingly burdened with growing numbers of wounded, tried to arrange for the Luftwaffe to land on a makeshift field and take out 650 wounded soldiers. However the rescue operation could not be organized.[2]

Between dawn and early afternoon the Soviets began strong attacks upon the southern wing of "Leibstandarte" between Petschenegi and Skripai. Soviet rifle battalions supported by heavy artillery, attacked the positions of SS-PzG.-Rgt. 2 "LAH" "LAH" repeatedly. At Gniliza, an entire Soviet rifle regiment and several tanks attacked the SS positions during the late morning and afternoon. A counterattack by assault guns and mobile Flak cannons broke up the most serious of these attacks and knocked out two T-34s. North of Andrejevka at Petschenegi, the 248th and 350th Rifle Divisions repeatedly assaulted positions of SS-PzG.-Rgt. 1 "LAH." The right flank of the regiment, held by SS-Sturmbannführer Max Hansen's battalion, came under especially heavy attacks. Several small assault groups of Russian infantry were able to gain toeholds in the front lines. The situation was finally restored by a counterattack of elements of III./SS-PzG.-Rgt. 1 "LAH," under the leadership of battalion commander SS-Hauptsturmführer Hubert Meyer.[3]

Later in the day it became apparent to the Germans that sometime during the night large columns of Russian cavalry had crossed the Donets south of Andrejevka and were advancing into the undefended gap south of Kharkov. The presence of the Russian cavalry was detected by German air reconnaissance which estimated that one cavalry column was 6000 men strong. Based on its direction of advance, the Soviet objective appeared to be the Losovaya-Kharkov rail line. At 1300 hours, reconnaissance reported the presence of a second Russian cavalry group, advancing west and strung out in a long column. These columns belonged to the 6th Guards Cavalry Corps, which had been brought up behind the 12th Tank Corps on 5 February. Its mission was to cross the Donets and thrust west to-

Werner Ostendorff was the 1a (Chief of Staff) of the SS-Panzer-Korps in the winter of 1942-43. Before the war, Ostendorff served in the German Army from 1925 until 1934. In 1934 he took flight training in the Luftwaffe and in the following year transferred to the SS Verfügungstruppe. Due to his experience and obvious talents, Ostendorff served as an instructor at Junkerschule Bad Tölz. He was selected by Hausser to be the 1a of "Das Reich" and won both classes of the Iron Cross while in that position. After leaving Hausser's staff he assumed command of 17. SS-Panzer-Grenadier-Division in November of 1943. In late 1944, Ostendorff took command of "Das Reich." While in that post he was struck by an incendiary shell and suffered severe wounds from which he never recovered. He died of complications and infections on May 4, 1945. (Credit National Archives)

ward the Merefa area, where it was to link up with troops of the 40th Army and encircle Kharkov. The forward elements of the corps intended to reach its first objective, the small town of Bereka, on 9 February. Bereka lay near the Kharkov-Losovaya railroad at a point 20 kilometers directly south of Kharkov. This penetration threatened the vital railroad and communication lines that ran into the southern sector of the city. It also meant that elements of the 6th Guards Cavalry Corps were between Andrejevka and 320. Infanterie-Division.

In "Das Reich's" sector, combat was generally light throughout the course of the day, although during the night a Soviet recon-

[2] Glantz, page 97 and *Befehl des Gewissens*, pg. 57.
[3] Lehmann, pg. 54-55.

naissance force penetrated between the positions of I./and III./Regiment "Deutschland." A counterattack was organized and SS Panzergrenadiers closed off the base of the gap, trapping the Russian infantry. The Soviet troops in the sealed penetration area filtered out of the boundary sector under cover of darkness.

South of the right flank positions of "Leibstandarte," near the town of Proletarskoje, SS patrols detected a column of Soviet troops moving to the west and in the open. This column was also probably a part of the 6th Guards Cavalry Corps, moving into the gap south of Zmiev. This information was reported to Dietrich's division Headquarters and the divisional artillery laid down a number of heavy barrages on the column, breaking it up and causing considerable casualties. On its threatened northern flank, a few tanks of the division supported a counterattack by SS-Aufklärungsabteilung 2, cleaning up another crisis east of Voltschansk.[4]

It was obvious to Lanz that the situation was reaching a critical point. He boarded his Fieseler Storch and conferred with both Cramer and Hausser. Of particular concern were the northern and southern flanks of the Armeeabteilung. To the south, the 6th Guards Cavalry Corps thrust was making good progress through the undefended gap. In the north, the advance of the Soviet 40th Army and the resulting collapse of 168. Infanterie-Division had made "Grossdeutschland's" position untenable. The infantry division was split into several groups, all of which were retreating westward. There was no possibility that Korps Raus could regain Belgorod and subsequently Lanz decided to shorten his defensive lines and prepare to hold Kharkov. He ordered "Grossdeutschland" to pull back and canceled the attack by "Das Reich" planned for the afternoon. Instead of attacking the SS division was ordered to withdraw behind the Northern Donets in two stages. Keppler was to pull back from the Veliky Burluk salient in the first stage and complete the withdrawal on 9 February, when the entire division was to cross over the river and take up new defensive positions. Protected by Regiment "Der Führer" on the north flank, Regiment "Deutschland" was to begin its pull back under cover on 8 February.[5]

Lanz planned to reorganize his divisions on 9 February, hoping to establish a solid defense of Kharkov to the north while the SS-Panzer-Korps was to assemble its mobile group at Merefa. Both "Das Reich" and "Leibstandarte" were to contribute mobile formations to the counterattack. Under command of Dietrich, the mobile group was to be used to counterattack the 6th Guards Cavalry Corps and prevent its further advance to the west. At the same time, "Leibstandarte" was to hold its positions on the Donets and assist

the breakout attempt of Postel's 320. Infanterie-Division, which was still delayed at Balakleja. Given the Soviet forces building up to its front, these multiple missions stretched the division's capabilities to the utmost. Any one of the three would have been difficult by itself. "Das Reich" had to complete a hazardous withdrawal, in the face of heavy pressure by the Russians and establish a new defensive position on the Northern Donets.[6]

On 9 February, the SS-Panzer-Korps took over command of the city of Kharkov. In response to Lanz' order regarding the threat of the 6th Guards Cavalry Corps Hausser ordered the assembly of the battle group at Merefa. The SS-PzG.-Rgt. 2 "LAH" was ordered to retake the town of Andrejevka, in order to establish a bridgehead closer to the breakout attempt of 320. Infanterie-Division. Postel's division was then about thirty kilometers from Andrejevka. "Leibstandarte" was ordered to pull all of its battalions back to the west bank of the Donets, in order to shorten the front and enable the division to free up forces for the Merefa Kampfgruppe.[7]

The morning reports from the Belgorod area were brief and dismal on 9 February. Those troops of 168. Infanterie-Division which had been able to escape the Russians still retreated westward, away from the advance of Soviet mobile groups. Elements of the division were already reported to have arrived at the town of Tomarovka, twenty-five kilometers west of Belgorod. Detachments of the Führer-Begleit-Bataillon and elements of "Grossdeutschland" fell back to the town of Dolbino, south of Belgorod, where they made contact with other troops of their division. By the afternoon, Grenadier-Regiment "Grossdeutschland" occupied blocking positions along the road entering the northern approaches to Kharkov from Voltschansk.

The Russians continued their probes of "Leibstandarte" defensive positions on the eastern bank of the Northern Donets during the night of 8-9 February. It is possible that the Russians realized the division was pulling out of its positions east of the river because shortly after first light on 9 February, attacks commenced against these positions. The strongest efforts were launched against the towns of Malinovka, Petschenegi and Skripai where "Leibstandarte" Grenadiers had held forward defensive positions east of the Donets. The Soviets launched regimental strength assaults, which were supported by armor and heavy mortar and rocket fire. The 160th Rifle Division, strengthened by armor of the 15th Tank Corps attacked Petschenegi just as the last "Leibstandarte" units were beginning their withdrawal to the west bank of the Donets. Under cover of a quickly organized counterattack launched by ele-

---

[4] NA/T-354, roll 120, 1a KTB, Darstellung der Ereignisse, 8.2.1943, frame 3753571.
[5] *Befehl des Gewissens*, pg. 55-57.
[6] Ibid. pg. 60-61.
[7] Lehmann, pg. 54-55.

ments of SS-PzG.-Rgt. 2 "LAH," most of the SS Grenadiers were able to reach the western bank safely. At Malinovka, two fifty ton KV-1 tanks were knocked out by Flak guns utilized in an anti-tank role. "Leibstandarte" emplaced many of its 88mm guns in positions to cover the division's withdrawal. Their flat trajectory and deadly accuracy at long range made them extremely dangerous to Soviet tanks and vehicles. The western banks of the Northern Donets are generally higher than the more marshy and flat eastern banks. Using the additional elevation provided by the western bank, 88s could hit Russian tanks moving over the flat, snow covered steppe at distance far beyond the range of T-34 cannon fire.[8]

While the two SS divisions completed the first phase of their withdrawal during the night of 9-10 February, the SS-Panzer-Korps gathered its forces for the counterattack upon the 6th Guards Cavalry Corps. Kurt Meyer's Aufklärungsabteilung was the first unit to reach the Merefa area. The I./SS-PzG.-Rgt. 1 "LAH" began its march to join the battle group being formed at Merefa. However, the only available roads were clogged with formations of "Das Reich" as well and the resulting traffic snarls slowed movement considerably. The entire attack group could not be formed at Merefa as scheduled, due to the delays of main units of the force, primarily caused by poor traffic control and bad weather conditions. As a result it was clear that the attack scheduled for 10 February could not be launched on time.

In the morning, 320. Infanterie-Division continued its agonizingly slow withdrawal toward the Andrejevka area, reporting that it was carrying 800 wounded. The increasing number of casualties strained the division's capacity to fight and move effectively. Postel requested that the Luftwaffe conduct Stuka attacks on Soviet forces north of Andrejevka in order to support the division's efforts to reach the town. Ammunition and medical supplies were very low and the men were totally exhausted. Generalmajor Postel told Lanz that he did not believe his men could fight through the Soviet forces blocking their retreat without strong support. However, the Stuka mission could not be organized in time and very little aid was given to Postel. "Leibstandarte" was occupied in its difficult withdrawal to a new defensive line and had sent main elements of the division to the Kampfgruppe assembling at Merefa.

Due to these factors, the breakout operation had to be postponed until the next day. The distance between the lead units of the division and the closest German position, Kampfgruppe Guhl at Andrejevka, was too great for Postel's increasingly less mobile division to cover in a single day burdened as it was with its wounded. It was hoped that after the move pulling back across the Donets the

The commander of II./SS-Panzer-Regiment 2 as of February 10, 1943 was SS-Obersturmführer Hans-Albin von Reitzenstein. He assumed leadership of the battalion after the former commander, Herbert Kuhlmann, took command of the regiment when Herbert Vahl replaced Georg Keppler as division commander. (Courtesy of Mark C. Yerger)

front held by the SS-Panzer-Korps was shortened sufficiently to free up some strength for a rescue operation. However, by that time the 6th Guards Cavalry Corps, led by the tanks of the 201st Tank Brigade had reached the rail line that ran southwest from Kharkov to Merefa. It then pushed on to the town of Novaja Vodolaga. The threat posed by this Soviet group to the two key rail lines leading into the southern sector of the city outweighed the rescue of 320. Infanterie-Division personnel. This decision was obviously the correct one because the danger of an encirclement west of Kharkov was far more serious than the threat to Postel's division. To Postel however, watching the agonies of his men, it must have felt that his division was being abandoned to its fate by Armeeabteilung Lanz.

In thirty degree below zero weather, elements of three Soviet divisions fought to destroy the battle groups of 320. Infanterie-Di-

───────────
[8] Lehmann, pg. 55-60.

vision. The numb German infantrymen stumbled through knee deep snow, while emaciated horses pulled the few remaining artillery pieces. Assault guns were absolutely vital and all efforts were made to keep them running even if other vehicles had to be left behind for lack of fuel. Exhausted officers tried to keep their weakening men and horses moving as they approached Andrejevka.

East of the town a Russian regiment blocked the division's path, intending to allow other Russian troops to catch up and destroy it. While Postel's rear guard held off their pursuers the men of the lead regiment, sensing that safety was close, assaulted the Russians with the ferocity of desperation. Led by a half dozen assault guns, the German infantry attacked the Russian regiment and smashed through it. Postel reported that his division destroyed three T-34s, six anti-tank guns and inflicted serious casualties upon a regiment of Soviet infantry.

During the later morning hours, General Lanz flew over the Kharkov sector with his Chief of Staff. As he traveled by air over the city's road net, he realized how badly the roads were jammed with German motorized units. He subsequently ordered an Army Feldgendarmerie-Kompanie to take control of the roads and regulate traffic in the sector. After conferring with Hausser, Dietrich and Keppler, Lanz stressed the importance of a quick assembly of the battle group at Merefa. However, Keppler was seriously ill with a chronic condition which had troubled him earlier in the war and was evacuated to Germany. SS-Standartenführer Herbert Vahl, the commander of SS-Panzer-Regiment 2, was given the command of the division. Vahl's place was taken by SS-Sturmbannführer Hans-Albin von Reitzenstein the commander of I./SS-Panzer-Regiment 2.[9]

The new division commander was a former Army officer transferred from the Army to take command of the "Das Reich" panzer regiment when no suitably trained SS officer was available. Vahl was a veteran combat commander, having served with an infantry regiment during World War I. During the war he was wounded twice and won both classes of the Iron Cross. Vahl remained in the Army between the wars, first commanding a motorcycle battalion and then serving as commander of a tank battalion in 4. Panzer-Division. By spring of 1942, he attained the rank of Oberst (Colonel) and took command of the Panzer regiment of 12. Panzer-Division. In August of 1942, Vahl was transferred to "Das Reich" to command the division's Panzer Regiment. He served as division commander until wounded near Belgorod on 18 March.[10]

Korps Raus was to assist in covering the operations of Dietrich's attack group by blocking the Soviet advance toward Kharkov, while the Luftwaffe was requested to give all possible support to Dietrich's counterattack south of the city. The attack group was to advance in three columns, with the center column made up of Otto Kumm's Regiment "Der Führer" and I./SS-Panzer-Regiment 1." On the right flank was Kurt Meyer's reinforced Aufklärungsabteilung "LAH" and on the left flank was I./SS-PzG.-Rgt. 1 "LAH," under the leadership of the regimental commander, Fritz Witt. The attack group was supported by most of Pioniere-Bataillon "LAH, assault guns of Sturmgeschütze Abteilung "LAH" and elements of the "Leibstandarte" Flak battalion. The rest of the Panzergrenadier battalions of both SS divisions were left to defend the sector from east

---

[9] Yerger, pg. 125 and Weidinger, vol. 3, pg. 482.
[10] Yerger, pg.126.

A knocked out Soviet T-70 light tank which appears to have suffered an internal explosion after being struck by a German shell. The T-70 was designed to be primarily an infantry support tank although it did not have a sufficiently heavy main gun to be more than marginally adequate in this role. It was lightly armored and the shells of Panzer IIIs and Panzer IVs could penetrate its frontal armor even at moderately long range. (Credit National Archives)

A KV-1 Soviet heavy tank burns after being put out of action during the fighting north of Kharkov in February of 1943. The KV-1 was a sound design and was heavily armored. It caused the Germans a great deal of difficulty when first encountered because its frontal armor was impervious to the 5cm gun of the Panzer III and the short barreled 7.5cm infantry gun that the Panzer IV was initially equipped with. (Credit National Archives)

of Voltschansk to Zmiev without most of the mobile battalions or armor then available.

Armeeabteilung Lanz fought to maintain a coherent defense of Kharkov during 10 February in order to secure a base of supply and prevent penetrations into the assembly area of the SS attack group. Of great concern was the advance of the Soviet 40th and 69th Armies, which approached Kharkov from the north and northeast. However, Armeeabteilung Lanz did not have sufficient resources to counterattack both the 6th Guards Cavalry Corps and the Soviet armies advancing on the city from the north. Lanz had to choose which threat he judged to be most dangerous and eliminate that one first. Since the 6th Guards Cavalry Corps was judged to be the most immediate threat, Lanz chose to deal with it. The challenge to the Armeeabteilung consisted of holding the perimeter around Kharkov while most of the mobile fire power of the two SS divisions was tied up in the south. Lanz hoped that "Grossdeutschland" could delay the 40th Army long enough to allow SS-Panzer-Korps to strike the Soviet cavalry south of Zmiev. It was hoped that 168. Infanterie-Division could at least hold Tomarovka since the Russian infantry attacking the town was not supported by Soviet tanks.[11]

However, the division proved unable to mount any effective resistance at Tomarovka. Infantry of the Soviet 107th Rifle Division shoved remnants of the division out of Tomarovka and pushed them westwards. The regimental group retreated to the southwest, in the direction of the nearby town of Borisovka. This served only to widen the gap west of Kharkov. Although a few isolated detachments of the division were southwest of the rail line from Kharkov to Belgorod these troops were able to provide little help and were brushed aside by the Russian advance. Moskalenko wheeled three divisions of the right wing of his army to the southwest, pushing into the undefended void between Kharkov and Tomarovka. A regiment of the 107th Rifle Division turned south after reaching the Tomarovka area and its column followed in the wake of the Soviet armor. Moskalenko's 303rd Rifle Division moved into a parallel position on its right flank. South of the 107th's route of advance the 305th Rifle Division marched into the area west of the Lopan River Valley. The lead elements of that division approached the town of Zolochev, which was twenty-five kilometers northwest of Kharkov, on 10 February.[12]

"Grossdeutschland," with the support of the remains of the Führer-Begleit-Bataillon, continued to delay the advance of Soviet armor north and east of Kharkov. Along the main road leading from Belgorod to Kharkov, Aufklärungsabteilung "GD" and the Führer-Begleit-Bataillon, manned weak blocking positions along the roads

leading into Kharkov. There was no contact with friendly forces on either flank of the battalions. To the right and left of the German troops there was only flat, snow covered steppe, stretching into the distance. To the west, long dark columns of marching Russian troops could be seen slowly winding southwards. "Grossdeutschland" could not extend its left flank to fill the void to the west of the city because it no longer had sufficient forces to do so. The main elements of the division occupied positions blocking roads leading toward Kharkov from the north and east. The I./Gren.Rgt. "GD," reduced to a combat strength of only 216 men, held the area around Dolbino, which was ten kilometers southwest of Belgorod and about the same distance west of the river. There were reports that Soviet troops had occupied the town of Zolochev, far to the south of Dolbino but these reports were not confirmed in the morning.[13]

Other elements of the division remained east of the Northern Donets on the night of 9-10 February. The Füsilier-Rgt. "GD" remained heavily involved in fighting for possession of the town of Schebekino, located about fifteen kilometers southeast of Belgorod. The regiment, commanded by Oberst Kassnitz, had a total of combat strength of 786 men. Under command of Oberst Lorenz, the main elements of Grenadier-Regiment "GD" held the town of Golovino, located along a main road twelve kilometers south of Belgorod. Lorenz' regiment had 996 men, including I./Gren.Rgt. "GD" at Dolbino.[14]

On the afternoon of 10 February, the regiment held an eight kilometer wide front stretching from Dolbino on the east to Staraja Nelidovka on the west. The Russians attacked the regiment with infantry reinforced by fourteen tanks but the attack was stopped by well directed artillery fire which disabled several T-34s. Twenty kilometers to the south, Fusilier-Rgt. "GD" (Gruppe Kassnitz) crossed the Northern Donets west of Voltschansk and reached the village of Archangelskoje, which was approximately five kilometers west of the river. The Füsiliers were attacked several times during the afternoon by a Russian infantry force estimated at two regiments in size. During the last attack, a group of 300 to 400 Russian infantry emerged from a nearby wooded area and assaulted a determined attempt to take Archangelskoje. Kassnitz immediately launched a counterattack that destroyed the Soviet attack group which lost two hundred casualties as well as a large amount of weapons. Kassnitz withdrew to Lipzy, a town about ten kilometers to the west with Russian reconnaissance patrols shadowing the German troops in the distance. In the late afternoon Soviet tanks and large masses of Russian infantry were reported just east of Lipzy by air

---

[11] *Befehl des Gewissens*, pg. 66.
[12] Glantz, pg. 176-178.

[13] NA/T-314, roll 489, 1a KTB Corps Cramer, Tagesmeldung an 10.2.1943, frame 000630-000635.
[14] Op cit.

reconnaissance. The division's Aufklärungsabteilung arrived at 1600 hours and prepared to block the Russian advance along a main road that led from Lipzy to the outskirts of Kharkov.[15]

While "Grossdeutschland" parried thrusts by the Soviet 40th Army during the day, the situation remained unsettled in the south primarily because of the snarled traffic which delayed the assembly of Dietrich's Kampfgruppe. Frustrated SS officers and Army Gendarmerie, tempers flaring, tried to establish some degree of order to the massive traffic jam south of Kharkov. Vehicles had become separated from their units and fell in with trucks and half tracks of another division or regiment. The columns moved forward in fits and starts. At each halt bone weary drivers stared at the rear of the truck in front of them, trying to stay awake while when the column was halted by vehicles that had become stuck in the snow or had broken down.

Late in the day, the first columns of SS troops and vehicles began to arrive in Merefa and the attack group assembled during the night and early morning hours of the next day. The SS columns converged on Merefa, after struggling for most of the day over roads covered in deep snow and jammed with long columns of vehicles. Weary SS Grenadiers, exhausted by hours of travel in freezing cold and cramped vehicles, tried to get a few minutes of rest before the beginning of the attack. The bitter cold forced many of them to remain awake, stamping their numb feet to keep them from freezing, while some of the more fortunate found a small fire to crowd around. While the rest of the two SS divisions organized their new defensive lines, Kampfgruppe Dietrich slowly assembled. The delays as a result of the traffic situation forced the attack against the 6th Guards Cavalry Corps to be postponed until 11 February.

While Dietrich put together his attack group on the night of 10-11 February, Moskalenko's 40th Army continued its advance during the early morning darkness. The right or western wing, consisting of the 107th, 309th and 305th Rifle Divisions marched south in roughly parallel attacks on 11 February. On the left flank the Army's 340th and 183rd Rifle Divisions moved down the shallow, flat bottomed Kharkov River Valley. The lead elements of the divisions approached Lipzy from the north, bypassing Grenadier-Regiment "GD" positions in the Dolbino-Staraja Nelidovka area. The Russians simply moved around the regiment's blocking position and continued to the south. This action was typical of the combat between Belgorod and Kharkov, along the main road and rail line and the smaller roads leading through the river valleys that ran generally from north to south. After stopping a Soviet column, the Germans were often forced to withdraw when the Russians moved off the road to both sides and bypassed the road block.[16]

Panzergrenadiers of "Leibstandarte" in a SdKfz 251, a lightly armored halftrack that was used by the Germans from the beginning of the war. German industry could never turn out enough of these versatile vehicles and even the primary SS divisions only had one Panzergrenadier battalion which was fully equipped with half tracks. (Credit National Archives)

In the south, Rybalko's 3rd Tank Army advanced against the "Leibstandarte" defenses along the east bank of the Northern Donets River while the SS division was withdrawing. Russian infantry of the 15th Tank Corps crossed the river, following SS rear guard detachments as they withdrew from Petschenegi and occupied the abandoned town. As the Soviet armor and infantry continued their advance westward, the battalions of SS-PzG.-Rgt. 1 "LAH" withdrew to new positions flanking the Rogan-Kharkov road, which entered Kharkov on its southeastern corner.

The Soviet 12th Tank Corps, with a rifle division in support, crossed the Northern Donets at Chugujev after finding the town nearly empty of Germans. When the lead troops encountering nothing stronger than light small arms fire the column continued westward in a parallel advance to that of the 15th Tank Corps. Moving along the Rogan road, the main 12th Tank Corps column pursued the SS Grenadiers while a second Russian column moved on a parallel course and reached a point less than ten kilometers southeast of Kharkov.

Company strength SS rear guard detachments, with a Sturmgeschütze III or several automatic Flak guns, ambushed lead units of the Soviet columns, forcing them to halt. When the Russians deployed to attack, the SS troops pulled back to another concealed position. Throughout the afternoon, the Russians lost tanks to ambushes by German assault guns and 88s and suffered infantry losses as well. After nightfall, the main bridge over the river that flowed through Rogan was blown by SS Pioniere. This caused further delays to the Russians who were forced to search for an alter-

---

[15] Ibid. Tagesmeldung an Armeeabteilung Lanz am 10.2.1943, frame 000634.
[16] Spaeter, pg. 32.

nate crossing site. Elements of SS-PzG.-Rgt. 1 "LAH" pulled back to the western section of Rogan and waited for the Russians to attempt to force their way across the river. The night was bitter cold, causing much suffering to the men of both sides. The temperature dropped so far below freezing that sausage and bread had to be cut with an axe before the rations could be distributed to the men.[17]

Directly east of Kharkov, "Das Reich" and "Leibstandarte" fought the lead divisions of the 69th Army. Squeezed into a narrow front southeast of Kharkov, Rybalko's 3rd Tank Army tried to smash its way through the German defenses in costly frontal assaults. Major elements of Regiment "Deutschland" and elements of the two Panzergrenadier regiments of "Leibstandarte" fought stubbornly to hold the city's eastern approaches. The tiring SS Panzergrenadiers, with most of the armored fire power of their divisions assembled south of the city, were assaulted by three rifle divisions of the 69th Army and armor and infantry of the 3rd Tank Army. On the left wing of the 69th Army the 180th Rifle Division crossed the river at Stary Saltov and advanced north of Petschenegi. South of Rogan "Leibstandarte" Panzergrenadiers under command of Wisch, fought bitter defensive engagements against the 3rd Tank Army's 160th and 62nd Rifle Divisions. The attacks were supported by tanks of the 12th and 15th Tank Corps and infantry reinforcements from two other rifle divisions of Rybalko's army. Although having local superiority in numbers, the two Soviet armies had lost the advantage of maneuver and were forced to fight a determined opponent occupying good defensive positions. German records do not mention Russian artillery, which may be an indication of a common failing of Russian operations once penetrations had been made. The inability to speedily relocate artillery to support successful attacks often resulted in slowing of forward progress and serious infantry casualties. Attacking Russian infantry undoubtedly sustained increased losses in their assaults upon SS positions due to the lack of sufficient artillery preparation and support. The German troops fired from well concealed firing positions in the ruins of towns and villages, amply equipped with the new MG-42 machine gun. The curtain of steel cut down assaulting Soviet infantry in droves, quickly reducing regiment to the strength of weak battalions.

The Russian rifle divisions were not at full strength when the offensive had begun and many had been reduced to 1000 to 3500 combat effectives by February. The heavy losses sustained in offensive actions during the first ten days of the month had reduced their combat value even further. This lack of sufficient infantry seriously affected the rate of progress of the Russian assault upon Kharkov, just as the same deficiency had hamstrung the assault upon

A Flakvierling (four barreled) 2cm anti-aircraft gun of the "Das Reich" Flakabteilung. Stacked beside the base of the gun are spare magazines. The 2cm shells were available in high explosive, incendiary and armor piercing. The Germans used these guns in various configurations, either single guns or the four barreled mount in both anti-aircraft mode or against ground targets. They were extremely effective in both roles. (Courtesy of Mark C. Yerger)

1. Panzerarmee on the southern reaches of the Northern Donets. Although the Russian infantry probably still outnumbered their German counterparts by 3.5 to 1, that numerical superiority was not sufficient to overcome good quality German troops fighting from defensive positions. This was particularly so because the quality of Soviet infantry declined markedly by the beginning of February, due to the heavy losses to experienced combat officers, NCOs and trained infantry. Only an adequate supply of armor and German weakness enabled the Russians to make any progress at all. By 10 February, there were only two notable sectors where the Soviets had penetrated German defenses with any depth.

The most destabilizing Russian advance was that made by the 40th Army, which had reached the northern and western approaches to Kharkov. Moskalenko's army threatened to outflank Armeeabteilung Lanz in the first days of Operation "Star." This had major consequences for both "Grossdeutschland" and "Das Reich." "Grossdeutschland" had to take over the defense of a sector much to wide for it to defend after 168. Infanterie-Division fell apart and retreated westward without delaying the Russian advance. This situation left "Grossdeutschland" without sufficient forces to decisively counterattack Soviet penetrations on its own front, which subsequently resulted in the division being forced to withdraw steadily to the west. When it did so, the northern flank of "Das Reich" was uncovered and this ultimately led to the failure to hold the Veliky Burluk-Belyi Kolodes salient.

The second penetration was the attack by the 6th Guards Cavalry Corps south of Kharkov, which had a decisive influence upon the defense of the city, because it attracted a large portion of the

---

[17] Lehmann, pg. 58-59.

striking power of the SS-Panzer-Korps. The advance of the Soviet cavalry toward the railroad lifelines into the city forced Lanz to act immediately. He utilized as much SS armor and mobile battalions as could be spared in order to block the advance of the 6th Guards Cavalry Corps. This substantially weakened the SS division's defensive strength east of the Northern Donets because there were no mobile reserves of sufficient strength to counterattack Russian penetrations. Although the SS regiments fought with great determination and inflicted heavy losses upon the Russians, there was no defensive depth and even tactical Russian penetrations forced the Germans to withdraw because they could not be eliminated by tactical reserves. The Russian thrusts north and south of Kharkov were the fatal blows to the German defense of the city.

Both of these attacks struck sectors which were not defended adequately because Armeeabteilung Lanz lacked the divisions necessary to defend its flanks. At any point which the Germans actively defended, the Russians were stymied and their casualties were debilitating regardless of their strength. During the first week of the month, parts of four Soviet rifle divisions were held at bay by Regiment "Deutschland" in the Veliky Burluk salient. "Grossdeutschland" delayed the advance of the most of the 69th Army and portions of the 40th Army as well. "Leibstandarte" denied the Northern Donets to the 3rd Tank Army until it was forced to deal with the 6th Cavalry Corps south of Zmiev. The Russian command found that the Germans could not defend either flank and took advantage of the situation. The Soviets were able to effectively use their armor to repeatedly overextend already thinly stretched German divisions both to the north and south of Kharkov. The Germans did not have the mobile reserves to deal with the situations simultaneously and were forced to choose which flank to defend. The decision to counterattack in the south meant that the army did not have sufficient strength to counter the advance of the armor of the 40th Army north of Kharkov.

Fortunately for the Germans, the T-34s were less effective when they operated in wreckage clogged urban streets. It proved necessary to use tanks to assist the debilitated Russian rifle regiments. The armor support was necessary because the Russians did not have the required artillery to provide close support. The Russian tank crews had to be cautious and always have adequate infantry support, because tanks fighting alone in city streets were easy prey for experienced infantrymen. The SS Grenadiers attacked Russian tanks with magnetic mines or improvised anti-tank weapons such as grenade bundles or Molotov cocktails. Assault guns and 88s proved deadly when firing from well concealed positions, which could have been eliminated with well coordinated artillery support.

East of Kharkov, Regiment "Deutschland" was under lighter Soviet pressure during its phased pullback out of the Veliky Burluk salient because the main effort and most of the armor of the 3rd Tank Army was then in the south. The army's rifle divisions were bloodied by the hard fighting at Veliky Burluk and Belyi Koledes and the survivors were not as aggressive. The divisions of the 69th Army, fighting against "Grossdeutschland" and SS-Kradschützen-Bataillon on the northern flank of "Das Reich," were worn down from the costly fighting as well. However, when it became evident that the Germans had abandoned their positions, the Soviet 180th, 270th and 161st Rifle Divisions followed steadily and at nightfall on 10 February were within twenty kilometers of the northeastern corner of Kharkov.[18]

On the following day, the 40th Army continued to make progress. Moskalenko brought up the 5th Guards Tank Corps, commanded by General A.G. Kravchenko and inserted it along the course of the Lopan River. The tank corps was the former 4th Tank Corps but was renamed the 5th Guards "Stalingradski" Tank Corps on 7 February as a reward for its valor during the Stalingrad fighting. Kravchenko was one of the Soviet tank brigade commanders who benefited from experience gained in the first year of the war and emerged in 1942-1943 as a skilled tank commanders. He habitually led from the front and had a knack for effective improvisation. Kravchenko understood the twin weapons of maneuver and surprise and how they could be utilized by armor commanders. By the end of the war he was promoted to the command of the 6th Tank Army.[19]

The attack of the 5th Guards Tank Corps illustrated Kravchenko's ability as a tank commander. He was able to achieve tactical surprise when his tanks passed through an undefended gap in the German line, then rolled into the northern end of the Udy River Valley. This valley ran southward until it entered the northwest section of Kharkov. Kravchenko's tanks succeeded in rapidly moving down the length of the valley in spite of the deep snow and bad roads. It forced aside weak German defensive forces at the southern edge of the Udy valley and stormed toward the Kharkov perimeter.[20]

The defenses east of Kharkov still held relatively firm, benefiting from the now shortened front. Frustrated by his lack of progress, Rybalko ordered the 12th Tank Corps, the 15th Tank Corps

---

[18] Glantz, pg. 172-175.

[19] The 5th Guards Tank Corps was originally equipped with an odd mixture of tank types, including thirty British "Matilda" Mark II tanks, which were issued to its 102nd Tank Brigade. The other two tank brigades were issued T-34s and the heavy but less mobile KV-1 model as well as a number of T-60 light tanks. How many tanks of each type it possessed by 11 February is not known. Sharp, Charles C. *Soviet Order of Battle - School of Battle.* (West Chester: 1995) pg. 17.

[20] Armstrong page 397-400 and 450.

A "Marder" or self propelled anti-tank gun belonging to the Panzerjäger Bataillon of "Das Reich." The picture was taken on February 21, 1943, while the division was heavily engaged in fighting southwest of Kharkov. The gun was nicknamed "Alves" by its crew and is shown shortly before it knocked out its 13th Soviet tank. (Courtesy of Mark C. Yerger)

and the 62nd Guards Rifle Division to renew their attacks upon the German perimeter east of Kharkov. The 111th Rifle Division resumed its attacks on Zmiev in support of the 12th Tank Corps' line of advance. These attacks were bitterly resisted by the Germans and Soviet infantry and tank losses were again high. This operation aided the advance of the Soviet cavalry group when the left flank of Gruppe Dietrich, still organizing to attack, was struck hard by Soviet armor, causing it to turn its attentions to the east.

"Grossdeutschland's" left flank remained open and the Udy River Valley was essentially undefended. This was the fatal flaw in the German defensive system on the northern flank of the Armeeabteilung and negated the staunch defensive efforts of the Germans east and south of Kharkov. Kravchenko's tank corps passed through the gap toward Ljubotin, which was directly west of Kharkov. At Ljubotin, the 5th Guards Tank Corps hoped to link up with the 6th Guards Cavalry Corps and the 201st Tank Brigade and completely encircle the city. However, on 11 February, the SS-Panzer-Korps counterattack finally began south of Merefa and it immediately threatened the lead units of the 6th Guards Cavalry Corps.

The right wing, Meyer's reinforced Aufklärungsabteilung "LAH," reached the northern approaches to Novaya Vodolaga by 1230 hours on 11 February. In the center, the attack by Regiment "Der Führer" and I./SS-Panzer-Rgt. "LAH" proceeded as planned and reached the main rail line east of the small town of Borki. The left wing however, consisting of Frey's reinforced I./SS-PzG.-Rgt. 1 "LAH," was not able to begin its advance on time because it was attacked by the 62nd Guards Rifle Division and the 12th Tank Corps along the Kharkov-Chuguyev road. The center and right wing columns continued to make some progress during the afternoon. Meyer's reinforced battalion penetrated southwest of Novaja Vodolaga and reached a road leading toward the Kharkov-Losovaja rail line by 1430 hours. Kumm's Regiment "Der Führer" and the Panzers of Max Wünsche's I./SS-Panzer-Rgt. "LAH" approached the railroad station on the outskirts of Borki from the north. Wünsche immediately attacked Borki, but did not conduct an adequate battlefield reconnaissance before the beginning of the attack. This proved to be a serious failure and led to the loss of German armor.[21]

---

[21] Armstrong, pg. 397-400 and 450.

The Russians had situated a number of well camouflaged anti-tank guns covering the northern approaches to Borki. The guns were placed on the southern edge of a snow covered swampy area north of the town. Wünsche's tanks advanced toward the town parallel to the railroad and did not spot the Russian anti-tank guns until it was too late. A number of the SS tanks ran headlong into the marsh and became bogged down. One Panzer sank until only its turret was visible, forcing the crew to abandon the tank and scramble to safety. Several others were able to flounder out of the marsh and reach solid ground. The Russians opened fire on the SS tanks with anti-tank guns and rifles. One tank burned out, another was destroyed by an internal explosion and a third could not be pulled out of the morass until after nightfall. SS personnel losses were seven dead and eight wounded.[22]

---

[22] Tiemann, Ralf, *Chronicle of the 7. Panzer-Kompanie- 1. SS-Panzer-Division "Leibstandarte"* (Atglen: 1998) pg. 32-33.

When the swamp and anti-tank gun fire halted the SS tanks, they were unable to support Regiment "Der Führer's" assault upon Borki. Kumm's Panzergrenadiers attacked the town as scheduled but heavy Russian machine gun and mortar fire broke up their advance. The momentum of the attack was destroyed when the tanks were unable to find a way through the marshy ground north of Borki. After the failure of the infantry attack, Kumm and Wünsche decided that the town could not be taken by frontal assault without armor support due to the strength of the Russian defenses. They decided to move past Borki to the east in order to get the attack moving again.

Meanwhile, on the left flank of the counterattack, Witt's Kampfgruppe remained involved in difficult defensive fighting against the attack of the 12th Tank Corps and its supporting infantry. Witt reported that Soviet pressure slackened somewhat by late afternoon, but he was still too heavily engaged to resume his ad-

On February 12, 1943 the first tanks of "Totenkopf's" Panzer Regiment were unloaded from flat cars in the Poltava rail yards. On the next day the tanks started on the journey to Krasnograd. The first losses of tanks occurred almost immediately, but they were not due to enemy action. Snow and ice and hazardous road conditions resulted in running gear damage and mechanical breakdowns. (The author's collection)

vance. The debacle at Borki was a setback to Dietrich and cost him lost time, which he could not afford due to the situation east of Kharkov. Any hope that the penetration of the Soviet cavalry could be cleared up easily, disappeared in the swamps north of Borki.[23]

While Dietrich's attack made uneven progress south of Kharkov, the Russians exerted constant pressure on "Leibstandarte's" defensive front east of the city. Their main effort was centered on the town of Rogan. The Russians attacked Rogan with elements of two rifle divisions and tanks of the 15th Tank Corps. At 0200 hours a strong attack was launched on the reinforced SS Grenadier company that occupied defensive positions south of Rogan, at the town of Ternovo. Russian infantry supported by tanks broke through the German perimeter and began to work their way into the town. A detachment of SS Panzergrenadiers and a few assault guns were hastily brought up from a neighboring sector to clean up the penetration. Led by Obersturmführer Rudolf Dix, the Kampfgruppe sealed off the penetration and drove the surviving Russians out of the town.

At Rogan itself, Soviet tanks and two battalions of infantry attacked 1./Kompanie of SS-PzG.-Rgt. 1 "LAH," which was commanded by SS-Hauptsturmführer Heinrich Springer. The SS Grenadiers were dug in behind the course of a balka (ravine or shallow valley) on the western section of the town and supported by a platoon of four barreled 2cm guns. The rapid firing Flak cannons, firing explosive shells, were devastating against infantry attacks. The Russians brought up T-34s to cover the advance of their infantry while other Russian tanks pulled up close to the balka in order to support the attack. The T-34s opened fire upon German positions, while Soviet assault groups attempted to work their way across the balka. In difficult fighting, which lasted until daylight, the Russian infantry were thrown back time after time. An SS infantry gun was able to knock out two T-34s by firing high explosive shells at point blank range across the ravine. At dawn, the attacks stopped and it appeared that the Russians were regrouping for a stronger attack. Columns of motorized infantry and tanks could be seen approaching the town from the east. At 1300 hours Springer reported that since the Russians had assembled more tanks and infantry in front of his position, he was unsure if his company could hold the town. He requested reinforcements and additional heavy weapons, but there were no significant reserves available at that time.[24]

This was a direct result of the SS-Panzer-Korps lack of sufficient forces to carry out defensive and offensive missions simultaneously. Most of the mobile elements of both SS divisions were committed to the counterattack south of Kharkov. Lanz had recog-

nized the troublesome situation several days earlier and remained deeply concerned about the consequences of failure at either task. This was particularly true after it became apparent that the counterattack would not have the desired degree of success. In a radio communication to Heeresgruppe Don, Lanz made it clear once again that he felt that his army could attack or defend but could not successfully do both. To make matters worse he had just learned of serious setbacks in another sector of the front which endangered not only the divisions holding Kharkov, but the entire army group. While the situation around Kharkov remained in the balance, events in 1. Panzerarmee's area threatened to unhinge the entire southern wing of the Eastern Front.

The Fall of Krasnoarmeiskoye

On 10 February, ten days after Vatutin had launched Operation "Gallop," the opinion of the Soviet Stavka was that the progress of the attack was less than satisfactory in the Slavyansk sector. Although the 1st Guards Army and 3rd Guards Army had driven the Germans to the southern bank of the Northern Donets River, Slavyansk had not fallen and the Soviet advance remained stagnated on a Slavyansk-Voroshilovrad-Kamensk line. The 6th Army reached the Losovaya-Merefa-Kharkov railroad line but had not made a decisive breakthrough at any point. The entire offensive was far behind schedule. The original concept had called for an advance of three armies of the Southwestern Front to smash through the German lines along the Northern Donets and make a decisive breakthrough by the seventh day of the attack. However, the Russians had not broken through the German defenses in sufficient depth to make a concentrated armored thrust south of the river.

At least some of the conditions that limited the success of the attack between Slavgorod and Voroshilovgrad can be traced back to the stubborn resistance of German troops during January in the sector north of Voroshilovgrad. The German troops even though weakened and off balance, remained dangerous and stubborn opponents. The arrival of Panzer divisions in the 1. Panzerarmee area was an unexpected development and their effective fighting performance proved to be a shock to the Soviet command. The Russians compounded the situation when they grossly misinterpreted their intelligence information. Armeeabteilung Hollidt had begun a retreat to the Mius River. The withdrawal was a difficult operation, as the Russians continually pressured Hollidt's tiring divisions and forced him to keep his weak Panzer divisions busy counter-attacking breakthroughs. To make matters worse, there were already Soviet forces operating behind his army. Hoth's 4. Panzerarmee was also moving from east to west.

---

[23] *Befehl des Gewissens*, pg. 74 and Lehmann, pg. 60.
[24] Lehmann, pg. 60-65.

Of course, Hoth's army was not preparing to retreat across the Dnepr but was withdrawing to establish new defensive positions from which a counterattack could be launched. Secure behind the cover of the positions along a Slavyansk-Voroshilovgrad line, Manstein planned to concentrate XXXXVIII., XXXX. and III. Panzer-Korps and launch a counteroffensive with Hausser's SS-Panzer-Korps as the main attack group. The Russians interpreted the withdrawal of the two armies as the beginning of a general retreat and decided that the Panzer divisions had arrived in order to cover a general retreat to the Dnepr River. As a result of their mistaken analysis of the situation, the Soviet High Command issued new directives which sent their armies into a trap.

The Stavka urged Vatutin in no uncertain terms that he was to cut off the German line of retreat to the Dnepr River. These orders spurred Vatutin into attempting to break the stalemate at Slavyansk by sending the 4th Guards Tank Corps on a rapid thrust into the gap west of Slavyansk. Vatutin hoped to accomplish two objectives with this attack. The first was the blocking of the vital railroad net extending from the Dnepr crossings to the east. He intended to sever these lines of communication by the capture of the town of Krasnoarmeiskoye with Popov's 4th Guards Tank Corps. Secondly, the 1st Guards Army was to shift its direction of advance to the west with the objective of capturing the main crossing on the Dnepr River at Dnepropetrovsk and Zaporozsche. The 6th Army was ordered to cut the railroad net extending south from Kharkov by first cutting the Losovaja-Kharkov line and then severing the Krasnograd-Merefa-Kharkov line. The proposed thrusts by Rybalko's 6th Guards Cavalry Corps and the 40th Army mobile groups would cut the remaining rail lines into the city from the west.[25]

The 6th Army pushed into the large gap south of Kharkov in the area between the western bank of the Northern Donets and the Kharkov-Merefa-Losovaya-Pavlograd rail line. The 172nd, 6th and 267th Rifle Divisions advanced shoulder to shoulder to a point about fifteen kilometers west of the Donets and approached the rail line near the town of Losovaya. The only German forces of any consequence in the sector was a battalion of infantry belonging to 333. Infanterie-Division, which was just arriving at the rail way station at Barvenkovo. Barvenkovo was about thirty kilometers due west of Slavyansk and lay on a secondary rail line that connected Slavyansk and Losovaja.

The 1st Guards Army's reinforced 35th Guards Rifle Division, after crossing the Donets south of Izyum, assaulted Barvenkovo on 6 February. After giving up the town on 7 February, the Germans fell back to Losovaya with the Russians close on their heels. On 10 February, the 35th Rifle Division attacked Losovaja and quickly drove the defenders out of the town. The Russian infantry joyfully liberated large quantities of stores and supplies at the rail station yard. These stores included a great deal of food and alcohol and this may have helped the routed German infantry to escape. The 35th Division spent the next several days in Losovaya, not stirring to action again until 14 February. When the German troops retreated from the town, the Russians did not follow and lost an opportunity to destroy part of 333. Infanterie-Division.[26]

The advance of the 35th Rifle Division formed the western or right wing of the 1st Guards Army advance into the large, undefended gap that existed between Slavyansk and Kharkov, which was approximately 100 kilometers in width. The 7. Panzer Division and elements of 333. Infanterie-Division still held Slavyansk, although they were under assault by two Soviet rifle divisions and the 3rd Tank Corps. The western flank of 1. Panzerarmee was anchored at Slavyansk, while the eastern flank was defended by XXX. Armeekorps at Voroshilovgrad. Beyond Slavyansk there remained the large and undefended gap, which Vatutin decided to utilize in an attempt to outflank 1. Panzerarmee west of Slavyansk and then seize the vital Dnepr River bridges.

Although the planned direction of attack for Mobile Group Popov was to have been generally south, the void between Slavyansk and Kharkov proved irresistible to the Russian command after the southward progress of the offensive was halted. The decision to abandon attempts to break through the German defenses along the Slavyansk-Voroshilovgrad line, eliminated a potentially devastating threat to the existence of Armeeabteilung Hollidt and 1. Panzerarmee. Although the Soviet 8th Cavalry Corps conducted a raid into the rear area of the army on 12 February, Hollidt was spared the disastrous consequences of a thrust by a Soviet tank corps that severed all major supply lines to his army. The Soviet decision contributed to a set of circumstances that were ultimately fatal to both Operation "Gallop" and "Star."

On the night of 11 February, Poluboyarov's 4th Guards Tank Corps struck out from Kramatorsk after leaving the defense of the town to the 3rd Tank Corps. Led by the 14th Guards Tank Brigade, the 4th Guards Tank Corps lunged to the southwest and encountered little resistance by German forces. Poluboyarov's objective was the town of Krasnoarmeiskoje, an important rail station on the Dnepropetrovsk-Stalino railroad line. Advancing in the icy cold, early morning darkness the Soviet tank brigade, along with a motorized battalion of infantry surprised a small German garrison at Grishino, a small town north of Krasnoarmeiskoye. After a short fight, the surviving German supply and security troops abandoned

---

[25] Glantz, pg.108-109.

[26] Op cit.

the town to the Russians and fled. The armored group quickly re-formed and continued toward its primary objective, Krasnoarmeiskoje, which was occupied by 0900 hours.

The loss of this critically important line of communication for Armeeabteilung Hollidt and 1. Panzerarmee electrified the German command. The shocking news fell like a thunderbolt on the HQ of Heeregruppe Don and 1. Panzerarmee. Both commands had thought that the terrain north and east of Krasnoarmeiskoje, which passed through the Krivoy Torets Valley, was impassable for tanks due to the nature of the road net and the winter conditions. However, the wide tracked T-34s as well as some T-60s proved able to traverse the frozen terrain in the valleys and cross the open ground.[27]

The Germans immediately began to withdraw panzer units from the defense of the Slavyansk-Voroshilovgrad front, in order to attack Krasnoarmeiskoye and reopen the rail line. Manstein voiced great concern about the immediate affect of a reduced fuel supply

which could restrict mobile operations at an critical time for the survival of the entire southern portion of the Eastern Front. Only one other major railroad line that crossed the Dnepr River remained in German hands. As a result the line which crossed the Dnepr at Zaporozsche would immediately be overloaded and unable to meet the demands placed upon it as long as the Russians remained in control of Krasnoarmeiskoje.

However, the problems associated with operating mobile groups at the ends of precarious supply lines were felt once again by the Russians. The lack of sufficient trucks to transport fuel, ammunition and troops remained critical. Shortage of trucks forced some of the Soviet infantry to ride on top of tank decks, exposed to the elements both night and day. Although the Russian troops were extremely hardy and could survive these conditions, there were drawbacks to this necessary expedient. When attrition reduced the number of tanks available for battle, the number of platforms to transport infantry was correspondingly reduced. The risks posed to infantry mounted on tank decks went beyond the effects of the cold.

---

[27] Sharp, pg. 74.

SdKfz 250 light half tracks and Marders of "Leibstandarte" east of Kharkov. This model of half track was lighter than the SdKfz 251 that the armored battalion of the division was equipped with. The SdKfz was produced in a number of configurations, including a command version. (Credit National Archives)

Riding into battle atop armored vehicles was commonly practiced by the German army as well, but the passengers were exposed to small arms fire and vulnerable to shrapnel and high explosive shells. A near hit by medium artillery shells or mortars generally left the tank undamaged but any soldiers riding on the turret or deck could be butchered by the explosion or flying shell fragments.

It may seem that the Soviet logistical problems and the resulting limitations should have been apparent and ought to have tempered Soviet ambitions and optimism. However, once the belief that the Germans were giving up the Donbas became fixed in the minds of the upper command it fueled an already heady mixture of strong optimism and aggressiveness. Undoubtedly the Russian command realized that there were gambles attached to "Gallop" and "Star." Obviously the Stavka believed that the potential gains were worth the inherent risks of the operations. There were many reasons for the determined optimism of the Russian High Command and its Front commanders, all of whom were strong personalities and not easily given to changing their minds.

There was the ever present pressure from the Stavka or Stalin himself, who was seldom reluctant to approve offensive action. In addition, since November of 1942 the German 6. Armee and two Axis armies were completely destroyed and other German armies had been severely damaged. Operations "Star" and "Gallop" were pressuring the Germans and the Russians had cut a main line of supply to Heeresgruppe Don. Soviet spearheads were driving toward the Dnepr crossings at Zaporozsche and Dnepropetrovsk, which were the sole remaining major lines of supply to Armeeabteilung Hollidt and 1. Panzerarmee. Stalin (and Manstein) knew that if the Russian armies destroyed Heeresgruppe Don, Germany would probably not be able to recover and would be in serious danger of losing the entire war.

Even given the delays and setbacks, the decision to strike out for Krasnoarmeiskoje was not unsound given the beliefs held by the Russians. The German mobile divisions at Kharkov and on the Northern Donets were all involved in heavy fighting. The German mobile divisions had been involved in unrelenting, brutal combat for weeks, if not months. With few exceptions, they were mere shadows of their normal strength. Most had no more than twenty to thirty operational tanks and some had less than a dozen. The 5. SS Panzergrenadier Division, "Wiking," had only five tanks left by the first week of February. All of the available German Panzer and Panzergrenadier divisions were in action, with the sole exception of "Totenkopf."

To make matters worse for the Germans, many of their Panzer divisions were committed to holding sectors of the front, an inappropriate role for armored divisions. However, there were not enough combat worthy infantry divisions available and 1. Panzerarmee and Armeeabteilung Lanz had to use its Panzer divisions to hold ground. This forced the Panzer divisions to take part in debilitating defensive combat which wore down their Panzergrenadier regiments. The Panzergrenadier companies of these divisions quickly were reduced to twenty-five to forty men. In addition, the Panzer and assault gun battalions were ground down by incessant combat.

Two of the three relatively fresh German Panzer divisions were already tied down in the Kharkov area and "Totenkopf" was just arriving. "Leibstandarte" and "Das Reich" were nearly encircled and seemed to be destined to fight to destruction at Kharkov. With the Soviet 40th Army pushing steadily southward, the Russian command was probably confident that the SS Panzer divisions would soon be trapped in Kharkov and destroyed. There were no more German armored reserves available.

On the Russian side, the situation was somewhat different. Although combat losses in the weeks prior to the beginning of Operation "Gallop" were significant, there were some mobile reserves available to Vatutin. These reserves consisted of the 1st Guards Tank Corps, the 25th Tank Corps and the 1st Guards Cavalry Corps. Golikov had additional armor reserves as well. The Russians were aware that some German reinforcements were arriving, in the form of a few infantry divisions and "Totenkopf," but they did not consider it likely that the slow trickle of reinforcements from the west would swing the balance in favor of the Germans.

In fact, there were substantial questions in Manstein's mind as to whether the situation could be salvaged, due to the difficult tasks that Heeresgruppe Süd had been assigned. Hoth's 4. Panzerarmee was still regrouping west of 1. Panzerarmee's left flank, a move made more difficult by the weather. The roads were miserable and the rail lines were often blocked by snow drifts or sabotage. This relocation was subsequently endangered by the Soviet advance toward the Dnepr, which threatened to shut off the flow of supplies to Hoth and Hollidt as well.

In addition to these concerns, Manstein had been ordered by Hitler to hold Kharkov. He also had find a way to defend the railroad net stretching to Kharkov from the river crossings at Zaporozsche and Dnepropetrovsk, while regrouping his forces to launch his planned counteroffensive. Since Hitler would not allow the withdrawal of Armeeabteilung Hollidt nor give up the Northern Donets sector between Voroshilovgrad and Slavyansk, Manstein was forced to find a way to achieve these missions simultaneously, essentially with the forces that he already had. He received only one additional full strength Panzer division ("Totenkopf") and was expected to accomplish all of the tasks facing his army group with the threadbare Army Panzer divisions already in battle and the three

SS divisions. Of those, "Das Reich" and "Leibstandarte" had already experienced bloody fighting in the defense of Kharkov and had experienced significant tank losses.

At first, Manstein did not believe that he would even have Eicke's division, because it seemed that "Totenkopf" would have to be committed in a counterattack against the Soviet 6th Army which was marching westward, toward the important rail center at the town of Krasnograd. Manstein intended to assemble "Totenkopf" and "Das Reich" at Krasnograd and from there the two divisions were to begin the opening phase of his counteroffensive. However, the advance of the 6th Army threatened to throw these plans into disarray by cutting both of the remaining main rail lines that extended from Dnepropetrovsk to Kharkov. After the rail road crossed the Dnepr at Dnepropetrovsk it split into two main branches. One branch ran north and passed through Krasnograd before entering the southern edge of Kharkov. This line remained clear on February 11. The second main line ran east from Dnepropetrovsk for a distance of about fifty kilometers before reaching the rail center at Pavlograd which was still in German hands. However, the Russians had cut this line further to the north on 10 February, when Russian infantry occupied Losovaja. Thus the Dnepropetrovsk-Krasnograd-Kharkov line was the sole remaining branch of the rail-road still available to supply Armeeabteilung Lanz and the SS-Panzer-Korps.

It was critically important to the survival of Armeeabteilung Lanz to keep this line open at this critical stage of the defense of Kharkov due to its vital importance to the counteroffensive. It appeared that the only German unit available to block the 6th Army advance toward Krasnograd from the southwest was "Totenkopf," which began to arrive on 11 February. The first unit of "Totenkopf" to arrive consisted of a battalion of motorized SS-Regiment "Thule," which arrived at Poltava on 11 February. On the next day, the first train carrying tanks of SS Panzer-Regiment 3 rolled into the Poltava rail yards.[28] The I./Regiment "Thule" began the sixty kilometer road march toward the threatened rail center at Krasnograd, while the tanks were being unloaded.

On that same morning, Manstein sent an appraisal of the situation to Hitler in which he was critical of the lack of aid that he had received from his neighboring army groups. He stated that the ratio of German to Soviet forces in the area defended by Heeresgruppe Don was an unfavorable 8 to 1, while Heeresgruppen Mitte and Nord, both less critical areas of the front, faced odds of only 4 to 1. Manstein emphasized the fact that the decisive Russian effort was in the south and that collapse in the south would be fatal. Subsequently Hitler wrung promises of aid from Heeresgruppe Mitte but there was little actual change in the situation other than a reorganization of forces. Armeeabteilung Lanz was placed under command of Heeregruppe Süd and the HQ of Heeregruppe B went into reserve.

The decision to remove Heeresgruppe Bs command and communication structure from Russia resulted in a temporary communications problem because Heeresgruppe Süd did not have adequate communications links established to the divisions in the Kharkov sector. This rearrangement of the front defensive structure eventually benefited Manstein, giving him more control of the German forces in the Kharkov area but did not solve his core problem which was lack of sufficient infantry and armored reserves to carry out the missions assigned to the army group.

Manstein commented on the situation in *Lost Victories*:

> I therefore suggested to Hitler that Army Detachment Lanz should forego Kharkov for the time being and try instead to beat the enemy south of the city. By this means the danger of the Army Group's being enveloped across the Dnepr on both sides of Kremenchug would be temporarily eliminated. On the other hand, it was reasonable to suppose that by throwing in Fourth Panzer Army, we could cope on our own with the enemy making for the Dnepr crossings at Zaporozsche and Dneropropetrovsk.[29]

Manstein went on to say that it was obvious that Armeeabteilung Lanz did not have the strength to successfully conduct both offensive and defensive operations simultaneously. Given this fact, he believed that it would be best to secure the flank of the army group first and then retake Kharkov when the situation stabilized. This path was both logical and militarily sound, because it was the most likely course of action to succeed. Manstein understood that the possession of Kharkov was not the most important issue at the time. Hitler did not agree with his assessment of the military situation.

> This solution, however, did not suit Hitler, for whom Kharkov, as the fourth biggest city in the Soviet Union, had already become a symbol of prestige, . . . he again passed a strict order to Army Detachment Lanz, through Army Group B, to hold Kharkov at all costs.[30]

[28] Vopersal, pg. 36-37.

[29] Manstein, pg. 422.
[30] Manstein, pg. 422.

Armeeabteilung Lanz in Crisis

While Hitler and Manstein wrangled over strategy, the fighting for possession of the city and the resulting carnage continued. The life or death struggle of 320. Infanterie-Division drew closer to a climax as it battled westward along the rail line leading westward to safety. On 11 February the division reported that it now had a total of at least 1000 wounded. This included hundreds of walking wounded, many of whom were still fighting. The stretcher cases were carried by wagon, sledge or piled on the few vehicles still remaining mobile. The tiring division gathered its strength once again in the late morning, lunged forward and by 1600 hours reported that it had taken the town of Liman with substantial help from the Luftwaffe. Repeated Stuka attacks ahead of the line of march destroyed Soviet gun positions and assembly areas or broke up infantry attacks. The ragged German infantrymen stumbled westward, fighting with the ferocity of desperation. The division was instructed to prepare for one last effort, which would take place on the following day. The SS-Panzer-Korps was ordered to aid the breakout of the division. Dietrich quickly organized a relief group

for the dangerous assignment. The rescue group had to seize Zmiev, cross the Northern Donets bridge there and fight through any Russian troops between them and their army comrades. Stukas were to fly continuous support missions and blast a path through the Russian troops between the division and German lines.[31]

Peiper's half track battalion was chosen to carry out the rescue. The battalion was reinforced with two Sturmgeschütze and a few mobile flak guns. A sixty vehicle ambulance train was assembled in order to transport the many wounded of the division. The ambulance column was to follow behind the battalion as it plunged forward, driving through Soviet occupied territory. Peiper's battalion was the armored battalion of the division and was equipped with SPW 251s, which were lightly armored half tracks. Platoon leader vehicles had additional armament such as short barreled 7.5 cm infantry howitzers or 3.7cm light anti-tank guns. These heavy weapons were extremely valuable in furnishing close support for the SS Grenadiers.

---

[31] *Befehl des Gewissens*, pg. 66-68.

A dramatic picture of a Sturmgeschütz III in action during the winter of 1942-43. In the distance a large artillery shell burst sends a fountain of frozen clods and smoke high into the air. The assault gun has a large German flag draped over its deck, in order to identify it to German ground attack aircraft. (Credit National Archives)

The mission called for daring leadership, confidence and determination and Peiper was ideally suited to carry it out. He was one of the young, aggressive unit leaders of "Leibstandarte" who had been hardened by years of fighting, first in the west and then in the fiery furnace of Russia. He was a product of the SS Junkerschulen, graduating with one of the first classes to complete the course of instruction designed by Hausser. In 1938, he was posted to Himmler's staff as a Liaison officer to the SS-Verfugungstruppen, the first formation of field troops of the SS. He did not rejoin his division until 1940 and then fought in the Western campaign and in Greece. Peiper distinguished himself repeatedly during the Kharkov fighting, winning the Knight's Cross as a result of several notable exploits. The first of these operations was the mission to rescue 320. Infanterie-Division.[32]

In order to succeed, Peiper's Kampfgruppe had to surprise and defeat the Russian troops defending Zmiev, capture and cross two bridges (the Udy and Msha Rivers) and then make contact with 320. Infanterie-Division. Then it had to lead the division back through the alerted Russians and find safety. Speed and surprise were absolutely essential, as was a generous helping of luck. With Russian infantry and armor in close pursuit and harassing the infantry division, the situation promised to be difficult. It was also important that the attack succeed quickly, because the men of 320. Infanterie-Division were at the end of their rope. If the Russians blocked Peiper's rescue attempt, many of the wounded could not be expected to survive sub-zero temperatures for much longer, given their weakened state.

Peiper's attack was planned for the pre-dawn hours of 12 February. The battalion's route of attack was almost entirely behind Russian lines, as it had to pass through the rear areas of the 6th Guards Cavalry and fight through strong Russian rifle forces. Southwest of Zmiev, the 6th Army's 350th Rifle Division had established a bridgehead over the Northern Donets by 11 February. Thus Peiper's raid had to be conducted through the rear areas of at least one rifle division as well as the communications zone of the Soviet cavalry corps.

On the night of 11-12 February, while Peiper's group assembled, the rattle of machine gun fire and the explosions of artillery shells echoed all around the perimeter of Kharkov. The Rogan-Krassnaya Polyana sector of the southeastern perimeter of the city defenses, manned by Wisch's SS-PzG.-Rgt. 2 "LAH," was tested by a number of Soviet reconnaissance attacks during the night. Russian infantry slipped forward in silence, probing the German lines, seeking a gap in the SS defenses. Sometime these groups contacted alert German positions and short, vicious fire fights erupted. In the icy

darkness, machine pistols rattled and grenades were hurled toward Soviet muzzle flashes. Deadly, close range combat raged at each point, until the battleground grew quiet again. Afterwards, when the battlefield once again became silent, the German forward outposts could hear the ominous noise of heavy motors and the metallic squeals and rattle of tank tracks in the night. This signaled the steady arrival of masses of Russian infantry and armor.

It was plain that the Russians were preparing for a major attack against "Leibstandarte" positions on the following day. Wisch's SS Grenadiers braced themselves for a hard fight, following on the heels of the fierce defensive fighting around Rogan on the previous day. The Rogan garrison had faced as many as 20 Soviet tanks, including the heavy KV-1s, during the fighting for Rogan area. Two Soviet tanks were destroyed or disabled and many dead Russian infantry lay in front of the German trenches and strong points. When dawn came, the Germans still held their positions and no Russian infantry had infiltrated the front. However, while "Leibstandarte" held firm east of Kharkov, the situation to the north of the regiment threatened to once again develop into a crisis.

In a sector of the northern perimeter, defended by 213. Sicherungs-Division, a Russian attack overwhelmed the overage security troops and broke through their defensive positions at several points. These penetrations could not be eliminated by the division, as it did not have adequate mobile reserves nor sufficient artillery support. Late in the day, the only uncommitted reserve of "Das Reich," SS-Aufklärungsabteilung 2, led by SS-Hauptsturmführer Weiß, arrived at the threatened sector. Weiß led his men in a savage attack that blunted the Russian advance temporarily but could not wipe out the Soviet penetrations. German counterattacks in the northern sector were hampered due to a lack of heavy weapons. Nearly all of "Das Reich's" artillery and armor was committed to the eastern perimeter supporting Regiment "Deutschland" and SS-PzG.-Rgt. 2 "LAH" or was assigned to Gruppe Dietrich. Neither "Das Reich" or "Leibstandarte" had any significant mobile reserves not already in action.[33]

On the left or northern flank of the sector held by Regiment "Deutschland," the Russians penetrated the SS front in the area near the villages of Privolje and Michailovski on 11 February. These Russian troops were counterattacked and eliminated by a battle group led by SS-Sturmbannführer Christen Tychsen, commander of II./SS-Pz.-Rgt. 2. North and northwest of Kharkov, Füsilier Regiment "GD" and Grenadier Regiment "GD" were engaged in an exhausting series of delaying actions which forced them backwards into the city's northern environs. The Aufklärungsabteilung "GD" was ordered to assemble for a reconnaissance in force to be con-

---

[32] Information from Mark C. Yerger archives.

[33] *Befehl des Gewissens*, pg. 67.

ducted to the northwest of Kharkov, on 12 February. The reconnaissance was to proceed into the Udy River valley in order to locate the 5th Guards Tank Corps, which had been seen by German air reconnaissance on 11 February. The much weakened battalion was expected to stop Kravchenko's tank corps. Armeeabteilung Kempf expected a series of concentric attacks on the morning of 12 February. Intelligence reports from all sectors indicated that the Russians were preparing to make a major effort.

As expected, a series of attacks rippled without pause along the entire front of Armeeabteilung Lanz on 12 February. Rybalko's 12th and 15th Tank Corps, supported by infantry, made repeated attacks on the positions of Regiment "Deutschland" and Wisch's regiment. Fortunately for the Germans, Rybalko experienced problems in coordinating his artillery support and concentrating his forces at the main point of attack along the Chuguyev-Kharkov road. Due to these difficulties and the continued stubborn defense of the Rogan area by "Leibstandarte" Grenadiers, the main Soviet attacks failed to successfully penetrate the German lines. The Russian infantry once again experienced grievous losses. However, because of the determined efforts made by the Russians, the Germans were hard pressed everywhere and all reserves remained tied up in heavy fighting. As a result, many small Russian penetrations were eliminated with great difficulty and sometimes necessitated the use of risky tactics.[34]

Such a situation occurred on the south flank of SS-PzG.-Rgt. 2 "LAH," when a company of Russian infantry fought its way through the regiment's positions at a village named Borovoje. Elements of two companies of the regiment were withdrawn from the line and formed into a Kampfgruppe, leaving only a few outposts and machine gun crews to cover the sector. The small detachment was supported by an assault gun or two and 2cm Flak guns. The two companies of Grenadiers, a total of about 150 men, launched its counterattack on the Russian infantry in several assault teams. The Russian infantry were in open ground west of Borovoje and without armor support. The SS Grenadiers, advancing behind the massive, squat Sturmgeschütze IIIs, pushed the Russians back into the small town.

However, once the Russian infantry took shelter in the buildings the situation changed. It was difficult and costly to root out the Russians, who were in their element fighting defensive engagements in towns and cities. They speedily occupied huts and buildings in the village and skillfully found concealed firing positions. Faced with this situation, the SS Grenadiers had to conduct methodical attacks to eliminate the Russians, battling from house to house. However the defenders could not be cleared out quickly and

their presence in Borovoje remained a potential problem, due to the Soviet penchant for reinforcing even small penetrations and building them quickly into a reinforced bridgehead.

Later in the day, an attack by the 12th Tank Corps and a regiment of Soviet infantry, penetrated a section of the line at Rogan between II. and III./SS-PzG.-Rgt. 1 "LAH." As there were no immediately available reserves in the sector, the commander of SS-PzG.-Rgt. 2 "LAH," SS-Standartenführer Wisch, took two companies from another section of the front and stationed them to the rear of the two endangered battalions in case the Russians broke through. This Soviet bridgehead could not be sealed off or eliminated because the Russians were able to reinforce their position and dig in before Wisch could launch a counterattack of sufficient strength to quickly eliminate the penetration. As a result, the Russians were able to use this bridgehead as a staging area for the next assault. Rybalko inserted tanks, infantry and additional heavy weapons into the bridgehead. At 1800 hours, the Soviets attacked out of the penetration area, assaulting the reinforced III./SS-PzG.-Rgt. 1 "LAH." Behind rocket and heavy mortar fire, Russian tanks burst out of the bridgehead, followed by shouting Russian infantry. T-34s moved up to blast the SS Grenadiers out of their trenches and buildings. High explosive tank shells reduced German strong points to ruins as the fighting dissolved into a series of bitterly fought, small unit actions. Flights of screaming rockets slammed down, blanketing an area with awesome displays of high explosive. Russian 12cm mortars laid down a heavy barrage of shells that made movement difficult and costly.[35]

Russian troops wormed their way forward, concealed by the debris of buildings and other wreckage and infiltrated between SS positions. Half strength German squads and platoons fought to hold buildings against attacks by depleted Russian companies and battalions. A few T-34s and T-70s cautiously made their way through the debris clogged streets with Soviet infantry clustered behind them. The Russians hurled grenades and fired automatic weapons to protect the tanks from close quarter attacks by SS Grenadiers. Supported by their tanks and artillery, Soviet assault teams began to force Weidenhaupt's men out of the town at the same time as another Soviet attack began.

At 1930 hours the Soviet 111th Rifle Division launched an attack south of Rogan, at Ternovo, which was supported by a thrust from out of a nearby forest . Both attacks were temporarily halted by fierce German counterattacks. After the collapse of the attack, many of the Russian infantry disappeared into the woods, which were south of the town. German artillery and mortars blasted the small forest with high explosives and fragmentation shells, hoping

---

[34] Glantz, pg.176.

[35] Lehmann, pg. 58-59.

to catch the Russians before they could dig in. SS infantry worked their way up to the woods after the artillery had forced the Russians to take cover and set up defensive positions at the woods edge. Due to quick reaction by the Germans, each Soviet thrust was at least temporarily blocked but neither could be eliminated.[36]

Rybalko skillfully switched his point of main effort from one area to the other. When his attacks were stopped at one place, he hammered at the SS positions in another area. He was determined to punch through the Germans and concentrated all of his armor and artillery against the "Leibstandarte" Panzergrenadiers. The battle for the Rogan sector became a costly slugging match, which was finally won through the application of brute force, constant pressure and superior numbers.

At 2200 hours, the 15th Tank Corps and its supporting infantry launched an effort to capture Bahnhof Rogan (railroad station) and penetrated the defensive positions of II./SS-PzG.-Rgt. 1 "LAH." Battalion commander Max Hansen organized a counterattack that stopped the attack, but under cover of darkness the Soviets regrouped and swung to the north and south of the station. Given that development, Hansen was forced to withdraw and find more favorable defensive ground. His battalion dug in about a kilometer west of Bahnhof Rogan and waited for the inevitable attacks.

In Rogan, Hubert Meyer's battalion was assailed by Soviet assault squads that stormed its perimeter relentlessly. In spite of heavy losses the Russians secured a number of footholds in the western edge of the town. T-34s found approaches that were shielded from SS anti-tank guns and infantry howitzers and fired point blank at German positions. Soviet snipers took up positions in houses opposite the SS defensive line and began to fire at anyone who dared raise their head. High explosive shells from 7.6cm anti-tank guns slammed through building walls, while 12cm mortar shells crashed through the roofs. Casualties steadily mounted and this storm of fire forced the SS Grenadiers to abandon the burning, smoke filled buildings and pull back to more sheltered firing positions.[37]

Immediately the Russians bridged the balka and began to funnel T-34s across the ravine. Soviet armor motored cautiously down the narrow streets, followed by Russian infantry and sharp shooters. Later in the war, the Panzerfaust and bazooka like Panzerschreck were common, but in early winter of 1943, the Germans did not have many of these effective infantry anti-tank weapons. More Soviet tanks entered the town and SS defenses began to collapse. After getting pushed out of their first defensive positions, the Germans tried to reach cover in another row of houses, carrying their

wounded with them. A hail of small arms fire caused additional losses and forced the SS Grenadiers to pull back. They discovered a Pak 40 anti-tank gun and its crew and attempted once again to make a stand but machine gun fire killed or wounded several defenders. The squeal and clank of tank tracks could be heard advancing toward them and abruptly three T-34s rumbled into sight while the gun crew frantically tried to pivot their gun. The first shot struck the lead Russian tank and damaged it. To the utter amazement of the SS men, the other two tanks broke off the attack and withdrew leaving the disabled tank behind.[38] In spite of this small victory, the unrelenting Soviet assault on Rogan pushed Meyer's Grenadiers out of the town. The SS battalion pulled back and occupied another position straddling the Kharkov-Rogan-Chugujev road.

The battles of both the 3rd Tank Army and 69th Army on the eastern approaches to Kharkov were extremely costly to the Soviets. Although they were forcing the Germans to slowly retreat toward the city, Russian infantry casualties and tank losses were high. Kazakov's 69th Army was forced to combine the remnants of its various decimated regiments, in order to form rifle battalions with a functional strength. After days of fighting, the two armies remained unable to break the three SS regiments that held the eastern approaches to the city. However, the SS Grenadiers were stretched to their limits and could no longer eliminate Russian penetrations.[39]

Rybalko was spurred on by directives from his Front commander and ordered one assault after the other in order to overwhelm the Germans defending the eastern approaches of the city. The 3rd Tank Army was squeezed into a narrow attack sector and had little choice but to make costly frontal assaults. The bitter fighting further reduced the strength of the Soviet rifle regiments and cost Rybalko tanks that he could not afford to lose. While Rybalko fought a bitter war of attrition, the situation remained more fluid in the area west and north of Kharkov.

Moskalenko's 40th Army retained freedom of maneuver because it exploited the gap west of Belgorod that had been created by the withdrawal of 168. Infanterie-Division. On the morning of 12 February, "Grossdeutschland" pulled back its overextended western flank. Threatened with encirclement at several points, the division withdrew to the towns of Zolochev and Olshanny, which were northwest of Kharkov. At Dergatschi, a few kilometers directly north of Kharkov, the Aufklärungsabteilung "GD" was outflanked and forced to withdraw to the northern outskirts of the city in order to avoid encirclement and destruction. This was in spite of orders by Lanz that the town was to be held to the last man. The exhausted men of the Führer-Begleit-Bataillon, which was reduced

---

[36] NA/T-354, roll 120, 1a KTB, Darstellung der Ereignisse, 9.2. to 10.2.1943. frame 3753575.
[37] Lehmann, pg. 65.

[38] Lehmann, pg 67.
[39] Glantz, pg. 177.

to company strength, were sent to Losovenka as reinforcement to the reconnaissance battalion.[40]

The breakthrough at Dergatschi was a serious threat to the "Grossdeutschland" Grenadier Regiment, which had two battalions stationed along the Belgorod-Kharkov road. The Russian forces at Dergatschi were in position to outflank the Grenadier Regiment's left flank. The division ordered the Aufklärungsabteilung "GD," strengthened by an SS anti-tank gun platoon, to either recapture Dergatschi or force the Soviet spearhead away from the area. Already Russian ski troops were infiltrating the area south of Dergatschi and a few solitary Soviet tanks could be seen scouting around the hills in the distance. In order to add armored support to the battalion, a few assault guns and tanks were assigned to the battle group. A supporting attack was to be made by III./Grenadier-Regiment "GD." Joined by a battery of self propelled artillery, the Führer-Begleit-Bataillon, led by one tank and a single assault gun, attacked Dergatschi at 0900 hours. One squadron of the reconnaissance battalion assaulted the town from the west, while another squadron remained in reserve. One battalion of "Grossdeutschland" Grenadiers was sent marching toward Dergatschi with orders to support the attack.

As the Führer-Begleit-Bataillon approached the town the assault gun was hit twice in succession by anti-tank gun fire and damaged. It remained in action, however and pulled back in order to find a sheltered firing position. A Russian tank then opened fire from the edge of the town but it was hit immediately by SS anti-tank gunners and put out of action. The two attack groups assaulted the town, forcing the defending Soviet infantry to withdraw to the northwest. The Germans occupied the southern edge of Dergatschi, when suddenly, several Russian tanks appeared on the crests of a range of hills to the northwest and began shelling the German troops.

Within a short time Soviet artillery and Stalin's Organs were brought to bear on the Germans and shells and rockets began to impact inside the town perimeter. Soon houses and building were burning vigorously, sending banks of smoke drifting about, which reduced visibility. The "Grossdeutschland" Grenadier battalion arrived while the Soviet shelling was in full swing but they charged into the town and secured it. There was no immediate counterattack by the Russians and the Führer-Begleit-Bataillon was able to regroup and withdraw, leaving the Grenadiers in possession of the town. The Aufklärungsabteilung "GD" was ordered to immediately pull back into Kharkov and prepare to carry out its previously ordered operation against the 5th Guards Tank Corps advance. In the meantime, infantry of the Soviet 25th Guards Rifle Division as-

sembled at Dergatschi and at nightfall launched attacks on the town which continued until morning. The Russian mobile spearheads, having met strong resistance, left the capture of the town to the infantry of the 25th Guards and bypassed Dergatschi.

During the night of 13-14 February, "Grossdeutschland" attempted to consolidate and reorganize its crumbling defenses north of Kharkov. The Grenadier Regiment and Füsilier Regiment were able to build up a front consisting of battalion strong points extending from west of Dergatschi to the area near the town of Zirkuny, where contact with Regiment "Deutschland" was established.[41]

The fragments of 168. Infanterie-Division still faced portions of the Russian 107th and 309th Rifle Divisions. The division was ordered to assemble combat groups of regimental strength in the town of Bogodukhov, which lay almost 40 kilometers to the northwest of Kharkov. However, the demoralized division had lost the will to fight and the withdrawing regiments made every effort to avoid combat as they retreated before the advance of Soviet infantry and tank forces. This was noted by the army because a report sent by Armeeabteilung Lanz to Heeresgruppe Süd stated that the division had given way too quickly (zu schnell wegläugt).

This was in stark contrast to the determination exhibited by the SS divisions and "Grossdeutschland," as well as the 320. Infanterie-Division. The lack of fighting motivation exhibited by the division was noted a second time by the officer writing the Kriegstagesbuch (war diary) of Armeeabteilung Lanz, who remarked on the 'unusual' (exzentrisch) movements made by the regiments of the division.[42]

Early in the morning, there were again reports of a Russian tank column moving south, following the course of the Udy River. These report undoubtedly refer to the leading detachment of the 5th Guards Tank Corps which was driving down the length of the narrow, flat bottomed river valley. In response to this threat, the Aufklärungsabteilung "GD" was again ordered to check the advance of the Russian tank column by establishing a blocking position at Peresetshnaya. This village was located just north of the larger town of Olschany. It is instructive that Lanz could do no more than send a depleted reconnaissance battalion to oppose the advance of an entire Soviet tank corps.

The combat north of Kharkov remained characterized by a series of blocking actions. "Grossdeutschland" switched its mobile battalions from one hot spot to the other, while stretching its left flank westward in a futile attempt to avoid being outflanked by Kravchenko's tank corps. Main elements of the 40th Army forced the defenders relentlessly back toward Kharkov. The hard fighting

---

[40] *Befehl des Gewissens,* pg. 85.

[41] Spaeter, pg. 38.
[42] *Befehl des Gewissens,* pg. 92-93.

German troops exacted a high price for the Soviet advance, but could not stop it.[43]

Soviet rifle divisions concentrated in the area north of Kharkov throughout the day, as long columns of sleds and marching infantry continued to arrive. Soviet armor rumbled and skid over the icy roads, rolling toward Kharkov from all directions. They passed long march columns of brown uniformed Russian infantry, trudging alongside sleds and horse drawn artillery and anti-tank guns.

The Grenadiers and Panzerjägers of "Grossdeutschland" were able to destroy 5 Soviet tanks in actions along the roads leading into the northern edge of Kharkov during 12 February. Northeast of the city, along the Kharkov River valley, the Füsilier Regiment "GD" temporarily blocked roads leading into the town of Lipzy. However, the 25th Guards, 340th, 183rd and 309th Rifle Divisions bypassed or outflanked the isolated German blocking positions. The stolid columns of Russian troops steadily marched southward toward their objective, Kharkov.[44]

The fighting for Lipzy raged throughout the night of 12-13 February and into the early morning hours of the next day. Soviet infantry broke into the German perimeter several times but were driven out. The Füsilier Regiment turned back all attempts of the Russians to take Lipzy itself, inflicting heavy losses on the Russian infantry. However, after pulling back, the Russians regrouped and within hours began to march around the town. On either side of Lipzy, Russian columns could be seen in the distance, pushing inexorably onwards towards the south and Kharkov. Forced to hold a front too wide to establish a continuous defensive line, the division had no other choice but to pull back again and again. The German rear guard troops fought back with skill and determination as they retreated and the division reported the destruction of 9 T-34s and 1 KV-1 for the day, but always they moved backwards. By the morning of 13 February "Grossdeutschland" was forced back into the northern environs of Kharkov.

Fritz Ehrath's I./"Deutschland," holding the SS division's left flank, was left with an open flank after the breakthrough made by the 40th Army's 340th Rifle Division east of Dergatschi, which had forced "Grossdeutschland" units to withdraw from the town. By the afternoon, the last few reserves of SS Grenadiers that remained available to Regiment "Deutschland" were committed to the fighting. The 3rd Tank Army and 69th Army threw their infantry and tanks at the SS defensive front in relentless frontal assaults and succeeded in penetrating the regiment's perimeter at several points.

[43] NA/T-314, roll 489. Tagesmeldung Generalkommando z.b.v. Cramer an "Grossdeutschland" frame 000655 to 000658.
[44] Glantz, pg. 177-178.

Heinz Macher, pictured here at the rank of SS-Untersturmführer. On February 13, 1943 Macher led his Pioniere company in a successful counter attack against a Russian rifle battalion that threatened to overrun a battalion of "Das Reich" artillery. (Courtesy of Mark C. Yerger)

One such penetration occurred near a small village where the advance of a Soviet rifle regiment threatened an artillery position of II./SS-Artillerie-Regiment 2. SS-Untersturmführer Heinz Macher's 16./"Deutschland," the regiment's Pioniere company, was ordered to counterattack the lead battalion of the Soviet rifle regiment. The Russians had occupied the village and begun to organize the defense of the area. A company of Soviet infantry dug in on a nearby hill to the north of the village and emplaced several machine gun positions in front of a small woods to the northwest.

Once he conducted a reconnaissance of the area, Macher ordered one platoon of the company to approach the village from the west, using a small ravine to conceal its advance. The company was then to make a quick surprise attack from the ravine and knock out the Russian machine gun outposts and an anti-tank gun position defending the edge of the forest. After eliminating the machine gun positions the platoon was to clear the forest and attack the Russians in the village from the flank. Simultaneously, a second platoon was to attack Soviet forward positions located on the hill north of the village. After taking the hill, the platoon was to attack the main Soviet position in the village, in support of the flank attack from the woods. Due to previous combat losses the company numbered only sixty-two men, with four non-commissioned officers and one officer.[45]

At 0800 hours the two platoons began their attack. The flanking attack toward the forest captured several machine guns and a anti-tank rifle, reached the woods and pushed to within a 100 meters of the village. It set up a machine gun position that was able to rake the length of the Russian position from the flank. The second platoon of the company routed the Soviet detachment holding the hill north of the village and advanced down the reverse slope. At that time they came under such heavy fire from the town that they were forced to pull back behind the hill crest. Macher's company suffered serious casualties, losing eight dead and nineteen wounded. As a result of the heavy casualties the company was reorganized into two combat groups with three MG 42s in each group and was ordered to serve as the security detachment of the artillery battalion. However, the Soviet battalion had suffered heavy losses as well and its advance was halted

In the area defended by "Leibstandarte," to the southeast and east, there was also a great deal of activity. The operation to rescue Generalmajor Postel's embattled division occupied a great deal of the division's energy, while the fighting south of the city grew in intensity as well. The two Panzergrenadier regiments were hard pressed to hold their positions without any appreciable mobile reserves due to the fact that the division's remaining tanks were in action against the 6th Guards Cavalry Corps thrust past its southern flank.

Kampfgruppe Peiper and the Rescue of 320. Infanterie-Division

While fighting raged southeast and east of Kharkov, particularly in the Rogan area, Kampfgruppe Peiper began its operation to reach 320. Infanterie-Division at 0330 hours. After assembling in the pitch black, bitter cold night, the SS Grenadiers stood around the half tracks, stamping their feet and clapping their frozen hands in futile attempts to stay warm. The SPW exhaust pipes sent out clouds of vapor while the men and drivers gathered in small groups, quietly talking while they waited for the order to begin the attack. To shut a motor off risked not being able to get it started again because of the intense cold. As a result there was a constant dull rumbling of idling motors throughout the assembly area. Finally the NCOs returned from a last mission review and the men clambered aboard the vehicles clutching their weapons. The Kampfgruppe moved off toward the south while to the rear the long line of ambulances also got under way, following at a distance behind the combat troops.

Led by two assault guns, the lead elements of the relief column drove southward toward the Udy River. At 0515 hours, Peiper's lead detachment surprised a Russian security force on the bridge over the river at Krassnaya Polyana. The bridge was in German hands before it could be destroyed by the surprised Russian troops. Those who were not killed or captured fled into the night and disappeared. After mopping up the area, Peiper left a platoon behind to protect the bridge and quickly pushed on. The following column of vehicles snaked through Krassnaya Polyana and crossed the bridge after a brief halt due to a Soviet counterattack that destroyed several vehicles and caused havoc for a time before it was driven off. Burning vehicles were pushed off the road into the deep snow and the lead vehicles left the river and its platoon of guardians behind. A few minutes later intense firing suddenly was heard once again from Krassnaja Polyana. The detachment guarding the bridge had been attacked once again and were fighting for their lives, but no help could be sent back to aid them because the column had to keep moving.

An hour later Peiper's Kampfgruppe reached Zmiev and crossed the Northern Donets River on a still intact rail road bridge, at first meeting no Russian resistance on the eastern bank. However, the Russians were alerted to the presence of the SS column and after Peiper's spearhead moved on, Soviet infantry mounted several attacks against the SS troops guarding the bridge. Machine gun fire snapped overhead and mortar shells began to impact around the bridge. Several small groups of Russian infantry attacked the bridge guard detachment, firing machine pistols and hurling grenades.[46]

Peiper received word that 320. Infanterie-Division battle groups were on the move, making their way toward their rendezvous with the SS troops. A reconnaissance plane spotted the first regimental group of the division traveling along the rail line only a few kilometers southeast of Zmiev. A trail of dead horses, discarded equipment and abandoned vehicles marked the passage of Postel's troops. Peiper sent patrols to establish contact with the division, while the main body of his battalion remained near Zmiev.

Shortly before noon, the first element of the infantry division could be seen in the distance. At 1230 hours, the lead group of the division, with its commanding officer, Generalmajor Postel at its head, made the first contact with Peiper's men. The regiment serv-

---

[45] Information from privately held KTB courtesy of Mark C. Yerger.

[46] Lehmann, pg. 60-65.

ing as the divisional rear guard was still several kilometers away in the Liman area. Peiper reported that the appearance of the men of the first group was shocking and brought to his mind visions of the retreat of Napoleon's Grand Army from Russia.[47]

Shortly after the link up was established, elements of a Russian rifle regiment occupied Krassnaja Polyana and took possession of the bridge. The Russians killed the last surviving men of the guard detachment, thus cutting Peiper's line of retreat. While Peiper had waited for Postel's division to reach Zmiev, one of the bridges in his rear had fallen into Soviet hands. There was nothing to be done however, except carry out the mission and then find a way to fight their way back to their own lines.

Throughout the night the assembly of bone weary German infantry continued, as the exhausted men of the three regimental groups called on their last mental and physical reserves in a final effort to reach safety. Columns of exhausted men reached the SS lines, unshaven, wrapped in rags and half frozen. Along the way they had collected all manner of animals to help drag their guns and equipment. Scores of little Russian panje horses had been taken from Russian civilians and hooked up to sleds or supply wagons. Officers rode horses on makeshift saddles of blankets, while cattle or oxen had been commandeered to drag the division's remaining artillery pieces. The men staggered past the SS soldiers wrapped in layers of tattered blankets, ice hanging from beards and eyebrows. Sleds and wagons rolled up to the river, loaded with wounded and dead. But regardless of their appearance, the men had kept their order and discipline and had not collapsed in the face of a terrible mental strain. They had brought out their wounded, retained the ability to fight and had occupied elements of three Soviet rifle divisions during its march west.

This was an amazing achievement in itself and before all of the division had even reached safety, Armeeabteilung Lanz considered several assignments for it. This included a probably unrealistic role as reinforcements for the SS-Panzer-Korps attack south of Kharkov. Only the lead group of the division had actually reached Peiper's position on the afternoon of 12 February in any event. The entire division did not assemble in time to contribute to the attack before other events completely changed the situation in Kharkov. The last regimental group, made up of the survivors of the division's 585. Grenadier Regiment, did not reach the rescue assembly area until 14 February. With the arrival of the rear guard detachment, the nightmarish withdrawal of the division was at an end.

Peiper's battalion spread out on each flank to protect the march route and the column got under way, with the long trail of ambulances carrying their cargo of wounded. When the leading detachments of the column neared the bridge at Krassnaja Polyana, they were fired on by a Russian ski battalion. The bridge was partially destroyed and the small German guard detachment, as well as a number of German medical personnel and wounded had all been killed. Their bodies lay in the snow, strewn in piles along the town streets. Peiper launched an immediate assault and took the town from the Russians. Little imagination is required to guess what happened to any Russian survivors after the dead SS Grenadiers and medical personnel were discovered. The remains of the bridge were used to construct a fragile temporary bridge and the wounded of the division were taken across. For those men, their ordeal ended when they crossed over to the north bank of the river in the ambulances and trucks. While the wounded and sick were taken across the makeshift crossing, the rest of the division gathered on the southern bank.

However the improvised bridge was not strong enough to hold the assault guns and SPWs of Peiper's battalion. One of Postel's surviving assault guns attempted to cross the frozen ice but fell through and had to be abandoned. After the entire 320. Infanterie-Division crossed the river to safety, Peiper was to assemble his battalion at Merefa. In order to reach Merefa as soon as possible, Peiper decided on a bold course of action and raced back to Zmiev. After reaching the town the battalion turned west and drove down a road on the northern bank of the Msha River. Passing through the towns of Sidki and Mirgorod, Peiper was able to slip between Russian forces in the area and reach Merefa, which lay about 15 kilometers southwest of Kharkov. The first of Peiper's remarkable operations during the winter of 1942-43 had reached a successful conclusion. Meanwhile, to the south, while the men of 320. Infanterie-Division marched into safety, the drama of the battle for Kharkov was reaching a climax.[48]

The Attack against the 6th Guards Cavalry Corps

Postel radioed Armeeabteilung Lanz and reported that his division 'stood ready for new deployment,' an optimistic assessment of the capabilities of the division, considering its recent ordeal. Armeeabteilung Lanz considered pulling the remnants of his division back to Merefa, where it could recover and serve as the army reserve. Another proposed course of action, transport of the division to Poltava, was mentioned to Heeresgruppe B, but the army group replied that this was not possible. The roads from Poltava to Krasnograd and the road net west of Kharkov already had march columns on them and there were no rail cars available for transport of the division. The division was ordered to continue its withdrawal

---

[47] Op cit.

[48] *Befehl des Gewissens*, pg. 79-87 and Lehmann, pg. 60-65.

A column of SS assault guns and half tracks moving across flat terrain typical of the area around Kharkov. The frozen steppe was often featureless as far as one could see in all directions. Characteristically, balkas (ravines) of varying size cut through the area of the Ukraine around Kharkov, some of which were large enough to conceal tanks and artillery. (Credit National Archives)

northwards toward Kharkov but it was not capable of helping the counterattack of SS-Panzer-Korps south of Kharkov. In the meantime, the first combat units of "Totenkopf" began to deploy in the Kharkov area. Regiment "Thule" was en route from Krasnograd to Novaja Vodolaga by late afternoon and other elements of the SS division, including the last units of SS-Panzer-Regiment 3, continued to arrive and unload at Poltava. Eicke's SS-Artillerie-Regiment 3 and support units of the division began to arrive by road from Kiev on the night of 12-13 February.[49]

While the third division of the SS-Panzer-Korps assembled, Dietrich's counterattack had continued with some success. The advance of the 6th Guards Cavalry Corps toward Ljubotin was halted and the Soviet cavalry column was sliced into several fragments by the SS attacks. The largest group withdrew to Novaja Vodolaga and organized a strong defense, reinforced by a number of anti-tank guns. The SS-Kradschützen-Bataillon 2, under command of SS-Sturmbannführer Fick, arrived in the area on the night of 11-12 February and was ordered to take the town, which was defended by the Soviet 11th Cavalry Division.

Supported by Panzer IVs of II./SS-Pz.-Rgt. 1, the Kradschützen-Bataillon captured a range of hills northeast of the town, after diffi-

cult fighting. After regrouping behind the hills the battalion assaulted Novaja Vodolaga itself and penetrated into the town but the motorcycle troops were immediately counterattacked and thrown out. Twice more Fick's motorcycle troops fought their way into Novaja Vodolaga but were driven back by ferocious Soviet counterattacks. Each time, Russian infantry, supported by T-34s, launched determined assaults upon the battalion before it could consolidate its gains. After darkness, Fick withdrew his battered men and reassembled east of the town.

At day break on 13 February, Fick's battalion, supported by III./Regiment "Der Führer" and "Leibstandarte" tanks, attacked Novaja Vodolaga once again. This time the SS Grenadiers fought through the Soviet defensive perimeter and drove the Russians out of the town, although the Germans lost three tanks in the process. After being forced out of Novaja Vodolaga, the Soviet cavalry withdrew in good order to the southeast. While III./Regiment "Der Führer" mopped up the remaining Soviet troops in the town, Fick's battalion cautiously pursued the withdrawing Russians and reached a crossroads south of the town.[50]

---

[49] Vopersal, pg. 98-100.

[50] T-354, Roll 118 Fernschreiben SS- Div. L-SS-AH an SS-Panzer-Korps, 2000 Uhr 13.2.1943. Weidinger, Otto, *Kameraden bis zum Ende*, (Göttingen: 1962) page 118.

After the loss of Novaja Vodolaga and Borki, major elements of the 6th Cavalry Corps withdrew eastwards. The cavalry detachments remained largely intact and in possession of their heavy weapons and made were able to keep their tanks running. The 11th Cavalry Division crossed the Udy River valley and made its way to Ochotschaje. Other well armed detachments, including the majority of the 201st Tank Brigade, pulled back further eastward, reaching the village of Bereka. Fick's battalion was ordered to stop its advance and prepare to support Regiment "Der Führer," which was approaching Ochotschaje, where the Soviet cavalry had taken up new positions.

Earlier that day, at 0500 hours, Regiment "Der Führer" began its advance, supported by the Stukas of Stukageschwader 77. A Luftwaffe officer was assigned to the command group in order to coordinate the air support. Before noon, the regiment occupied the town of Rjabuchino, which was a few kilometers north of Ochotschaje. The poor roads and bad weather slowed the Germans down considerably, while the Russian cavalry divisions and T-34s seemed to have less difficulty moving over the snowbound terrain. Soon afterwards, the Kradschützen-Bataillon reached the town of Starowerowka, which was east of Ochotschaje, after leaving behind a security detachment to guard its supply lines.[51]

While the center group lagged behind, both flanking groups made good progress and closed in on two different groups of Russian cavalry. By the afternoon the right wing spearhead, Meyer's Aufklärungsabteilung approached the town of Alexejevka, which was west of Ochotschaje. However, due to a lack of fuel Meyer's Kampfgruppe was forced to halt its attack and take up defensive positions after occupying the town. Albert Frey's I./SS-PzGren.-Rgt 1 "LAH," on the left or eastern flank, finally began to make steady progress and reached the outskirts of Bereka, which was east of Ochotschaje. At Bereka, Witt's advance once again came to a halt when he found that the Russian cavalry troops were entrenched in considerable strength in and around the town. His first attacks were thrown back with substantial losses and very little gain. The men of the 6th Guards Cavalry Corps proved to be tough opponents, although the corps was sliced up into isolated fragments which were forced to try to escape to the east. The cavalry combat groups remained full of fight and dealt out heavy casualties whenever they were cornered by the SS. The largest cavalry group remained entrenched at Ochotschaje, while at Bereka strong forces of the corps continued to fight off Witt's Grenadiers. Although the Soviet cavalry was still south of the city in some strength and occupied main elements of the available SS mobile forces, its thrust towards

Ljubotin and the vital railroad lines was stopped. If the cavalry group had not been stopped, the SS-Panzer-Korps would have been cut off by 14 February, due to the presence of Soviet armor west of Kharkov.

Russian tanks, probably from the 5th Guards Tank Corps, were reported to have reached the Ljubotin-Bogodukhov road, about ten kilometers west of Kharkov on 13 February. This was only about twenty kilometers northwest of Novaja Vodolaga. A Soviet link up at Ljubotin would have severed the last rail line into Kharkov and created additional difficulties for Hausser at a critical time. The SS counterattack prevented the encirclement of the city by breaking up the attack of the Soviet cavalry corps but the commitment of the mobile forces of the two divisions prevented the use of the entire SS-Panzer-Korps in defense of Kharkov itself. Although the attempt of the 3rd Tank Army to encircle Kharkov from the south failed, the eastern defenses of the city were about to crack. By the time that the 6th Cavalry Corps attack was stopped it was too late to redeploy the SS mobile units to the east and north of the city. Just as the flanking movement by the 40th Army had unhinged the German front north of Kharkov, the thrust of the 6th Guards Cavalry Corps fatally weakened the SS defenses east of the city. Lanz correctly predicted the outcome several days earlier but his reports fell on deaf ears and the Armeeabteilung received orders to continue to hold the city, regardless of the circumstances and the SS-Panzer-Korps was to continue Dietrich's attack against the Soviet cavalry corps.

Lanz hoped to accomplish several limited objectives on 14 February, the first of which was the mopping up the remaining battle groups of Soviet cavalry. The day also saw a change in leadership of Korps Cramer. General der Panzertruppen Erhard Raus took over command of the corps, which was redesignated as Korps Raus. Optimistically, Lanz hoped that the SS Kampfgruppe would be able to drive further south after accomplishing their first task and clear Soviet troops off the Dnepropetrovsk-Pavlograd-Kharkov rail line between Kharkov and Losovaja. This stretch of railroad had been lost to the Germans when columns of the 6th Guards Cavalry Corps crossed the line in their thrust to the west.

The 83rd Cavalry Division held the town of Taranovka, which was ten kilometers west of the rail line and near Ochotschaje, which was held by major elements of the 11th Cavalry Division. Elements of the 201st Tank Brigade, the armored spearhead of the Soviet cavalry corps, occupied Bereka and parts of the surrounding area. These towns would be consumed in the bitter fighting that was to come in the following days.[52]

---

[51] T-354, Roll 118, Fernscreiben SS- Div. L-SS-AH an SS-Panzer-Korps, 2000 Uhr 13.2.1943 and Weidinger, pgs. 119-120.

[52] NA/T-354, roll 120, 1a KTB, Darstellung der Ereignisse, Morgenmeldung an SS-Panzer-Korps, frame 3753591.

Lanz also hoped to hold the approaches to the southeastern sector of Kharkov, anchored in its center by the tractor works at Lossevo. However, by the following day, the northern and eastern defenses were crumbling and could not be saved. On 13 February Hausser had already given warning orders for the first demolition of bridges and roads in preparation for a withdrawal from the city. Some demolition was begun at that time and Lanz was informed of this fact. On 14 and 15 February a confusing series of orders, counter orders and conflicting command intentions embroiled Lanz and Hausser. While the officers debated the proper course of action and Hitler wielded his influence upon their decisions, the Soviet ring closed ever tighter on the German troops fighting and dying in the icy cold steppe and ruined buildings of Kharkov.

At midnight on 14 February, Armeeabteilung Lanz officially became part of Manstein's army group, which was then designated Heeresgruppe Süd. It was to be a day of crisis not only for Lanz, but for the SS-Panzer-Korps and its commander, Paul Hausser as well. On the previous night, Manstein was notified by OKH that a new German army was to be built up west of Poltava, although this proposal never took any substantive shape. It is possible that Manstein's affirmation of Hitler's orders to hold the city on that date, regardless of military realities, were based upon the belief that new forces would be available in a short time.

In his book *Lost Victories,* Manstein remarked that the realignment of Armeeabteilung Lanz served only 'one useful purpose.'

> By bringing Army Detachment Lanz under Southern Army Group, it enabled our headquarters to exercise exclusive command at the decisive place and the decisive time . . . this contributed substantially to the final success of the winter campaign of 1942-43.[53]

This is a strange comment, especially considering the remarks made by Manstein in the following paragraph, in which he described the 'fresh source of anxiety' caused by Hitler, who 'by dint of his personal interventions – remained in command there for a few days yet.' Apparently Manstein did not consider himself to be in exclusive command because he further stated that he demanded to be informed whether he would be bound by orders previously issued to Lanz by the Führer, through Heeresgruppe B.

It appears that Manstein decided that he was still bound by these directives. At 0510 hours, according to the records of the Armeeabteilung, Lanz received orders from Heeresgruppe Süd that reiterated the Führer Befehl, which stated that the city of Kharkov

was to be held under all circumstances, even if it became necessary to stop the attack south of the city. The order added that local breakthroughs were to be dealt with by "mobile defensive operations." This suggests that Manstein was not immediately aware of the realities of the situation in Kharkov and the condition of the defending divisions, particularly regarding their lack of any strong mobile reserves on the eastern and northern sectors of the city perimeter. It is possible that the poor communications net contributed to the lack of proper understanding of the manpower situation faced by Armeeabteilung Lanz. Otherwise, it is hard to understand how Korps Raus could have been realistically expected to utilize mobile defensive operations in its defense of the city. Lanz issued a number of orders to the SS-Panzer-Korps a few hours later, stating that according to Hitler's directive, the city was to be held and that destruction of bridges and roads was to be halted.

Recognizing the critical situation on the eastern perimeter, Lanz first directed that Regiment "Deutschland" should pull back closer to the city, essentially confirming Hausser's previous orders to the regiment. Secondly, Sepp Dietrich was directed to finish the operation against the remains of the 6th Guards Cavalry as soon as possible, in order to free up the mobile units for use in the defense of the city. All available anti-tank weapons, assault guns and armor was to assemble at Merefa and prepare for assembly at an enormous tractor factory at the town of Lossevo which was located between Kharkov and Rogan and produced T-34 tanks.[54]

Lanz also ordered Postel's 320. Infanterie-Division to assemble southeast of Kharkov and serve as the reserve of the SS-Panzer-Korps. Korps Raus was ordered to use elements of the division to build up a blocking position south of the city, in order to delay the attack of the 12th Tank Corps and the 62nd Guards Rifle Division, which were slowly pushing up the Kharkov-Rogan road. The remainder of 320. Infanterie-Division was to attack across the Udy River and strike the flank of the Soviet forces moving west on this road.[55]

Korps Raus took over responsibility for the front west and north of the city and attempted to establish a strong defensive position at Olschany in order to prevent Soviet forces northwest of Kharkov from penetrating farther south and completing the encirclement of the city. The 168. Infanterie-Division was to assemble a reinforced regimental group at Bogodukhov and cover the west flank of Korps Raus. This was a very optimistic plan, given the dispirited condition of the division's soldiers. There was little hope that the division could establish contact with the western flank of

---

[53] Manstein, pg. 421.

[54] *Befehl des Gewissens,* pg. 94-96
[55] NA/T-314, roll 489, Armeeabteilung Lanz an Korps Raus und Gen.Kdo. SS-Panzer-Korps, frame 683.

"Grossdeutschland" judging from the situation map reproduced in *Befehl des Gewissens.*[56] Soviet units surrounding the city are stacked in columns above the northwestern perimeter of Kharkov. Arrows marking the thrust of Soviet armor west of the city with slashes of red slice between the two divisions and also show Soviet cavalry south of Kharkov. It is clearly evident how perilous the situation was for the German troops defending the city on 13-14 February.

The situation reached a climax on the following morning when orders and counter orders were issued and Hitler and his generals wrangled over the proper course of action. In the midst of this crisis, Paul Hausser made a fateful decision regarding his former division and the SS-Panzer-Korps as a whole.

Hausser's Order to Abandon Kharkov

The day began with the German commanders conferring with each other regarding the proper course of action. At 0800 hours, Lanz flew to Merefa, where the headquarters of the SS-Panzer-Korps was located, in order to personally speak with Hausser concerning Hitler's directives and the situation in general. After conferring with the SS commander he sent a radio message to Heeresgruppe Süd describing the critical nature of the situation. Lanz made it clear that there was no hope that the gap to the west could be closed as it was too wide and only fresh divisions could hope to fill it. The sole new division was "Totenkopf" and only the lead elements of the division's Regiment "Thule" were actually on hand on 14 February. The rest of "Totenkopf" was still on trains or just beginning to unload at various railheads many kilometers west of Kharkov.[57]

To make matter worse, Krasnograd and its vital railroad line was endangered by the advance of the Soviet 6th Army. Forward units of the Army's 106th Rifle Brigade had already been seen along roads east of the town. It was absolutely critical that the rail line be kept open if Armeeabteilung Lanz was to survive, because it was the last rail road still running into Kharkov. Korps Raus reported that it could no longer protect the northwest perimeter of Kharkov and that by nightfall Soviet troops could be expected to enter the city.

Manstein replied to the information received from these messages with several directives. First, SS "Totenkopf" was ordered to assemble near Valki, which was about 40 kilometers west of Kharkov. From there the division was to be used to strike at the Soviet forces west of the town or attack southward in defense of Krasnograd. Secondly, Manstein approved the relocation of the HQs of Armeeabteilung Lanz, from Kharkov to Poltava, obviously real-

izing at that point, that the city was seriously endangered. Third, he ordered the SS-Panzer-Korps to stop sending direct communications to higher SS command structures, by passing the normal channels of the army. He apparently believed that SS communications sent directly to the SS Führungshauptamt or main headquarters, were responsible for Hitler's belief that the city could still be held. As adhering to these Führerbefehle might cost him his only strong Panzer reserve, Manstein issued instructions that the SS-Panzer-Korps was to cease transmitting reports directly to the SS Führungshauptamt.

It would appear that Manstein was almost surely mistaken in his belief that Hausser would have ever told Hitler that the city could still be held. It would be interesting to know if Himmler, who was anxious for his newly built up SS-Panzer-Korps to cover itself with glory, had any role in encouraging Hitler to order the SS troops fight to the death in Kharkov. However, no record exists of any influence he might have had on Hitler in this regard. It can logically be assumed that Hausser would not have encouraged decisions that would have resulted in the destruction of his corps, particularly in light of his subsequent decisions.

By the afternoon of 14 February, Hausser no longer believed that he could still hold the city. At 1530 hours he had received a message from the commander of "Das Reich," Herbert Vahl, reporting that the division's last reserves had been committed and the defensive front could no longer be held. Vahl stated that if the order to withdraw was not received by that evening, the division could not be saved. Hausser informed Lanz that if the division was not allowed to withdraw by nightfall, the Panzergrenadier Regiments defending the eastern perimeter would be lost. Hausser radioed Armeeabteilung Lanz, requesting that a decision to withdraw be made by 1630 hours. He also reported that riots and civil disturbances had broken out in the city itself and that Soviet civilians were firing upon German troops in the city. Hausser then stated that if a decision to withdraw was not issued by the Armeeabteilung at 1630 hours, then he would give it himself. Kinzel replied at 1620 hours, reminding Hausser of Manstein's earlier directives which reaffirmed the directive from Hitler, stating that the city was to be held regardless of the circumstances. He also reminded Hausser that if the eastern perimeter was given up and the two hard pressed SS regiments withdrew, it would leave "Grossdeutschland's" flank hanging in the air (in der Luft) and that if he gave the order to withdraw, he (Hausser) must accept the consequences. This was not strictly correct as "Grossdeutschland" had already been pushed back along its entire front.[58]

---

[56] *Befehl des Gewissens*, pg. 92.
[57] *Befehl des Gewissens*, pg. 94.

[58] Ibid. pg. 96 and NA/T-354, roll 120, 1a KTB, Darstellung der Ereignisse, 14.2.1943. frame 3753593.

In reality, "Grossdeutschland" could not have halted the Russians regardless of what positions were held by Regiment "Deutschland." Considering the penetrations in strength already existing between "Grossdeutschland" and the SS troops the flank security of "Grossdeutschland" was probably a moot point by that time. At 1645 hours, SS-Panzer-Korps records document that Hausser notified Armeeabteilung Lanz that he had given "Das Reich" the order to withdraw from the eastern approaches of Kharkov and that he had notified Korps Raus of his order. He intended to begin a retreat toward the city on the night of 14-15 February and establish new positions behind the Udy River, southwest of Kharkov.[59]

Forty minutes later, Headquarters Armeeabteilung Lanz replied to Hausser's communication. At 1725 hours, the Armeeabteilung reiterated Hitler's order to hold the city to the last man. Armeeabteilung Lanz records state that at 1800 hours, Lanz then personally called Hausser at SS-Panzer-Korps HQ by telephone and repeated the order from Hitler to hold the city to the last man. Lanz discussed Hausser's decision to evacuate the city and as it was contrary to Hitler's order to hold Kharkov, he quite properly asked Hausser to rescind the order. Hausser replied that once such an order was given and troops began to abandon positions, it was difficult to cancel. The SS-Panzer-Korps records acknowledge the reception of the Gegenbefehl (counter order) at 1810 hours. The SS-Panzer-Korps records state that at 1815 hours Hausser radioed an order to "Das Reich" stating that the city was to be held to the last man.[60]

This was an hour and a half after Hausser had transmitted his first order for the pullback to begin. By that time, it can be assumed that both men knew that it was already too late to easily or safely cancel the withdrawal. After receiving Hausser's directive to remain in position, "Das Reich" reported that its withdrawing units were no longer in radio contact with the division HQ and thus could not be notified that the previous order was canceled. At 2200 hours, "Das Reich" reported that disengagement was in progress and that it could only be stopped with great difficulty. Of course, it proved too late to stop "Das Reich" from abandoning its exposed defensive positions east of Kharkov.[61]

Lanz' clearly stated transmission of Hitler's orders to Hausser could have been intended to provide evidence that Armeeabteilung Lanz and its commander had done their duty to the Führer. Lanz

The commander of Regiment "Deutschland," Heinz Harmel is the officer on the right of this picture. The man standing on the left is SS-Sturmbannführer Hans Bissinger, the commander of II./Regiment "Deutschland." (Courtesy of Mark C. Yerger)

was providing a documented record of his own actions while Hausser chose to suffer the consequences of acting contrary to a direct order from Hitler, regardless of how militarily correct that act might have been. Of course, it can be assumed that Lanz knew he would ultimately be held responsible for the actions of his officers. It can be speculated that Lanz intentionally delayed countermanding the order because he knew that withdrawal was the militarily correct decision and that once begun, a pull back conducted under close contact with an aggressive enemy could not be stopped without undue danger to the withdrawing force. This might explain Lanz' delay in responding to Hausser's 1630 hour deadline and suggests that Lanz may have tacitly agreed with Hausser's action and allowed events to take their course. If that were so, it can be speculated that during Lanz's visit to Hausser the generals worked out their strategy to save the army but of course no documentation exists to even suggest that this was so. However, such a scenario could perhaps explain why Lanz waited for such a long time before dutifully reminding the SS commander of Hitler's order.

Hausser gave the order to withdraw and it was carried out. He assumed the responsibility and the possible consequences, taking all of the blame squarely on his own shoulders. This was a decision that carried more than a hint of personal danger, in addition to potentially ending his career. Hitler was not one to suffer such incidents quietly. Once the withdrawal had been irrevocably begun, Hausser returned to the fold and at 2130 hours, the SS-Panzer-Korps assured the army that its objective on 15 February was to hold Kharkov to the last man, according to the Führer's order. Of course, by that time, the exposed positions of "Das Reich" had been abandoned and the Panzergrenadiers were pulled back.

[59] Op cit. The order stated. 'Ich habe am 14.2.1943 16.45 Urh den Befehl zur Räumung von Charkow und zum Ausweichen hinter den Udy Abschnitt in der Nacht vom 14./15.2 gleichzeitig an Korps Raus gegeben. Beurteilung der Lage folgt schriftlich.'
[60] NA/T-354, roll 120, 1a KTB, Darstellung der Ereignisse, frame 3753595.
[61] Op cit.

Lanz continued to formulate plans for the defense of the city in accordance with Hitler's orders. He instructed Dietrich to assemble one Panzer battalion, Peiper's SPW battalion and a battalion of motorcycle troops for an attack toward Valki, along the Kharkov-Poltava rail line and road. After clearing the Russians from the key supply line immediately west of the city, Gruppe Dietrich was to reassemble at Valki and join "Totenkopf" units there, in preparation for further action. This order was given in response to the presence of Soviet forces in unknown strength in the Ljubotin – Olschany area and the threat they posed to the communications lines of Korps Raus and SS-Panzer-Korps.

Lanz also wanted 320. Infanterie-Division to attack Soviet forces southeast of Kharkov and relieve the pressure on the SS defensive positions east of Kharkov but Hausser knew better than to count on any help from that division so soon after its ordeal. In any event, he told Lanz that major elements of the division were still near Zmiev and the desired attack by the division was not possible. Lanz replied that it could be immediately made available to the SS-Panzer-Korps but Hausser knew from first hand reports that the army division was not yet ready to conduct offensive operations and had little mobile striking power. Hausser told Lanz that the surviving horses of the division were too weak to be able to transport the remaining divisional artillery and the division was not in any condition to conduct an effective attack. The conversation ended without any further recorded remarks by either officer.[62]

While "Das Reich" pulled back toward Kharkov, "Leibstandarte's" two Panzergrenadier regiments continued their defense of the southern and eastern perimeters of the city. The Soviet 62nd Guards Rifle Division, supported by a fresh tank formation, the 179th Tank Brigade, broke through German defenses north of Kampfgruppe Weidenhaupt. The Soviet thrust drove to the west and approached the town of Ossnova, threatening the rear of Kampfgruppe Weidenhaupt.[63] This advance represented a critical threat not only to the "Leibstandarte" defenses west of Rogan but also to both "Grossdeutschland" and Regiment "Deutschland." The attack laid the foundation for a further Soviet armored attack penetrating into the center of the city. Ossnovo was only five kilometers from the southeastern outskirts of Kharkov and a Soviet thrust beyond that point and continuing into Kharkov could have blocked the divisions from withdrawing through the city. Regimental commander Wisch quickly gathered a few Panzergrenadiers and a Sturmgeschütze battery and assaulted the flank of the 179th Tank

Brigade. The fierce attack cut through the Soviet line of advance and temporarily halted the Russian attack as the brigade regrouped to meet this threat. However Wisch's Kampfgruppe lacked the strength to eliminate the penetration and even though the Soviets were temporarily forced to go over to the defensive, new forces were brought up by the 3rd Tank Army and thrown into the fight. Wisch was forced to retreat by the appearance of Russian tanks and infantry on his eastern flank. Covered by the assault guns, the SS Panzergrenadiers pulled back and the Russians regrouped for the next assault.

Simultaneously, the Russians renewed their pressure upon the SS troops south of Rogan, where the 12th Tank Corps again tried to break through the defenses of Kampfgruppe Linden in the Lisogubovka area. T-34s and infantry attacked SS lines east of Lisogubovka at 1650 hours whereupon SS anti-tank gunners hit and damaged four of the Soviet tanks, forcing them to withdraw from the fighting. The Russian infantry attack collapsed without the support of the tanks and was not immediately repeated. At the same time, on the extreme southern flank of the German defenses east of Kharkov, infantry of the 111th Rifle Division assaulted SS positions in the Konstantinovka-Bahnhof Sidki area. This attack was turned back also and a Soviet heavy tank, a KV-1 was destroyed.

The drive toward the city's center by the 179th Tank Brigade, supported by the 62nd Guards Rifle Division and the threat of encirclement west of Kharkov were fatal blows to the German defenses. Without any reserves to meet these threats, Hausser had no choice but to withdraw "Das Reich" from the eastern section of the city, in order to avoid the destruction of the division. During late afternoon and into the evening hours of 14 February, the Soviets brought up additional fresh troops and armor and threw them against the Germans at Ossnovo. "Leibstandarte" reported to SS-Panzer-Korps HQs that it was not able to clean up the penetration at Ossnovo with the forces at hand. Peiper's battalion, with reinforcement by a Sturmgeschütze battery, was ordered to counterattack the Soviet force after assembling under cover of darkness.

Further to the south, remnants of the 6th Guards Cavalry Corps continued to filter out of the area and back into the lines of the 111th Rifle Division although a large number of the cavalrymen remained surrounded at Ochotschaje. The German attempts to eliminate this force on 14 February met with little success. The Russian cavalrymen, although encircled, continued to fight fiercely and inflicted considerable casualties and vehicle losses upon the SS troops.

[62] *Befehl des Gewissens*, pg. 100.
[63] According to Sharp (*Soviet Order of Battle - World War 2: School of Battle*, pg. 79), the 179th Tank Brigade was an independent unit, made up of two tank battalions and one motorized rifle battalion. It was assigned to the 3rd Tank Army as an infantry support unit.

Gruppe Dietrich in Action Against the 6th Guards Cavalry Corps

On the night of 14 February, while Hausser and Lanz wrestled with the burden of command and responsibility, Kumm's Regiment "Der Führer," with III./"Der Führer" leading the attack, assaulted Ochotschaje from assembly areas in a wooded area north of the town. The II./Regiment "Der Führer," under Stadler, was held in reserve. Kumm's attack was supported by a battery of artillery and a company of "Leibstandarte" Panzers. Three companies of the SS Grenadiers assaulted the town under cover of fire from the German tanks and mobile artillery. They were met by accurate fire from Russian infantry, anti-tank guns and dug-in tanks.

The Russians skillfully concealed their anti-tank guns and the tanks of 201st Tank Brigade, some of which were camouflaged in stacks of hay. Other Russian tanks were hidden in the ruins of buildings and were extremely hard to see. The Russian defenders held their fire until the German soldiers nearly reached the outskirts of Ochotschaje and then unleashed a storm of close range machine gun, mortar and anti-tank gun fire. Caught in the open, many of the advancing SS Grenadiers were killed or wounded in short order. The survivors threw themselves into shallow depressions and small ravines and the attack came to a halt.

The 9./Kompanie of Regiment "Der Führer" was particularly hard hit, suffering the loss of several officers and became pinned down by the heavy Soviet fire. Unable to advance or retreat, leading elements of the battalion took cover in houses along the northern edge of the town while the SS Grenadiers to the rear fell back through a hail of artillery and mortar fire. The attack came to a complete halt after the commander of III./"Der Führer," SS-Sturmbannführer Fritz Horn, was wounded and two company commanders were also lost.

Kumm, upon receiving the report that Horn was out of action, sent the regimental adjutant, SS-Hauptsturmführer Friedrich Holzer to take over command. Kumm then ordered II./"Der Führer," led by SS-Sturmbannführer Sylvester Stadler, to attack from the west simultaneously with the resumption of the attack led by Holzer. After hours of hard fighting, the two battalions were able to take the town. Most of the Russian armor and cavalry escaped, however and it is likely that they withdrew only because they were threatened with encirclement by SS-Kradschützen-Bataillon 2 and Meyer's column from the south, as well as Witt's thrust to the southeast of the town.[64]

Late in the day, Fick's battalion of motorcycle troops had cleaned the Russians out of the towns of Paraskoveja and Melchovka

which lay just to the west of Ochotschaje. From there, the battalion motored eastwards along the Paraskoveja-Alexejevka road and linked up with elements of Kurt Meyers Aufklärungsabteilung "LAH" at Jefremovka. Meanwhile, Meyer's main detachment, having left troops in Jefremovka, advanced to the east of Ochotschaje. After reaching the village of Alexejevka, Meyer was forced to stop due to a shortage of fuel and ammunition, taking up positions in the town.

At that point the Russian troops in Ochotschaje, consisting mainly of the 11th Cavalry Division, were nearly encircled. Witt's attack upon Bereka threatened to close off the division's route of withdrawal directly to the east although the 201st Tank Brigade still held a narrow corridor between Bereka and Jefremovka. When Meyer's Aufklärungsabteilung pushed into the Jefremovka area, the corridor between the two villages was constricted to a width of about 5 kilometers. In order to cover the retreat of the 11th Cavalry Division, Bereka had to be held and the Russians reinforced the 201st Tank Brigade with additional infantry and heavy weapons. Rybalko also launched an attack on Meyer's battalion with strong detachments of Soviet infantry, probably from either the 184th Rifle Division or the 111th Rifle Division. This attack was designed to hold open the corridor and allow the 6th Cavalry Corps elements in the Ochotschaje and Bereka areas to pull back to safety.

The Russian attacks, combined with lack of fuel, forced Meyer to remain on the defensive and he could not close the encirclement around the Soviet cavalry withdrawing from Ochotschaje. In the midst of a blinding snowstorm Meyer organized the battalion into an all round defensive perimeter and awaited further Russian attacks which were not long in coming. A penetration into the town could not be prevented but a counterattack of the battalion's SPWs threw the Russians out. SS armored cars and half tracks, spitting 2cm explosive shells and a hail of machine gun fire, chased Russian infantry down the narrow, smoke filled streets while buildings burned around them. Although many Russian troops were killed or wounded in the bitter, close quarter fighting, the SS troops suffered losses as well, including SS-Hauptsturmführer Gustav Knittel, who was wounded and put out of action.

Meyer's hard pressed battalion could not defend the entire perimeter of the elongated village and Russian infantry continued to infiltrate into Alexejevka, taking shelter in its houses and buildings. During pauses in the fighting, far in the distance, both west and east of Alexejevka, the SS troops could see long columns of Russian infantry marching to the west. These were probably columns belonging to either the Soviet 184th Rifle Division or the 111th Rifle Division. Lacking the fuel to move and carry out the final phase of the encirclement, the situation rapidly became even

---

[64] Weidinger, pg. 79.

more critical when Meyer's battalion began to run low on ammunition. Meyer urgently requested resupply by air but the SS-Panzer-Korps replied that it could not be done at that time.

In order to get the attack of the reconnaissance battalion moving again, a combat group was organized, consisting of three Panzer IIIs and three Panzer IVs which were supported by a dozen half tracks of SS Panzergrenadiers. The Kampfgruppe was led personally by Max Wünsche, commander of I./Panzer-Regiment "LAH." The tanks and half tracks were piled high with all the fuel and ammunition that was available. This made each half track a potential firebomb, which could not have made the Grenadiers in each vehicle very happy. The fuel had to be delivered however and Wünsche's small Kampfgruppe set out to rescue Meyer's battalion.

About two kilometers from Alexejevka the column came under light mortar fire and Russian troops were observed in the distance, but Wünsche did not allow this distraction to delay his mission. The column rolled on and soon entered the town where it was joyously greeted by the reconnaissance troopers. Meyer embraced Wünsche in gratitude for successfully delivering the precious cargo. Having just observed Russian infantry gathering for an attack in a nearby balka, Meyer immediately proposed to launch a preemptive attack on the assembly area. Striking out quickly from the town, Meyer's SPWs seemingly appeared out of nowhere and overran the Russian assembly position. The German half tracks and armored cars, firing machine guns and 3.7cm guns, ran straight through the Russian troops, who scattered in all directions. From their overwatch positions, the tanks secured the attack from flank attacks and gunned down the Russians when they floundered helplessly over the open, snow covered steppe. The attackers suffering only light losses in wounded while many dead and dying Russians lay like dark blotches in the snow, scattered throughout the assembly area.[65]

Unfortunately for Meyer and his men, the attack expended much of the ammunition and fuel that had been provided by the rescue column and it was necessary to have additional supplies dropped from a Heinkel 111 on the following morning. This was not entirely successful and many of the supply canisters ruptured, spilling fuel and ammunition over the snow. The SS reconnaissance troops drained fuel from the gas tanks of a number of their armored cars and half tracks to provide enough fuel for several assault guns. Meyer decided to conduct a company sized thrust toward Bereka in order to link up with Witt's regiment.[66]

Under cover of mortar fire, the assault company, personally led by Meyer, flew down the road at maximum speed in order to hit the Russians before they could react. With assault guns firing shell after shell, the company broke through the Russian detachment defending the road and fought to the southern edge of Bereka. Witt's battalion had been ordered to close the ring around the Russian cavalry encircled in Ochotschaje by taking Bereka. But hampered by chest deep snow drifts and determined Russian resistance Witt's troops could not take the town. Unable to make contact with the main body of Kampfgruppe Witt, Meyer had to pull back to Alexejevka. In order to complete the encirclement before the Soviet cavalry was able to escape, Dietrich moved SS-Pioniere-Bataillon 1 from Taranovka and ordered it to reinforce Kampfgruppe Witt at Bereka.

Since the SS pincers were unable to close around the Russian troops in Ochotschaje, major elements of the 11th Cavalry Division escaped the impending encirclement. The Soviet cavalry withdrew from Ochotschaje, despite the pressure from Regiment "Der Führer" and escaped without being pursued during the night of 14-15 February. This signified the end of the Soviet attempt to complete the encirclement of German forces in Kharkov from the south. Although the Russian troops were able to escape Ochotschaje and most of the corps eventually reached safety south of Kharkov, the 6th Guards Cavalry Corps thrust to complete the encirclement of Kharkov was over.

The Effects of the Attack of the 6th Cavalry Corps

Although the 3rd Tank Army's cavalry attack was unsuccessful in linking up with the 40th Army west of Kharkov, it served to attract almost all of the mobile reserves of Hausser's SS-Panzer-Korps at a critical time. Although the German counterattack forced the withdrawal of the Russian cavalry corps, it was a hard won victory. Even though the SS counterattack inflicted significant casualties on the Soviets, the 201st Tank Brigade and the tough Soviet cavalry troops had bloodied an SS tank battalion and severely battered Regiment "Der Führer." In addition, the Russians then conducted a skillful retreat eastward, saving most of the tanks of the 201st Tank Brigade, which escaped and reached Russian lines. The Germans estimated that the Russians had about 25 tanks in Ochotschaje, which was probably a realistic number. Afterwards, only a few were found abandoned in the town, having been knocked out by Regiment "Der Führer." Thus it can be logically assumed that about 15 to 20 Russian tanks were able to escape destruction in the town. The Russian cavalry had not panicked when their communication lines were cut, and instead conducted an orderly, difficult withdrawal, which occupied major elements of SS-Panzer-Korps for several days.

In addition to the absence of most of the SS armor and mobile units from the front east of Kharkov, the commitment of Regiment "Der Führer" removed substantial infantry strength from the pe-

---

[65] Lehmann, pg. 95.
[66] Lehmann, pg. 95.

rimeter as well. If the two SS divisions had been able to commit all their strength to the eastern defensive front, without having to deal with the cavalry corps south of the city, the Russians obviously would have had a more difficult time breaking through from that direction. As the battle developed, two reinforced regiments, Regiment "Deutschland" and SS-Pz.Gren.-Rgt. 2 "LAH" were opposed by two entire Soviet armies. Of course, Lanz had little choice but to react to the penetration in the south, because the 6th Guards Cavalry had already cut the important Losovaya-Kharkov rail line and was approaching the area west of Kharkov. If the Russian cavalrymen had been allowed to reach Ljubotin, and establish contact with the 5th Guards Tank Corps, the city would have been completely encircled, possibly as early as 10-11 February.

The German Dilemma

The problem for the Germans was that they had insufficient forces to defend the city, a situation that had been obvious to Lanz and Hausser from the start. There had been other distractions and problems as well. The tortured withdrawal of Postel's 320. Infanterie-Division occupied the army for many days, as well as requiring a rescue effort. However, 168. Infanterie-Division's rapid retreat to escape the Soviet 40th Army's advance did much more damage to the coherence of the German defense of Kharkov. Throughout the withdrawal of 320. Infanterie-Division, Postel's troops remained full of fight and actually tied up significant numbers of Soviet troops. In contrast, after fighting for several days, 168. Infanterie-Division collapsed and withdrew as quickly as possible toward the Vorskla River Valley. Instead of conducting a delaying action while withdrawing into Kharkov, 168. Infanterie-Division allowed itself to be pushed west, exposing "Grossdeutschland's" west flank. As a result, the Lopan and Udy River valleys were essentially undefended and open to exploitation by the 40th Army.

The Russian command quickly discovered these routes of advance towards Kharkov and pushed the 5th Tank Corps into the valleys, which were like twin daggers aimed at the northwest quadrant of the city. "Grossdeutschland" was forced to throw out screening detachments farther and farther to the west, in attempts to block the Russian advance through the river valleys. This weakened the division's already overextended perimeter northeast of Kharkov and fatally stretched the defense of the northern flank of the Regiment "Deutschland" salient. The elite, hard fighting Army division, like the two SS divisions found itself with inadequate mobile reserves with which to counter the 40th Army's spearheads. The fighting gradually wore down the division and by 14 February, many of the Grenadier and Füsilier companies were reduced to a strength of only 20-30 men.[67]

The defenses of the city continued to deteriorate during the night of 14-15 February. The next day brought fresh setbacks and continued Soviet pressure from the east, southeast and north. West of the city, the 5th Guards Tank Corps remained astride the Ljubotin-Kharkov road. A narrow rail corridor from the southwest corner of Kharkov was the sole remaining line of communication and supply into the city. There was little that Lanz or Hausser could do about the situation, as the Russians had the initiative and the reserves necessary to continue to hold it. The Germans had no chance of holding the city with the forces available to them, regardless of Hitler's orders. This situation was a microcosm of the fighting on the Eastern Front in which German forces were stretched too thinly to successfully defend the territory that it had occupied. Whether militarily correct or not, due to the orders of Hitler, often German armies were ordered to remain rooted in place, defending their ground until their destruction. As we have seen, the lack of mobility of German infantry divisions made alternative courses of actions risky, a fact which is often ignored by historians anxious to always criticize Hitler's directives to hold ground at all costs. There is no question that the orders cost the Germans many thousands of casualties during the fighting in Russia. However, the alternative, which was often the conduct of a withdrawal during winter, carrying an ever increasing number of wounded with ever decreasing numbers of vehicles, is hardly appealing. This was the German dilemma which existed after the first year of the war in Russia failed to produce a victory for Hitler's armies. As often as not, the German divisions were destroyed or nearly useless after escaping from Russian encirclement. Fortunately for the Germans, the SS divisions avoided this fate. On 14 February, Paul Hausser made the decision to pull back to the Udy River and thereby saved the SS-Panzer-Korps, as well as "Grossdeutschland" and 320. Infanterie-Division. As a result, Manstein was provided with the divisions that enabled him to plan a counterattack only a short time after Kharkov fell.

Manstein's counter stroke provided Hitler with a major victory on the Eastern Front, temporarily reversing the tide of the war. The divisions that provided the main impetus to this counter stroke were the SS divisions of Hausser's SS-Panzer-Korps. If Hausser had not had the courage to oppose Hitler's directive to hold Kharkov to the last man, Hoth's 4. Panzerarmee could not have conducted the counteroffensive envisioned by Manstein. The handful of Army Panzer divisions available to Hoth had all been involved in heavy fighting for months and were far below full strength. None had more than 20 to 25 tanks and their Panzergrenadier companies often had less than 50 men each. Although the costly fighting for

---

[67] *Befehl des Gewissens*, pg.100.

Kharkov had inflicted severe losses on the SS divisions as well, they remained much stronger than any of the emaciated Army divisions.

"Leibstandarte" was in much better shape, while "Das Reich's" heavier casualties reflected the losses incurred during the fighting in the Belyi Kolodes-Velikyj Burluk salient as well as the costly withdrawal operations. By 13 February, "Leibstandarte" reported that its battalions had an average battle strength of 750 men, a total that was certainly above that of the Army infantry divisions or "Grossdeutschland." The Panzer regiment had fifty-three Panzer IIIs and Panzer IVs, in addition to twenty-one Sturmgeschütze. The division still had most of its artillery.

On the same date, "Das Reich" reported that it had only twenty-one German tanks left, a total that included only one Panzer IV. However, the division utilized a number of operational Russian tanks which had been captured during the fighting. One KV-1 and 5 T-34s were captured and manned by SS crews, in order to supplement the tank strength of the division. There were eighteen operational Sturmgeschütze IIIs and the division had been able to retain most of its artillery. The motorcycle, reconnaissance and combat engineer battalions had suffered extensive casualties due to their constant use. Fick's Kradschützen Bataillon had only 290 combat effectives and the Aufklärungsabteilung was reduced to a strength of 450 men. The division's Pioniere-Bataillon was in a little better condition, listing a total of 550 men.[68]

"Totenkopf" remained essentially at full strength, as it had not yet been actively involved in the fighting for Kharkov and it arrived too late to prevent the fall of the city. The conduct of the defense of the entire southern sector of the Eastern Front hung in the balance on 15 February, 1943, as Hitler, intending to take matters into his own hands, prepared to make one of his infrequent trips to the front. As he did so, he surely would have been surprised to know that at one point in the coming days, only a few kilometers of undefended steppe would lay between him, the supreme commander of Germany and a spearhead detachment of T-34 tanks.

---

[68] NA/T-354, roll 118. 1a KTB, Nr. 208/43. Combat report by General-kommando SS-Panzer-Korps to Armeeabteilung Lanz on 13.2.1943.

6

THE CITY IS LOST

The SS-Panzer-Korps Withdraws from Kharkov

An atmosphere of tension continued at the headquarters of Armeeabteilung Lanz and Heeresgruppe Süd, early on 15 February. At 0240 hours, Manstein radioed Lanz and reminded him of Hitler's order to hold Kharkov under all circumstances. Evidently, at that point, Manstein considered that the orders given to Armeeabteilung Lanz previous to its coming under the command of Heeresgruppe Süd, were binding upon him. However, he also stated that the conduct of the battle should be characterized by mobility and that encirclement was to be avoided. It seems clear that Manstein believed the city was to be held if at all possible, but he took into account the possibility of rapidly changing circumstances that might alter the situation. His directive to avoid encirclement and destruction was militarily justified, if for no other reason than to preserve the strength of the SS divisions, the only armored force available to him that was capable of carrying out the planned counteroffensive.[1] The order to avoid encirclement was consistent with German military doctrine, which placed considerable reliance on commanders making correct decisions according to their estimation of the situation on the spot. It also essentially provided justification for Hausser's decision to pull back and give up the eastern perimeter in order to avoid encirclement.

Early in the morning, the SS-Panzer-Korps reported that its eastern front remained under heavy Soviet pressure at all points. During the night, the Russians had brought up additional infantry and armor at Ossnovo, in order to reinforce their breakthroughs. In the early morning, infantry of the 62nd Guards Rifle Division pushed German troops out of their positions on both sides of the road leading into Kharkov. At 0415 hours, Russian infantry, with many tanks in support, resumed their assault on the SS positions north and west of Rogan. To the north, the 69th Army continued determined assaults upon "Das Reich" and "Grossdeutschland" positions. Throughout the night and early morning hours, the 69th Army's 270th, 161st and 219th Rifle Divisions stormed forward through a deadly hail of machine gun and mortar fire. Casualties were heavy, but the resolute Russian infantry continued to push forward and forced the exhausted Grenadiers to give ground. In "Grossdeutschland's" sector, Korps Raus reported several breakthroughs in battalion strength, in the northwest quadrant of the city. The fighting cost "Grossdeutschland" further losses in men and equipment. Soviet combat groups, belonging to the 40th Army's 183rd Rifle Division, supported by the 5th Guards Tank Corps, pushed into the western edge of the city.

At 1100 hours, Lanz sent a teletype message to Manstein regarding the situation. He described the heavy pressure the Russians were exerting on his exhausted men and the additional casualties. He emphasized his lack of reserves and the shortage of armor, in contrast to the Russians who were pouring tanks and infantry into attacks upon the city from three directions. Lanz clearly stated that

---

[1] *Befehl des Gewissens*, pg. 103. In full the transcript states, 02.40 Uhr <u>teilt H.Gr. Süd durch Funkspruch mit</u>, daß auf die heutige Anfrage Generalfeldmarschall v. Manstein der Führer entschieden habe, daß Charkow unter allen Umstanden zu halten ist, die Kampfführung im Gebiet von Charkow aber so beweglich zu gestalten ist, daß eine Einschließung von Charkow vermieden wird.

if the present lines were held, Manstein could expect heavy losses in men and equipment, with no guarantee the city could be held even given the further sacrifices of the troops. Lanz recommended that the defensive front should be abandoned and the battered divisions withdrawn from defense of the city and pulled back to the southwest. In closing, he urgently requested a prompt decision from Manstein.[2]

Shortly afterwards, Lanz received a telephone call from General der Infanterie Kurt Zeitzler, Chief of Staff OKH. After listening to Lanz, he inquired how many troops could be pulled from the south and used to reinforce the city's defenses. Lanz's reply was that no more than a regiment could be spared, a force that was inadequate to significantly affect the situation. He clearly stated that "Das Reich" would be encircled and destroyed if the division was not allowed to continue to pull back. Then Zeitzler asked Lanz if it was still possible, at that time, for the SS division to withdraw quickly enough to escape the Russian pressure. Lanz, perhaps feeling that Zeitzler was fishing for a justification to leave the SS division where it was, strongly insisted that "Das Reich" must be withdrawn in order to prevent its destruction. In closing, Zeitzler promised that an answer would be forthcoming shortly. Heeresgruppe Süd transmitted Hitler's reply just after noon, stating that the order to hold the city to the last man remained in effect.[3]

At 0750 hours, Korps Raus sent a pessimistic radio transmission to Lanz, reporting several major Russian penetrations. However, according to Hitler's affirmation of his previous order to hold the city to the last man, Lanz responded that the eastern perimeter of the city was to be held, regardless of the situation. It was decided that "Totenkopf" formations were to be fed into the battle as available, even though it was clear to Lanz and Hausser that the arrival of the division would not alter the essential facts of the situation at that late hour. One division could not be expected to change the basic German shortcoming, which was lack of sufficient forces to defend the city against three Soviet armies.

It was not even certain whether all of "Totenkopf" would arrive before the city fell, in any event. The plight of the German command was further complicated by the approach of Russian troops east of Krasnograd. That town could not be allowed to fall into Soviet hands, because it was the railhead and assembly area that the SS-Panzer-Korps was to use for launching its counterattack. At that time, the only troops available to defend Krasnograd belonged to "Totenkopf." Since Krasnograd had to be held and the Eicke was also to send troops to Kharkov, the division faced the prospect of being split up into fragments, a course of action that had already

The bodies of German troops in the street of a Russian village. On February 15, 1943 supply and security troops of Regiment "Harmel" were attacked by Russian infantry at Taranovka. Most of the troops were shot down and their bodies were still in the street when the regiment recaptured the village. (Credit National Archives)

resulted in heavy losses for "Das Reich" and "Leibstandarte." Although Hitler had specified that the SS divisions were not to be committed piecemeal, he had also ordered that Kharkov be held to the last man. Once again, Lanz and Hausser were faced with either disobeying a direct order from Hitler or watching the probable destruction of their commands.

Hausser's course of action remained as clear to him as it had been the day before. He was already close to the front, having gone to the HQ of Regiment "Deutschland," in order to see the fighting for himself. What he saw only confirmed his estimation of the situa-

OPPOSITE: The positions of "Grossdeutschland" and the SS divisions on 15 February, 1943, after Kharkov was abandoned. The operations of Kampfgruppe Dietrich against the 6th Guards Cavalry Corps are shown at bottom of map, in the Bereka-Alexejevka area. Note the gaps to the south and north of the city, which were undefended by German troops.

---

[2] Op cit.
[3] *Befehl des Gewissens*, pg. 108.

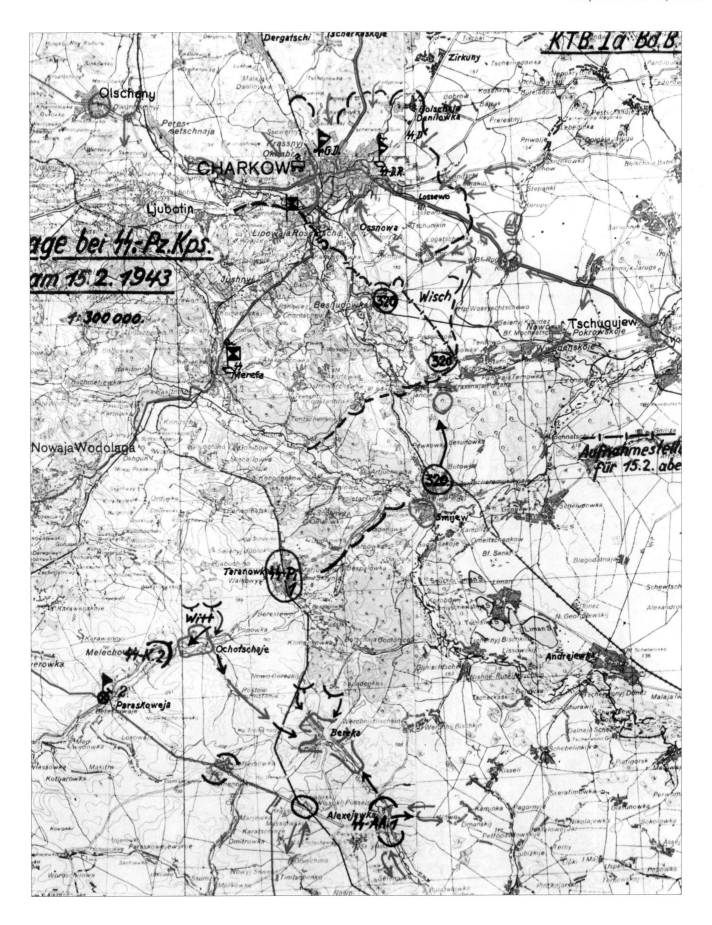

ation and at 1300 hours he radioed Ostendorff and told him to issue the order for the SS-Panzer-Korps to completely withdraw from Kharkov and fight its way out of the city. Ostendorff expressed his surprise and reminded his superior officer of Hitler's order, but Hausser did not want to be a part of another Stalingrad. Knowing full well the possible consequences of his actions, Hausser issued the orders that saved his former division and the SS-Panzer-Korps from destruction for the second time in as many days. At 1305, Hausser informed Armeeabteilung Lanz that he had just given the order for the SS-Panzer-Korps to withdraw and that Korps Raus had been made aware of this decision as well. He later notified the Armeeabteilung that his intention was to cross the Msha River and establish a new defensive line west of Merefa. By that time, Lanz was airborne, flying in his Fieseler Storch toward Kharkov, having decided to speak with Raus and Hausser personally.

In the meantime, Armeeabteilung Lanz reported this development to Manstein at Heeresgruppe Süd headquarters. Manstein requested Lanz's opinion as to whether the steps taken by Hausser could be approved or at least justified, since due to the situation, it was no longer possible to carry out Hitler's order to hold the city. He also asked if Hausser should offer to resign his command. Armeeabteilung Headquarters replied that after Lanz returned from his flight into Kharkov, he would make his decision on the basis of his visits to the two corps headquarters. Meanwhile, the fighting continued to rage in Kharkov and the situation steadily deteriorated for the Germans. The SS-Panzer-Korps again reported that civilians had taken up arms and that the population of the city was in revolt. Germans soldiers were being shot at behind the front lines and sabotage was reported in many areas. At 1332 hours, Korps Raus reported that in the opinion of the corps it was no longer possible to hold Kharkov and that the corps HQs was already moving to Merefa, south of the city.

In the Regiment "Deutschland" sector, Hausser conferred with Heinz Harmel and personally gave him the order to withdraw and fight back through Kharkov to the southwest. Harmel gathered the battalion and company commanders at his HQ and gave them their instructions. Conducting an orderly withdrawal was not an easy task, because since early in the day, the regiment had been under heavy frontal attack at one location or another. A number of subsequent Soviet penetrations could not be eliminated before the Soviets launched attacks from these bridgeheads. Heinz Macher's 16. "Deutschland," now reduced to just thirty-three men and three non-commissioned officers, was attacked three times by massed Russian infantry during the day. Each time, the SS Pioniere threw the Russians back, laying down heavy machine gun and mortar fire. Soviet dead covered the ground in front of the company and the

Pioniere held their positions. However, in other sectors of the front, the Russians made deep penetrations that couldn't be cleaned up.[4]

At 1500 hours, Harmel issued the order to his regiment to begin its withdrawal. Two hours later, the tired men of Regiment "Deutschland" climbed aboard whatever vehicles were available and pulled back into the burning city. Strings of Soviet rockets impacted all around the column, the rockets striking one after the other in a series of explosions. In the darkness ahead, thunderous blasts rocked Kharkov as German engineers destroyed bridges and military installations with explosive charges. Along the way, the SS troops helped themselves to rations, grabbing cases of cigarettes, candied hams, champagne and other supplies from massive supply warehouses, which were being prepared for destruction.

While Regiment "Deutschland" pulled back through Kharkov, Kumm's Regiment "Der Führer" and Fick's SS-Kradschützen-Bataillon 2 remained on the attack south of the city, operating in support of Witt's attack on Bereka. However, Kumm's attack to close off the route of retreat of the 11th Cavalry Division, following its withdrawal from Ochotschaje, bogged down. In any event, it was too late to trap the 201st Tank Brigade because most of its tanks had already been able to escape. Kampfgruppe Witt, having rested for a few hours during the night, attacked Bereka again at 0700 hours, hoping to establish contact with Meyer's battalion, which was near Jefremovka.[5]

The Grenadiers advanced through thick, early morning fog, which greatly hampered observation and limited the effectiveness of supporting German artillery. In spite of the poor conditions, the attack succeeded in penetrating the village perimeter, until it met a curtain of machine gun and infantry fire, which inflicted substantial casualties on the assaulting Grenadiers. All of the platoon commanders in the attack force were either killed or wounded and the attack foundered temporarily. At that time SS-Oberscharführer Herman Dalke took over command of the assaulting company and led it in a ferocious attack that penetrated into the center of the village. Dalke was awarded the Knight's Cross for his leadership and personal bravery in the assault on Bereka.

While Dalke's men were involved in the bitter close quarter fighting, SS-Pioniere-Bataillon 1 encircled the village from the east and other elements of the Panzergrenadier regiment pushed around the perimeter to the west. However, the stalwart Russian troops, fighting from hastily fortified positions amongst the houses and buildings in the center of Bereka, refused to be driven out. Savage house to house combat continued into the night. Reconnaissance

---

[4] Information from privately held unit KTB from Mark C. Yerger archive.
[5] Lehmann, pg. 99.

patrols reported the steady arrival of Soviet troops during the hours of darkness. To make matters worse, while the regiment was fully occupied in the fighting for the possession of the village, its supply lines were attacked by the Russians. [6]

Witt left only supply and security troops at the nearby town of Taranovka which was north of Bereka. Russian infantry attacked Taranovka after dark and occupied the town, capturing stores of supplies and a few vehicles. Most of the SS supply troops were killed and left lying where they fell in the streets. With Russian forces at Taranovka, stubborn Soviet infantry still resisting in Bereka and increasing pressure from the east, the attack scheduled for 16 February had to be called off. The regiment withdrew northwards, towards Taranovka, during the predawn hours, while the Pioniere Bataillon took up a blocking position west of the town and covered the retreat. At first light, Kampfgruppe Witt attacked Taranovka. Supported by several assault guns, the SS Grenadiers seized the southern section of Taranovka, but could not clear the Russians out of the rest of the village.[7]

While "Das Reich" withdrew through Kharkov, and "Leibstandarte" continued to fight in the southeast, "Grossdeutschland" conducted its own difficult fighting in the north and northwest sections of the city. During the night of 14-15 the Russians broke through the division's defensive positions along the rail line leading into the city through the Udy River Valley. The 340th Rifle Division, with tanks of Kravchenko's 5th Guards Tank Corps, drove German troops out of a wooded area on the western perimeter, but the tanks had difficulties moving through the deep snow in the forests. As a result, the Russian infantry pushed on without armored support and their advance slowed. The Führer-Begleit-Bataillon and Aufklärungsabteilung "GD" were quickly ordered to block this new Russian advance and moved to intercept it. Near Ljubotin, there was a large divisional medical clearing station packed with casualties and the two battalions fought resolutely to keep their wounded out of the hands of the Russians. North of Ljubotin, near Hill 182.6, Russian infantry moving along the rail line, collided with the hastily occupied position of the reconnaissance battalion.

At first, light artillery shelling fell on the defensive positions of the battalion, signaling the beginning of the Russian attack. Then long rows of Soviet infantry emerged from the shadows of the forest and began to charge toward the German positions, with bayonets fixed. Machine gun fire rattled and the ever present German 2cm automatic guns cracked, sending a hail of deadly projectiles at the brown figures silhouetted against the snow. Fountains of white snow and black earth were sprayed into the air as the explosive shells struck among the Soviet infantry. After suffering heavy losses, the attack fell apart under the intense German defensive fire.

However, to the east and west of the battalion, the Soviet advance continued to move toward the vital Kharkov-Ljubotin road. In the distance, the men of the battalion could clearly see long, dark columns of Russian troops and sledges moving south, toward the road, which was the last main line of communication entering the city from the west. Meanwhile, the column of T-34s struggled to find a way through or around the wooded area, a few laboriously moving down narrow forest trails with great difficulty. Eventually some Soviet tank crews began to find their way through the forest and were able to support the next attacks against "Grossdeutschland."[8]

At 0943 hours, Korps Raus reported that more than a battalion of Russian infantry had broken through the northwest perimeter of the city and stated that the Kharkov-Ljubotin road was likely to be blocked at any time. "Grossdeutschland" reported that it did not have sufficient forces at hand to clean up the penetration and that the order to hold the city was no longer possible. Raus made it clear that if the order to withdraw was not given soon, it would be impossible to save the units of either "Grossdeutschland" or "Das Reich." By 1100 hours, the 40th Army's 183rd Rifle Division broke through German defenses in the Dergatschi area and reached the northern section of the city. Under pressure along its entire front, with several deep penetrations having fragmented its defensive perimeter, "Grossdeutschland" disengaged from the Russians, in order to save itself. The division reported that at 1400 hours, it had begun to pull its isolated blocking groups back to the south, while trying to maintain its hold on the Ljubotin-Kharkov road. By radio the division notified Armeeabteilung Lanz of its decision to withdraw to positions west of the Udy River. It is probably not coincidental that "Grossdeutschland's" decision to pull back was made at approximately the same time that "Das Reich" withdrew into the city.[9]

All of the German divisions pulled back into Kharkov during the afternoon of 15 February. Regiment "Deutschland," covered by anti-tank detachments and assault guns, pushed slowly through wreckage strewn streets and over bridges along a designated route of retreat. Grim faced SS and Army Pioniere watched silently while the vehicle columns passed, waiting to destroy the bridges when the regiment finally crossed over. The German troops nervously watched the surrounding buildings, with their darkened windows

---

[6] Op cit. and Schneider, Jost W., *Their Honor was Loyalty - An Illustrated and Documentary History of the Knight's Cross Holders of the Waffen-SS and Police*, (San Jose: 1993) pg. 54.
[7] Lehmann, pg. 103-104.

[8] Spaeter, pg. 39.
[9] Glantz, pg. 179.

and peered down shadowy streets, expecting T-34s to emerge at any time. To the east, enormous demolition charges blew up commissaries and nonessential bridges, signaling that the tail end of the columns were approaching. Everything of value that could not be taken out was supposed to be burned or destroyed by explosion.

With German troops withdrawing before them, the Soviet armies converged upon the center of the city, flooding into Kharkov from all directions. West of Ossnova, on the main road leading into Kharkov from the southeast, the 62nd Guards Rifle Division and the 179th Tank Brigade entered Kharkov, meeting little resistance other than delaying actions conducted by small rear guard detachments. When Regiment "Deutschland" abandoned its defensive perimeters, the Soviet 15th Tank Corps and the 160th Rifle Division occupied the positions for which they had expended a great deal of blood during their unsuccessful attempts to break through the SS defenses. Concealed "Das Reich" Panzers ambushed pursuing Soviet tanks that pursued the withdrawing regiment and the division reported that it destroyed some 15 Russian tanks during the withdrawal. Meanwhile, in the southern sector of the city, the 62nd Guards Rifle Division and the 12th Tank Corps pushed forward and threw a bridge head over the Udy River near Lizogubovka. Elements of the 111th Rifle Division also crossed the Udy further south, reaching the west bank. As "Grossdeutschland" and the SS regiments continued to make their way to the south and west, the complete occupation of the city was only a matter of time.[10]

By nightfall, Lanz had conferred with Hausser and hoped to have found a way out of his dilemma regarding the conflict between Hitler's orders and the realities of the military crisis confronting his army. He referred to Manstein's early morning radio message to the Armeeabteilung and its statement that an encirclement at Kharkov was to be avoided. Lanz told Hausser that he agreed with the decision to withdraw over the Udy River, in order to avoid destruction of the units fighting east of the city. Lanz also sent his congratulations to Sepp Dietrich for his destruction of the 6th Guards Cavalry Corps. In fact, the Soviet corps had not been destroyed although it had been battered during the fighting 11-15 February. Considering the casualties it inflicted on the SS formations south of Kharkov and its disciplined withdrawal, it was hardly destroyed.

Later in the day, at 1700 hours, evidently after conferences with Hausser and Raus, Lanz radioed Manstein and gave him a report on the situation in Kharkov. In his message to Manstein Lanz informed the Feldmarschall that the last corridor out of the city was barely two kilometers wide when "Das Reich" withdrew from its positions in the eastern section of the city and that in view of the

military situation and the danger of encirclement, the Armeeabteilung agreed with the decision of Hausser to withdraw the SS-Panzer-Korps from Kharkov. The withdrawal to the Udy sector represented the only possibility to save the forces of the Armeeabteilung and allow it to continue the battle. Apparently, Manstein relayed this report to Berlin, because later in the evening, OKH communicated with Lanz by radio, demanding an immediate written report regarding the situation in Kharkov, particularly regarding the withdrawal by elements of "Das Reich." Lanz referred to his earlier reports, in which he had stated that given the double missions assigned to his army, he did not believe Kharkov could be held past 15 February with the forces available.[11]

Lanz's acceptance of Hausser's decision to withdraw, even though it was an option specifically mentioned by Manstein, cost him the command of the army. Adolf Hitler viewed Kharkov as politically and personally important and its loss was a bitter affront to his pride. In this situation, Hitler's decision to hold ground at all costs, although somewhat valid in other contexts, cannot be defended. The SS divisions and "Grossdeutschland" were completely mobile and of critical importance to Manstein's plans for a winter counterattack, not to mention the summer offensive operations. Unaccountably, given their value, Hitler would have had the highly mobile SS divisions and "Grossdeutschland" fight to destruction to hold the city. Had Hausser not had the courage to oppose Hitler's orders, the SS-Panzer-Korps and "Gross-deutschland" would have been destroyed or at least seriously weakened and may not have been available to Manstein for the Kharkov counteroffensive.

Late evening reports by Armeeabteilung Lanz for the critical day of 15 February stated that "Leibstandarte" had taken Ochotschaje and remained in the Bereka area. "Das Reich" was still in the process of pulling back through Kharkov, covered by its tanks and rearguard detachments, supported by assault guns. The division reported that it had damaged or destroyed fourteen Russian tanks in the bitter street fighting. The reports mention a request from OKH for a written statement about "Das Reich's" withdrawal without orders. To his credit, Lanz did not place the blame for the loss of the city upon Hausser's withdrawal. Refusing to blame the SS-Panzerkorps for the loss of the city, Lanz reiterated that because of the double missions assigned to his army, Kharkov could not be held. He then stated that "Das Reich," "LAH" and "Grossdeutschland" had been faced by twenty Soviet rifle divisions, ten tank brigades, two tank regiments and two cavalry divisions. He added that because of the danger of encirclement facing the two divisions, he agreed with Hausser's decision to pull back.[12] Since

---

[10] Op cit.

[11] *Befehl des Gewissens,* pg.110.
[12] Ibid. pg. 111.

he made that statement as Hausser's superior, he essentially gave his approval of the actions of a subordinate officer who had disobeyed the supreme commander, Adolf Hitler.

Subsequent reports stated that two regimental groups of 320. Infanterie-Division had occupied a section of the line west of the Udy River at Wodjanoje, which was south of the city and were astride the Kharkov-Chuguyev rail road line. A third regimental group of the division was marching west from the Msha River, towards Merefa. "Grossdeutschland" continued its withdrawal, with rear guards detachments covering the retreat. "Totenkopf" elements that had assembled in Valki were to attack Soviet forces on the Ljubotin-Kharkov road and establish contact with "Grossdeutschland." However, at that time, only a company of "Totenkopf" Panzergrenadiers had unloaded at Valki, although they were reinforced by a Sturmgeschütze battery, a battery of 10cm howitzers and a platoon of anti-tank guns.

Heeresgruppe Süd sent a radio message to Lanz at 2205 hours, outlining the several very optimistic missions for the Armeeabteilung on 16 February. Lanz was expected to tie up the Soviet 6th Army, 3rd Tank Army, 69th Army and the 40th Army. Reconnaissance groups were to strike out from Krasnograd to the east and southeast, in order to locate the Russian advance. "Leibstandarte" was to hold its positions south of Kharkov, while 320. Infanterie-Division, "Grossdeutschland" and "Das Reich" took up their new positions along the Udy River between Ljubotin to the west and Borowoje to the east. Dietrich was to assemble a force in Valki in order to attack to the northeast, and clear the main road west of Ljubotin. The 168. Infanterie-Division was to delay the Russian advance through the Vorskla River Valley.[13] Surprisingly, the four divisions were essentially able to accomplish these tasks, with help from "Totenkopf's Regiment "Thule."

After the Germans abandoned Kharkov, the Russians poured into the city, following close on the heels of the withdrawing troops and reached the center of the city. From the south and east, the 62nd Guards and 160th Rifle Division pushed down debris strewn streets. Tanks of the 5th Guards Tank Corps rolled cautiously down the broad main streets from the west, making their way toward the huge main square in the northern quadrant of the city. The 183rd Rifle Division occupied the former positions of "Grossdeutschland" as it entered the city from the north. Soviet infantry penetrated between "Grossdeutschland" rear guards elements and ambushed Pioniere demolition teams. In the darkened, burning city, Russian troops unexpectedly made contact with groups of the retreating troops and the situation became very confused. After difficult fight-

A detachment of I./Regiment "Thule" soon after arriving in Krasnograd. Immediately upon detraining the battalion sent out reconnaissance patrols to find the Russian troops advancing toward the town. Krasnograd was the assembly area for "Das Reich" and "Totenkopf" before the two divisions led Manstein's counterattack upon the Soviet 6th Army spearheads threatening the vital Dnepr crossings. (The author's collection)

ing the division was able to complete its withdrawal, but was hard pressed to save its rear guard detachments.[14]

The division ordered the assault gun battalion to assemble at the enormous Red Square and escort the last rear guard unit, a battalion of the Grenadier Regiment, out of Kharkov. The battalion had just received 20 brand new Sturmgeschütze IIIs, giving the battalion a total of more than 30 vehicles. While buildings burned around them and tremendous explosions rocked the dark, rubble strewn streets, the assault guns positioned themselves around the square and anxiously awaited the Grenadier battalion, which was commanded by Major Otto Remer. Machine gun fire and explosions could from every direction and the crews grew more and more nervous. Russian infantry or tanks could arrive at any minute, unseen in the darkness, which was lit only by the flickering of distant fires or the occasional shell burst. Huge shadows darkened the many large streets converging on the square and they knew that a gun or tank could set up in the shadows unobserved. Hours passed and the rear guard still had not arrived, while the apprehension of the soldiers grew by the minute.[15]

Thinking that it was possible Remer had been forced to use another exit from the city, Hauptmann Frantz, the assault gun battalion commander, radioed the division, hoping to receive news about the Grenadiers. There was no additional information, however, and the situation grew more tense when light small arms fire was directed at the assault guns from nearby roof tops. Frantz was

[13] Op cit.

[14] Spaeter, pg. 42.
[15] Spaeter, pg. 42.

faced with a dilemma, as he did not want to abandon the square before his comrades arrived, but the awful waiting and lack of information was difficult. Finally, he decided to send out a single Sturmgeschütze III, which was instructed to maintain constant radio communication with the battalion command vehicle. The assault gun rolled northwards down a long street, disappearing into the maelstrom of explosions, fire and artillery fire, while Frantz and his men waited, eyes straining to spot any approaching enemy. At the same time, the men knew that Remer and his vehicles might appear at any moment and without warning. More than once, situations like this had ended tragically, when a nervous, frightened gunner fired on friendly vehicles or men.

Finally Remer and the main element of the SPW battalion emerged from the darkness, escorted by the very relieved crew of the solitary assault gun that had located them. However, Frantz's battalion could still not leave, because they found that they had to wait for Remer's rear guard platoon, which was bringing up the

rear. At last, this detachment arrived also, the drivers exhausted from the stress of hours of driving through the dark streets. With Frantz's command vehicle bringing up the rear, the column got underway, stopping only to pick up the remaining Pioniere troops, who detonated explosive charges that collapsed the last bridge behind them. After a two hour long journey, the assault guns and the SPWs reached a forward outpost of the division west of Kharkov.

The main elements of the Füsilier Regiment "GD," which had left Kharkov's western sector, had moved along the main road toward Ljubotin, spearheading the breakout of the division. However, near Ljubotin, the Füsiliers had been ambushed by Soviet armor, probably belonging to the 5th Guards Tank Corps. The German column was forced to halt and move back, after losing many vehicles and men to heavy Russian fire. It was unable to find a way past the Russian tanks and the column became pinned down near the village of Kommuna. The assault gun battalion was once again ordered to rescue a detachment of the division.

A "Das Reich" Marder in the Kharkov area in late February, 1943. The assault guns and self-propelled anti-tank guns of the division provided vital protection when the division regrouped at Krasnograd. Mobile rear guard detachments, usually made up of Sturmgeschütze, Marders and Flak guns, covered the pull back of the division. (Courtesy of Mark C. Yerger)

Frantz and his 30 Sturmgeschütz IIIs were ordered to attack the Russian troops blocking the road in order to get the column moving again. Supported by a few mobile anti-tank guns and several SPWs with Grenadiers, the assault gun battalion moved west and without warning, struck the flanks of the Soviet position. The main attack elements of the battalion deployed on either side of the road and motored forward, the churning tracks throwing up sprays of snow and chunks of ice. Under covering fire of anti-tank guns and the overwatch detachment of Sturmgeschütze, the racing assault guns overran the Soviet positions around Kommuna and routed the Russian infantry. Within a short time the road was at least temporarily open and the Füsilier Regiment continued on its way toward Ljubotin, which was held by Aufklärungsabteilung "Grossdeutschland." [16]

While the three divisions pulled back to the Udy sector and began to organize a defensive line southwest of Kharkov, 168. Infanterie-Division remained essentially isolated to the west and of very little value to the army. Cut off from contact with "Grossdeutschland" by the advance of the 5th Guards Tank Corps to the west of the city, elements of the division had remained in the Bogodukhov and Graivoron-Borisovka area. On 16 February, Russian forward elements attacked division positions at Graivoron and Bogodukhov, forcing the division to withdraw even farther west. This created a gap north of the Ljubotin-Kharkov road. Between Graivoron-Bogodukhov and Valki, where SS "Totenkopf" was assembling, there were no German forces other than local security detachments. Within days Soviet divisions began to fill the void west of Kharkov but they drove primarily to the west, and although this remained a serious problem, this direction of attack was less dangerous than an advance south would have been.

Moskalenko's 40th Army had received orders to regroup after the fall of Kharkov and advance west, towards Bogodukhov and from there to take the town of Achtyrka. Achtyrka was about ninety kilometers west of Kharkov, slightly farther north and just east of the Vorskla River. The Soviet advance to the west was relatively unhindered by the Germans because there were no significant forces in the area. Armeeabteilung Lanz was given defensive missions concerned primarily with building a defensive line southeast of Kharkov in order to prevent a further Russian advance into the assembly areas of the SS-Panzer-Korps and other than the ineffectual 168. Infanterie-Division, had no troops to spare in any event.

Heeresgruppe Süd stressed that a move by the 6th Army to threaten the deep flank of 1. Panzerarmee must be blocked. Exactly what force that Lanz was to use to block this threat was not speci-

fied. Given that the right flank of the 6th Army's area of attack was thirty kilometers south of Kharkov and that the 3rd Tank Army was between Armeeabteilung Lanz and the 6th Army, it is difficult to understand what Heeresgruppe Süd expected Lanz to accomplish. At that point, it was not certain that the Armeeabteilung would even be able to hold the Udy River Valley, much less take and hold a defensive sector thirty kilometers to the south.

However, the extremely dangerous threat posed by Kharitonov's 6th Army was clear and Manstein's concern was justified. By 16 February, the fighting entered another critical phase for the Germans and was further complicated by the fall of Krasnoarmeiskoye. On Kharitonov's right flank, three rifle divisions continued to advance west of the Northern Donets, shoulder to shoulder, toward the railroad line Dnepropetrovsk-Krasnograd-Kharkov. One of the Soviet divisions, the 6th Rifle Division, was only twenty-five kilometers from Krasnograd by 16 February. Further to the south, the 106th Rifle Brigade and 267th Rifle Division approached the same rail line, at a point farther to the south, at Pereshschepino. In addition, rifle divisions of the Soviet 1st Guards Army, advancing south of the left flank of the 6th Army, threatened to occupy sections of the Dnepropetrovsk-Pavlograd-Krasnoarmeiskoye railroad, which had already been severed at Krasnoarmeiskoye-Grishino by Poluboyarov's 4th Guards Tank Corps.[17]

The loss of the Dnepropetrovsk-Krasnograd-Kharkov line would have left only the Poltava-Ljubotin railroad open to Armeeabteilung Lanz, and this rail line was already being intermittently cut by Soviet forces between Ljubotin and Kharkov by 16 February. The threats to the remaining German lines of communication leading into Kharkov were thus extremely critical for both Armeeabteilung Lanz and 1. Panzerarmee, which was still fighting hard for the Slavyansk-Voroshilovrad line south of the Northern Donets. Manstein spoke about the situation in *Lost Victories* and commented about the potential dangers of posed by the Soviet advance.

> In the meantime 4. Panzerarmee was still moving by road and rail from the lower Don to the western wing, its progress being considerably delayed by the bad state of the roads. Thus, apart from the fact that the enemy was already in 1. Panzerarmee's deep flank at Grishino and able to send in fresh forces to reinforce those temporarily held up there, the danger in the yawning gap between the left wing of 1. Panzerarmee and the Kharkov region remained desperate as ever. In this area the enemy had complete freedom of action . . . The enemy

---

[16] Spaeter, pg. 44-46.

[17] Glantz, pg. 179-184.

was capable – while ensuring that he was covered in the direction of Kharkov – of moving down on Pavlograd with the forces reported to be advancing westward from Izyum From Pavlograd he could go on to the Dnepr crossings . . . thereby severing the Army Groups communications across the river.[18]

Hitler and Manstein at Zaporozsche

That same day, Hitler flew from Germany by Fw 200 Condor transport, with several fighters in escort, in order to meet with Manstein. He arrived at Heeresgruppe Süd headquarters at Zaporozsche, along with a retinue that included a cook and Generaloberst Alfred Jodl. Hitler wanted to see the situation at first hand and he was not happy with Manstein's conduct of the fighting, nor with a matter that was discussed earlier in the month. Manstein had explained his plans for a mobile defense of the area between Kharkov and Slavyansk in their earlier meeting of 6 February and this type of tactics did not sit well with Hitler. He was a veteran of World War I and the enormous physical cost of taking even ridiculously small amounts of enemy territory was burned into the psyche of all infantry soldiers familiar with the slaughter of trench warfare. Once such a terrible price had been paid in blood for territory, it was to be defended to the last man, a cost less than the butcher's bill for regaining lost ground. As a result, the surrender of vast amounts of territory, as advocated by German generals who understood modern mobile war, was a foreign concept to him and one that he was never comfortable with.

In addition, a previous proposal by Manstein to unite the high command responsible for conducting the war in Russia under a single, supreme commander, had disturbed the Führer, according to Joseph Goebbel's account of a meeting in which the subject was discussed. Hitler did not trust anyone to conduct the war as he saw fit, believing that he was uniquely suited for that role. Manstein of course, had himself in mind for the post, and had he assumed such a position, would have been a dangerous, skilled commander. However, Hitler arrived at Heeresgruppe Süd headquarters having essentially decided to sack Manstein, if we are to believe Goebbels.[19] The military reports reaching Berlin painted a picture of crisis everywhere in the Heeresgruppe Süd area and Hitler may have been wondering about Manstein's ability to bring the situation under control.

Everywhere on the situation maps of the Eastern Front, a desperate situation seemed to exist. Armeeabteilung Hollidt had been

Manstein greets Hitler upon the Führer's arrival at Heeresgruppe Süd HQ in Zaporozsche on 16 February. Hitler flew to Russia because he was still angry over the loss of Kharkov and was determined to find a scapegoat for the embarrassment. Some sources suggest that he intended to remove Manstein from command. (Credit National Archives)

forced to retreat behind the Mius River, with the Russians pressuring the exhausted army every step of the way. In addition, Soviet forces had already penetrated behind the Mius positions, before the army was even able to settle into its new positions. Several days earlier, the Soviet 8th Cavalry Corps had reached Debalt'sevo, which was on the Voroshilovgrad-Stalino railroad line and in the rear of 304. Infanterie-Division positions south of Voroshilovgrad. The capture of Debalt'sevo had disrupted the supply situation, causing the army to use alternate, longer rail routes, thus delaying the delivery of fuel, what meager replacements were available and the flow of supplies.

Mackensen's 1. Panzerarmee was threatened with a deep penetration by Mobile Group Popov on its western flank, while Hoth's 4. Panzerarmee was still in the process of assembling for an attack to close the gap between 1. Panzerarmee and Armeeabteilung Lanz. Into this very gap the Russians were pouring rifle divisions and tanks and there was little standing between them and the important crossings of the Dnepr River. The Soviet advance threatened to cut the last remaining supply lines to the southern wing of the army group by capturing the bridges over the Dnepr. The loss of these crossings would block the railroad supply routes to the armies of Hollidt, Hoth and Mackensen. For his part, Manstein did not look forward to Hitler's visit as it presented security problems and was a distraction at a critical time. To Manstein, it seemed that Hitler did not understand the gravity of the situation, from his Headquarters in Berlin or East Prussia. In fact, Hitler did not trust his generals and did not believe their estimations of the desperate situations existing on the Eastern Front.

---

[18] Manstein, pg. 418.
[19] *The Goebbel's Diaries*, edited by Lochner, Louis P. (London: 1948) pg. 265.

The one positive factor of Hitler's visit, regardless of all the potentially negative aspects, was the opportunity to personally explain the situation and talk one on one with the dictator. By the time that Hitler's entourage descended upon his Headquarters, Manstein was only days away from beginning his counterattack and the last preparations were already begun. To Hitler's credit, his misgivings began to dissipate once Manstein described his plan to destroy the Soviet forces in the gap by a counterattack of all available Panzer divisions. When the bold offensive actions were described, Hitler became intrigued in spite of himself, particularly when it became clear that his SS divisions were to play a major role in the operation. Manstein wanted to block the Russian advance toward the Dnepr first and then continue the attack into an assault upon the flanks of the Soviet armies in the gap between Slavyansk and Kharkov. Once this threat had been eliminated, the victorious Panzer divisions could sweep north and envelop Kharkov, recapturing the city that Hitler desperately coveted. The dictator's obsession with taking Kharkov led to difficulties from the start and resulted in marathon, exhausting arguments.

It was clear to Manstein that the threat to the Dnepr crossings had to be eliminated first. If the Soviets captured the crossings and cut the railroad lines stretching eastward, 1. Panzerarmee and Armeeabteilung Hollidt would perish from lack of fuel, food and ammunition. However, Hitler wanted to take Kharkov at once, with no regard for the military situation and the threat to the Dnepr crossings. Always glib in supporting his ideas, Hitler used a number of arguments to support his proposal. He was skeptical that there were actually Russian tank corps and entire divisions threatening the Dnepr. Paul Carell described the scene at Heeresgruppe Süd headquarters in his classic account of the Eastern Front, *Scorched Earth*. Hitler expressed incredulity at Manstein's plan to strike into the gap with all of the Panzer divisions that were available, even those pulled from Armeeabteilung Hollidt.

"No," he said. "Why such a concentration of forces against an imaginary enemy?" Hitler wanted Kharkov recaptured first. Kharkov! He just could not swallow the fact that Hausser had abandoned this metropolis, this great administrative center of

Hitler and the dignitaries of his party inspect several German and Russian tanks at Zaporozsche. The tank in the picture is a Panzer III, equipped with a 5cm main gun. A longer barreled gun of the same caliber was in extensive use already, although even the improved gun was inferior to both the 7.6cm gun of the T-34 and the L42 (7.5cm) gun of the Panzer IV. (Credit National Archives)

Ukrainian heavy industry, against his express orders . . . he refused to let Manstein use the SS Panzer Corps for a mobile flanking attack against the Soviet Sixth Army and demanded . . . a locally limited counterattack against Kharkov. Not until that was accomplished was Manstein to proceed against the Sixth Army.

Hitler forcefully demanded that all three of the SS divisions should immediately recapture Kharkov. Manstein had to engage in a painstaking discussion to justify his plan and finally persuaded the Führer to delay making a final decision until the next day. Fortunately for the Germans, the events of that day persuaded Hitler to allow Manstein to conduct the planned counteroffensive as he saw fit. Early reports to Heeresgruppe Süd painted an exceedingly grim picture in the morning. The 1st Guards Army's 35th Guards Rifle Division, after advancing from Losovaja, had captured Pavlograd, supported by a tank brigade of the 25th Tank Corps. Remnants of a division of Italian troops had put up a brief, largely token resistance and then fled. After consolidating their hold on the town, the Russian division thrust west, reaching Novo-Moskovsk, which lay on the Dnepropetrovsk-Krasnograd-Kharkov railroad line. The capture of this railroad was a major blow to operations of Armeeabteilung Lanz and Korps Raus at the worst possible time. The divisions of Lanz' battered army had just arrived on the Udy River and he was trying to organize some semblance of a defense west of Kharkov. With the loss of the Dnepropetrovsk line, all supplies had to be routed through Poltava and one rail line didn't have adequate capacity to carry a sufficient number of trains.

At the same time, on the right flank of the 1st Guards Army, the 6th Army had advanced even further west, pushing to the Orel River. The Orel meandered generally east to west, and passed roughly halfway between Poltava, where "Totenkopf" was assembling, and Dnepropetrovsk. On the northern flank of the Soviet 6th Army, the 350th, 172nd and 6th Rifle Divisions moved westward, roughly shoulder to shoulder, moving toward the key assembly point of Krasnograd. The 6th Rifle Division was only about 30 kilometers east of the town on 17 February. To the south, the 267th Rifle Division advanced on a broad front, and approached the town of Pereshschepino. Pereshschepino was an important station on the Dnepropetrovsk-Krasnograd-Kharkov railroad line and was located on the Orel River.

In addition, there was a report that Soviet troops and armor were approaching Sinel'nikovo, which was less than thirty kilometers east of Dnepropetrovsk. There were only weak German security and police units between the forward elements of the Soviet 25th Tank Corps at Sinel'nikovo and the HQ of Heeresgruppe Süd

Hitler inside Manstein's Headquarters at Zaporozsche. For several days Hitler suspiciously grilled Manstein and his staff, not entirely believing how serious the military situation was until Soviet tanks appeared about thirty kilometers west of Zaporozsche. At that point, there were only security troops and supply personnel between Hitler and the Russian tanks. (Credit National Archives)

at Zaporozsche. Thus, on 18 February, a determined thrust by the 25th Tank Corps could have endangered the HQ of Heeresgruppe Süd, where Hitler and Manstein were in conference. There were also a series of negative reports from Armeeabteilung Hollidt, whose plight was directly related to orders given by Hitler. His reluctance to give up territory had delayed the decision to pull Hollidt's army back to its new positions behind the Mius River until the last minute. This procrastination ultimately threatened to result in Russian troops reaching the Mius River before Hollidt's weary troops could organize new defenses on the western bank. The Soviet 8th Cavalry Corps was already in the rear areas of Hollidt's army, at Debalt'sevo and during the course of 18 February, the Soviets crossed the Mius River at several places. The most serious penetration was made by forward elements of the 3rd Guards Mechanized Corps, which threatened to roll west and seize Stalino.

Hitler became fixated on this fact, objecting to using all of the Panzer divisions to the north when Hollidt's army was in such a critical situation. He also became concerned that Manstein's counteroffensive might get bogged down in a late winter thaw, a development that Manstein admitted was a possibility. However, the whole operation was a carefully calculated gamble and Manstein stated that he was prepared to risk the possibility of a short period of warm weather. A thaw was only a potential problem, while the Soviet presence on German supply lines was a reality that had to be dealt with immediately, before it strangled Heeresgruppe Süd. Hitler

Hitler leaves Manstein's HQ shortly before boarding his plane for the return flight to Germany. Hitler became caught up with excitement when he learned about Manstein's counteroffensive. Part of his enthusiasm was no doubt because his SS divisions, especially Sepp Dietrich's "Leibstandarte," had the major role in the attack. (Credit National Archives)

continued to argue interminably, as he still remained unconvinced of the dangers presented by the reported advance of the Soviets toward the Dnepr. He suspiciously questioned the 1a of Heeresgruppe Süd, Oberst Theodore Busse, perhaps thinking that some reports had been exaggerated in order to support Manstein's arguments.

Hitler glanced suspiciously at Colonel Busse, the chief of operations of Army Group South. Was he being bluffed? "I'd like to know more about that," he grunted . . . Busse began to reel off the details. The Soviet 267th Rifle Division is here, south of Krasnograd," he said, pointing to a map. His finger then came down on Pavlograd: "A tank battalion of 35th Guards Rifle Division has taken Pavlograd."[20] (actually the armor belonged to the 25th Tank Corps – author's note)

After receiving the information regarding the advances of the 6th and 1st Guards Army, and the immediate dangers posed by the presence of the Russians on key railroad lines, the gravity of the situation finally became clear to Hitler. He also realized that this was not the time to change commanders of Heeresgruppe Süd. It must have been clear to Hitler that Armeeabteilung Hollidt and major elements of 4. Panzerarmee would be immobilized by lack of fuel and supplies if the railroads were not secured quickly. This was a fact that could not be debated or explained away with rationalizations, because an army unquestionably needs fuel and ammunition to fight. However, Hitler still advocated a thrust to regain Kharkov by the SS divisions as the first order of business. He may have gotten his way, if not for a change of the weather along the route of march assigned to SS-Panzer-Regiment 3, which was on the way to its assembly areas, after leaving train stations at Kiev. By late morning, an uncharacteristically bright sun burned through the morning fog and mist after which the temperature rose above freezing. Within a short time, all of the roads were churned into meter deep muck by

---

[20] Carell, pg. 185.

the regiment's vehicles. Trucks and half tracks sunk to their axles in the sticky, clinging black mud, reducing the speed of the column to a crawl.

Heeresgruppe Süd received a report from Armeeabteilung Lanz that the mobile elements of "Totenkopf" were bogged down in deep mud on the roads between Poltava and Kiev, as the result of temporary thaw. Since the third division of the SS-Panzer-Korps was not immediately available for the strike north to Kharkov, Manstein was able to reason with Hitler. He explained that if two SS divisions could not hold the city in defensive operations, it was extremely unlikely that the same two divisions, now considerably weakened, would be able to take the city from several Russian armies. The logic of this argument was not disputed after Hitler put aside his obsession with Kharkov after he became engrossed in the discussion of the upcoming offensive operations. His enthusiasm grew and he became greatly animated during discussions regarding the counteroffensive described by Manstein.

The boldness of the operation won Hitler over, especially after it became clear that the Soviet forces approaching Dnepropetrovsk and Krasnograd were the most dangerous threat to the army group and by extension, the entire southern sector of the Russian front. The Russian armies to the north, although they had occupied Kharkov, had failed to destroy either the SS divisions or "Grossdeutschland," or even for that matter, 320. and 168. Infanterie-Divisions. The 3rd Tank Army, having been dealt serious losses by "Das Reich" and "Leibstandarte," no longer had sufficient strength to break German defenses west of Kharkov and was then engaged in fighting against SS-Panzer-Korps in the Udy River Valley area, southwest of the city.

Manstein explained his bold plan to concentrate all of the available Panzer divisions on the flanks of the penetrations of the Soviet armies. Strong mobile elements of the SS-Panzer-Korps were to first block the Soviet advance toward the Dnepr. Armeeabteilung Lanz would cover the northern flank of the SS attack and prevent the 40th or 3rd Tank Army from attacking the SS supply lines. Korps Raus, with "Grossdeutschland," 168. Infanterie-Division, Regiment "Thule" and the remnants of 320. Infanterie-Division, would continue their defensive operations west of the city, in order to prevent the Russians from driving into the SS-Panzer-Korps assembly areas southwest of Kharkov. After the SS divisions secured the Dnepr River, they would turn north and destroy the Soviet forces along the railroad lines running to Kharkov. Hoth's XXXXVIII. Panzer-Korps would close up on the right or eastern flank of the SS divisions and support the advance towards Kharkov. Armeeabteilung Lanz, strengthened by 167. Infanterie-Division, would launch an attack on Kharkov from the west, thus tying down the Russian forces

in and around Kharkov, while the SS and Army Panzer divisions of Hoth's army destroyed the Soviet forces south of Kharkov. After accomplishing this task, Heeresgruppe Süd could turn its attention to the recapture of the city.

On the night of 18-19 February, Hoth and the Headquarters detachments of 4. Panzerarmee finally arrived at Heeresgruppe Süd Headquarters. Manstein and his staff immediately began to brief Hoth and his staff on their role in the offensive, explaining that 4. Panzerarmee was to be reinforced with the three SS Panzergrenadier divisions. According to Manstein, his daring operation was finally sanctioned by Hitler in its entirety, after the very real dangers of the critical situation in the East had at last become clear to the dictator.[21]

On 19 February a further conference took place, and this time Field Marshal von Kleist had been asked to attend. Apparently Hitler's stay at my headquarters had quite impressed him after all as to the dangers on the German southern wing, for he announced that Army Group A was henceforth to transfer whatever forces it could possibly spare to Southern Army Group. In his own words, Army Group A would henceforth be regarded as an adjacent reservoir of forces for the Southern Army Group.[22]

Persuading Hitler to accept his plan had been arduous task and had put a great strain on Manstein and his headquarters personnel. Manstein later commented that, "We lived, it seemed on two entirely different worlds." The Führer's presence at Zaporozsche was particularly nerve wracking since the Russians were so close to the army group headquarters. Fortunately for Manstein and his staff, some of Hitler's entourage were also getting quite disturbed by their close proximity to actual combat, and they urged Hitler to leave as soon as possible. After Hitler boarded his transport plane and took off toward the west, every officer from Manstein down to the lowest lieutenant of the Headquarters Staff must have breathed a sigh of relief. At the moment when the planes left the ground, Soviet tanks were less than 20 kilometers miles from Zaporozsche.

Manstein remained in command of his army group and surprisingly, Hausser retained his command of SS-Panzer-Korps. However, everyone did not escape so cleanly. Lanz was made the scapegoat for Hitler's embarrassment over the loss of Kharkov, presumably for not being able to compel the SS divisions to commit military suicide in the doomed city. As a result, the command of the

[21] Ziemke and Bauer, pg. 92.
[22] Manstein, pg. 427.

Armeeabteilung passed to General der Panzertruppen Werner Kempf.[23]

The Voronezh Front Regroups

On 16 February, troops of the 15th Tank Corps entered Dzerzhinsky Square, in the center of the northern quarter of Kharkov. The tankers embraced infantry of the 40th Army, celebrating in delirious triumph, while farther south, Kravchenko's 5th Guards Tank Corps met tanks of the 3rd Tank Army. While the fragmented elements of Lanz's army withdrew and tried to build up a new defensive front southwest of the city, there were already Soviet troops crossing the Udy River. The Soviet command hoped to establish bridgeheads for a subsequent advance from out of the city to the south, before the Germans could organize their battered divisions into a coherent defense. However, as we have seen, the main push of the Voronezh Front was not to the south.

Several days earlier, the commander of the Voronezh Front, Golikov, received directives from the Stavka that changed the direction of his attack at a critical time and sent his armies to the northwest of Kharkov. Accordingly, he issued orders directing the 40th Army to march toward Graivoron and Slavgorod. The 69th Army was to attack Bogodukhov, almost directly west of Kharkov, where 168. Infanterie-Division elements were in position. Rybalko's 3rd Tank Army was ordered to assemble southwest of Kharkov. The 5th Guards Tank Corps, after extricating itself from Kharkov, which was crowded with Soviet troops and vehicles, was to secure the left wing of the 3rd Tank Army.[24]

The city had become snarled in one giant traffic jam, its streets packed with trucks, tanks and tens of thousands of men from three armies that were trying to move through the congested streets at the same time. Confusion reigned as each army commander issued orders that his corps and division commanders attempted to follow. Lack of traffic control, inadequate logistical organization by the Front command and the destruction of bridges and roads prevented the Soviet armies from sorting out much of their formations for several days. The two tank corps of Rybalko's 3rd Tank Army were not in the city, and avoided most of the congestion and confusion caused by the complicated realignment of the armies. Due to the chaos that reigned in the city, even the Soviet command was not sure exactly where each army was.

The Voronezh Front chief of Staff, General Mikhail Kazakov, met Rybalko in Kharkov and actually reproached him for still having his tank corps in the city, when they had been ordered to assemble for an attack toward Ljubotin. Rybalko explained to the skeptical Kazakov, that only his rear elements were still in Kharkov, and that his main elements were already west and south of Kharkov. The 15th Tank Corps was in battle at that time, fighting with "Grossdeutschland" formations in the Ljubotin area. The 12th Tank Corps, which had never been in the center of the city, approached the Udy River from the east, supported by the 111th Rifle Division. The tough survivors of 6th Guards Cavalry Corps, with the 201st Tank Brigade still attached, reassembled west of Zmiev in order to secure the approaches to the town from the south. The regrouping of the three armies took three more days before it was complete and was complicated by the capture of vast stocks of German supplies. The Russian troops liberated and enjoyed enormous amounts of food, drink and other materials, which had not been destroyed by the Germans before leaving the city.[25]

Moskalenko's 40th Army began to shift its zone of attack to the area northwest of Kharkov on 17 February. On the northern flank, the 107th and 309th Rifle Divisions continued their advance westwards, reaching the area north of Bogodukhov by 17 February. In the wake of their advance, three other Soviet rifle divisions exited Kharkov from the northern quarter of the city and marched north towards Zolochev, passing through the attack sector just vacated by the 107th and 309th divisions. From there they turned to the northwest and drove due west, towards the town of Slavgorod, about 75 kilometers west of Belgorod. These three divisions became the northern wing of the 40th Army, while the 69th Army occupied the former 40th Army sector west of Kharkov.

Kazakov's 69th Army exited the city from its western perimeter and began an advance toward Krasnokutsk, which was 75 kilometers west of Kharkov. The path of the army passed through the Merla and Merchik River valleys, on both sides of the town of Bogodukhov. The first echelon of the army's attack consisted of the 180th and 219th Rifle Divisions. North of the Merla River, the 219th Rifle Division passed near Bogodukhov during its advance west. On the south bank, in the terrain between the Merla and Merchik, the 180th Rifle Division moved over the snow covered dirt roads just north of the railroad that ran from Poltava, through Vysokopol'ye and Ljubotin, before entering the western edge of Kharkov. In reserve, following in the second echelon of the attack, were the 270th and 161st Rifle Divisions. The advance of the 69th Army was opposed by 168. Infanterie-Division and "Gross-

---

[23] In the summer of 1943, the Germans lost Kharkov again, for the last time. Kempf, like Lanz before him, would be held responsible for the loss of the city and be removed from command of the army by Hitler.

[24] Glantz, pg. 180.

[25] Armstrong, pg. 172-173 and Glantz, pg. 180-181.

deutschland," which was reinforced by SS Regiment "Thule." Lammerding's motorized regiment did not join the main body of SS-"Totenkopf," as it would remain assigned to Korps Raus during the Kharkov counterattack. The fresh SS troops of Regiment "Thule," well equipped and confident, were a welcome addition to Korps Raus. The mobility and fire power made the mobile regiment a potent force, whether on the offensive or in a defensive role.[26]

Rybalko's 3rd Tank Army resumed its attack on 17-18 February, while the 40th and 69th Armies were still regrouping for their new mission and direction of attack. On the left or southern flank of the 3rd Tank Army, the 6th Guards Cavalry Corps and an accompanying rifle division, advanced toward the area south of Novaja Vodolaga. Again Rybalko thrust toward into the area south of Kharkov, seeking to cut the key railroads and gain control of the stations. In the center of the army, the 12th Tank Corps spearheaded the attack, with the objective of capturing Novaja Vodolaga itself. was supported by the 111th Rifle Division. The right or northern flank of the army's attack was led by the 15th Tank Corps and was the primary attack zone. Accordingly, Rybalko assigned three rifle divisions to support 15th Tank Corps. The objective of the right wing was the capture of the key rail center at Valki, where "Totenkopf" troops and equipment were still arriving.

Two of the three Soviet armies of Golikov's Voronezh Front in the Kharkov area continued their movement westward, because the Soviet command remained oblivious to the danger of the Panzer divisions gathering on the flanks of the gap south of Kharkov. The armies of the front had been seriously weakened by the fighting for Kharkov and the rifle divisions of both the 40th and 69th Armies were greatly under strength. The 69th Army, which had been forced into frontal attacks on narrow, strongly defended sectors, had a number of rifle divisions which did not number more than about 1500 combat effectives. The 40th Army was in somewhat better condition, since it had been involved in operations of maneuver for the most part and had not been involved in the brutal slugging match east of Kharkov. Its rifle divisions had an average strength of about 3500 to 4000 men. Only the 3rd Tank Army attacked to the south, slowly pursuing the withdrawing German divisions.[27]

Rybalko's tank army had suffered severe losses as well, having lost about 60 of its 165 tanks by 18 February. In fact, Rybalko had requested a three day rest for his army before resuming offensive operations, but this request was denied by Golikov. The need for rest, replacements and fresh tanks was ignored by the Stavka

An SS half track plows through deep snow on a road in the southern Ukraine in early 1943. In the distance behind the vehicle is an elevated rail road embankment which were common in that area. The spring and fall rainy seasons caused such wide spread flooding that a rail line at normal ground level was flooded or washed out completely. (Credit National Archives)

and the Front commanders, who must have been aware of the exhaustion of their armies. However, the Soviet command could only see the opportunity to fatally cripple German forces in southern Russia, an opportunity worth any risk and any sacrifice. Many, if not all, high level Soviet commanders were convinced that the Germans were finished and had no other alternative but to withdraw behind the Dnepr. The Germans had done nothing to contradict this conviction and the mistaken notion was strengthened by the movements of the armies of Heeresgruppe Süd during the first two weeks of February.

It appeared that 1. Panzerarmee was defending the Slavyansk-Voroshilovgrad line in order to cover the retreat of 4. Panzerarmee and Armeeabteilung Hollidt, both of which were in fact, withdrawing. Hollidt's halt on the Mius River was interpreted as part of a phased withdrawal by his army. Armeeabteilung Lanz had withdrawn from Kharkov and was also retreating to the west and southwest of Kharkov. Lower level Russian commanders, however, were more aware of the factors that affected the combat performance of their armies and corps. In addition to the losses suffered by the rifle divisions, the tank corps, beyond suffering normal attrition of armor, were affected by the lack of sufficient amounts of fuel and ammunition, as well as mechanical breakdowns.

The constantly lengthening lines of supply and insufficient numbers of transport vehicles, resulted in shortages that hampered operations severely. At times the tank corps of Group Popov were immobile due to lack of fuel. Orders from Front commanders bordered on the ridiculous at times. While the 4th Guards Tank Corps,

[26] Glantz, pg. 181.
[27] Armstrong, pg.173.

reduced to less than twenty tanks, was surrounded and fighting for its life at Grishino, Poluboyarov received orders demanding that his corps should encircle and destroy the German forces in the area. He was further instructed that he was 'not in any case, to permit an enemy withdrawal.' Since it was his tank corps that were attempting to withdraw, while fighting desperately to avoid destruction due to the concentric attacks by German armor, this order must have seemed incredible to Poluboyarov.

General of the Russian Army, S.M. Shtemenko, in his history of the Soviet General Staff during World War II, discussed some of the reasons for the aura of unreality permeating the highest level of the Soviet command. Describing Operation "Gallop," Shtemenko gave a surprisingly frank description of how overconfidence affected the good judgment of the Stavka:

> . . . at that time, the Front, the General Staff and GHQ as well were convinced of the correctness of their assessments and calculations. This was of course, unforgivable, but it is a fact. The victorious reports that had been coming in from the fronts blunted the vigilance of both GHQ and the General Staff, although I must add, for truth's sake, that we did have some doubts and did tell Vatutin about them, and afterwards reported them to the Supreme Commander as well, in the presence of Marshal Zhukov.[28]

Shtemenko further described the difficulties of supply that affected the operations of the attacking armies, in particular the tank corps spearheads. Vatutin's Front began the operation with an insufficient number of trucks and many of those still running were in need of repair and overhaul. He stated that the maximum fuel capacity of the trucks available to the Southwestern Front was 900 tons, while an average of 2000 tons was needed by the front's vehicles. This enormous shortfall in fuel supply capacity makes it clear why at one point in the battle, the 10th Tank Corps desperately sent a message requesting additional fuel, stating that 'no wheel was turning.' On another occasion, lack of fuel limited the mobility of the 4th Guards Tank Corps after it occupied Krasnoarmeiskoye. Furthermore, a shortage of ammunition impaired its ability to fight even if it had been supplied with sufficient amounts of fuel. These supply problems were beyond the powers of the Russians to correct at that period of the war. Even during the following summer, in August of 1943, when the tide had turned against the Germans for the last time, the Russians were still short of enough trucks to supply and move troops, artillery, fuel and ammunition. Late in 1943,

General der Panzertruppen Werner Kempf, who took over command of Armee-abteilung Lanz on February 19, 1943. The army was subsequently designated Armeeabteilung Kempf until August of 1943, when Kharkov fell to the Russians for the last time and Kempf was relieved by Hitler for the loss of the city. (Credit National Archives)

the flood of equipment from Lend Lease swelled to a torrent and supplied many hundreds of thousands of American jeeps, trucks and motorcycles to the Soviet army, but still only partially alleviated the situation.

There would never be enough trucks and supply vehicles, not even at the end of the war. Of course, by that time, the Germans were beaten and so weak that the shortage was not an important factor. However, in the late winter of 1942-43, the lack of sufficient vehicles to move men, supplies and guns, combined with poor roads and an inadequate logistics organization, had a debilitating effect on Russian mobile groups. Fuel, ammunition and supplies became increasingly scarce in direct proportion to the distance from the nearest supply centers or rail heads. The results of these deficiencies were loss of mobility, ammunition shortages and reduction of

---

[28] Shtemenko, pg. 105.

fighting power. These factors contributed to a steady erosion of Soviet combat strength that in effect, grew worse with Russian success. The farther the tank corps penetrated into the German rear areas, the worse their logistical situation became. However this was ignored in the flush of blinding post-Stalingrad optimism that colored the judgment and hopes of the Soviet command on many levels.

The Southwestern Front Chief of Staff, Lieutenant General S.P. Ivanov, incorrectly concluded that the German armor concentrating on the flanks of the front's armies was assembling in order to cover a general German withdrawal from the southern Ukraine. Ivanov's report concluded that 'all information affirms that the enemy will leave the territory of the Don basin and withdraw his forces from the Donbas across the Dnepr.' Incredibly, as late as 20 February, Ivanov still insisted that XXXXVIII. Panzer-Korps' relocation to the east of 1. Panzeramee's left flank, was a preparation to cover a general withdrawal from the Donbas.[29]

Vatutin also continued to believe the Germans were finished, even when additional air reconnaissance reported that a number of Panzer divisions were massing to the east of Krasnoarmeiskoye (XXXX. Panzer and XXXXVIII. Panzer-Korps) and that large concentrations of German armor had assembled near Krasnograd. The presence of enemy armor on each flank of the Southwestern Fronts advancing divisions was ignored. Shtemenko commented on the mistaken assessment of information by Vatutin and his staff.

> To this day it remains a riddle how Vatutin, who certainly had considerable powers of circumspection and always paid due attention to reconnaissance, should on this occasion have been so long in appreciating the danger that had arisen in the path of his front. The only explanation seems to have been his utter conviction that the enemy was no longer capable of marshaling his forces for decisive battle.

Vatutin was not the only Front commander affected by faulty interpretation of intelligence information. The intelligence and reconnaissance information gathered by Vatutin's staff, and more importantly, their interpretation of this material, was transmitted to Golikov and his command staff at Voronezh Front. Golikov accepted both the information and the conclusions drawn by Vatutin and his staff, which stated that the Germans were preparing to conduct a general retreat behind the Dnepr. These assumptions were confirmed in Golikov's eyes, by the actions of Armeeabteilung Lanz in the second half of February. After losing possession of Kharkov, the retreat of 168. Infanterie-Division to the west of Kharkov and

SS-Panzer-Korps withdrawals southwest of the city, reinforced the mistaken Soviet evaluation of the situation. Later in the war, Golikov admitted that, 'It is necessary to recognize that at that stage I had an incorrect evaluation of the intent and capabilities of the enemy.' The Stavka continued to issue orders that were influenced by the reports issuing from Vatutin and Golikov's fronts. This state of affairs delayed a prompt response to German counterattacks when they began to occur, because the Russians interpreted the attacks as the beginning of covering operations for the withdrawal.

Stalin, with a sixth sense of danger that had served him well many times in the past, may have begun to feel that something was not right. On 21 February, the Stavka's deputy chief of operations, Lieutenant General A.N. Bogolyubov, was sent to the Southwestern Front headquarters, in order to report on the situation. He told Stalin, that according to information from Major General Varennikov, Southwestern Fronts chief of staff, 'solid enemy columns were pulling out of the Donbas.' Bogolyubov had been ordered to find out what was going on by Stalin, an indication that perhaps Stalin may have awakened to the potential dangers of German armor assembling on the flanks of the advance.[30]

However, Vatutin continued to order his army and tank corps commanders to attack and committed his last armored reserves, the 1st Guards Tank Corps and the 1st Guards Cavalry Corps. The two corps were ordered to drive to the west, towards the Dnepr and destruction. Vatutin also sent a message to Popov, urging him in no uncertain terms that he was to get his attack moving again. By that time, Popov was painfully aware that his tank corps possessed a fraction of their original strength and were at the end of logistically shaky supply lines. He tried to make Vatutin aware of the situation, but the Front commander did not want to see reality.

Popov protested his new orders to no avail, and was told to attack in terms which he could not ignore. A request to withdraw Poluboyarov's 4th Guards Tank Corps from the Krasnoarmeiskoye area was turned down vehemently. Vatutin angrily reproached Popov and brusquely demanded that he carry out his orders. Other generals tried to explain the weakened state of their armies and the unrealistic expectations of their Front commanders and the Stavka. Kuznetsov, commander of the 1st Guards Army, tried to explain the reduced combat capability of his army and the difficulties of supply, which restricted the effectiveness of his army's operations. He explained that artillery shells were in short supply and food and ammunition were not consistently available in the necessary amounts. His reports and recommendations were ignored. As a result, his worn out rifle divisions, supported by fractions of the army's former tank strength, marched ever westward.

---

[29] Glantz, pg.120-121.

[30] Erickson, pg 50.

By 21 February, it was too late for the Russians to prevent a disaster. The 4. Panzerarmee had brought the SS-Panzer-Korps and XXXXVIII. Panzer-Korps on line, supported by LVII. Panzer-Korps. Mobile Group Popov was surrounded and cut off, with German armor closing in from all directions. The Northern Donets between Voroshilovgrad and Slavyansk was secured by 1. Panzerarmee. Manstein had completed his regrouping and the trap had been sprung. The last great victory of the German Army in Russia, indeed of the war itself, was about to take place. The conditions that existed in the area of the coming storm were in large part because of the determination and resiliency of the German soldier during a time of extreme stress and hardship. Perhaps the most important contribution to the victory took place in the Voroshilovgrad-Kamensk sector. If Armeeabteilung Fretter-Pico had not been able to prevent the Russians from driving south from the Northern Donets and reaching Stalino or the Sea of Azov, another German disaster would have resulted.

Armeeabteilung Fretter-Pico and 1. Panzerarmee on the Northern Donets

To a significant extent, some of the conditions that existed in the gap between Slavyansk and Kharkov, were due to the efforts of Armeeabteilung Fretter-Pico and later, 1. Panzerarmee. Improbably as it was, given the odd assortment of military units in his army, Fretter-Pico had successfully held the vital Millerovo-Donets-Voroshilovgrad area during the month of January. Fortunately for the Germans, the Russians were handicapped by their own logistical shortcomings and the extremely poor road net. The Soviet failure to cross the Northern Donets was due in large part to these factors and not just the efforts of the Germans. However, Armeeabteilung Fretter-Pico gallantly fought against a much stronger foe and did not collapse, even given its own shortcomings in armor, experience and strength. The efforts of Kreysing's 3. Gebirgs-Division Kampfgruppe, Gruppe Schuldt and the other units that battled the Russians in the Voroshilovgrad-Kamensk sector certainly played a significant role in preventing a catastrophic collapse.

By the time that Operation "Gallop" began, Fretter-Pico's 'army' had been absorbed by 1. Panzerarmee, and reverted to its original designation of XXX. Armeekorps. Commanded by Generaloberst Eberhard von Mackensen, 1. Panzerarmee had three infantry divisions and two weak Panzer corps. Mackensen had served in the German Army since 1908, with his first posting as a Leutnant in the Hussar Regiment 1. At the start of the war he had reached the rank of Generalmajor and was the 1a of 14. Armee. He took command of 1. Panzerarmee on 11 November, 1942. The 1a of 1. Panzerarmee was Oberst Wolf-Rüdiger Hauser, also a former cavalryman who had been regimental adjutant with Reiter-Regiment 18. Hauser served as 1a of the army from November of 1941 to November of 1943.

Mackensen's army had about 40,000 men and less than 50 tanks when it took over defense of the Northern Donets. While the SS-Panzer-Korps and Armeeabteilung Lanz fought to secure the northern shoulder of the Kharkov-Slavyansk gap, Fretter-Pico and subsequently, 1. Panzerarmee, held the southern shoulder until 4. Panzerarmee could launch its counterattack. During the fighting in the Slavyansk-Voroshilovgrad-Kamensk area, Mackensen's divisions fought a determined battle against superior forces from late January, until the German counterattack began on February 20-21.

If the Germans had failed to prevent the Soviets from crossing the Northern Donets between Slavyansk and Voroshilovgrad and subsequently breaking out to the south, the recapture of Kharkov would have been superfluous. If the Russians had been able to thrust to Stalino, a major portion of the German southern wing would have been sliced away from the remainder of the front. Coming so soon after the loss of Paulus' 6. Armee, the destruction of the Axis armies and the attrition of early 1943, such a defeat could have been the death knell of Hitler's armies in southern Russia. It is unlikely that the Germans could have recovered from a further mangling of Armeeabteilung Hollidt, 1. Panzerarmee and Hoth's 4. Panzerarmee. What course the war would have taken in that event can not be known.

However, the Russians were not able to strike that potentially fatal blow. In December and January, Manstein threw what ragtag resources he could find into the breach north of the Northern Donets, and astonishingly, the fragments of German divisions, detached SS and Army battalions and ad hoc combat groups of Armeeabteilung Fretter-Pico, held the river. In February, the emaciated Panzer divisions of 1. Panzerarmee arrived to take up the fight and once again managed to prevent the Russians from breaking free of the Northern Donets and lunging directly south, to Rostov or the Sea of Azov. The stubborn resistance of the German troops in the Slavyansk area forced the Stavka to try to outflank 1. Panzerarmee to the west. This thrust was eventually blocked, after it cut the vital rail line at Krasnoarmeiskoje. However, this last gasp attempt by the Soviets to get their attack moving again was too late. The Germans blocked the final thrust of Mobile Group Popov and began to systematically destroy the isolated Russian tank group as a supporting operation of the counterattack of 4. Panzerarmee.

While 1. Panzerarmee fought off the attacks of Vatutin's Southwestern Front and Malinovsky's Southern Front, Manstein had assembled his counterattack force, while the 6th Army and the 3rd Tank Army pushed ever westward, into the gap between Slavyansk and Kharkov. Manstein had no troops to oppose them without fatally weakening either 1. Panzerarmee or the counterattack by 4. Panzerarmee, but his military genius was never more evident than at that time. He astutely realized which areas had to be held at all costs and did not waste his limited strength opposing the Russian advance in less critical areas. The two absolutely essential areas were the Northern Donets sector and the railroad net and assembly areas southwest of Kharkov. These areas were held by Armeeabteilung Lanz/Kempf and 1. Panzerarmee.

The Northern Donets had to be held to prevent the destruction of Armeeabteilung Hollidt and 4. Panzerarmee before these two embattled armies could complete their withdrawal. The railroad net and assembly area southwest of Kharkov, in the Poltava-Krasnograd sector, had to be held in order to allow the SS-Panzer-Korps to assemble for the counterattack. Manstein committed all of his resources toward holding these two areas, risking that the Russian armies pouring into the gap between Kharkov and Slavyansk would not reach the Dnepr before he could begin the counterattack. Unlike Hitler, Manstein saw with crystal clarity where his true priorities lay. He understood that the Russian armies driving west, into the gap, were the least dangerous threat and he did not commit major forces to block their advance. Manstein knew that it would take time for them to reach the Dnepr and he planned to block their advance with the opening riposte conducted by the SS-Panzer-Korps. If all went according to plan, the overextended Soviet forces marching toward the west, would be cut off and destroyed by the counterattack of 4. Panzerarmee. Manstein realized that his gamble could have resulted in disaster and it is certain that the capture of Krasnoarmeiskoje gave the German command in the south a scare, but ultimately this success came too late to help the Russians.

It still proved to be a close race, because the Russians nearly reached the Dnepr crossings at Dnepropetrovsk and Zaporozsche by the end of the second week of February. By 20 February, the leading divisions in the center of the Soviet 6th Army had advanced over 160 kilometers west of Slavyansk. Forward elements of the 25th Tank Corps approached Zaporozsche, the Headquarters of Heeresgruppe Süd. This was an advance of some 100 kilometers west and southwest of Krasnoarmeiskoye. At the same time, the 1st Guards Tank Corps had plunged further to the west and was in the area west of Losovaja, 80-90 kilometers west of a Kramatorsk-Slavyansk line. Throughout the first two weeks of the month of February, the 130 kilometer wide gap, which stretched from Merefa on the north, to Slavyansk on the south, filled up with Soviet troops. Kharkov had fallen and the handful of German divisions that had defended the city were bloodied by days of costly fighting. Armeeabteilung Kempf had pulled back to the Msha River, but had open flanks and had received no significant reinforcements, other than "Totenkopf."

The Southwestern Front and the Stavka still believed that the stubborn defense conducted by 1. Panzerarmee throughout the first weeks of February was meant to cover the retreat of Armeeabteilung Hollidt and 4. Panzerarmee. Once behind the Mius River, however, Hollidt occupied the old German positions on the western bank of the river with every intention of holding his ground. Hoth's 4. Panzerarmee continued to assemble to the west, covered by 1. Panzerarmee, but only to take up positions from which to launch Manstein's counteroffensive. Remaining confident that the Germans were all but beaten, the Soviet Front and high command drove their troops further and further to the west. Although it is clear, in hindsight what was happening, it is understandable why the Soviet command still believed that the Germans planned to withdraw out of the Donbas.

However, on 19 February, the SS-Panzer-Korps had regrouped in preparation for the first phase of its counterattack. "Das Reich" and "Totenkopf" were in position to strike the overextended Russian spearheads approaching the Dnepr crossings east of Dnepropetrovsk. The timing was nearly perfect, thanks to the efforts and blood of the German troops that had held the Northern Donets and provided a screen behind which Heeresgruppe Süd was able to carry out its regrouping. Manstein had counted upon the steadfast bravery of the men and officers of Armeeabteilung Fretter-Pico, and 1. Panzerarmee. Beginning on 21 February, their sacrifices paid handsome dividends, as Manstein wielded the divisions of the SS-Panzer-Korps like an armored bludgeon, cutting off and smashing the Russian forces approaching the Dnepr crossings. The XXXX. and XXXXVIII. Panzer-Korps attacked much of the remaining Soviet forces in the gap west of Slavyansk, smashing Mobile Group Popov and striking the southern flank of the 6th Army.

During the last days of February Manstein began to collect what would be considerable winnings from his successful gamble. The 4. Panzerarmee had completed its regrouping under shelter provided by Armeeabteilung Kempf, just as Rybalko's 3rd Tank Army was running out of steam. The 6th and 1st Guards Armies had driven into the void west of Kharkov, while Mobile Group Popov was surrounded by German Panzer divisions. The bulk of the 3rd Guards Army was held up on the Northern Donets and Armeeabteilung Hollidt turned back attacks from the 5th Tank Army and settled into positions behind the Mius River it would hold until the end of summer of 1943. The overextended 40th and 69th Armies, ordered to continue their attacks ever westward, could only look with discomfort at the events unfolding to the south. The SS-Panzer-Korps was surging northward, leaving a wake of death and destruction after it passed. It goal was the city of Kharkov.

7

MANSTEIN'S COUNTEROFFENSIVE BEGINS

Critical Days

While 1. Panzerarmee fought its key battles along the Slavyansk-Voroshilovgrad line, Armeeabteilung Lanz delayed the Russian advance past Kharkov. Only by the remarkable efforts of the ordinary German soldier was a disaster avoided, although at the cost of high casualties and the loss of Kharkov. The two SS divisions, "Leibstandarte" and "Das Reich," as well as "Grossdeutschland," were bloodied in the hard fought defensive battles of February. The 168. and 298. Infanterie-Divisions were fragments of their former strength while 320. Infanterie-Division was weakened from its debilitating retreat. "Das Reich" had suffered particularly severe losses in armor, due to the fact its tanks had been engaged in the bitter fighting on the eastern outskirts of Kharkov. The battle in that area was a costly slugging match because the German troops faced superior numbers of Soviet tanks, in extremely tough fighting at close range in the city streets. The SS Panzers damaged or knocked out many Soviet tanks in the fighting but suffered losses of their own. On 17 February "Das Reich" had only twenty tanks still in action, a total that included fourteen Panzer IIIs, two Panzer IVs and four "Tigers." Apparently during the next several days, the division either received new tanks or was able to repair a number of its previously damaged tanks because on 20 February, it listed thirty-three Panzer IIIs, seven Panzer IVs and one "Tiger" as ready for action. The division still had an impressive amount of heavy weapons, possessing thirty-five towed anti-tank guns of either 5cm or 7.5cm caliber and thirty-seven other anti-tank guns, including captured 7.62cm and self-propelled 7.5cm guns. It also was equipped with forty-eight 8.8cm Flak guns and fifteen Sturmgeschütze IIIs.

The Panzer regiment of "Leibstandarte" was somewhat stronger, as it had been more often engaged in operations in open territory and had retained the advantages of mobility, thus suffering fewer losses of tanks. On 19 February, the regiment had forty-five Panzer IVs, ten Panzer IIIs and twenty-one command tanks, in addition to twelve Panzer IIs. Many of the 'command tanks" were probably Panzer IIIs and IVs. Clever old soldiers like Dietrich had learned from war time experience to accumulate 'unofficial' vehicles and weapons and hide their presence in order to avoid having to give them up. The division also had a substantial additional fire power in the form of thirty-two towed or self-propelled 7.5cm Pak 40s, forty-five 5cm Pak 38 guns and twenty-two Sturmgeschütze IIIs. It also had nineteen light, 3.7cm anti-tank guns, either towed or self-propelled.

The combat around the city had also cost the Russians dearly. The momentum of Operation "Star" diminished due the casualties and vehicle losses inflicted upon the Russians and Golikov's offensive was well behind schedule by 19 February. The Soviet attempt to completely encircle Kharkov was delayed and the German divisions defending the city were able to escape. The Russians had not destroyed Armeeabteilung Lanz and had not been able to cut the remaining communications corridors still open to the southwest. As a result, the Germans were able to organize a new line of defense behind the Udy River and bring up and begin to deploy "Totenkopf" and the newly arrived 15. Infanterie-Division. German air activity in the sector was on the increase, further reducing the amount of supplies reaching the Soviet tank corps. Russian supply columns, unprotected by the Soviet air force, were shot up and left burning on the roads with increasing frequency.

To the south however, the Russians approached the Dnepr crossings with little between them and the river. It appeared that Operation "Gallop" was on the verge of a decisive success. The 6th Army had smashed through the thin German defenses between Kharkov and Slavyansk and then advanced through the undefended gap. By

15 February, Soviet infantry columns were only fifty kilometers east of the vital bridges across the Dnepr at Dnepropetrovsk and Zaporozsche. Forward elements of the 25th Tank Corps and the 35th Guards Rifle Division had occupied the Pavlograd-Sinel'nikovo area, cutting the rail line that ran from Dnepropetrovsk to Pavlograd. Only the timely arrival of a fresh German infantry division prevented the Russians from advancing further west and seizing the Dnepr bridges over which the supplies flowed east to 1. Panzerarmee and Armeeabteilung Hollidt.

The first units of 15. Infanterie-Division, which was under the command of Generalmajor Erich Buschenhagen, reached Dnepropetrovsk on 18 February. The division had seen first significant combat while serving with Heeresgruppe Mitte in Russia, during 1941. It was sent to France in late 1942, to be rebuilt after sustaining over 50% casualties after the fighting for Yelna. The division left La Rochelle, France on 9 February, carried in seventy trains. The first units arrived at Dnepropetrovsk just in time to be thrown into action. By 19 February the 25th Guards Tank Corps pushed south of Sinel'nikovo, reaching the town of Slavgorod. From Slavgorod, the 111th Tank Brigade drove further to the south and approached Zaporozsche, the second main crossing over the Dnepr River. If the Russians were allowed to capture the bridges over the river, the German forces east of the Dnepr would die a slow death, strangled by lack of fuel, food and ammunition.

A Catastrophe Narrowly Averted

Manstein's headquarters first established communications with Generalmajor Buschenhagen on 18 February but discovered that he could not take charge of the situation. Buschenhagen was forty miles west of the Dnepr crossings and his plane could not take off due to thick fog and a heavy snowstorm. In the absence of the divisional commander, the Chief of Staff (1a) of the division, Oberstleutnant Wilhelm Willemer, took charge of the division on his own initiative. Willemer decided upon a daring and risky tactic which he felt was called for considering the situation. A train carrying three companies of infantry, equipped with heavy support weapons was sent hurriedly across the bridge at Dnepropetrovsk. Commanded by a Hauptmann Berckel, it arrived at a point west of Sinel'nikovo late in the night of 19 February and halted while Willemer reviewed his plan with Berckel. The train was to steam right up to the outskirts of Sinel'nikovo at which point the three companies of Grenadiers were to spring out of the train and launch their attack, hoping to take the Soviets by surprise. A second train with the battalion command group, three more companies of Grenadiers and a few self-propelled anti-tank guns, was to follow the

Sepp Dietrich was a wily old soldier and veteran who knew how to accumulate extra tanks and heavy weapons for his division. The tank strength records of II. SS-Panzer-Korps frequently show that "Leibstandarte" often had larger than normal amounts of command tanks. These were most likely tanks that were scrounged from one source or another and hidden by calling them command tanks. (Credit National Archives)

lead detachment. Berckel briefed his company commanders while the train steamed through the darkness toward Sinel'nikovo.[1]

The tense German infantrymen clutched their weapons, eyes straining to see through the blowing snow as they peered into the night. Not knowing if the rail line had been destroyed or blocked by Russian troops, Berckel and his men were ready to spring into action at any moment. However, the line was undamaged and the train pulled into the outskirts of the town without incident. As the cars slowed, the German infantrymen leaped out and quickly assaulted along the rail line, capturing a few very surprised Russian troops, who were asleep along the siding. The three companies took up positions near the tracks and organized a defensive perimeter. A short time later the second train steamed into the station and swarms of dark figures leapt out of the rail cars before they squealed to a halt. Grenadiers scrambled to take up positions alongside their comrades, while machine gun teams set up their guns. The crews of three self-propelled anti-tank guns hurriedly unloaded their vehicles and positioned them to defend the Grenadiers from attacks by Russian armor. Once the area was secured, Berckel quickly organized an attack and swept the remaining Soviet troops out of Sinel'nikovo. Infantry of the 35th Guards Rifle Division, supported by elements of the 1st Guards Cavalry Corps and the 41st Guards Rifle Division, assaulted the town later in the evening but were turned back. The Grenadiers in Sinel'nikovo repelled several other Soviet attempts to recapture the station during the night.

---

[1] Carell, pg. 186.

By the following day, the Germans had thrown an entire fresh infantry regiment in the sector and occupied a solid position inclusive of Sinel'nikovo and the town of Novo Moskovsk. At dawn the weather cleared slightly and Buschenhagen flew to the town in a Fieseler Storch. He personally directed the organization of defensive positions around the Sinel'nikovo area. Before nightfall the main elements of three Grenadier Regiments and the divisional Pioniere battalion occupied strong points blocking the main roads and manned a defensive position north of Dnepropetrovsk, at Novo Moskovsk. The positions were reinforced by anti-tank guns of the divisional anti-tank battalion, 15. Panzerjägerabteilung, which was a high quality unit according to Carell. He stated that it was fully equipped with self-propelled 7.5cm guns, which was unusual for an infantry division at this time in the war.[2] When the Russians were able to bring up additional forces and attack once again, they ran up against solid defensive positions at both Sinel'nikovo and Novo Moskovsk. The Soviet attacks were thrown back by heavy firepower from well organized defensive positions.

The quick reaction by Willemer averted a possibly disastrous situation for the Germans. Without his bold decision to push troops down the line in order to seize Sinel'nikovo, the Russians could have reached the river and seized the rail bridges at Dnepropetrovsk. It would then have been necessary to clear up that situation immediately, in order to restore the flow of supplies eastward to 1. Panzerarmee and Armeeabteilung Hollidt. The only mobile divisions available to quickly deal with such a setback would have been the SS divisions. The use of "Totenkopf" and "Das Reich" to rectify the situation would have unavoidably delayed the launching of Manstein's counteroffensive. This might have allowed the Russians time to bring up additional forces to block the attack of Hausser's SS corps. However, due to the timely arrival and commitment of 15. Infanterie-Division, the SS-Panzerkorps was able to assemble undisturbed at Sinel'nikovo on 19-20 February and begin its attack as scheduled.

---

[2] Carell, pg. 186-188.

Marders move through a Russian village with bunches of SS Grenadiers riding on their decks. These vehicles probably belonged to SS-Panzerjäger Bataillon 3, commanded by SS-Hauptsturmführer Armin Grunert. (Credit National Archives)

Manstein's Counterattack

"Das Reich" and "Totenkopf" began a relocation to assembly areas after nightfall on 17 February. Regiment "Der Führer" was the last formation of the two divisions to move to its new assembly areas. The leading combat element of "Das Reich," Harmel's Regiment "Deutschland," reached its staging area at Krasnograd by 1650 hours. According to orders from Heeresgruppe Süd, the first priority of the SS-Panzerkorps was to block the advance of the Soviet 6th Army toward the Dnepr and relieve the hard pressed 15. Infanterie-Division. Manstein ordered 4. Panzerarmee to take command of "Das Reich" and "Totenkopf" as well as 15. Infanterie-Division.

After seizing a bridgehead over the Orel River at Pereshchepino, "Das Reich" was to advance to Novo Moskovsk and prepare for a further advance to the rail center of Pavlograd, supported by a simultaneous advance by "Totenkopf." Subsequently, the divisions were to detach a regimental Kampfgruppe to the south and fall upon the rear of the 41st Guards Rifle Division at Sinel'nikovo in order to strike the Russian troops opposing 15. Infanterie-Division from the rear and destroy them. After joining forces at Pavlograd, the two divisions were push northwards, along the railroads that led to Kharkov.[3]

While the other two SS divisions were preparing to attack, all purely offensive operations of "Leibstandarte" were suspended in order to cover the relocation movements to the south. Witt's 1. Panzergrenadier-Regiment "LAH" was ordered to withdraw from the Taranovka area after sustaining very heavy casualties without being able to secure the town. Soviet infantry, probably from the 184th Rifle Division, attacked Witt's regiment several times during the course of the day and the regiment remained involved in heavy fighting in the town. The battalion in the town itself, Albert Frey's I./SS-PzG.-Rgt. 1 "LAH" had over 100 wounded and could not withdraw without leaving their wounded behind. There were no longer enough able bodied men to provide sufficient covering fire for a retreat and not enough vehicles to transport the battalion's casualties. Witt had no intention of abandoning Frey's wounded to the Russians, as he had no illusions as to their fate. However, with every passing hour streams of Russian infantry were entering Taranovka from the north and east. Frey's battalion was pushed into a steadily shrinking perimeter and their only remaining avenue of retreat passed through a narrow, flat expanse of snow covered terrain that offered no concealment.[4]

With Russian troops in position to cover the corridor with machine gun and mortar fire, it was suicidal to attempt a retreat in that direction, especially when burdened with stretcher cases. Frey realized that he had only two choices. He could break out with his able bodied men, leaving the wounded to the Russians or continue fighting until overrun by the steadily massing Soviet infantry. Since abandoning his casualties was out of the question, the second, grim choice seemed to be inevitable. Fortunately for the battalion, help arrived in the form of a column of SPWs from Kumm's Regiment "Der Führer." The half tracks of a company of the regiment raced through a gap in the Russian forces surrounding Taranovka and entered the town. The men of Frey's battalion were understandably elated, as all had been aware of the seriousness of the situation. The column broke out of the town and withdrew successfully, its load of wounded delivered to safety.

After the evacuation of Frey's wounded, Witt was able to withdraw the rest of the regiment and pull back to the Novaja Vodolaga area, where it established contact with troops of 320. Infanterie-Division. That division's three regiments had taken up positions southwest of Kharkov on 17 February, on a front about 10 kilometers in width. In the afternoon of that same day, the Soviet 12th Tank Corps probed "Leibstandarte" positions at two points, but did not follow up either attack with any great effort and the penetrations were eliminated.

On the following day, Wisch's regiment took over a section of the front formerly held by Regiment "Der Führer." The I./SS-PzG.-Rgt. 2 "LAH," under command of SS-Sturmbannführer Rudolf Sandig and II./SS-PzG.-Rgt. 2 "LAH," commanded by SS-Sturmbannführer Hugo Kraas, took up defensive positions southwest of Kharkov. Peiper's battalion, with its half tracks and self-propelled heavy weapons, moved to the Krasnograd area, serving as the division reserve. A battalion of the divisional artillery, reinforced with a battery of heavy howitzers, supported Wisch's regiment. North of this sector, Witt took over a section of the line in the Novaja Vodolaga area, supported by artillery of nearly two battalions of howitzers and guns of Artillerie-Regiment "LAH."

While the Panzergrenadier regiments organized their defenses, the divisional Pioniere battalion was ordered to patrol the divisional boundary to the north, in order to screen a gap between "Leibstandarte's" northern flank and 320. Infanterie-Division's southernmost regiment. The gap was to have been defended by Postel's infantry but that division was slow to take over responsibility for the area and Dietrich was forced to use SS troops to block any Soviet attack in the sector. Meyer's Aufklärungsabteilung was also in reserve at Starowerovka, several kilometers behind the front. The remaining artillery was moved into a position where it could reinforce the other battalions where necessary.[5]

[3] NA/T-354, roll 118, Oberkommando der 4. Panzerarmee an SS-Panzerkorps, 20.2.1943. 1a Tgb. Nr. 264/43, frame 3751740.

[4] Lehmann, pg. 106.

[5] Lehmann, pg. 106-107.

LEFT: SS-Sturmbannführer Albert Frey commanded I./SS-Pz.Gren.-Rgt. 1 "LAH" on 19 February 1943 when the battalion was surrounded in Taranovka. With over 100 men disabled by wounds, the battalion could not fight its way out of the town and still save its wounded. However, shortly before being overrun, a "Das Reich" half track company fought its way into Taranovka and rescued the battalion and its wounded men. (Courtesy Mark C. Yerger) RIGHT: SS-Sturmbannführer Hugo Kraas, pictured here as an SS-Hauptsturmführer, was the commander of I./SS-Pz.Gren.-Rgt. 2 during the Kharkov fighting. He won the Knight's Cross for his actions during the Kharkov fighting. (Courtesy Mark C. Yerger)

Korps Raus defends Ljubotin and Merefa

While "Leibstandarte" took over defensive positions southwest of Kharkov, "Grossdeutschland's" Füsilier Regiment defended the section of road leading out of Kharkov to the west, between the city itself and Ljubotin. At the town of Korotisch, the division's line bent southward, where it tied in with the northern flank of 320. Infanterie-Division. This created a salient at Korotisch, which was held by III./Grenadier Regiment "GD." The other two battalions of the regiment occupied the line south of Korotisch, facing the east toward Kharkov. The western flank of the division ended at Ljubotin, which was still defended by the division's assault gun battalion and Aufklärungsabteilung "GD." West of Ljubotin, the flank of the division remained open, the undefended gap stretching to the positions of 168. Infanterie-Division, in the Graivoron area. Had the

40th Army struck south, through this gap and thrust toward Valki, there would have been no German forces that could have kept them from cutting the Poltava-Ljubotin-Kharkov railhead. The halt due to the realignment of the attack direction of the Soviet 40th and 69th Armies prevented the complete collapse of the western flank of the army and a major disruption of Manstein's counterattack.[6]

As the 40th and 69th Army completed their realignment, Rybalko's 3rd Tank Army was engaged in trying to break through the new Korps Raus line of defense southwest of Kharkov. On the morning of 18 February, the 15th Tank Corps and elements of several rifle divisions attacked "Grossdeutschland" salient position at Korotisch. One such attack took place near a collective farm on the

---

[6] Glantz pg. 182.

outskirts of the town. At that point, about twenty Russian tanks, supported by a regiment of infantry, approached a position defended by two companies of III./Gren. Rgt "GD," which were dug-in on a series of small hills along the Korotisch road. The German infantry had been alerted by sounds of approaching fighting in the early morning hours before daylight. Artillery flashes lit up the night and the rattle of machine gun fire was heard in the distance. As the noise of battle grew louder, the defenders waited in their shallow holes, trying to restore feeling to frost bitten hands and frozen feet.

Just before dawn, motor noise could be heard in the distance. More ominously, tank tracks squealed and clanked in the darkness, signaling the arrival of Russian armor. Shortly after dawn, the dark, massive shapes of T-34s and KV-1s became visible, deployed on the road to the east. Soon the huge machines began to grind up the hillsides toward the German Grenadiers. Russian infantry, huddled on the tank decks, fired automatic weapons furiously in order to keep the Germans heads down. Behind the bulk of the tanks, waves of brown coated Soviet infantry trudged forward, rifles and long, needlelike bayonets ready.[7]

The two German companies had no anti-tank guns and were not supported by assault guns and had no defense against tanks. With nothing to fear from German heavy anti-tank weapons, the Soviet armor rolled toward the foxholes. The "Grossdeutschland" infantry tried to smother the accompanying Russian infantry with small arms fire, in a hopeless effort to stop the attack. The MG-42s ripped out streams of bullets and machine pistol fire sprayed the attackers. Brown uniformed figures fell off of tank decks and crashed to the earth but the T-34s rumbled closer to the line of shallow foxholes. From time to time a tank fired at a German machine gun position with high explosive shells. Direct hits flung body parts, frozen turf and pieces of machine gun spinning into the air. One after another, the machine gun positions fell silent. The volume of German fire lessened and the Russian infantry surged forward with a shout.

When the T-34s reached the first holes, they turned and rolled down the length of the German positions, crushing the foxholes and the terror stricken men in them. The tanks left only bloody patches of snow after the tracks finished their work. A few of the Grenadiers leapt up at the approach of the tanks, wild eyed with terror and made futile sprints toward the rear. Some reached safety but most were gunned down as they struggled to run through the snow. In minutes, the hill was nearly cleared of German troops. The shaken survivors fled down the reverse slope of the hill and reached safety. After the first company was overrun, a half dozen

SS-Sturmbannführer Ernst Häussler's III./Regiment "Totenkopf" made contact with "Das Reich" troops near Pereshschepino on 21 February. The picture shows trucks carrying the battalion as it passes through a village on the road between Poltava and Pereshschepino. ((The author's collection)

Soviet tanks left the road and raced up the hill toward the other company. The T-34s destroyed this position as well, machine gunning any Germans who tried to run from the armored giants.

The men who survived the slaughter made their way away down from the bloody hills and regrouped after they were joined by other detachments of the regiment. The second company lost five dead and two wounded, with one missing. After shattering the companies defending the road, the Russian tanks milled around for a time, possibly unsure about what to do next. Another Russian column of tanks and infantry arrived but continued down the road to the west without stopping.[8]

At that time a few German tanks appeared, accompanied by additional infantry. This small force assembled and a hastily organized counterattack was launched in order to seal off the penetration. The attack was repulsed by accurate cannon fire from the Russian tanks, which immobilized two of the German tanks. The survivors of the two companies, with the remaining three operational tanks, fell back toward Ljubotin.

Meanwhile, south of the Korotisch salient, at Merefa, 320. Infanterie-Division was under attack as well on 18 February. Merefa was attacked by the 12th Tank Corps and infantry of the 111th Rifle Division. Supported by tanks and artillery, Russian infantry advanced across the snow toward the town, while mortar fire and rockets smothered German front line positions. German artillery fire blasted holes in their ranks and machine gun fire flickered out in streams at the Soviet troops. At points where German anti-tank guns were knocked out, T-34s and KV's roared over the defenders, opening gaps in the defensive perimeter. Soviet battle groups passed through these gaps and were able to break into the town. They en-

[7] Spaeter, pg. 47.

[8] Spaeter, pg. 48-49.

gaged the defending German infantry in house to house fighting. Always superb in fighting in built up areas, the Russians drove the Germans from their perimeter defenses.

T-34s edged cautiously down streets, poking their gun barrels around corners, with crowds of Russian soldiers taking shelter behind them. Under cover of fire from the tanks, Russian assault teams crept through houses or masses of rubble and infiltrated into the town. The Russian infantry cleared one block after the other in fierce and brutal street fighting which lasted the entire day. Merefa fell into Russian hands at midnight but the 12th Tank Corps was not able to cross the Msha River to the north or south of the town because the defenses of 320. Infanterie-Division held firm at all other points.

The next day, Rybalko decided to accelerate his efforts to break through Korps Raus' defense of the Ljubotin-Korotisch-Merefa salient. Although the 111th Rifle Division had been able to capture Merefa, the rest of the army had difficulty breaking through the German front running south from Merefa to the town of Korotisch. "Grossdeutschland" successfully defended its defensive line which

extended from Ljubotin to the Korotisch salient angle and southwards toward Merefa.[9]

The Russian rifle divisions had lost so many men, their rifle regiments were a fraction of their normal strength and had lost much of their fighting power. The difficult combat had worn down Russian tank strength as well and the tank corps no longer had enough armor to support large scale infantry attacks and conduct effective offensive operations at the same time. Rybalko decided to break the stalemate by maneuver, rather than suffer additional casualties simply trying to bludgeon through Korps Raus defenses. He decided to eliminate the "Grossdeutschland" salient at Korotisch with a two prong encirclement of the town, chopping off that section of the front. The 12th Tank Corps formed the southern prong of the encircling jaws and the 15th Tank Corps was the northern prong.

On 20 February, Rybalko directed the 12th Tank Corps to attack between Korotisch and Merefa, break through and drive to the

---

[9] Glantz, pg. 194 and NA/T-314, roll 490, 1a KTB Korps Raus, Tagesmeldung vom 19-20. 2.1943. frames 000098 to 000108.

A crew of a Sturmgeschütz III firing at Russian infantry in the distance. The flat terrain offered little concealment and the Germans were frequently able to use artillery, Flak guns and machine guns against columns of Russians at great distances. (Credit National Archives)

west. The 48th Guards Rifle Division was brought up to furnish additional infantry strength. Also supporting the attack were infantry and artillery of the 25th Guards Rifle Division. The 15th Tank Corps, reinforced by infantry of the 160th Rifle Division, formed the northern jaw of the attack. The plan of attack was to penetrate the German front on both sides of Korotisch and encircle the stubborn defenders. When the two tank spearheads linked up west of the Ljubotin-Korotisch salient, the "Grossdeutschland" troops in the salient would be trapped.

Rybalko planned to occupy the Germans with strong frontal attacks from the east, while the armored groups enveloped the town. Both of the Soviet mobile groups achieved some success on 20 February, breaking through the German front without great difficulty. By the next day, the 12th Tank Corps had fought its way across the Msha River, penetrated five kilometers and reached the town of Ogulsky, which was southwest of Ljubotin. The 15th Tank Corps 195th Tank Brigade broke through the German front at the town of Stary Merchik and drove south, easily reaching its first objectives. However, it unexpectedly came into contact with Regiment "Thule," which occupied defensive positions west of Ljubotin. A series of bitter battles began for possession of the railroad line.[10] However, by 20 February, Armeeabteilung Lanz had accomplished its main objective. Its dogged defense of the area southwest of Kharkov shielded the assembly of the SS-Panzerkorps until Hausser's divisions were ready to launch the counteroffensive. Korps Raus delayed the Soviet advance west of Kharkov sufficiently so that the Russians were not able to threaten the supply lines of Hausser's SS divisions. South of the Korps Raus sector, "Leibstandarte" protected the assembly of "Das Reich" at Krasnograd and made possible the safe arrival of "Totenkopf" at Poltava.

There were several tense moments for the army however. On 18 February, due to confusion regarding the location of the boundary between 320. Infanterie-Division and "Leibstandarte," a dangerous situation was created. On the previous day, 320. Infanterie-Division had been removed from the order of battle of the SS-Panzerkorps and assigned to Korps Raus. At that time, Raus gave the division defensive responsibilities which changed the division's southern boundary. As a result, troops of the division were withdrawn from a sector of the front along the boundary shared with "Leibstandarte." This adjustment was made without informing SS-Panzerkorps and resulted in the creation of a gap in the German lines at the divisional boundary. The Russians, who always patrolled aggressively, found the gap and soon approached the town of Borki.

---

[10] Glantz, pg. 184-185.

Without hesitation, the Soviets moved a battalion of infantry into Borki itself and began to dig in. The bridgehead provided an assembly area for an exploitative attack toward the railroad leading out of Poltava. The penetration had to be cleared up immediately.

After it had discovered and subsequently reported the threat to its flank, "Leibstandarte" was ordered to remedy the situation in cooperation with Postel's division. A battalion of Grenadier-Regiment 586, reinforced with a battery of SS assault guns and 1./SS-Pioniere-Abteilung "LAH," immediately attacked the Russians. At 1630 hours, the SS Kampfgruppe reported that Borki was in German hands again. However, the Soviet troops occupying the town were able to pull back intact and make their escape. A reinforced company took up a position in a rail road station north of town while the rest of the Soviet troops withdrew into a number of nearby wooded ridges north of Borki. When the Germans attempted to follow the retreating Russians into the woods, they were hit by heavy machine gun fire and a curtain of mortar shells. The Germans were forced to halt their pursuit and lost contact with the Russians. This allowed the Russians to dig in along the ridge tops. Without adequate information about the layout of the Russian defenses the Germans did not want to make a night time assault and pulled back.

The battalion from 320. Infanterie Division took up new positions to the west of the town and the SS Pioniere company remained in Borki itself. However, the Soviet bridgehead could not be allowed to exist without risking detection of the movements of the last elements of Regiment "Der Führer." On 19 February, Dietrich was ordered to retake the railway station at Borki, supported by III./Grenadier-Regiment 586. At the same time, the division was directed to throw out screening detachments east of Krasnograd. In order to secure the line of departure, Dietrich was directed to conduct an active defense along his division's entire front. He decided to recapture the towns of Jefremovka and Ochotschaje, which were just east of the positions held by SS-PzG.-Rgt. 2 "LAH."

Peiper's battalion was to conduct the attack upon Jeremejevka and seize the area south and east of the town in order to prevent the Russians from using them as launching areas for attacks. At 1650 hours on 19 February, under a cold, clear sky, Peiper began his attack upon Jeremejevka. To the north, Albert Frey's battalion, supported by SS assault guns and the "Leibstandarte" Pioniere Abteilung, assaulted the Borki railway station. By 1800 hours the station was captured and the Russians were put to flight.

Peiper's SPWs converged on their attack objective from two separate directions. One group approached from the south and one from the north. Near the village of Ziglerovka, the southern column overran a force of Soviet infantry, destroying a number of guns and mortars, as well as three tanks. The fighting for Ziglerovka lasted several hours. Although Peiper was soon on the move again, the attack upon Jeremejevka was delayed.[11]

During the time that "Leibstandarte" fought to hold its ground south of Kharkov, reinforcements from 167. Infanterie-Division, under command of Generalleutnant Wolf Trirenberg began arriving on 20 February. The 167. Infanterie-Division had fought in Russia in 1941 and was decimated by combat losses. In early 1942 it was pulled out and sent to Holland to rebuild. The division remained in the west until January, 1943 when it boarded trains bound for the Eastern Front. On 18 February the first elements of the division arrived at Poltava and prepared to help take over the undefended sector of the front west of Ljubotin. The division was to occupy the gap on the western flank of Korps Raus. At that point the Russians had lost their best opportunity to easily outflank the Armeeabteilung to the west.

While Korps Raus secured the supply lines and rear areas of the Armeeabteilung, the SS divisions assembled in Krasnograd. They prepared to drive to Pavlograd, sweep the Russians off the railroad network south of Kharkov and make contact with XXXXVIII. Panzerkorps. Once having linked up with the Army divisions, the two Panzer corps were to attack north, slicing through the entire forward communications zone of the Soviet 6th Army west of the Northern Donets. After severing the front half of the army from its supply bases, the next objective was the 3rd Tank Army and Kharkov. The 15. Infanterie-Division was to advance in the wake of the Panzer divisions and eliminate any remaining strong points which were bypassed by the mobile spearheads. Manstein's counterattack had begun!

The SS-Panzerkorps Attacks

On the night of 19-20 February, the counterattack of Hoth's 4. Panzerarmee was launched. It would be almost like the old days of blitzkrieg once again, as the Panzer divisions struck with speed and concentrated, overwhelming firepower. Led by flights of Stukas and ground attack planes, they sliced through the communication lines of Russian tank corps and infantry divisions, smashing the advanced units of the Russian armies. In this type of attacking, mobile warfare, the SS divisions were involved in a type of combat that suited their nature perfectly. They were led by experienced, hard bitten company, battalion, and regimental commanders, many of whom had three to four years of combat experience. A significant number of these officers were products of the prewar SS Junkerschulen, organized and administered by Hausser, trained by

teachers such as Steiner and inspired by legendary leaders such as Dietrich. They were supremely confident in their own abilities and the capabilities of their men.

These men understood the values of surprise, concentration of firepower and combined arms assault. Most recognized that mobility was a weapon, and that firepower combined with mobility could be a deadly weapon. Like all German troops, they were trained to be aggressive, whether attacking or defending. Led by dynamic and often charismatic combat commanders, from corps down to company level, the SS-Panzerkorps went in to battle believing in its superiority to anything the Russians could throw against them. These divisions, instilled with the confidence of the elite, well trained soldier and hardened by bitter combat experience, launched the opening phase of the counterattack by Hoth's 4. Panzerarmee.

Generaloberst Hermann Hoth, the commander of 4. Panzerarmee. Hoth was one of the outstanding tank commanders of the war. He was a blunt spoken Prussian who was very demanding with his staff officers. He was not afraid to speak his mind, even to Hitler. The dictator removed him from command late in the war after Hoth gave him a realistic appraisal of Germany's dim prospects for victory which did not suit Hitler's view of the war situation. (Credit National Archives)

---

[11] Lehmann, pg. 112.

The first task of Hausser's corps was to block the advance of the Soviet 6th Army from Krasnograd to Zaporozsche and to re-open the railroad net which stretched eastward from the two main Dnepr River crossings at Dnepropetrovsk and Zaporozsche. East of the Dnepr, Soviet troops remained in possession of sections of the Dnepropetrovsk-Pavlograd-Stalino railroad net at a number of places. The Dnepropetrovsk rail line, after crossing the river, extended eastward for about 50 kilometers, passing through Sinel'nikovo and then running east until it reached Pavlograd. At Pavlograd, the line split into two main branches, one running to the north, the other to the south. The northern line ran from Pavlograd and then due north towards Kharkov. The southern section exited Pavlograd on its eastern edge, passing through Krasnoarmeiskoje and on to Stalino. The Pavlograd-Krasnoarmeiskoje line was entirely in possession of the Russians on 19 February, with Soviet troops holding key rail stations at Krasnoarmeiskoje, Petropawlovka and Rasdory. The 1. Panzerarmee's XXXX. Panzerkorps, in cooperation with XXXXVIII. Panzerkorps, was to clear the Russians from the railroad net between the Northern Donets and the flank of the SS-Panzerkorps. This area was approximately 80 kilometers in width. It was absolutely vital to the continued existence of 1. Panzerarmee and Armeeabteilung Hollidt to regain control of the railroad system from the Dnepr River crossings to Stalino.

However, the Russians were still in position to threaten the Dnepr bridges at both Dnepropetrovsk and Zaporozsche. East of Dnepropetrovsk and its vital bridges, Buschenhagen's 15. Infanterie-Division remained involved in bitter battle against the Soviet 4th Guards Rifle Corps. Meanwhile, the 25th Guards Tank Corps forward group approached Zaporozsche, unopposed by any significant German forces. In effect the two opponents had been involved in a race to see if the Soviets could seize the entire railroad system from the Dnepr River to Stalino before the Germans could launch their counterattack. In the midst of nearly unbridled optimism, the Russian high command spurred on its forward elements, unaware that it had already lost a race it was never aware of participating in.

"Das Reich" Leads the Attack to Pereshschepino

Vahl's "Das Reich" assembled at Krasnograd and prepared to launch the opening thrust of Manstein's counteroffensive, the drive to block the Soviet advance toward the Dnepr bridges. SS-Standartenführer Heinz Harmel's reinforced regiment led the attack of the division, departing from the town on the night of 19 February. From Krasnograd, Kampfgruppe Harmel thrust south towards Pereshschepino, which was occupied by rear echelon detachments of the Soviet 267th Rifle Division. Pereshschepino was located on

SS-Sturmbannführer Christian Tychsen in his command tank. Tychsen was the commander of II./SS-Panzer-Regiment 2 during the Kharkov fighting. Tychsen later commanded "Das Reich" in the summer of 1944. He was killed after being captured by American troops a matter of days after assuming command. (Courtesy Mark C. Yerger)

the banks of the Orel River about 60 kilometers north of Dnepropetrovsk. The town lay on the Dnepropetrovsk-Krasnograd-Kharkov section of rail line and was an important rail center. The lines of communication of the Soviet 267th Rifle Division extended through this sector. The division's route of attack would slice through the supply lines of the division and would also cut through the rear areas of the 106th Rifle Brigade, which was in the area northwest of Pereshschepino.

Kampfgruppe Harmel advanced in two columns, one of which was built around Fritz Ehrath's I./Rgt. "Deutschland" and II./SS-Pz.Rgt 2, under the leadership of Christian Tychsen. The battle group was reinforced with assault guns and Panzerjäger batteries. On the morning of 19 February, I./Rgt. "Deutschland" was to lead the attack, driving southwest from Krasnograd, until it reached the village of Otrada. Once it had assembled at Otrada, which lay only a

SS-Sturmbannführer Jakob Fick, the commander of SS-Kradschützen-Bataillon 2, which was the "Das Reich" motorcycle battalion. Fick's battalion was extremely mobile and screened the western flank of "Das Reich" after it began its attack from Krasnograd on February 19-20, 1943. (Courtesy Mark C. Yerger)

Heinz Harmel, the commander of Regiment "Deutschland" in early 1943. Harmel was an aggressive and effective commander of troops. He was a highly decorated soldier and won the German Cross in Gold, the Knight's Cross and subsequently the Oakleaves and Swords to the Knight's Cross. (Courtesy Mark C. Yerger)

few kilometers from Pereshschepino, the battalion was to immediately assault the town. The division's Kradschützen-Bataillon, led by SS-Sturmbannführer Jakob Fick, covered the western flank of the division's attack, screening it from attacks by Soviet infantry.[12]

The second column was commanded by SS-Sturmbannführer Hans Bissinger and consisted of his battalion reinforced by Flak guns and Sturmgeschütze. The regiment commander, SS-Standartenführer Heinz Harmel, accompanied Bissinger, riding near the front of the column in a light armored car. Behind the leading battalions, SS-Sturmbannführer Günther Wisliceny's III./"Deutschland" was echeloned to the rear, serving as the regimental reserve. Harmel directed Bissinger's Kampfgruppe to attack

Pereshschepino from the north, in support of Ehrath's attack from the west. Regiment "Der Führer" was follow the advance of Regiment "Deutschland." The regiment was still without the detached I./"Der Führer" which remained in action with Kampfgruppe Schuldt. The regiment was to drive south in the wake of Regiment "Deutschland" and attack the Russians opposing 15. Infanterie-Division at Novo-Moskovsk. "Das Reich" had forty-one operational tanks at the beginning of the attack, including thirty-three Panzer IIIs, seven Panzer IVs and one "Tiger." It also had fifteen Sturmgeschütz IIIs available for action and still possessed a large number of anti-tank guns, either towed or self propelled. While the "Das Reich" columns departed from Krasnograd, "Totenkopf" troops began to enter the town and assemble in preparation for the division's attack. On 22 February Eicke's division was to attack on

---

[12] Weidinger, page 27 and Regiment "Deutschland" pg.184-185.

a roughly parallel course to "Das Reich's" attack and cooperate in the capture of the key railroad center at Pavlograd.

The weather was bitter cold. Heavy falling snow and freezing rain made movements difficult, while thick fog restricted visibility. Regardless of the miserable weather conditions, the attack went ahead as scheduled and at 0500 hours, the right flank battalion, I./"Deutschland," left Krasnograd. The lead vehicles felt their way forward, their drivers barely able to see the vehicle in front of them. The column moved along a narrow track, passed through a wooded area and arrived at the town of Natalino. This initial advance cut through supply routes of the Soviet 6th Rifle Division and alerted Russian supply and security units, who promptly spread the alarm.

The poor visibility slowed the column and by noon, I./Regiment "Deutschland" was only twelve kilometers southeast of Krasnograd. At that point, infantry of the Soviet 6th Rifle Division launched a battalion strength counterattack on the column from the southwest. The battalion of Soviet infantry attacked without armor or artillery support and was driven off by the heavy firepower of the SS Kampfgruppe after suffering heavy casualties.

To the east, Bissinger's Kampfgruppe began its attack on the left flank of the division after a brief delay when the lead detachments encountered a shallow Soviet minefield. A squad from Macher's company came forward quickly to remove the mines. Using mine detectors and bayonets as probes, the Pioniere troops cleared a path through the mine field. After removing more than thirty mines, a sufficiently wide lane was opened and marked, at which point Harmel signaled for the column to get rolling again.[13] Bissinger's battalion passed through the gap in the mine field and Wisliceny's III./Regiment "Deutschland," followed close behind.

Just north of Otrada, II./Regiment "Deutschland" ran into its first determined resistance from Soviet infantry occupying the village of Beseka. By 1100 hours, the weather had cleared up and the fog been burned off by the morning sun. After the skies cleared, the Luftwaffe was able to lend its support to the attack. Stukas began to circle in the sky above Beseka as targets were identified and Luftwaffe forward observers prepared to direct air attacks upon the village. The Stukas climbed into the sky and plunged downward upon their targets, releasing their bombs before swooping back into the sky. The 250lb bombs exploded on the outskirts of the village, throwing up black clouds of smoke and debris. Columns of greasy dark smoke began to climb into the cold morning sky.

After the flight of Stukas droned away, the amount of fire coming from the defenders of the town lessened considerably. Supported by fire from self-propelled artillery, 2cm explosive shells from the

[13] Weidinger page 27-28.

Bissinger's II./Regiment "Deutschland" led the advance of Harmel's regiment on 19-20 February. Soon after setting out from Krasnograd the lead vehicles ran into a shallow Soviet minefield that blocked the road. A troop of the Pioniere company came forward and removed the mines. The Russians often used wooden cased mines in order to prevent the Germans from easily finding them with a magnetic mine detector. The picture shows SS Pioniere probing for mines with bayonets on a snow covered Russian road. (Credit National Archives)

Flak guns and accompanied by assault guns, the SS Grenadiers assaulted the village. The Soviet defenders gave way before the violent attack. Assault guns rolled past destroyed machine gun nests and the smoking ruins of Russian huts, pushing into the village. Resistance quickly collapsed at all points and at 1600 hours, Beseka was in German hands.

Throughout the day, both wings of the regiment's advance were closely supported by Stukas of Luftflotte 4, which was commanded by Generalfeldmarschall von Richtofen, son of the legendary World War I pilot known as the "Red Baron." The gull winged Stukas

A Junkers Ju 88 Stuka ready to be loaded with bombs on a typically foggy Russian morning. In the distance beyond the guard, another Stuka came be seen a short distance away. When the dive bombers were allowed to operate undisturbed in support of the SS columns they furnished invaluable support, eliminating Soviet gun positions and strong points. They were a key element of German offensive tactics, supplementing artillery, close support by assault guns and Flak guns. (Credit National Archives)

droned lazily over head, shadowing the battalion's advance until Soviet resistance was encountered. Then the deadly machines plummeted downwards in steep dives, dropping their bombs with pinpoint accuracy upon Russian positions.

Less than an hour later, the larger town of Otrada was captured also and the advance halted briefly. Shortly afterward, Tychsen's battalion of tanks arrived. After taking on additional ammunition and refueling, the tankers waited for the arrival of Wisliceny's battalion. The tanks were to support III./"Deutschland's" attack on the town of Pereshschepino. After the arrival of the battalion, the tanks and half tracks pushed on. Just before midnight on 19 February, III./Regiment "Deutschland" arrived in the area north of its initial objective, Pereshschepino. In addition to the tanks, the battalion was reinforced by a battery of self-propelled howitzers, two Sturmgeschütz batteries, self-propelled anti-tank guns and a few 2cm Flak guns.

Accompanied by Tychsen's Panzers, which slid and scraped along on the icy roads, the column reached the outskirts of Pereshschepino and halted. Tychsen and Wisliceny conferred for a time, deciding upon their plan of action. In the center of the town was a bridge across the Orel River, which had to be captured intact if the column was to quickly cross the river. In an audacious decision, typical of the aggressive leadership exhibited by officers of the elite SS divisions, Wisliceny and Tychsen decided upon a daring plan to capture the bridge before it could be destroyed. They did not utilize preparatory artillery fire or otherwise alert the Russians. Instead, they decided to race at full speed directly into the town and over the bridge before the defenders could react or even recognize that the troops and vehicles appearing out of the night were German.

The German column raced by Russian vehicles and soldiers standing along the road leading toward the town. Because of the darkness and poor visibility, the Russians in the outlying posts took the German vehicles for Soviet tanks and trucks. Not a single shot was fired at them and the SS column plunged into the outskirts of Pereshschepino at full speed. Without stopping, the Germans roared across the bridge before the Russians at the bridge guard posts understood what was happening. Once the lead vehicles of the SS column reached the opposite bank, SS Grenadiers leaped over the sides of their SPWs. Machine pistol fire stuttered and grenade explosions shattered the quiet of the night. The stunned bridge guards were quickly killed or put to flight. Other Russian troops stumbled out of nearby buildings and ran toward the sound of fighting, uncertain as to exactly what was happening. When they approached the bridge, a storm of fire greeted them.

The Russians were stunned by fire from tanks, half track mounted guns and automatic Flak guns, firing at close range. The confusion caused by the sudden appearance of German soldiers and tanks and the shock of violent firepower destroyed any hope of launching an organized counterattack. After a short time, the Russians abandoned the fight and withdrew from the bridge area. Wisliceny later described the audacious capture of the town and bridge, as his most 'adventurous' (abenteuerlichsten) success of the whole war.[14]

Harmel soon arrived and ordered Wisliceny and Tychsen to continue the attack. A company of SS Panzergrenadiers, along with the HQ group, remained behind in order to secure the bridge. From Pereshschepino, Wisliceny's Kampfgruppe and the division's tanks continued the advance toward the town of Novo-Moskovsk, in order to link up with the infantry of 15. Infanterie-Division. After establishing contact with the Army troops, the regiment was to destroy the Russian troops in the sector and secure the town. While Harmel's regiment plunged southward, Regiment "Der Führer" began its advance, following in the path of destruction left by the passage of Regiment "Deutschland."

By 0500 hours, 20 February, Kampfgruppe "Der Führer," led by the half track equipped III./Regiment "Der Führer," roared over the bridge at Pereshschepino. The battalion, commanded by SS-Hauptsturmführer Vincenz Kaiser, was reinforced with a battery of assault guns and several "Wespe," a 10cm self-propelled howitzer. The battalion raced south until reaching the village of Gubinicha, which was a short distance north of Novo-Moskovsk. Kaiser discovered that a garrison of Russian infantry held the town and the battalion quickly deployed for battle. The seemingly ever present Stukas appeared on cue and screeched down to bomb Russian troops holding positions along the flank of the attack. Kaiser placed the mobile artillery on nearby high ground, while the armor and Grenadiers deployed for the attack.

Bombs from Stukas and 10cm artillery shells exploded inside the town, striking Russian gun positions and vehicles. Huts and houses disintegrated in clouds of smoke, shattered by bombs or shells. A hail of 2cm explosive projectiles and tank shells blasted the town perimeter. While this combined arms fire kept the Russian's heads down, SPWs and half tracks sped over the snow on either side of the road leading into the town. They were supported by close range fire from assault guns, whose wide tracks threw up plumes of snow as they raced toward the town perimeter. The assault guns stopped, fired upon Russian gun positions and moved closer, supporting the advance of the Grenadiers. Under cover of

---

[14] Weidinger, pg. 31-32.

this fire, the SS Grenadiers leaped from their half tracks and worked forward. Soon the lead company reached the first houses and penetrated the village perimeter.

The shocked Russian troops, hammered by a storm of German fire power, were overwhelmed by the violent assault and gave way at the point of attack. The SS Grenadiers were able to reach the interior of the town quickly. They fought down narrow streets, which were filled by thick smoke rolling out of burning houses. After a brief firefight, the defenders withdrew and pulled back down the length of Gubinicha. The town was secured by 0635 hours and mopping up began. However, a short time later the Russians brought up a battalion of infantry and attempted to regain possession of Gubinicha. Supported by a few tanks, the Russian infantry surged forward, long bayonets fixed to their rifles. SS tanks and assault guns, firing from concealed positions, directed an accurate fire on the Russian tanks. Two T-34s were quickly hit and destroyed. Several others were damaged, although they were able to limp away to safety. After the Soviet armor was forced to pull back, the infantry attack failed to gain any additional ground, and fell apart. The Russian infantry could not move forward through the wall of German machine gun, mortar and artillery fire that fell upon them. The disheartened survivors retreated over the bloody snow, dragging their wounded to shelter and leaving their dead littering the snow around blazing Soviet tanks.[15]

Wisliceny's battalion quickly regrouped after securing the village and continued on towards Novo-Moskovsk, where it was to link up with elements of 15. Infanterie-Division. The column raced through a number of small villages without delay. The battalion was opposed by little more than supply and support troops, who were not armed with anything heavier than small arms. At 1400 hours the leading units of the SS column approached positions occupied by men of Grenadier Regiment 52, northwest of Novo-Moskovsk. After the arrival of the SS mobile column, elements of the Soviet 35th Guards Rifle Division could be seen withdrawing from positions west of the town and pulling back to the east, toward the Samara River.[16]

At the same time that the two Panzergrenadier regiments approached Pereshschepino, the Kradschutzen-Bataillon protected the right flank of the division's advance. After leaving Krasnograd, Fick's motorcycle troops sped south on a secondary road west of the main route of attack. The battalion reached the area west of Pereshschepino by 1600 hours, without making contact with any

SS-Hauptsturmführer Vincenz Kaiser, the commander of "Das Reich's" III./Regiment "Der Führer," which was the division's half track battalion. The badges on his right arm signify the single handed destruction of a tank. He was a highly decorated solder of the division, winning the German Cross in Gold, both grades of the Iron Cross and the Knight's Cross, as well as the Oakleaves. (Courtesy Mark C. Yerger)

Soviet troops. However, just as Fick's forward detachment approached the town, it received small arms and heavy mortar fire from an isolated pocket of Russian infantry located on a hilltop southeast of the town. These troops were men of the Soviet 106th Rifle Brigade or the 267th Rifle Division, both of which were in the area.

The SS motorcycle troops took pulled back and called for help from the SS armor, which they knew were already in the town. After an hour or two, a few Panzers motored up to the battalion and the tank commanders climbed down to meet with Fick. After a short consultation, the dismounted Grenadiers assaulted the hilltop supported by the German tanks. The Russians were driven out of their position and fled to the south. The battalion then continued on towards Pereshschepino and entered the town.

---

[15] Weidinger, pg. 32 and NA/T-354, roll 118, 1a KTB, "Das Reich" Tagesmeldung an Generalkommando SS-Panzerkorps, 20.2.43. frame 375749.

[16] Glantz, pg. 126 and NA/T-354, roll 120, Darstellung der Ereignisse, frame 3753613.

Although the road between Krasnograd and Pereshschepino was temporarily free of Russian troops, there were still large numbers of Russian infantry west of the road. Some of these troops continued to cause problems for the Germans for some time, fighting as guerrilla forces behind German lines. Forward elements of the 267th Rifle Division realized that strong German columns had cut through its lines of communication and began to fight their way toward the east. During the afternoon of 20 February, the Russians reacted to the SS columns slicing through the area between Krasnograd and Novo-Moskovsk. The main body of the 267th Rifle Division launched attacks upon German positions in and around Pereshschepino and blocked the road south of the town.

Throughout the course of the day, Soviet infantry made a number of attacks in the area with the intent of clearing the Germans from the roads north of Pereshschepino. The attacks by the Russian infantry were halted. Regiment "Deutschland" launched counterattacks which were supported by a flight of Stukas that conducted a number of devastating attacks upon the Russians. The SS troops overran several defensive positions, capturing a number of anti-tank guns and artillery pieces. By late 20 February, "Das Reich" and 15. Infanterie-Division were in control of the Novo-Moskovsk area north and east of Dnepropetrovsk.

The next objective of the attack was to secure the railroad net between Dnepropetrovsk and Pavlograd. The first task of the SS-Panzerkorps was to clear the segment of the railroad between Novo-Moskovsk and Sinel'nikovo, where 15. Infanterie-Division still held a perimeter around the railroad station in the center of the town. After driving the Russians away from Sinel'nikovo, the next objective was to drive northeast to the important rail center at Pavlograd. "Das Reich" was assigned both of these tasks because "Totenkopf" was still on the road between Krasnograd and Pereshschepino.

The division had already accomplished a great deal. During its seventy-five kilometer advance from Krasnograd, "Das Reich" had smashed through the tactical communication zones of the 267th Rifle Division and 106th Rifle Brigade. The two columns of the division had captured or destroyed a number of artillery and anti-tank guns and disrupted Soviet communications. The Panzer regiment had suffered moderate losses, but had only twenty-seven Panzer IIIs, eight Panzer IVs and three command tanks still in operation.

Losses in the Panzergrenadier battalions were light, thanks primarily to well coordinated attacks with combined supporting fire from artillery, Flak guns and assault guns. The devastating Stuka attacks were particularly effective. The heavy weight of firepower effectively suppressed Russian defensive fire and allowed the Germans to quickly overwhelm Russian positions along the route of

A self-propelled howitzer belonging to "Leibstandarte's" artillery regiment. This particular model was known as the "Wespe" and featured a 10cm light field howitzer mounted on a Panzer II chassis. The gun crew was protected by light armor in an open topped configuration. (Credit National Archives)

Two Waffen-SS Grenadiers involved in street fighting in an unknown Ukrainian town. Many towns and villages in the area of Kharkov were very long and narrow. Sometimes the houses and huts stretched along both sides of the road for more than a kilometer, with narrow side streets randomly branching off from the main road. (Credit National Archives)

advance. The violence of the sudden assaults by the rampaging German mobile columns must have been a significant shock to the Soviet infantry. For months, German troops had been driven back by the Russians in one campaign after the other. Not surprisingly the Russians troops and more significantly, their commanders, assumed that they were pursuing a beaten enemy. The only Axis troops many Soviet columns encountered were ragtag German and Hungarian/Italian columns, moving on foot and intent only on escaping the Russian onslaught. Imagine the shock when powerful German mobile columns appeared as if out of thin air and smashed through the Soviet line of advance.

To their credit, the Russians reacted very quickly at the divisional and army level and elements of the Soviet 1st Guards Tank Corps were immediately diverted toward Pavlograd by the 6th Army. The armor was sent to support the 35th and 41st Guards Rifle Divisions, which were defending the town. This armor arrived before "Das Reich" was able to launch its attack upon the town. Unknown to the Russians, a second SS Panzer Division was about to make its presence felt. While "Das Reich" moved out of Novo-Moskovsk, advancing toward the western edge of Pavlograd, "Totenkopf" prepared to begin its attack.[17]

The Attack of "Totenkopf"

The main combat units of "Totenkopf," except for Regiment "Thule," assembled around Krasnograd by 20 February, although I./SS Panzer- Regiment 3 was still in Poltava on that date. At 1820 hours, the division received the order that it was formally placed at the disposal of Heeresgruppe Süd. During the night, the tanks of I./SS Panzer-Regiment 3 began their advance to the battlefield, passing through the vast, desolate Russian steppe. One of the veterans of the battalion, SS-Oberscharführer Steiger, described the journey through the starkly, empty and hostile terrain.

> "Make ready," came the order . . . A sharp wind blew from the west, out of the pitch black darkness. From the lead vehicles one could see the red hot glow of the exhaust pipes. It was an extraordinary moment that each man would remember. There was no village, no tree, no bush or shrub to break the monotony of the lonely road. In the darkness several vehicles became lost, but by the morning of 21 February, we arrived at Karlovka.[18]

Another unit of the division, IV./SS-Artillerie-Regiment 3, was also on the march to Krasnograd on the early morning of 20 February. Its new men received their first taste of the peculiar nature of war on the Eastern Front. At 0300 hours the long column was suddenly shelled by Russian mortars, the explosions bracketing the column. Without warning, a Russian infantry battalion attacked out of the darkness, advancing toward the column with fixed bayonets and wild yells. Two howitzer crews calmly unlimbered their guns, swung them around and fired into the advancing mass of Russians at point blank range. The resulting carnage shocked the Russian troops, and destroyed the momentum of the charge for a moment. The hesitation was just long enough for two Flakvierling (4 barreled) 2cm Flak guns to swing into action. Streams of tracers from the explosive 2cm shells sparkled through the night, smashing into the Russians when they attacked again. The horrific volume of shells from these guns cut down the charging Soviet infantry in droves

SS-Sturmbannführer Günther Wisliceny, the commander of III./Regiment "Deutschland." On 20 February, 1943 Wisliceny's battalion took over leading the advance of Regiment "Deutschland." Upon reaching the outskirts of Pereshschepino, Wisliceny decided upon a daring course of action to capture a key bridge located in the town. He ordered his battalion to speed down the road past unwary Soviet troops and drive right up to the crossing site, seizing the bridge before the Russian security force could destroy it. (Courtesy Mark C. Yerger)

---

[17] Glantz, pg. 126-127.
[18] Vopersal, pg. 121.

"Das Reich" Panzer IIIs in a Russian town during February of 1943. Tychsen's battalion of tanks supported the advance of Regiment "Deutschland" toward Pereschschepino. (Credit National Archives)

and shattered the attack. When the battle was over, the "Totenkopf" gun crews counted over 100 Russian dead and dying laying in the bloody, trampled snow.

The rest of SS-Panzergrenadier-Regiment 3 and the entire SS-Panzerjägerabteilung 3, left Poltava for Krasnograd on the morning of 21 February. Eicke and his 1a, SS-Sturmbannführer Schneider, drove ahead and reported to Hausser at the Headquarters of the SS-Panzerkorps in Krasnograd. Once there, Eicke received further orders for the deployment of his division. One column of "Totenkopf" was to follow in the tracks of "Das Reich's" right wing and sweep the road from Krasnograd to west of Pereshschepino. After reaching Pereshschepino, the Panzer regiment and Regiment "Totenkopf" was to attack Pavlograd from the north in support of the assault of "Das Reich," which was to be launched simultaneously from the west. Hellmuth Becker's SS-"Totenkopf" Grenadier-Regiment 3 was to advance eastward from Pereshschepino and drive toward a point about 25 kilometers north of Pavlograd. The objective of the regiment was to seize the railroad line north of the town and prevent the Soviets from using it to bring up supplies or reinforcements.

The first "Totenkopf" unit to arrive at Pereshschepino was SS-Sturmbannführer Ernst Häussler's III./Regiment "Totenkopf," which made contact with "Das Reich" troops at 1800 hours on 21 Febru-

ary. After arriving at the east edge of the town, SS-Sturmbannführer Max Kuhn's III./SS-"Totenkopf" Panzergrenadier-Regiment 3 took over control of the area, replacing Fick's motorcycle battalion. Häussler's troops had encountered a few small Russian detachments south of Krasnograd, but had not been faced with any significant resistance and arrived without suffering any casualties. The regiment prepared to resume its attack on the next day, when the division's tanks were able to support the advance.

However, Eicke's tanks had a difficult time in the march from Krasnograd, due to bad road conditions and lost half a dozen tanks due to accidents on the treacherous road. The "Totenkopf" tank crews were inexperienced in moving over frozen Russian dirt roads. The journey was a nightmare of collisions, damaged tanks and bruised egos. The SS tank column became strung out on the road and was repeatedly delayed when vehicles slid off the road or collided with one another. "Totenkopf" possessed many more tanks than either "Leibstandarte" or "Das Reich" because it had been spared the brutal fighting for Kharkov which cost the other SS divisions much of their armored strength. "Totenkopf's" Panzer regiment was the only SS or Army Panzer regiment that was at full strength on the eve of the great counteroffensive. However, it would be several days before "Totenkopf" Panzers could join the battle at Pavlograd. Eicke's tanks slowly and painfully inched their way southward, falling behind the Panzergrenadier regiments. In the meantime, "Das Reich" was once more on the attack, driving toward Pavlograd.

Regiment "Der Führer" attacks Novo-Moskovsk

During the night of 21 February, Regiment "Der Führer" assaulted Russian positions along the Samara River, east of Novo-Moskovsk. The self propelled III./SS-Artillerie-Regiment 2, commanded by SS-Sturmbannführer Friedrich Eichberger, moved into position near the edge of Novo-Moskovsk, in order to furnish fire support for the attack. The Samara River was a shallow stream that meandered along the eastern edge of the town, where the railroad crossed the swampy river over three bridges. To the German's surprise, patrols reported that the bridges were still standing. The SS troops prepared to capture the crossings by storm but this crossing proved to be difficult.

The attack was made by II./Regiment "Der Führer," led by the battalion commander SS-Obersturmbannführer Sylvester Stadler. Supporting the battalion's attack was a battery of Sturmgeschütze IIIs belonging to SS-Hauptsturmführer Walter Kniep's assault gun battalion. At 0300 hours, the attack began with the assault guns advancing at the head of the column. The Grenadiers stormed across

the first bridge and caught the Russians completely by surprise. The bridge guard detachment was shot down before they could set off demolition charges and destroy the crossing. The bridge was cleared of demolitions by SS Pioniere and captured intact. At the second bridge Russian fire began to grow in intensity and the SS Grenadiers were pinned down by intense machine gun fire that swept the length of the bridge. Soviet artillery fire then began to sporadically fall upon the west bank of the river although it was largely inaccurate at that point. The attack was in danger of stalling, but at that critical moment, the battery commander, SS-Hauptsturmführer Ernst Krag, provided the spark that got the attack moving again.

The first assault gun that cautiously rolled onto the bridge was forced to withdraw because of a barrage of Soviet anti-tank gun shells, which struck all around it but did not disable the vehicle. On his own initiative, Krag ordered his 2./Batterie to charge across the bridge and take the Russian positions under fire at point blank range. The assault guns roared forward and with cannons blazing, raced across the bridge, through a storm of high explosives and machine gun fire. This sudden, aggressive tactic evidently caught the Russians by surprise and the startled gunners did not aim well. None of the anti-tank gun shells seriously damaged any of the assault guns before they were across the bridge. Once on the opposite bank, Krag's men knocked out several machine gun positions as well as 3

Karl Kloskowski was one of most highly decorated men of "Das Reich's" Panzer Regiment. In January of 1943 Kloskowski was an SS-Hauptscharführer and commanded a tank platoon of 4. Kompanie. He won the Knight's Cross and Oakleaves before his death in action in the last days of the war. (Courtesy Mark C. Yerger)

SS-Sturmbannführer Ernst Häussler, commander of III./ Regiment "Totenkopf." Häussler led the battalion in the early fighting south of Pereshschepino until he was wounded on 21 February. (Courtesy Mark C. Yerger)

On the night of 21-22 February II./Regiment "Der Führer," led by SS-Obersturmbannführer Sylvester Stadler, assaulted a bridge across the Samara River near Novo-Moskovsk. Stadler was an excellent battalion commander and showed great aggressiveness and good tactical knowledge in his attack preparations. He is shown in the picture as an SS-Oberführer. (The author's collection)

anti-tank guns. The hail of fire that had pinned down the SS Grenadiers fell away and the Grenadiers stormed forward again. Once across the first two bridges, SS assault teams forded the river in Schwimmwagen and attacked the defenders of the last span from behind. Shortly afterward, the last bridge was in the hands of the Germans, completely undamaged.[19]

As a direct result of Krag's actions, the SS Grenadiers had been able to seize all three bridges before they could be blown up. The column quickly reorganized and then pushed quickly to the east. Less than two hours later, the town of Petschanka, which lay several kilometers east of the river, was assaulted by Stadler's battalion. While the SS Grenadiers entered the edge of the town, Stukas attacked a number of Russian tanks which were in the center of Petschanka. The dive bombers were able to hit a number of the Soviet tanks, leaving 6 T-34s burning in the streets. After their armor was destroyed, elements of the 35th Guards Rifle Division pulled out of the town and withdrew towards Pavlograd, accompanied by surviving elements of the 1st Guards Tank Corps, which had supported the infantry division. Once the bridgehead over the river was secured by Stadler's battalion, Tychsen's Panzer battalion crossed the river, followed by Eichberger's self-propelled howitzers. By 0800 the entire Kampfgruppe, in three assault columns, raced to the attack again, and reached the eastern edge of Pavlograd by late morning. The sun had evaporated the normal early morning fog and although it was cold, the day was sunny and bright.

A few kilometers east of Pavlograd, the main column, which was moving along a primary road, ran into a Soviet rear guard position. Tychsen's Panzers were called forward, and the tanks clanked to the head of the column, then deployed on either side of the road. The 10cm self-propelled howitzers got into position and began blasting away at the Russians, their high explosive shells shattering the Soviet defensive position. Supported by Eichberger's guns, the SS Panzers quickly smashed through the Soviets and rolled on. The SPWs of the battalion took the lead again and sped to the front of the main body of the column. The battalion met no other significant resistance, because the Soviet infantry and tanks continued their retreat to the north, in an attempt to link up with other elements of the 35th Guards Rifle Division that were withdrawing from Novo-Moskovsk.[20]

By 1000 hours, Stadler's II./Regiment "Der Führer," along with Eichberger's battalion of self-propelled guns, reached the outskirts of Pavlograd, where the columns halted in order to study the ap-

Ernst Krag, commander of 2./Batterie SS-Sturmgeschütz-Bataillon 2. Krag personally directed his battery of assault guns in several key actions during the advance of "Das Reich" from Krasnograd to Sinel'nikovo and Pavlograd. He was awarded the German Cross in Gold on 20 April, 1943 for these and other accomplishments. (Courtesy Mark C. Yerger)

proaches to the town. Kumm arrived shortly afterward and caught up with Stadler's men near an elevated rail road bridge which crossed over the main road near the edge of the town. The SS Panzers were some distance behind, as they had fallen behind the speedier SPWs and had not yet arrived. However, while Kumm was still conferring with his battalion commander, the first tanks began to roll into sight and the columns began to deploy for the attack. From the bridge, the edge of the town lay only 500 meters to the east, spread out on the floor of a wide, flat valley. Kumm, after looking the situation over, requested a Stuka attack for 1300 hours.[21]

In the streets of the town, the Germans could plainly see many Russian soldiers and numerous vehicles moving about. Just over

---

[19] Yerger, Mark C. *SS-Sturmbannführer Ernst August Krag - Träger des Ritterkreuzes mit Eichenlaub und Kommandeur SS-Sturmgeschützabteilung 2.* (Atglen: 1996) pg. 11.
 [20] Glantz, pg. 127 and Weidinger, pg. 37.

---

[21] Weidinger, pg. 38.

167

100 meters from the bridge, there was a large collective farm, which was obviously fortified and had been occupied by the training battalion of the 35th Guards Rifle Division. The Russians gave no evidence that they had detected the presence of the Germans. There was no visible reaction or fire from the town and at one point two heavily laden trucks crossed the bridge directly in front of the Panzers. Two rounds from a tank and both trucks exploded in flames. Although the Russians were obviously alerted at that point, there was still no reaction from the town or its defenders. Shortly afterward, German air support arrived and the assault began.[22]

Promptly at 1300 hours, three waves of Stukas plunged down from the clear blue skies, dropping their bombs on forward positions of the town. At the same time, all guns of the self-propelled artillery battalion opened up and pumped shell after shell into Pavlograd. Tychsen's Panzers moved into firing positions and added their cannon fire to the storm of explosives striking the town and farm. Stadler's armored cars and SdKfz. 251s, with Grenadiers firing machine guns and machine pistols, sped to the attack. The fast moving, violent assault, launched just as the last bombs from the Stuka's struck the Soviets, overwhelmed the defenders manning the defenses on the perimeter of the town. Once having penetrated into the outskirts of the town, the SS Grenadiers dismounted and pushed down the narrow streets, meeting little resistance at first. The SS combat teams, covered by cannon fire from the tanks, blasted a path through the town. Whenever isolated detachments of Russians put up a determined fight, the Stukas and artillery blasted the defenders into submission. By 1600 hours, the southern sector of the town was in German hands, although fighting continued in the northern half of Pavlograd, where Russian infantry held on to a strong defensive perimeter. Tanks and well concealed anti-tank guns made the Soviet position very formidable and gradually Stadler's attack ground to a halt. "Totenkopf" was to attack the northern section of Pavlograd, in support of Regiment "Der Führer," but Eicke's division had not arrived on 21 February, because its supply line had been attacked and the division was forced to deal with that problem first. Before nightfall, Hausser arrived at the town and found the battalion Headquarters. Stadler gave him his report regarding the successes of the day, while his men began to occupy defensive positions around the perimeter of Pavlograd. Mop up fighting continued in the town during the night and throughout the following day, as pockets of surrounded Russians continued to fight back stubbornly.[23]

While Regiment "Der Führer" established control over Pavlograd and prepared for further action, elements of Regiment "Deutschland" took over security of the main road (rollbahn) passing through Pereshschepino, Novo-Moskovsk and into Pavlograd. The road had been defended by a hastily thrown together guard detachment, which consisted of a Flak battery and SS-Panzerkorps security units. But this small force proved inadequate to guard the long stretch of road by itself, because sizable groups of Soviet troops who had been cut off west of the SS line of attack, crossed the road frequently. These troops, in groups of company size or larger, ambushed German supply columns, which disrupted the flow of supplies. More substantial forces were required to deal with the situation and eliminate the Russians along the road. The divisional headquarters and the Headquarters support group moved south of Pereshschepino, to the town of Gubinicha. There was still scattered fighting going on in that area also, as Russian troops continued to move through the sector in attempts to escape to the east. These were probably elements of the 267th Rifle Division or the 35th Guards Rifle Division. The main portion of Regiment "Deutschland" assembled just across the Samara River, at Petschanka, a few kilometers east of Novo-Moskovsk.

On the following day, 22 February, both SS divisions resumed their operations. The morning was cold, -20 degrees Celsius and as usual in the early hours of the winter months, a thick fog lay over the area. During the night "Totenkopf" assembled north of Pavlograd, as the division readied itself to support the attack of "Das Reich." Just before the attack began however, the division was forced to defend its supply route from a threat at Pereshschepino.

At 0600 hours, a Soviet infantry attack suddenly materialized out of the damp fog, which had only slightly dissipated after sunrise. The 106th Rifle Brigade, which had been cut off by the advance of "Das Reich" along the Krasnograd-Pereshchepino road, assaulted the northwest and western edge of the town. The brigade attempted to break through the German lines in order to reopen its lines of supply and communication. With the support of infantry howitzers and small arms fire, a battalion of Russian infantry attacked defensive positions of III./Rgt. "Totenkopf," then commanded by Obersturmbannführer Joachim Schubach. The combined fire of Flak guns, assault guns and heavy weapons, as well as small arms fire, decimated the Russian battalion as it struggled over the snow fields toward the German guns. Machine gun fire cut down

---

[22] NA/T-354, roll 118, Fernschreiben SS-Panzergrenadier-Division "Das Reich" an Generalkommando SS-Panzerkorps, frame 375749 and Weidinger, pg. 37-39.
[23] Weidinger 38-39 and NA/T-354, roll 120, 1a KTB- Darstellung der Ereignisse 22-23.2.1943. frame 3753627.

OPPOSITE: While Regiment "Der Führer" fought for Pavlograd, Regiment "Deutschland, under Harmel, thrust southward from Pavlograd, into the rear of the Soviet troops opposing 15. Infanterie-Division. Only quick action by the Army division prevented a possible loss of the vital Dnepr bridges and gained time for Hoth to set Hausser's counterattack into motion. Simultaneously, "Totenkopf" advanced from Pereshchepino toward the towns of Kotschereski and Wjasovok, which were north of Pavlograd.

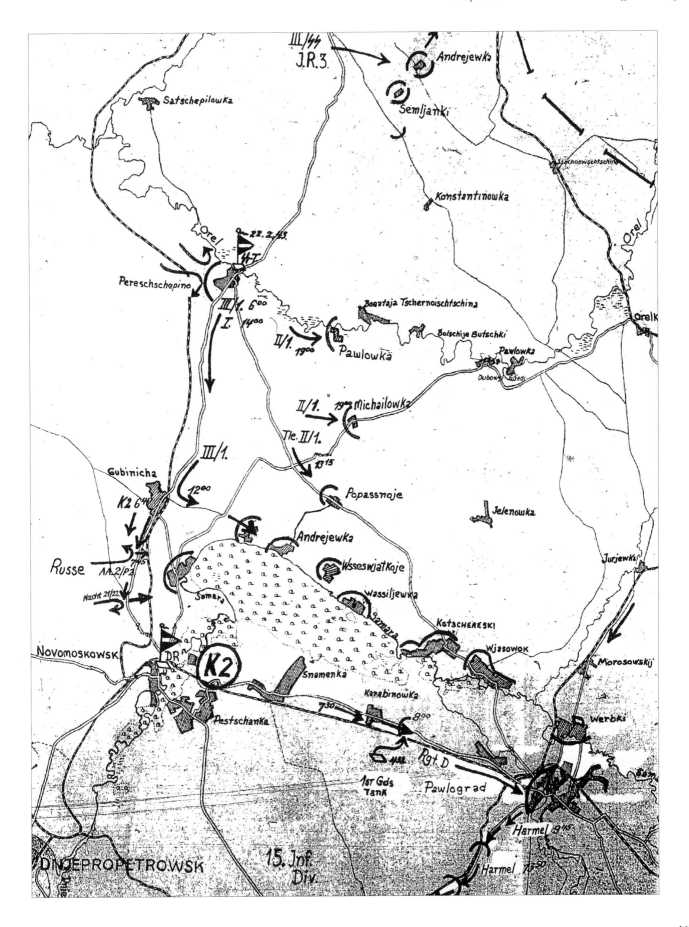

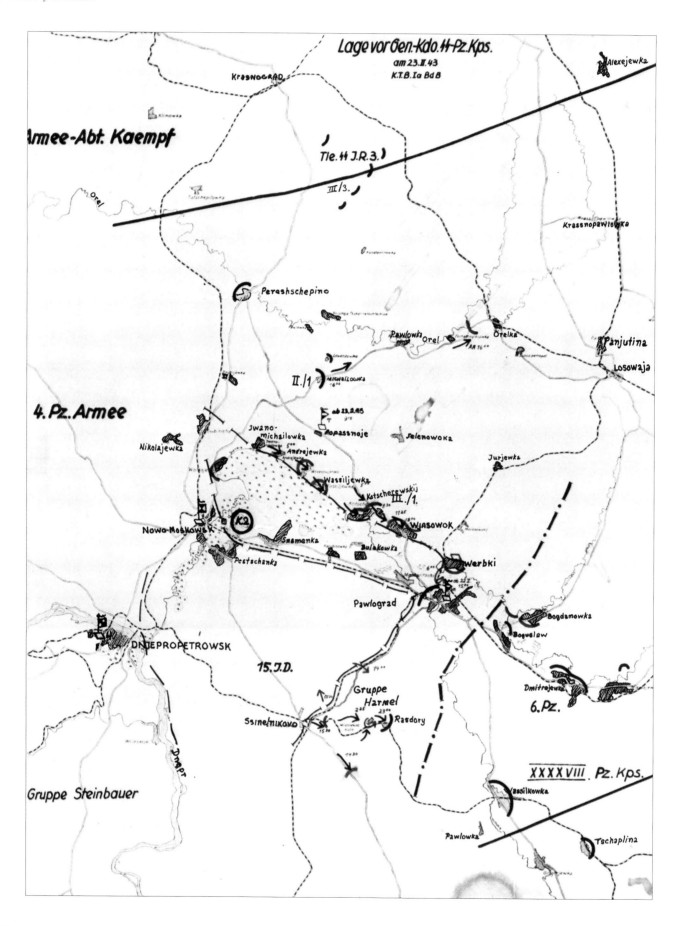

many of the charging, brown uniformed figures and artillery shells burst among the waves of attackers, sending sprays of black earth and ice fragments into the air. The quad-barreled 2cm automatic guns pumped shell after shell into the mass of Russian infantry, wreaking terrible damage when they struck flesh. The leading wave of attackers faltered in the face of this firepower and the attack lost its momentum. Many of those Russians who were still alive scrambled and crawled back to safety, leaving one hundred and fifty of their dead spread upon the snow. Others threw down their rifles and surrendered or lay in the snow behind the bodies of their dead comrades until the Germans took them prisoners.[24]

The SS men took sixty prisoners, gathering them up from the gruesome battlefield and sending to the rear. At 1400 hours the Russians brought up another battalion of infantry and tried again to overrun the German positions on the northwest edge of the town. Once again, the attack foundered in the face of heavy German fire, which inflicted heavy casualties upon the charging Soviet infantry. The MG-42s ripped out long bursts of rounds, which knocked down Russians by the score.

After the attack was stopped, the surviving Russian infantry began to pull back, once again leaving mounds of their dead piled up in the snow. Not content to allow the Russians to withdraw to safety, SPWs of Baum's I./Regiment "Totenkopf," supported by tanks and assault guns, charged after the withdrawing Soviet troops. With motors roaring, the tanks and half tracks raced over the snow covered steppe in pursuit of the fleeing Soviets. After a short chase, the SS Panzers and assault guns caught up with the helpless, stumbling Russians and massacred them as they fled over the featureless snowfields.[25]

After turning back these Soviet attacks, the division once again turned to the task of preparing for its advance from Pereshschepino toward Pavlograd. At 1130 hours, III./Regiment "Totenkopf" was replaced by half track battalion, which took over defense of the town. A half hour later, after a quick assembly, III./"Totenkopf" departed from the southern edge of Pereshschepino and began the journey in the direction of Gubinicha. After reaching Gubinicha, the battalion advanced toward the towns of Werbki and Wjasovok,

"Das Reich's" Sturmgeschütz Bataillon was commanded by SS-Hauptsturmführer Walter Kniep, shown here later in the war after attaining the rank of SS-Sturmbannführer. Kniep was awarded the first German Cross in Gold won by a member of "Das Reich." He won the Knight's Cross during fighting in the summer of 1943, while the division was involved in fighting north of Belgorod. Kniep did not survive the war, although he did not die of combat wounds. He was accidentally shot and killed during target practice with a pistol. (Courtesy Mark C. Yerger)

which were on the north bank of the Samara, just north of Pavlograd. Schubach's battalion followed the course of the Samara, moving along the bank until it encountered a small Russian garrison in the village of Ivano Michailovka. This detachment of defenders was quickly routed and the village secured. However, just after the fighting ended, a larger Russian force attacked the battalion while it was still regrouping. As a result, several squads of Russian troops were able to fight their way into the village and occupy hastily organized defensive positions. It took some time before the Germans could eliminate the Russian infantry and clear the town. Later in the afternoon, the battalion got under way once more, moving toward the village of Andrejevka, which was found to be occupied by a com-

---

[24] NA/T-354, roll 120, 1a KTB SS-Panzerkorps, Darstellung der Ereignisse, frame 3753625.

[25] Vopersal, pg. 128 and NA/T-354, roll 118, Tagesmeldung SS-Panzergrenadier-Division "Totenkopf" an Generalkommando-SS-Panzerkorps, 22.2.1943, frame 3751768.

OPPOSITE: While "Das Reich" was involved in the fighting for possession of Pavlograd, "Totenkopf" continued to attack eastward toward the railroad junction at Orelka and south, toward the area north of Pavlograd. Soviet tanks and infantry occupied the towns north of Pavlograd and proved to be difficult and stubborn opponents.

pany of Russian infantry. There were a number of forward defensive positions controlling the approaches to the village from the west and they held up the battalion until nightfall. After eliminating these defenders and driving the main body of Russians out of the town, Schubach rested and reorganized his battalion, planning to resume his attack at 0100 hours.[26]

Meanwhile, SS-Hauptsturmführer Wilhelm Schulze's II./Regiment "Totenkopf" had begun its advance toward Pavlograd after the departure of Schubach's battalion from Pereshschepino, taking a different road out of the town. Schulze's objective was to assemble in the area to the north of Pavlograd, in preparation for attacking the town from the northwest. The battalion was reinforced by motorcycle troops, an artillery battery and the division's Panzer-Pioniere Kompanie, led by SS-Obersturmführer Georg Kinzler. The long column, moving over narrow, icy roads, advanced slowly to the southeast of Pereshschepino, although its passage through the darkness was unimpeded, until just after midnight. At that point it ran into a detachment of Soviet cavalry troops, at the village of Popassnoje, fifteen kilometers northwest of Pavlograd. The column deployed for battle and assaulted the village, supported by fire from a battery of 10cm howitzers. By daylight Popassnoje was in German hands and the Soviet cavalrymen had been put to flight, but the battalion was delayed and could not support "Das Reich's" attack on Pavlograd.

When the advance resumed Russian cavalry, numbering about 150-200 men, appeared on the flank of the march route, forcing Schulze to deal with them. A Kampfgruppe of the SS Panzer-Pioniere-Kompanie, two assault guns, an SPW and the howitzer battery, set off in pursuit. The commander of the battery, SS-Hauptsturmführer Friedrich Messerle, remembered the chase as a 'crazy hunt out of the wild west." Following the tracks of the Russian horses, the Germans made their way to a Soviet town, which was typically spread out along the road which ran through its center. By this time, nightfall was approaching and the Germans did not want to risk entering the village and stumbling into an ambush in the dark. The small Kampfgruppe circled its vehicles like wagon train threatened by Indians and positioned its howitzers along the perimeter, ready to go into action at a seconds notice.[27]

Just before the dawn, the SS Pioniere cautiously entered the village, feeling their way down both sides of the main street. This flushed out the Soviet cavalry, which suddenly took off across the snow, galloping hard for a hill behind the village. Messerle's howitzers fired into their midst, but within seconds the Russians reached the edge of the hill, after suffering only a few casualties. The Germans tried to follow the horsemen and raced out of the village in pursuit. However, they immediately found themselves in the midst of a rough, uneven field which was traversed by many small, steep banked ravines and depressions. The German vehicles crashed and bounced violently over the broken terrain. Wheels and tracks smashed against rock hard, frozen ruts or slammed into icy ditches, which damaged suspensions and steering gear. In this race the hardy, sure footed little Russian horses proved superior to the motorized mounts of the SS battalion. While the German troops could hardly keep avoid being thrown from their seats, the cavalry ponies easily outdistanced their pursuers, disappearing over the hill crest.

Shortly after the Russians made their escape over the hilltop, a Fieseler Storch swooped down out of the sky and alighted in a small smooth area near the German vehicles. To the surprise of everyone, out of the plane stepped the commander of the SS-Panzerkorps, Paul Hausser, who had been watching the action from above. Wryly noting the comical difficulties of the vehicles as the Russian horses quickly outdistanced his frustrated troops, Hausser could hardly keep a grin off his face. Soon however, the moment passed and Hausser conferred with the commander of the small Kampfgruppe. After a short conference Hausser's plane lifted off again.[28]

There was no humor in the situation that afflicted "Totenkopf's" tanks, which had set out early on 22 February. More than 100 Panzers were stretched out in a long column along the frozen ribbon of ruts and frozen slopes. The speed of the regiment was dictated by the progress of the lead vehicles. When the tanks reached steep downward inclines which were frozen and slippery, the slope had to be negotiated one vehicle at a time, while the rest waited. If a tank slid off the path, it had to be towed back on to the road, a task which sometimes resulted in thrown tracks or another tank becoming stuck in deep snow along the sides of the road. Approaching tight turns proved another obstacle which often resulted in collisions when tracks slid on the black ice. At several difficult points there were collisions between skidding tanks which crashed into other vehicles. Four Panzers became disabled through damage sustained during these collisions and had to be left behind. Tank commanders were furious, bellowing in frustration when their vehicles were disabled before even seeing combat.[29]

Many hours later, it was evident that the column, led by 1. Kompanie, was approaching the front and fighting was close at hand. In the distance, the dull thumps of artillery shells could be heard, signaling the fighting going on around Pereshschepino. Motorcycle messengers made their way by the column and ambulances passed, bearing their load of wounded to the rear. Suddenly, the 1. Kompanie

---

[26] Vopersal, 128-29.
[27] Ibid. pg. 129-130.
[28] Op cit.
[29] Vopersal, pg. 130-131.

tank commanders heard a order crackle over the headphones, "Clear for battle." The Russians were attacking the northwest edge of Pereshschepino again, trying to break through German lines. The SS tanks soon reached the first houses of the town, taking up position in a line that faced to their right flank. In the distance, a long line of Russian infantry appeared, advancing over the flat, snow covered fields. Soon the flash of Russian anti-tank rifles could be seen and the projectiles struck armor and whistled off into the air, or buzzed past the ears of the tank commanders.

The order was given to the tank gunners to load the guns with high explosive. The cannons of the Panzer IIIs and IVs roared time and again, firing high explosive shells into the mass of Russian infantry. Artillery began to fall around the tanks, but most of the shells struck behind them, exploding harmlessly. The Soviet attack was thrown back, but the delays caused by the horrible condition of the roads and the resulting difficulties for the Panzer regiment, caused it to arrive much later than expected. The regiment's tank crews, in combat for the first time, were inexperienced with the problems associated with moving over Russian roads in winter. The delay meant that the Panzergrenadier regiments had been forced to go into action without the support of the division's armor.

Late on 22 February, while "Totenkopf" Panzers still struggled along the icy roads, Regiment "Totenkopf" continued its advance, driving toward Pavlograd. The division had two immediate objectives. First was to support the attack upon Pavlograd, where "Das Reich" remained in action against Soviet tanks and infantry of the 35th Guards Rifle Division. The second objective was the capture of the rail center at Panjutina and an important railroad station at Orelka.

Elements of the Soviet 35th Guards Rifle Division, reinforced by supporting armor, occupied the towns of Wjasovok and Werbki, which guarded the approaches and rail lines leading out of Pavlograd to the north. Schulze's II./Rgt. "Totenkopf" advanced on the right or eastern flank of the regiment's attack, moving on a broad front to the east and southeast. One Kampfgruppe of the battalion moved along the bank of the Orel River, pushing toward the railroad stations at Orelka and Panjutina, which lay on the Kharkov-Losovaja-Pavlograd rail line. Panjutina was an important railhead hub in the region and was located at the center of the railway communications net south of Kharkov. From Panjutina, one rail line ran north to Kharkov, while other lines ran east, west and south. Its capture was an important part of restoring supply by rail to the entire region south of Kharkov. Meanwhile, a second battalion group continued along the road which led to Wjasovok and occupied the towns of Wassiljevka and Michailovka. Schubach's III./"Totenkopf" turned east, approaching Wjasovok along a different road.

On the extreme left or northern flank of the division's advance, III./SS- "Totenkopf" Rgt. 3 (Sturmbannführer Kühn) left the Krasnograd area and pushed along a secondary road toward the east. Small detachments of Russians, occupying the villages of Andrejevka and Semljanki were driven out by the advance of the SS battle groups and withdrew to the north, toward the Kegitschevka area, which was occupied at that time by formations of "Leibstandarte." Late in the afternoon of 22 February, "Leibstandarte" reconnaissance troops made contact with Kühn's battalion. This union with Dietrich's division was to be strengthened on the following day by establishing contact with Peiper's half track battalion in the Otrada area.

"Totenkopf" continued its attack, led by the Panzergrenadier regiments of the division, while "Das Reich" remained on the offensive. A Kampfgruppe built around Harmel's Regiment "Deutschland" was to attack southwest from Pavlograd, with the objective of striking the Soviet forces opposing 15. Infanterie-Di-

Joachim Schubach, pictured in a prewar photo as an SS-Hauptscharführer. Schubach took over the command of III./Regiment "Totenkopf" on 22 February, 1943 after Ernst Häussler was wounded. Schubach remained in command until 17 March, when he too was wounded. Schubach was later severely wounded and lost his vision during fighting near Krivog Rog. He survived the war however, passing away in Hannover, Germany in 1980. (Courtesy Mark C. Yerger)

vision at Sinel'nikovo. Harmel planned to attack the Russians from the rear, while Buschenhagen's infantry launched a supporting attack from the front. On 21 February, the stalwart army division, like the SS divisions, had been placed under command of Hoth's 4. Panzerarmee.

Hoth was one of the outstanding armor commanders of World War II. In May of 1942, he had assumed the command of 4. Panzerarmee, his last command of the war. Hoth led the army through the second winter of the war, the subsequent Stalingrad relief operation and the battles for Kharkov in 1943. Hitler later removed him from his command of the army, amidst accusations that Hoth had a defeatist attitude. In reality, Hoth was a blunt spoken realist who let Hitler know his opinion on the conduct of the war in no uncertain terms. Although he was subsequently awarded the Swords to the Knight's Cross, he was forced to retire from active service. However, these events were far in the future during February of 1943. On 22 February, Hoth was orchestrating the beginning of the counteroffensive, perfectly implementing the grand plan envisioned by Manstein. That day saw the continued whirlwind of mobile operations that characterized the Kharkov counteroffensive.

Harmel's Regiment "Deutschland" Kampfgruppe left Novo-Moskovsk during the early hours of darkness. By midnight, the regiment had traveled nearly half the distance between Sinel'nikovo and Pavlograd, assembling at the village of Snamenka. After only a few hours rest, the regiment was on the move again, leaving Snamenka at 0245 hours and arrived at its assembly areas in Pavlograd by 0915 hours. Kumm's Regiment "Der Führer," which had been reinforced by two platoons of Flak guns, firmly held its defensive positions on the north and east edge of the town, in order to shield the assembly and attack of Harmel's regiment. Meanwhile Fick's Kradschutzen-Bataillon sent reconnaissance detachments through the town and to the east, in order to screen the road in the direction of the attack route. During the afternoon, the motorcycle battalion established contact with a forward detachment of SS-Panzergrenadier-Division "Wiking," which was a part of 1. Panzerarmee's XXXX.Panzerkorps.

When the main body of Regiment "Deutschland" arrived at Pavlograd, II./"Deutschland" replaced Kaiser's III./"Der Führer," occupying that battalion's defensive positions on the east edge of town. Kaiser's battalion was then assigned to Harmel's Kampfgruppe for the attack upon Sinel'nikovo.[30] After this reorga-

Horst Gresiak was a tank commander in "Das Reich's" Panzer Regiment when the division was reorganized as a Panzergrenadier Division during the latter part of 1942. Later in the war, he won the Knight's Cross while commanding a tank company during the fighting in France after the Allied invasion of Normandy. (Courtesy Mark C. Yerger)

nization, Kampfgruppe Harmel consisted of I. and III./Regiment "Deutschland," III./Regiment "Der Führer and two battalions of artillery. The ability of the Germans to efficiently and seamlessly combine various battalions and companies into specialized battle groups was one of the reasons that they were so effective during the war. This trait characterized German operations throughout the war, on all fronts and contributed to the often startling effectiveness of offensive and defensive efforts by regimental and battalion sized battle groups. It is clearly in evidence when the mobile operations of the SS-Panzerkorps during the Kharkov battles are studied. Allied armies did not often share this ability because the British and Americans often had a distinct aversion to serving under unfamiliar officers of a "strange" unit.

---

[30] Kaiser's III. (gepanzerte)/Regiment "Der Führer" was the halftrack battalion of the division. The Germans never had enough halftracks to equip more than one Panzergrenadier battalion of even their elite divisions. The other battalions were transported by truck or heavy car, although some had a number of light armored cars.

The objective of Harmel's attack was to destroy the remaining Soviet forces around Sinel'nikovo. This operation was part of a coordinated operation to clear Soviet forces from the railroad in order to completely secure the communication and supply routes from Dnepropetrovsk into Pavlograd and thereafter, east to Stalino. After the Pavlograd-Ssinel'nikovo-Dnepropetrovsk rail net was again in German control, the SS divisions could turn north and attack toward Kharkov. The direction of attack would follow the rail lines north, toward Panjutina and Losovaja.

After Harmel and Buschenhagen's troops eliminated the remaining Soviet troops from the stretch of rail line between Sinel'nikovo and Pavlograd, the rail line from Dnepropetrovsk into Pavlograd would be operational again. The 15. Infanterie-Division was then to be responsible for mopping up remaining Soviet troops and securing the rear areas of the SS-Panzerkorps. The division would follow behind the SS divisions, clearing up pockets of resistance and securing the railroads. This would allow an uninterrupted line of supply for Hoth's Panzer corps as they advanced northward, toward Kharkov. After 1. Panzerarmee cleared the Russians out of Barvenkovo and pushed them away from Slavyansk, the entire rail net from east of the Dnepr crossings to the Northern Donets, would once again be secure. The operations of 4. and 1. Panzerarmee during the next phases of the counterattack reflect the importance of the rail net, which was especially vital during the winter, due to the road conditions.

Less than an hour after reaching Pavlograd, Harmel's column left the southwest edge of the town, moving along the railroad and parallel road leading toward Sinel'nikovo. The movement of Kampfgruppe Harmel was made under the same poor road conditions that had plagued "Totenkopf's" Panzers and it could move only as fast as its slowest vehicles. However, the column proceeded without undue delays and again benefited from the support of Stuka dive bombers and ground attack planes. The importance of air support to the operations of the German Panzer spearheads cannot be overemphasized because close air support was a vital component of German offensive actions. The Stukas were extremely effective and dropped their bombs with pinpoint accuracy, paralyzing or destroying opposing forces, which were then assaulted by a stunning weight of combined arms fire power. An example of the close cooperation of the Luftwaffe with the ground troops occurred during Harmel's advance towards Sinel'nikovo.

At 1110 hours the lead formations suddenly ran into three Soviet T-34s that had taken up a concealed defensive position astride the road, blocking the path of the German column. The leading German vehicles were suddenly hit by high explosive shell fire which threw them into confusion. The SS half tracks scattered in all directions and pulled back out of the line of sight of the T-34s. The Russian tanks could have delayed the attack significantly, if the column would have been forced to deploy against the blocking position, but several Stukas arrived immediately and attacked the T-34s, destroying all three tanks in a matter of moments. After passing the destroyed Soviet armor, the lead elements of the column arrived north of Sinel'nikovo at about noon. Here again Harmel's Kampfgruppe encountered a small, but determined detachment of Soviet troops blocking the road. The Russians had little chance of creating a significant delay, however and after a brief fight, Saizevo was taken at 1430 hours. The Kampfgruppe pushed on to Sinel'nikovo, where contact was established with 15. Infanterie-Division elements. Throughout the rest of the day, elements of the Kampfgruppe remained in action, cleaning out Russian troops from both sides of the road running into Sinel'nikovo from the north.

Meanwhile, during the night of 22-23 February, most of the tanks of "Totenkopf's" Panzer regiment managed to assemble south of Pereshschepino. The tanks that had gotten stuck or damaged during the move were gradually dragged out of the snow and repaired if necessary. One by one they followed after the regiment and most rejoined their comrades, although some were commandeered by supply officers in order to keep the roads clear of Russian infantry. Other main elements of the division had begun to assemble as well. The majority of SS-Standartenführer Hellmuth Becker's regiment, including I./and II./SS-Pz-Gren. Rgt. 3. reached Krasnograd on the night of 22-23 February. With dawn on 23 February, Eicke's division prepared to take a larger role in the 4. Panzerarmee counteroffensive, fighting for the first time as a full fledged Panzergrenadier division. The attack of the SS-Panzerkorps, led by "Das Reich" during its opening stages of the operation, benefited from the energy and strength of the fresher "Totenkopf" troops during the following weeks.

Already, forward units of the Soviet 6th Army had been dealt a serious blow during the first two days of the attack by the slashing advance of "Das Reich." The 35th Guards Rifle Division had been chopped into several pieces and hammered significantly. However, in spite of its losses, the units of the division retained their will to fight and made every effort to sever German supply lines or regain contact with the 6th Army. In some areas, the division managed to launch counterattacks upon the German mobile groups, as did elements of other Russian divisions. An organized response could not be coordinated however and the swift moving SS columns continually bloodied isolated Russian attacks along the route of advance of "Das Reich."

At Sinel'nikovo "Das Reich" and 15. Infanterie-Division eliminated the threat to Dnepropetrovsk by the 35th Guard Rifle Division, which was forced to withdraw when it could not be reinforced. The 41st Guards Rifle Division was also struck hard by 15. Infanterie-Division and "Das Reich" in the area between Pavlograd and Sinel'nikovo. The division suffered severe casualties and lost contact with other Soviet units. The 267th Rifle Division and 106th Rifle Brigade had their lines of communication severed by "Das Reich" and both were subsequently hit hard by "Totenkopf" when the SS division followed in the wake of "Das Reich."[31]

In spite of the developments at Novo-Moskovsk and east of Sinel'nikovo, at the Headquarters of the Southwestern Front, the level of confidence remained high. Vatutin ordered the 6th Army to introduce the 25th Tank Corps and 1st Guards Tank Corps into the offensive and continued to prod the army to drive to the Dnepr. Lieutenant General Kharitonov, 6th Army commander, realized the dangers of the course of action which the Front had insisted upon. Instead of blindly throwing the 1st Guards Tank Corps forward to the Dnepr as well, he utilized two tank brigades of the corps to react to the German attacks at Pavlograd and the advance of "Totenkopf" east of Pereshschepino. The Soviet army and corps commanders immediately sensed that German attacks were not the actions of a rear guard covering a withdrawal. However, the commanders of both the Southwestern and Voronezh Fronts stubbornly maintained their view that the Germans were a beaten foe and were retreating out of the region. This delay in assessing the actual danger to their overextended columns played into German hands and contributed to the coming disaster. The mobile groups were in particularly vulnerable conditions. Most were far advanced from their army, unsupported by adequate infantry and artillery forces and were steadily weakened by attrition of their tank strength. In contrast to well coordinated German air operations, the Soviet air force did not consistently supply the tank corps with good air support. However, these problems were ignored by the Soviet command, which was still buoyed by what it interpreted as completely positive intelligence reports and remained under the false impression, as late as 21-22 February, that all was going well. In fact, on the night of 21 February, Vatutin received an intelligence report which stated, " We have exact data that the enemy in the evening is withdrawing from the Donbas." That night, Vatutin ordered Kharitonov's 6th Army to drive further west and carry out its mission at any cost.[32]

To the north, Golikov's Voronezh Front, also received evidence that seemingly confirmed the prevailing Soviet command view that the Germans were beaten and withdrawing from the Kharkov area. In Golikov's defense, there was little conclusive evidence to sug-

A small Ukrainian railroad station located along a rail line south of Kharkov during the winter of 1942-43. The direction of attack during Manstein's Kharkov counteroffensive was often determined by the location or possession of key segments of the rail network surrounding Kharkov. (Courtesy Mark C. Yerger)

gest that this view of the situation was incorrect. Kharkov had been abandoned and German forces were damaged heavily during the fighting. The picture in the Kharkov area definitely seemed to favor the Russians. The SS divisions and "Grossdeutschland" were dealt severe losses and had withdrawn to the west and southwest. The 168. Infanterie-Division was fragmented and continued to withdraw westward under pressure by forces of the 40th Army. Therefore, Golikov continued to prod his army commanders to push further west, driving toward the Vorskla River west of Bogodukhov. The right flank divisions of the 69th Army drove westwards, into the gap above Armeeabteilung Kempf's northern flank, threatening to outflank Korps Raus from the Bogodukhov area. The corps bent back its northern flank to the west, but lacked the forces to further extend the flank to any significant length. The gap remained between Bogodukhov and Ljubotin. However, some help had arrived, in the form of "Totenkopf's" Regiment "Thule," which was quickly thrown into the gap.

At first glance, Regiment "Thule" seemed inadequate to effectively change the situation, but the unique mobility of Lammerding's regiment and its ability to form effective mobile battle groups allowed it to be used very effectively. The regiment was a welcome addition to Korps Raus, which was entering a critical stage in its defense of the sector southwest of Kharkov. It was imperative to hold the Poltava-Krasnograd supply hub in order to supply the SS-Panzerkorps while the SS divisions made their initial thrust to the south. Armeeabteilung Kempf had to secure the rail supply net until the 4. Panzerarmee offensive turned and pushed north along the railroad lines which ran into Kharkov from the south. Kempf's tired men had to hold their ground until the SS division's struck the Soviet's southern flank.

[31] Glantz, pg. 126.
[32] Ibid. pg.121.

8

KORPS RAUS SHIELDS THE SS-PANZERKORPS

During 19-23 February, while "Das Reich" and "Totenkopf" were engaged in offensive operations south of Krasnograd, "Grossdeutschland," Regiment "Thule" and 320. Infanterie-Division, under command of Armeeabteilung Lanz's Korps Raus, conducted defensive operations north and east of Krasnograd. The 168. Infanterie-Division was driven farther west by the Soviet advance, its will to fight severely damaged by the losses and psychological costs of the fighting around Kharkov in January and early February. During this period, the Soviet 3rd Tank Army moved its 160th and 25th Guards Rifle Division into position on the Merchik River, west of Kharkov. The army's intention was to secure bridgeheads on the southern bank, from which further attacks could be launched upon the Poltava-Ljubotin-Kharkov railroad. The Merchik ran roughly parallel to this rail line. Once across the river, the Russians could advance southward and cut the sole remaining railroad available to Korps Raus. This stretch of railroad exited Poltava, ran roughly to the northeast and then entered Ljubotin, which was only a few kilometers west of Kharkov. There were a number of smaller rail yards and stations along this segment of the key railroad, notably at the towns of Vysokopol'ye and Kovjagi. During the next weeks the Russians attempted to cut the railroad between Ljubotin and Poltava, which was the primary railhead and supply hub of Armeeabteilung Kempf. Once having captured Poltava, the Russians planned on driving further south and taking Krasnograd, which would have hamstrung the attack of the SS-Panzerkorps.

If Korps Raus lost the sector, the operations of Hausser's SS-Panzerkorps would have been seriously disrupted just as the offensive had gotten underway. If the Soviets had been able to seize the rail head at Poltava, the supply lines to Hoth's main armor group would have been cut off at a critical time. It would have been necessary to regain possession of the rail line. "Totenkopf's" assembly would have been delayed and it might have been necessary to commit "Das Reich" to the restoration of German control of the Poltava-Ljubotin railroad. This would have given precious time to the Soviet command, perhaps allowing them to make a correct assessment of the situation and react accordingly.

A great deal of the responsibility for holding the sector rested with "Leibstandarte," Regiment "Thule" and "Grossdeutschland" because the army infantry divisions did not have the necessary mobility or firepower. Although the attacks by Voronezh Front were losing steam, the Armeeabteilung remained under considerable pressure. Golikov drove his armies toward the area west of Kharkov, toward the rail centers of Poltava and Achtyrka, while Rybalko's 3rd Tank Army screened the southern flank of the 40th and 69th Armies. In order to carry out this assignment Rybalko pushed his army to offensive action, despite having suffered severe losses in armor and men during the battle for Kharkov. Rybalko's weakened army tried to smash the Krasnograd salient, which was defended by "Leibstandarte," while the other two armies marched west. Fortunately for the Germans, the Soviet rifle divisions were not motorized and the snow and ice slowed their rate of advance.

It had been necessary for "Das Reich" to launch the counteroffensive before "Totenkopf" arrived, due to the threat to the Dnepr bridges. Beginning the attack with only one tired division was risky, but Manstein gambled that "Leibstandarte" could defend Krasnograd long enough for "Totenkopf" to arrive and join "Das Reich." Even then considerable danger remained because Korps Raus had to hold the supply lines while the two SS divisions took Pavlograd and then drove north in order to strike the 3rd Tank Army. While "Das

Reich" raced toward Sinel'nikovo, Russian columns plodded onward, pushing to the west and south of Kharkov like a relentless flood.

Behind the Soviet forward detachments, long columns of infantry, artillery and horse drawn sledges slowly marched out of the assembly areas northwest of Kharkov. Soviet forces were pouring into the gap and toward the Vorskla. On the northern flank of the gap, Heeresgruppe Mitte's 2. Armee weakly defended the area north of the threatened Vorskla River sector, while to the south, Korps Raus held a thin line stretching 15 to 20 kilometers west of Kharkov. Regiment "Thule" was given the responsibility for defending a line of strongpoints west of the town of Olshanny. On its right or southern flank, "Grossdeutschland" still held on to its positions around Ljubotin. The right wing of the SS regiment tied in with the left wing of Füsilier Regiment "Grossdeutschland" near Ljubotin. The left or western flank of Regiment "Thule" was essentially open beyond the regimental positions at the village of Bairak. There was no contact with any German forces to the west and other than weak elements of 168. Infanterie-Division, spread out between Achtyrka and Bogodukhov, the gap remained undefended.

Early on the morning of 19 February, several marching Russian columns were detected by air reconnaissance in this gap, north of Regiment "Thule" positions at Bairak. This indicated that the Soviets planned to conduct an attack with the intention of trying to turn the Korps Raus defensive line on its western flank, in order to cut the Poltava-Ljubotin-Kharkov railroad line, which ran through Bairak. Other intelligence information seemed to indicate that a Russian attack could be expected at Bairak within a short time. A strong breakthrough in this area would quickly cut the railroad and with 167. Infanterie-Division still arriving the Russians threatened to launch an attack before the Germans could extend the defense of the western flank of Korps Raus. As the German command had expected, on the night of 19-20 February, the Russians attacked the right flank of Grenadier Regiment "Grossdeutschland." This attack was thrown back and the defenders were able to launch a counterattack, which knocked out a T-34 and destroyed several anti-tank guns. The counterattack by the Grenadiers also captured sixty horse drawn sleds of a Soviet column. However, Rybalko's army kept up heavy pressure all along the defensive positions around Ljubotin, while Golikov moved men and supplies behind Rybalko's army, towards the undefended gap. Other Russian assaults fell on II./Regiment "Thule" positions north of the Merchik River, while I./Rgt. "Thule" was still assembling in Krasnograd.

Three companies of Georg Bochmann's II./Regiment "Thule," under command of regimental commander Lammerding, held the town of Bairak on the western flank. Kampfgruppe "Schulze," con-

The commander of II./Regiment "Thule" was SS-Sturmbannführer Georg Bochman. The entire regiment was detached from the rest of "Totenkopf" during the majority of the fighting for Kharkov. It fought primarily as part of Armeeabteilung Kempf's Korps Raus, supporting 320. Infanterie-Division in defensive fighting southwest of Kharkov. (The author's collection)

sisting of several companies of II./SS-"Totenkopf" Rgt. 1, reinforced by heavy weapons, held the eastern flank which was loosely tied in with "Grossdeutschland" defenses at Ljubotin.[1] The regiment was assigned a broad sector which was too wide to establish a continuous defensive line. Its "front" consisted of dispersed strong points, each defended by a platoon, which were unable to support each other by direct fire. Behind the screen of platoons were strongpoints manned by companies, serving as sector reserves. There were numerous gaps in the regimental front, although the main roads were defended.

At 0400 hours on 19 February, concealed by early morning fog and heavy snow fall, infantry of the Russian 160th Rifle Division burst out of the darkness in the sector held by II./Regiment

---

[1] Named for the commander of the Kampfgruppe, SS-Sturmbannführer Wilhelm Schulze.

"Thule." Heavy artillery fire fell upon several key German defensive positions located on hills along the main roads. T-34s of the 195th Tank Brigade led the main thrusts, sliding and careening over narrow, icy roads, while columns of Soviet infantry trudged along behind them. This attack was in conjunction with the attempt by the 12th Tank Corps to break through the front of the 320. Infanterie-Division southeast of the Ljubotin salient. The 195th Tank Brigade was to cross the Merchik at a point northwest of Ljubotin and drive south, toward the town of Kovjagi, which was located on the railroad line leading out of Ljubotin's western edge. After penetrating the German front southeast of Ljubotin, the 15th Tank Corps was to drive west and reach Kovjagi by advancing along the railroad. This link up would chop off the Ljubotin salient and trap the "Grossdeutschland" troops defending the town.[2]

The regimental strength attack began from assembly points north of the Merchik River and was supported by divisional artillery. The Soviet columns penetrated between the villages of Bairak and Selenji Gai and drove German troops off of two key hills south of Bairak. Lammerding was initially able to retain possession of Bairak itself, but was forced to pull back to the south to avoid being cut off. Meanwhile Soviet infantry reached the outskirts of the town of Novy Mertschik, which was south of Bairak and defended by 7. Kompanie of Regiment "Thule."[3]

It was obvious that the objective of the Soviet attack upon Regiment "Thule" was the Kovjagi-Ljubotin section of railroad, south-

---

[2] Glantz, pg. 185.
[3] Vopersal, pg. 117.

LEFT: SS-Hauptscharführer Rudolf Säumenicht was a company commander in Regiment "Thule." He led the company through the bitter fighting south of the Ljubotin-Kharkov rail road and was awarded the German Cross in Gold in April of 1943 for his leadership during this fighting. (The author's collection) RIGHT: SS-Sturmbannführer Franz Kleffner, the former commander of "Totenkopf's" Kradschützen-Bataillon, took command of I./Regiment "Thule" in the summer of 1942. Kleffner was an outspoken officer and his blunt comments regarding the conduct of the higher command landed him in hot water more than once. After he spoke his mind to Himmler on one such occasion, he was relieved as commandant of "Totenkopf's" Panzer training and replacement battalion and returned to a combat command. He was killed in action while leading Regiment "Eicke." (Courtesy Mark C. Yerger)

west of Bairak. From initial reports it became apparent that a Soviet rifle regiment was on the move through the breakthrough sector. The attack was moving in a southwestern direction, toward a bridge across the Merchik River at Novjy Merchik. Once across the river, it was an easy march to the railroad line and another important rail center, which was located at Kovjagi. Kovjagi was a railroad station on the key Poltava-Ljubotin-Kharkov rail line, Armeeabteilung Lanz's primary supply route. Thus the Soviet attack represented a very serious danger to Armeeabteilung Lanz, because it endangered the ability of Korps Raus to supply its formations west of Kharkov. By extension, this threatened the most important mission of Armeeabteilung Lanz, the protection of the assembly areas and supply lines of Hausser's SS divisions.

The 7./Kompanie of Regiment "Thule," under command of SS-Obersturmführer Alfred Arnold, defended Novyj Merchik and the important crossing site over the Merchik River. Arnold's company was part of Kampfgruppe "Schulze" and held the main defensive position on the regiment's left flank. The Russian rifle regiment on the march from the Bairak area reached the town at 0830 hours and immediately launched a full scale assault on the German positions. During heated fighting at close quarters, the SS company quickly suffered heavy losses, including all three of Arnold's platoon commanders. Company commander Arnold fell to a severe wound also and the company was taken over by SS-Hauptscharführer Rudolf Säumenicht. Overwhelming the German company, Soviet infantry broke into the perimeter at several points and outflanked company strong points. With Russians infiltrating behind and between their forward positions, the SS defenses began to fall apart. After the Russians exploited these breakthroughs by throwing another battalion into the attack, the Germans were forced to give up the town entirely. Säumenicht and the remains of his company, dragging their wounded with them, pulled back to the south.

While the left flank of the regiment's front fell back, the center of Regiment "Thule" also came under attack. At 0900 hours, a Soviet rifle battalion pushed due south, toward the town of Stary Merchik, which was located on the Merchik River between Novyj Merchik and Ljubotin. This breakthrough threatened the western flank of "Grossdeutschland" and Armeeabteilung Lanz issued immediate orders to the division to clean up the dangerous situation. From Bairak, one company of Kampfgruppe "Lammerding" was to attack to the south, and hit the Russian penetration on its right flank. Simultaneously a "Grossdeutschland" battlegroup was to advance from Kovjagi Station and stop the Soviet penetration before it cut the railroad line.[4]

SS-Sturmbannführer Otto Kron studied law at Würzburg University before the war. He commanded SS-Flak-Abteilung 3 during the time the division was encircled in the Demyansk pocket. Kron won the Knight's Cross during the Demyansk fighting for his leadership while commanding a Kampfgruppe built around the remnants of his battalion. (Courtesy Mark C. Yerger)

The "Grossdeutschland" Kampfgruppe consisted of the divisional Aufklärungs-abteilung and the Pioniere Abteilung "Grossdeutschland," which were reinforced with an assault gun battery and attached self-propelled artillery. The Kampfgruppe was ordered to assemble in Kovjagi, conduct an attack to the north and block the Russian advance from Novyj Merchik, while the SS troops attacked the flank of the breakthrough. The "Grossdeutschland" soldiers had added incentive to stop the Russians, because their divisional medical clearing station was located in Kovjagi. The town was full of their wounded comrades, who could not be evacuated at that time and it was inconceivable to allow their wounded to fall into the hands of the Russians.[5]

The situation quickly became critical at other points along the front as well, when the Russians exerted pressure on the division's

---

[4] Vopersal, pg. 117.

[5] *Befehl des Gewissens*, pg. 123.

These pictures show German soldiers training in methods of destroying Russian tanks by placing explosive devices on the tanks by hand. The top photo shows an SS Grenadier placing a mine under the forward edge of the turret of a captured T-34. The bottom picture illustrates the use of a magnetic hollow charge mine which was placed on the side of a tank or on the thin armor over the upper deck. Either of this methods required great courage and were obviously extremely hazardous. By mid-1943 the Germans developed rocket propelled hollow charge anti-tank weapons that could be fired by one man. These extremely effective weapons were known as Panzerfaust and a direct hit could penetrate the armor of any tank produced during World War II. The Germans also developed a bazooka type weapon that was not as commonly used. (Credit National Archives)

front. With the removal of the Aufklärungsabteilung from the front lines at Ljubotin, personnel from supply units, bakeries and security detachments were thrown into the line to take the battalion's place on the line. As a result, when the Russians conducted strong probes upon the thinly held lines, these inexperienced German troops gave way in several areas. The Russians were able to break through in the sector just west of Ljubotin, and reached the main road coming into the town from the west. Since this was a major supply route, and ran parallel to the railroad, the Aufklärungsabteilung was ordered to clear up this situation before assembling at Kovjagi for the planned counterattack. While this situation unfolded, additional Regiment "Thule" detachments, brought up from reserve, halted the Russian breakthrough between Novyj Merchik and Stary Merchik. A small Kampfgruppe, under command of SS-Hauptsturmführer Albert Voight, counterattacked a battalion of Russian troops in Novyj Merchik in the early afternoon, driving them out of the town with a fierce assault. The Russian infantry withdrew to the northeast but regrouped and the situation remained unresolved late in the afternoon, because Voight's force was not strong enough to destroy the Russian battalion.[6]

Other elements of the SS Grenadiers recovered also and began to fight back at Stary Merchik. Elements of Kampfgruppe Schulze regrouped, launched a counterattack and fought their way back into the town. At 1530 hours, the main body of the Russians was forced out of the town and the SS soldiers began to mop up the remaining pockets of resistance. Within an hour, the last Russians were cleared out and the town was secured. This victory significantly changed the tactical situation in the breakthrough area at the Merchik River between Novyj Merchik and Stary Merchik. The threat to the railroad and main road, as well as the casualty clearing station in Kovjagi was temporarily eased, even if it was not eliminated entirely. Korps Raus was able to focus its attention upon the Bairak sector.

Subsequently, the "Grossdeutschland" Aufklärungsabteilung received orders to assemble near Novyj Merchik and counterattack toward the Soviet forces in the Bairak area. The first attack objective was to recapture Hill 209.5, located just a few kilometers south of Bairak, which had been lost earlier in the day. After regaining the hill, the Aufklärungsabteilung was to break through to Bairak and link up with Lammerding's companies. Subsequently, Lammerding received orders to support this counterattack by a thrust upon the hill from his positions near Bairak. However, before the attack group under Lammerding could assemble, the Russians launched a number of attacks on the remaining German forces holding Bairak. Soviet forces estimated to be regimental strength,

launched concentric attacks on German positions on the southern and northern perimeters of the town in the afternoon.

By late in the day, the remaining elements of Kampfgruppe Lammerding were forced out of the town and withdrew to the west, toward the village of Grigorovka. Soviet pressure increased between Stary Mercik and Novyj Merchik and by nightfall the Russians had taken possession of a bridgehead on the river between the two towns, at the village of Dobropolje. Fortunately for the Germans, this Russian penetration was not immediately exploited because there were no reserves left to close any gaps in the lines. The situation was so desperate that "Grossdeutschland's" Werkstatt Kompanie (repair company) sent three disabled and barely mobile tanks to help block the new Soviet thrust, which again threatened Kovjagi.

Lammerding's battalion withdrew to the south of Bairak and organized a new defensive position just north of the Merchik during the evening of 20 February. Lammerding's hard pressed battalion had taken heavy casualties during the day, including the commander of II./Regiment "Thule," SS-Sturmbannführer Georg Bochmann, who had been wounded and was unable to remain in the field. SS-Hauptsturmführer Wilhelm Deege took over command of the battalion at that point. The reported losses of the battalion for the day included 36 dead, 41 wounded and 36 missing.

The I./Regiment "Thule," commanded by SS-Sturmbannführer Franz Kleffner, was still in Krasnograd, when it received orders to replace the companies of II./Regiment "Totenkopf" which were with Regiment "Thule," under command of Kampfgruppe Schulze. During the night of 20-21 February, the first elements of I./Regiment "Thule" reached the Stary Merchik area and began to take over the defensive positions of Kampfgruppe Schulze. Schulze immediately set out to march south to rejoin the main body of his regiment, but at that time another emergency arose and the weary SS soldiers were thrown into another difficult situation, literally off the march.[7]

A crisis had arisen on the right flank of "Grossdeutschland," which adjoined 320. Infanterie-Division. Once again Postel's division experienced difficulties defending its flanks, as had happened earlier with "Leibstandarte" at the Borki railroad station. A gap was created between the two divisions by an inexplicable and unreported withdrawal of a company of the division. The Russians promptly discovered the gap and exploited the situation by launching a battalion sized attack into the gap which penetrated the German lines northwest of the town of Jushny.

At that time, Schulze's battalion was marching south, and by chance passed near the breakthrough area at the critical time. The battalion was ordered to march toward the west, occupy blocking

---

[6] NA/T-314, roll 490, 1a KTB, Tagesmeldung Korp Raus vom 21.2.1943 and Vopersal, pg. 118-119.

[7] Vopersal, pg. 119-120.

A disabled SS "Tiger" camouflaged with brush and snow. The 8.8 cm gun of the "Tiger" was very effective and could penetrate the frontal armor of any Soviet tank. However, there were limitations upon their use, particularly in the southern Ukraine, where bridges were often too weak to bear the weight of the huge tanks. The "Tiger" was also a more complex tank than the robust and simple Russian T-34. As a result, sometimes there were more of the heavy Panzers out of action due to mechanical problems than through combat damage. (Credit National Archives)

positions and block the Russian thrust along the main rail line leading into Ljubotin. During the night of 20 February, the Russians assaulted the SS positions with infantry supported by tanks. Although the battalion suffered heavy losses during the bitter night fighting, the line was held and the Russian advance was temporarily blocked until "Grossdeutschland" took over defense of the gap. On the following morning, II./Regiment "Totenkopf" resumed its trek to the rear, receiving new orders to assemble in Krasnograd.

On 21 February, Regiment "Thule" and "Grossdeutschland" counterattacked the Russian bridgeheads on the Merchik River. A "Grossdeutschland" Kampfgruppe advanced against Russian positions near Novyj Merchik and the village of Krasnopolye. A company of the Pioniere Abteilung, supported by fire from a battery of heavy howitzers, assaulted Krasnopolye, while the main force assaulted Novyj Merchik. By 1030 hours the Kampfgruppe reported that it had broken into Novyj Merchik and was involved in bitter house to house fighting. Shortly afterward the Russians were completely driven out of the village and withdrew to positions on Hill 209.2, several kilometers north of Novyj Merchik. The battle left

the village in ruins, with half of its houses and buildings destroyed or burning.

In the meantime, Deege's II./Regiment "Thule" assembled south of the Merchik and assaulted Soviet forces in the Dobropolje bridgehead, after using a nearby woods to conceal the approach of the battalion. Simultaneously, "Grossdeutschland" assault guns and troops of the Aufklärungsabteilung attacked the village from the east. The main Russian force was expected to be encountered in Dobropolje. Faced with attacks from two directions, the Russians could not defend their perimeter and the German infantry fought their way into the center of the village. Destroyed or abandoned Soviet artillery pieces and trucks were still in position here and there, with dead members of the gun crew lying around them. Many dead horses, killed by German artillery or small arms fire, were strewn over the narrow roads and streets. However, while a great deal of small arms and other material was captured or destroyed, the main body of the Russian force advancing toward Kovjagi was not in Dobropolje or Novyj Merchik. To the disappointment of the Germans, the attack had caught only supply columns and transport troops in Dobropolje. This unexpected development meant that the main body of the Soviet attack had slipped between the two prongs of the German counterattack and was advancing on Kovjagi Station, with its important railroad and the German wounded.[8]

While the 69th Army pushed westward, rifle divisions of Rybalko's 3rd Tank Army fought to break "Grossdeutschland's" hold on Ljubotin. South of Ljubotin, the 12th Tank Corps attempted to expand the gap between the right flank of "Grossdeutschland" and the left flank of 320. Infanterie-Division, an opportunity presented to the Soviets by the army division's failure to properly defend its boundary. Russian infantry, supported by a few tanks, tried to enlarge the penetration but were initially delayed by the hasty counterattack launched by Schulze's II./Regiment "Totenkopf." The attack completely broke up when the "Grossdeutschland" Aufklärungsabteilung smashed into its flank and routed the Russian infantry. The hard fighting battalion knocked out two Soviet tanks, including one of the massive KV-1 heavy tanks, which was put out of action by a magnetic anti-tank mine. German artillery furnished considerable support, breaking up a strong attack by two battalions of Russian infantry and several tanks.[9]

The Soviets kept up the pressure on the Ljubotin salient itself throughout 20 February, attacking the German perimeter with armor and infantry. At Kasarovka, which was located on the northern edge of Ljubotin and defended by elements of the Füsilier Regiment, the Russians broke through the defenses on the north edge of the town. Nine tanks rolled into the town, but counterattacks sealed off the penetration, destroying one tank and disabling another. After being separated from their infantry support, the T-34s raced out of the town and pulled back to the north. However, the Russian infantry accompanying the tanks, had entrenched themselves in low ground only 100 meters in front of the town and refused to abandon their positions. A subsequent Soviet attack, consisting of another group of Soviet tanks, lost six T-34s to German anti-tank weapons and foundered due to these losses.[10]

The new Russian attacks around Ljubotin became a very serious concern of Armeeabteilung Lanz by 20-21 February, particularly with the 160th and 25th Guards Rifle Divisions exerting steady pressure against Regiment "Thule." These forces were temporarily blocked by the commitment of Aufklärungsabteilung "Grossdeutschland," and the stubborn fighting of the SS infantry along the Merchik. However, it was only a matter of time before they bludgeoned their way through the thin line of German troops

An interesting picture of German troops in a Ukrainian village during the Kharkov fighting. The soldier on the left is firing what appears to be a Russian sniper rifle while the men behind the barricade of debris appear to be observing the effect of his fire.(Credit National Archives)

and linked up with the 12th Tank Corps south of Ljubotin. When this occurred Ljubotin would be encircled and the remnants of "Grossdeutschland" would have to fight their way out of the pincers of another collapsing pocket.

The remaining weak reserves available to Armeeabteilung Lanz were insufficient to support a breakout attempt by "Grossdeutschland." With the SS-Panzerkorps counteroffensive already underway, there could be no help expected from Heeresgruppe Süd either. When Lanz communicated with Manstein about the situation, he asked about the objectives of the SS-Panzerkorps after the corps arrival at Novo-Moskovsk. Doubtless Lanz wanted to have the corps back under his control in order to clean up the situation west of Kharkov. Manstein of course, had more important purposes in mind for the SS divisions. Accordingly, the 1a of Heeresgruppe Süd replied that the two SS divisions were to conduct further attacks on Pavolograd and drive out the Russian troops in the Samara River area. Lanz replied that in his opinion, the more pressing problem was on the northern flank. West of Bairak there was a gap of about 60 kilometers and there was little available to defend it, except the dispersed regimental battle groups of 168. Infanterie-Division. Even if these forces put up a credible defense, which was extremely doubtful, gaps would remain through which the Soviets could pass through relatively unhindered and advance to the south or further west. Heeresgruppe Süd informed Lanz that Manstein's intention was to deal with the situation in the south first, meaning the 6th Army and 1st Guards Army forces south of Kharkov, before dealing with the situation north and west of Kharkov. Armeeabteilung Lanz was to be left to solve the situation with the forces at hand and could not expect any help. In any event, Lanz's command of the Armeeabteilung was nearly at an end.

[8] Ibid. pg. 120-121.
[9] NA/T-314, roll 490, 1a KTB Korps Raus: Tagesmeldung vom 21.2,1943, frame 00080.
[10] Op cit.

Later in the day, Lanz was informed by the Feldmarschal that he was being replaced by General der Panzer-Truppen Werner Kempf. In *Lost Victories*, Manstein does not go into great detail regarding this decision. He stated that the reason for the change was that Lanz was trained in mountain warfare (he had commanded 1. Gebirgs-Division earlier in the war) while Kempf was a Panzer general and better suited for the demands of the situation. Undoubtedly however, the real reason for Lanz' dismissal was the abandonment of Kharkov. The loss of the city infuriated Hitler and although it was Hausser who had disobeyed his orders, apparently it was Lanz who was to pay the price of the embarrassing defeat.

Kempf was a capable leader, with extensive combat experience. During World War I he served with Infanterie-Regiment 149 and reached the rank of Oberst in the pre-war Reichswehr. Kempf began his service during World War II at the rank of Generalmajor and his first divisional command was given to him on 1 October, 1939 when he took command of 6. Panzer-Division. Kempf was promoted to General der Panzertruppen effective 1 July, 1941 and he later commanded XXXXVIII. Panzerkorps. He was also familiar with the SS troops and many of the SS officers because he had commanded Panzer-Division Kempf during the Polish campaign. Mobile elements of that division were used to form "Das Reich."[11]

After the decision to replace Lanz was communicated to the Armeeabteilung, efforts continued to find some help for Korps Raus and its depleted infantry divisions. In a radio communication to Werner Ostendorff, the 1a of the SS-Panzerkorps, the Armeeabteilung requested that "Leibstandarte" take over complete responsibility for the Borki sector, relieving 320. Infanterie-Division of a task it obviously felt it could not handle. Secondly, the Armeeabteilung requested that all self propelled 4.7cm anti-tank guns in possession of the corps, be sent to Achtyrka, in support of the northern regimental group of 168. Infanterie-Division. Panzerjäger Kompanie 106 was also directed to support the division, as was the "Tiger" company of "Grossdeutschland." The elements of the division located around Achtyrka, continued to withdraw before the methodical advance of the 69th Army. Meanwhile, the regimental battle group southwest of Bogodukhov held its positions, at least temporarily, which was more an indication of Russian exhaustion rather than German strength.[12]

The situation both west and south of Ljubotin remained critical, particularly due to the depth of the penetration made by the 12th Tank Corps. By the night of 20-21 February, the penetration, located between Ljubotin and Merefa, had expanded to 2 kilometers in width and an additional 1.5 kilometers in depth. The situation at Borki remained a concern as well, because what reserves were available had to be used to limit the Russian efforts in that sector. Although "Leibstandarte" troops recaptured the Borki and railroad station, Russian infantry remained in defensive positions in the woods north of the town. The Russians used this bridgehead to assemble additional forces in the wooded area and push back 320. Infanterie-Division infantry, widening the gap to the north. There were simply few adequate reserves available to clear up the situation.

---

[11] Privately held KTB, information courtesy of Mark C. Yerger.

[12] *Behehl des Gewissens*, pg. 134.

In the midst of house to house fighting in an unknown Russian village, two German infantrymen sprint toward a damaged Russian house. The two men appear to be under fire or expect to be fired upon because the man in the rear runs in the crouch familiar to any soldiers who have crossed an open area under fire. (Credit National Archives)

A German Pak 38 anti-tank gun in position with its crew ready to fire. This gun came into service as a replacement for the inadequate 3.7cm Pak 35/36. The Pak 38 basic anti-tank round weighed nearly five pounds and could penetrate the frontal armor of a T-34 at about 500 meters. Later in the war, a shell with a tungsten carbide core was developed which was effective at longer range. (Credit National Archives)

In recognition of the seriousness of this crisis, Armeeabteilung Kempf issued orders to its divisions in the Ljubotin area to pull back to a more defensible line. At 2230 hours, Manstein radioed the Armeeabteilung with further instructions for Kempf. The 168. Infanterie-Division, with its southern regimental group, was to block the Vorskla Valley. The importance of the prompt assembly of all of "Totenkopf's" forces for the SS-Panzerkorps offensive was emphasized strongly. Heeresgruppe Süd emphatically stated that II./Rgt. "Totenkopf" was not to be made available to the army again and it was to continue its march to Krasnograd without delay.[13]

"Grossdeutschland" ordered its regiments to withdraw southward during the night of 21-22 February. Regiment "Thule" was ordered to pull back from the Merchik River and establish defensive positions north of Kovjagi. From there, it could cover "Grossdeutschland's" western flank while the division withdrew from Ljubotin. The Füsilier Regiment pulled out of Ljubotin and established new defensive positions southwest of the city with its western flank tied in with the right wing of Regiment "Thule." All noncombat personnel and any vehicles that could be spared by the SS regiment were ordered to assemble at Kovjagi in order to aid in the evacuation of the wounded from the rail center. In the meantime, motorized reconnaissance detachments of "Grossdeutschland" constantly roved the extensive gap west of the SS regiments left flank. The reports from these patrols furnished sketchy but disturbing information about the Russian forces moving into this area. Long columns of Soviet infantry, tanks and artillery were observed marching westward, further stretching the Armeeabteilung's left flank.

While "Grossdeutschland" pulled back to its new positions, the main elements of I./Regiment "Thule" moved into positions formerly occupied by II./Regiment "Totenkopf" near Stary Merchik. The battalion had a combat strength of 17 officers, 94 NCOs and 758 men. Most of II./Regiment "Thule" occupied the town of Vysokopol'ye, which was west of Kovjagi. Two companies of the battalion, reinforced with a battery of assault guns and two batteries of infantry howitzers, remained in the Novyj Merchik area. Later in the day this group was pulled back south of the railroad and was designated as the regimental reserve. The main element of II./Regiment "Thule" reached Vysokopol'ye in the evening and prepared to attack toward the Merchik River crossings at first light on 22 February.

In the morning, the battalion began its attack from assembly areas north of Vysokopol'ye, striking northwards toward crossings of the Merchik River. The attack was made with the purpose of blocking the expected Russian attacks upon Kovjagi. Progress was slow because of deep snow and poor road conditions. At 1615 hours, a company of the battalion reached Marino, which was several kilometers south of the river. A second company approached the village of Mirnoje, which was on the southern bank of the Merchik. Mirnoje was known to be occupied by Russian troops although no information was available as to their strength. Russian troops were encountered at several villages and sharp fighting broke out during the advance.

Elements of the Soviet 69th Army, including the 161st, 219th and 180th Rifle Divisions had advanced north of the Merchik, moving at a right angle across the front of the SS advance. Further to the north, moving in a roughly parallel direction, 40th Army's 309th Rifle Division approached Achtyrka, as the army pushed forward on a broad front. Grenadier-Regiment 246 of 88. Infanterie-Division, belonging to the German 2. Armee was ordered to occupy the town of Kupjevacha, in order to block this advance. Kupjevacha had been assaulted by Russian infantry, probably of the 219th Rifle Division on 20 February, and the Russians fought their way into the town while Grenadier-Regiment 246 was still en route. When the new regiment arrived, it provided greatly needed infantry strength to 168. Infanterie-Division, which had lost 4465 total casualties from the period of 15 January to 18 February, 1943. The division had also lost much of its artillery and had only a handful of anti-tank guns still in action. While Korps Raus fought to hold its positions along the Merchik and protect Poltava, the Soviets continued to pressure "Leibstandarte" in the Borki area.[14]

On the morning of 21 February, "Leibstandarte" received orders from Korps Raus to clear up the situation at Borki, as soon as practical, with troops of III./2.SS-Pz.-Gren.-Rgt."LAH" and supporting elements of SS-PzG.-Rgt. 1 "LAH." Peiper's half track battalion occupied Borki shortly before nightfall, replacing a company of SS-Pioniere-Bataillon 1. The Russians still occupied the forested area near the town in considerable strength and remained a potential threat. Since Peiper lacked sufficient strength to launch a full scale assault on the formidable Russian defenses, the bridgehead was to be contained by spoiling attacks. While Dietrich's Panzer-grenadiers prepared to block the Russians from expanding the Borki bridgehead, the division continued active defensive operations along its center and southern flank.

Dietrich's division was relatively strong in regard to the number of operational tanks it possessed on that date. It had a total of seventy-one tanks and possessed twenty of what were described as command tanks although not specifying what type of tanks these vehicles were. Of the seventy-one operational tanks, twelve were Panzer II light tanks which were primarily used for reconnaissance

---

[13] Ibid. pg. 130.

[14] NA/T-314, roll 490,1a KTB Korps Raus, frame 00051 and 000077.

and observation missions. Contrary to the popular belief that the SS divisions always received the newest tanks before the Army Panzer divisions, the division still a number of Panzer IIIs. The Panzer III remained a mainstay of the SS divisions until late in 1943. "Leibstandarte" did have a "Tiger" company, however, the heavy tanks often could not use the small bridges found in the Ukraine and were prone to mechanical difficulties because of the snow and ice. As a result of these limitations the "Tigers" were not always available to play a major role in the operations of the SS-Panzerkorps during February-March 1943.[15]

"Panzermeyer" wins the Oakleaves

At dawn on 22 February, Wünsche's I./SS-Panzer-Regiment 1, along with Meyer's reinforced Aufklärungsabteilung, attacked from Krasnograd, thrusting toward Soviet positions near the villages of Kegitschevka and Ziglerovka. When the SS column approached a ridge near the village of Jeremejevka, Meyer and Wünsche's battalions surprised a battalion of Soviet infantry which had just entered the elongated village. The Russian column was moving without adequate flank security and never suspected the presence of the Germans until it was too late. On the reverse slope of the ridge the tanks and the vehicles of the reconnaissance battalion waited in ambush for the unsuspecting Russians. Meyer quickly decided on a bold course of action, using speed and surprise as a weapon and personally led the attack. When the leading troops of the Soviet column emerged from Jeremejevka a wave of Schwimmwagens and SPWs charged toward the village firing every weapon. Several of the first German vehicles hit mines which had been laid along the flank of the route of march, but the following SPWs plunged ahead through the gaps created by the destruction of the lead vehicles. Instantly, Wünsche's Panzers motored to the ridge top and shelled the tail end of column at close range. Before the startled Russians could react and organize a cohesive defense, Meyer's attack group struck the center of the column and split it in half.

The Russian troops that were in the village disintegrated and panic stricken groups of Soviet soldiers fled in all directions. A hail of 2cm and mortar shells showered debris along the entire length of the muddy streets, flinging shards of shrapnel in every direction. The German vehicles raced into the village, careening down narrow lanes which ran between the Russian huts. SS Grenadiers fired automatic weapons from all side of the vehicles and tossed hand grenades into houses. A few of the Soviets took shelter in buildings

On 22 February, Meyer's reinforced Aufklärungsabteilung attacked from Krasnograd, reinforced by Wünsche's I./SS-Panzer-Regiment 1. The Kampfgruppe was moving toward Soviet positions near the villages of Kegitschevka and Ziglerovka when it discovered a large Russian infantry column moving into a village. During the ensuing attack the column was destroyed. For this and other actions during the Kharkov fighting Meyer was awarded the Oakleaves to the Knight's Cross. (Courtesy of Mark C. Yerger.)

and attempted to fight back, while others fled in disorder across the snow covered fields. Many of the Russian soldiers who ran across the snow were pursued by SS SPWs and mowed down by machine gun fire. The rear half of the column recoiled from this violent assault.

Exploiting the chaos that resulted when the reconnaissance troops assaulted the column, the SS tanks rolled down the hill toward the rear half of the column. A number of anti-tank guns and artillery pieces were still hooked up to teams of horses or oxen, having been abandoned by their crews. Here and there a crew tried to get its gun into action, while all around them pandemonium reigned. Terror stricken horses raced wildly up and down the road, dodging the SS half tracks and SPWs that charged through the vil-

[15] NA/T-354, roll 118,1a KTB Tagesmeldung Panzergrenadier - Division "Leibstandarte-SS-Adolf Hitler" an SS PzKorps 21.2.43.

lage. Before most of the Russian guns could be put into action, their crews were shot down or run over by SS tanks, the tracks grinding gun and crew into piles of bloody, twisted metal.

The rear section of the column tried to make an orderly withdrawal to the east. However, Meyer quickly regrouped his men and while the last Russians were still being cleaned out of building and houses, the battalion sped off in pursuit of the retreating Russians. Wünsche's tanks roared down the ridge and moved along both sides of the road. The tank gunners methodically slammed shell after shell into the mass of Soviet infantry. Faced with a wave of tanks moving toward them, discipline evaporated in the Russian ranks and the infantry and gun crews fled in panic as the SS Panzers rolled toward them. Those in the rear ranks were engulfed by the mob of running men, as officers vainly tried to stem their flight. The SS tanks and SPWs caught the horrified Russians from behind, knocking them into the snow with machine gun fire or running them down as they fled. The Soviet battalion was destroyed as a fighting force and nineteen anti-tank guns were destroyed or captured. Meyer received the Oak Leaves to his Knight's Cross for leading this attack.[16]

While the "Leibstandarte" Panzers and Aufklärungsabteilung were in action on the right on southern flank, the center of the division was under assault throughout the day. There were several Russian attacks against the boundary line between the two Panzergrenadier regiments. The main attack was centered in the area of Ochotschaje and was accompanied by tanks. These attacks were turned back after inflicting heavy losses upon the Russian infantry. "Leibstandarte" positions near Rjabuchino were struck by supporting attacks and the Soviets were able to make a small penetration of the defensive line. This local breakthrough was eliminated by counterattack later in the day.

At noon on 21 February, "Leibstandarte" was informed that it was assigned to the command of Armeeabteilung Kempf, which pleased the command group of the division because both Dietrich and his 1a, SS-Sturmbannführer Rudolf Lehmann, had a good relationship with the new commander. Dietrich radioed Kempf and gave him a report on the situation, informing him that the division was being hard pressed to hold its ground. Kempf knew the courage and toughness of the rough and ready divisional commander and trusted Dietrich's estimation of the situation. Subsequently, given the dangerous developments west of Ljubotin and the Russian penetrations westward along the course of the Merla River, he gave the order to withdraw a short distance in order to shorten the defensive lines of his army. Kempf directed Raus to create a mobile group for

---

[16] Lehmann, pgs.115-116.

Max Wünsche, here as an SS-Sturmbannführer. Wünsche and Meyer often worked together during the defensive fighting in the Kharkov area in the winter of 1942-43. The two officers trusted each other completely and formed an extremely effective command team on many occasions. (Courtesy of Mark C. Yerger.)

use against the Russian forces southwest of Bogodukhov, near Krasnokutsk.

The town of Krasnokutsk, which lay on the Merla River at a point nearly 60 kilometers west of Ljubotin, was reported occupied by Russian troops at 1700 hours. The German forces in the area consisted only of security troops and supply units and were unable to stem the slow, but steady Soviet tide. However, help was arriving in the form of fresh battalions belonging to 167. Infanterie-Division. By 1830 hours, II./Grenadier-Regiment 315 was marching to take over the defense of the Krasnokutsk area but Kempf knew that a single battalion would not remedy the situation. Besides a few extra tanks and anti-tank gun batteries which were already on their way west, there was little that Kempf could do. The

Luftwaffe was requested to make extra efforts to aid the defensive operations of Korps Raus and at least harass the march route of the Soviet columns. The Aufklärungsabteilung "Grossdeutschland," reinforced by the Führer-Begleit-Battalion, was sent racing toward Krasnokutsk with orders to help block the Soviets if they turned to the south once they were able to assemble in force at Krasnokutsk.[17]

On the following morning 168. Infanterie-Division continued its withdrawal to the west, driven ahead of the Soviet spearheads. One Kampfgruppe retreated to the Parchomovka area, which was north of Krasnokutsk and near the important rail center of Kotelva. Two other weak regimental groups, one based on Grenadier-Regiment 242 and the other on Grenadier-Regiment 442, also took up new positions. Into the void marched columns of Russian troops, trudging through snow and ice, moving westward through the Merla and Merchik river valleys. One of these column reached the town of Kolontajev which was located on the Merla River north of Krasnokutsk.[18]

The situation in the Merla-Vorskla area greatly concerned Kempf, as it had Lanz, particularly after the new commander realized the limited strength of his Armeeabteilung. In communication with Manstein during the mid-morning he voiced the opinion that the Armeeabteilung had insufficient resources available to do much about the situation. Kempf's justifiable concern was that the Russians would outflank his army to the west and then turn south and sever his lines of communication by the capture of Poltava before Hausser's corps was able to strike the Russians south of Kharkov. Manstein understood that Kempf's problems were real, but unlike Adolf Hitler he realized that he had to make a decision based upon cold appraisals of military priorities.

One of Hitler's failings was that he frequently tried to accomplish too much with too little and more often than not this led to failure. Manstein understood that he could conduct the counterattack in the south or aid Kempf, but not both at the same time. He chose to launch the counterattack in the south, knowing that if it was successful, the pressure on Kempf would be relieved also. It was a clear cut question of priorities to Manstein. In one sector, a weak Armeeabteilung was at risk while in the other sector, the entire southern wing of the Eastern Front was endangered. Therefore, Manstein realized that the situation in the south would have to be dealt with first before Kempf could expect substantial help from Heeresgruppe Süd. Manstein knew that the success of his planned offensive would eventually result in cutting the communication and supply lines to the Soviet forces that concerned Kempf. Accord-

ingly, he urged Kempf to keep his nerve and do everything possible to delay the Russian advance and wait for the counterattack to drive farther to the north and begin to bear fruit in the Kharkov area. He also informed him that 332. Infanterie-Division was to be sent into the gap between his Armeeabteilung and Heeresgruppe Mitte's 2. Armee. The 332. Infanterie-Division was essentially at full strength since it had been in France but it was inexperienced and was expected to undergo the same difficulties of adjustment to the war in the East as all green divisions. Fortunately for Kempf, more experienced help was already at hand. A reinforced battalion of the battle tested 167. Infanterie-Division was nearing the town of Rublevka, which was west of Kolontajev and Krasnokutsk. The battalion was in position to block the advance of Soviet forces from Krasnokutsk. Kempf would have to be content with what he had and trust that the situation did not collapse before the effects of the SS-Panzerkorps counteroffensive struck the 3rd Tank Army south of Kharkov.

The Luftwaffe was doing its part also and reported that it had attacked a 1000 man column east of the Kotelva area, forcing it to turn back, at least temporarily. Virtually non-stop Stuka and fighter bomber attacks had damaged the Russian troops in Kolontajev and Krasnokutsk. In other developments, the reinforced Aufklärungsabteilung "Grossdeutschland" was directed to assemble south of Kolontajev. From there it would also provide assistance should the Russians advance toward Poltava or the railroad line at Kovjagi.

During the night, when the temperature plunged to -20 degrees, "Grossdeutschland's" withdrawal initially proceeded smoothly until the aggressively patrolling Russians discovered that the Germans were withdrawing. They immediately launched a number of reconnaissance probes against the positions of "Leibstandarte" and 320. Infanterie-Division. Covered by rear guard detachments, the right flank of "Leibstandarte" was able to pull back west of Jeremejevka, the scene of Meyer's rout of the Soviet column on the previous day. In "Grossdeutschland's" sector the Russians made several stronger attacks, including one supported by several tanks, which caused problems to the troops pulling back to new positions.

At 0500 hours, the I./Grenadier Regiment "Grossdeutschland" had reached the village of Malaja Lichovka when Soviet tanks carrying mounted infantry caught up with the end of the column. T-34s came into sight behind the last vehicles and began to fire at the battalion, hitting several trucks and causing wild confusion. The Russian infantry dismounted from the tanks and advanced along both sides of the road, entering the village. The rear of the column was smashed and the Germans were forced to turn and defend themselves. Point blank fire from an anti-tank gun battery and infantry howitzers finally halted the Soviet advance in the western end of

---

[17] *Befehl des Gewissens*, pgs.134-135.
[18] NA/T-314, roll 490,1a KTB Korps Raus, Tagesmeldung 168. Infanterie-Division, frame 000108.

the village. At nightfall, the Russians regrouped and attacked the village again. T-34s and infantry attacked under cover of darkness but were not able to penetrate the battalion perimeter and pulled back into the darkness.[19]

Controversy Again: "Leibstandarte" and Heeresgruppe Süd

The night passed similarly in "Leibstandarte's" sector, where close pursuit by the Russians complicated the withdrawal of the division. Elements of the Pioniere Abteilung "LAH" were inadvertently left behind in the pull back from Borki and were cut off by Russian infantry. A small Kampfgruppe, consisting of several Panzers and assault guns was organized and raced back toward Borki, hoping to reach the trapped German troops before they were overrun. The SS armor broke through Soviet lines and fought its way into the village, rescuing the Pioniere troops.

SS-Standartenführer Witt's SS-PzG.-Rgt. 1 "LAH" was aggressively pursued by the Russians west of Borki, forcing the regiment to turn and cover its withdrawal. When the Russians threatened to overtake the retreating battalions Max Hansen's battalion was ordered to halt and strike back at the pursuing enemy. After a sharp engagement, which cost the Germans a number of casualties, the Russians pulled back to regroup. The brief respite gained by Hansen's attack allowed the regiment to reach its new positions safely. SS-Sturmbannführer Albert Frey's battalion also had to fight off several Russian reconnaissance attacks during its move. However, the regiment reported that it occupied the designated positions by 0530 hours. The new line stretched from Novaja Wodolaga on the north, to Melechovka in the south. Frey's battalion anchored the southern half of the line, while Hansen's battalion defended the northern sector. The III./SS-PzG.-Rgt.1 "LAH," under Hubert Meyer, was stationed behind the main defensive positions as regimental reserve. Soon after daylight the positions of both battalions were probed by a series of Russian attacks in platoon or company strength. By late afternoon the reconnaissance probes were conducted by battalions, a sure indication of growing Russian strength.

Wisch's SS-PzG.-Rgt.-2 "LAH" defended the southern half of the division's front, adjoining the "Totenkopf" attack sector. Reconnaissance patrols reported that an uninterrupted flow of heavy weapons and Soviet troops were on the march through the area several kilometers to the east. This development suggested a potential threat not only to the southern flank of "Leibstandarte" but endangered the tenuous contact with "Totenkopf." It was decided

"Leibstandarte" Panzergrenadiers in foxholes waiting for the Russians. Both Panzergrenadier regiments of the division defended the approaches to Krasnograd while "Das Reich" and "Totenkopf" assembled in the town and prepared to launch the first phase of the counterattack. (Credit National Archives)

to block this assembly with an attack by Meyer's Aufklärungsabteilung and Wünsche's Panzer battalion. However, both units were in need of vehicle repair and maintenance and the attack was postponed until the next day. SS mechanics worked around the clock to repair and refit the vehicles of both battalions by dawn of the following day.

While the division prepared to launch its attack upon the Soviet columns assembling on its southern flank, Dietrich and his staff were puzzled when they received a message from Heeresgruppe Süd, as transmitted by the 1a of Armeeabteilung Kempf, Major i.G. Heidenreich. The message stated that the army desired that 'the principle of offensive combat finally prevail with this strong and mobile unit.' After many days of successfully defending a broad front against aggressive and superior forces it was understandable that the tone, if not the content of this message did not sit well with Dietrich. Inquiries to Armeeabteilung Kempf resulted in an explanation of sorts. Manstein had sent a telegram message to the army on 22 February, directing that it was 'emphatically to bear responsibility that the principle of offensive combat prevail.' Heidenreich's order to the division evidently was derived from the Manstein message, the wording of which led Kempf to defend the division's per-

---

[19] Spaeter, pg. 52.

Halftracks filled with "Leibstandarte" Panzergrenadiers and a Sturmgeschütz III speed over a snow covered Ukrainian steppe in pursuit of Russian troops. Peiper's halftrack battalion and Meyer's reconnaissance battalion were frequently combined with a battalion of the division's tanks to form battle groups with mobility and great firepower. (Credit National Archives)

An SdKfz 251 with a 7.5cm short barreled infantry gun mounted in the space behind the driver. These vehicles and others equipped with a variety of heavy weapons furnished firepower for close support of the Panzergrenadier battalions. (Credit National Archives)

formance. He quickly sent a reply to Manstein and listed the most recent examples of the mobile actions of "Leibstandarte." After being made aware of the difficult and costly fighting that the division had been involved in, Manstein replied that the "Leibstandarte SS Adolf Hitler" successes were not apparent from the reports sent to the army group. This answer seemed to provide a grudging recognition by Heeresgruppe Süd of the efforts of the division but was tempered when Manstein felt it necessary to deliver a tactical lecture to the division regarding the beneficial effects of concentration of forces. This is an indication that the higher command was not sufficiently aware, even at that date, of the breadth of front defended by the German divisions nor the strength of the Soviet attacks. It chose to ignore that the Armeeabteilung was not strong enough to conduct large scale offensive operations to the south and defend against attacks by three Soviet armies in the north. Each of the division's Panzergrenadier regiments had a battalion detached and all of the division's armor and mobile battalions were operating with Kampfgruppe Dietrich against the 6th Guards Cavalry Corps. Exactly what divisional assets remained available to concentrate and where they were to be deployed is not clear. This incident may have been a simple case of lack of sufficient information. It may have been an example of Army prejudice against the Waffen-SS or Dietrich himself.

"Grossdeutschland" and Regiment "Thule" defend the Poltava-Ljubotin Rail Line

During the night of 22-23 February, the sector held by "Grossdeutschland's" Grenadier Regiment was generally quiet. However on the left flank of the division the sector held by the Füsilier Regiment and Regiment "Thule" was more active. The contact between the left flank of the Füsilier Regiment and the right flank of the SS regiment was not still not solid. This situation was promptly identified by the Soviets, who were always adept at finding and exploiting the weakness of unit boundaries. The pressure of Russian attacks at the regimental boundary threatened to split the German front when the Russians renewed their efforts to cross the Merchik River and drive to the railroad. The right flank of the SS regiment, held by elements of II./Regiment "Thule" at the small town of Mirnoje was attacked by two companies of Russian infantry that assaulted the northern perimeter of the German position. This was the beginning of a battle that continued to grow more fierce throughout the morning.

More Russian infantry joined the battle and passed through the gaps on both sides of the village, attacking the German strongpoints from the rear and flank. At 1200 hours contact with the Füsilier Regiment "Grossdeutschland" was lost completely after II./Rgt.

"Thule" was forced to abandon its positions under heavy Soviet pressure. Most of the battalion was able to withdraw to the south, toward the railroad town of Vysokop'ye. However, one company of the battalion was encircled at the town of Dergatschi and had to fight its way to freedom. After reaching the railroad, the company was able to disengage from the Russians and rejoined the remainder of the battalion at Vysokopol'ye.

The Füsilier Regiment "Grossdeutschland" also came under attack during the night of 22-23 February and these assaults continued after dawn on the morning of 23 February. Masses of Russian infantry, supported by heavy artillery fire, tried to overrun the regiment's defensive positions but it managed to repel all attacks during the day. One company counted over 100 dead Russians in the snow in front of its position. However, the right flank of the regiment was threatened by the penetration at Dergatschi.[20] The Russians exploited their initial success in the boundary area by bringing up more infantry and thrusting farther to the south. Subsequent Soviet attacks fell upon II./Rgt. "Thule's" new positions at Vysokopol'ye just before darkness. This attack failed, with the Russians again suffering heavy infantry losses, but SS patrols reported the movement of long Soviet columns moving south toward the rail line.

In spite of the importance of maintaining control of the section of railroad between Vysokopol'ye and Ljubotin, there was little that Armeeabteilung Kempf could do to strengthen the forces holding the area. A few small combat groups were cobbled together and used to support the SS regiment and Aufklärungsabteilung "Grossdeutschland." One such ad hoc unit was designated as Panzerzug 62. This small Kampfgruppe consisted of a handful of hastily repaired tanks pulled out of tank repair workshops and a few armored cars. The detachment patrolled the rail line from Vysokopol'ye west to the town of Schelestovo by utilizing a small parallel service road. Panzerzug 62 reported that several Soviet battalions crossed the railroad during the day, however since it lacked any infantry strength, the unit could not secure the line. The detachment attempted to disrupt and delay the Russian advance by making repeated sorties along the section of road between the two towns. Meanwhile, I./Rgt. "Thule" received a new defensive mission from Korps Raus. It was to hold a line between Vysokopol'ye and the town of Schelestovo, on the left flank of the Füsilier Regiment sector. Schelestovo was to be the scene of intense fighting near the key rail line on the following day.[21]

---

[20] This is not the village of Dergatschi that has been mentioned before, which is north of Kharkov. The names of Russian villages often are identical, even in the same area and this can be confusing.

[21] Vopersal, pg. 136-37 and NA/T-314, roll 490, Tagesmeldung Korps Raus an Armeeabteilung Kempf frame 000144.

In the widening gap west of Regiment "Thule's' positions, the "Grossdeutschland" Aufklärungsabteilung and reserve elements of I./Regiment "Thule" were directed to block Soviet forces that were expected to try and outflank the SS regiment and turn the Armeeabteilung western flank. The "Grossdeutschland" battalion was ordered to make a thrust against any Russian columns advancing into the gap from the Krasnokutsk area. Reinforced by a few vehicles of the Führer-Begleit-Bataillon, the battle group got underway in the morning and made good progress toward its first objective which was the town of Kolontajev, which lay on the Merla River near Krasnokutsk. The main body of the Führer-Begleit-Bataillon was not able to get underway immediately due to a shortage of fuel, but caught up with the battalion later in the day. However, the Kampfgruppe met no significant resistance other than scattered shots directed at its forward units by partisans, who were never actually seen by the German troops. Kolontajev was occupied without trouble and the Aufklärungsabteilung sent a number of platoons on reconnaissance missions covering a 25 kilometer wide area, in order to detect any Soviet advance through the area. A squadron of the battalion made contact with units of 167. Infanterie-Division at the village of Rublevka, located on the Merla River west of "Grossdeutschland" positions at Kolontajev.

The I./Regiment "Thule," after leaving the Alexejevka assembly areas, drove north toward the Merla River crossing at Krasnokutsk to support the "Grossdeutschland" Aufklärungsabteilung attack. The SS column, led by two assault guns and supported by a battery of 10cm howitzers had to contend with deep snow drifts which covered the road north of Alexejevka. In spite of the weather conditions by 0850 hours the battalion reached the village of Kustarevka. After a short battle with a small Russian detachment occupying the town, Kustarevka was taken and cleared by 0910 hours. At this point, the battalion was a few kilometers east of the "Grossdeutschland" attack but contact was not established with the other column. After securing Kustarevka, the lead elements of the battalion advanced on its primary objective, Katschalovka which was reached shortly before noon. The town was found to be strongly defended and the battalion commander, SS-Hauptsturmführer Wilhelm Deege requested Stukas to support his assault upon the town and the Grenadiers prepared to attack. However, before the attack could be launched Deege received orders that the battalion was to immediately return to Alexejevka. From there it was to help clean up the widening penetration between the Füsilier Regiment and II./Regiment "Thule." As the Kampfgruppe marched back through the snow, a passing ambulance driver informed them that the Russians were now between them and Alexejevka. He also gave them the bitter news that a bat-

talion aid station had been overrun by the Russians and informed them that the medical personnel and all of the wounded had been shot and the station burned. As the column continued its march, the men trudged by the charred bodies of their comrades sprawled in the smoking wreckage of the aid station.[22]

Hours later, in the dead of night, contact was made with a Russian strong point blocking the road. Machine gun fire broke out in the darkness and the SS men flung themselves into the snow, seeking shelter while the two assault guns moved forward. Quickly, the howitzers were unlimbered and swung around to furnish direct fire upon the Soviet position. Shells from the howitzers slammed into the road block at close range, exploding with bright flashes in the darkness and shattered the Soviet positions. The two Sturmgeschütze IIIs clanked forward, firing at the muzzle flashes of Russian machine guns, which fell silent quickly. Behind them, the SS infantry took shelter behind the armored hulks, while they laid down suppressing fire with automatic weapons and hurled grenades to the left and right. Surviving Russians fled into the dark after the column blasted its way through the Russian position. One can imagine the fate of any Russian attempting to surrender to the SS Grenadiers after they had seen the bodies of their comrades lying in the burned out aid station. The column continued south, meeting little further resistance and reached Alexejevka in the early morning.

However, there was to be little rest for the battalion, because it was quickly assigned a new mission. Under cover of darkness during the previous night, elements of a Soviet rifle regiment had occupied the village of Ssurdovka, which was a short distance from the German occupied town of Schelestovo, which was located on the Poltava-Ljubotin railroad line. Just after dawn, these Russian troops surrounded and attacked the German garrison at Schelestovo. By 0815 hours, the Russian infantry had broken into the lightly defended town and fierce house to house fighting began. Outnumbered heavily, the surviving German railroad security troops were squeezed into the center of Schelestovo. The 2./Kompanie of Regiment "Thule," which was equipped with Schwimmwagen, raced toward Schelestovo and arrived while the fighting still raged in the center of the small town.

A veteran of the division gave the following account of the fighting at Schelestovo, illustrating the plight of the Russian civilian population, who were often unwillingly caught up in the horrors of the war.

The Schwimmwagen arrived at Schelestovo and moved into cover. The infantry leaped out of the vehicles and assaulted

---

[22] Vopersal, pg. 136.

down the center of the main road. Under covering fire from their machine guns, they moved from house to house on both sides of the street. One group kept the Russians heads down with fire while another group rushed forward in short bounds. Soviet infantry leapt away from the street into the little gardens behind each house, falling back toward a crossroads on the northern edge of the town. With the Schwimmwagen following behind at a distance, the attack moved forward until the SS infantry reached the railroad embankment.

Storage buildings burned . . . To the right a road crossed the railroad. The Russian troops ran across the tracks over open ground in order to take shelter behind the embankment. Our machine guns got into position near the crossing and fired belt after belt after the fleeing Russians.

Suddenly a fur capped figure was visible behind the tracks. The machine gun sighted in on the target. The shots bounced off the tracks and ricochets sizzled by our ears. Then we suddenly realized, that the figure was too small to be a soldier. It was a child, running between the tracks. The small figure ran a little farther, staggered and fell, and disappeared from our sight. A moment later, the small bundled up child gathered himself and jumped up again in front of us. We shouted and yelled in mortal fear for the child. However, the air was filled with the noise of battle, and he could not hear our warnings.

Untersturmführer Müller sprang on to the road and signaled the machine gun to stop firing. Finally, after what seemed to be an eternity, the gun fell silent. We leapt on the road and in an instant brought him away from the railroad bank. Miraculously, the little rascal was unhurt.[23]

By 1040 hours, the village was back in German hands, however a reconnaissance patrol had to be sent out toward Ssurdovka in order to gain further information about the presence of any remaining Soviet troops in the area. The patrol returned at 1420 hours, and reported that the Russians still had considerable forces in Ssurdovka. Other elements of the company, led by two assault guns, met elements of Aufklärungsabteilung "Grossdeutschland" moving back along the rail line leading into Schelestovo. However, there was another emergency brewing and the two battalions were ordered to clean it up.

A Russian battle group had penetrated to the area around the town of Iskrovka, which was located directly on the Poltava-Ljubotin section of railroad line southwest of Schelestovo, where the line turned southwest and ran toward Poltava. Each new threat to the railroad stretched the German defenses a little further to the west. It

became apparent that Russian troops of several different divisions were moving nearer to Poltava and only Regiment "Thule" and Aufklärungsabteilung "GD" stood in their path.

In order to block the Soviet advance at Iskrovka, the Grenadiers of I./Rgt. "Thule" were sent off along the railroad, with orders to take the town. When the column approached Iskrovka, it came under fire from a Russian forward position entrenched in a wooded area near the town. The main body of the Russian detachment was in Iskrovka itself. While the SS troops deployed to assault the forward position on the forest edge, the "Grossdeutschland" battalion attacked the town from the south.

"Totenkopf" assault guns carefully found good firing positions and knocked out three Russian howitzers that were emplaced in the woods. After silencing the guns, the assault guns moved forward again and the SS Grenadiers assaulted the tree line. After brief fighting the Russian forward position was overrun. The survivors withdrew to the southwest, leaving behind 60 of their dead. Shortly afterward, at 1730 hours, the SS infantry linked up with the "Grossdeutschland" troops on the outskirts of the town. The combined force assaulted Iskrovka from two directions. The bitter fighting continued for several hours before the last resistance was crushed. The town was virtually obliterated, as most of its structures were either destroyed during the fighting or were on fire after being set alight by tracers bullets or high explosives. Many of the small houses burned to the ground, while German infantry mopped up the last pockets of resistance.[24]

After Regiment "Thule" and "Grossdeutschland" blunted the Russian attacks at Iskrovka and Schelestovo, the Russian advance seemed to run out of steam. After the battles south and west of Schelestovo and at Iskrovka, there was a lessening of Soviet pressure in the area. On 23 February, patrols of 167. Infanterie-Division found that Krasnokutsk had been abandoned by the Russians. A further reconnaissance north of the town found little other evidence of Soviet troops in that sector. Several groups of Russian troops remained in the area north of the Schelestovo-Vysokopol'ye-Kovjagi section of the rail line. However, these troops became less active, possibly due to supply deficiencies or sheer fatigue and casualties. There were still significant Russian forces in the gap west of Kovjagi, but by 25 February the situation west of Kharkov seemed to have become slightly less critical.

With the lessening of activity in the sector, Korps Raus was able to withdraw elements of "Grossdeutschland" to rest and recovery areas near Krasnograd, beginning on 24 February. Armeeabteilung Kempf ordered Korps Raus to again fall back to a new, more compact line of defense around Krasnograd. This short-

---

[23] Vopersal, pg.143.

[24] Op cit.

ening of the front allowed Korps Raus to withdraw the remainder of "Grossdeutschland" by 27 February. The recuperation period was necessary in order to prepare the division for its role supporting the 4. Panzerarmee counteroffensive when the SS divisions reached the area south of Kharkov.

To the north of the Merchik River area, the Soviets continued to drive west and there remained some worry that they could turn south and attack the communications lines of Kempf's army. Of particular concern was the presence of the Soviet 5th Tank Corps, north of Achtyrka, however, Heeresgruppe Süd knew that the counterattack of the SS-Panzerkorps and XXXXVIII. Panzerkorps was in the process of closing the gap between Pavlograd and Kharkov and would reach Kharkov in a matter of days. Manstein had gambled that Kempf's embattled troops would find a way to block the Soviet advance west of Kharkov long enough to shield the 4. Panzerarmee counterattack. Thanks to the efforts of Regiment "Thule" and the mobile units of "Grossdeutschland" this confidence was rewarded. Their sacrifices allowed Manstein to concentrate the two SS divisions and focus his attention on the 4. Panzerarmee counterstroke. Once Hoth's divisions reached Kharkov, the German Panzers were to swing to the west of the city and threaten the lines of supply to the Soviet forces west of Kharkov. Manstein knew that the Russians would not allow their forces to remain in their overextended western positions when the SS advance threatened to strike into their communications zone.

On the northern shoulder of the Kharkov-Slavyansk gap, Armeeabteilung Lanz/Kempf had performed about as well as could have been expected, given its limitations. Between Kharkov and Bogodukhov, the Russian 40th, 69th and 3rd Tank Armies had been delayed sufficiently by the handful of German divisions of Armeeabteilung Kempf to secure the supply lines of the SS-Panzerkorps until "Das Reich" and "Totenkopf" could be withdrawn and subsequently launch their counterattack. To the east, Armeeabteilung Fretter-Pico and then 1. Panzerarmee had defended the Slavyansk-Voroshilovgrad line and forced the Soviets to attack farther and farther west of Slavyansk, instead of to the south and Rostov. The stubborn resistance of Fretter-Pico's threadbare divisions and the dogged defensive actions of 1. Panzerarmee had resulted in a situation that ultimately proved fatal to Soviet forces in the Kharkov-Slavyansk gap. While the continued Soviet march toward Achtyrka and the Dnepr seemed at first glance evidence of Russian successes, particularly to the Soviet high command, it laid the ground work for a massive disaster. The German Landsers and Panzer troops, fighting with a tenacity seldom surpassed by soldiers of any army, slowed down an overextended Soviet colossus long enough for Manstein to gather his meager mobile forces and

launch one of the most remarkable turnabouts of the war. By 25 February, his counterattack was well underway, still anchored west of Kharkov by Armeeabteilung Kempf and Korps Raus, who completed withdrawals to new positions between 23-24 February.

When the rest of 167. Infanterie-Division arrived on the western flank, there seemed to be little evidence of heavy Russian pressure. The division's Grenadier-Regiment 339 unloaded on 24 February, while the division experienced little significant combat along its front. The regimental group near Rublevka, south of Krasnokutsk, reported no Russian pressure on its positions. Reconnaissance patrols from Grenadier-Regiment 339, scouting to the north of their unloading station, reported weak Soviet forces in that sector. This was the first evidence that the effects of the attack of the SS Panzer divisions were being felt in the gap west of Kharkov. Just as the Russians had seemed ready to push around the western flank of Korps Raus and advance to Poltava, Manstein's offensive began to have the desired affect. Combat still occurred in the area, but there was no longer a concerted Soviet push to drive south. The commanders of the 40th and 69th Armies cast a nervous eye to their supply lines and began to pull back.[25]

Early on 25 February, 168. Infanterie-Division reported its Pioniere Battalion, which was supported by a few tanks, was attacked by a Russian rifle battalion at Sinkiw. The Russians were able to get a foothold in the northern and western edges of the town, while the Pioniere and their supporting Panzers held on to defensive positions in the southern half of Sinkiw. In order to hold this strongpoint, the entire division was ordered to assemble in the area south of Sinkiw. The division's Grenadier-Regiment 442 numbered barely a hundred men, while the other two regiments had about 200 men between them. The Pioniere battalion, reduced to forty men, held the town of Sinkiw only because it was reinforced by two Panzer IVs and two Panzer IIIs. However, at that strength, it could not be expected to hold out if there was any sustained fighting for the town. To make matters worse, partisans in the area had made contact with Russian army troops and were exploiting the unit's weakness. Their sabotage and ambushes are often noted in Armeeabteilung Kempf reports after 23 February. The 167. Infanterie-Division was ordered to take over defense of the gap in the Krasnokutsk area, given the obvious inability of 168. Infanterie-Division to hold any large area.[26] The "Grossdeutschland" "Tiger" company was ordered to proceed to Sinkiw.

[25] NA/T-314, roll 490, Tagesmeldung Korps Raus an Armeeabteilung Kempf, 25.2.1943. frame 000184.
[26] *Befehl des Gewissens*, pg. 142.

At 1115 hours on 25 February, 168. Infanterie-Division reported that it still held Sinkiw, although fighting continued. Unfortunately, Armeeabteilung Kempf was informed that "Grossdeutschland's" company of "Tigers" was having difficulty traversing the roads leading to the north and had additional trouble with weak bridges. Normally this problem was quickly solved when German engineers conscripted civilian labor to strengthen bridges, open roads or shovel snow. However, Armeeabteilung Kempf records mention that was no longer possible, because the male civilian population was conspicuously absent from many towns in the rear areas of Korps Raus. Undoubtedly, some may have joined partisan bands and others may have fled from the fighting. However, it is most likely that most of the men had been forced to join the Russian Army. It had become common practice for the Russians to conscript every available male between sixteen and sixty years of age. These men were forced to fight, sometimes with only a piece of a uniform and rudimentary training. The more fortunate received a few days training in the use of their weapons. Most of these men were killed or wounded but the few that survived gained hard won battle experience. The conscription of untrained civilians is probably one explanation for German reports about unimaginative massed frontal attacks which resulted in heavy Soviet casualties.

Later in the day, 167. Infanterie-Division elements at Rublevka were attacked by two Soviet rifle companies, without tanks or artillery support. Most of the attacking force was killed and the attack accomplished nothing. It was evident that the Soviet advance west of Kharkov was running out of steam even before a somewhat tardy realignment of the Heeresgruppe Süd-Heeresgruppe Mitte boundary helped Kempf shorten the length of his front. The VII. Armeekorps took over defense of the area northwest of Achtyrka and when 4. Panzer-Division elements arrived beginning 23 February the remnants of 168. Infanterie-Division were assembled at Sinkiw. The westward advance by the Soviet 107th Rifle Division and the 5th Tank Corps came to a halt after counterattacks by 4. Panzer-Division.[27]

There were no serious problems on the western flank of Armeeabteilung Kempf during 25 February. The right flank of 320. Infanterie-Division was attacked by Russian infantry supported by artillery and a few tanks, but the penetration was sealed off and two T-34s were destroyed. The division had a fairly strong anti-tank capability at that time because the earlier heavy equipment losses had been replaced. Postel had twenty anti-tank guns at his disposal by 24 February. Five of them were the adequate 5cm guns, but there were also fifteen of the more effective 7.5cm PaK 40s available by that date. German defensive efforts were also aided by the Russian's

failure to concentrate what little armor they still possessed. Many of the Soviet tanks were wasted in support of infantry attacks which accomplished little. Instead of concentrating their armor in an attempt to create a decisive point of main effort, tanks were gradually dissipated in piece meal attacks. By 25 February, Rybalko's 3rd Tank Army possessed only fifty to sixty operational tanks. About a third of the tanks remaining in action were the lightly armored T-70s or T-60s.[28] It was also observed that the Soviet infantry had lost much of their resolve to fight. This could have been due to a high percentage of untrained conscripts in the Russian rifle battalions or just plain battle fatigue. However there were still occasions when stronger attacks were mounted by more determined and skillful Russian units.

One such incident occurred north of Novaja Vodolaga where 320. Infanterie-Division was hard pressed by the attacks of the Soviet 111th Rifle Division. These attacks were directed at the town of Staraja Vodolaga. A counterattack launched by a hastily thrown together Kampfgruppe blocked the first Soviet attack temporarily but fighting continued until the late afternoon hours when the fighting gradually subsided. In spite of this situation the division began its planned withdrawal on schedule because Soviet pressure remained surprisingly light except at Novaja Wodolaga. After dark the Russians renewed their attack upon Staraja Vodolaga with tanks and infantry. An anti-tank gun battery knocked out one T-34 and the rest pulled back. The garrison evacuated the town, covered by a rear guard detachment.

Active Defense! Max Wünsche wins the Knight's Cross

Meanwhile, "Leibstandarte" continued its relocation and reported little Soviet pressure during the pullback. The division's two Panzergrenadier regiments re-established firm contact along the designated regimental boundary line near Staroverovka. This position was modified slightly during the course of the day upon recommendations from SS-Sturmbannführer Lehmann after he inspected the sector. Along its boundary adjoining the "Totenkopf" sector, the division was active, conducting attacks by Max Wünsche's I./SS Panzer-Regiment "LAH" and Peiper's half track battalion. Peiper conducted a reconnaissance east of the regiment's positions and found that the Soviets were fortifying a ridge line that ran parallel to the front. West of the Bogataja River, which was little more than a large stream, the Aufklärungsabteilung troops observed infantry of the 350th Rifle Division busily constructing earthworks and fortifications. Air reconnaissance also reported the

---

[27] Glantz, pg. 186.

[28] Armstrong, pgs. 172-173.

presence of Soviet artillery along a second low ridge behind the infantry positions. Dietrich did not want Russians to build up a solid bridgehead and ordered Wünsche to eliminate the Soviet artillery before the infantry finished digging in and anti-tank guns were brought up.

Advancing from near Jeremejevka the SS tanks, supported by a few self-propelled howitzers and a battalion of Grenadiers, mounted a devastatingly effective assault on the Soviet division. Wünsche intended to make a lighting fast attack while artillery hammered the Soviet infantry in their forward defensive positions. He decided to quickly penetrate through the first line of defense and then to the Russian artillery positions which lay approximately five kilometers behind the front lines. The attack proceeded according to plan and its great success resulted in the award of the Knight's Cross to Wünsche.[29]

Reconnaissance revealed that there were no Russian tanks supporting the defensive line and this allowed the German tanks to attack with little fear of danger to their flanks. Most of the Russian anti-tank guns were knocked out or suppressed by German artillery or Stuka attacks. The rest were destroyed by high explosive fire from the Panzers themselves. The attack quickly reached the forward positions without the loss of a single tank and drove toward the east. After achieving this breakthrough, Wünsche wasted no time attempting to destroy Russian defensive positions. Instead he pushed his battalion into the depths of the Soviet defenses, with the intention of destroying the Soviet artillery. The speed of the attack evidently took the Russian artillerymen by surprise.

When the SS tanks appeared suddenly out of a nearby valley, the Russians were still in the process of pulling their artillery out of their emplacements. The artillery crews were busy hooking up teams of oxen and horses to their guns when suddenly German shells exploded in their midst. Startled horses fled in panic, frightened by the shell impacts, while the crews frantically tried to get them under control. German machine gun fire washed over the hilltop and killed men and draft animal alike. While many of the Russian gun crews were still trying to free the piles of dead and wounded animals from their harnesses, the Panzers roared up the ridge and overran the position. Several Soviet gun teams were able to get their guns hooked up to their teams and attempted to make their escape, but it was too late. The SS tanks gunned down men and animals alike and then crushed the guns or blasted them into pieces.

After destroying the Russian artillery, Wünsche then turned his attention to destruction of the enemy infantry who were then withdrawing from the forward defensive positions. While Wünsche's

Sepp Dietrich arrives at Witt's regimental headquarters during the division's defense of the Krasnograd salient in late February, 1943. Witt is on the left, shaking hands with Dietrich. (Credit National Archives)

tanks assaulted the artillery in the Soviet rear, other elements of the Panzer regiment and SS motorcycle troops conducted a frontal attack on the Soviet front line positions. Supported by a steadily advancing artillery barrage, they drove the stunned Russians out of their trenches. Masses of fleeing Russian infantry, already demoralized by the tank assault, abandoned the main defensive line. To their horror these doomed men saw Wünsche's Panzers racing back toward them from the rear. Defenseless against the SS Panzers the panic stricken Russians scattered in all directions, with tanks and SPWs in pursuit. When the slaughter was over more than 800 dead Russians littered the battlefield. Fifty guns were destroyed and many lighter weapons were collected, while no prisoners were reported taken.[30]

The destruction of the Soviet artillery position along the Bogotaja River temporarily delayed Russian offensive plans in the sector east and southeast of Krasnograd. "Leibstandarte's" active defense continued to throw the Russians off balance. This activity probably contributed to the lack of aggressive pursuit when Korps Raus pulled back to its new defensive positions by the end of the day on 25 February. Other than normal patrol activity, there was no concerted follow up to the German withdrawal.

By 23 February the Soviet Stavka began to uncomfortably realize that they had underestimated the capabilities of the Germans, although the true dimensions of the looming disaster were not yet clear. The SS divisions had turned north, striking through the rear areas of the 6th Army. When the Stavka grudgingly realized that this was not an attack to cover a withdrawal it made several adjust-

---

[29] From Wünsche's recommendation for the Knights Cross. Courtesy of Mark C. Yerger.

[30] Lehmann, pg. 129 and *Befehl des Gewissens*, pg. 158.

An SS Marder similar to the self propelled anti-tank guns of SS-Panzerjägerabteilung 1, commanded by Jakob Hanreich. On 23 February, a battery of the battalion attacked and destroyed tanks of Rybalko's 3rd Tank Army while they were moving through the sector east of the Krasnograd salient. (Courtesy of Mark C. Yerger)

ments in reaction to the changing situation. Kazakov's 69th Army slowed its westward advance through the sector northwest of Bogodukhov and began to move rifle divisions directly south. It was these divisions that had attacked Regiment "Thule" and "Grossdeutschland" along the Ljubotin-Poltava railroad. The 40th Army had to fill the void left by the shift of 69th Army rifle divisions towards the Merla River with the result that several of its rifle divisions left the Achtyrka area and marched south, toward positions then held by 167. Infanterie-Division.[31]

The 3rd Tank Army began a regrouping of its armor designed to put it into position to block the advance of Hausser's SS divisions. Rybalko was to attack and occupy the Krasnograd sector in order to create a bridgehead from which to launch an attack on the SS-Panzerkorps. Due to this extensive shift of forces, the Soviet push to the west finally slowed due to the effect of the attack of the SS-Panzerkorps. Of course, Manstein had gambled that this would happen which was the reason he had requested Kempf to have patience for just a little while longer. In reaction to the Soviet relocation of forces and the 3rd Tank Army threat to Krasnograd, Armeeabteilung Kempf pulled back from the Msha area. Valki and Novaja Wodalaga were given up on 26 February as the army's front contracted to the southwest. Kempf intended to withdraw to a shorter defensive line which shielded Krasnograd from attacks originating north or east of the town which remained the base of operations for the SS-Panzerkorps.

After the withdrawal to its new line was complete, the Armeeabteilung Kempf defensive sector ran in a southwest direction from the area north of Poltava to the town of Valki where it bent southward to form a protective arc around Krasnograd's key railroad net. On the left or western flank of this line the remnant of 168. Infanterie-Division, reinforced by two fresh infantry battalions, held Sinkiw which blocked one road passing through the Vorskla River Valley. Sinkiw was approximately forty kilometers north of Poltava. The 167. Infanterie-Division defended a thirty kilometer section of the front between Sinkiw and the Poltava-Schelestovo-Vysokopol'ye area. To its west, Regiment "Thule" held a sector between the right flank of 167. Infanterie-Division and the left flank of 320. Infanterie-Division. The SS regiment occupied the salient position at Valki where the front turned toward the southeast. From Regiment "Thule's" sector this defensive line extended fifty kilometers in length and was held by 320. Infanterie-Division and "Leibstandarte." Postel's division held a twenty kilometer sector extending from Valki to a point northeast of the town of Staroverovka. "Leibstandarte's" two Panzergrenadier regiments held a thirty kilometer section of the front that bent back to the south-

"Leibstandarte" commander Sepp Dietrich with Max Wünsche, here pictured at the rank of SS-Hauptsturmführer. Because of his lower class origins and the German Army's disdain for the SS, some of the Army officers who came into contact with the plain spoken and earthy Dietrich did not initially appreciate his talents as a leader of combat troops. (Credit National Archives)

west and ended west of Kegitschevka. The SS division protected the eastern and southeastern approaches to Krasnograd. Its southern flank was essentially open, except for a tenuous contact with reconnaissance detachments of "Totenkopf." Dietrich's division faced elements of the 3rd Tank Army, 6th Guards Cavalry Corps and the 184th, 350th, 172nd and 6th Rifle Divisions.[32]

While the Germans settled into their new defensive alignment on 26 February, Rybalko's 3rd Tank Army received new orders once again. Rybalko, although he had less than 50 operational tanks, was ordered to halt its preparations to attack Krasnograd and realign to the south. This new operation was designed to mount a relief attack to rescue the 6th Army from the attack of the SS-Panzerkorps. The 12th Tank Corps' 106th Tank Brigade was ordered to remain in the Ljubotin area while the rest of the army's tanks turned to the south. On 25 and 26 February, the main bodies of the 12th and 15th Tank Corps began to move southward, moving roughly parallel to "Leibstandarte" positions. German air and ground reconnaissance detected some of these armor movements, reporting Soviet tanks and other vehicles traveling along roads east or north of Krasnograd.

A group of twelve Russian tanks and several trucks carrying infantry were observed approaching the town of Nikolskoje. The division decided to intercept the Russian battle group with an attack by SS-PzG.-Rgt. 1 "LAH," supported by armor. Regimental commander Witt quickly assembled a small Kampfgruppe made up of four assault guns and a company of Panzergrenadiers. He ordered the battle group commander to locate and then destroy the Soviet tanks, which were probably traveling towards assembly positions designated by the 3rd Tank Army.

---

[31] Glantz, pg. 185-187.

[32] Glantz, pg. 134 and map, pg. 135.

The Kampfgruppe left Nikolskoje at 1400 hours with the SS infantry riding on top of the assault guns, intending to ambush the Russian column at the village of Minkovka. After a three hour trip in sub-zero temperatures the column entered a village a short distance from Minkovka. The SS men found all the villages to be nearly deserted and the few Russians that could be found gave them no useful information. The assault guns and Grenadiers pushed on cautiously and arrived at Minkovka a short time later. However, a reconnaissance patrol failed to find any evidence of the presence of Russian tanks. After failing to locate the Russians, the column returned to Nikolskoje.[33]

The T-34s were in the area however, and another reconnaissance patrol spotted them near a railroad station. Rather than taking a chance that the tanks might slip by the other Kampfgruppe and escape, Witt ordered a second battle group formed. The division's Panzerjäger company was stationed east of Nikolskoje at that time and battalion commander, SS-Sturmbannführer Jakob Hanreich was ordered to detail a battery of self-propelled anti-tank guns to attack the Soviet armor, which had been spotted at another location, some distance to the east of Minkovka.

Accompanied by a company of Panzergrenadiers, the Panzerjäger company moved into position on a nearby low ridge without being observed by the Russians. The SS anti-tank guns, firing from hull down positions behind the ridge crest, destroyed eleven T-34s and one KV tank. With burning Russian tanks sending up columns of black smoke, the SS Panzergrenadiers moved into the village and wiped out any remaining Soviet troops.[34]

That same day German air reconnaissance detected what was probably part of the 3rd Tank Army moving in a long column toward the south, but did not recognize it for what it was. Armeeabteilung Kempf received a report from a Luftwaffe reconnaissance plane stating that a 1000 vehicle column was moving to the southwest on a course parallel to the "Leibstandarte" front. However, no conclusions regarding the movements of such a large numbers of vehicles were made in the army report. There is a hint that the accuracy of the report may have been in question because the copy of the records shows a ? mark written in parentheses beside the number 1000, as if the number was doubted. However, later information which included radio intercepts, indicated the presence of a number of Russian headquarters that were new to the sector. This information eventually helped form a picture of what was happening east of "Leibstandarte" positions.[35]

It became obvious from the reports of numerous groups of Soviet tanks and long infantry columns that the Russians were moving a sizable amount of men and equipment into the Kegitschevka area. Gradually a picture began to emerge, but Dietrich and Kempf were not completely sure of Russian intentions and incorrectly suspected that the Russians were planning to make another attack toward Krasnograd.

In fact Rybalko had no intention of thrusting eastward and was preparing to block the advance of Hausser's SS-Panzerkorps. On 26 February, the forward elements of Rybalko's tank army, further weakened by "Leibstandarte's" attacks, collided with Hausser's SS divisions in the sector around the town of Kegitschevka in a futile attempt to block the advance of the SS-Panzerkorps.[36]

[33] Lehmann, pg. 130-132.
[34] Op cit.

[35] *Befehl des Gewissens*, pg. 158.
[36] After his reproach by Manstein, Kempf was careful to record the division's successes, which were due to the constant attacks conducted by mobile and Panzer units, exactly the tactics Manstein desired. For example, on 25 February, Armeeabteilung Kempf records specifically mentioned Wünsche's attack, stating that it resulted in the following losses to the 350th Rifle Division. According to the records of the army, 47 anti-tank guns of 7.6cm or 4.5cm were captured or destroyed, in addition to 10 howitzers of 12.2cm caliber. A German 10cm gun was recaptured, over 300 sleds destroyed and many heavy and light weapons were taken. The total of Russian dead was listed as 800-900. Wünsche's attack on 25 February is also described in the Vorschlag (recommendation) for his Knight's Cross, which also stated that his tank personally destroyed 2 Russian howitzers in the attack, while his own losses were only 5 dead and 14 wounded. Wünsche had been recommended for the German Cross in Gold, by regiment commander Georg Schönberger, only a week earlier, for actions during the first weeks of February.

9

THE SS-PANZERKORPS TURNS NORTH

While Armeeabteilung Kempf fought to protect Poltava and Krasnograd, the SS-Panzerkorps remained involved in heavy fighting in the Sinel'nilovo and Pavlograd area. On 23 February, Kumm's Regiment "Der Führer" continued its defense of Pavlograd, turning back Soviet attacks from the north and east. At Sinel'nikovo, Kampfgruppe Harmel fought to clear the Russians out of villages located on the several rail lines that passed through the town. The main line ran into Pavlograd from Dnepropetrovsk and split off into several branches, one of which ran eastward to Krasnoarmeiskoye and the other to Stalino. This branch was the major line of communication to 1. Panzerarmee.

In the morning, Harmel tirelessly moved among the men of his regiment, encouraging the exhausted soldiers to greater efforts. The regiment had been on the attack for several days without rest and the men were becoming mentally and physically tired. However, the attack had to be continued because there were Soviet troops still in the area. A regiment of the 124th Guards Rifle Division had earlier been driven to the east of Sinel'nikovo by the attacks of 15. Infanterie-Division and "Das Reich" on the previous day. The Soviet regiment had taken up positions in the towns of Razdory and Marievka and was reinforced by stragglers from other units in the area. Supported by Stukas and assault guns, the regiment assaulted Marievka and encountered solid resistance. Harmel's personal leadership carried his regiment through prolonged, hard fighting at Marievka which lasted many hours. When the town finally fell, most of the two Soviet regiments which had fought stubbornly throughout the day were destroyed.[1]

Reconnaissance elements of the regiment established contact with 6. Panzer-Division, which had driven to the north from the area southeast of Sinel'nikovo against light resistance from the 244th Rifle Division. It established two bridgeheads across the Samara River east of Pavlograd at the towns of Petropawlovka and at Boguslav. At that point, the two primary Panzer corps of Hoth's 4. Panzerarmee had linked up and were ready to advance north, sweeping through the communications lines of the 6th Army and driving toward a collision with Rybalko's 3rd Tank Army.

The Soviet 25th Tank Corps, which had driven westward towards the Dnepr, was cut off by the SS advance into the Sinel'nikovo-Pavlograd area. Vatutin had repeatedly ordered it to drive westwards, even after the German counteroffensive had begun and its main body was strung out between Sinel'nikovo and Zaporozsche, with a forward detachment even further south. Supplies had been short even before the corps was cut off but after 23 February they dried up completely. There was no air supply, as all available Soviet aircraft were needed to drop supplies to encircled units with a better chance of survival. Elements of 15. Infanterie-Division pressed in on the trapped Russians from Novo-Moskovsk, driving them toward "Das Reich." To the immediate east, columns of 6. Panzer-Division filled the roads, driving north from the Samara. Since Soviet air support was totally lacking, German planes found the helpless columns of Soviet vehicles and men easy targets. A political officer of the corps reported that his tank brigade was 'subjected to intense bombardment from the air. We have lost seven tanks and a large number of personnel.'[2]

Eventually the 25th Tank Corps was ordered to break through the German encirclement and rejoin the main body of the 6th Army. What little fuel remained was scavenged from nearly empty tanks and used to keep a few T-34s and trucks running. Eventually even

---

[1] Weidinger, pgs. 49-50.

[2] Glantz, pg. 129.

this paltry amount of fuel was used up and trucks and tanks were abandoned when they sputtered to a halt. Armed with little more than machine guns and rifles, the survivors made their way to the east in small groups, infiltrating past columns of German infantry and vehicles, all of which were speeding to the north. Behind the Russians lay a trail of useless vehicles, piles of equipment and spiked guns. Tanks were left where they ran out of fuel and then blown up. Here and there artillery pieces remained standing along roads, still hooked to trucks which had no fuel to move them.

Meanwhile, Regiment "Der Führer," reinforced with Macher's 16./"Deutschland" and SS armor, cleaned the last Russian stragglers and pockets of resistance out of Pavlograd. At the completion of this task, the regiment organized a new defensive ring around the north and northeastern perimeter of the town. After pulling out of the town and crossing the Samara River, battered regimental groups of the 35th Guards Rifle Division established themselves in the nearby towns of Wjasovok and Werbki. The division was joined by tanks of the 16th Guards Tank Brigade which was sent to reinforce the division. The Russian command intended to establish a strong defensive position to prevent "Das Reich" from crossing the Samara. While the Soviets dug gun positions and entrenchments facing south, towards Pavlograd, elements of "Totenkopf" approached Wjasovok and Werbki from the west.

While "Das Reich" prepared to attack across the river, the Kradschützen Bataillon took over the task of keeping the road leading from Pavlograd to Novo-Moskovsk open.[3] This was a difficult task because groups of Russian infantry or rear area troops in various strengths, crossed the road continually as they tried to escape to the east. These roving bands sometimes blocked the road when they occupied villages or crossroads at locations west of Pavlograd. Company sized groups of Soviet infantry, sometimes with a tank or two, represented a real threat to SS security or supply troops. Hermann Buch, a company commander in "Das Reich's" Kradschützen-Bataillon, remembered these actions.

On 23 February, my company received the mission of cleaning the Russians out of a village north of the Novo-Moskovsk-Pavlograd road. The company was equipped with Schwimmwagen. About half of the vehicles mounted machine

A patrol of SS-Grenadiers, probably belonging to "Leibstandarte," move through scrub brush. The men are dressed in the mouse gray, fur lined SS anorak and carry a variety of weapons. The man on the right is armed with the semi-automatic Gewehr 43, while in the center a Grenadier is equipped with the MP-40 with folding stock extended. On the left, the third man carries an MG-42 and is followed by his loader with extra ammo boxes. (Credit National Archives)

guns. Of the 64 Schwimmwagen which we arrived with at Kiev, at the end of January, 1943, that were only 45 still operational.

As I was at the point of my company, through my binoculars I could clearly see enemy movements on the east edge of the village and a dug-in T-34 tank. Between us and the village lay about two and a half kilometers of level ground with a light covering of snow.

I had the company deploy on a wide front, with about 20 machine gun vehicles in the first line, with the other vehicles behind them as a second wave, advancing on the village at a speed of 50-60 kilometers an hour. The Schwimmwagen bounced over the snow filled ditches and small ravines. When we came within a hundred meters, we let go a volley of machine gun fire while going at top speed.

The actual tactical effect was practically nothing, but the effect on enemy morale was considerable and the Russians fled from their positions, leaving the T-34 behind. The hunt through the village was short and we did not suffer any losses. From the amount of weapons left behind and the number of Russian dead, it was apparent that the enemy had been much stronger in numbers than we were.[4]

On 23 February, while "Das Reich" and 15. Infanterie-Division troops fought Soviet forces around Sinel'nikovo and in Pavlograd, "Totenkopf's" Panzer regiment left the Pereshschepino area, accompanied by Otto Baum's I./Regiment "Totenkopf." At 0100 hours, Regiment "Totenkopf," in two reinforced battalion columns, began its attack towards Wjasovok and Werbki, the two villages north of Pavlograd. Infantry of the 35th Guards Rifle Divi-

---

[3] Fick's motorcycle battalion, of which Buch's company was a part, was a combined arms unit and had been equipped with a variety of weapons and vehicles. Buch's 3. Kompanie had the amphibious Volkswagen light car called the Schwimmwagen, many of which mounted machine guns. The 5. Kompanie was the battalion heavy company and had a Panzerjäger Zug (anti-tank platoon) as well as a Infanterie-Geschütz Zug which was equipped with 7.5cm infantry howitzers. The company also had a Pioniere Zug, with demolition charges, mine removal equipment and other heavy weapons. Fick's battalion was a formidable unit, possessing great firepower. Yerger, *Knights of Steel*, vol. 2, page 26 to 30.

[4] Weidinger, pg. 49.

sion held Wjasovok, which was a few kilometers northeast of Pavlograd. The 17th Guards Tank Brigade, detached from the 1st Guards Tank Corps, occupied Werbki, which was directly north of Pavlograd. The mission of Regiment "Totenkopf" was to clear the two villages of Soviet infantry and armor in order to support "Das Reich's" attack to the north.

The southern column, SS-Sturmbannführer Joachim Schubach's III./Regiment "Totenkopf," was slowed after warm temperatures created a temporary local thaw. The once frozen roads rapidly softened and became muddy due to the passage of many wheels and tracked vehicles. The battalion moved with difficulty on a small road that was roughly parallel to the north bank of the Samara River. The Samara flowed from west to east, passing through

both Wjasovok and Werbki. Schubach's column took several hours before it was able to slog through the mud and reach a nearby village, which was defended by a small infantry detachment.

By midmorning, the Russian troops were driven out and the battalion pushed through a succession of villages that dotted the road north of the Samara. Led by its motorcycle company, it was just a few kilometers west of Wjasovok when a reconnaissance patrol of Russian troops in trucks and motorcycles collided with the battalion near the village of Kotschereshki and was wiped out. After the elimination of the Russian motorcyclists, reconnaissance patrols found that Kotschereshki was defended by Soviet infantry. The SS column deployed west of the village and assaulted the Russian positions, supported by well directed artillery support. By 0830

SS-Unterscharführer Hans Hirning, an NCO in 6. Kompanie Regiment "Totenkopf" who won the Knight's Cross for bravery during the fighting in the Demyansk pocket. Hirning fought with the regiment until 1945, when he was killed in Czechoslovakia on April 30, during the last few days of the war. (Courtesy of Mark C. Yerger)

Hermann Buchner, a company commander in Regiment "Totenkopf," later served as a battalion commander in the regiment. He won the Knight's Cross in June of 1944. Buchner was killed in November of the same year, during fighting near Warsaw. (The author's collection)

hours, after a brief period of house to house fighting, the town was in German hands. The bulk of the surviving Russians fled across the river to the south, finding shelter in densely wooded areas covering the southern bank.

At 1100 hours the battalion reached the edge of Wjasovok, where it immediately launched an assault upon the town, which was stubbornly defended. A hill north of Wjasovok had been fortified and was occupied by the Russians, giving them a good position from which artillery forward observers could see all of the surrounding area. The Russian troops already in the town were receiving reinforcements from the northeast and east, which arrived just as the Germans attacked the west edge of the town. A number of hidden T-34s fired upon the attackers from concealed positions in the town, their presence signaling that the town would be stoutly defended. The SS troops realized that they were in for a fight after Soviet artillery, firing from south of the Samara, shelled the advancing SS Grenadiers so heavily that the attack fell apart when the assault group went to ground.

The SS self-propelled howitzers deployed and fired on the Russian defenses in the town, while the Grenadiers began working their way forward again under cover of their own artillery fire. The fighting continued into late in the day and it was not until 1800 hours that III./Regiment "Totenkopf" fought its way close to the edge of the town, against determined resistance by elements of the 267th Rifle Division and the 19th Tank Brigade of the 1st Guards Tank Corps. Several T-34s were concealed between the houses, forming strong points around which infantry fought from well camouflaged firing positions. The SS Grenadiers fought their way toward the center of the town as the Russians bitterly contested every foot of ground. A total of five T-34s were knocked out during the fighting and two others were damaged, forcing them to leave the town. However, at nightfall parts of the town still remained in possession of the Russians and house to house fighting continued. Information provided by prisoners revealed that Werbki was also strongly held and was reinforced with as many as thirty tanks. While III./Regiment "Totenkopf" fought for Wjasovok on the southern wing of the regiment's advance, the northern wing of the regiment began its push toward Losovaja.[5]

From assembly positions southeast of Pereshchepino, II./Regiment "Totenkopf" began a broad advance eastward toward the town of Orelka, which was near the key railroad center at Losovaja. Schulze's battalion advanced on a broad front along several roughly parallel roads leading toward Orelka. The battalion's northern column was led by the division's reconnaissance battalion, SS-Aufklärungsabteilung 3, commanded by SS-Sturmbannführer Walter Bestmann. Bestmann's battalion pushed rapidly forward, with the intention of reaching the town of Tschernoglasovka in order to prevent any Russian force in Orelka from attacking Schulze's northern flank. A small forward detachment of the reconnaissance battalion pushed forward and occupied Tschernoglasovka.[6] In this sector also, the division's operations and supply were plagued by marauding Soviet columns seeking to pass through the German lines. The forward detachment, consisting of SPWs armed with 2cm guns, ran into one such group southwest of Orelka and completely de-

SS-Sturmbannführer Walter Bestmann, the commander of SS-Aufklärungs-abteilung 3. On 23 February, Regiment "Totenkopf" attacked toward the towns of Wjasovock and Werbki, which were located north of Pavlograd, where "Das Reich" was involved in heavy fighting. The II./Regiment "Totenkopf" was reinforced by Bestmann's battalion during the advance. (Courtesy of Mark C. Yerger)

---

[5] NA/T-354, roll 118, Tagesmeldung SS-Division "Totenkopf" an SS-Panzerkorps, 23.2.1943, frame 1781-1784 and Vopersal, pg. 131-133.

[6] Op cit.

stroyed the column. Several Russian light tanks, a large number of prisoners and various guns and other heavy weapons fell into the German's hands.[7]

Hellmuth Becker's regiment left Krasnograd at 0600 hours and moved south, with Kühn's III./SS-"Totenkopf" PzG.-Rgt. 3 covering the regiment's northern flank, while the main body proceeded to Pereshchepino. By 1400 hours, the column had moved through Pereshchepino and turned east after reaching a road that entered the Orel River Valley. The column passed through a number of small villages before halting for the day a few kilometers south of the Orel River. There was little resistance to the regiment's advance.

In spite of the uncontested advance, by the end of the day "Totenkopf" still had not linked up with "Das Reich" at Pavlograd. Eicke's northern flank was secure and under little pressure, but Regiment "Totenkopf" remained delayed west of Wjasovok. The division had not suffered any tank losses due to enemy action, although a number of vehicles were again scattered along the route of the night movement from Krasnograd. SS-Panzerkorps records state that the Panzer regiment had eighteen Panzer IVs and sixty-two Panzer IIIs in operation on 23 February, as well as nine "Tigers." The heavy tanks had great difficulties moving over poor roads that did not have sufficiently sturdy bridges.[8]

Becker's SS-"Totenkopf" PzG.-Rgt. 3 secured the northern flank of the corps advance on 23 February, blocking the Orel River Valley between Krasnograd and Orelka. The objective of Regiment "Totenkopf" for the following day was to sweep the Russians out of the towns along the northern bank of the Samara, assemble north of Pavlograd and attack the Russians in Wjasovok and Werbki. Once the Russians were cleared from the two towns, both divisions could turn north and attack along the railroad toward their next objective, the town of Losovaja. Throughout the day "Das Reich" remained under attack by Soviet tanks and infantry thrusts out of Werbki. Late in the evening, a group of fifteen to twenty T-34s, accompanied by infantry, penetrated the German defensive perimeter. At 0100 hours, fighting suddenly flared in the northwestern section of the town. The Russians broke through the German defenses and caused a brief crisis when they pushed down the streets into the center of the town. Quick action by Heinz Macher and his company, which by that date was reduced to three NCOs and thirty-eight Pioniere, helped restore the situation.

Alerted by the sounds of battle, Macher led a squad of Pioniere and quickly moved through the dark streets toward the fighting. The brisk rattle of machine guns firing and tank motors could be heard in the distance. In the pitch black darkness, additional Russian tanks crept down the streets of the town, moving cautiously forward. Russian infantry accompanied the T-34s, slipping like ghosts through the rubble, with machine pistols and grenades held ready. Groups of SS Grenadiers ran toward the sounds of combat until they collided with the Russian infantry and sudden fire fights erupted. Over the blast of grenades and automatic weapons fire, tank noises could be heard in the distance, their tracks squealing and clanking in the dark. It became clear that the situation was quickly growing very serious.

Creeping through the shadowy back alleys, lit only by the flashes of gun fire and explosions, Macher's group spied two T-34s that were halted a short distance from a 8.8cm Flak gun position. The German gun crew had been taken by surprise when Soviet tanks appeared suddenly out of the night and hastily abandoned the gun. After Macher sent a messenger to the nearest battalion command post describing the situation, he organized two tank destruction groups, one of which he led himself. As they felt their way forward, cautiously approaching the tanks, the sound of fighting swelled in volume all around them.[9]

One detachment of the Pioniere provided cover against Russian infantry on the flank, while Macher and his group worked stealthily forward. Under cover of the darkness, the small group worked their way closer to the Russian tanks. Flares lit up the streets from time to time, throwing a harsh light upon the houses and momentarily creating deep shadows on the streets. An Oberscharführer crept to within 10 meters of the T-34s, before it became apparent that there were many Russian infantry protecting the tanks. Unable to get closer to the Russian tanks the leading group withdrew and two of the Pioniere returned to the abandoned 88 gun. However, they were unsure how to operate and fire the unfamiliar weapon at the Russian tanks, which were less than 100 meters from their position. Four T-34s, a KV-1 and seven Christie light tanks were visible by the time the two men managed to load and fire the gun. The 88 roared and the shell whistled off somewhere into the night, missing all of the tanks. From out of the night, a Rottenführer of the gun crew suddenly leapt back to his gun, in order to help the two Grenadiers operate the unfamiliar weapon. With the guidance of the Rottenführer the gun was loaded and fired again. This shell struck a T-34, which immediately lurched to a halt and caught fire. This unexpected threat caused the Soviet infantry to race for cover instead of directing small arms fire on the gun crew. The T-34s scurried into alleys or behind buildings. In the confusion a Grenadier was able to get close enough to place a mine under the turret edge

---

[7] Vopersal, pg. 134.
[8] NA/T-354, roll 118, Tagesmeldung der SS-Panzerkorps an 4. Panzerarmee, 23.2.1943, frame 3751784.

---

[9] Yerger archive and Weidinger, pg. 51.

of a T-34 and pull the cord on a grenade placed with the mine. When the grenade detonated, the mine exploded and blew the turret off the tank.[10] With two of their tank in flames, the Russian attack petered out and the remaining tanks withdrew into the cover of darkness.

After the attack was over a squad of the Pioniere company remained behind to support the 88 position. The quick reaction and personal leadership of Macher cleared up a situation that could have been very serious. However, although the first attack did not succeed the Russians were not finished yet. At 0415 hours a second attack of Russian infantry, supported by 10 tanks hit German positions in and around a graveyard near a church, which was in the defensive sector of 16./Rgt. "Deutschland." Once again Macher personally led the counterattack, which struck the flank of the Russian attack. The tough Pioniere troops engaged the Russian infantry in close combat and drove them out of the graveyard. Over 40 Russian dead were left behind among the shattered and splintered grave markers, while Macher's counterattacking force suffered no significant casualties. Although the Germans halted the Russian attack on the graveyard position itself, the Soviets were able to pull back and establish a defensive position between the graveyard and the church. This had to be cleaned up promptly, as it inevitably would be used as a staging area for further attacks.[11]

A battery of assault guns, under the leadership of SS-Hauptsturmführer Ernst Krag, supported a company of "Der Führer" Grenadiers in a counterattack on the Russian positions. Skillfully maneuvering into position, Krag's assault guns knocked out an anti-tank gun position and destroyed six machine guns with close range fire from their 7.5cm main guns. With this effective support, the SS Grenadiers collapsed the Soviet perimeter and eliminated the dangerous strong point, inflicting heavy casualties on the Russian infantry.[12]

On the morning of 24 February, after the night of hard fighting in Pavlograd, "Das Reich" began a determined push to eliminate Russian forces in Werbki. Regiment "Totenkopf" did not support "Das Reich" because it was held up by Russian troops in Wjasovok. The Russian infantry refused to be driven out of the town and their determination showed no signs of weakening. Furthermore, "Totenkopf" still had not been able to concentrate all of its forces for the attack on the town in the early morning hours. The Panzer Regiment and I./Rgt. "Totenkopf" (Baum) were behind schedule and did not reach Wjasovok until later in the morning. The regiment's attack, which was scheduled to have begun at 0700 hours, was therefore postponed.

Debris of war on a roadside in the Kharkov area, in late February, 1943. A Russian anti-tank gun lies in the foreground, while a T-34 is in a ditch beside the road. On the side of the turret, a black German cross can be seen. This T-34 was one of a number of captured Russian tanks that were put to use by the SS divisions during the Kharkov fighting. In fact, "Das Reich" equipped an entire company with captured T-34s and used the Soviet tanks until late summer 1943. (Credit National Archives)

Just after receiving word that the attack had been postponed, III./Rgt. "Totenkopf" was attacked suddenly by Soviet infantry supported by tanks. This Russian force was probably elements of the 35th Guards Rifle Division and some of the remaining vehicles of the 1st Guards Tank Corps, which had been cut off by the attack of "Das Reich" in the area east of Pavlograd. The Russian force crossed the Samara River unobserved and attacked the SS battalion from the southwest after assembling in the village of Kotschereshki. However, the Germans reacted swiftly and III./Rgt. "Totenkopf" launched a ferocious counterattack against the flank of the Russian force. The aggressive SS assault forced the Russian infantry to withdraw into Kotschereshki. German casualties were light, but the Russians lost sixty-eight prisoners and a large number of dead and wounded.[13]

After the Russian attack from Kotschereshki was repelled, the Germans regrouped and prepared to attack Wjasovok once again. In the meantime, the Panzer Regiment and Baum's Panzergrenadier battalion assembled at Wassiljevka, which was about ten kilometers west of Kotschereshki. At 0930 hours, III./Rgt. "Totenkopf" attacked Wjasovok from the north while a company of II./ "Totenkopf" moved toward the town from the south. The tanks of

[10] Information from Mark C. Yerger archival documents.
[11] Weidinger, pg. 51-52.
[12] Yerger, Ernst Krag biography, pg. 13.

[13] Glantz page 132 and Vopersal, pg. 138.

OPPOSITE: *Following several days of fighting "Totenkopf" drove through the Soviet troops defending the towns of Wjasovok and Werbki and then launched its attack upon Pavlograd from the north. After the withdrawal of the Russian troops defending the town, leading elements of "Das Reich" and "Totenkopf" moved toward each other, unaware of the other division's presence. Forward elements of the divisions narrowly avoid firing upon each other when they unexpectedly collided north of Pavlograd.*

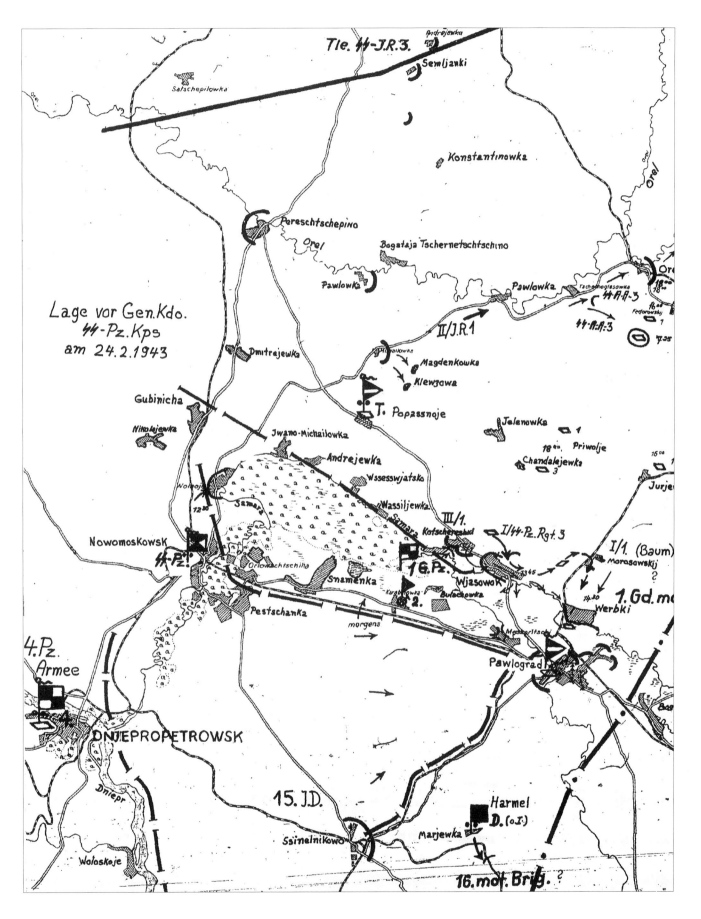

the Panzer Regiment moved forward in three waves, with Baum's half tracks arrayed behind them, and assaulted a Soviet defensive position located on the hill north of Wjasovok. Advancing behind a storm of artillery, the SS tanks and half tracks rolled over entrenchments and machine gun nests and reached the crest. The Russian infantry streamed down the other side of the hill and were decimated by machine gun fire.

The Grenadiers and tanks then assaulted Soviet defensive positions on the perimeter and then fought their way into the town. The defenders, which were composed of elements of the 244th Rifle Division and the 17th Tank Brigade, fought back stubbornly and skillfully. Several T-34s were dug into the sides of houses or emplaced in camouflaged entrenchments and were supported by machine guns and mortars. The combat was costly to both sides. However, the SS Grenadiers methodically rooted out the Russians, first smothering each strong point with heavy firepower and then assaulting the positions with grenades and machine pistols. After hours of bitter fighting, most of the Soviet infantry were driven out of the town. They left behind piles of their dead in the streets and three burning T-34s. Wjasovok was declared solidly in German hands by 1345 hours. While the two battalions cleaned up the last pockets of resistance, "Totenkopf" Panzers and Baum's battalion swept the remaining Russians out of the hills north of Wjasovok.

Immediately assembling in the southeast section of the town, Schulze's II./Rgt. "Totenkopf" pursued the retreating Soviet forces and pushed into the western outskirts of Werbki.[14] Shortly afterward Kampfgruppe Baum established a bridgehead over a small river that branched off from the Samara a few kilometers east of Werbki. By 1430 hours, Baum's battalion and the Panzers reached the northern outskirts of the town. The "Totenkopf" tanks passed over a small hill and immediately spotted a number of vehicles and infantry moving toward them in the distance. The SS tanks began firing at the oncoming force when to their astonishment, over the headsets of the "Totenkopf" tank commanders came the cry, 'Don't shoot! This is the forward elements of SS Reich.'

The tanks and vehicles were Kumm's Kampfgruppe, advancing to the north out of Werbki, which the regiment had captured earlier in the day. A laconic voice answered from one of the "Totenkopf" tanks, "We only fire at worthwhile targets!" Fortunately for the "Das Reich" tank crews, the shells that were fired did not strike their intended targets. Contact between the two SS divisions was established although injuries and equipment loss due to "friendly fire" had been narrowly avoided. Although Werbki had already fallen to Regiment "Der Führer," no one had informed the armored group of "Totenkopf" and as a result it was only by chance that casualties from German shells were avoided.[15]

The final attack by II./Regiment "Deutschland" and its supporting Panzers had been launched on Werbki just before noon. Several flights of Stukas provided direct support to the advance, bombing with their usual deadly, pinpoint accuracy. The Russian defenders fought back until the approach of "Totenkopf" from the north forced them to withdraw from the town to avoid encirclement and destruction.

After the fall of Werbki and Wjasovock, Pavlograd was finally secured for the continuance of the offensive northwards along the vital railroads which stretched towards Kharkov. The II./Rgt. "Totenkopf" regrouped in order to cover the advance of the armored elements of both divisions toward the next objective, the towns of Panjutina and Orelka. Meanwhile, SS-Aufklärungsabteilung 3 held the main road leading southeastwards out of Orelka, in order to block any Soviet counterattack originating from the town. Further to the north, Hellmuth Becker's SS-"Totenkopf"-PzG.-Rgt. 3 held defensive positions in the Orel River Valley west of the line of advance of the two divisions, securing their flank.[16]

XXXXVIII. Panzerkorps

While the SS divisions cleared Pavlograd, 6. and 17. Panzer Division of 4. Panzerarmee's XXXXVIII. Panzerkorps, began a drive to the north in an advance roughly parallel to the attack of the SS-Panzerkorps. The attack struck forward elements of the 1st Guards Army, which held a 140 kilometer wide front extending from Losovaja on the west to a point south of Lisichansk on the east. The Soviet 58th Guards Rifle Division held Losovaja, while the 195th Rifle Division held a large sector that extended nearly forty kilometers east of Losovaja to Barvenkovo. The 195th Rifle Division had suffered extensive casualties during the fighting for Slavyansk and was too weak to adequately defend its extended front. The 3rd Tank Corps was the sector reserve, but had only a handful of tanks still running.

The 1st Guards Army was aligned on an east to west axis, with its divisions facing generally south. The southern flank of the army had been collapsed by the attack of 1. Panzerarmee's XXXX. Panzerkorps and driven away from its positions at Krasnoarmeiskoje. The 44th Guards Rifle Division occupied a twenty-five kilometer wide sector, from Barvenkovo to Kramatorsk, supported by the 10th Tank Corps, which was located in Barvenkovo.

---

[14] NA/T-354, roll 118, Tagesmeldung SS-"Totenkopf" Panzergrenadier-Division an SS-Panzerkorps, 24.2.1943. frame 3751795.

[15] Weidinger, pg. 53.

[16] Glantz, pg. 132 and NA/ T-313, roll 367, Tagesmeldung der SS-Panzerkorps an 4. Panzerarmee, 24.2.1943, frame 8653026.

Two other Soviet rifle divisions were situated in the Slavyansk sector, while the 52nd and 78th Rifle Divisions defended the extreme eastern flank of the army's front. There were essentially no uncommitted army reserves and ammunition supplies were low. In spite of the army's deficiencies, it was vital for the Russians to prevent XXXXVIII. Panzerkorps from penetrating its front and striking the southern flank of the 6th Army, whose primary direction of attack was westward and at right angles to the front of the 1st Guards Army.

On the eastern flank of the corps attack, the 17. Panzer-Division organized two weak attack columns and moved northward. It was able to reach the Samara River at a point twenty-five kilometers east of Pavlograd, but only a handful of its tanks and assault guns were still running. After passing through Pavlograd the Samara extended to the southeast for about twenty kilometers, then turned north at the town of Petropawlovka. By 23 February the division reached Petropawlovka and tried to establish two bridgeheads across the river. In the meantime, 6. Panzer-Division arrived at the Samara and entered the town of Boguslav which was less than ten kilometers east of Pavlograd. By the afternoon, the division crossed the river and was involved fighting to capture a nearby village defended by Russian infantry.[17]

Farther to the east, 1. Panzerarmee's XXXX. Panzerkorps attacked with its three divisions from the Krasnoarmeiskoye region and advanced northward. SS "Wiking," 7. Panzer-Division and 11. Panzer-Division moved in parallel columns driving through the area east of Slavyansk. Along the rest of the front, south of the Northern Donets, III. Panzerkorps and Fretter-Pico's XXX. Armeekorps held a 100 kilometer long defensive sector that stretched from near Slavyansk to just west of Voroshilovgrad. On the far eastern flank, Gruppe Kreysing and reinforced I./Regiment "Der Führer" defended a section of the front where the line bent to the south just west of Voroshilovgrad. Kreysing's neighbor to the west of his division was 335. Infanterie-Division, which faced elements of the 60th Guards Rifle Division. The Soviet division was in little better condition than its German counterparts, having been reduced to a fraction of its strength through the battles of the winter campaigns. Combat between the two divisions had essentially stopped and consisted primarily of patrol activity and artillery fire.

The western flank of Mackensen's army was anchored by 333. Infanterie-Division elements, which still held the town of Kramatorsk. The 3. Panzer-Division and 19. Panzer-Division held the remainder of the front, which stretched from Slavyansk east-

SS-Sturmbannführer Herbert Kuhlmann, the commander of I./SS-Panzer-Regiment 2. Kuhlmann took over the battalion after Hans-Albin von Reitzenstein assumed command of the regiment when Herbert Vahl became division commander on 10 February. (Courtesy of Mark C. Yerger)

wards to Pervomaisk, a distance of seventy kilometers. South of Voroshilovgrad, Armeeabteilung Hollidt held a continuous defensive line behind the Mius River, which ran at a 90 degree angle to the eastern flank of XXX. Armeekorps positions in the area west of Voroshilovgrad. Significant Russian attacks had essentially ceased along the army's defensive frontage by this time because both opponents were exhausted by the hard fighting of the earlier weeks.

Thus by 24 February the Germans had established solid shoulders on both boundaries of the gap between Armeeabteilung Kempf's southeastern flank and 1. Panzerarmee's western wing. The 1. Panzerarmee, having fought hard for the Slavyansk-Kramatorsk salient, had furnished itself a solid position from which to launch a counterattack in support of 4. Panzerarmee's main effort. Its Panzer divisions were very weak, but the largest burden was carried by Hoth's SS divisions. The attack had been launched

---

[17] NA/T-313, roll 367, 1a KTB Tagesmeldung XXXXVIII. Panzerkorps an 4. Panzerarmee, frame 8653042 and Glantz, pg. 132-133.

at the right moment, because Russian strength was dissipated by attrition, weakened by poor supply and endangered by mistakes in command. In these circumstances, even the weak Army Panzer divisions were able to conduct effective offensive operations.

The Destruction of Mobile Group Popov

While the shattered spearheads of the Soviet 6th Army and the 1st Guards Army tried to fight their way back through attacking German columns, remaining elements of Mobile Group Popov prepared to defend the railroad line between Losovaja and Slavyansk. The Russian defensive line was essentially strung out along this rail line, in an attempt to protect it from the German advance. By this time it had become clear to the Soviet high command that the Germans were mounting a counteroffensive that threatened not only the flank of the 6th Army but major elements of the 1st Guards Army and what was left of Popov's Mobile Group as well.

Popov's tank corps were all a fraction of their former strength by the end of February, each possessing about fifteen to twenty operational tanks. Although the four corps had more tanks than any single Panzer division of XXXX. Panzerkorps, they lacked the combined arms combat organization of the German divisions. While a Soviet tank corps might have some additional engineers, a few Flak guns or an additional rocket battalion attached to its order of battle, German divisions were true combined arms formations. In addition to its tank regiment, the assault gun battalion gave the German divisions an additional armored formation that was valuable in furnishing close support to infantry operations and was also extremely effective in a defensive role as well. The reconnaissance battalion was a versatile combat formation, equipped with armored cars, half tracks or Schwimmwagen. Battalions of self propelled artillery, anti-tank guns and Flak guns were versatile formations that could be used to effectively support offensive or defensive operations. In addition, the component units of German divisions could be quickly combined and utilized to form specialized battle groups of varied structure according to the given assignment. This capability made German Panzer Divisions flexible and formidable opponents not solely dependent on the strength of their Panzer regiment. In fact, most German Panzer Divisions often operated effectively with significantly less than fifty operational tanks.

In addition to the quantitative difference, there was a significant gap in command quality, tactical skills and communications. German tank crew training was generally superior to that which was received by their Russian counterparts. The German tank commanders were trained to be flexible, aggressive and to use their personal initiative in combat situations. Russian tank unit command-

The gesturing man on the right is SS-Sturmbannführer Wilhelm Schulze, the commander of II./Regiment "Totenkopf." He led the battalion during the attack upon Wjasovock, when armored elements of Kampfgruppe Baum accidentally fired upon "Das Reich" tanks north of the town. (Credit National Archives)

ers had much less freedom of action and were trained to carry out simple orders, in an inflexible manner. This was at least partially a result of the enormous casualties suffered by the Russian tank arm in the first years of the war, when Soviet tank corps were often utterly destroyed by the Germans. These losses resulted in a shortage of trained tank crews and officers with the necessary skills to operate effectively.

A second limiting factor was that the Soviets did not routinely equip many of their tanks with radios and sometimes a battalion or company commander had the only radio in his unit. As a result, Russian tank unit commanders had much less control over the tanks in their company or battalion once fighting began. Russian tank attacks were often characterized by single minded adherence to a linear direction of attack, regardless of the conditions encountered. Russian tank tactics were forced to remain simple, rigid and unimaginative because the Russian formations could not react quickly due to the lack of a sufficient communications capability. In contrast, all German tanks were equipped with radios and intercoms and a German tank commander could talk with any crew member or with the commanders of any of the tanks under his command. This enabled the unit commander to quickly direct his tanks and react immediately to the course of the battle around him. This inflexibility of command often resulted in enormous Soviet tank losses, even though the T-34 tank was essentially superior to the German Panzer III and IV in many ways.

There were other deficiencies as well. While the T-34 was a robust and dependable tank with well sloped frontal armor and very good maneuverability there were technical flaws in its design that detracted from its combat performance. The first models had no turret command cupola and thus T-34 commanders were unable to see very well when buttoned up. In contrast, German tanks had well designed cupolas with excellent periscopes which gave a German tank commander 360 degree vision while remaining relatively well protected. Perhaps the most serious shortcoming, aside from the lack of radios, was the turret design.

The Panzer III and IV had turrets which housed the gunner, loader and tank commander. The early T-34s had cramped, two man turrets and the Soviet tank commanders had to help operate the gun, which detracted from their ability to command the tank. When involved in firing the gun, the tank commander could not spot enemy tanks or give directions to the driver. The German tank commanders only responsibility was to direct the combat operations of the vehicle.[18]

In the first years of the war Russian command and technical deficiencies were at least partially compensated for by producing massive numbers of tanks. The enormous Soviet factories produced 40,000 to 50,000 T-34s of all types by 1945. In contrast, the Germans produced about 30,000 main battle tanks of all types from 1939 to the end of the war.[19]

However, Popov no longer had a numerical advantage and his four tank corps were down to their last few dozen tanks, had little motorized infantry and were short of ammunition and fuel. Popov's weary tankers and understrength infantry detachments prepared to stem the German tide flowing towards them. However, when XXXX. Panzerkorps brought its three Panzer divisions on line and drove north, the German divisions rolled over the thin screen of Russian infantry. In their debilitated state, the tank corps could not prevent the Germans from advancing toward the 6th Army lines of communication northwest of Slavyansk. There was no question of Popov resuming offensive operations due to his lack of mobile infantry, armor and artillery strength and supply shortages. The higher Soviet command did not yet realize the realities of the situation, nor how the tide of war had turned against them.

When Popov radioed Vatutin in order to request that he be allowed to withdraw his disintegrating mobile group to the north, the Front commander rebuked him. He told Popov that if he withdrew northwards, it would allow the Germans to withdraw to

An early model Soviet T-34. The T-34, although a robust and durable tank with good sloped frontal armor and an adequate gun, had several design flaws. The tank commander had to help operate the gun and could not devote his entire attention to the command of the tank. In addition, the absence of a turret cupola hindered the ability of the commander to see well. The most serious problem was the lack of a radio other than those of the company or battalion commander. This prevented individual tanks from communicating with each other and more critically, did not allow commanders to direct the tanks of their unit once combat began. In contrast, German tanks were equipped with radios and a tank commander could talk with each member of the crew and any other tank. (Credit National Archives)

Dnepropetrovsk and the Dnepr. Vatutin brusquely ordered Popov to accomplish his attack objectives, which were to cut off all avenues of a German retreat to the Dnepr. With his devastated tank corps tied up in desperate defensive battles and preparing to fight for their very survival, the Stavka's concern regarding the possibility of a German withdrawal was doubtless not shared by Popov.

Not only did the Stavka misinterpret German intentions and troop movements, but it also did not understand the realities of why Popov's attack had begun to fail. A deputy chief of the operations staff of the Stavka, who was a trusted subordinate of Stalin, offered the opinion that the failure to advance was primarily due to the fact that the Mobile Group was not attacking 'with sufficient vigor.' After his request to withdraw was refused, Popov grimly went about the task of preparing for the German attack.[20]

On 21 February, after bypassing the last Russian forces in the area around Krasnoarmeiskoye, 7. Panzer-Division assaulted Russian strong points north of the town, which were located south of Dobropol'ye. The town and environs were defended by the remains of the 10th and 18th Tank Corps. The Germans knew that Popov's situation was serious, because they had intercepted a radio transmission requesting permission to withdraw northward. Popov wanted to pull back from Dobropol'ye, to the area southwest of Stepanovka, where he expected to link up with elements of the 3rd

---

[18] The Russians did not correct this defect until late 1943, when the T-34/85 began to come into service. This much improved tank had a completely redesigned three man turret, as well as a more powerful 8.5cm main gun. The Soviets made great strides toward correcting tactical as well as technical shortcomings during the last year and a half of the war.

[19] Production numbers of German tanks vary slightly according to different sources but the following figures can be considered to be representative:

Panzer III 15,300
Panzer IV 8,100
Panzer V 5,500
Tiger I 1,350
Tiger II 485

[20] Glantz, pg. 133 and Carell, pg. 191.

A Panzer III supports white camouflaged SS infantry during an attack on a village typical of the type found in the Ukraine in the Kharkov area. (Courtesy of Mark C. Yerger)

Tank Corps. However, Sinenko's 3rd Tank Corps was under assault itself, having been attacked by 11. Panzer-Division's Kampfgruppe Balck. Balck was ordered to tie up the Russians with aggressive attacks and not allow the 3rd Tank Corps to withdraw towards Dobropol'ye and unite with the other two tank corps.[21]

While Balck blocked Sinenko's armor at Stepanovka, "Wiking" and 7. Panzer-Division were to advance past Krasnoarmeiskoye, and penetrate the Russian defenses south and southeast of Barvenkovo. This was to prevent the Soviets from crossing the Samara at Petropawlovka and striking 1. Panzerarmee in the flank. The XXXX. Panzerkorps was clearly instructed that this could not be allowed to happen under any circumstances. Therefore the possession of the crossings of the Samara at Petropawlovka were viewed as absolutely critical by 1. Panzerarmee.

The three Panzer divisions of XXXX. Panzerkorps advanced on parallel lines of attack northwards while 333. Infanterie-Division moved in behind the tanks and cleared out the last remaining Soviet troops in Krasnoarmeiskoye on 23 February. The Germans reported that they captured or destroyed many T-34s and a great deal of other war materials in the burned out and flattened town. After finishing the mopping up operations, the main force of the division was to set out for the sector held by III. Panzerkorps, in order to take over defense of the area west of the Krivoy Torets River.

During the night of 22-23 February, Kampfgruppe Balck launched a determined attack, swinging to the north and driving northwards along the roads leading into Stepanovka from the north. This operation effectively blocked the 3rd Tank Corps line of retreat. Subsequently, on the following day, "Wiking" attacked the town itself from the west and southwest and 7. Panzer-Division struck from the south, rolling up the roads leading into Stepanovka

---

[21] NA/T-313, roll 46, 1a KTB, Darstellung der Ereignisse, 1. Panzerarmee, frame 7279499.

from that direction. Statements made by prisoners revealed that there were elements of the 18th Tank Corps, a motorized rifle brigade, a Flak detachment, Ski troops and the 57th Guards Rifle Division in the town. The 11. Panzer-Division Kampfgruppe continued its attack, advancing to the north and approaching Barvenkovo, while the other two divisions encircled the Russians and began to assault the town perimeter. After several hours of hard fighting, "Wiking" broke into the town from the southwest, however the Russian troops continued to fight stubbornly, forcing the SS Grenadiers to take the town block by block. Later in the afternoon, 7. Panzer-Division turned back a counterattack by a battle group of the 3rd Guards Tank Corps, which tried to break through German lines and reach the encircled defenders.[22]

The fighting continued at Stepanovka through 24 February, with both "Wiking" and 7. Panzer-Division slowly pushing toward the center of the town. While the house to house fighting raged, 11. Panzer-Division bypassed the city entirely, driving toward Barvenkovo. Just before reaching a range of hills that lay south of the town, Balck ran into a group of Soviet tanks, which were caught by surprise. The T-34s were outflanked from the march by the swift moving German tank column and quickly knocked out. After regrouping, the column continued rolling toward Barvenkovo. Balck attempted to maximize the element of surprise by advancing to the attack as fast as possible, hoping to catch the Russians unaware. However, the Soviets were alerted and well dug in, as usual and had laid rings of mines around Barvenkovo. Having failed to surprise the Russians, 11. Panzer-Division pulled back in order to regroup for a renewed assault on the following morning.

Soviet radio security was poor on frequent occasions during this period of the war and the 1. Panzerarmee daily battle reports often refer to intercepted Russian radio orders and conversations, many of which were communications to and from Popov's headquarters. The Germans monitored these messages and got a great deal of valuable information from them. It became clear that Popov was ordered to concentrate his remaining forces for the defense of Barvenkovo, with his primary objective being to delay the further advance of XXXX. Panzerkorps and to hold the railroad. Directives from Vatutin were also intercepted and the Germans gained the knowledge that the Southwest Front planned to move all available forces into the Barvenkovo-Slavyansk-Isyum sector with the

intention of holding this area at all costs. It was also learned that reinforcements were on the march from the east to that area. This indicated that Russian offensive operations in the Kharkov-Slavyansk gap were over and that the Soviet high command had gone over to defensive operations designed primarily to keep open an escape route for the retreating remnants of the 1st Guards Army and the 6th Army.

The last Russian resistance in Stepanovka was eliminated during the night of 24 February by 7. Panzer-Division Panzergrenadiers. "Wiking," which had regrouped and left the final operations in the town to the army division, swung toward the Samara valley. The first elements of the SS division reached the river in the Petropawlovka area, where they made contact with elements of 17. Panzer-Division. In cooperation with "Wiking," the division drove Russian forces to the north, forcing them to retreat across the Samara. Mobile Group Popov no longer had any offensive capability, and the tattered remains were entirely on the defensive.[23]

The XXXX. Panzerkorps had successfully concluded 21 days of hard fighting, having held the western bastion of 1. Panzerarmee, defeated 5 tank corps and launched a counterattack on schedule to support Manstein's offensive. It had inflicted heavy losses on the Soviets during these three weeks. By its own accounting, it had destroyed 251 Russian tanks, 17 armored cars, 73 artillery pieces, 135 anti-tank guns and captured or destroyed 475 other vehicles. The total Soviet casualties recorded by the corps were 3000 dead and 569 captured. As the SS-Panzerkorps and XXXXVIII. Panzerkorps assembled in order to drive north and retake Kharkov, XXXX. Panzerkorps prepared to assault the Soviet defenses south of Barvenkovo as quickly as possible, hoping to break through to Izyum and the Northern Donets before the Russians could build up a solid defensive front and bring up strong reserves. With the elimination of Popov's armored force as a threat, Hausser's SS Panzer divisions were able to devote their entire attention to the advance on Panjutine and Losovaja, with a secure eastern flank. The Panzer divisions of 4. Panzerarmee and 1. Panzerarmee were aligned on roughly parallel lines of attack, on a front that extended from Pavlograd in the west, to Slavyansk in the east. Spearheaded by Hausser's SS divisions, the Panzer divisions prepared to drive north, turning toward Kharkov, in a series of attacks that would hammer the Soviet armies against the anvil of Armeeabteilung Kempf.

[22] NA/T-313, roll 46, 1a KTB 1. Panzerarmee, Darstellung der Ereignisse, 23.2.1943. frame 7279502.

[23] NA/T-313, roll 46, 1a KTB 1. Panzerarmee, Darstellung der Ereignisse, 23.2.1943. frame 7279509.

10

THE DRIVE TO KHARKOV

In the early morning cold and fog, typical for that time of year in the Ukraine, the SS-Panzerkorps began its drive north from Pavlograd on 25-26 February. Supplies were flowing over a somewhat tenuous road net, which was still not entirely secure. Due to roving bands of Soviet troops, the icy, snow covered roads were an uncertain conduit for the enormous amount of fuel, ammunition and supplies that was needed to keep the SS divisions moving. Russian forces that had been cut off by the attack of the SS divisions were still infiltrating through the area and caused severe disruptions when they occupied a section of the road or ambushed a German detachment. On the night of 24-25 February, one of these detachments made contact with a contingent of "Totenkopf" rear area troops at the village of Nageshdovka.

Neighboring HQ and supply units of I./SS-Panzer-Regiment 3, billeted at nearby Kotschereshki, were suddenly awakened before dawn by gunfire and the unmistakable sounds of battle. Flashes of explosions could be seen in the distance, illuminating the dark shadows of buildings in Nageshdovka. The alarm was sounded and sleepy men rushed out into the damp, chilling morning air. An ad hoc battle group was formed and immediately set off toward the sound of the fighting. The small battle group was supported by a number of eight wheeled armored cars and a single Panzer IV. A second Kampfgruppe of Pioniere and supply troops followed the lead group, echeloned to the rear, in order to protect the flank of the leading group. In the distance, they could see several vehicles burning in the streets of Nageshdovka. When they approached the outskirts of the town, which was lit by the flickering fires from the burning vehicles, the German troops saw many dark shapes scurrying down the streets, outlined against the flames in the center of the town.

Suddenly, muzzle flashes lit up the darkness in front of the first group and the German troops immediately suffered several casualties. After an answering volley of fire and an exchange of grenades, Soviet return fire slackened and then stopped entirely. The armored vehicles moved cautiously forward once again and the Kampfgruppe entered the town, finding many of their comrades lying dead in the street. The SS men ran to the edge of Nageshdovka and in the distance they saw a rear guard detachment of a long Russian column hurrying away into the cover of darkness. Mounting their vehicles, the infuriated Pioniere raced after the Soviets until they closed to within range of the rear elements of the column. The automatic 2cm guns of the SPWs fired, machine gun tracers flew in streams across the snow and the tail end of the fleeing Soviet column was thrown into an uproar. In the distance, there were screams from horses and men, and several trucks burst into flames. The Russian detachment recoiled from the SS gun fire, fleeing toward a nearby small village.

When the SS troopers reached the spot where the burning vehicles lay abandoned, they found six anti-tank guns left by the roadside and a number of dead or dying horses, lying twisted in their harnesses. Among the debris scattered over the road, several mortars were discovered. After searching furiously, ammunition was found and hastily assembled mortar crews fired shell after shell into the darkness, until the last shell was used. After collecting their booty of Russian weapons, the patrol returned to Kotschereshki.[1] Before dawn, stronger battle groups were organized from Headquarters personnel and security detachments, reinforced by personnel from the Pioniere battalion. Several of these ad hoc battle groups

---

[1] Vopersal, pg. 145.

left Kotschereshki at first light in order to secure the surrounding roads. By 0950 the area was cleared of any remaining Russians and the road was again open temporarily. In the meantime, III./Rgt. "Totenkopf" had arrived and set out in pursuit, hoping to intercept the Russian column before it reached safety.

The rest of the division resumed its attack as the overcast morning sky turned gray with the break of dawn. The main corps objective was the towns of Panjutina and Losovaja which were only a short distance apart. "Das Reich" was to attack Losovaja from the south, while "Totenkopf's" reinforced Panzer Regiment struck from the southwest. Two battalions of Becker's SS-PzG.-Rgt. 3 assembled at Orelka in preparation for attacking Panjutina from the west, in support of the attack upon Losovaja. The 15. Infanterie-Division moved into the Pavlograd area, and began operations to secure the rear areas of the two divisions. The division cleared out a number of small detachments of Soviet troops and reduced isolated strong points left behind. It also provided forces to secure the road net south of Pavlograd, relieving the SS combat units of this task. An unintended result of the division's operations was that Soviet troops were unable to move eastward, toward their own lines and crossed the Samara west of the town. As a result, the flow of supplies into the town was disrupted from the west and Soviet troops threatened the "Totenkopf" supply units from unexpected areas.

In spite of these disruptions and other problems in the rear, the division launched its attacks on 25 February, although shortages of supplies caused numerous difficulties. Becker's regiment, still led by SS-Aufklärungsabteilung 3, rolled out of Orelka toward its first objective, which was a low hill about ten kilometers north of Panjutina. However, before the column had gone very far, a Russian attack boiled out of a wooded area northeast of the road. Tanks emerged from the woods, accompanied by Russian infantry who were urged on by shouting officers. The advance of the regiment came to an abrupt halt as it deployed to meet the Russian attack. After an hard fought battle, the Russian infantry began to withdraw to the north.

The German casualty toll mounted during the morning and Becker did not pursue the Russians aggressively after they pulled back. At that moment, the SS Grenadiers were buoyed by the sudden arrival of their division commander, the man they called "Papa." Theodore Eicke, perhaps frustrated at his division's lack of progress, had flown to the battlefield in a Fieseler Storch. The plane landed and Eicke got out. His arrival gave the Grenadiers and Becker an emotional lift and both responded to his presence. They did not want to incur his scorn by not attacking with sufficient enthusiasm and by 1500 hours, the regiment, spearheaded by Walter Bestmann's Aufklärungsabteilung, captured the village of Fedorovka. That night,

"Totenkopf" division commander Theodore Eicke (right) with Otto Baum. Baum was one of the division's most outstanding regimental commanders and one of the most decorated German soldiers of the war. He was awarded both grades of the Iron Cross, the German Cross in Gold, the Wound Badge in Silver and the Knight's Cross by mid-1942. In the latter years of the war he was presented with both the Oakleaves and Swords to the Knight's Cross. (Courtesy of Mark C. Yerger)

Becker ordered two companies of the battalion to push east of Fedorovka, toward Hill 177. By the early morning, the exhausted companies reported that they had reached the village of Barbaschevka, but were still short of their primary objective. In the meantime, "Das Reich" and "Totenkopf" began their advance northward.

After assembling his battle group in Wjasovok, SS-Sturmbannführer Karl Leiner led the attack of II./SS Panzer-Regiment 3, supported by Baum's battalion. With the half track battalion in the lead, the column drove north along the course of a small river until it reached the village of Kondratjevka, where it was delayed briefly by light Russian resistance. By 1000 hours, the column was on the move again, moving north along the bank of the frozen stream. At 1415 hours, the forward elements of Kampfgruppe Leiner arrived south of the town of Alexejevka, where it encountered a stronger Russian defensive position. The advance of the SS column was brought to an abrupt halt when the leading vehicles were fired upon by Soviet anti-tank guns and heavy weapons. The Russian guns were concealed in well constructed earthen entrenchments located behind a tank ditch south of Alexejevka.[2]

The SS column was stopped and the lead half tracks pulled back into cover. As the column tried to regroup it was attacked by a number of T-34s and a tank battle broke out between German and

---

[2] This is one of a number of villages with the name of Alexejevka located in the area south of Kharkov.

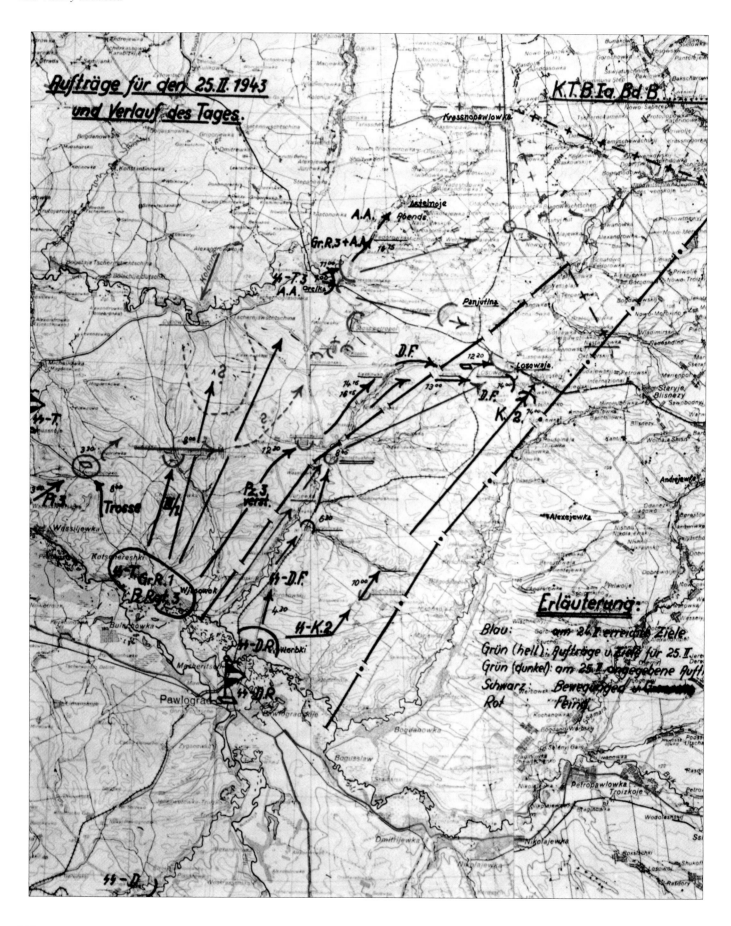

Russian tanks. The Panzergrenadiers leapt from their half tracks and a detachment of Pioniere began to bridge the ditch. However, before the crossing site could be secured, Leiner issued an order calling a halt to the attack and directed the Kampfgruppe to go over to the defensive. The Panzergrenadiers abandoned their attempt to assault the guns and dug in around the edge of the tank ditch. The attack had been halted because the tanks were low on fuel, undoubtedly caused by the interruptions in supply caused by the Russian forces disrupting the division's communications lines.

From Alexejevka, it was only a few kilometers to the north before reaching the main road running between Orelka and Losovaja. However, Leiner's battle group did not move again until the refueling and resupply operations were accomplished. The Russians exploited German inactivity and they launched an attack on the spearhead of the column. In the middle of the night, T-34s suddenly appeared out of the darkness and began racing wildly through German lines. At least one of the T-34s was knocked out after its commander was shot and killed by a "Totenkopf" squad leader and several grenades were tossed into the open hatch. After the Soviet tanks disappeared back into the darkness, Leiner was stung into action and decided to make an ill advised thrust past the Soviet defenses at Alexejevka. He ordered a company of tanks to bypass Alexejevka and block the elevated railroad between Orelka and Losovaja.

Shortly before midnight, 6./Kompanie of SS-Pz.Rgt. 3, commanded by SS- Hauptscharführer Fritz Biermeier, was ordered to make a reconnaissance attack toward Losovaja. Biermeier was ordered to reach the elevated roadway west of the town and seize it. However, Leiner did not send any supporting infantry or mobile artillery with Biermeier and there was no preliminary reconnaissance of the terrain leading to the objective. Biermeier's unsupported company was sent out into the darkness, without any information about its objective. The company was to pay a stiff price for Leiner's failure of command.

To make matters worse, Biermeier's Panzer IIIs had not been able to complete their resupply and did not have adequate fuel or shells for their main guns. They had received an inadequate supply of machine gun ammunition as well. Since Biermeier and his men were unfamiliar with the featureless snow fields, the Panzer company predictably became disoriented. However, just as several tanks were about to run out of fuel, Biermier finally stumbled upon the elevated road west of Losovaja, shortly before daybreak. A member of a tank crew under Biermeier's command described the situation.

Knight's Cross winner Fritz Biermeier, a company commander of "Totenkopf's" Panzer Regiment. On 25 February he was ordered to make an ill-advised night time attack on an elevated roadway between the towns of Orelka and Losovaja, after the regiment's attack was blocked by Russian armor. (Courtesy of Mark C. Yerger)

We had totally lost our bearings. When a driver voiced concern that his tank was nearly out of fuel, Biermeier's sharp response was barked over the radio. 'Weiterfahren!' (Drive on!) . . . It was about 0500 hours. We peered through the armor slits at the snow covered land . . . A shudder passed over us. The road embankment became visible at 500-600 meters and near it were T-34 after T-34. There was little time to think over the situation, since we suddenly saw the muzzle flashes of the 7.62cm tank cannons. I waited nervously for the order to fire from my platoon commander, Unterstürmführer Offner. Instead Offner, who was from Innsbruck, screamed over the microphones, "Biermeier, your tank's on fire!"

I yelled at the driver to quickly pull off to the side of the high railroad embankment . . . In my gun sight I could see three T-34s with their flank toward us, less than 100 meters in front of us.

Without waiting for the order to fire, I hit one of the T-34s halfway up the turret. The first T-34 caught fire. The second one began to smoke also. Its hatches flew open. The crew jumped down and ran for safety. I also hit the third Russian tank. This time however, the crew did not abandon the tank. Although it was burning, the T-34 turned to the right and disappeared to the rear. Then the rest of the Russian tanks also turned away.[3]

[3] Vopersal, pg. 151.

OPPOSITE: On 25 February, "Das Reich drove from the area north of Pavlograd, attacking toward the railroad junction at Losovaja. "Totenkopf" struck out in a northeast direction from the town of Orelka and reached the sector near Artelnoje, which was just south of the vital railroad station at Krasnopawlovka. This was the final step in securing the railroad net north of Pavlograd and provided a supply line for the SS-Panzerkorps assault upon Kharkov.

The trials of Biermeier's company were not over when the Russian armor withdrew. A number of the German tanks had been knocked out or disabled and the crew members were trying to assemble near the elevated road. With his tank disabled and burning, Biermeier stood with the surviving members of his crew near one of the undamaged tanks, when they suddenly heard the unfamiliar sound of horses pounding over the snow. The shocked German tank crews turned to see swift, strange shadows speeding toward them. A moment later they were overrun by a large group of Russian cavalry. The Soviet horsemen swooped down on the Germans, sabers drawn and shouting at the top of their lungs. Fortunately for the dismounted crews, the tanks had received fresh stocks of machine gun ammunition and were able to defend themselves at close quarters. A few of the Soviet cavalrymen and horses were chopped down by streams of bullets as they dashed among the men, slashing and shooting wildly. The Germans on foot scattered and the Russians pursued them, cutting them down with sword or gun. Biermeier and his crew survived the mounted onslaught, but others were not so lucky, and were found dead in the snow, ridden down by the cavalry. After the fighting Russian civilians told the SS men that several other Germans, dressed in the black uniform of Panzer troops, had been taken prisoner and taken away.[4]

In other areas, much of the division remained involved in chaotic fighting against marauding columns of Russians who had been pushed north by 15. Infanterie-Division. These troops continued to cause havoc along the roads west of Pavlograd creating an uncertain supply situation. SS-Hauptsturmführer Max Seela arrived from Pereshschepino with his SS-Pioniere-Bataillon 3 and immediately was thrown into heavy fighting against elements of these Soviet troops. At 0850 hours, a stronger Russian battle group crossed the Samara west of Pavlograd and attempted to fight its way through "Totenkopf" lines.

The situation became disturbing to the SS-Panzerkorps command. At mid-morning, Eicke was ordered to clean up the situation along the Rollbahn with Regiment "Totenkopf" while the Aufklärungsabteilung and Becker's regiment were to push from Orelka and reach Krasnopawlovka, on the railroad line north of Panjutina-Losovaja. Regiment "Totenkopf" found itself involved with the smaller Russian column which had forced its way into the town of Wassiljewka, driving out SS supply and security troops. Immediately, II./Regiment "Totenkopf" sent a reinforced company marching to the town. After a short battle, the Russians scattered to the four winds, leaving eleven of their number behind as prisoners. Meanwhile III./Regiment "Totenkopf," had pursued the larger column and remained on the trail of the Soviets. Schubach's battalion

---
[4] Op cit.

An SS Panzer III knocked out by two apparently tremendous impacts on both the frontal armor and the armor in front of the driver. The force of the explosions completely ruptured the steel plate and left gaping holes in the frontal armor of the tank. (Credit National Archives)

cornered them later in the afternoon and reported that it was involved in fighting with a force of approximately 1000 Russians south of the elevated road embankment, near Biermeier's tank company. The SS-Panzerkorps ordered the division to destroy the Russian forces south of Orelka by nightfall and secure the communication lines of Becker's regiment and Leiner's Panzer Regiment 3.[5]

Throughout the night fighting continued in the rear areas of the division. Various sized groups of Russians passed through the road network of the division, maintaining the disruption in the rear areas. The Russian command had instructed the fragments of their encircled divisions to fight their way through the German lines in order to man a new defensive line farther to the north. The Soviets had finally awakened to the realization of the impending catastrophe and planned to delay the advance of the SS-Panzerkorps long enough for major elements of the 6th Army and 1st Guards Army to withdraw to the east.

The numerous small battles fought along the Samara and north of Wjasovok hindered "Totenkopf's" advance on the following day. Most of two battalions of Regiment "Totenkopf" remained involved in cleaning up the road net west and north of Pavlograd. More critically, many of the division's tanks were still in the Losovaja area, due to ammunition and fuel shortages, as well as poor command decisions. Biermeier's attack toward the elevated road was made without proper reconnaissance or adequate infantry support and the company lacked sufficient stocks of ammunition and fuel. The end result was that the division's armor was dispersed and was not able to support "Das Reich's" attack upon Losovaja.

---
[5] NA/T-354, roll 120, 1a KTB, Darstellung der Ereignisse, frame 3753641-3753643 and Vopersal pg.148.

At 0430 hours, Regiment "Der Führer" moved to the north from Pavlograd, with Regiment "Deutschland" in the second echelon of the advance. The division's attack was screened on its right flank by the Kradschützen-Bataillon, which encountered little resistance. By 1400 hours, Regiment "Der Führer" reached the southern outskirts of Losovaja, where it quickly became evident that the Russians meant to defend the town vigorously. The units defending the town included the 58th Guards Rifle Division, tanks of the 1st Guards Tank Corps and elements of the 41st Guards Rifle Division. The latter unit had just conducted a costly and grueling withdrawal from the area east of Pavlograd.

The division had been driven north by the attack of 6. Panzer-Division. After Pavlograd fell to the SS-Panzerkorps, the 41st Guards Rifle Division began a withdrawal northward to Losovaja. During its retreat, the division was attacked by German aircraft and encountered 6. Panzer-Division mobile columns. The withdrawal was a disaster which cost the division substantial losses in men and equipment. SS artillery spotted the division moving in the open east of Pavlograd and shelled the defenseless columns. The casualties included the division commander, his executive officer and the division political officer, as well as a regimental commander. The survivors of the division finally reached Losovaja and found themselves in action against the Germans very shortly afterward.[6]

The II./"Der Führer," under Stadler, fought its way into Losovaja along a railroad line which passed through a factory district on the southern edge of the town. After pushing into the midst of the factories and storehouses, the battalion was brought to a halt by a hail of machine gun bullets and heavy mortar fire. T-34s emerged from concealment and fired upon the Germans, forcing Stadler to pull his battalion back. The attack foundered and came to a halt. Kaiser's III./"Der Führer" penetrated into the town from the west but was stopped by determined Russian counterattacks. Then a series of ferocious infantry counterattacks, supported by T-34s, struck Stadler's battalion and threatened to drive it out of the town. The battalion was so hard pressed that it held its position only due to the close support of II./SS-Artillerie-Regiment 2.

The artillery battalion laid down a barrage of shells a few meters in front of the German lines, breaking up repeated Russian assaults with a storm of high explosives. The counterattacks upon both battalions were finally halted by the German artillery. Stadler's battalion immediately launched a counterattack and pursued the Soviet infantry so closely that they were not able to take up new defensive positions. The SS Grenadiers destroyed two T-34s and continued to

Wolfgang Gast, a former battery commander of "Das Reich's" artillery regiment, was staff adjutant to regiment commander Kurt Brasack in 1943. He later commanded II./SS-Artillerie-Regiment 2. During the war he won the Knight's Cross, both classes of Iron Cross and the Close Combat clasp in Silver. (Courtesy of Mark C. Yerger)

advance, supported by Sturmgeschütze and Stuka attacks. At the end of the day, in spite of Russian counterattacks later in the day, Regiment "Der Führer" occupied secure defensive positions in both the southern and western sectors of the town. The fighting died down after dark, perhaps because both combatants were exhausted from the ferocious close quarters combat that had raged throughout the day.[7]

---

[6] Glantz, pg. 132.

[7] Weidinger, pg. 56.

"Das Reich" fights for Losovaja

Fierce house to house fighting began again with first light on 26 February. Two companies of the Kradschützen-Bataillon, accompanied by Ernst Krag's assault gun battery attempted to outflank the Russian defensive positions in the southern and eastern portions of Losovaja. The motorcycle troops launched their attack and almost immediately, the two companies became bogged down in front of stubbornly held Russian positions. Shortly afterward, Russian infantry, supported by a few T-34s, furiously counterattacked the German motorcycle troops, who were hard pressed just to avoid being thrown completely out of the town.

While Fick's troops battled the Russian tanks and infantry, giving ground under the ferocious assault, Stadler's battalion was also counterattacked by three T-34s, supported by a company of Russian infantry, which struck the battalion flank and created a dangerous situation. The company on the threatened flank was forced to withdraw and the Russian tanks rolled down the narrow streets firing their 7.6cm guns and on board machine guns. Russian infantry followed close behind the tanks, blasting away with submachine guns and hurling hand grenades. The flank of the battalion was on the verge of collapse when the assault gun battery commander, SS-Obersturmführer Ernst Krag, intervened. On his own initiative, Krag placed his assault guns into a position from where they could fire upon the T-34s from the flank. The Sturmgeschütze were not seen by the Russian tanks and two went up in flames, after which the lone survivor hastily retreated. Encouraged by the destruction of the Russian armor, Stadler's Grenadiers counterattacked and the Russian infantry melted away, using the buildings and back alleys to make their escape.[8]

Supported by Krag's assault guns, the SS Grenadiers regained the initiative and began to methodically eliminate one Russian strong point after the other. The Sturmgeschütze IIIs moved up to point blank range and fired 7.5cm high explosive shells at Russian machine gun positions. When daylight allowed SS artillery spotters to coordinate artillery fire, medium and heavy batteries of the division supported the advance. After several flights of Stukas arrived and dropped bombs on Soviet positions with pin point accuracy, resistance diminished somewhat in the south. By the afternoon, Stadler's men fought their way into the center of the town, reaching a position near a large church. However, III./Regiment "Der Führer" was not able to make much progress on the western sector of the town.

At 1430 hours, Regiment "Deutschland" arrived and Oberführer Vahl ordered the regiment to attack the town from the east and north-

Heavily laden "Leibstandarte" Grenadiers march past a half track with a 2cm automatic Flak gun mounted behind the driver. The man at the rear, in addition to his rifle, canteen and food pouch, carries an ammo box and a spare machine gun barrel. (Credit National Archives)

west, supported by the division's remaining tanks. At that time, the Panzer regiment had only nineteen operational tanks, fourteen of which were Panzer IIIs. The II./Regiment "Deutschland" assembled north of where Fick's battalion remained pinned down, while on the northwest corner of the town, I./Regiment "Deutschland" pushed into the first buildings. Both battalions encountered bitter resistance from the Russian troops holding the town. Soviet tanks were hidden in piles of rubble or ruined buildings and were extremely difficult to spot or knock out. Often the Germans did not see the T-34s until they fired.

Anti-tank guns could not be brought to bear on the T-34s, because Russian infantry directed machine gun or mortar fire on any gun that was wheeled into position. The SS Grenadiers had to first eliminate the Russian infantry protecting the hidden tanks in order to get in close, where they could destroy the T-34s with grenade bundles or magnetic anti-tank mines. By 1600 hours, after extremely difficult fighting, the two battalions had gained a solid foothold in the town. During the period from 24-25 February, "Das Reich" troops destroyed a total of fourteen Russian tanks in Losovaja.[9]

In spite of the German ring of steel closing in upon them, the Russians still fought back aggressively. At 1900 hours, T-34s and infantry of the 1st Guards Tank Corps launched another attack on

[9] NA/T-354 118, Tagesmeldung an Gen.Kdo. SS-Panzerkorps zum 26.2.1943, frame 3751876.

OPPOSITE: "Das Reich" and "Totenkopf" captured the towns of Panjutina and Losovaja, driving northwards along a section of the railroad net south of Kharkov. The Armeeabteilung Kempf sector begins in the upper northwest corner of the map. "Leibstandarte" held the sector west of the town of Alexejevka, successfully defending the Krasnograd salient until it was once again placed under command of Hausser's SS-Panzerkorps.

[8] Yerger, Ernst August Krag biography, pg. 13.

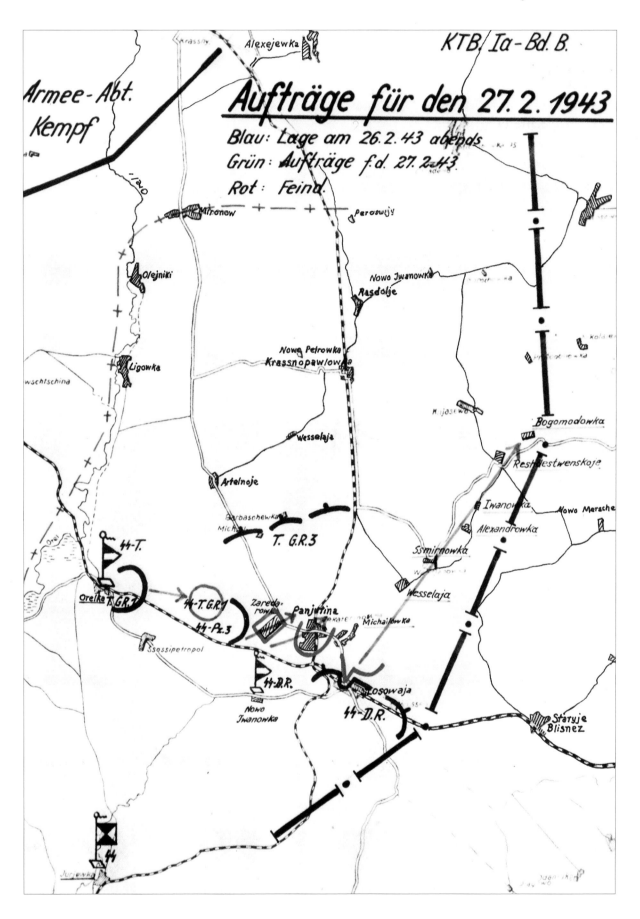

the positions of Regiment "Der Führer" and Fick's motorcycle troops. The ferocious attacks made some progress after Russian infantry detachments infiltrated the SS regiment's front by crawling through interconnected basements. Russian troops began firing from unexpected directions in the German rear and Soviet armor suddenly roared into sight and supported their infantry with machine gun and cannon fire. However, SS tanks and assault guns, in cooperation with infantry of Regiment "Deutschland," attacked from the flank and put six T-34s out of action. The Soviet infantry were forced to fall back slowly, past the knocked out tanks. The regiment sealed off the attack, pushing the Russians out of the penetration or encircling and destroying them. By evening, the German counterattacks had closed the gap between the battalions of Regiment "Der Führer" and restored the regiment's front.[10]

"Totenkopf" endured another day of dissipating combat in its divisional communications zone. These actions tied much of its infantry strength and slowed its advance once again. The I./SS-"Totenkopf"-PzG.-Rgt. 3, under SS-Sturmbannführer Fritz Knöchlein, was engaged in defensive fighting against Russian troops attempting to cross the Orel River, in order to link up with the Soviet elements moving to the northeast. The battalion established a defensive perimeter at the village of Tschernoglasovka, blocking access to a bridge over the river. Large and small groups of Soviet infantry, survivors of supply detachments and even isolated tanks, continued to move through the area between the Orel and the Samara Rivers. Seela's Pioniere-Bataillon fought a series of battles along the main road in the Nageshdovka sector, east of Pavlograd.

South of Wjasovok, II./Regiment "Totenkopf" cleared remaining elements of Russian troops out of a forest a short distance from the town. The SS troops made contact with lead elements of 15. Infanterie-Division, who had crossed the river near Wassiljewka. A company of Wilhelm Schultze's battalion unexpectedly ran into a Soviet supply battalion moving along a road, sparking a wild but one sided fight. When the firing subsided, 92 Russians, including a colonel, were taken prisoner. To the surprise of Schultze's Grenadiers, they found large amounts of German supplies and equipment in the Soviet trucks. Evidently it was booty captured when Kharkov fell on 14 February. The III./Regiment "Totenkopf" was also involved all day mopping up the remnants of the Russian column it had cornered on the previous day. Reconnaissance elements of Becker's regiment finally reached Hill 177, which was located on the road north of Panjutina.[11]

SS-Obersturmbannführer Fritz Knöchlein, commander of I./Regiment "Totenkopf." Knöchlein's battalion was engaged in extensive fighting against Russian troops passing through the division's communications zone on February 25-26. The disruptive situation hindered the combat operations of the division for days before the last remnants of Russian troops were finally eliminated. (Courtesy of Mark C. Yerger)

Leiner's Panzer regiment finally got on the move again and renewed its attack toward the elevated road at first light. By 1000 hours, its lead elements approached the town of Zaredarovka, which was a short distance west of Panjutina and northwest of Losovaja. In the distance to the east, the sounds of fighting could be heard as "Das Reich" battled for possession of Losovaja. However, Leiner's advance halted when he requested medical supplies, ammunition and rations. Leiner reported that he was involved in fighting against Soviet tanks, but the location of the regiment was unclear. During this delay, division headquarters sent new orders for Leiner's regiment, ordering him to support the advance of Regiment "Deutschland" after that regiment moved northward from the Losovaja area. At that inopportune moment, radio communications between the division headquarters and the Panzer regiment ended. According to Vopersal, the regiment had lost some of its radios through battle damage and others had simply broken down and could not be repaired. At noon the Panzer regiment still remained out of radio contact with division headquarters. This situation set in motion events that resulted in the death of Theodore Eicke on 26 February, 1943.[12]

"Totenkopf" loses its Commander

Eicke decided to leave his headquarters in his Fieseler Storch, accompanied by his Ordonnanzoffizier, Hauptsturmführer Otto Friedrich, and fly toward Zaredarovka. He intended to find Leiner and convey the new order personally. After leaving Orelka, the light plane appeared in the air above Michailovka, where Eicke expected

---

[10] Ibid, frame 3751864-3751876 and Weidinger, pg. 59.
[11] NA/T-354 118, Tagesmeldung an Gen. Kdo. SS-Panzerkorps 26.2.1943, frame 3751866-3751869.

[12] Vopersal, pg. 154.

to find the headquarters of the division Aufklärungsabteilung. The small HQ security detachment was expecting him, as it had received a radio message informing them that Eicke was en route. About 1300 hours Eicke and Friedrich circled the village and after the correct signal flare was fired into the air, landed in a nearby flat section of ground. The division commander received a report about the local situation and was informed that Zaredarovka was still strongly held by the Russians. An officer of the division's Auflärungsabteilung informed him that he had personally reconnoitered the town and seen Soviet road blocks and T-34s. Eicke seemed to disregard this information, and after giving some cigarettes to the "Totenkopf" troops, flew off again. Some time later, Eicke located forward elements of the Aufklärungsabteilung northeast of Orelka. He landed there also but was not able to learn anything about the location of the Panzer regiment and was informed that radio communication was still not established. The light plane took off once again and continued searching for the regiment. At that time, it was probably near the road that ran between Artelnoje and Panjutina.

About 1600 hours, the plane was observed by SS troops to turn and fly in a long sweeping curve south of Artelnoje. Shortly afterward, it flew over a Soviet Flak position and tracers were seen striking the plane, which immediately caught fire and fell to the ground in flames. At once "Totenkopf" troops tried to reach the crash site to see if there were any survivors of the crash. SS-Hauptsturmführer Arzelino Masarie (Aufklärungsabteilung) set out with several half tracks of Grenadiers and attempted to reach the crash site. About 1000 meters from the blazing wreck, a lone tank, commanded by an SS-Unterscharführer Schindler, joined the attempt to reach Eicke. A Panzerjäger officer, SS-Untersturmführer Hans Jendges, leaped on the tank deck, in spite of Russian small arms fire and accompanied it. Russian anti-tank guns began to fire at the tank and struck it several times. Although damaged, it was able to keep moving. Flak guns opened up on the small rescue detachment and a hail of projectiles struck the SS vehicles, forcing the half tracks to find cover.

On orders from Masarie, the tank approached within fifteen meters of the fiery crash site, where Jendges recognized Eicke's body, which had been thrown clear. He could see that all of the plane's passengers had been killed. None of the dead could be recovered at that time because the Russians near Artelnoje continued laying down a tremendous volume of fire on the area. The tank was hit several additional times and Jendges, as well as most of the crew were wounded by steel splinters. Unable to do more with the forces at hand, the detachment reluctantly pulled back, leaving the dead by the burning plane. During the night, the division organized an operation to recover Eicke's body on the following day.

A Fieseler "Storch" similar to the plane carrying "Totenkopf" division commander Theodore Eicke when he and an adjutant were shot down. Eicke was concerned about the location of the division's Panzer Regiment, which remained out of radio contact with his HQ throughout the morning of 26 February. While searching for the regiment the plane flew over a town occupied by a Russian anti-aircraft unit which shot the plane down, killing all aboard. A divisional Kampfgruppe tried to fight their way to the crash site and recover the bodies, but was forced to withdraw because of heavy Russian fire. Eventually a stronger battle group, supported by divisional artillery reached the bodies. (Credit National Archives)

Eicke's grave in Russia. Eicke was initially buried in a division cemetery near the town of Orelka. When the Germans were forced out of Russia several division staff officers led a group to Orelka, exhumed the body and moved it to Kiev. (The author's collection)

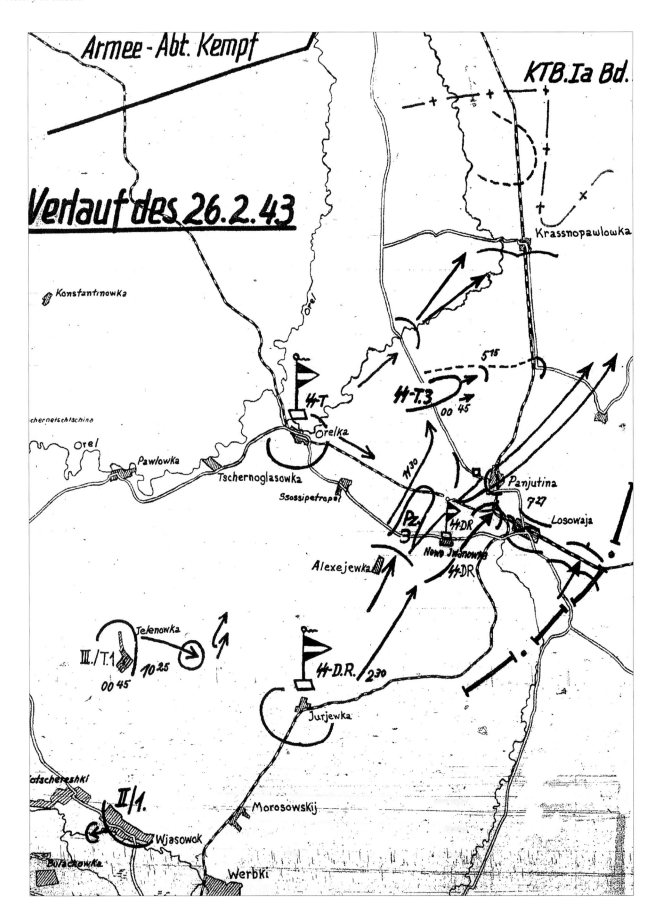

At first light, a Kampfgruppe commanded by SS-Hauptsturm-führer Arzelino Masarie set out for Artelnoje. It consisted of two Sturmgeschütze IIIs, three SPWs and two platoons of motorcycle troops After the Kampfgruppe arrived near the crash site, "Totenkopf" artillery laid down a heavy barrage to cover the vehicles as they advanced toward the wreckage of the plane. The artillery fire knocked out at least some of the Soviet anti-tank guns in the village and forced the Russians to abandon Artelnoje. The Kampfgruppe reached the plane and recovered the bodies of Eicke, Friedrich and the pilot, an Oberfeldwebel named Werner. The bodies had been stripped of their boots and some of their insignia and decorations. Artelnoje was searched in hopes of finding some of Eicke's personal effects. After looking through the wreckage and debris of the Flak gun position, Eicke's Knight's Cross with Oak Leaves was recovered, along with other articles taken from the plane.[13]

Eicke was buried at a nearby village on 1 March, with full honors. He was genuinely mourned by the members of the division. The death of Eicke hit the old veterans particularly hard, especially those who had been with the division through its first battles, the invasion of Russia and the eleven month ordeal at Demyansk. These men, as well as the young soldiers, called him "Papa Eicke" and revered him because of his toughness, as well as his rough humor and affection for them. He shared their hardships and won their respect by being present near the front lines throughout the worst of the division's difficult battles. Later in the war, the body was removed when the Germans were being forced out of the Ukraine and Eicke was reburied at Zhitomir.[14]

While Eicke's body was being recovered, Kampfgruppe Leiner remained west of Zaredarovka, unable to take the heavily defended village. At about 1000 hours, Leiner reported that he had deployed his regiment against overwhelming numbers of enemy tanks (überlegenen Panzerfeind) and was involved in heavy tank vs. tank combat. This was an interesting report, because "Totenkopf" had at least 75 tanks still in action at this time and there was no Soviet armored formation with comparable tank strength in the area. Elements of the Soviet 1st Guards Tank Corps were scattered in small

[13] From a report by Masarie, sent to Simon on 28.2.43, Vopersal, pg. 159.
[14] Sydnor, Charles W., *Soldiers of Destruction: The SS Death's Head Division, 1939-1945.* (Princeton: 1977).

OPPOSITE: On 26 February, both "Das Reich" and "Totenkopf" pushed northeast, toward the Krasnopawlovka sector, in preparation for turning due north and beginning the assault upon Kharkov. The Soviet 3rd Tank Army, under command of General P.S. Rybalko, awaited the advance of the SS divisions in the area north of Krasnopawlovka, setting the stage for the destruction of Rybalko's army.

SS-Oberführer Max Simon took command of the division after Eicke's death. Otto Baum took his place as commander of Regiment "Totenkopf" on 27 February, 1943. Simon was a long time subordinate of Eicke from the prewar days and had commanded the division once before. During the second half of 1942, Simon was appointed temporary commander of "Totenkopf" after Eicke was evacuated with severe leg wounds. (Courtesy of Mark C. Yerger)

groups of tanks from Losovaja to west of Pavlograd. In any event, the Soviet corps had less than a total of fifty tanks remaining in action on that date and it is unlikely that they all were concentrated against Leiner. It is more probable that Leiner did not have local superiority in the Zaredarovka area.

Whatever the reason for the delays west of Losovaja, the division could not take its objectives for 26 February. On the next day, according to orders from 4. Panzerarmee, "Totenkopf" was to encircle the Soviets by thrusting to the north of Losovaja and capturing Zaredarovka. In this manner, "Totenkopf" would cut the road leading out of the town to the north and block the escape of any

Russians trying to withdraw along that route. "Das Reich" was to destroy Soviet forces in the Losovaja-Panjutina area, drive north and push the remaining Russians into "Totenkopf." From there, the two divisions were to attack farther northwards and take Krasnopawlovka as soon as possible. The 15. Infanterie-Division was to follow in their wake, mop up any pockets of Soviet resistance and secure their supply lines. Another Kampfgruppe, designated Gruppe Steinbauer, was assigned the task of finishing off the remaining Russian troops cornered in forests northeast of Novo-Moskovsk.[15]

At 0430 hours on 27 February, Max Simon, who commanded Regiment "Totenkopf," assumed command of the division and Otto Baum became the new commander of the regiment. Baum's half track battalion (I./Regiment "Totenkopf") was taken over by SS-Hauptsturmführer Walter Reder.[16] During the morning, Kampfgruppe Leiner assembled west of Zaredarovka, preparing to attack the village again. The Panzers were to be supported by a simultaneously launched attack by I./Regiment "Totenkopf." The Panzergrenadier battalion got tied up in fighting near its assembly area and could not disengage in time to take part in the assault upon Zaredarovka. However, when Leiner's tanks assaulted the town, Soviet resistance abruptly collapsed and by 0740 hours Zaredarovka was in German hands.

After occupying Zaredarowka, Leiner thrust toward Panjutina, blocking any exit from the town. At 1135 hours, the regiment attacked in two columns, one approaching from the west and one from the north. There it encountered stiff resistance from Russians entrenched along both sides of the rail line leading out of the town to the north. The division's artillery moved up to support the attack of the Panzer Kampfgruppe, assembling in new firing positions. Under cover of their artillery, the Panzer-Pioniere-Kompanie cleared the Russians from the section of railroad leading out of the northern section of Panjutina. The Pioniere troops set up a blocking position, buttressed by several anti-tank guns, to prevent Soviet armor from moving behind the shelter of the railroad embankment. In the meantime, I./Regiment "Totenkopf" finally arrived and was able to join the attack. The Panzergrenadiers dismounted from their half tracks and assaulted Soviet positions on the northern edge of Panjutina.[17]

In the afternoon, SS-Standartenführer Werner Ostendorf, the Ia of the SS-Panzerkorps, arrived at the division's headquarters. It is likely that Hausser had instructed him to find out what was de-

laying the Simon's attack. He directed Simon to concentrate his forces and get the division moving again in short order. At 1330 hours, I./Regiment "Totenkopf" and the supporting tanks renewed the attack, supported by well directed artillery. By 1615 hours, the battalion had fought its way into the outskirts of Panjutina, led by SS tanks, which clanked forward while a barrage of high explosive shells pulverized the village. Shortly afterward, II./SS-"Totenkopf"-PzG.-Rgt. 3 arrived to reinforce the attack. German tanks and assault guns eliminated Soviet strong points with close range cannon fire, allowing the SS Grenadiers to reach the middle of the town by nightfall. Isolated groups of Russians continued to fight back, tying up the SS troops in house to house fighting. The "Totenkopf" troops had to methodically blast the Russian infantry out of their hiding places before securing the middle section of Panjutina. Fighting continued until dark, but by then the SS troops had taken half the town.

The fighting suddenly slackened when the Russian infantry abruptly withdrew from the town and attempted to retreat to the north or northwest. The remaining troops, now probably less than regimental strength, had been ordered to break through German lines and escape encirclement. The Soviet 15th Rifle Corps had been ordered to organize a new defensive line northwest of Losovaja, with orders to hold this line at all costs. Accordingly, the corps directed the two divisions to pull back to the town of Krasnopawlovka, where it hoped to build up a new defensive line and block the SS advance. However, Hausser did not intend to let the Russians reach Krasnopawlovka undisturbed.

Early in the morning of the following day, Kampfgruppe Becker (reinforced SS-"Totenkopf"-PzG.-Rgt. 3) left Artelnoje and headed toward Krasnopawlovka. By 1600 hours, the first detachment of the column, Max Kühn's battalion, had covered about 1/2 the distance between the two towns. Reconnaissance detachments of the Aufklärungsabteilung screened the flanks of the regiment, reporting that villages west of the road were occupied by Russian troops. Becker assembled his battle group in the Krasnopawlovka area by the early afternoon and attacked the western edge of the town with Kühn's battalion. By 2000 hours, the SS troops had pushed most of the Russians out of the town and reached the eastern edge. During the night, the regiment cleaned out the remaining Soviet stragglers and organized defensive positions on the northern perimeter of the town.

Meanwhile, III./and II./Regiment "Totenkopf," and the division's SS-Pioniere-Bataillon 3, destroyed the last Soviet troops threatening the communication lines of the division north of the Samara and west of Wjasovok. Seela's Pioniere battalion (not to be confused with the Panzer-Pioniere-Kompanie of the Panzer regi-

---

[15] T-354, roll 118, 4. Ia KTB 1253/56, Panzerarmee Oberkommando 4, Befehl Nr. 28. Received by SS-Panzerkorps on 1930 hours, 26.2.43.
[16] Vopersal, pg. 157.
[17] Ibid, pg. 163.

ment) destroyed another group of Soviet troops near Nageshdovka on the morning of 26 February. The battalion then followed in the wake of Kampfgruppe Becker, reaching Orelka and establishing defensive positions in the town by late in the day. After the end of the fighting, "Totenkopf" reported that it had seventy-six tanks still in operation, including sixty-one Panzer IIIs and fifteen Panzer IVs. The nine "Tigers" of the division were apparently not in action with the Panzer Regiment, probably due to the lack of sufficiently strong bridges to enable them to keep up with the rest of the lighter tanks.[18]

While Regiment "Totenkopf" fought through Panjutina, the sounds of fighting at Losovaja could be heard during the morning of 27 February. Regiment "Deutschland" began a flanking assault at 0800 hours, swinging toward a railroad line that exited the east edge of Losovaja. The advance bogged down in the face of heavy Russian fire and at 1000 hours, Fick's Kradschützen-Bataillon was ordered to disengage from the fighting in its sector and reinforce the attack of Regiment "Deutschland." The Russians were dug in at the base of the embankment of the railroad line and defended it tenaciously. Soviet machine gun and mortar fire swept the flat terrain south of the embankment, forcing the SS Grenadiers to take cover, utilizing whatever concealment was available. They could not get close enough to the embankment to assault the position and were taking casualties steadily. At that time, a battery of SS assault guns arrived, took up hull down firing locations and began to pound the Soviet positions along the railroad line with direct fire.

Then Stukas appeared over head, droning slowly above the battlefield until targets could be identified. After forward observers radioed instructions to the circling Stukas, they screamed down to drop their bombs. Soviet gun positions and machine gun nests disintegrated in a spray of frozen earth chunks and ice splinters. Gradually, the volume of defensive fire weakened and the Sturmgeschütze ground forward, with SS Grenadiers following close behind. Squads of SS Grenadiers reached the Soviet defensive line in several places.

Once gaps were created, the squat Sturmgeschütze rumbled to the embankment and moved parallel to the rail line, eliminating Russian defensive positions. Stukas continued to support the Grenadier combat groups and assault guns as they rolled up the Soviet position. Farther down the line, many of the defenders scrambled out of their bunkers and holes and took flight, running over the snow covered fields in the distance. Immediately, Macher's Pioniere-Kompanie, which was motorized and elements of Ehrath's I./Regiment "Deutschland," set off in pursuit. The circling Stukas pounced on the helpless Russians also, strafing them as they ran across the snow. Most were cut down before reaching safety and lay sprawled in bloody heaps on the snow.

After taking the embankment, the Germans moved closer toward the edge of the town. Ehrath's battalion reached a point near the northeastern corner of Losovaja, near the village of Michailovka. With "Totenkopf" closing in from the north and northwest and "Das Reich" threatening to encircle the town from the east, the Russians began to abandon the town. Stadler's II./"Der Führer," led by Ernst Krag's assault gun battery, blasted its way into the northern section of Losovaja, driving retreating Russian infantry before it. Simultaneously, III./"Der Führer," supported by SS-Obersturmführer Dr. Wolfgang Röhder's assault gun battery and SS-Aufklärungs-abteilung 2, drove the remaining Soviet troops out of the industrial sector on the western edge of the town.[19]

By 1500 hours, Stadler's battalion arrived at the Regiment "Deutschland" attack sector. At that point, effective Soviet resistance had largely ended, because most of the surviving Russians had melted away to the north, trying to escape before the ring closed around the town. Losovaja was secured by 1600 hours, although snipers and small groups of isolated Russian troops were still active in the southeastern sector of the town. Abandoned and destroyed Soviet vehicles were strewn along the streets. A few fire blackened T-34s smoldered in the ruins of camouflaged firing positions or lay interspersed with burnt out trucks and abandoned equipment. Reconnaissance patrols reported that the Soviets had pulled out of the surrounding villages as well. The tough fighting had been costly to "Das Reich" in men and material, particularly tanks. By the end of the day on 27 February, "Das Reich's" Panzer regiment had only eleven operational tanks, in addition to two command tanks. The assault gun battalion was in somewhat better shape, with twelve Sturmgeschütz IIIs.[20]

During the night of 27-28 February, Kumm's Regiment "Der Führer" and Harmel's Regiment "Deutschland" assembled north of Losovaja, in preparation for the resumption of the attack on the morning. The SS division's direction of attack was roughly parallel to the railroad tracks that ran northward toward Krasnopawlovka. "Das Reich" advanced on the eastern side of the railroad and "Totenkopf" attacked through the sector west of the rail line. The initial objective for the following day was Krasnopawlovka itself, which lay directly on the railroad line, about ten kilometers south of the town of Alexejevka. From Alexejevka it was only thirty kilometers to the southern edge of Kharkov.

18 NA/T-354, roll 118, Tagesmeldung der SS-"Totenkopf" Division an SS-Panzerkorps, 1715 hours, 28.2.1943, frame 3752002.

19 Weidinger, pg. 62.
20 Op cit and NA/T-354, roll 118, Tagesmeldung SS-Division "Das Reich" vom 27.2.1943, frame 3751901.

"Das Reich's" attack got off to a good start on 28 February. Regiment "Der Führer" swung around Krasnopawlovka and reached the nearby town of Rasdolje before noon. The regiment launched its attack upon Krasnopawlovka from Rasdolje. The SS Grenadiers were supported by Krag's assault guns and once again the battery of Sturmgeschütze IIIs was vitally important to the success of the attack. Several Russian tanks were entrenched on the edge of the town, interspersed along a defensive front studded with anti-tank guns and machine gun positions. After conducting a battle reconnaissance, Krag found an uncovered gap in the Russian perimeter, through which his assault guns were able to approach several of the Soviet tanks without being seen. Krag got his Sturmgeschütze in position to fire at the Russian tanks from the flank. Two of the T-34s were hit with the first rounds and put out of action, after which a third backed out of its position and scuttled away.

The SS Grenadiers quickly followed up Krag's success with an assault on that section of the perimeter. After hours of hard fighting, the SS Grenadiers forced their way into the town and SS assault groups began to stalk the rest of the entrenched Russian tanks. In support of the advance, Krag personally directed the vehicles of his battery into positions where they were able to destroy four additional T-34s, three anti-tank guns and a number of infantry positions. The fighting continued until the afternoon hours, when most of the Russians defending the town withdrew to the north. Regiment "Der Führer" cleaned up the last resistance by nightfall.[21]

Harmel's Regiment "Deutschland," on the right flank of the division's line of advance, made quicker progress to the north. Meeting little resistance, forward elements of the regiment reached the town of Otradava at 1600 hours. Several hours earlier, 6. Panzer-Division, advancing to the right of Regiment "Deutschland," had reached a range of hills a short distance east of Otradava. The remaining elements of the SS regiment closed up with the forward detachments later in the day and made contact with the Army troops. The Germans encountered generally light resistance and by nightfall, Harmel's regiment had completely assembled at Otradava, capturing large stores of Russian supplies, weapons and ammunition. At the end of the day, the division had reached its objectives, however "Totenkopf" did not experience a similar degree of success.

On 28 February, while "Das Reich pushed north in the Krasnopawlovka area, Max Simon experienced initial setbacks on his first day in command of "Totenkopf."[22] Simon was not able to concentrate all of the scattered tanks of the division at Panjutina, where Baum's Regiment "Totenkopf" awaited them in assembly

SS-Sturmbannführer Hans Weiss. At the rank of SS-Hauptsturmführer, Weiss commanded SS-Aufklärungs-abteilung 2, the reconnaissance battalion of "Das Reich." On 26 February Weiss' battalion supported III./"Der Führer's" attack on the important railroad center of Losovaja. (Courtesy of Mark C. Yerger)

areas east of the town. Sufficient armor did not begin to arrive until the late morning hours. Earlier in the day, Baum's regiment was also delayed while it cleared Soviet troops out of Jekaterinovka, a village on the railroad line, north of Panjutina. Baum then regrouped his regiment near Artelnoje, preparing to continue the attack as the division's left flank column. The Kampfgruppe drove north, without Leiner's tanks, advancing parallel to the course of the Orel River, rolling over a narrow, frozen dirt track. Russian infantry occupied several towns along the road and strong positions were encountered at the small villages of Ligowka and Lissowinovka.

In order to soften up the defenders of the two towns, Stukas bombed and strafed the Soviet positions during the afternoon and artillery shelled the Russians after the planes had completed their work. At 1230 hours the first elements of the regiment brushed past the stunned surviving defenders and crossed the Orel River at Ligowka. Reconnaissance patrols reported that large numbers of Russians occupied the area north of the village. Meanwhile, Leiner's tanks finally assembled on the road leading out of Panjutina's northwest quadrant. This road ran westward for a short distance until turning due north. It intersected a stretch of road and elevated railroad embankment south of Alexejevka.

Meanwhile Becker's SS-"Totenkopf"-PzG.-Rgt. 3, which will be called Regiment "Eicke" from this point on, finished cleaning out the remaining Russian troops in Krasnopawlovka and moved into several outlying villages north of the town. Later in the day, the regiment renewed its advance, traveling on a road that ran parallel to the railroad. Becker's regiment formed the right flank attack column of the division.

Sturmbannführer Max Seela's Pioniere-Bataillon 3 moved into Orelka where it served as the security detachment for the division's

---

[21] Weidinger, pg. 64, and Yerger, Ernst August Krag biography, pg. 14.
[22] Op cit.

Headquarters. Seela's Pioniere Bataillon had been relieved of its rear area security duties by elements of 15. Infanterie-Division. He was then ordered to proceed to Krasnopawlowka and serve as the corps mobile reserve. Russian resistance, which had been expected to be strong, weakened considerably, because the 1st Guards Army was in the process of withdrawing to the north. However, the Russians were not able to concentrate their efforts solely upon the SS divisions, because the XXXXVIII. Panzerkorps remained on the move also. The fast moving German spearheads smashed through the first Russian blocking positions and broke through the Russians lines before they could establish more organized defenses.

The XXXXVIII. Panzerkorps Attack

East of the SS-Panzerkorps attack sector, XXXXVIII. Panzerkorps, under Generalleutnant Gotthard Heinrici, began a parallel drive north after establishing bridgeheads over the Samara River on 25 February. The two divisions of the corps reached the area on both sides of the town of Stary Blisnezy, which was fifteen kilometers southeast of Losovaja. While "Das Reich" battled for Losovaja, 6. Panzer-Division encountered little effective resistance from the Russians and reached the village of Stary Blisnezy which was due east of Losovaj-Panjutina. Many demoralized Soviet troops began to surrender and the division soon had to secure over a thousand Russian prisoners. In addition, twenty-five cannons and anti-tank guns were captured or destroyed on 25 February. By late afternoon, the Stary Blisnezy sector was cleared of Russian troops. Other elements of the division were delayed by fighting to the southwest of the town.

Meanwhile, 17. Panzer-Division, commanded by Generalleutnant F.M. von Senger und Etterlin, operating on the right flank of the corps, crossed the Samara River at the town of Dobropolje which was defended by troops of the 195th Rifle Division. After a short fight, organized Russian resistance in the town was broken and the Germans occupied the entire town by 0915 hours. The remnants of the Soviet troops fled to the north in several columns, while the Panzer division rapidly pushed on, compensating for its relative weakness with speed, mobility, and audacity. The Luftwaffe conducted relentless and well coordinated air attacks on Soviet positions and supply detachments, smashing roadblocks and attacking troop columns.

The 17. Panzer-Division constantly pressured the Russians, launching attacks only split seconds after the last bombs fell upon the Soviet positions. Driving northward in an advance parallel to 6. Panzer-Division, Von Senger's handful of tanks and assault guns, reinforced by a few mobile anti-tank guns and the divisional Flak battalion, wreaked havoc upon the retreating Soviet soldiers. Riding into the midst of several hapless Russians formations, the SPWs and Panzers motored through the panic stricken infantry columns, blasting away at close range. One of the Soviet detachments contained the divisional Headquarters group of the 195th Rifle Division, including the commander and portions of his staff. For a time, the Russian command group was separated from the rest of the division. Fortunately for the Russians, von Senger's division could not afford to stop and the command group eventually rejoined the remainder of the division, which had been led to safety by the chief of staff. By midday, 17. Panzer-Division reached a range of low hills in the area twenty-five kilometers due east of Losovaja. They could hear the sounds of fighting, because "Das Reich" was still fighting to take the town.[23]

On 26 February, the two divisions turned the direction of their advance to the northwest. This was done in order to maintain contact with the SS-Panzerkorps which began to shift its line of advance in the same direction. The 17. Panzer-Division began operations at 0430 hours, advancing northward from Stary Blisnezy. After a brief encounter with a small Russian detachment, the forward elements of the division pushed on. The eastern flank of the division was covered by artillery fire directed upon known Soviet positions and bridges or key crossroads. The 6. Panzer-Division reached the railroad line between Losovaja and Stary Blisnezy, where it was halted by a Russian battalion which was dug into the railroad embankment. The elimination of the Soviet infantry took some hours. but once underway again the division continued its drive to the northwest.

The progress of the entire corps slowed at that point due to several reasons. The two divisions encountered positions manned by Russian rifle divisions which had arrived from the north. The Soviet 245th and 197th Rifle Divisions initially held strong, prepared positions although they were very weak in manpower. Another factor that contributed to the lack of progress by the two divisions was their almost nonexistent tank strength. By 26 February, 6. Panzer-Division had only six operational tanks and 17. Panzer-Division had only two Panzers still running. It was only due to the excellent coordination with the supporting Stukas and aggressive leadership of the German battalion commanders, that the two weakened divisions had enjoyed their surprising success. The Stukas efficiently blasted defensive positions of the Russians time and again, clearing a path for the lead elements the columns. Neither division was strong enough to quickly overwhelm determined resistance without such effective close support.[24]

---

[23] Glantz, pgs. 136-137 and NA/T-313, roll 367, Tagesmeldung 4. Panzerarmee vom 25.2.1943, frame 8653065.
[24] NA/T-313, roll 367, Tagesmeldung 4. Panzerarmee vom 27.2.1943, frame 8653095.

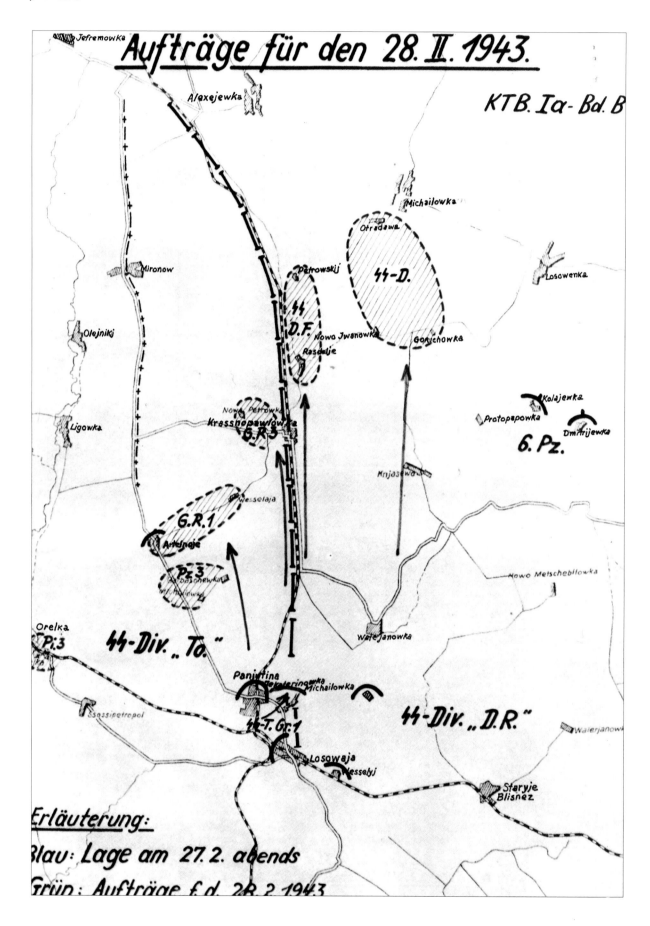

Aufträge für den 28. II. 1943.

KTB. Ia- Bd. B

Erläuterung:

Blau: Lage am 27. 2. abends

Grün: Aufträge f. d. 28. 2. 1943

Both divisions were engaged in tough fighting on the night of 26-27 February, because the Russians made a determined effort to hold their defensive line that ran from the area north of Stary Blisnezy and then eastward to Barvenkovo. However, the Russian rifle divisions were overextended and not able to hold the Germans for long. By 27 February, 17. Panzer-Division had shoved the 195th Rifle Division far to the north of the Stary Blisnezy railroad. The advance of the division created a dangerous penetration in the Soviet defensive line west of Barvenkovo. Von Senger's division kept moving north and approached the Northern Donets near Izyum, in the area where 320. Infanterie-Division had begun its long and grueling retreat early in February. However, the 6. Panzer-Division remained tied up in prolonged fighting and remained about fifteen kilometers behind the most forward elements of 17. Panzer-Division.

In the meantime, the XXXX. Panzerkorps, operating in the sector east of 17. Panzer-Division, approached Barvenkovo. Kuznetsov, the commander of the 1st Guards Army, placed the 38th, 44th and 52nd Guards Rifle Divisions in new defensive positions south and west of Barvenkovo. He ordered them to hold their line at all costs, in order to allow the debilitated Soviet tank corps and remnants of rifle divisions of the 6th Army to escape destruction. The line was buttressed with nearly fifty tanks, although most had little or no fuel. Dug in along the line, they served as steel pillboxes and proved to be a significant obstacle to the Germans in the Barvenkovo area.[25]

The 1. Panzerarmee's XXXX. Panzerkorps, with "Wiking" on the left, 11. Panzer-Division in the center and 7. Panzer-Division on the right, assaulted Russian defenses south of Barvenkovo on 26 February. The 7. Panzer-Division fought for possession of several fortified villages east of Barvenkovo, which were defended by elements of the 18th and 10th Tank Corps, were supported by infantry and artillery. The main attack group of the division was led by division commander, Generalleutnant von Funck. It was composed of the division's remaining tanks, supported by PzG.-Rgt. 6 and Kradschützen-Bataillon 7. During the afternoon, the division fought off counterattacks by small groups Russian tanks, unsupported by infantry or artillery. The Germans destroyed two T-34s and a KV-1. However, even after several Stuka attacks upon the line of defended Russian villages, the Panzergrenadier regiment, reduced to a strength of less than 500 men, was unable to make a breakthrough. At night-

fall the fighting continued in that sector without any German success. In a supporting attack, PzG.-Rgt. 7 established a small bridgehead over the Torets River near the town of Novo Alexandrovka.[26]

Meanwhile, 11. Panzer-Division found the going hard east of Barvenkovo, where the Russian defensive line was studded with numerous anti-tank guns. Again Stuka attacks were unable to break Soviet defenses and the attack remained stalled. Late in the day, the Russians launched a strong tank counterthrust that forced the division to halt its attack and go over to the defensive. "Wiking" had more success during its attacks west of Barvenkovo. The division's assault groups established a bridgehead over the Suchoj Torez River. By late afternoon, "Wiking" tanks and Panzergrenadiers pushed out of the bridgehead and attacked Soviet defensive positions about ten kilometers northwest of Barvenkovo. The XXXX. Panzerkorps reported that it destroyed a total of twenty-one Soviet tanks during the fighting between Barvenkovo and Stary Blisnezy. However, the corps made no decisive breakthrough until the following day.[27]

The Soviet defense of the Barvenkovo area began to weaken under the steady attack by the three divisions which threatened to envelop the town. The 11. Panzer-Division battled steadily forward, driving toward Barvenkovo from the south in spite of a Soviet counterattack by ten to fifteen tanks. Division anti-tank guns knocked out six of the T-34s and the counterattack failed. After this last ditch attempt to throw the Germans back, the Soviet defenses began to collapse on either side of Barvenkovo. Although the town itself remained strongly held, there were signs of weakening Soviet resistance.

A group of eleven Russian tanks attempted to escape from Barvenkovo along the Barvenkovo-Izyum road, but was intercepted by 11. Panzer-Division. Several Russian tanks were knocked out and rest raced back into the town. The 1. Panzerarmee accounts report unexpected, disorderly Soviet withdrawals in several areas. Abruptly the division began to break into the Soviet perimeter and make penetrations. By the end of the day, XXXX. Panzerkorps reported that it destroyed a total of forty-five Russian tanks. The 1. Panzerarmee estimated that the majority of the tanks belonging to the 4th Guards, the 18th and 10th Tank Corps had been largely eliminated. On the western flank of the corps, "Wiking" elements made contact with XXXXVIII. Panzerkorps' 17. Panzer-Division. On the basis of Soviet tank losses, as well as accurate intelligence about the Russian's fuel situation, the army correctly concluded

[25] Glantz, pg. 137.
[26] Hasso von Manteuffel, *Die 7. Panzer-Division im Zweiten Weltkrieg, 1939-1945,* (Freidberg: 1986) page 327.
[27] NA/T-313, roll 46, 1a KTB - Darstellung der Ereignisse:1. Panzerarmee, frame 000514.

OPPOSITE: The two divisions attacked parallel to the section of railroad between Krasnopawlovka and Alexejevka on 28 February. After reaching the Alexejevka area "Das Reich" and "Totenkopf" linked up with "Leibstandarte" and swung to the west of Kharkov, in preparation for beginning the attack upon the city. North of Alexejevka, the 3rd Tank Army was crushed between the attacking columns of SS-Panzerkorps and pushed into a pocket near the town of Kegitschevka.

Half tracks and motorcycles of "Das Reich" on a frozen, snow covered road south of Kharkov during February, 1943. With few exceptions, the roads in the Ukraine were not paved and proved to be very hard on the motor vehicles of the German divisions. "Das Reich's" tanks and vehicles were so worn out by March that division commander Ernst Vahl sent a message to Himmler personally, in hopes that he could get new vehicles for the division. Himmler was not able to rectify the situation. (Courtesy of Mark C. Yerger)

that Mobile Group Popov had lost virtually all of its heavy weapons tanks. German intelligence intercepted Russian radio reports that clearly detailed the serious loss of tanks in Popov's disintegrating Mobile Group. It became evident that the danger of a Russian armored strike against "Wiking" and 7. Panzer-Division was negligible, because the few surviving Soviet tanks were without fuel. As a result of this intelligence and to avoid squandering time as well as limited resources of men and machines, 1. Panzerarmee decided to envelope Barvenkovo rather than attack it directly. While 11. Panzer-Division conducted holding attacks upon the town from the south, the other two divisions were to swing past the strongpoint and continue toward the Northern Donets and Izyum confident their flanks were secure.[28]

On 28 February, XXXX. Panzerkorps carried out its plan to encircle the remaining Soviet forces in Barvenkovo. The 7. Panzer-Division attacked successfully during the night of 27-28 February.

The forward elements of the division reached the Barvenkovo-Izyum road in the afternoon. The division advanced along this road, toward the northwest and reached a point approximately halfway between Izyum and Barvenkovo. Meanwhile, "Wiking" drove even farther to the north, against steadily disintegrating Soviet resistance. The forward elements of the division caught up with and passed 17. Panzer-Division, which by that time was reduced to a strength of less than 2000 men, six tanks and a few assault guns. SS security detachments replaced the elements of 17. Panzer-Division at a crossing of the Bereka River north of the town of Gruschevacha in the early hours of the day. A "Wiking" Kampfgruppe reached the southern bank of the Northern Donets River after dark.[29]

The 11. Panzer-Division continued its infantry assaults upon the southern and eastern perimeter of Barvenkovo. A small mobile battle group swung to the east and attacked the northern edge of the town, knocking out or capturing a number of Soviet tanks. Resis-

[28] Glantz, pg. 140 and NA/T-313, roll 46, 1a KTB-1. Panzerarmee, Darstellung der Ereignisse, frame 000521.

[29] NA/T-313, roll 46, 1a KTB-1. Panzerarmeee, Darstellung der Ereignisse, frame 000521 and Glantz, pg. 140.

tance rapidly melted away after the destruction of the Russian armor, although in the southern sector of the town, fighting continued to be bitter because the Russian troops could no longer withdraw. A stubbornly defended bridge north of the town was captured intact after German Pioniere troops rushed across the span and disarmed the explosive charges that had been placed upon it. Late in the afternoon, the fighting in the town began to wind down as the Germans rooted out the last stubborn Russian infantry. Small groups that could escape filtered out of the town to the northeast, accompanied by surviving tank crews.

By nightfall on 28 February, Russian forces were in full retreat from Barvenkovo. Some of the Soviet columns were able to move between the advancing elements of "Wiking" and 7. Panzer-Division. These troops and vehicles streamed northwards along roads leading to Izyum. The XXXX. Panzerkorps directed its divisions to drive north and link up at a point on the west bank of the Donets River, about twenty kilometers west of Izyum in order to block the crossings of the Northern Donets north of Barvenkovo. If successful, this would close the remaining routes of escape between the sectors already controlled by elements of "Wiking" and 7. Panzer-Division.

The Withdrawal of the 6th and 1st Guards Army

The Panzer divisions of the SS-Panzerkorps, XXXXVIII. Panzerkorps and 1. Panzerarmee's XXXX. Panzerkorps advanced on a front fifty kilometers in width. The fact that the contact between the divisions was tenuous and that most of the Army divisions were hardly more than regimental battle groups did not matter.

As we have seen, Soviet operations prior to 28 February still showed a failure by the Russian high command echelons to understand the capabilities of its depleted armies and the German threat. The Stavka apparently discounted or ignored the potential danger of continued German advances past Kharkov and issued directives to Voronezh Front that reflected a false optimism. Golikov was ordered to continue his attack. He directed his 40th and 69th Armies, although both were worn down and short of all supplies, to continue attacks west of Kharkov and push forward on a broad front. Kazakov, the commander of the 69th Army, had very few tanks still running and his rifle divisions were considerably weakened. They had suffered crippling losses of infantry and artillery during the fighting in February. Kazakov responded to the orders to renew his attacks by questioning the advisability of continuing to advance west. Although his concern was obviously legitimate, the Voronezh Front headquarters responded with a sarcastic rebuke. Golikov sourly noted the distance remaining between Kazakov's spearheads and his primary objectives and the time remaining before the onset of the spring muddy season. He ended the brief conversation with the caustic comment that Kazakov should make the necessary 'conclusions.'[30]

Apparently, however the full extent of the approaching disaster began to dawn on the Stavka, Golikov and the eternal optimist, Vatutin after 28 February. Many of the remnants of the fragmented 6th Army, cut to pieces by Manstein's offensive, were being destroyed by 15. Infanterie-Division and elements of "Totenkopf." The 1st Guards Army was no longer capable of offensive action. The Soviet command, finally recognizing that the remaining elements of the 6th Army and 1st Guards Army could be destroyed by the advance of the three German Panzer corps, ordered the two armies to attempt to pull back to the Northern Donets area. The withdrawal was to be covered by 3rd Tank Army, which was to assault the strongest German formation, the SS-Panzerkorps. At that point, Rybalko's army no longer had the resources to conduct a successful counterattack on Hausser's Panzer divisions. In spite of its weakness, the Soviet command ordered Rybalko's 3rd Tank Army to block the German advance by launching a counterattack upon the SS-Panzerkorps. However, after the severe losses of men and tanks sustained during the hard fighting of February, the army was nearing exhaustion. Only a trickle of replacement tanks reached the army and few if any infantry replacements were available. The counterattack had little hope of success and would result in the destruction of the 12th and 15th Tank Corps.

---

[30] Erickson, pg. 55.

11

THE DESTRUCTION OF THE 3RD TANK ARMY

In the days preceding its reception of the order to attack the SS-Panzerkorps, the 3rd Tank Army had maintained steady, if weakening pressure on Korps Raus. In these operations, the Russians slowly pushed the Germans back, making tactical gains, but suffered a steady attrition of precious tanks, artillery and men. Rybalko was never able to gain a decisive advantage. The Germans always managed to escape or immediately counterattacked and regained their losses. During the last days of February, Armeeabteilung Kempf conducted a phased retreat, steadily inflicting losses upon the Russian, draining the army of offensive strength. The Russian attacks struck at one point or another, creating only temporary gaps, which were blocked and then sealed off by the Germans. Aggressive German counterattacks struck at the flanks of the Russian thrusts, eating away at Rybalko's manpower and armor. By the end of the month, the 3rd Tank Army no longer had the resources to make a significant penetration in the German lines. The Soviet armor and infantry had been so reduced that assaults the Germans believed to be combat reconnaissance attacks, were attacks made with all the strength that Rybalko could then muster.

As of 28 February, Armeeabteilung Kempf had successfully maintained its defensive bastion around Krasnograd until the attack of the SS-Panzerkorps reduced the Soviet pressure on the salient. The previous shortening of the front allowed the creation of a German operational reserve for the first time. Kempf's army had often been hard pressed, but had maintained a coherent defense and was no longer in danger of suffering a collapse. In fact, it had weathered the strongest part of the Russian storm, because the counterattack by 4. Panzerarmee soon effectively removed the 3rd Tank Army from its sector.

In order to establish a reserve, "Grossdeutschland" had been withdrawn from the fighting and assembled near Poltava. New trucks, tanks and hundreds of replacements, as well as tons of equipment arrived daily. The division received a second battalion of tanks, including a company of "Tiger" tanks which were organized into Panzer-Regiment "Grossdeutschland." The regiment commander was Oberst Graf von Strachwitz, a highly competent, Silesian professional soldier of noble birth who was nicknamed the "Panzer Count." Some elements of "Grossdeutschland" remained involved in fighting, where their aggressiveness and mobility were key factors in blocking weakening Soviet thrusts toward the Poltava-Kolomak-Kharkov railroad line. Screening the rest area of the division was the Aufklärungsabteilung, supported by II./Grenadier Regiment "GD," the Führer-Begleit-Bataillon and the division's Sturmgeschütz Bataillon. Providing artillery support for these detachments were two batteries of the artillery regiment.[1]

From 25 to 28 February, the Soviets continued their efforts to push westward and cut the key railroad between Polatava and Kharkov, but attrition had reduced the strength of 40th and 69th Armies. The Russians continued to maintain a weak presence farther to the west but it was obvious their strength had declined markedly. The Russian 69th Army's support and supply system became more strained every day, a situation aggravated by increasing frequent Luftwaffe attacks, which destroyed valuable trucks and wagons. The 40th Army attacked the main remnants of 168. Infanterie-Division at Sinkiw and was not able to overrun even that weak collection of survivors. The "Grossdeutschland" Aufklärungs-abteilung and Sturmgeschütz Bataillon turned back Russian thrusts toward the Poltava-Ljubotin railroad in the area around Kolomak. While "Grossdeutschland" units secured the gap between the right wing of 167. Infanterie-Division and 320. Infanterie-Division, Regi-

---

[1] Spaeter, pg. 57.

ment "Thule" reinforced 320. Infanterie-Division and helped the division defend its assigned its section of the Krasnograd bastion.

The most dangerous attacks were mounted against German defensive positions between Kolomak and the town of Schelestovo, both of which were located on the Poltava-Ljubotin railroad about thirty kilometers west of Ljbotin. At Schelestovo, the Soviet 69th Army was able to break through the German lines in the sector between units of 320. Infanterie-Division and the "Grossdeutschland" detachments on its flank. Regiment "Thule" immediately launched counterattacks during the night of 25-26 February and blocked the Russian breakthroughs in the 320. Infanterie-Division sector. On the following day, Regiment "Thule" took over most of the sector and allowed 320. Infanterie-Division to reorganize in new defensive positions. Other elements of the regiment supported the "Grossdeutschland" Aufklärungsabteilung in the heavily forested area around Kolomak.[2]

On the following morning, 320. Infanterie-Division was still on the march out of the Valki area, covered by Regiment "Thule" and rear guard detachments of the division, which knocked out two T-34s during the course of the morning. German dive bombers and fighter planes were active over the battlefield, striking the supply lines of the 3rd Tank Army's 12th Tank Corps. The German planes were essentially unopposed by the Soviet air force and operated without interference, other than from small arms fire from infantry. The Soviet maintained light pressure on the division in the form of reconnaissance attacks in company or platoon strength, but did not mount any strong attacks. The 320. Infanterie-Division was strengthened by a few tanks of Panzerzug 62, the ad hoc unit thrown together from scavenged tanks and assault guns. The detachment possessed eight Panzer IIIs or IVs, one Sturmgeschütze III and a mix of light armored vehicles. Farther west, the 15th Tank Corps, supported by infantry units of the 111th Rifle Division attacked Novo Vodolaga, attempting to push around the town to both sides. After the withdrawal of the last German rear guard detachments the Russians occupied the town under continuous attacks by the Luftwaffe.[3]

Near Valki, a company of the Pioniere Bataillon of 167. Infanterie-Division re-established contact with the "Grossdeutschland" Aufklärungsabteilung west of Kolomak restoring the situation west of Kolomak. Other troops of the division held a defensive line stretching westward from the town of Rublevka which was on the western border of the disputed gap. The division remained under attack by Russian infantry and the fighting contin-

SS-Obersturmführer Ralf Tiemann, the adjutant of SS-Panzer Regiment 1. On 1 March, 1943 the Russians attacked toward Krasnograd from the Olkhovatka area. This attack created a potential crisis situation when the Russians established a bridgehead from which division commander Dietrich feared they could mount an attack upon the Poltava-Ljubotin rail road. Tiemann led an attack group of tanks, assault guns and Panzergrenadiers which blocked the Soviet advance and stabilized the situation. (Courtesy of Mark C. Yerger)

ued throughout 26 February. However, the Soviet attacks did not have tank or strong artillery support and these attempts to take the division's positions were defeated. On 27 February, the division began to conduct aggressive reconnaissance attacks to the east, into the Jeremejevka-Kegitschevka area, where its patrols discovered strong Russian defensive positions.

Into the Maelstrom - The 3rd Tank Army Turns South

In the 3rd Tank Army sector, which extended roughly from Valki to east to Krasnograd, Rybalko planned a last major effort to take Valki

---

[2] NA/T-314, roll 490, 1a KTB, Tagesmeldung Korps Raus, 25.2.43, frame 000184.
[3] Ibid. frame 000185-000195.

with his remaining armor, while on his southern flank several rifle divisions tried to take Krasnograd. After the 12th Tank Corps forced the Germans out of the area north of the town, the Soviet tanks and supporting infantry assembled north and east of Krasnograd. Russian guns began shelling the town and strong patrols probed the perimeter. Often these patrols were accompanied by two or three tanks. Fortunately for Korps Raus, the 320. Infanterie-Division had a more than adequate anti-tank capability and was able to knock out many of these tanks. Korps Raus records list the division as possessing five 5cm guns, three self-propelled 7.5cm guns and twelve PAK 40s, the newest model German anti-tank gun. The Panzerjäger Kompanie of Regiment "Thule" added a mobile anti-tank capability that was available to the division. Rybalko's plans were disrupted after he received orders to relocate his army and counterattack the SS-Panzerkorps.

By 27-28 February, Russian pressure in the 3rd Tank Army area began to decrease, as more and more of Rybalko's army began the relocation to the south. Luftwaffe reconnaissance reported Soviet columns leaving the Valki area and moving toward the Kegitschevka area, which was east of the defensive positions held by "Leibstandarte." Kegitschevka was to be the assembly area for the major armored elements of the army, which began to arrive in the area by 28 February. After giving up two of his rifle divisions to 69th Army, Rybalko concentrated his tank corps between Kegitschevka and Jefremovka, in preparation for their attack.

The 15th Tank Corps began to reach the Kegitschevka assembly area after marching throughout the night of 28 February. The 12th Tank Corps followed with lead elements of the corps arriving in the same area by the morning of 1 March. The 6th Guards Cavalry Corps concentrated at the town of Jefremovka to protect the assembly area from German attacks. The Russian infantry immediately began to dig in and prepare a screen of defensive positions stretching across the path of the SS divisions. At Kegitschevka, infantry of the 111th, 184th and 219th Rifle Divisions occupied defensive positions around the town. Behind the thin screen of rifle divisions, although having only thirty operational tanks, the 3rd Tank Army prepared to launch its counterattack on 2 March. However, fuel and ammunition shortages forced Rybalko to postpone the army's attack until the morning of 3 March. A counterattack was never actually launched and the tanks were kept in reserve or dug in to reinforce the defensive positions of the army.[4]

The Germans were aware of significant Russian troop movements passing through the area bordered by the Berestovaja and Orel Rivers. Armeeabteilung Kempf had detected long columns of infantry, sleds, vehicles and tanks, marching south through the area

east of the front of "Leibstandarte." Stukas and fighter-bombers struck repeatedly at these columns, harassing the marching Russians and causing additional casualties and vehicle destruction. "Leibstandarte" conducted raids on the columns which further reduced the number of tanks Rybalko had in action by the time his emaciated army assembled around Kegitschevka. The Luftwaffe also harassed supply columns attempting to reach the assembly areas and these actions may have contributed to the postponement of Rybalko's attack. The Germans were also aware that the Russians were digging in east of the SS division, but did not know what these development signified, although it was apparent a major relocation was in progress. While "Das Reich" and "Totenkopf" drove north, towards Kegitschevka and a collision with the 3rd Tank Army, "Leibstandarte" received orders to conduct a reconnaissance operation in force toward Kegitschevka and the other assembly areas around Jeremejevka.

On 28 February, Meyer's Aufklärungsabteilung, I./Panzer-Regiment "LAH," and an attached battalion of self-propelled howitzers assembled west of Kegitschevka. To the northeast of Krasnograd, III./SS-PzG.-Rgt. 2 "LAH," supported by a company of assault guns, was to defend the left flank of Meyer's reinforced Aufklärungsabteilung. Before the mission departed, a Soviet break through northwest of Krasnograd, near the village of Olkhovatka caused a temporary crisis. Dietrich became concerned that if the Russians attacked in strength at that point, the supply line of the division extending to Poltava would be endangered. The critical sector was defended by SS-PzG.-Rgt. 1 "LAH" and Dietrich ordered regiment commander Witt to clean up the situation, destroy the attacking Soviet force and occupy Olkhovatka.[5]

A Kampfgruppe commanded by SS-Obersturmführer Ralf Tiemann, the 1a of the Panzer regiment, was assembled to deal with the situation on 1 March. At 0445 hours, with sixty Panzergrenadiers riding on his tanks, Tiemann began the attack. He intended to rendezvous with a battery of assault guns. The Kampfgruppe reached the area south of Olkhovatka without incident and Tiemann sent out two reconnaissance groups. One patrol was to establish contact with the assault guns while the main attack group, made up of six Panzer IIIs and Panzer IIs, approached Olkhovatka itself. Under cover of the Panzer IIIs, a forward recon group, consisting of two of the light tanks, approached the town. Almost immediately, the Panzer IIs came under Russian tank and anti-tank gun fire but were able to pull back. The covering group of Panzers spotted the position of a Russian tank and destroyed it while covering the withdrawal of the patrol. However, one tank of the patrol detachment was struck and burned out.

---

[4] Glantz, pg. 189.

[5] Lehmann, pg. 134.

At 1200 hours, Tiemann was informed that a company of "Leibstandarte" tanks and assault guns, supported by Frey's battalion, was preparing to attack the town from the east. Tiemann's mission was to support their assault by attacking from the south and west. Just before the attack was to jump off, SS artillery began to pound Olkhovatka, catching some of the Russian tank crews when they were refueling. A few minutes later Tiemann's Panzer IIIs opened fire on the western edge of the town. The Grenadiers and Sturmgeschütz IIIs moved into position to assault the town perimeter.[6]

The rolling hills east of Olkhovatka were still icy and the Sturmgeschütze had difficulties getting into position for their attack. After the last assault guns reached the ridge crest, they deployed and advanced in battle order toward Olkhovatka. SS Grenadiers perched on the assault gun decks, ready to leap off as soon as firing began. There was no reaction from the Russians until the Germans were less than 500 meters from the outskirts of the town and then a storm of fire broke out. Heavy weapons fire, mortar

---

[6] Ibid. pg. 137.

shells and small arms fire lashed out at the advancing Sturmgeschütze. The Grenadiers dived off the assault guns and tumbled into whatever depression or ravine was available. At least one Sturmgeschütz was damaged and the Grenadiers could not advance. The attack stalled in the face of this stout resistance.

After dark, the Germans brought up 15cm infantry guns and under the personal leadership of Fritz Witt, assaulted the village again. The heavy 15cm shells passed above the half frozen Panzergrenadiers, who had scrabbled shallow holes in the frozen earth and impacted on the village perimeter. The high explosives blasted Russian huts apart, suppressing defensive fire and knocking out several anti-tank gun positions. With additional covering fire from their tanks, the Panzergrenadiers moved forward again, sheltering behind their assault guns. Two Sturmgeschütz IIIs and one tank were hit and knocked out of action by Soviet anti-tank gun fire but the SS infantry broke into Olkhovatka and began to systematically root the Russians out of their positions.

Uncharacteristically, Soviet resistance collapsed suddenly and the Russians pulled back from the western edge of Olkhovatka. Several Soviet tanks and about two companies of infantry tried to

Knight's Cross winner Martin Gross, pictured here as an SS-Sturmbannführer. Gross commanded II./SS-Panzer Regiment 1 in early 1943 and won the German Cross in Gold after the Kharkov campaign. He was awarded the Knight's Cross for his battalion's performance during the fighting around Prochorovka on 12 July of 1943. In a single day, the battalion destroyed more than ninety Russian tanks west of the town. Gross survived the war and did not pass away until 1984. (Courtesy of Mark C. Yerger)

SS-Obersturmbannführer Albert Frey, the commander of I./SS-Panzergrenadier-Regiment 1 "LSSAH." Frey's battalion was in the thick of the defensive fighting east of Kharkov in February, 1943 and played a key role in the recapture of the city after "Leibstandarte" went over to offensive action in early March. He was awarded the Knight's Cross on 3 March, 1943. (The author's collection)

SS-Oberscharführer Alfred Günther, an assault gun battery commander in "Leibstandarte." Günther won the Knight's Cross on 3 March, 1943 for his combat leadership during the Kharkov fighting and earlier engagements. He was killed in action in June of 1944 during fighting in France, shortly after the Allied invasion of Normandy. (Courtesy of Mark C. Yerger)

SS-Hauptsturmführer Ernst Dehmel, commander of "Totenkopf's" 1./Batterie SS-Sturmgeschütz-Bataillon 3. During late February and early March of 1943, Dehmel's battery supported Regiment "Thule" during the fighting for the Poltava-Valki-Kharkov railroad southwest of Ljubotin. He later took command of the battalion and led it until shortly before the end of the war. He died in August 1945, due to severe wounds he had received in late April. (Courtesy of Mark C. Yerger)

SS-Hauptsturmführer Walter Gerth, the commander of 7. Kompanie SS-Artillerie-Regiment 3. He was awarded the Knight's Cross for his unit's performance in support of Regiment "Thule" when it was subordinated to 320. Infanterie-Division. (Courtesy of Mark C. Yerger)

cross the Ortschik River and escape into a nearby marsh. Two of the tanks became bogged down in the soft ground and were destroyed. Some of the Russian infantry were killed or wounded as they floundered through the icy cold mud and water of the Ortschik but many of the Russians were able to reach safety. Four tanks somehow successfully navigated the marsh and also escaped.[7]

During the night of 28 February-1 March, "Leibstandarte" received new orders for the following day. It was to attack to the east from its positions around Krasnograd, thus striking the flank of the 3rd Tank Army just as it was engaged to its front by the attack of the SS-Panzerkorps. However, some reconnaissance information indicated that the Russians were withdrawing to the north. Of course,

the 6th Army rifle divisions were withdrawing northward. What was unclear to the Germans was that Rybalko's army was moving into the area at the same time. Russian columns were moving in two different directions and this contributed to seemingly contradictory reports from air reconnaissance.

At 1000 hours, Armeeabteilung Kempf ordered "Leibstandarte" to assemble a Kampfgruppe for an attack designed to cut Rybalko's lines of communications north of Kegitschevka. Dietrich suggested sending out a strong reconnaissance force due north of Kegitschevka, in order to keep pressure on the Russian rear guard if they were withdrawing. The main attack was to continue toward Jefremovka.

Dietrich also proposed to use the reinforced SS-PzG.-Rgt. 2 "LAH" in an attack against Russian positions in the Staroverovka-Taranovka sector. The army agreed with these proposals. Dietrich

---

[7] Lehmann, pg. 137-138.

On 1 March, 1943 Regiment "Deutschland" spearheaded the attack of "Das Reich" upon positions held by Rybalko's 3rd Tank Army. The regiment was led by II./Regiment "Deutschland" commanded by Fritz Ehrath. Its attack was supported by Heinz Macher's Pioniere company which rode into the battle on the decks of Marder's from the division's Panzerjäger battalion. (Courtesy of Mark C. Yerger)

The crew of an SS half track with a 7.5cm anti-tank gun mounted in what was probably a field modification, watches as a target burns in the distance. The picture shows a typical expanse of the snow covered terrain in the Kharkov area. (Credit National Archives)

was aware that the SS-Panzerkorps advance was expected to link up with his division if all went well over the next few days. It was hoped that "Leibstandarte's" attack would reduce the resistance of the 3rd Tank Army to the advance of "Totenkopf" and "Das Reich," which were driving north, toward Kegitschevka.[8]

On the night of 1 March, the last of the 3rd Tank Army forces gradually completed their assembly near the Kegitschevka-Jeremejevka area. Portions of these troops occupied extensive trench systems, positioned to block the advance of the SS-Panzerkorps. In the morning, elements of Witt's regiment attacked to the northwest from the town of Jarotin. The objective of this attack was Krutaja Balka, which was directly on the supply lines of the remaining Russian forces around Nagornaja-Olkhovatka. The attack was successful and Frey's battalion reached its objective by mid-afternoon, also reestablishing contact with the eastern flank of 320. Infanterie-Division by 1650 hours.[9]

At first light, Wisch's Kampfgruppe began its advance on Kegitschevka. However, muddy roads and strong Russian defenses thwarted any significant progress in that area after early morning. The initial attack ran into a Russian column east of Ziglerovka, which Peiper's battalion attacked and destroyed. However, when the temperature gradually rose, the roads became nearly impassable due to deep mud. Several of "Leibstandarte's" tanks became bogged down or broke down mechanically. After the armor was delayed and was not able to support the infantry, the attack foundered in the mud. Dietrich was on the scene and was of the opinion that little would be gained by trying to attack strong, entrenched Soviet positions with unsupported infantry. He ordered the divisional artillery to shell Soviet position around Kegitschevka and

---

[8] *Befehl des Gewissens*, pg. 182-183.
[9] Op cit.

SS-Hauptscharführer Adolf Peichl, a platoon commander in III./Regiment "Der Führer" who was particularly adept at destroying tanks in close assault. On his right sleeve he wears badges for the single-handed destruction of a number of tanks. He was one of the most highly decorated soldiers of the regiment, receiving the Knight's Cross, German Cross in Gold and various other medals including the extremely rare Close Combat Clasp in Gold and both classes of the Iron Cross. (Courtesy of Mark C. Yerger)

SS-Standartenführer Otto Kumm, commander of Regiment "Der Führer" during the Kharkov fighting, strikes a relaxed pose for the camera. Kumm remains active in regimental and divisional veterans groups as of this writing. (Courtesy of Mark C. Yerger)

the SS artillery maintained harassing fire throughout the day. Reconnaissance patrols found that the Russians had dug in and emplaced many anti-tank guns around the perimeter of the town. The Panzer regiment and Meyer's reinforced battalion regrouped during the afternoon and night, preparing for a renewal of the attack on the following day.

Manstein was following the progress of "Leibstandarte's" operations and had a radio conversation with Kempf late on 1 March which seemed to indicate either a lapse in command or lack of effort by Dietrich's division. He stressed the importance of "Leibstandarte" in relation to the success of the counterattack of Hausser's SS-Panzerkorps. The assumption of criticism due to the failure of "Leibstandarte's" attack upon Kegitschevka and Manstein's inquiries appear to have agitated Kempf and he communicated to Heeresgruppe Süd that Dietrich had been issued absolutely correct verbal and written order. However, the Ia of Armeeabteilung Kempf stressed that the weather and road conditions in the entire sector east of the Vorskla River made operations of mobile units very difficult, if not impossible. In no uncertain terms, the Armeeabteilung supported Dietrich's estimation of the situation at Kegitschevka and Manstein pressed the matter no further. He then turned to other matters and inquired about "Grossdeutschland," wanting to know when it was to be available for further mobile operations. Kempf replied that it would be 4 March before the division would be able to complete its refitting and stressed that the division's advance could be expected to be more successful if it was conducted in support of a strong attack by the SS-Panzerkorps from south Kharkov.[10]

Korps Raus Defensive Operations

In other areas, the three infantry divisions of Korps Raus experienced little significant Russian activity. The 320. Infanterie-Division maintained contact with the northern flank of "Leibstandarte" in the Krutaja Balka area. The division's heavy weapons situation had improved markedly. It then possessed thirty-nine anti-tank guns, as well as six Sturmgeschütze and eight tanks of Panzerzug 62. It was reinforced with Regiment "Thule," II./Grenadier Regiment "Grossdeutschland" and the heavy Panzerjäger company of "Grossdeutschland," as well as additional artillery.

However, in spite of the increased fire power assigned to the division, the SS troops and "Grossdeutschland" were continually called upon to help the division restore its front. It seems that Postel regularly had difficulties establishing exactly where his divisional

Otto Kumm and SS-Obersturmbannführer Karl Ullrich, the SS-Panzer-Korps chief of Pioniere. On 2 March, Ullrich was with "Totenkopf's" SS-Pioniere-Bataillon 3, which was working non-stop to keep rear area roads serviceable. Ullrich formerly commanded the battalion during the fighting in the Demyansk pocket. He returned to the division on 17 March, 1943 after Joachim Schubach, the commander of III./Regiment "Totenkopf," was wounded and Ullrich took over the battalion. (Courtesy Mark C. Yerger)

boundaries were located and even more trouble defending them. The Borki situation was an earlier instance of the division calling on its SS neighbor to help clear up a situation of its own making.

A company of Regiment "Thule" had to counterattack a small Russian break through near the divisional boundary between 320. and 167. Infanterie-Division, when Postel informed Raus that his division could not deal with the penetration. In co-operation with a platoon of II./Infanterie-Regiment 331 from 167. Infanterie-Division, 6./Kompanie, II./Regiment "Thule," supported by two assault guns and a platoon of SS Pioniere, attacked Russian positions around the village of Skebivka. With the Pioniere troops on the left flank, the SS troops and assault guns in the center and the Army platoon on the right, the Kampfgruppe advanced on Skebivka from a neighboring village. The Germans received effective flanking fire from Russian mortars and small arms, which inflicted casualties on the attackers when they approached the southwest edge of Skebivka. After the army platoon suffered losses from this flanking fire, they went to ground and fell behind. The 6./Kompanie and the SS Pioniere continued to advance, although the Kampfgruppe lost one Sturmgeschütze in the process.[11]

---

[10] *Befehl des Gewissens*, pg. 185.

[11] Vopersal, pg. 171. The SS Pioniere Zug (platoon) had 2 killed, 3 missing in action and 7 wounded, significant losses for a platoon. The Zug from II./Infanterie-Regiment 331, lost 13 men to wounds.

"Leibstandarte" Sturmgeschütz IIIs moving with difficulty up an ice and snow covered road. By early March, the first signs of the spring thaw were sometimes evident, but temperatures still plunged to below freezing after dark. Mud and slush froze overnight and road conditions in the early morning hours were often very difficult. (Credit National Archives)

Fighting from house to house, the SS troops pushed the Russians down the length of Skebivka and were then joined by the Pioniere Zug. However, just as it looked as if the village would fall into German hands within a short time, one of the Sturmgeschütz IIIs, without orders, swung out into an open field beside the village, in pursuit of a group of fleeing Russian troops. This unwise maneuver exposed its flank to a 4.7cm Russian anti-tank gun crew. It was instantly hit by a round that penetrated the engine compartment and put it out of action. A subsequent hit struck the ammunition storage compartment and the Sturmgeschütze exploded in a thunderous roar. At that moment, Palm's Kampfgruppe, then reduced to only 20 men, was attacked by Russian infantry who were encouraged by the destruction of the assault gun. After repulsing the Soviet attack, the SS troops had very little ammunition and the remaining assault gun had no shells for its cannon or machine guns. Palm sent it to the rear to bring more ammunition and took the opportunity to evacuate a number of the wounded, which were piled on to the assault gun deck.

Russian heavy mortar fire began to fall on the SS Grenadiers, who were rejoined by the platoon of army troops. With this welcome reinforcement, Palm built up an organized defensive position, supported by the fire of a battery of "Totenkopf" artillery, which was well directed by a forward observer accompanying the battle group. The Sturmgeschütz returned with its precious cargo of ammunition, which was distributed under continuous fire from the

Russian mortars and heavy weapons. The II./Regiment "Thule" commander, Georg Bochmann was on hand, having returned to command after his earlier wound. He received a report from Palm who proposed to continue the attack and take the eastern edge of the town. However, at that time, Bochmann received a report that the army platoon had left its position and withdrawn without orders to do so. To make matters worse, the forward observer lost radio contact with the artillery battery. Since it was near dark, Bochmann decided to pull Palm's company out of Skebivka. Russian losses were listed as thirty-one dead, with one 4.7cm anti-tank gun and several machine guns captured or destroyed.[12]

Along the fronts of 168. and 167. Infanterie-Divisions, there was similar activity, consisting primarily of combat reconnaissance probes in less than battalion strength, which were conducted by both sides. A few of the Soviet patrols were supported by one or two tanks, but the intensity of the fighting declined in the sectors of both divisions, as Russian casualties and unit fatigue increased daily. At Sinkiv, where elements of 168. Infanterie-Division had been engaged in heavy fighting for several days, the Russian presence faded away altogether. Reconnaissance patrols scouting the areas northeast and west of the town revealed that the Soviets had completely abandoned several nearby villages. The withdrawal of the Russian troops was a tangible result of the advance of the SS-

---

[12] Ibid. pg. 172-173.

Panzerkorps and its threat to the lines of communication of the 40th and 69th Army. The battered 168. Infanterie-Division had given its final effort and was exhausted by the defensive fighting around Sinkiv. The division numbered less than 1500 men on that date. Although a company of "Grossdeutschland's" tanks, consisting of five Panzer IVs and three Panzer IIIs, was attached to the division, as well as a few other support troops, it had reached the end of its rope and Korps Raus decided to withdraw it beginning on 2 March.[13]

The battle situation stabilized in the Korps Raus sector on 1 March, although "Leibstandarte" remained immobilized by the mud. In spite of the less than ideal situation in "Leibstandarte's" sector, the SS-Panzerkorps renewed its offensive operations. Hoth ordered the divisions to advance into the Alexejevka sector, which was due east of Krasnograd. "Totenkopf" was to attack along the Orel River, advancing toward Jefremovka, while "Das Reich" advanced on a parallel course, in order to smash Russian resistance along the railroad line leading out of Krasnopawlovka. The division was to drive further north, through Ochotschaje and into the area just south of Kharkov.

"Totenkopf's" objective was to slice through the 3rd Tank Army's front east of Kegitschevka, then turn west and cut through the roads leading into the area from the north. This would trap the 3rd Tank Army between "Leibstandarte" on the west and "Totenkopf" on the east. While this portion of Rybalko's army was engaged, "Das Reich" and "Leibstandarte" were to join hands further to the north of Kegitschevka, in the area of Staroverovka. This would create a small pocket, encircling the heart of Rybalko's army, the 12th and 15th Tank Corps.

With the three SS divisions once again under command of the SS-Panzerkorps and Manstein intended to crush Rybalko's army and then drive north to Kharkov. In conjunction with the advance of the SS-Panzerkorps, XXXXVIII. Panzerkorps, which had been strengthened by the addition of 11. Panzer-Division, was ordered to destroy Russian forces south and southwest of Kharkov, below the Msha River. After crossing the Msha, it was to clear the Merefa sector, in order to block a Soviet attack on the eastern flank of the SS-Panzerkorps that could originate from bridgeheads on the Northern Donets River. The XXXX. Panzerkorps' role was to hold the crossings site over the river in its sector and prevent the Russians from attacking the eastern flank of 4. Panzerarmee's attack.

On 1 March, the three divisions of Hausser's SS-Panzerkorps crashed into the 3rd Tank Army. The SS-Panzerkorps had realized by that time that a regrouping of Soviet forces was in progress because German intelligence had identified troops from both tank corps and three rifle divisions of Rybalko's 3rd Tank Army in the area

east of Krasnograd. Hoth ordered his Panzer divisions to strike north, taking advantage of the weakness of the Russian forces opposing his army's advance to Kharkov. The SS-Panzerkorps was ordered to concentrate its strength and advance northward, along the railroad lines that passed through the Staroverovka-Ochotschaje sector.[14]

"Das Reich" began its attack on 1 March, finding ways to keep its columns moving, even in the deepest mud. On the right wing of its advance, the reinforced Regiment "Deutschland" began its advance early in the morning while roads were still frozen solid. The regiment's troops assembled at 0300 hours and at 0600, the unit commanders reported to Harmel for their last briefing. At 0800 the regiment began its attack, rumbling north over the frozen roads leading toward Alexejevka. The leading battalion of the regiment was II./Regiment "Deutschland," commanded by SS-Sturmbannführer Fritz Ehrath. Regiment commander Harmel, accompanied by an escort detachment and Macher's 16./"Deutschland," was near the head of the column. Some of the SS Pioniere rode on the decks of "Das Reich" tanks and were equipped with mine detection and removal equipment and anti-tank weapons. Macher and the rest of the Pioniere rode on eight wheeled Panzerspähwagen or on the decks of several Marders.[15]

There was little effective Soviet resistance at first and the column took a number of prisoners who quickly surrendered when they encountered the SS troops. For a time, the tanks were held up due to a weak bridge which threatened to collapse under their weight. Macher's Pioniere, using materials at hand, shored up the bridge and the crossing site and the attack continued. When the lead detachments reached Alexejevka, they encountered brief resistance from weak Russian defensive positions on the southern perimeter of the town, which were supported by several anti-tank guns. Harmel realized that the Soviet position was not organized in depth and had no flank protection. From the march, the lead battle group immediately swung into action and detachments attacked the town from two sides.

Harmel accompanied Macher's company in a thrust past Alexejevka and attacked the Russians from the rear, while the rest of the column assaulted the town's eastern and western perimeters. The Russian defenses collapsed quickly after the SS Pioniere broke through the roadblocks in the northern section of Alexejevka and entered the center of the town. Quickly Macher led his company forward and attacked the Russian positions from behind. Soviet gun crews panicked and abandoned their guns when the SS Pioniere

---

[13] NA/T-314, roll 490, 1a KTB Tagesmeldung Korps Raus, frame 000279.

[14] Weidinger, pg. 67 and T-354, roll 118, frame 3752054- 1a KTB der SS-Panzerkorps- 4. Panzerarmee Befehl nr. 30. 1.3.1943 an 2225 Uhr.

[15] Privately held unit account, excerpts courtesy of Mark C. Yerger.

attacked from this unexpected direction without warning. Many of the unnerved Russians troops abandoned the town, scattering in all directions, with machine gun fire knocking down many of them as they fled over the open, flat steppe. A column of Russian vehicles abandoned Alexejevka, following roads that led to the north and northeast, in order to escape from the advance of the SS column. The war journal of Macher's company described total Russian casualties as 12 prisoners and 240 dead, as well as listing the capture of several machine guns, mortars and many small arms. By 1150 hours, the town was in the hands of Harmel's regiment, at a cost of only four German wounded, although two were seriously injured and died shortly after the town was secured.[16]

After regrouping in the town, Harmel led the regiment out of Alexejevka to the west, following a good road until it intersected the railroad embankment that ran north, to Bereka. A good road ran parallel to the tracks, affording the SS vehicles two lanes to travel. Soon after the German column began to move north again Harmel's command detachment, consisting of Macher's Pioniere Kompanie and four tanks, made contact with 3rd Tank Army units at a railroad bridge northwest of Alexejevka. Near the village of Krassnyj the regiment reported that "rear guard" units, supported by tanks offered strong resistance from positions along a range of wooded hills northwest of Krassnyj. However, when the regiment assaulted the Russian defenses, supported by heavy artillery fire, the tanks withdrew and the Russian infantry pulled back quickly. By 1800 hours the remaining pockets of Soviet infantry were mopped up and the hills were reported in German hands. Many of the fleeing Soviet troops could be seen assembling near a wooded hill northwest of Bereka. Macher's company and the four SS tanks continued along the road, then turned east, pursuing another withdrawing Soviet column. After dark it became too dark to move safely and Macher's men occupied a small forest northeast of Bereka, spending a nervous night in the woods.[17]

The attack of Regiment "Der Führer," on the left wing of the division, made similar progress. After assembling in the Rasdolje area in the cold, damp morning hours, the regiment roared off along a secondary road parallel to the advance of Regiment "Deutschland." The regiment encountered no Russian troops until it reached the village of Pervomaisky and a nearby railroad station, where it made first contact with the defensive positions of the 3rd Tank Army at 1300 hours. The regiment's opponents were elements of the hard fighting 6th Guards Cavalry Corps, who responded with what was described as 'energetic resistance.' After brief, but tough fighting, Regiment "Der Führer" was on the move again by 1500 hours but

then ran into another Soviet strong point at the village of Wassikovsky.

Kumm decided to bypass Wassikovsky and the column turned west onto a good road and reached the outskirts of Jefremovka before 1700 hours. Shortly afterward Regiment "Der Führer" assaulted Soviet defensive positions in villages south of Jefremovka. The Russians had a number of T-34s, heavy mortars and anti-tank guns in the village, but after the first assault, many of the Russian troops withdrew, according to the Regiment "Der Führer" reports. The fighting took on a familiar pattern for most of the day in front of the SS-Panzerkorps. After brief and sometimes spirited fighting, the Russians usually quickly abandoned their position and withdrew. Within an hour after the attack began, the area south of Jefremovka was reported occupied by the regiment.[18]

On the left or west flank of the SS-Panzerkorps advance, "Totenkopf's" Kampfgruppe Baum drove northward through the Orel River valley unopposed by strong resistance. Only a few small detachments of the 3rd Tank Army were encountered as the division pushed through the area east of Kegitschevka. Becker's Regiment "Eicke," in a parallel advance, drove northwards and reached the Alexejevka area. The division's attack was screened by detachments of Bestmann's Aufklärungsabteilung operating on the corps eastern flank.

The "Totenkopf" march routes passed through a sector that had very poor roads and bridges. Many bridges had to be reinforced and flooded areas had to be filled in before they could be used by vehicles. During the night of 28 February-1 March, SS-Pioniere-Bataillon 3 had been hard at work strengthening bridges and making the roads more passable. In a report submitted to the SS-Panzerkorps, battalion commander Seela described the actions of his battalion. The battalion repaired or reinforced two bridges north of Krasnopawlovka and filled in large mud holes in the road with stones or gravel, one of which took seven cubic meters of fill materials. Meanwhile, Seela's 3./Kompanie, joined by a few "Totenkopf" Panzers, reconnoitered north along a road that ran parallel to railroad line running into Alexejevka. When the battle group approached a small Russian village, it began receiving mortar and anti-tank gun fire from a strong Russian defensive position at the edge of Alexejevka. Seela and his Pioniere, having located the enemy and identified a number of firing positions, returned to Krasnopawlovka.[19]

On the division's right flank, Regiment "Eicke" left its assembly areas north of Krasnopawlovka and rolled northwards to a cross-

---

[16] Privately held unit account, excerpts courtesy of Mark C. Yerger.
[17] Yerger, Weidinger, pgs. 68-69 and NA/T-354, roll 120, frame 3753660.

[18] NA/T-354, roll 120, 1a KTB der SS-Panzerkorps, 1.3.1943, frame 3753660.
[19] NA/T-354, roll118, Meldung über Einsatz des SS Totenkopf-Pioniere-Btl by its commander Sturmbannführer Max Seela, frame 3752055.

roads located between Jefremovka and Alexejevka. The regiment made good progress in spite of the extremely bad road conditions. By early afternoon the lead elements reached the town of Mironovka and occupied it before pushing further to the north. It encountered little significant Russian resistance until reaching the area southwest of Alexejevka. By nightfall, the regiment arrived at a range of hills just south of Jefremovka and stopped for the night.[20]

Regiment "Totenkopf" formed up for its attack in the Orel River valley at the village of Novo Vladimirovka. The first line of attack of the regiment was toward the river, in order to reach a road running northward which paralleled the course of the river. After two hours of uneventful travel the forward elements of the division approached Alexejevka. The regiment launched its attack and quickly broke into the town. Schubach's III./Regiment "Totenkopf" took Alexejevka at 0845 hours. Following a brief conference with Baum and his battalion commanders, the advance continued along the river road, led by the SPWs of SS-Hauptsturmführer Walter Reder's I./ Regiment "Totenkopf." Reder's half tracks raced through several villages until the battalion ran into Soviet infantry in the village of Oleiniki just before noon. By 1350 hours, Oleiniki was captured and the surviving Russians withdrew to the north. Further to the north, Reder's battalion ran into what it thought was a rear guard detachment at Lissowinovka. The reports of the division indicate that the rear guard included tanks and these troops probably belonged to the 3rd Tank Army. Reder's Grenadiers deployed to attack the road block position and encountered tough fighting initially, but the Soviet tanks and infantry suddenly attempted to pull back to the north.

The Russians were pursued by part of the SS battalion and several assault guns. What began as a withdrawal turned into a rout when the Sturmgeschütze and 2cm automatic guns took the slower elements of the retreating Russians under fire. With many horse drawn sleds loaded with wounded and equipment, the tail end of the Russian column was too slow to escape the SPWs, who caught up with them north of Oleiniki. The Germans pulled up parallel to the fleeing columns, firing at close range and gunning down scores of Russian troops. Many dropped their weapons, threw up their hands and attempted to surrender or took to their heels in all directions. Panicked horses ran wild, turning over sledges and spilling their cargoes of wounded onto the ground. The SS Grenadiers took no time with prisoners, but continued their pursuit of the retreating Russian tanks and vehicles.

Shortly afterward, the "Totenkopf" forward elements caught up with the main body of the Russian column and opened fire at a distance of 500 meters. All order and discipline disintegrated when the assault gun shells and streams of 2cm explosive rounds shattered the column. Russian troops fled over the icy, muddy steppe, while a solitary Russian on horseback, with a long cape fluttering from his shoulders, spurred his mount and raced away to the north. A crew of one of the 2cm guns spotted him and fired several rounds after the galloping horseman, who was obviously an officer. However, the rider soon reached a low hill in the distance and disappeared safely over the crest. Under interrogation, Soviet prisoners identified the lone rider as the regimental commander. After regrouping, Baum pressed on several kilometers farther to the north, reaching his objective, the village of Nishnjy Orel, before dark. To their surprise, the SS troops found that battery of an Army Flak battalion already occupied the hamlet. How the German troops had come to be that far behind Russian lines was not explained.[21]

By nightfall, Regiment "Totenkopf" was assembled in the Alexejevka area and Regiment "Eicke" occupied positions south of Jefremovka. Reder's reinforced I./"Totenkopf," continued its advance after darkness fell and reached a spur of the Krasnograd-Panjutina railroad line which branched off from the main line at a point north of Kegitschevka. The battalion surprised a small Russian rail road guard detachment at Schljachovoje Station, which was north of Kegitschevka. When the SS column roared out of the pitch black night the astonished guards were not able to put up much resistance. After taking the survivors prisoner, the battalion organized a defensive perimeter and halted for the night. The occupation of the village cut an important supply line of the Soviet troops in the Kegitschevka area. At dawn on 2 March, the battalion perimeter was struck by an attack of Russian infantry, led by a handful of T-34s. After three of the Russian tanks were hit by anti-tank gun fire and partially disabled, the attack faded away. Reder's capture of the railroad station almost sealed the northern border of the Kegischevka pocket, leaving only a narrow corridor extending out of the pocket. The fate of the Soviet 12th and 15th Tank Corps was sealed with this success.

While "Das Reich" and "Totenkopf" slashed into the Jefremovka area, pushing the Russians before them, "Leibstandarte" remained largely immobilized by the mud in its sector, west of the Kegitschevka pocket. Peiper's battalion, reinforced with a company of assault guns, occupied defensive positions west of Kegitschevka. Just a few kilometers separated his battalion from Reder's position on the railroad north of Kegitschevka. Peiper's positions were struck by repeated attacks by tanks and infantry of the 15th Tank Corps, while several strong Russian columns were spotted by German air reconnaissance approaching the Kegitschevka area from the north.

---

[20] Vopersal, pg. 167-168.

[21] Vopersal, pg. 167-168 and NA/T-354, roll 120, 1a KTB, Darstellung der Ereignisse, frame3753662.

These troops were probably the last 12th Tank Corps columns, assembling for the counterattack planned for 3 March. These additional forces moved into position northeast of the SS battalion, arriving just soon enough to be encircled by "Totenkopf."

By early afternoon, Russian pressure on Peiper forced him to withdraw a short distance and the battalion was pulled back to better defensive positions. Patrols reported that strong Russian forces remained dug in along its entire front east of Krasnograd. The defenses on the front and eastern flank of the 3rd Tank Army had given way, driven back by the advance of "Das Reich" and "Totenkopf." However, in the Kegitschevka sector, Rybalko's army held good defensive positions between the Orel and Berestovaja Rivers, facing "Leibstandarte." While this blocked an eastward advance by Dietrich's division, it had the end result of allowing these forces to be encircled.

Rybalko knew that his army was being sacrificed, because Armeeabteilung Kempf's war diary reports that Luftwaffe and ground reconnaissance units observed Russian infantry columns pulling out at the same time that Rybalko's columns were marching into the pocket. It is certain that Rybalko's columns must have passed at least some of these retreating columns, and this situation could not have been good for the confidence of his troops. In fact, Rybalko's army continued to march into the trap that was closing behind them until the last moment. It is little wonder that the troops of the 3rd Tank Army often put up little more than token resistance to the columns of "Totenkopf" and "Das Reich." This gave the Germans the impression that these forces were little more than rear guard detachments, covering a general withdrawal. At 0855 hours on 2 March, Armeeabteilung Kempf received intelligence reports indicating that heavy vehicle traffic was still moving south from Valki, heading toward Kegitschevka. Meanwhile, a second column of 2000 infantry and several hundred vehicles was spotted in the Jeremejevka sector, heading into the pocket.

On 2 March, the battle south of Kharkov entered a new phase. The two Panzergrenadier divisions of the SS-Panzerkorps, as a result of their advance parallel to the Orel River, had penetrated the right flank of Rybalko's army east of Krasnograd. The "Das Reich" spearheads were well north of Kegitschevka and the main armored elements of the Russian tank army. "Totenkopf" columns pressed in from the east, with I./Regiment "Totenkopf" already blocking Russian lines of communication north of Kegitschevka. At that point, Rybalko's two tank corps and the three supporting infantry divisions were nearly completely encircled, except for the narrowing corridor that remained open north of Kegitschevka. Most of the army held positions between Jeremejevka and Kegitschevka. Hoth planned to deal with Rybalko's remaining armor and infantry as-

A Russian T-26 light tank with the armor covering its motor blown off by an internal explosion. The body of one of its crew lies behind the tank. The T-26 was used for reconnaissance and infantry support but was no match for even the up gunned Panzer III. (Credit National Archives)

sets with Meyer's reconnaissance battalion and "Totenkopf," while still pushing northward with "Das Reich" and the main elements of "Leibstandarte" on 3 March.

Seela's "Totenkopf" Pioniere Bataillon remained in Krasnopawlovka, where it served as the corps mobile reserve while it continued to work improving the poor roads and bridges in the communication's zone of the corps. The SS-Panzerkorps chief of Pioniere, SS-Sturmbannführer Karl Ullrich, was with Seela's battalion in order to observe the operations of the Pioniere. Ullrich was the former commander of the battalion and led it during the eleven months that the division was in the Demyansk pocket. He was soon to return to his old division.[22]

---

[22] After Schubach was wounded on 17 March, Ullrich took command of his battalion. Ullrich had been a company commander in "Das Reich's" Pioniere Bataillon 2 in 1939 and served with the division during the fighting in France. In 1941, he took over command of SS Pioniere-Bataillon 3 of "Totenkopf" and served under Eicke. He was a highly decorated combat veteran, who won both grades of the Iron Cross, the Knight's Cross and the Oak Leaves to the Knight's Cross. Ullrich's former regimental commander, Otto Baum, told the American historian Mark Yerger that he considered Ullrich the finest officer he had ever had under his command.

The SS-Panzerkorps issued orders directing its divisions to encircle and destroy the 3rd Tank Army forces beginning on 3 March. In co-operation with "Totenkopf," mobile elements of "Leibstandarte" were to finish off the remaining elements of the 12th and 15th Tank Corps and their supporting rifle divisions. Dietrich was informed that his division would come under the command of the SS-Panzerkorps once again on 3 March. "Das Reich," supported by a reinforced Kampfgruppe of Regiment "Eicke," was to take Novaja Vodolaga and establish contact with "Leibstandarte" spearheads when they reached the town.[23]

"Das Reich" was instructed to prepare to attack to the northwest from Jefremovka. The division was to establish bridgeheads over the Berestovaja River. After assembling on the northern bank, the division was to attack the town of Staroverovka in order to capture a secure assembly and supply base for the assault on Novaja Vodolaga. However, Russian resistance at Jefremovka became considerably stronger and the town remained in Soviet hands. This was due to the arrival of the additional 3rd Tank Army columns moving into the pocket and so the first task of the division was to eliminate Russian defensive positions in the town. During the night of 1-2 March, II./ and III./Regiment "Der Führer" were engaged in fighting for Jefremovka. The Russians fought stubbornly to keep the town, mounting effective counterattacks several times during the night. The sounds of machine gun fire and muffled explosions of grenades bursting inside houses and buildings, echoed throughout the night as bitter house to house fighting continued without a decisive success by either side. The main elements of "Totenkopf" became occupied with the task of destroying the Jeremejevka-Kegitschevka pocket and could not support the attack upon Jefremovka. Hoth feared that the Russians might escape the pocket and so "Leibstandarte" was ordered to assemble a mobile group for an attack which was to close the last remaining corridor out of the pocket and prevent the escape of Rybalko's army.

The Destruction of the Kegitschevka Pocket

The early morning hours of 2 March were cold and the ground was covered with a light frost, enabling the Germans to move over still frozen roads and ridge tops. However, by early morning, a bright sun burned through the clouds and the temperature began to rise. The quickly softening roads degenerated into quagmires of thick, black mud. The exhausted German troops, who had been in action with little rest for almost ten days, were tested by the demands of traversing the rapidly deteriorating Ukrainian roads. Vehicles some-

times damaged their running gear while trying to extricate themselves from the mud. At times, while attempting to pull other vehicles out of the morass, an overtaxed transmission failed and two vehicles were thus lost.

In spite of the difficulties moving over the rapidly deteriorating roads "Regiment "Totenkopf," assisted by Panzermeyer's Aufklärungsabteilung, began operations to destroy the 3rd Tank Army elements between Jeremejevka and Kegitschevka. "Leibstandarte" mounted attacks along both sides of the Berestovaja River, early on 2 March, driving to the north parallel to the other two SS divisions. A battle group consisting of the reinforced I./SS-PzG.-Rgt. "LAH" moved along the southeastern bank of the Berestovaja River, supported by a few SPWs from Peiper's battalion and a company of "Leibstandarte" Panzers. Their objective, the village of Berestovaja, was reported captured by 1020 hours. The village did not remain secure for long however, because just after noon, a group of Russian tanks rolled into Berestovaja from the northeast. The T-34s attacked the forward elements of the regiment, firing cannons and machine guns as they charged into the village. This attack was not supported by infantry or artillery and it was quickly halted. The SS Panzers and assault guns engaged the Russian tanks and knocked out two T-34s. The remaining Soviet tanks broke off the attack and returned to Paraskoveja. Four other tanks were disabled or abandoned and left behind. These were significant losses for the 3rd Tank Army as it probably had fewer than thirty tanks after the armor losses inflicted on it during the last week of February. Later in the afternoon, "Leibstandarte" troops made contact with reconnaissance patrols of "Das Reich" west of Losovaja and Rudolf Lehmann, the division 1a, notified Armeeabteilung Kempf of the link up at 1640 hours.[24]

Peiper's SPW battalion, advancing on the northern bank of the Berestovaja River, encountered several long Russian motorized columns retreating from the area west of Paraskoveja and pursued them. The battalion harassed the Russians throughout the afternoon, firing at the columns of trucks and sledges with long range machine gun fire or 2cm automatic guns. At 1600 hours, Peiper's troops reached the town of Melechovka, which was only a few kilometers west of the main body of "Totenkopf," which had remained in the area between Melechovka and Jefremovka.

The divisional attack group on the northern flank of the division, II./SS-PzG.-Rgt. 2 "LAH," led by battalion commander Rudolf Sandig, pushed along a stream that branched off the Berestovaja to the northeast and flowed through the town of Staroverovka. The column first made contact with 3rd Tank Army troops, supported

[23] NA/T-354, roll 118, Fernschreiben SS-Panzerkorps zu "L-SS-A.H." an 2.31943. frame 3752058.

[24] *Befehl des Gewissens*, pg. 190.

by a few tanks, at Staroverovka. In the fighting, one Russian tank was put out of action and a second was captured when its crew abandoned their undamaged T-34. After leaving Staroverovka, the battalion attacked due east, approaching the Berestovaja River at a point just west of Peiper's battalion in Melechovka. At 1400 hours, Sandig's battalion occupied several surrounding villages after light fighting.

In the meantime, Meyer's Aufklärungsabteilung observed Russian troops moving into and out of the Kegitschevka area during the entire day. A very long column of marching infantry, sleds and horse drawn artillery snaked out of the sector and trudged northeast, toward Jefremovka. Throughout the day, "Leibstandarte" attempted to establish a firmer contact with "Das Reich" near Jefremovka, where Kumm's Regiment "Der Führer" still battled Russian infantry.

The II./ and III./Regiment "Der Führer," after many hours of bitter fighting against 6th Guards Cavalry Corps troops, were able to reach a point south of Jefremovka. Russian artillery and anti-tank gun fire was heavy and the SS attacks were thrown back by concentrated mortar and machine gun fire. Finally the SS Grenadiers took cover in a long ravine south of the town. Just after midnight, the commander of II./"Der Führer," SS-Sturmbannführer Stadler, conferred with regiment commander Otto Kumm and was ordered to immediately carry out a thorough reconnaissance of the Soviet defenses. Kumm told Stadler that the town had to be taken by the following day and that he was decide whether it would be best to launch a surprise attack that night or wait until daylight. By the following day, the divisional artillery would be able to provide its full support, but the guns were not in position yet.

When the reconnaissance patrols reported back to Stadler, they told him that the entire Soviet eastern perimeter was studded with machine gun positions and was reinforced by dug in tanks. Stadler knew that a day time attack, conducted over the flat terrain east of Jefremovka, would be very costly. Accordingly he decided to attack the western perimeter immediately, while it was still dark. His battalion deployed in three attack groups, each supported by two of Krag's assault guns. Krag personally directed the positioning of the Sturmgeschütze in order to provide the most effective supporting fire for the infantry.[25]

Fortunately for the German Grenadiers, a sudden, blinding snow storm helped conceal the advance of the battalion, although the Russian lines erupted in what Weidinger described as a 'murderous' fire when the attack began. Due to darkness and the snow, the Russian defensive fire was ineffective and the SS assault groups crossed the open ground and reached the western perimeter without heavy losses. SS Grenadiers leapt into the Russian trenches out of the snowstorm, hurling grenades and firing MP-40 submachine guns. The SS assault teams fought through the perimeter and battled their way down wreckage strewn, smoke shrouded streets. At first, the Russian infantry fought back stubbornly from strong points that were built up around about a dozen entrenched tanks. However, the T-34s and T-70s were immobile, possibly due to lack of fuel and once again the SS Sturmgeschütze were able to maneuver into position to hit them from the flank or rear. Krag's battery knocked out several tanks and destroyed a number of anti-tank gun positions.

Russian guns and tanks began to fall silent, their crews lying dead or wounded beside their weapons. The Soviet infantry wavered and began to abandon their fortified houses and camouflaged positions. The remaining T-34s were easy pickings for the SS Grenadiers after their supporting infantry withdrew. The Germans placed bundles of hand grenades or satchel charges on the tank hulls. The charges exploded with thunderous roars, disabling turrets or igniting engine compartments. Fiery explosions incinerated a number of tanks and their unfortunate crew as well. Soviet tankers who attempted to abandon their burning tanks were shot down.

By the first hours of daylight most of the Soviet infantry had pulled out of Jefremovka and at 0800 hours, a large portion of the town in possession of the regiment. The SS Grenadiers pushed through Jefremovka and reached a stream on the northern edge of the town later in the morning. Inside the blasted, smoking town, the Germans counted ten destroyed or abandoned tanks and Kumm estimated that his troops had destroyed a regiment of Soviet infantry.[26]

Shortly after the town was taken III./Regiment "Der Führer" was on the move again, driving westward along the road leading to Paraskoveja. To the south, the battalion could see "Totenkopf's" Panzers and SPWs, all of which were rolling in the same direction. Later in the day, the "Das Reich" troops linked up with elements of I./SS-PzG.-Rgt. 2 "LAH" which were driving east. The two columns met on the west bank of the Berestovaja River northwest of Paraskoveja, making contact at 1600 hours and closing the Kegitschevka bottleneck.[27]

Earlier, while Regiment "Der Führer" still fought for possession of Jefremovka, Regiment "Deutschland" drove west from Bereka, passing south of Regiment "Der Führer's" advance. The SS-Kradschützen-Bataillon 2 pushed toward the town of Losowaje. At 1430 hours, the motorcycle troops arrived at their objective and

[25] Yerger, Ernst August Krag biography, and Weidinger, pg. 70.

[26] NA/T-354, roll 120, 1a KTB, Darstellung der Ereignisse, frame 3753664 and Weidinger, pg. 70.
[27] Weidinger, pg. 70.

drove the Russians out of the southern section of the town. From Losowaje, the battalion continued west, toward the Berestovaja River, leaving only a few security detachments behind.[28]

"Totenkopf" began its offensive operations on the morning of 2 March by thrusting through the northern half of the Kegitschevka pocket, advancing in two regimental battle groups. The right flank attack group was Regiment "Eicke" and its objective for the day was to reach the Berestowaja River near Medwedovka. There it was to link up with elements of "Leibstandarte," and begin a general move by the entire Panzer corps to swing to the northwest. If successful, the attack by Regiment "Eicke" would cut the Kegitschevka pocket in half. Simultaneously, Regiment "Totenkopf" was to smash the bulk of Soviet forces in the southern half.

The two "Totenkopf" regiments assembled just before dawn and were scheduled to jump off at 0800 hours. The division faced the same quickly deteriorating road conditions as the other two SS divisions. Roads that were frozen solid during the night turned first to icy slush. The tracks of the SPWs and Panzers ground the quickly thawing roads into black mush. The dirt roads became nearly impassable at points where runoff from melting snow created deep mud holes. At some points, small streams became rushing torrents that washed out bridges and road embankments. However, the SS Grenadiers and Panzer crews found ways to keep moving throughout the morning and by afternoon, had reached their attack objectives. The temperatures continued to rise all day. Long columns of German vehicles plowed through the ever deepening mud and resupply as well as movement became increasingly difficult.[29]

On the right flank of the division, Regiment "Eicke" began its attack from assembly areas south of Jefremovka. The jump off was delayed a half hour due to the late arrival of supply columns carrying fuel and ammunition. The I./SS-Pz.-Rgt. 3 was to have supported the attack of the regiment, but the tanks remained immobile until 1400 hours, because their assigned fuel trucks did not reach them until noon. While Regiment "Der Führer" was still involved in clearing Jefremovka, Becker's regiment pushed west until it reached a smaller road that led toward the Berestovaja River valley. The two columns of SS troops could see other in the distance. At about 1430 hours, I./and III./Regiment "Eicke" reached the Berestovaja River's eastern bank. The northern corridor leading out of the Kegitschevka-Jeremejevka pocket was closed. Although it was not an airtight seal, the main roads leading north from Kegitschevka were solidly blocked by SS battle groups.

---

[28] NA/T-354, roll 120, 1a KTB, Darstellung der Ereignisse, frame 3753666-3667.
[29] Vopersal, pg. 174-175.

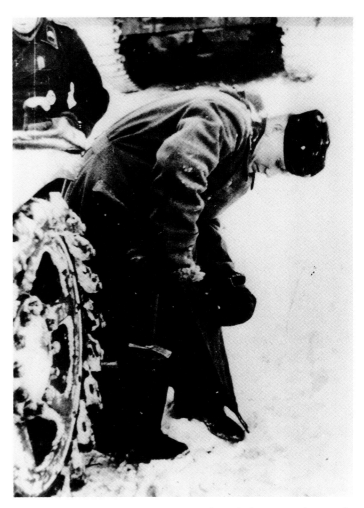

A heavily clad soldier of "Totenkopf" works on the track of a Sturmgeschütz III. The man pictured was probably a member of the Werkstattzug of the Division's Sturmgeschütz Abteilung. The Germans were often able to salvage and repair damaged vehicles in the field, returning them quickly to action. The Russians did not have the same capability in the first years of the war because they generally lacked anything more than rudimentary repair facilities, although the Russian tankers themselves often found ingenious ways to keep their tanks running. (Credit National Archives)

After regrouping, Regiment "Totenkopf" formed up to begin its attack to destroy the Soviet forces in the pocket, although the regiment was delayed slightly due to resupply problems and did not begin its attack at the scheduled time. From the western bank of the Orel River, around Nishny Orel, its three battalions attacked on a narrow front. On the northern flank, Schubach's III./"Totenkopf" advanced quickly, in spite of weather conditions, and took the town of Pissarevka after a sharp battle. The other two battalions approached Kegitschevka where they collided with 3rd Tank Army formations trying to break out of the pocket and escape. The desperation of the Soviet troops was evident to soldiers of the SS divisions. One of them described the determined lunges of the Russians, as 'wild breakout attempts.' The fighting to block Russian escapes from the pocket occupied the regiment for most of the day. After destroying six T-34s and blocking the escape of several Russian columns, elements of the regiment converged on Jeremejevka at 1430 hours. "Leibstandarte's" Aufklärungsabteilung, led personally by Kurt Meyer, attacked from the southwest.[30]

Reder's I./Regiment "Totenkopf" deployed east of Jeremejevka, which sprawled for several kilometers along the floor of a shallow, flat valley. The SS SPWs drew closer to the long line of huts and small houses that lay in the distance. A long column of Russian troops was visible in the distance, leaving the northern edge of the town. Many sleds, horse drawn artillery and hundreds of stolid, marching infantry were trying to escape to the north, their retreat covered by elements of the 3rd Tank Army. As the SS vehicles approached the outskirts of town, the Germans began to take fire from a number of anti-tank guns on the eastern edge of the town. Dismounting from their troop carriers in a nearby depression, the SS Grenadiers deployed in open order and began to advance over the floor of the shallow valley. Self-propelled guns and infantry howitzers laid down supporting fire on the perimeter, while assault guns found hull down firing positions and shelled the town. High explosive shells slammed again and again into the trenches and machine gun nests, throwing up bursts of black smoke and clumps of frozen black earth. Flakvierling 2cm guns smothered Russian infantry positions with a hail of explosive shells.[31]

Under cover of this fire, the Grenadiers stormed toward the village, closing on the perimeter, but the Russians held their fire, exhibiting superb fire discipline. The assault teams approached to within 200 meters and there still was no response from the Russians. Suddenly, at a distance of 100 meters, the village perimeter erupted with gun fire. Machine gun bullets swept the ground and anti-tank guns barked. The dense, sweeping machine gun fire forced the Grenadiers to quickly take cover in any available ditch or fold in the ground. Squad leaders got their MG-42 crews into action, laying down suppressing fire on the Russians, while small groups of Grenadiers rushed forward in quick bounds. Casualties were heavy, but the assault detachments reached the edge of the town and assaulted the first defensive positions. After breaking through the perimeter the SS Grenadiers engaged the Russians in costly house to house fighting. The trapped Russians fought furiously to hold Jeremejevka and casualties were numerous on both sides.[32]

While Regiment "Totenkopf" was involved in the fighting for the possession of the town, elements of the 3rd Tank Army began to slip over the Orel River to the east. By this time most of Rybalko's army was either desperately trying to escape encirclement or was heavily involved in fighting with the SS division spearheads. On the southern perimeter of the pocket Meyer's reinforced battalion rampaged through retreating Russian columns, destroying them as they rolled over the snow covered steppe. Late in the afternoon, Meyer made firm contact with Regiment "Totenkopf" at Jeremejevka, having pushed in the western edge of southern half of the pocket.

By that time, the 12th and 15th Tank Corps were in danger of being completely destroyed in the Kegitschevka pocket. Rybalko ordered their commanders to attempt an orderly withdrawal. At nightfall, Rybalko abandoned the Kegitschevka defensive positions, never having had any hope of mounting a real counterattack on the SS divisions. Some Soviet columns were able to pass between German units and reached safety. Other columns ran into SS defensive positions and fighting flared throughout the sector during the night.

The 12th Tank Corps was able to maintain some unit cohesion during its withdrawal. At midnight on 3 March, pulling back behind stubbornly fighting rear guard detachments, the corps began a disciplined retreat. However, many of its tanks and most of the heavy equipment had to be left behind due to lack of fuel or mechanical breakdowns. Led by their commander, General M.I. Zinkovich, the main group of the corps to fight through the German lines. They carried little more than their small arms and the clothes on their back. Only a handful of tanks still had fuel and could support the escape effort. The 15th Tank Corps was not as fortunate because command control and discipline failed. In contrast to the relatively orderly withdrawal of the 12th Tank Corps, the various groups of the 15th Tank Corps began uncoordinated escape attempts.

The destruction of the Kegitschevka-Jeremejevka pocket marked the end of the first stage of the counterattack by Hausser's SS-Panzerkorps. While "Totenkopf" hunted down the remaining Soviet troops in the pocket, Hausser prepared to begin the advance upon Kharkov itself. Late in the day, the SS-Panzerkorps was informed that Adolf Hitler had decided to change the unit designation of SS-"Totenkopf" Panzergrenadier-Regiment 3. He renamed the regiment 3. SS-Panzergrenadier-Regiment "Theodor Eicke," in honor and remembrance of the division's slain commander. Hoth's 4. Panzerarmee also received a message from Manstein, thanking the officers and men of the army and Waffen-SS for their efforts during the counteroffensive. Hausser was given new directives from 4. Panzerarmee for the next day.

"Totenkopf" was to finish off the encircled Russian forces in the Kegitschevka-Jeremejevka pocket between the Berestovaja and Orel River. "Leibstandarte" and "Das Reich" were to drive north

---

[30] Op cit.

[31] The Flakvierling was a four barreled configuration of 2cm automatic guns. It was originally intended as an anti-aircraft weapon but the German troops soon discovered that it was deadly against troops and soft vehicles on the ground.

[32] Vopersal, pg. 176.

from the Novaja Vodolaga area and attack the 3rd Tank Army and 6th Army forces that had escaped from the pocket and taken up new defensive positions southwest of Kharkov along the Msha River. By nightfall on 2-3 March, the 3rd Tank Army had ceased to exist as a tank army. All that were left of Rybalko's two tank corps were bands of exhausted survivors and a few tanks. It had lost most of its artillery and heavy weapons.

However, even as the remnants of his tanks corps hobbled northward or fought to destruction in the pocket, Rybalko received orders to build up a new defensive line south of Kharkov. He had few resources with which to accomplish this task other than the very weak rifle divisions that had not been encircled in the pocket. Rybalko's task would have been impossible had he not received reinforcements. However, the Stavka was able to furnish additional troops to the decimated army, including some armor. Rybalko received two tank brigades, a rifle division and a rifle brigade, although none were fresh units. All had been in combat for a long time and were not at established strength, although the 179th Tank Brigade had twenty-four T-34s and T-70s. Between 3-5 March, Rybalko tried to organize the fragments of his army into a coherent

defensive line protecting the Msha River line and blocking the southern approaches to Kharkov.[33]

While Rybalko built up a patchwork defensive line, XXXXVIII. Panzerkorps' 6. Panzer-Division assembled northwest of Jefremovka. While the SS divisions battled the 3rd Tank Army in the Kegitschevka area, 6. Panzer-Division and 17. Panzer-Division advanced against the army's eastern flank. The two divisions attacked shoulder to shoulder, through a narrow corridor bounded on the west by the SS-Panzerkorps sector and on the east by the Northern Donets River. Barely thirty kilometers remained between the leading units of the corps and the Msha River line. The 1. Panzerarmee's XXXX. Panzerkorps closed up to the right flank of XXXXVIII. Panzerkorps.

The XXXX. Panzerkorps reached the Donets after pursuing the Russians to the banks of the river itself. "Wiking" and 7. Panzer-Division drove Russian troops over several crossing sites into a large bend of the river west of Izyum and occupied positions to block any Soviet counter thrust out of the Izyum area. As the main

---

[33] Glantz, pg. 193.

This is a striking picture that conveys a sense of the enormous expanse of Russia and provides a reminder of the vast scale of the conflict. An unknown SS tank commander, standing erect in the cupola of his turret, signals his unit to advance, while in the distance stretches the seemingly endless Russian steppe, as featureless as an ocean. No village or road is visible as far as the eye can see. Only an indistinct gray sky that falls onto the distant horizon. The tank can be identified as a commander's vehicle by the special antenna. (Credit National Archives)

offensive thrust was to be made by the SS-Panzerkorps, Manstein gave Hoth one of Mackensen's Panzer divisions. The battle tried and experienced 11. Panzer-Division was directed to disengage from combat and transfer to the XXXXVIII. Panzerkorps as the third division of the corps.

As Manstein moved his final chess pieces into place, he could look back with satisfaction on the last days of February. Just a few weeks earlier, in the aftermath of Stalingrad, Heeresgruppe Süd had been enmeshed in continual crisis, giving ground everywhere. It had few reserves to halt the Soviet steamroller and those that were available were in danger of being encircled and destroyed at Kharkov. By the third week of February, Kharkov was lost, Armeeabteilung Lanz was being pushed out of the area and the 6th Army had seized control of key sections of the railroad net south of Kharkov.

The Russians had crossed the Mius with the 4th Guards Mechanized Corps and penetrated Armeeabteilung Hollidt's front. Mobile Group Popov had cut off through the railroad supply lines to Armeeabteilung Hollidt and 1. Panzerarmee. A huge undefended gap yawned between Kharkov and Slavyansk and two Soviet armies were pouring into the gap. The Soviet 40th Army was west of Kharkov and needed only to link up with Rybalko's 6th Guards Cavalry to encircle Armeeabteilung Lanz.

However, by 3 March an amazing reversal had begun. Hoth's 4. Panzerarmee had shattered Rybalko's 3rd Tank Army and approached the southern edge of Kharkov. The 1. Panzerarmee was holding firm on the Northern Donets and had blocked all Soviet attempts to thrust south from the river. Mobile Group Popov was fighting for its life and the vital railroad network between the Dnepr and the Donets was secured. Armeeabteilung Hollidt had turned back all attempts by the Russians to cross the Mius River the Russian troops in its rear areas were surrounded and destroyed. The Soviet 1st Guards and 6th Armies were bloodied and in retreat. One of the most remarkable turnabouts in the history of World War II was well underway.

The point where a looming disaster was halted can be traced to the SS-Panzerkorps operations beginning on 19-20 February. "Das Reich" and "Totenkopf" first blocked the Russian threat to the Dnepr bridges, then cut through the entire front of the Soviet 6th Army. Subsequently the two divisions turned north and crushed the Soviet 3rd Tank Army. Manstein had masterfully allowed the Russians to advance into the Kharkov-Slavyansk gap until Hoth's 4. Panzerarmee unleashed its Panzer corps on the Russian's overextended southern flank. Hausser wielded his SS divisions aggressively and relentlessly. The SS divisions attacked a surprised, and subsequently disheartened opponent. The Russian soldier was gradually becoming demoralized by the unrelenting, sledge hammer blows and slashing attacks of the SS divisions. The fact that the Germans had been so close to utter defeat and had literally risen from the ashes and mud, made the inexplicable reversal all the more devastating to Russian morale. By 3 March, the opportunity to recapture Kharkov was at hand. Hausser's SS divisions were returning to the city where a few short weeks ago they had been forced to withdraw in order to save themselves from utter destruction.

12

THE ADVANCE TO KHARKOV

By 3 March, the initiative in the southern Ukraine rested firmly in German hands. The 3rd Tank Army was smashed, the 6th and 1st Guards Armies were in retreat and the Panzer divisions of 4. Panzerarmee rolled northward, closing in on Kharkov. Manstein described the situation in *Lost Victories*:

> After thus regaining the initiative by the victory between the Donets and the Dnepr, Southern Army Group proceeded to deliver the stroke against the 'Voronezh Front' – i.e. the enemy forces located in Kharkov area – in accordance with an order already issued on the 28th of February. The intention was to attack these forces in their southern flank with the aim either of turning the latter or – if at all possible – of later driving into the enemy rear from the east. Our object was not the possession of Kharkov but the defeat – and if possible, the destruction of the enemy units located there.[1]

After culmination of the 4. Panzerarmee's operation to destroy the 3rd Tank Army, Armeeabteilung Kempf launched an attack on the 69th Army with the main effort directed against the boundary it shared with the 3rd Tank Army. Kempf's objective was to occupy the Russians west of the city by a frontal attack which would fix them in place while Hoth's Panzer Division struck their flank and rear areas from the south. "Grossdeutschland," after completing its rest and reequipping, was to supply the major offensive power of Kempf's attack. Regiment "Thule" also played a key role in the attack. These two mobile formations were ideally suited to the operations that followed. The infantry divisions of Korps Raus were of less offensive value, but were to be utilized in supporting attacks.

According to German Army doctrine, in preparation for a frontal counterattack, the necessary mobile reserves should be moved into assembly areas close behind the breakthrough area. The positioning of such a mobile reserve was crucial, for it had to be quickly available, but far enough removed from the front lines so that its flexibility of movement was not compromised by an unexpected enemy penetration.[2] It was essential for maximum effectiveness, that the reserves be located in a secure area, so that they were not exposed to the attrition of debilitating local actions and enemy air strikes. The screening actions of the Korps Raus infantry divisions provided this security for "Grossdeutschland." Regiment "Thule" also remained in combat, providing valuable mobile firepower to 320. Infanterie-Division.

The Poltava-Krasnograd salient remained intact after the departure of the SS divisions, due to two factors, the first of which was the decline in Russian strength. By the time that the SS-Panzerkorps and XXXXVIII. Panzerkorps were ready to assault the Kharkov area on a united attack frontage, the Russian forces opposite Armeeabteilung Kempf had lost most of their tanks and artillery. Supply was increasingly hampered by German air attacks and Russian infantry strength was greatly reduced.

The second factor was that the Germans were able to operate on interior lines, with supply assured and were not hampered by orders restricting the army's freedom to make adjustments in the front. Thus Armeeabteilung Kempf was able to make tactical withdrawals when necessary, as justified by the situation. Both Lanz and Kempf conducted phased withdrawals that allowed them to

---

[1] Manstein, pg. 433.
[2] Raus, Erhard, (commander of Korps Raus): German Defense Tactics against Russian Breakthroughs, contained in *The Anvil of War - German Generalship in Defense on the Eastern Front.* pg 135.

exhaust the Russians and maintain defensive integrity, while keeping their losses to an acceptable level. At the same time they inflicted consistent losses upon the Russian rifle divisions which debilitated them.

Due to the above factors, the situation was ideal for Korps Raus to launch a supporting attack when the SS-Panzerkorps closed in on Kharkov. The potential threat to the flank of the 69th Army was clear, certainly so after the shattering of Rybalko's armor in the Kegitschevka pocket. Golikov, possibly surprised at the quick collapse of the 3rd Tank Army, belatedly reacted to the threat looming from the south after 28 February. Kazakov's suspended all offensive operations by the 69th Army and pulled his rifle divisions back. He placed all of his remaining armor and most of the available anti-tank guns in defensive positions on his southern flank, in order to provide protection from the SS advance. This realignment spelled the end of any significant offensive pressure against 320. Infanterie-Division and 167. Infanterie-Division units between the Merchik and Merla Rivers, north of the Poltava-Ljubotin-Kharkov railroad line.

After having been misinformed by the optimistic reports and misleading situation reports received from Vatutin it had become clear to Golikov that his armies were in real danger. He recognized the threat posed by the SS divisions and ordered Moskalenko to withdraw three rifle divisions from the 40th Army and assemble them in the Akhtyrka area, so that they could be available to support the 69th Army, if necessary. After this realignment of his army, Moskalenko was left with only three depleted rifle divisions and a handful of tanks. These meager forces were stationed along the Psel River, some 70-80 kilometers west of Achtyrka.[3]

In the meantime, Rybalko hurriedly tried to put together a new defensive line. He moved reinforcements to his flanks, while in the center, he deployed the remnants of the divisions which had escaped the Kegitschevka pocket, including tank troops utilized as infantry. On the west flank of the 3rd Tank Army, adjacent to the 69th Army boundary, the 48th Guards Rifle Division held positions near Novaja Vodolaga. The 253rd Rifle Brigade and a few tanks of the 195th Tank Brigade held the town itself. In the center of the army, the 62nd Guards Rifle Division defended a line between Novaja Vodolaga and Ochotschaje. The east flank was defended by the 25th Guards Rifle Division and the 179th Tank Brigade, which occupied a line from Ochotschaje eastwards to Zmiev. In Ochotschaje Rybalko stationed a 900 man Czechoslovakian volunteer battalion.[4]

<hr />

[3] Glantz, pg. 193.
[4] Op cit.

A knocked out American M3 Stuart light tank, which was provided to the Russian army through Lend-Lease agreements with the western Allies. The Russians did not like the tanks sent by either Britain or the United States because they considered them undergunned and too lightly armored. Note the interesting camouflage scheme, which resembles one of the patterns seen on Waffen-SS smocks. (Credit National Archives)

"Totenkopf" Mops Up the Kegitschevka Pocket

Regiment Eicke was subordinated to "Das Reich" on 2 March, while the remainder of the division remained in action in the Kegitschevka area. The night of 2-3 March saw the last frantic attempts of the Russians to break out of the Kegitschevka-Jeremejevka area. There were equally intense efforts by "Totenkopf" and Meyer's Aufklärüngsabteilung to block their escape. Soviet columns repeatedly ran into SS troops along the perimeter of the encirclement throughout the night and the following day. Weather again played a significant role in the combat operations of the day, because a very heavy snow that had fallen during the night, melted in the morning when daytime temperatures climbed quickly. The deluge of runoff water left many main roads almost impassable to wheeled vehicles and were often completely flooded with swift moving, muddy water.

On the night of 2-3 March, led by its commander, Major General M.I. Zinkovich, a column of the 12th Tank Corps broke out of the northeastern edge of the pocket. Zinkovich's column assaulted German troops in the village of Paraskovejewsky. At 0130 hours, the Russian column struck "Totenkopf" positions, catching the Germans troops by surprise. Shortly after midnight, the night was suddenly alive with explosions and the shouts of charging Russian soldiers. Houses began to burn after shells exploded along the northern edge of Paraskovejewsky and shadowy Russian vehicles raced east, toward a small village a short distance down the road. SS Pioniere and supply troops, suddenly awakened, stumbled out of their vehicles and huts, grabbing rifles and machine guns. A company of the Panzer regiment was also in the town, and the tank crews quickly tried to get their bearing and direct fire on the Soviets.

However, by that time, many of the Russians had made their escape and were charging away down the road or had dispersed into forests east of Paraskovejewsky. The tail end of the column came under fire when it attempted to pass through the town after the Germans had were alerted. A hastily organized Pioniere Kampfgruppe, supported by a few tanks, attacked the Soviet column and broke it up. Flares and blazing trucks cast a flickering light over the narrow roads and dense forests. The Russians abandoned vehicles which were disabled and scattered into the protective cover of night and forest, pursued by tracers and tank shells.[5]

A breakout attempt by the 15th Tank Corps struck German positions near Losovaja, on the Jefremovka-Paraskoveja road. The town was occupied by troops belonging to SS Kradschützen-Bataillon 2, while III./Regiment "Der Führer" held nearby positions on the Berestovaja River at Medvedovka. In the area southeast of the two towns were II./and III./Regiment "Eicke," as well as units of I./SS-Panzer-Regiment 3, under Erwin Meierdress. In a force estimated by the Germans to be about two regiments, the Russians attacked Losovaja and Medvedovka in the early morning hours of 2-3 March, trying to escape to the north.[6]

The breakout attempt was launched just before daylight on 3 March, hoping to catch the Germans napping. However, in this sector, the Germans were more alert, probably having been aware of the situation by reports from Regiment "Totenkopf." Almost immediately the Russian columns ran into solid opposition at Losovaja and Medvedovka. There were several batteries of howitzers, supported by 88s in firing positions south of the towns. When the Russians began their attacks, the howitzers lowered their gun barrels parallel to the ground and fired shell after shell into the massed attackers with direct fire.

After the early morning sun came up, the 88s were put into action also and several Russian tanks were disabled by hits from high explosive shells. With their tanks knocked out, the attacking Soviet infantry was decimated by German fire. The columns recoiled backwards at both villages, the survivors retreating to the southeast or east. One large group veered off toward the town of Kotljarovka, which was occupied by II./Regiment "Eicke." Other groups, fleeing to the southeast, suddenly appeared in the rear of III./Regiment "Totenkopf" west of Jeremejevka.[7]

A "Totenkopf" Panzer III in a Russian village street. During the night of 2-3 March the Soviet troops surrounded in the Kegistschevka pocket tried to fight their way out of the encirclement and withdraw to the north or east. A significant number of "Totenkopf" tanks were distributed throughout its rear areas in order to protect supply and support troops. (Credit National Archives)

Arriving at Kotljarovka at approximately 0700 hours, the Russians found the road blocked by II./"Eicke." Desperate to find their escape path blocked, the Russians furiously assaulted the town, seeking to ram their way through the SS troops and escape. The startled men of the SS battalion were immediately involved in house to house fighting. Soviet infantry charged into the village, fighting with the intensity of desperation. The battalion commander, Kurt Launer, was concerned that the furious assault would overwhelm his men and called for help. Kaiser's III./"Der Führer" launched a counterattack from Losovaja, in order to break up the Russian assault. When the "Der Führer" battalion suddenly appeared on their flank the Russians broke off their attack and withdrew to the southeast. German air reconnaissance reported a Russian column leaving the Kotljarovka area at 0845, moving in the direction of Jeremejevka and this was almost certainly troops of the 15th Tank Corps. The survivors of this group ran into I./"Totenkopf" northwest of Jeremejevka at 1500 hours and was reported destroyed by the battalion. During one of these breakout attacks, the corps commander, Major General V.A. Koptsov, was killed. The corps essentially disintegrated, losing or abandoning all of its heavy weapons, although a number of the tank crews and other troops eventually made their way to safety. The rifle divisions assigned to the army were reduced to shattered fragments.[8]

While the fighting raged around Kotljarovka, I./and III./ "Totenkopf" began a concentric attack on the Soviet forces en-

---
[5] Vopersal, pg. 182 and Glantz, pg. 191.
[6] Weidinger, pg. 150 and Vopersal, pg. 191.
[7] NA/T-354, roll 120, 1a KTB: Darstellung der Ereignisse, frame 3753671.

---
[8] Vopersal, pg. 182 and NA/T-354, roll 120, 1a KTB: Darstellung der Ereignisse, frame 3753669-3670.

trenched in Jeremejevka. Attacking from the west and north, the two battalions immediately ran into heavy machine gun fire. After several machine gun nests were knocked out by assault gun fire the SS Grenadiers were able to push into the town from several directions. At 0800, a Russian battle group consisting of a few T-34s with mounted infantry attempted to reinforce the Russian troops holding Jeremejevka. The Soviet tank group approached the town from the south, where it ran into tanks of I./SS Panzer-Regiment 3. After a sharp fight in which one Russian tank was struck and damaged, a half dozen of the T-34s turned east, where they encountered supply troops of III./Regiment "Eicke." The Soviet tanks raced completely past the surprised rear echelon troops and disappeared down the road to the northeast. At 1100 hours, Jeremejevka was taken by the Germans, who found piles of dead and wounded Russians in the ruined houses and rubble strewn streets. SS losses were high as well and Vopersal mentions that the SS troops buried many of their comrades in a makeshift burial site located on the edge of the village.[9]

---

[9] Vopersal, pg. 182 and NA/T-354, roll 120, 1a KTB: Darstellung der Ereignisse, frame 3753669-3670, pg.182-183.

Several 15th Tank Corps columns were able to make their way through the pocket with relatively little difficulty and moved eastward until they crossed the Orel River. One of these groups ran headlong into Seela's Pioniere battalion, which was still reinforced by a number of "Totenkopf" tanks. The SS Kampfgruppe blocked the road, whereupon the Soviets turned and melted away into the countryside. The column split up into small groups who made their way through German lines to the east or north. "Totenkopf's" Panzer regiment assembled and moved toward the eastern edge of Kegitschevka, in support of SS Aufklärungsabteilung 3, which attacked from southeast of the town. The Kampfgruppe occupied positions east of the town during the later afternoon hours. Shortly before dark, a battalion or more of Soviet cavalry tried to break through positions of the "Totenkopf" reconnaissance battalion.

At first, only a few small cavalry patrol detachments were observed north and south of the battalion forward posts. Suddenly, however, a swarm of horsemen galloped into view, racing toward the Orel River. Before the alarm could be raised, the cavalry was in the midst of the German positions, hacking at anyone in their path with drawn sabers. The startled Germans grabbed their rifles and machine pistols and began firing on the horsemen speeding through their outposts. However, the Russians passed through the forward

A "Das Reich" Sturmgeschütz III with the L48 main gun during early March of 1943. The L48 gun, which fired a high velocity 7.5cm round, replaced the original short barreled infantry gun. The assault guns were designed to furnish infantry support but gradually they became an important part of the anti-tank capability of the German divisions. (Courtesy Mark C. Yerger)

positions so quickly, they did not suffer heavy losses at first. Once they had passed through the German lines however, a quick thinking German forward observer directed artillery fire on the cavalry as they galloped eastward. Within seconds high explosive shells erupted on the steppe, throwing up sprays of black earth and snow. Horses and riders spilled to the ground as shrapnel and rock hard clods of earth flew through the air and found them. SS SPWs pursued several groups of cavalry, who could be seen in the distance, spurring their horses furiously. The half tracks and armored cars fired machine guns and 2cm guns at the horsemen, but within minutes the surviving Russians disappeared.[10]

Meanwhile, "Das Reich" and Regiment "Eicke" were trying to coordinate a renewal of the attack toward Ochotschaje. However, the attack did not take place as planned, because containing the unpredictable Soviet breakout attempts occupied most of Regiment "Der Führer" and Regiment "Eicke" during the whole day. The weather and road conditions remained terrible and the road from Jefremovka to Ochotschaje was totally impassable for wheeled vehicles, while the road from Paraskoveja to Staroverovka became barely usable even for tracked vehicles when freezing sleet covered the black, deep mud. It proved impossible to get sufficient supplies and ammunition to the forward combat elements and the attack was postponed. While "Das Reich" and "Totenkopf" were tied up with the reduction of the pocket, "Leibstandarte" finally attempted to get moving once again.[11]

Elements of "Leibstandarte" blocked an escape attempt by a small group of Russians near Berestovaja. The division spent most of the day trying to assemble for the attack ordered for 4 March. The road conditions north of Staroverovka were somewhat better than in the "Das Reich" sector and "Leibstandarte" was able to conduct a reconnaissance attack north of the town during the afternoon. Peiper's SPW battalion left Staroverovka at 1500 hours and made its way northward. By 1700 hours, the battalion reached Nikolskoje, a small town northwest of Staroverovka. Peiper halted in the town and established defensive positions for the night.

When the day's action ended and night settled over the sector, many groups of Russians still tried to infiltrate past German positions throughout the hours of darkness. Most Soviet formations in the pocket above company strength had either escaped or been destroyed in the attempt. But many small groups of Russian troops were able to make their way out of the area and eventually reached Soviet lines.

Again the situation was chaotic in the communications zone of the division. Russians appeared out of the night at unexpected places and without warning. Throughout the area, gunfire and explosions could be heard all night long. Tracers sailed through the night sky, signaling a location where a Soviet column had bumped into German troops. A small Russian column even stumbled into the perimeter of the Panzerkorps Headquarters during the night. After losing one T-34, it was forced to withdraw and find another escape route, disappearing into the darkness as quickly as it had come.

While the night was periodically lit up by these small fire fights, the SS divisions attempted to repair their tanks and other vehicles, move up stores of supplies and fuel and make ready for the following day. The tank strength of all three divisions had declined markedly. However "Das Reich," which had only eight tanks, all of which were Panzer IIIs was in the worst condition. In contrast, its anti-tank gun strength was high, with twenty-eight 5cm Pak, sixteen 7.5cm guns and an assortment of eight captured Russian anti-tank guns of various calibers. "Totenkopf" still had forty-two operational Panzer IIIs (seventeen others being in various stages of repair) sixteen Panzer IVs and six "Tigers," a total of sixty-four tanks. The division also had sixteen assault guns and forty-seven 5cm or 7.5cm anti-tank guns, either towed or on various self-propelled mountings. "Leibstandarte" possessed seventy-four tanks, of which seven were light Panzer IIs, and twenty-one Befehlwagen. The division possessed an unusually high number of anti-tank guns (sixty), a total of thirteen 88s and sixteen Sturmgeschütz IIIs.[12]

The SS-Panzerkorps prepared for the continuation of its attack to the north and remained occupied with cleaning out the Kegitschevka pocket on 4 March. The weather was still miserable in the day time because heavy wet snow and freezing rain fell constantly. The temperatures fell to below freezing during the night and the muck froze solid. The weather remained very unpredictable however. During the night of 4 March, a raging snowstorm dumped a heavy snow over the entire sector and gale force winds piled up deep drifts. The snow turned into freezing rain and the drifts were transformed into banks of ice that glazed over the deeply rutted roads. Except for tracked vehicles, the roads were impassable and even tanks and assault guns had difficulty moving. In these conditions, merely arriving at the top of a hill was a triumph. However, in spite of these handicaps, for the first time, some elements of the corps were able to go over to offensive actions in the morning.

"Totenkopf" had organized ad hoc battle groups from supply personnel, flak crews and headquarters security units, in order to defend its supply lines. Although most of the larger formations of Russian rifle divisions or tank corps had been wiped out, smaller

[10] Vopersal, pg. 184.
[11] NA/T-354, roll 120, 1a KTB: Darstellung der Ereignisse, frame 3753671-3753672.

[12] NA/T-354, roll 118, Tagesmeldung Gen.Kdo. SS-Panzerkorps an Panzerarmee Oberkommando 4, 4.3.1943, frame 3752114.

groups of Soviet troops roamed through the entire rear area. These men, desperately seeking to escape, created havoc. The Russians had largely abandoned their useless vehicles and split up into small groups of men carrying only small arms.

During the course of the entire day, the improvised SS security groups were involved in actions against the Russians still passing through the division's communications zone. Some of the SS detachments were utilized to protect crossroads or supply depots, while others actively searched for Russian stragglers who often tried to hide in the numerous small villages throughout the area. These mopping up actions proved to be both a distraction to combat operations and contributed to further supply system problems. The interrupted supply of fuel and ammunition continued to cause delays and hampered the combat operations of "Totenkopf" and to a lesser extent, "Das Reich." One of the last groups of the 15th Guards Tank Corps, which still had a number of operational tanks, tried to break out and cross the Orel River north of Nishny Orel. Elements of II./SS-Panzer-Regiment 3, supply troops and a Pioniere detachment first blocked the escape of the Russians and then drove them into a small pocket. Artillery and Stukas help finish off the surviving Russian tanks and men.

At midday, division commander Simon was ordered by Hausser to finish cleaning out the pocket quickly, because the division remained so occupied in the task of fighting the Soviets infiltrating across their supply lines, that it could not devote full attention to offensive actions. Simon had allowed a significant portion of his division's tanks to be assigned to several of the small Kampfgruppen combating the Russian stragglers. This was a tactical mistake because the tanks needed to be concentrated in the main attack group of the division.

In order to carry out the orders which he had received from SS-Panzerkorps, Simon ordered SS-Hauptsturmführer Walter Reder to organize a Kampfgruppe built around his battalion, drive through the pocket and sweep it clean of any further Soviet resistance. Reder put together a group that included his SPW battalion, an assault gun battery, Flak detachments and Grenadiers detached from Regiment "Eicke." A few batteries of artillery, all of which were motorized or fully tracked, supported the operation. After receiving his new orders, Reder organized his Kampfgruppe near Jeremejevka.

Reinforced with this heavy firepower Reder's battalion swept through the pocket and crushed the last remaining Soviet resistance. On 3 April 1943 Reder received the Knight's Cross for this successful action. In his recommendation for the award, division commander Simon listed the material Reder's Kampfgruppe captured or destroyed in the period of time between 1 and 4 March. This included thirteen tanks, eighty-two guns, a Flak battery and over

An 88 ready for action against ground targets. "Totenkopf" brought its Flak guns on line around the perimeter of the Kegitschevka pocket and used them against Russian tanks and other vehicles which tried to break through the division's lines. (Credit National Archives)

three hundred vehicles, as well as innumerable sleds and wagons. Hundreds of Soviet soldiers were killed or captured.[13]

North of the pocket, "Das Reich" resumed offensive action. Stadler's II./"Der Führer" prepared for battle north of Paraskoveja, however, a divisional artillery battalion which had been assigned to support the battalion, was not able to reach the assembly area on time. To take the place of the mobile artillery, Stadler commandeered a battery of "Das Reich's" 8.8cm guns from the Flak battalion. After a difficult and tortuous trip over miserable roads, the battalion reached the northwest edge of Ochotschaje before mid-morning. The Germans found the town was occupied by elements of the 62nd Guards Rifle Division, supported by a few T-34s. Under cover of the 88s and the battalion's own heavy weapons, the SS Grenadiers stormed into Ochotschaje and seized the northern part of the town.

Four Soviet tanks were damaged or destroyed by shells from the 88s. After the Russian tanks were put out of action, the Germans were able to push the Soviets out of the center of the town. By later morning, the remaining Russians were isolated in the southern and western sections of Ochotschaje. Heavy fighting continued, because the trapped Russian infantry fought back with the desperation of men whose only hope lay in killing their attackers before they were killed themselves. Unexpectedly, the Russians in the town received help from outside the perimeter.

While the battalion was involved fighting the Russians in the town itself, Soviet tanks counterattacked, trying to break through to relieve their comrades in the village. On two separate occasions, groups of T-34s appeared on the road leading into the village and tried to force their way through into the center of the village, but

---

[13] National Archives, copies of Berlin Document Center records. Vorschlag Nr. 1680, für die Verleihung des Ritterkreuz des Eisernen Kreuze. Simon's recommendation was submitted on 4 April, 1943. Courtesy of Mark Yerger.

both times fire from the 88s turned them back. By late afternoon, after the Russians gave up trying to rescue their comrades, the SS troops crushed the last pockets of Russians in the town.[14]

Earlier, while the fighting still raged in Ochotschaje, elements of I./"Deutschland" struggled through waist deep snowdrifts in the morning and knee deep mud in the afternoon. The regiment was strung out along the road leading from Jefremovka to Ochotschaje. The lead elements began to straggle into the nearby town of Karavanskoje at 1615 hours. Karavanskoje was northwest of Ochotschaje and adjacent to the right or eastern flank of "Leibstandarte's" attack sector. Meanwhile, the other two battalions of Harmel's regiment assembled with difficulty, the roads behind them strewn with disabled trucks. The transmissions or running gear of many vehicles, already worn out through days of torturous use, finally gave out due to the demands placed on it by Russian roads.

"Leibstandarte" was also unable to continue its attack north of the Berestovaja River on 4 March. This was due partially to the road conditions and in part to the condition of its vehicles, which were breaking down at an alarming rate. Dietrich ordered Meyer's Aufklärungsabteilung and I./Panzer-Regiment "LAH" to move back to Krasnograd, for a much needed refitting and repair. Peiper's half track battalion was ordered to remain in Nikolskoje, until it was replaced by Max Hansen's battalion of Panzergrenadiers. After Hansen arrived, Peiper moved his battalion to the west, toward the town of Jarotin, where it assembled before attacking the village of Stanitschny. The battalion met little resistance and Stanitschny was reported occupied without difficulty by 1205 hours. During the rest of the day, the battalion conducted a number of reconnaissance probes along roads radiating from Stanitschny.

Late in the afternoon, Hoth radioed instructions to his Panzer corps for the next day. By the end of 5 February, the SS-Panzerkorps was to finish mopping up its rear areas, destroy all remaining Russian forces south of Paraskoveja. Hoth intended to move the divisions to assembly positions in preparation for the resumption of the attack on 6 March. All of the rest of 4. Panzerarmee would operate in support of the SS-Panzerkorps, protecting its eastern flank from attack originating from the Northern Donets area. The XXXXVIII. Panzerkorps was ordered to conduct a parallel attack to the north, with the objective of reaching the Merefa area and seizing crossings over the Msha River. Along with the newly arrived 11. Panzer-Division, the corps was to concentrate in the Ochotschaje area as soon as possible in order to maintain contact with the SS-Panzerkorps divisions. The 11. Panzer-Division reached the Orel River sector at 0500 hours on 4 March, making contact with elements of "Totenkopf's" Pioniere Abteilung south of Jefremovka.

The two extremes of Ukrainian weather conditions in early March. The top picture is a "Das Reich" column of tanks and trucks on a village road covered with snow and ice, while the bottom picture shows an SS motorcycle bogged down in mud. (Mark C. Yerger)

---

[14] NA/T-354, roll 120, 1a KTB: Darstellung der Ereignisse, frame 3753674 and Weidinger, pg. 76.

Seela's combat engineers were still fighting Russian troops trying to flee across the Orel River.

The LVII. Panzerkorps was to take over defense of the sector east of XXXXVIII. Panzerkorps right flank and which extended to the XXXX. Panzerkorps western flank. Hoth reorganized his divisions on 3 March, taking 17. Panzer-Division from XXXXVIII. Panzerkorps and giving it to LVII. Panzerkorps. The 15. Infanterie-Division, formerly under command of SS-Panzerkorps, was also placed under command of this headquarters, which had arrived with no divisions of its own. The introduction of the LVII. Panzerkorps on the army's eastern flank allowed the 6. and 11. Panzer-Divisions to concentrate their attack on a narrower front.

The objective of the next phase of the SS-Panzerkorps attack was to destroy Russian forces south of the Msha River between Bachmetjevka and Valki, in preparation for an attack on Kharkov itself.[15] The operations of the three divisions were hindered every day by poor road conditions, particularly after the sun rose and melted the ice and frozen mud. During the morning hours of 5 March, "Totenkopf" began to assemble in preparation for the next phase of the attack. Seela's Pioniere Bataillon was reinforced with a platoon of Panzer IIIs and was held as divisional reserve while one platoon was still building a reinforced bridge over the Berestovaja River, near Staroverovka. While "Totenkopf" finally secured its rear areas and began to regroup, the other two divisions of the SS-Panzerkorps tried to get on the move once again.

Regiment "Deutschland," advancing on the western (left) flank of "Das Reich," moved northward in two battalion columns from jump off points around the town of Staroverovka. Ehrath's I./ "Deutschland," reinforced with IV./SS Artillerie Regiment 2, pushed towards the town of Stanitschny. In the other column, III./ "Deutschland" made slow progress along a parallel mud track slightly to the east. Regiment "Der Führer" marched north from Ochotschaje, on the right (eastern) flank of the division, accompanied by fleets of Stukas. The Luftwaffe had been ordered to commit the bulk of its available planes to aid the advance of "Das Reich." This may have been due to the tank losses of the division, which had only eleven operational tanks on 5 March. Hausser had radioed an urgent request for additional armor to the SS Führungshauptamt (SS Main Office), stating that it was of decisive importance that "Das Reich" receive fifty Panzer IVs immediately. However "Das Reich" did not get any tanks because the SS Führungshauptamt itself did not have tanks of its own and was dependent on the armor that was supplied to the Waffen-SS by the Army.[16]

The SS divisions struggled forward on increasingly deteriorating roads during the night of 5 March. All movements were time consuming and stressful, draining the last strength from the men

and taxing limited fuel supplies as well. Tanks and assault guns used a great deal more fuel in bad weather and trucks carrying tins of fuel often had difficulty keeping up with the tracked vehicles. Both "Das Reich" and "Leibstandarte" did their best to keep on the move all through the night and attempted to reach their assigned jump off areas for the next day's attack.

There was no rest for the weary men, other than brief snatches of uneasy sleep while bouncing and sliding over the muddy tracks that passed for roads. Wedged into the backs of unheated trucks or half tracks, sitting on small benches, the Panzergrenadiers were thrown continually from side to side as the vehicles slid into mud holes or swerved up and down hills. When a truck slid off the road and became stuck, the cold and miserable men had to climb out into the freezing night and put their shoulder to the sides of the vehicle. Standing knee deep in icy slush, the exhausted Grenadiers shoved the trucks or half tracks out of the half frozen mud. Temperatures of twenty below freezing were still common in March.

Afterwards, the Grenadiers would climb back in, covered with cold mud and soaked with sweat, which froze once they were moving again. For most of the long hours of darkness before the attack was to begin, the Grenadiers of the two divisions spent the night in such a fashion. The drivers got even less sleep. One can imagine that more than one driver fell sound asleep while somewhere far ahead, a truck or tank was hauled out of a mud hole. Behind the spearhead columns, equally tired supply troops drove through the pitch black night, searching for their assigned assembly areas. Trucks became stuck or broke down with increasing frequency and many failed to deliver their precious cargo of fuel and ammunition. Inevitably, there were delays and in "Leibstandarte's" sector, most of the division's attacks could not begin at the scheduled time on 6 March.

"Leibstandarte" leads the Assault Upon Kharkov

Meyer's Aufklärungsabteilung, reinforced by a Panzerjäger company and Max Wünsche's I./SS Panzer-Rgt. 1 was to have begun its attack at 0700 hours. However, only four "Tigers" had arrived at assembly area by the jump off time. In addition, the artillery battalion supporting the attack was not in position at 0700 hours and could not deliver fire support. Due to similar problems, the attack of SS-PzG.-Rgt. 1 "LAH" was delayed also. Hours later, after the

[15] NA/T-354, roll 118, Funkspruch 4. Panzerarmee to 1a SS-Panzerkorps. Received 4.3.43 at 1954 hours and Sturmbannführer Max Seela's report of the actions of SS Pioniere Bataillon 3, which was corps reserve on March, frame 3752118-3752122.

[16] Weidinger, pg. 85.

last tanks arrived and the artillery was ready, the division finally began its attack. In spite of the delays, the advance by both attack groups was successful, primarily because the Russians were pulling back to their next defensive line. Only weak rear guards covered the withdrawal and the SS attack columns easily overwhelmed most of them. In the attack sector of SS-PzG.-Rgt. 1 "LAH," the III./and II./battalions fought their way into Bobrovka, while Frey's battalion took Michailovka at 1800 hours. Although Witt's regiment gained ground fairly quickly primarily due to the weakness of the opposition, Meyer's attack met more solid resistance.[17]

The "Leibstandarte" armored recon battalion struggled northward until it reached a village named Sneshkov Kut, which was occupied by Russian troops. Immediately the column deployed into assault formation, with Meyer personally leading the attack from the Panzer of 2. Kompanie commander, SS-Obersturmführer Wilhelm Beck. The tanks rolled to the attack with the half tracks and armored cars following behind. Wünsche ordered one company of tanks to swing east and attack the town from the flank. The remaining eighteen Panzers deployed on line and rumbled cautiously forward, the half tracks wallowing through the snow behind them, their engines racing as the drivers fought to keep up. The battalion's Schwimmwagen had no hope of navigating the mushy steppe terrain. Each one was filled with Grenadiers and were hauled behind each tank by a steel towing cable.

Soon the tanks approached to within a kilometer of Sneshkov Kut, cresting a low hill which had previously shielded their advance. As the elongated Russian village came into view, anti-tank gun fire immediately erupted from houses along the perimeter. Shells sizzled through the air past the SS Panzers, or threw up snow in front of them. The Soviet guns had opened fire prematurely and at too great a distance, making the fatal mistake of revealing their firing positions. The SS tank commanders turned into the nearest shallow depression or behind a low hillock, in order to find cover. Several tanks maneuvered forward into hull down positions and fired on the line of gun flashes, knocking out some of the Russian guns. The other Panzers sped forward to the next depression or hillock and covered the movements of their comrades. In this manner, the tanks were able to get closer to the village with minimal losses. At a point about 500 meters from the village, Wünsche ordered the tanks to accelerate their advance. The tanks plunged forward, the racing tracks throwing plumes of snow and ice into the air. However, when they left cover Russian shells hit two of Wünsche's tanks and set them on fire. Beck's Panzer was hit and disabled, forcing Meyer and the crew to bail out into the storm of fire that had burst from the position in front of them.[18]

The wall of anti-tank gun fire brought the main attack to a halt temporarily. However, shortly afterward, the flanking group, which included the "Tigers," radioed that it was approaching the village

---

[17] NA/T-354, roll 120, 1a KTB: Darstellung der Ereignisse, 6.3.12943. frame 3753684.

[18] Lehmann, pg.148-151.

"Leibstandarte" trucks and half tracks in a Russian village. While "Totenkopf" and Kurt Meyer's Aufklärungsabteilung were involved in reducing the Kegitschevka pocket, the rest of Dietrich's division regrouped for the assault upon Kharkov. Peiper's battalion was able to conduct a reconnaissance attack on 3 March, in order to locate the new line held by Rybalko's 3rd Tank Army. (Credit National Archives)

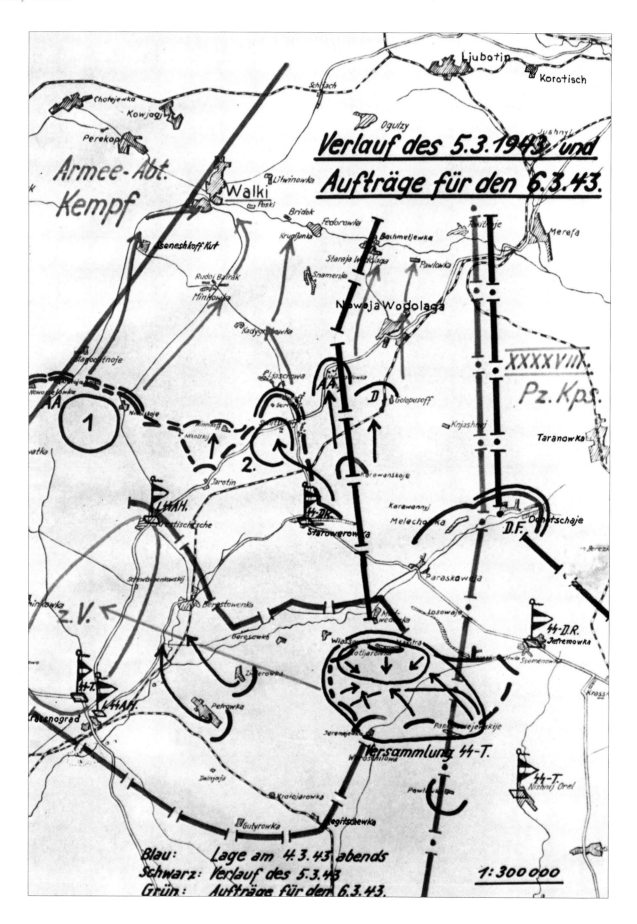

from the east. At that point, Wünsche directed the flanking group to accelerate and assault the village immediately. When the tanks came into sight in the distance, Wünsche ordered the rest of the battalion to follow him. He ordered his driver to instantly charge forward, directly toward the anti-tank gun positions. When the tanks got to within 200-300 meters of the village, a T-34 which was camouflaged in the ruins of a house, fired and knocked out another German tank. The stricken Panzer, trailing smoke, swerved to a halt and immediately burst into flame

At that point, both the SS and Russian tankers were given a lesson in the strength of the "Tiger's" frontal armor and the power of its 88mm gun. One of the armored monsters crawled slowly forward, heading directly toward the house which concealed the Russian tank. A shell struck the front of the "Tiger's" turret with a blinding flash, but there was no apparent effect. Again the T-34 gun barked, but shell glanced off of the thick turret armor, trailing a stream of sparks. The seemingly invulnerable German tank rumbled forward, its long barreled 88 slowly turning toward the house. The "Tiger" came to a halt and fired, rocked back on its suspension by the tremendous recoil of the gun. The front part of the house disintegrated after the shell plowed through the wall, struck the T-34 and blew its turret off.

A second "Tiger" moved up to support the first, just as a group of T-34s emerged from the village in a counterattack. Both "Tigers" pivoted toward the new threat and their guns turned toward the Russian tanks. The guns barked and the first 8.8cm shells punched through Russian frontal armor and turrets with ease, while the 7.6cm Russian guns could not penetrate the "Tiger's" armor. Even shells that struck the "Tiger's" armor dead on failed to penetrate the heavy steel plate. The stunned Soviet tank commanders who survived quickly realized that they were up against a new German weapon. After eight T-34s were put out of action the rest of the Soviet tanks quickly withdrew and raced away to the north until they were intercepted by the other tank company. Four additional Russian tanks were knocked out.

This encounter took the heart out of the Russians. Eight to ten T-34s were blazing just outside the village as the "Tiger's" rumbled into the town. Resistance collapsed and Russian gun crews fled when the monstrous tanks turned their guns toward their guns. The SS Grenadiers assaulted the village edge, capturing or knocking out a large number of anti-tank guns. Meyer quickly ordered his

battalion to keep moving and drove further to the north, occupying Bridok, a town on the Msha River. Immediately the battalion built a bridgehead over the small, frozen river.[19]

The SS-PzG.-Rgt. 2 "LAH" was not ready to begin its attack at sun rise, but became involved in fighting immediately, because its jump-off positions were discovered by the Russians. Soviet artillery and rocket fire was directed upon the regiment's assembly areas. However, the regiment made substantial gains in ground, in spite of the road conditions and the efforts of the Russians. Sandig's Panzergrenadiers opened a gap in the lines of the 48th Guards Rifle Division and Peiper's SPW battalion rolled through it, reaching the Msha River at Fedorovka by 1430 hours. From hills south of the town, the "Leibstandarte" troops could observe "Das Reich's" attack on Novaja Vodolaga.

The Soviet troops defending Novaja Vodolaga consisted of the 253rd Rifle Brigade and the 195th Tank Brigade, which had less than twenty tanks. After fighting through weak Russian positions south of the town, Regiment "Deutschland" neared Novaja Vodolaga in the early afternoon. It attacked the town from the south, while Stukas dropped out of the sky and bombed Russian strong points, facilitating the regiment's advance. The assault was also supported by 8.8cm guns of 1./SS-Flak Abteilung 2 and the handful of surviving "Das Reich" Panzers. While the Stukas destroyed Soviet forward positions, the 88s knocked out six Soviet tanks. By late afternoon the SS Grenadiers had reached the northern edge of Novaja Vodolaga. Those Russians that were able to escape, abandoned the town, fleeing in long columns to the north. Their withdrawal was covered by a rear guard made up of a few tanks and infantry with heavy machine guns. Mopping up operations continued into the night and it wasn't until morning that the town was cleared of Russians. While Harmel's regiment mopped up, Regiment "Der Führer" marched toward Novaja Vodolaga during the night of 6-7 March. Its leading units reached the area south of the town on the morning of 7 March.[20]

While "Das Reich" and "Leibstandarte" were involved in fighting south of the Msha River line, "Totenkopf" completed its regrouping on 6 February and was moving laterally behind the left wing of the SS-Panzerkorps, passing through the rear area of "Leibstandarte." The mission of Simon's division was to protect the western flank of the corps during the attack upon Kharkov. Meanwhile, south of the sector of attack, Russian partisans and small groups of Soviet infantry became very active again, probably having been reinforced with stragglers from the 6th Army who were

---

OPPOSITE: While a "Totenkopf" battlegroup and Kurt Meyer's Aufklärungsabteilung mopped up the remnants of Rybalko's ruined army in the Kegitschevka pocket, "Das Reich" and "Leibstandarte" broke through the shattered tank army and moved toward the Valki-Ljubotin sector, which was directly west of Kharkov. Armeeabteilung Kempf secured the western flank of the SS divisions, with its main effort in the "Grossdeutschland" sector.

[19] Lehmann, pg. 149-150 and NA/T-354, roll118, Tagesmeldungen der SS-Panzerkorps 6.3.43, frame 3752187.
[20] Weidinger, pg. 87-88.

bypassed by the German advance. The elimination of these troops was taken over by 15. Infanterie-Division and various rear area security detachments. Small battle groups were organized, reinforced with a few assault guns and directed to hunt down and eliminate the partisans. Several Partisan bands were cornered southeast of Sinel'nikovo and destroyed. Other anti-partisan operations continued against isolated detachments of regular troops hiding in the heavily forested hills in the area.[21]

As the SS divisions approached the Msha River, the XXXXVIII. Panzerkorps had slowly driven elements of Rybalko's 3rd Tank Army back toward the Msha River. Elements of the Soviet 25th Guards Rifle Division were pushed into a perimeter around the town of Taranovka, which was about 10 kilometers south of the Msha. The Russian infantry had fought stubbornly, bitterly contesting every foot of the way. On 6 March, 6. and 11. Panzer-Division attacked Taranovka. The Russian infantry in the town was supported by a dozen T-34s of the 179th Tank Brigade, which were entrenched along the perimeter of a strong point built up around a church. While the Panzergrenadiers of 6. Panzer-Division battled to take the town, the Panzer regiment of the division swung past Taranovka to the northwest. At the same time, the 11. Panzer-Division Kampfgruppe moved along the southern bank of the Msha, looking for a good crossing site. This line of advance put it on the eastern flank of "Das Reich's" sector.[22]

A large part of 6. Panzer-Division remained locked in the struggle for Taranovka, battling the Russian rifle division and its supporting tanks. Taranovka was an important rail center because a main railroad line ran from there to Merefa and continued into the southern section of Kharkov. Control of this rail line would allow the Germans to bring trains up from the southern crossings over the Dnepr and provided a direct rail line supply route for troops attacking Kharkov. A second railroad, which passed through Novaja Vodolaga, intersected with the Taranovka-Merefa line and crossed the Msha at Rakitnoje. The XXXXVIII. Panzerkorps was assigned the task of taking the segment of the railroad leading through Rakitnoje. The 11. Panzer-Division assaulted the Msha River line south of Rakitnoje and attempted to cross the river at that point. However, in bitter fighting, the Soviets prevented the Germans from establishing a bridgehead on the northern bank of the river. Throughout the rest of the day, the corps was unable to make a decisive breakthrough, with 6. Panzer-Division fighting for Taranovka and 11. Panzer-Division unable to get across the Msha at Rakitnoje.[23]

An interesting picture because it shows a German medical vehicle (note the red cross on the side of the truck) which appears to have been used to transport fuel instead of wounded. (Credit National Archives)

The German efforts to clear out the Kegitschevka pocket forced small groups of Russians to scatter in all directions and attempt to escape through German lines. "Totenkopf's" rear areas remained in a state of chaos and the combat strength of the division was tied up in attempts to secure its supply lines. Hausser ordered division commander Max Simon to finish mopping up the remaining Russian troops. The picture shows a German soldier cautiously entering a Russian home with pistol drawn. (Credit National Archives)

[21] NA/T-354, roll 118, 4. Panzerarmee Tagesmeldung an SS-Panzerkorps, 6.3.1943, frames 3752187 and 3752188.

[22] Paul, Wolfgang, *Brennpunkte - Die Geschichte der 6. Panzerdivision (1. leichte) 1937-1945*, pg. 293.

[23] Glantz, pg. 196-197 and NA/T-313, roll 367, Morgenmeldung 4. Panzerarmee, frame 8633251.

The Attack of Armeeabteilung Kempf - The Western Flank

Armeeabteilung Kempf began its supporting attacks against the boundary of the 69th and 3rd Tank Armies on 7 March, just as 4. Panzerarmee struck Rybalko's 3rd Tank Army. On the previous morning, the German 2. Armee's 332. Infanterie-Division (southern flank of the army) established tenuous contact with the north wing of Korps Raus, about fifty kilometers west of Achtyrka, at the town of Vesprik. Reconnaissance by the Luftwaffe during the night had detected signs of heavy motor traffic along the front, which could have possibly been the first arriving elements of the three rifle divisions transferred from the 69th Army. There was more direct evidence of the transfer of rifle divisions when the intelligence detachment of Armeeabteilung Kempf intercepted a radio communication between the 107th Rifle Division and the HQ of the 40th Army. The Germans were able to establish that the 107th was withdrawn from the northern wing of the army south of Sumy and was to be assembled in the Achtyrka area. A further indication that a planned and major realignment was underway was evident form Soviet measures to protect the march route, such as installing abnormally strong Flak detachments near bridges in the Achtyrka area. With Soviet forces in the midst of shifting their forces, the timing for the beginning of the Korps Raus attack could not have been better.[24]

The Armeeabteilung was given the mission of attacking the Russian forces west of Kharkov and occupying these forces while the SS-Panzerkorps enveloped the city. The objective was to block a withdrawal by the 3rd Tank Army out of the Msha sector by using the main roads passing through Ljubotin. "Grossdeutschland" was to make the main effort, supported by Regiment "Thule." The 320. Infanterie-Division was to support "Grossdeutschland's" attack by screening the division's western flank in the area north and west of Regiment "Thule's" direction of attack. "Grossdeutschland" was to jump off from assembly areas in the rear of 320. Infanterie-Division positions, attack through the infantry division and advance along the line of Valki-Kovjagi-Vysokopol'ye. The attack of Korps Raus was supported by I. Fliegerkorps, which assigned most its aircraft to support of "Grossdeutschland."[25]

"Grossdeutschland" was to advance westward until it reached the section of the Poltava-Valki railroad south of the Merchik River. At that point, it was to attack northwest along the railroad, in order to clear it of Soviet troops. After taking the railroad stations at Kovjagi and Vysokopol'ye, the division was to turn north and drive

"Totenkopf" tanks in a Russian village. Hausser needed "Totenkopf's" tanks to be available for the attack upon Kharkov, instead of being tied up securing the rear areas of the division. (Credit National Archives)

SS-Sturmbannführer Max Hansen, the commander of II./SS-Panzer-Grenadier-Regiment 1 "LAH." Hansen's battalion led one of the "Leibstandarte" attack columns that drove to the northern outskirts of Kharkov on 6-8 March. (Courtesy Mark C. Yerger)

---

[24] *Befehl des Gewissens*, pg. 216.
[25] NA/T-314, roll 490, Armee-Abteilung Kempf, 1a Nr. 331/43 g. Kdos: Armee-Befehl 2230 Uhr, 6.3.1943, frame 000349.

SS-Obersturmführer Georg Preuss, a platoon commander in Peiper's half track battalion during the Kharkov fighting. Preuss later won the Knight's Cross during the German Ardennes offensive in December of 1944. (Courtesy Mark C. Yerger)

Karl-Heinz Worthmann, shown here at the rank of SS-Untersturmführer, was an SS-Hauptscharführer in command of a platoon of tanks in 6. Kompanie of SS-Panzer-Regiment 2 in March of 1943.(Courtesy Mark C. Yerger)

Rudolf Enseling was the commander of "Das Reich's" Pioniere battalion in June, 1942. He later took command of I./SS-Panzer-Regiment 2 and by the summer of 1944 became the Panzer regiment commander. (Courtesy Mark C. Yerger)

across the width of the Merla-Merchik River valleys. It was to capture the key town of Bogodukhov on the Merla River, north of Kharkov. After the capture of Bogodukhov, the division was to turn east and support and protect the SS envelopment of Kharkov. Regiment "Thule" was attached to 320. Infanterie-Division on 7 March, along with Panzerzug 62, Sturmbataillon 393 and schwere Panzerjäger-Kompanie 517. The SS regiment was to advance between 320. Infanterie-Division and "Grossdeutschland. Lammerding planned to attack in two columns of reinforced battalion strength and strike north to the Merla.[26]

The 320. Infanterie-Division still had a strong anti-tank capability, possessing fifteen medium (5cm) and twenty-three (7.5cm) heavy anti-tank guns. After the attack began, Postel's division was to support "Grossdeutschland" in a parallel offensive operation. The division's objective was a crossing over the Merla River just a few kilometers west of Bogodukhov. The 167. Infanterie-Division was reinforced with 13./Panzer-Regiment "Grossdeutschland" (the "Tiger" company) and a battalion of Werfer-Regiment 55, a Nebelwerfer unit. It was to attack on the left (western) flank of Korps Raus, north of the Merla and drive to a point northwest of Bogodukhov.[27]

By late afternoon on 6 March, Kempf's preparations were complete. "Grossdeutschland" units arrived at their start positions. Armeeabteilung Kempf notified Manstein that it had completed its

preparations for the counterattack at 1700 hours. Some hours later, reports from the Luftwaffe reinforced the conclusion that the Russians were moving troops into the area from other sectors. The Soviet forces which had earlier been spotted passing through Achtyrka, had begun to move south towards Bogodukhov. Heeresgruppe Süd and Armeeabteilung Kempf speculated on this information, not certain whether it signaled a withdrawal of the Soviet forces in the sector between 2. Armee and Armeeabteilung Kempf or if it was a regrouping of forces for a counterattack upon the Poltava-Ljubotin railroad.

Manstein again communicated with Kempf later in the afternoon, expressing his concern that the army should take care to attack with forces concentrated on a narrow front. He was well aware of the army's shortage of armor and sufficient mobile reserves and wanted to be certain that Kempf concentrated the strength of his main attack group, in order to give "Grossdeutschland" and Regiment "Thule" their best chance of achieving a quick penetration of the Soviet defenses. Kempf replied that he was in complete agreement with Manstein and the proper concentration of the attack force had been taken into account during the planning stages of the operation. The attack start time was 0500 hours on 7 March.[28]

[26] NA/T-314, roll 490, 1a KTB: Korps Raus-Tagesmeldung vom 6.3.11943, frame 000347.
[27] Ibid. frames 000347-000351.
[28] *Befehl des Gewissens*, pg. 217.

Across from Armeeabteilung Kempf, the Russians were ripe for a counter strike. It appeared to the Germans that Russian morale had begun to suffer from the continual pressure. Reports from 4. Panzerarmee indicated that the Soviets were not fighting with their characteristic stubbornness. Instead of the usual fanatical defense of strong points and defensive positions the defenders often withdrew shortly after a German breakthrough or tactical penetration. It was clear that the Russians had little remaining armor strength in the Kharkov sector and what few tanks remained were often short of both fuel and ammunition.

While Moskalenko had been urged to strike further and further west only a few days before, he watched events on his southern flank with alarm, as the German advance approached the southern boundary of the 69th Army. It was apparent that Rybalko was not going to be able to stop the German thrust toward Kharkov, at least not with the forces at his disposal. As a result, Moskalenko's army was in a precarious situation. Not only was the army overextended and having severe supply difficulties, but it had been forced to give up three divisions, just when the Germans were beginning to regain their strength. The advance of Hoth's 4. Panzerarmee threatened to produce another disaster of the proportions of the defeat inflicted upon the 6th and 1st Guards Army. If the Germans struck the 69th Army and drove through it, penetrating to the north, the lines of communication of the 40th Army were at risk. The only encouraging factor for the Russians may have been the realization that the weather was due to change within weeks and bring large scale operations to a halt. Already temperature fluctuations signaled that the spring muddy season, the 'rasputitsa," was approaching.

On 7 March, as Korps Raus prepared to attack the boundary between the 40th and 69th Armies, 1. Panzerarmee closed up to the southern bank of the Donets. These operations secured the flanks of 4. Panzerarmee while the three divisions of the SS-Panzerkorps completed their assembly south of the Msha River and XXXXVIII. Panzerkorps approached the river on the eastern flank of the advance of Hausser's SS divisions. The LVII. Panzerkorps had linked up with XXXX. Panzerkorps, which created a solid front of German Panzer divisions from south of Kharkov to the Northern Donets River's western bank. At 0500 hours on 7 March, Manstein's 4. Panzerarmee, led by the SS-Panzerkorps and XXXXVIII. Panzerkorps, began the assault on Kharkov itself.

13

THE CITY BESIEGED

The SS-Panzerkorps Assaults the Msha River

"Leibstandarte" spearheaded the offensive operations of the SS-Panzerkorps beginning on 7 March, attacking in three reinforced regimental battle groups. Meanwhile, "Totenkopf" passed behind "Leibstandarte," in order to swing around "Leibstandarte's" western flank and shield it from Russian counterattacks. Regiment "Eicke" was on the move throughout the day, making slow progress due to traffic congestion and abysmal road conditions. The regiment continued its advance after darkness settled over the area, in order to reach its assembly point in Valki area by 8 March. Regiment "Totenkopf" was temporarily designated as the corps reserve and regrouped southwest of Kharkov. During this march, the commander of II./Regiment "Totenkopf," SS-Sturmbannführer Wilhelm Schulze and members of his staff were wounded by fragments of a Soviet shell that struck them while they were in conference under a tree. Schulze remained with his regiment despite his wounds.[1]

Wisch's regiment formed the eastern or right wing of "Leibstandarte's" attack. Peiper's SPW battalion prepared to lead the advance out of the Msha bridgehead in the morning, while the rest of the regiment was supposed to follow and reach the river later that day. Wisch's objective was to move past Valki and cut the main road exiting from the northeast corner of the town, preventing any Russians troops in the town from escaping via that route. Witt's regiment would attack the town from the south and destroy the Soviet defenders trapped by the flanking attack.

The first objective for Wisch's regiment was to cross the Msha River. His battalions had assembled in darkness west of Novaja Vodolaga, about ten kilometers south of the Msha bridgehead. Be-

fore first light, the regiment began its advance, with Peiper in the lead. Peiper's intention was to seize crossing sites on the Msha, secure them and wait for the rest of the regiment to arrive before pushing on to Valki.

The remainder of the regiment rolled toward the river in two columns, following Peiper's half tracks. On the left, Sandig's II./SS-PzG.-Rgt. 2 "LAH" attacked and captured its first objective, which was located on a secondary road south of Valki. To the right, Kraas' I./SS-PzG.-Rgt. 2 "LAH" faced little Russian resistance and reached its first objective south of Valki by 0730 hours. From there, the battalion pushed a few kilometers further northward, parallel to the attack of Regiment "Der Führer," which was advancing east of the "Leibstandarte's" sector. The two battalions reached the Msha River at the villages of Fedorovka and Bridok by noon, where they discovered that Peiper was already gone. Impatient to get moving, Peiper decided not to wait for the rest of the regiment to reach the river and ordered his battalion to move out at 0745 hours. He left a small security detachment at the river and pushed on.

While Peiper swung around Valki, meeting little opposition, Witt's regiment, supported by a battery of assault guns and Gross' tank battalion, prepared to assault the southern edge of Valki. The II./SS-Pz.Rgt. 1 and the 2./Sturmgeschützabteilung swung out to the west, with orders to first capture the town of Babirka. The Panzer battalion was to make contact with Meyer's reconnaissance battalion and support the battalion's attack after seizing Babirka. While Wünsche and Meyer moved their battalions into position, Witt's battalions deployed on a broad front, with III./SS-PzG.-Rgt. 1 on the right flank of the regiment's attack, the I./SS-PzG.-Rgt. 1 on the left and II./SS-PzG.-Rgt. 1 in the center.

Before dawn lit the gray, overcast sky, Kampfgruppe Witt's tanks and assault guns approached Babirka over the still frozen open

---

[1] NA/T-354, roll 118, Morgenmeldung vom SS-Reich an SS-Panzerkorps 7.3.1943, frame 3752197, and Vopersal, pg. 196.

terrain. After cautiously cresting a small hill, the assault gun detachment could see the town. It lay below them in a long shallow balka, about 300 meters away. Gross' tanks moved into cover behind the hill and reached a road which entered the town from the west. While the tanks deployed on either side of the road and rolled toward the town, the assault guns attacked Babirka from the south. The Sturmgeschütz battery advanced in bounds, one platoon furnishing covering fire while the other two moved up.[2] When the German assault guns rolled into sight over the hilltop, the Russians immediately began firing with small arms and anti-tank guns. The fire was not well directed and failed to inflict any significant losses on the Germans before the superior fire power of the attackers suppressed the Soviet reaction. Rapidly the SS assault guns came on line, finding hull down firing positions and began to shell the town. The high explosive shells from the Sturmgeschütze began to silence the Russian anti-tank guns. This allowed the tanks to move up and make their assault.

Meyer's Aufklärungsabteilung and Wünsche's battalion were assembled west of Babirka. Several hours before, during the usual, thick predawn fog and darkness, the Kampfgruppe had received a surprise as they prepared to begin its attack. The adjutant of the Panzer battalion, SS-Obersturmführer Georg Isecke, was conducting a tour of the battalion when a Grenadier burst into his presence with the unsettling news that motor and track noise from unidentified tanks could be heard to the west of the battalion's positions. Nothing could be seen at first, as the fog limited visibility to a distance of a few meters. However, the unmistakable sound of idling tank motors could be heard. Isecke cautiously moved forward and found to his relief that the tanks were elements of "Grossdeutschland's" Panzer regiment. Isecke went to the commander, Oberst Graf von Strachwitz and informed him of the presence of the SS Panzers, in order to avoid any friendly fire accidents. Strachwitz then met with Meyer and agreed to adjust his direction of attack farther to the north of Valki.[3]

Meyer began his attack as soon as the fog lifted. The Kampfgruppe scattered a small detachment of Russian infantry with little trouble soon after it got on the move. Just after noon the battalion, driving retreating groups of Russians before it, reached Valki and assaulted the town's western edge. Simultaneously Witt's Panzergrenadiers began their attack from the southeast. At this point the fighting quickly began to grow more intense because the Russian perimeter defense consisted of mutually supporting anti-tank gun positions which were manned in this instance, by disciplined

SS-Sturmbannführer Rudolf Sandig, the commander of II./SS-Panzergrenadier-Regiment 2 "LAH." Sandig led his battalion of Panzergrenadiers in the division's attack on the 3rd Tank Army units holding the Msha River line. (Credit National Archives)

gun crews under a unified command. The Germans called this arrangement a "Pakfront."

Wünsche sent SS-Obersturmführer Wilhelm Beck's company of tanks to strike the Russians from the rear while he led the rest of the battalion in a frontal assault. Several hundred meters of open ground lay between Wünsche's Panzers and the edge of the town. The Russian anti-tank guns could not be seen. They were placed in concealed fortified positions or in camouflaged locations inside houses. Beck's Panzers left their shelter assembly area, immediately firing with machine guns and cannons, hoping to force the Russian gunners to keep their heads down. The Aufklärungsabteilung raced to the attack, the Grenadiers firing over the sides of the half tracks and Schwimmwagen or clinging to tank decks.

Instantly the Russian Pakfront erupted and its gun crews directed a storm of accurate fire toward the tanks. Immediately shells struck three SS Panzers and knocked them out of action in short order. The reconnaissance troops flung themselves off the tank decks when Russian machine gun fire swept over the tanks. Beck's command vehicle was hit and put out of action, forcing the crew to bail out, although it did not burn. Beck ran across the open ground, leapt onto another nearby tank. He ordered the Panzer IIIs and IVs back into cover. In the meantime, the infantry attack had bogged down. Meyer's men were hugging the ground, in the face of heavy Russian fire. Machine gun fire swept the ground in front of the village and the SS Grenadiers flattened themselves in every available depression, seeking shelter rather than attacking.[4]

Meyer recognized that the attack was stalled and immediately took charge of the situation. In order to get his men moving once again, he grabbed a rifle and started blasting away at the Russians.

---

[2] Lehmann, pg. 143.
[3] Lehmann, pg. 151 and NA/T-354, roll 120, 1a KTB: Darstellung der Ereignisse, frame 3753692.

---

[4] Ibid. pg. 152-153.

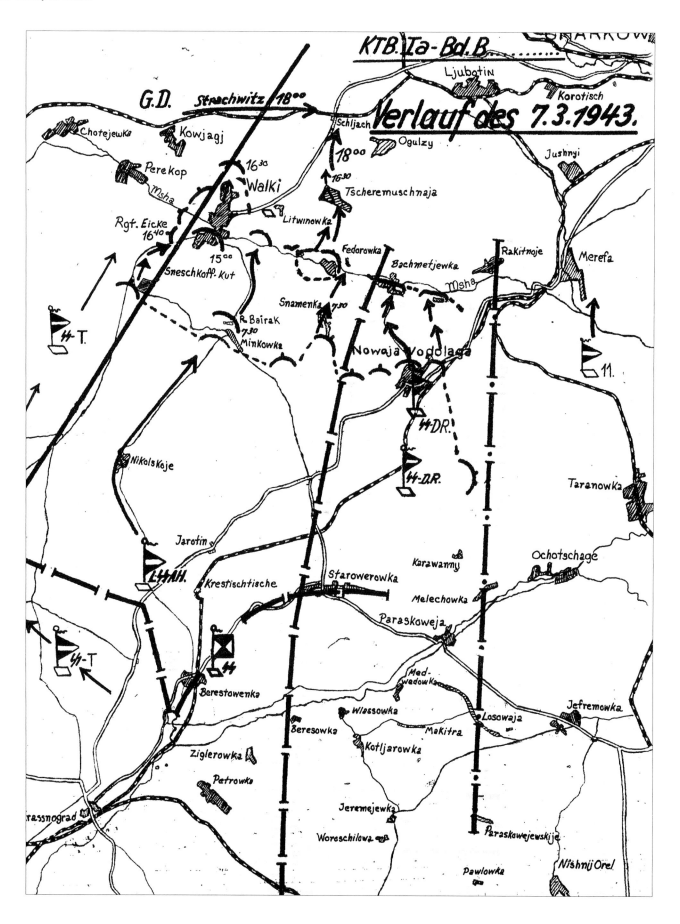

The Grenadiers pinned down in front of the village began to build up their fire just as two "Tiger" tanks made their appearance. The steel giants paused, fired and then rolled on toward the village. The anti-tank shells of the Russian guns had no effect on the "Tigers" to the consternation of the Russian gun crews. As the enormous tanks approached within the last few meters of the anti-tank gun front some of the Russian gun crews lost heart and took to their heels. The lumbering, seemingly invulnerable "Tigers" silenced one firing position after the other, their 88 shells turning Russian guns into piles of scrap metal. Beck's Panzer IIIs and IVs then attacked once again, followed close behind by the rest of the Aufklärungs-abteilung troops. Supported by 2cm automatic gun fire from the SPWs, the SS Grenadiers broke into the system of foxholes and trenches on the outskirts of Valki. The tanks remained on the outskirts of the town mopping up the last anti-tank gun positions while the Grenadiers of Weiser's company fought their way farther into the town.

When Meyer's lead company reached a small river which passed though the center of Valki, they discovered a bridge which was still intact. Suspecting that the Russians had mined the bridge, Meyer did not use it to cross the river. He was certain that if his men charged across the bridge it would be blown up by the Russians. The river was frozen but it was not known how firm the ice was. The attack was in danger of stalling once again. While Meyer contemplated his next course of action, the sound of a tank motor and squealing tracks could be heard from Valki. It was clear that the Russians were bringing up a tank. Meyer knew that if a T-34 took up a good firing position on the other bank before his men got across the river they would be slaughtered. Quick action was required, but the men were hesitant about making the assault. Meyer realized that he had to remedy the situation immediately. He then stood and shouted to the men that the first one across the river would earn a three week leave. The Grenadiers sprang to their feet and surged across the frozen river in a wild dash to the other side.[5]

After crossing the river, the bridge was secured and the German tanks rolled up and began to cross the river. No Soviet tanks opposed them. The Russian infantry's will to fight evaporated after the SS tanks entered the town and supported the attack of the Grenadiers. At close range the tanks blasted isolated strong points that still resisted and gunned down Russians who abandoned their fighting holes and tried to escape. The surviving Russian infantry withdrew in all directions and many of them ran into "Grossdeutschland"

Vincenz Kaiser and Karl-Heinz Worthmann standing together after the end of the fighting for Kharkov. Note the four tank destruction badges on Kaiser's right sleeve. Worthmann was awarded the Knight's Cross on 31 March, 1943 for his leadership during the Kharkov campaign. (Courtesy Mark C. Yerger)

troops on the road leading out of the town to the northeast. Witt's regiment swept up from the south and he reported that his lead battalion reached the northern edge of Valki at 1630 hours.[6]

While "Leibstandarte" enveloped and captured Valki, "Das Reich" troops were engaged in securing Novaja Vodolaga, after attacking the town in the early morning. Regiment "Deutschland" eliminated the last remaining pockets of Russians by the first hours of daylight, establishing complete control by noon. Forward elements of the regiment seized a bridge north of the town, again before the Russians were able to blow it up. Shortly afterward, Soviet planes were seen circling overhead, preparing to bomb the bridge and destroy it.

In order to protect the bridge from Soviet aircraft, Flak detachments were quickly brought up and stationed around the bridge.

OPPOSITE: After the final destruction of the Russian troops in the Kegitschevka pocket, "Totenkopf" swung westward, behind the advance of "Das Reich" and "Leibstandarte." The division regrouped near Valki, in preparation for a push northwards into the sector west of Ljubotin, where it served as the flank protection for the other two SS divisions during their attack upon Kharkov.

---

[5] Lehmann, vol. III, pg. 108-109.
[6] NA/T-354, roll 120, 1a KTB: Darstellung der Ereignisse, frame 3753692.

The four barreled automatic 2cm guns were a formidable defensive weapon against low flying planes and each time Russian planes made an attack, a storm of fire forced them away. The bridge remained standing, in spite of several Russians attempts to bomb it. While the Flak guns kept Russian planes at bay, Ehrath's battalion streamed over the bridge. Russian bombs exploded harmlessly in the river, throwing up geysers of water in the distance.

Ehrath organized a lead detachment that consisted of one company of Grenadiers, 5. Panzer-Kompanie and a Flak detachment. The small battle group led the battalion's thrust north toward the river, moving on the right flank of the regiment's attack. Bissinger's II./Regiment "Deutschland," advanced on the left and occupied the village of Pawlovka. Bissinger's battalion crossed the river also and secured a second bridgehead over the Msha River, east of the spot where Peiper crossed the river.

Regiment "Der Führer" received orders to move up and use the bridgeheads secured by Harmel's regiment. Once across the river, Kumm's regiment was to drive north toward the Merefa River south of Korotisch. From there the regiment was to proceed to Ljubotin and gain control of the road leading to Kharkov.[7] Leading the attack was Kaiser's III./"Der Führer." The battalion was reinforced with a battery of assault guns and self-propelled anti-tank guns. Shortly before 1500 hours, a Fieseler Storch had flown over the column and dropped a written message, informing Kaiser that the Russians were withdrawing toward Kharkov and did not appear to hold the Merefa River crossings in any strength. Kaiser decided to seize this opportunity to capture the Merefa River bridges south of Korotisch, ordering the thrust on his own initiative. He organized a small mobile assault group and directed it to seize a bridge before the Russians could destroy it. The mobile detachment was then to proceed to Korotisch, report on any Soviet troops that it discovered and block the road if possible.[8]

The assault detachment was made up of 9. Kompanie "Der Führer," a few assault guns and three self-propelled anti-tank guns of the Panzerjäger Abteilung. It set out at 1500 hours, with the SPWs leading the way. The assault guns and anti-tank guns followed, bringing up the rear of the column. The battle group crossed the Merefa River without incident, approaching the Ljubotin-Kharkov road at Korotisch after dark. At that time, the assault group commander, SS-Untersturmführer Gerhard Schmager, called a halt and radioed Kaiser, informing him that they had reached their objective. A detachments of SPWs edged closer to the main road, which ran along the edge of a woods. The pitch-black tree line gave no sign if there

[7] Weidinger, pg. 88 and NA/T-354, roll118, Tagesmeldung an SS-Panzerkorps vom 7.3.1943, frame 3752197.
[8] Weidinger, pg. 89.

Oberst d.R. Hyazinth Graf Strachwitz took command of the refitted Panzer Regiment of "Grossdeutschland" in January, 1943 and led the regiment until November, 1943. Strachwitz was a career soldier who had served in the German Army since 1912. He was wounded more than a dozen times during two wars and was one of the most highly decorated soldiers of the German Army in World War II. He was awarded the Knight's Cross in 1941 and the Oakleaves in November of the following year. Late in 1943 he won the Swords and became the 11th man to win the Diamonds to the Knight's Cross on 15 April, 1944. He was promoted to Generalleutnant in January of 1945. Strachwitz survived the war, in spite of his many wounds and a near fatal accident in the summer of 1944. (Credit National Archives)

were Russian troops or vehicles in the forest. Schmager ordered the drivers to turn off their motors in order to hear better.

They heard the sound of voices and the low rumblings of idling truck motors. The detachment fired their 2cm guns across the road, into the dark woods. Almost at once, a Soviet truck burst into flame, lighting up the entire area. In the next instant, a violent fire fight exploded, shattering the quiet of the night with cannon and machine gun fire. The 2cm automatic guns fired volleys of explosive shells at gun flashes near the road. Soviet return fire struck one of the SPWs, wounding two members of the crew and knocking out the vehicle. While the wounded crew members staggered away from the stricken vehicle, Panzergrenadiers leapt out of their armored personnel carriers, threw themselves to the ground and laid down machine gun on the tree line. Several men raced forward to pick up the wounded and hauled them to cover. The anti-tank guns took up positions on the flank to protect the half tracks and armored cars. The firing continued until the assault guns arrived and began to blast the edge of the woods. Faced with that superior firepower, the Russians withdrew. By morning the detachment established firm control of a section of the main road between Ljubotin and Korotisch.[9]

The 3rd Tank Army, battered by the hammer blows it had endured, was fighting back but not always with the normal Russian resilience in defensive operations. It had not conducted a counterattack against the SS-Panzerkorps because Rybalko undoubtedly recognized that he didn't have the strength to carry out an offensive operation. The army had little if any mobile reserves, lacked sufficient artillery and its remaining tank strength was quickly melting away. In spite of this situation, the 3rd Tank Army was not yet ready to collapse and in many areas, managed to delay the German attack upon Kharkov. Rybalko had received some infantry reinforcements and a little extra armor and these troops managed to stabilize the situation on the eastern half of the army's front, in the XXXXVIII. Panzerkorps sector. In contrast, the SS divisions met with success in all their attacks while Russian resolve showed more signs of weakening in that sector of the fighting. However, Rybalko's rear guard detachments made the SS columns stop and assault the villages that were defended. These defensive operations did not constitute a counterattack by any stretch of the imagination but were delaying actions that allowed the 6th Army rifle divisions to escape and bought time for the 69th Army. Rybalko's scant remaining armor and dwindling rifle divisions tried to hold its defensive front against Hoth's Panzer columns driving toward Kharkov from the south, however, when Armeeabteilung Kempf began its offensive west of Kharkov, the 69th Army gave way and Rybalko was threatened from the west as well the south. The most immediate threat was from the SS divisions, whose attack momentum seemed to be growing by the day.

By the night of 7-8 March, both "Leibstandarte" and "Das Reich" were across the Msha after establishing solid bridgeheads and had thrust beyond the river. Elements of "Leibstandarte" had captured Valki and a combat group of Regiment "Der Führer" was blocking the main road between Kharkov and Ljubotin. There were fresh rifle divisions on the way from the Stavka reserve, but these had not yet arrived. SS spearheads penetrated the 3rd Tank Army line at several points, regardless of the abysmal weather, Soviet resistance and poor roads. This determined pursuit and attack forced Rybalko's western wing to give up any hope of defending the river. There were no adequate Soviet reserves available to counterattack the German breakthroughs and once Rybalko's lines were penetrated, the battered rifle divisions were unable to block German mobile columns. With every victory, Russian will to fight was sapped to a greater degree and instead of gains measured by a hard fought kilometer or two, the SS spearheads began to break through and make deeper penetrations.

The 3rd Tank Army was under less intense pressure on its eastern flank by XXXXVIII. Panzerkorps, which was advancing toward the eastern flank of the army which was anchored at Merefa. Although the weaker Army Panzer divisions were not able to make dramatic breakthroughs, they exerted continuous pressure on Rybalko's eastern flank and did not allow Rybalko to transfer any strength to buttress the collapsing western flank. The situation became more serious when Korps Raus began its assault on the junction area between the 69th Army and Rybalko's 3rd Tank Army.

The Korps Raus Attack

"Grossdeutschland" assembled in three battle groups, launching its attack on the morning of 7 March. On the right was Kampfgruppe Strachwitz, named for the aggressive Oberst Graf von Strachwitz, nicknamed the "Panzer Count," who led the division's Panzer Regiment. Strachwitz's group was made up of II./Pz. Rgt. "GD" and Grenadier Rgt. "GD." It was reinforced with mobile artillery as well as Pioniere and Panzerjäger detachments. Kampfgruppe Beuermann, in the center, consisted of Füsilier Rgt. "GD," I./Pz. Rgt. "GD" and was similarly reinforced with heavy weapons. The third group, aligned on the divisions left flank, was Kampfgruppe Wätjen and was built around Aufklärungsabteilung "GD." It was supported by Sturmgeschütze Bataillon "GD" and additional self-propelled artillery and Flak units.

The division was on the move at 0500 hours, although in some areas the columns encountered very poor road conditions due to a wet snow which had fallen over a layer of icy sludge. A number of the roads in the attack zone of Kampfgruppe Strachwitz were fairly passable and this facilitated the progress of the attack. Gruppe Strachwitz advanced northward, met little Soviet resistance and gained about ten kilometers, arriving at the town of Jassenovy at 0840.[10] By 1020 hours, Strachwitz pressed further along the road and ran into a strong Russian position astride the road which was near the division's old medical station at Kovjagi. The Soviets fought

---

[9] Ibid. pg. 90.

[10] It was this column which had made contact with the "Leibstandarte" Kampfgruppe consisting of Meyer's battalion and elements of the Pz. Rgt. "LAH."

from good defensive positions reinforced with anti-tank guns and supported by artillery.

The strong resistance forced the column to halt and deploy. A detachment of Panzers swung off the main road, in order to attack the Soviet position from the flank. The "Grossdeutschland" tanks discovered that the Soviet position was not tied in with other supporting units and the tanks were able to assault an undefended flank from the west. Before noon the column smashed the Russians and was on the move again. It reached the area south of Perekop at 1330 hours, close enough to hear the sounds of fighting in the SS-Panzerkorps sector. The main part of Strachwitz's Kampfgruppe bypassed Soviet troops in Perekop, leaving strong elements of the Grenadier Regiment behind in order to reduce the position.[11]

The Panzer battalion led the attack out of the Perekop area by 1655 hours, while the Russians continued to fight hard for the town itself. The "Grossdeutschland" Grenadiers were unable to fight their way into the town without the support of their armor. North of Perekop the Panzer group ran into a large Soviet column and destroyed it, leaving dead Russians, horses and burning sleds on either side of the road. The battalion pushed further to the northeast, until arriving at a train station at the village of Schlach. At Schlach, the Kampfgruppe reached the main road which ran east towards Ljubotin. Strachwitz's tanks were only a few kilometers from the point where Regiment "Der Führer" had secured a section of the same road with its thrust to Korotisch.[12]

The left flank "Grossdeutschland" Kampfgruppe, Gruppe Wätjen, began its advance at 0500 hours, making good progress although the roads in its attack sector were covered with deep snow drifts. Gruppe Wätjen reached the Kolomak railroad station at 1020 hours and pushed farther up the rail line toward Schelestovo. South of the town, the Kampfgruppe encountered its first serious resistance, at the village of Iskrovka. Wätjen's troops quickly became tied down in heavy combat on the northwest edge of the town. The Soviet position could not be quickly outflanked because of difficult wooded terrain on either side of the road. A part of the column managed to bypass the town and pushed on toward Schelestovo. Lammerding received orders to make forces from his regiment available to assist Gruppe Wätjen's attack of the Iskrovka defensive position. A small SS assault group linked up with Wätjen's troops, however, the main elements of the SS regiment were delayed by Russian defensive positions in a wooded area south of Iskrovka.[13]

Lammerding's regiment had begun moving in two assault groups, parallel to Gruppe Wätjen's line of advance. The reinforced I./Rgt. "Thule," under Ernst Häussler, moved off the road into a forest and attempted to outflank the Soviet positions at Schelestovo. The battalion moved into the mass of dark trees and tangled undergrowth. Shortly after entering the forest, the SS Grenadiers stumbled onto a line of well concealed Soviet bunkers. Soviet mortar shells suddenly rained down upon them. Immediately, machine gun fire sprayed from the cleverly concealed, heavily timbered bunkers. The SS infantry threw themselves to the ground, taking shelter behind trees or in shallow depressions. Once the bunkers could be located, Häussler organized his attack. Covered by fire from MG-42s and machine pistols, assault teams began to eliminate knock out the cleverly concealed Russian positions. After several hours, Soviet fire began to slacken. The defensive line was not organized in depth, although other bunkers were encountered when the battalion advanced into the depths of the forest. It was a slow process and the combat continued until well after dawn. Snipers and machine gun nests continued to delay the advance. To the north, the sounds of combat gave evidence that Gruppe Wätjen had begun fighting to take Schelestovo.

Moving farther to the northeast, Häussler's men discovered a very large, well hidden Soviet camp. Captured documents and interrogations revealed that the camp was a partisan stronghold, used for training hundreds of civilian recruits. Immediately, the fortified camp was attacked and found to be occupied by a large number of Russian partisans. It was defended with determination, and Häussler left a company at the camp to occupy the Russians while the main part of the battalion pushed toward Iskrovka. About 800 meters south of the town, another line of fortifications delayed the advance of the SS Grenadiers. After assembling assault groups, the bunkers were stormed and the line taken. Häussler reassembled his battalion just south of Schelestovo. The attack was supported by a few tanks of Panzerzug 62, and the battalion prepared to support the attack of Gruppe Wätjen.

The Russians were dug in along an elevated railroad embankment on the southeast side of the town. The Panzers assembled in a shallow, flat bottomed balka near the railroad and waited for the "Grossdeutschland" troops.[14] Gruppe Wätjen, with Grenadiers of 3./Kompanie Rgt. "Thule" riding upon its assault guns arrived at 0800 hours. After regrouping, the SS and Army troops approached the town from an unexpected direction. After bringing the assault guns on line, the Kampfgruppe deployed to attack the town. The SS and "Grossdeutschland" Grenadiers advanced, their MG-42s spraying the line of houses and encountered only light defensive fire. However, the intensity of the firing soon picked up. Groups of

[11] *Befehl des Gewissens*, pg. 221-225.
[12] Op cit. pg. 221-225.
[13] Vopersal, pg. 198.

[14] *Befehl des Gewissens*, pg. 223-225 and Vopersal, pg. 197-199.

German troops assault an elevated railroad embankment, which were a common sight in southern Russia, keeping the above the spring floods. The embankments furnished means of travel for the Germans as well as convenient fortifications for the Russians, who often dug foxholes and machine gun positions into the earthen banks. (Credit National Archives)

Russian infantry could be seen rushing through the village to meet the attack. It was obvious that the Russians had not expected the attack to come from that direction. A Soviet gun crew manhandled a heavy (7.62cm) anti-tank gun into position near one end of the railroad embankment. Recognizing the danger that the gun posed to their armor, the SS Grenadiers directed a hail of machine gun fire on the Soviet soldiers pushing the anti-tank gun into place. The small arms fire kept its crew pinned down, until an assault group knocked out the gun. Soon tracers and shell fire set many of the houses on fire. When the Germans battled through into the center of the town, thick banks of smoke obscured the streets.

Sturmgeschütze IIIs cautiously moved into the town, with Grenadiers at their side, preventing Russian infantry from attacking with Molotov cocktails or explosive charges. Firing at close range, the assault guns blasted Russian strong points, stunning or killing the defenders. Then German assault teams leapt into action with grenades and machine pistols ready, while automatic weapons fire covered their sprint forward. Grenades were hurled into windows and door ways, exploding inside with muffled booms. The difficult street fighting in Schelestovo continued until darkness while the town burned down around the combatants. The fires and cannon flashes illuminated the village.[15]

Meanwhile, I./Rgt. "Thule" remained pinned down, until Häussler, who was with the leading company, recognized a weak point in the Soviet defensive system. The battalion commander personally led the attack which broke into the southern edge of the town. Once inside the perimeter, the SS troopers drove the stubborn Russian infantry slowly into the center of Schelestovo. After II./Rgt. "Thule" reached the western and southwest sectors of

Schelestovo, Gruppe Wätjen disengaged from the battle and continued their attack toward Kolomak. Meanwhile, in the woods south of the town, the elements of I./Rgt. "Thule" left behind in the woods remained involved in fighting to take the partisan training camp.[16]

While Regiment "Thule" and Gruppe Wätjen fought for Schelestovo, Gruppe Strachwitz crossed the Poltava-Ljubotin-Kharkov railroad. At the same time, the center group of "Grossdeutschland," Gruppe Beuermann, had been fighting its way from Chudovo towards Kolomak. The Kampfgruppe encountered little resistance, but had progressed slowly to the north throughout the morning. It was moving along muddy, snow covered roads which caused many difficulties. At 1550 hours, the battle group arrived at Kolomak, where it linked up with a patrol from Gruppe Wätjen. After reaching Kolomak, Gruppe Beuermann was ordered to march to the northwest and replace Grenadier Regiment "GD" which had been left at Perekop. For the remainder of the afternoon, Beuermann's Kampfgruppe attempted to carry out their mission. Slowed by the atrocious road conditions, the battle group became strung out and the last vehicles of the Kampfgruppe did not arrive until the following day. When about half of the battle group assembled at Perekop, Grenadier Rgt. "Grossdeutschland" followed after the tanks of Gruppe Strachwitz.

By evening, Gruppe Strachwitz's II./Pz. Rgt. "GD" had assembled in the Kovjagi area, halting while the Grenadier Regiment marched to rejoin it. A battalion of Gruppe Beuermann was in Perekop, but I./Füsilier Rgt. remained strung out on roads around Vysokopol'ye. Gruppe Wätjen, along with major elements of I./Rgt. "Thule," was still occupied clearing out the Schelestovo-Iskrovka sector.

[15] Vopersal, pg. 197-198.

[16] Ibid. pg. 199.

While the three "Grossdeutschland" columns attacked into the seam between the 69th and 3rd Tank Army, the infantry divisions of the Armeeabteilung had begun their attacks also. The 320. Infanterie-Division made adequate progress during the day, particularly in the area immediately west of the attack sector of Regiment "Thule" and Gruppe Wätjen, where it benefited from the Soviet attention focused on the two German mobile battle groups. However, the left flank of Korps Raus' attack, in the sectors of 167. and 168. Infanterie-Divisions, fell behind the more mobile SS and "Grossdeutschland" formations. Because of this, there was some concern at HQ of Armeeabteilung Kempf regarding the open flank of Gruppe Strachwitz, but unknown to the army command, there was little cause for worry, as the Russians had neither the intention or capability of making any significant counterattack in that area by 7-8 March. Kempf was justifiably concerned about the weather and its affects on his offensive operations, due to the obvious difficulty in moving over almost impassable roads. Poor flying weather had also resulted in the lack of Luftwaffe support but "Grossdeutschland" was able to make good progress on the first day of the attack in two of its three attack sectors.

In contrast to the situation west of Kharkov and in the SS sector, XXXXVIII. and LVII. Panzerkorps faced tougher going. To the east of the SS-Panzerkorps area, XXXXVIII. Panzerkorps continued to encounter stout Soviet defensive efforts. Between Zmiev on the east and Taranovka on the west, 11. Panzer-Division pushed forward against tenacious Russian troops equipped with abundant anti-tank guns and artillery. The division captured an intact railroad bridge southeast of Merefa and discovered evidence that the Russians were attempting to strengthen their defensive front east of the town. Reconnaissance reports indicated that the Soviets had brought twelve artillery batteries into position in that area. There was no arrival of significant new armored forces detected to oppose the forty-three tanks of the division.

On the right flank of XXXXIII. Panzerkorps, 6. Panzer-Division attacked the towns of Pervomajskij and Michailovka. After tough fighting, the division took the two towns, capturing a total of sixteen anti-tank and infantry guns. A number of Soviet tanks were reported in the Taranovka area, on the flank of the division's advance, but did not attack at that time, although corps records indicate that the presence of the Russian armor concerned the division. However, it continued to strike north and northwest, pushing toward the town of Ssokolovo, which lay on the southern bank of the Msha River, about twenty-five kilometers south of Kharkov. Both divisions remained involved in heavy fighting and made very little progress throughout the day.

The LVII. Panzerkorps, on the far eastern flank of the army, faced even more determined Soviet defensive efforts. The 17. Panzer-Division and 15. Infanterie-Division were both struck by multiple counterattacks a few kilometers south of the Donets River. The Russian attacks conducted against the center and right flank of the infantry division were particularly strong, especially near the town of Bairak. The division had only to cross the river and advance a few kilometers to the north before it could cut the key railroad line that ran from Izyum to Kharkov. However Soviet counterattacks prevented the division from reaching the river.

The infantry battalion defending Bairak was struck at day break by a strong Soviet infantry attack that originated from a bend of the river a short distance to the southeast. The Russians fought their way into the town and drove II./88. Infanterie Regiment and a bicycle equipped reconnaissance detachment out of the town. Aggressively following up their success, the Soviet advance threatened positions of the division near the town of Tschepel. The 106. Infanterie-Regiment, which was engaged in clearing the area southwest of Bairak, was then struck by the Russian attack. The forward elements of the regiment received effective flanking fire from the north and suffered significant casualties. Due to these losses and a shortage of ammunition, most of the regiment had to pull back. A battalion of the division counterattacked the Soviet force west of Bairak and was able to clear Russian infantry out of that sector. Supported by 15. Feld-Ersatz-Bataillon, the divisional training battalion, the regiment drove the Russians from the southern edge of Bairak, but could not reclaim the village entirely.

On the west or left flank of the corps, 17. Panzer-Division counterattacked a Soviet rifle regiment at the town of Werchnij Bischkin and drove the Russian infantry out of the town. However, the Russians remained in control of several sectors. A reconnaissance patrol reported that a strong Soviet infantry force remained solidly dug in a short distance east of Werchnij Bischkin. In addition to the intense fighting on the front lines, the division was also occupied with clearing groups of Russians out of its rear areas. A particularly strong detachment of Soviet troops, which had been bypassed during the earlier advance of the division, was encircled and destroyed during the afternoon. After having suffering heavy casualties and narrowly avoided being driven back by the Russian attack, the division regrouped for further action on 8 March.

The SS-Panzerkorps Encircles Kharkov

While the other two Panzer corps of the army drove north, towards Kharkov, the SS-Panzerkorps renewed its attack on 8 March. The main body of "Das Reich" crossed the Msha, while "Leibstandarte" advanced in three attack columns and "Totenkopf" took over the protection of the corps flank. The weather made one of its typically unpredictable changes, and temperatures plunged, whereupon the previously muddy roads froze into iron hard ruts and snow began to fall on top of the icy crust. All movements of the three divisions were hampered by below freezing temperatures and heavy snow-fall. Hoth did not allow the changed road conditions to affect his plans. The 4. Panzerarmee issued its main directive for the day, which was to first prevent the Russians from building up an orga-nized defense north of the Msha River and secondly, to advance further to the north from Valki. It was the intention of the army that the SS-Panzerkorps cut all main communications lines leading into Kharkov from the west and thus prevent elements of 69th or 40th Armies from withdrawing into the town.

Hausser's corps was to block the main roads and rail lines that exited the western side of Kharkov and connected the city with Ljubotin. Hoth ordered that two of the SS divisions assembled west of Ljubotin were to swing around the city's northern perimeter and then drive east, slicing through the main roads and railroads that entered the northern edge of Kharkov. Meanwhile, the remaining division was to fight its way eastward through the area south of the city. The encircling divisions were to link up east of the city in order to encircle the Russian forces in Kharkov and support the attack of XXXXVIII. Panzerkorps. Hoth felt that the 3rd Tank Army was too weak to conduct a credible defense any longer. He intended that XXXXVIII. Panzerkorps would be able to reach the southeast edge of Kharkov and cut the roads and rail lines leading out of the city from that direction. He was wrong, however, because the Army Panzer divisions proved too weak to carry out their mission and were not able to break through Soviet defenses southeast of Kharkov.

The three SS divisions carried out their attacks with typical aggressiveness and energy, smashing Soviet resistance as they at-tacked. It is interesting to note that just as the loss of Kharkov was controversial because of Hausser's withdrawal contrary to Hitler's orders, the attack upon the city resulted in additional disputed cir-cumstances involving the commander of the SS corps. Hausser has been accused of acting against orders and involving the SS-Panzerkorps in an unnecessarily costly battle for the city that re-sulted in enormous casualties for the three divisions. However, we will see that Manstein mentioned the possibility of taking the city by a quick strike if Hausser thought it was possible, thus opening the door for the controversy which occurred in the following days. Adolf Hitler himself expected Sepp Dietrich to directly attack the city and this was a directive that Dietrich could not ignore, espe-cially considering the manner in which the city was abandoned.

A "Leibstandarte" Sturmgeschütz III and Panzer II enter the outskirts of Dergatschi, on one of the main roads north of Kharkov that led directly into the center of north-ern section of the city. The huge Red Square was located in the northern third of Kharkov and on 10 February, 1943 three battle groups of "Leibstandarte" thrust toward the square in a controversial attack upon the city. (Credit National Archives)

"Totenkopf" was given the task of covering the outside flank of the SS-Panzerkorps. The division was to begin its attack from Valki and then drive to the town of Olshanny, which was about twenty kilometers northwest of Kharkov. Once having reached Olshanny, "Totenkopf" was to turn and attack due east and block the major roads leading into Kharkov from the north. In this man-ner the division would shield "Leibstandarte" attack groups from Soviet forces approaching Kharkov from the north. In simple terms, "Totenkopf" formed an outer defensive arc, protecting "Leibstandarte's" assault upon the northern perimeter of Kharkov. Meanwhile, "Das Reich" was to push through Soviet defenses south-west of Kharkov and drive eastward, forcing the Russians to allo-cate substantial strength to this attack. This operation would strongly support the attack of XXXXVIII. Panzerkorps, which was to cross the Msha River, drive to the southeastern corner of Kharkov and block a Soviet withdrawal from the eastern edge of the city. The corps was to accomplish this task by blocking the Kharkov-Chugujev road which exited the southeast section of the city.

Regiment "Eicke's" first objective was the town of Stary Merchik, which was located on the Merchik River west of Ljubotin. After clearing groups of Russian stragglers out of the area west of Valki, the regiment began its attack, although the road conditions remained very poor, due to deep snow drifts. The first attack objec-tive was the town of Stary Merchik. In spite of the difficult road conditions, the regiment reached Stary Merchik at 1700 hours. SS-Sturmbannführer Becker kept the regiment on the move after night-fall because the roads froze solid and the assault guns and SPWs were able to make better speed. However, any vehicles that were not tracked still had great difficulties, particularly towed artillery

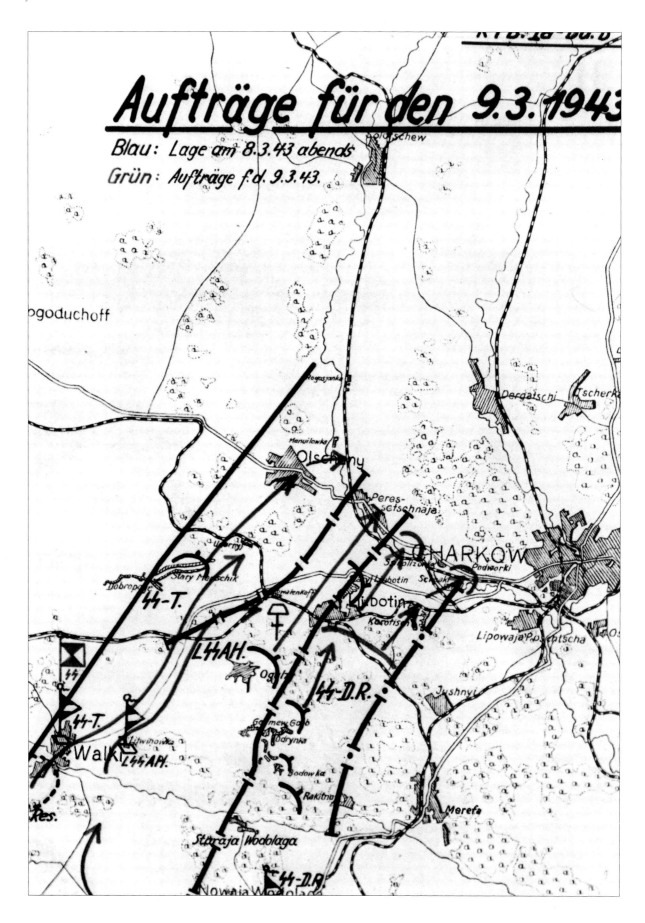

pieces and trucks. Becker was to secure Olschany as a supply base from which Baum's Regiment "Totenkopf" could launch its attack protecting "Leibstandarte's" rear.[17]

Baum's Regiment "Totenkopf" had been given the task of protecting "Leibstandarte's" attack on the northern perimeter of the city. The regiment was reinforced with assault guns and Walter Bestmann's SS-Aufklärungsabteilung 3, greatly increasing its mobility and firepower. The Kampfgruppe left its positions in the southern section of Valki before dawn and passed through the town during the morning. Bestmann's recon battalion led the advance and reported that large numbers of Russians were in the area. The regiment followed a railroad line that exited Valki and ran generally in a northwestern direction. The lead elements of the column reached Schljach, the rail station on the Ljubotin-Kharkov railroad, in the dark of the early evening. The SS troops found security detachments of "Grossdeutschland" still occupying the station. The regiment turned on to the road from Schljach which ran north towards Olshanny. Following behind the two Panzergrenadier regiments, Leiner's SS-Panzer-Regiment laboriously moved up to the area south of Valki.[18]

"Leibstandarte" columns were also moving on the morning of 8 March. The Panzer regiment had only thirty-six operational main battle tanks on that date, not counting the dozen or so Panzer IIs the division utilized as reconnaissance vehicles. From assembly positions north of Valki, with his Grenadiers riding on tank and assault gun decks, Witt began his advance on Ljubotin at 0730 hours. The attack moved relatively quickly along the road leading to the town because it was in better shape than other, smaller roads. The first detachment of the regiment arrived at a landmark church on the outskirts of Ljubotin by early afternoon.

The column was briefly held up by artillery and anti-tank gun fire, but passed through the town by 1500 hours. The column turned east along the main road and approached the western edge of Kharkov without serious interference. Barely five kilometers west of Kharkov, the column first met entrenched Soviet tanks and infantry. Soviet artillery fire increased in intensity and the advance was temporarily delayed while the column deployed to attack. The SS tanks left the road and maneuvered against each flank, under cover of fire from assault guns and Flak detachments. By nightfall, II./SS Panzer-Regiment "LAH," under command of SS-Sturmbannführer Martin Gross, had destroyed five T-34s and cap-

tured or destroyed thirty guns of various calibers.[19]

Later in the evening, the Kampfgruppe was ordered to halt its attack and pull back to new positions northeast of Ljubotin. The direction of attack that had been taken by Witt's Kampfgruppe after it passed through Ljubotin was deep into the "Das Reich" sector. Instead of proceeding to Olshanny as directed, Witt had headed straight for Kharkov. Whether he was ordered to attack Kharkov by Dietrich or made the decision himself, is unknown. In any event, the regiment had to retrace its steps and assemble at Kommuna, in order to be in position for "Leibstandarte's" attack on the next day.[20] Meyer's Kampfgruppe, still accompanied by Wünsche's tank battalion, crossed the Poltava-Kharkov railroad near Schljach and by day's end was northwest of Ljubotin, near the town of Peressetschnaja. Peressetschnaja was located on the Udy River, astride a railroad line that ran south until it entered Kharkov's northwestern corner.

Just east of Meyer's attack, Peiper's half track battalion again led Wisch's regiment. Peiper's objective was to cross the shallow Merefa River where it paralleled the Ljubotin-Kharkov road. The battalion assembled before dawn and got underway just after first light, encountering little Russian resistance. The column moved slowly due to the road conditions and was continually held up by vehicles mired in the snow, half frozen mud and slush. It did not reach Merefa until 1700 hours and Peiper's men were exhausted by the physical demands of the difficult journey.[21]

The other two battalions of the regiment, with II./SS-PzG.-Rgt. 2 in the center and I./SS-PzG-Rgt. 2 on the right, advanced toward their objectives, the towns of Odrynka and Ogultzy. Sandig's battalion encountered strong resistance at Ogultzy and did clear it until 1630 hours. At Odrynka, a battalion of Russian infantry initially checked the advance of I./SS-PzG.-Rgt. 2. Battalion commander Kraas assembled a company of Panzergrenadiers, along with a Flak detachment and a battery of self propelled artillery. This Kampfgruppe utilized the cover provided by a range of low hills to move around the village quickly. Supported by the fire of the 10cm guns of the self-propelled howitzers and accompanied by assault guns, the company of SS Grenadiers reached the cover of a dry stream bed near the town's northern edge by noon. The Russian troops defending the town abandoned it when they discovered the Germans were preparing to attack them from two directions. Unknown to Kraas he had received help from Otto Kumm's Regiment "Der Führer."

OPPOSITE: "Totenkopf" attacked toward the Olschany area on 8 March. After the division took control of the town, it blocked the roads leading into the area from the north, forming an outer ring of protection for the attack of "Leibstandarte." Dietrich's division moved completely around Kharkov's western edge and attacked from the north, pushing toward the large Red Square in the northern quarter of the city. "Das Reich" thrust eastward after reaching Korotisch, intending to strike the western edge of Kharkov by attacking along the Ljubotin-Kharkov road.

[17] Vopersal, pg. 200-204.
[18] Op cit.
[19] NA/T-354, roll 118,1a Tagesmeldungen SS-Panzerkorps am 8.3.43. frame 3752236.
[20] Ibid. frame 3752235-3752245.
[21] Vopersal, pg. 205.

At first light, Regiment "Der Führer" had advanced out of its bridgehead at Bachmetjewka, on the northern bank of the Msha River. Russian infantry in the forested terrain north of Bachmetjewka delayed the battalion for a short time, however, by 0930 hours, Kumm's regiment was north of the river, with II./"Der Führer" leading the way. After pushing through the forest, the battalion approached Odrynka before noon. The sounds of battle could be heard north of the town, where Sandig's men were fighting to clear the stream bed. The battalion immediately deployed and attacked Odrynka. Within an hour, Russian resistance collapsed and the remaining Soviet troops pulled out of the town and dispersed to the east and north. Forward elements of the SS battalion pushed through the town and were three kilometers beyond it by 1354 hours. By 1600 hours, II./"Der Führer" reported that it had reached a point five kilometers north of the town.[22]

Regiment "Deutschland" moved up into the Msha bridgehead area north of Pawlovka, but the regiment was ordered not to advance further to the north. This was due to a number of aggressive Soviet counterattacks launched against 11. Panzer-Division, the SS regiment's neighbor in the sector to its east. The Russian 195th Tank Brigade attacked out of the Merefa area and cut through the Army division's rear areas and threatened the SS crossings over the Msha River. For the remainder of the day, Regiment "Deutschland" aligned itself to protect the bridgeheads over the river. The two Panzer divisions of XXXXVIII. Panzerkorps continued to face difficulties in the area on both side of Taranovka. Using Taranovka as a base of operations, Soviet tanks thrust out of the town repeatedly over the next few days, tied down large parts of 6. Panzer-Division and prevented the advance of 11. Panzer-Division.

On 8 March, 11. Panzer-Division encountered stiff resistance north of Taranovka, which was defended by the Soviet 62nd Guards Rifle Division, reinforced by the 253rd Rifle Brigade and the 195th Tank Brigade. The division attacked with the objective of establishing bridgeheads over the Msha River, south of Merefa. The main attack was made by Kampfgruppe Schimmelmann, which consisted of Panzer-Rgt. 15, the division's half track battalion, which was little more than company strength and a battery of artillery. The objective of Kampfgruppe Schimmelmann was to cross the river about ten kilometers west of Merefa, bypass the strong Russian defenses on the southern perimeter and attack Rakitnoje from the rear. The Panzergrenadiers of the division were in position to launch a simultaneous attack upon the town from the front. Kampfgruppe von Bosse, consisting of II. and III./PzGren.-.Rgt. 111 and Panzer-Pioniere Bataillon 209, was to make the frontal attack. A small mobile group, designated as Kampfgruppe Henze was to screen the flank of the frontal attack.[23]

The 11. Panzer-Division's Panzer-Regiment 15 had thirty-six Panzer IIIs, seven of which mounted the short barreled 7.5cm infantry howitzer. It also had seven Panzer IVs with the long barreled 7.5cm gun. With a total of forty-three tanks, it was as strong in armor as it had been since before the fall of 1942. After moving past Taranovka to the west in the morning, Kampfgruppe Schimmelmann moved along the railroad line and parallel road that linked Taranovka with Merefa. After leaving the northern edge of Taranovka, the railroad gradually curved to the west until once again turning north near Rakitnoje. Kampfgruppe Schimmelmann followed the railroad, encountering difficult road conditions, but managed to keep moving. The division captured two lightly defended villages south of Rakitnoje.[24]

At 1000 hours, the Panzer group reached the Msha River near Rakitnoje and found the town strongly defended. There were two crossing sites at Rakitnoje, one of which was an ordinary bridge. The other was an earthen railroad causeway over the river. When the Germans reached the river, they found that both had been destroyed by the Russians. Soviet fighter-bombers and Sturmovik attack planes bombed and strafed the Germans throughout the day. Several Russian tanks and about 10 anti-tank guns were dug into the entrenchments defending the southern half of Rakitnoje, which was occupied by two battalions of infantry. It became apparent that the division would not be able to quickly force its way over the river, because Kampfgruppe Schimmelmann had been held up by the bad roads and was not in position to begin its attack upon Rakitnoje from the northwest. Without the support of the Panzers, the infantry attack was not able to establish a foothold on the north bank of the river and the Grenadiers were withdrawn. Meanwhile, 6. Panzer-Division continued to battle its way toward the river.[25]

One battle group of 6. Panzer-Division reached the area south of Sokolovo, a few kilometers from the southern bank of the Msha River. Sokolovo was defended by 900 men of the 1st Czechoslovakian Infantry Battalion, which had been assigned to Rybalko's 3rd Tank Army. Fighting from behind extensive tank ditches, the Czechs offered surprisingly tough resistance and blocked the German advance until late in the day. At 1500 hours the Germans took Sokolovo, with the Czechs leaving 30 guns and over 300 dead in the town. A second battle group of the division remained involved

[22] Weidinger, pg. 91 and NA/ T-354, roll 120, 1a KTB Darstellung der Ereignisse, frame 3753696.

[23] T-315, Roll 598,1a KTB, Darstellung der Ereignisse der 11. Panzer-Division 8.3.1943, frame 00034.

[24] NA/T-313, roll 367, 1a KTb Tagesmeldung 4.Panzerarmee, 8.3.43, frame 8753289.

[25] NA/T-313, roll 367, 1a KTB Tagesmeldung 4.Panzerarmee, 8.3.43, frame 8653288-8653300.

in fighting at Taranovka, where a Russian rifle regiment and some armor still held out. By that time, 6. Panzer-Division had only a half dozen operational tanks, although it had received additional six Panzer III flame throwing tanks. Some of the companies of its Panzergrenadier regiments were reduced to a strength of only ten to fifteen men.[26]

On the far right flank of the army, LVII. Panzerkorps' 15. Infanterie-Division and 17. Panzer-Division were inactive south of the Northern Donets River, on XXXXVIII. Panzerkorps right flank. The 15. Infanterie-Division brought up supplies and rested its troops during 8 March, preparing to resume its attack on the following day. While the two divisions regrouped from their covering operations on the eastern flank of the army, the Russians became more active on their front. Perhaps sensing the German's fatigue, the Russians sent out platoon to company sized reconnaissance attacks, seeking to locate gaps and weaknesses in the line. Several German positions were very heavily shelled throughout the day by rocket and artillery fire. At the village strong point of Tschepel, the Soviets pounded 15. Infanterie-Division positions with heavy artillery, blasting the village into rubble. German patrols reported a strong Russian presence on the front and right flank of the division on the southern bank of the Donets. The river itself proved no obstacle to Soviet troops, as it remained frozen solid enough to allow troops and heavy equipment to easily cross to the opposite bank.

Meanwhile, 17. Panzer-Division cleaned out Russian stragglers from villages and towns throughout its rear areas. The Soviets brought up reinforcements from east of the Donets and launched an infantry attack upon a Panzergrenadier battalion which had just begun to dig in at the town of Kobanka. The Soviet assault was accompanied by mortar and direct howitzer fire and the Russian troops, numbering about 500 strong, swept into Kobanka and drove the battalion out of the town. Disorganized by the heavy dose of firepower and the ferocity of the Russian infantry assault, the German infantry fled the village. The disorganized troops were not able to regroup until they reached a series of low hills southwest of the town. After reaching higher and more defensible ground, they recovered and were able to stop the Russian advance.

In other sectors, the division held its ground or made some progress northward. It pushed the Russians out of the village of Tscherkaskij and forced them to withdraw over a range of high ground to the north. The division's Kradschützen Bataillon attacked a Russian rifle battalion holding another small town and became involved in house to house fighting. The battalion received heavy

A tank commander of "Kampfgruppe Kunstmann" with Panzergrenadiers before the attack upon Kharkov. Due to "Das Reich's" heavy tank losses, Hausser assigned II./SS-Pz.Rgt. 3, led by Eugen Kunstmann, to support "Das Reich" on 10 March. Wilhelm Schulze's II./Regiment "Totenkopf" was also assigned to the battle group. The overall command of the "Totenkopf" battle group was given to Kunstmann. (Courtesy Mark C. Yerger)

fire on one flank, which brought its advance to a halt, until several tanks of the division arrived and lent their support. The cannon fire from the tanks silenced Soviet gun positions on nearby hills and allowed the motorcycle troops to reach the town's defensive perimeter. After additional hours of hard fighting, the Germans took the town, capturing several guns that the Russians were not able to remove.

As the day wore on, the situation in the corps area remained fluid. At Werchnij Bischkin, the Russians brought up large numbers of infantry reinforcements and attacked from assembly points in a wooded area north and northwest of the town. Fighting continued into the night at Werchnij Bischkin and nearby Kobanka. After the Sturmgeschütze Abteilung arrived with a company of Panzergrenadiers, the division tried to regain possession of Kobanka, but the first counterattack was repulsed by smothering machine gun

---

[26] Glantz page 197 and NA/T-313, roll 367, 1a KTB 4. Panzerarmee Tagesmeldung vom 8.3.43, frame 8653291.

fire. The Grenadiers fell back and launched a second attack that initially had some success. The attack stalled when the battalion became embroiled in house to house fighting in the western half of the town. The Russians launched repeated counterattacks, but could not eliminate the German penetration.[27]

At dawn on 9 March, while the advance of the other two Panzer corps slowed in the sectors west and south of the Donets, the SS divisions continued to sweep through the sector west of Kharkov. On the western flank of the SS-Panzerkorps, Baum's Regiment "Totenkopf" approached the Udy River at a point northwest of Kharkov. Reconnaissance elements reached the outskirts of Olshanny at about 0400 hours. Surprisingly, this key rail and road junction town was reported to be unoccupied by the Russians. Seizing this unexpected opportunity, Baum ordered his regiment to quickly follow its forward detachment and thrust to the banks of the Udy River. The small river ran parallel to a main railroad line which exited the western edge of Kharkov before turning north, towards Olshanny.

By 1155, Baum's troops had built bridgeheads across the river at the villages of Peressetschnaja, Jarotavka and Golowatscshtschev Station. Baum established contact with Witt's SS-PzG.-Rgt. 1 "LAH" and later in the afternoon pushed even farther northward, with I./Regiment "Totenkopf" occupying the town of Tschepelin. During the fighting, the battalion commander, Walter Reder, was struck by fragments of an anti-tank gun shell which shattered his left arm and pierced his right hand and throat. Command of the battalion was taken over by Reder's second in command, SS-Obersturmbannführer Rudolf Schneider.[28]

Regiment "Eicke" began its attack early on 9 March, advancing in a wide, arcing sweep to the west, which was designed to cover the communication and supply lines of Regiment "Totenkopf." The regiment reached a point ten kilometers south of Olshanny, at 0655 hours. By mid-afternoon, the regiment had reached its objective for the day and established a solid screening position southwest of the edge of Olshanny. Reconnaissance patrols moved forward and along roads to the north and northwest, looking for any sign of Russian troops. Contact was maintained with "Grossdeutschland" elements in the area to the west of Stary Merchik.

"Das Reich" began its advance on 9 March, slowed more by poor road conditions and exhaustion, than by any Soviet actions. Regiment "Der Führer" attacked Korotisch at dawn. At 1600 hours, III./"Der Führer," finally fought its way into the town and reported

Tanks of "Kampfgruppe Kunstmann" with SS Panzergrenadiers, probably assembled shortly before the 10 March attack by "Das Reich" on the western edge of Kharkov. (Courtesy Mark C. Yerger)

the capture of Korotisch at 1750 hours. Nearly two hours later, Stadler's II./"Der Führer," almost completely exhausted by its journey, began to straggle into the town. Meanwhile, Regiment "Deutschland" assembled at Ssinolizovka, a town on the Poltava-Ljubotin-Kharkov railroad line. Harmel's regiment prepared to attack Kharkov from the west on the next day.[29]

"Leibstandarte's" three attack columns were moving by 0600 hours on 9 March, with the divisional commander, Sepp Dietrich, traveling close behind the lead elements of the battle groups. On the right, Kampfgruppe Peiper passed through the southern section of Ljubotin at 0730 hours. The battalion moved east along the road and rail line that led towards the western edge of Kharkov. The I. and II./SS-PzGren.Rgt 2 "LAH" arrived later and cleared out the remaining Russian forces on the outskirts of the town. Peiper's battalion turned north and began the advance towards the town of Dergatschi, which was north of Kharkov's northwest corner.

Witt's regiment, attacking in the center, was able to drive north from Ljubotin and reached the southern outskirts of Peressetschmaja at 0730 hours. At 1000 hours, the regiment made contact with Baum's Panzergrenadiers on the southern perimeter of the "Totenkopf" bridgehead. On the left or western wing of the division, Meyer's reinforced Aufklärungsabteilung also advanced to Peressetschnaja, where it was ordered to reinforce Witt's regiment. In the later hours of 9 March, Kampfgruppe Witt, accompanied by the Aufklärungsabteilung, advanced northeast of Kharkov, driving toward the objective of Zirkuny, which was northeast of the city. Meanwhile, Peiper's battalion approached Dergatschi, which was

[27] NA/T-313 roll, 367 frame, LVII. Panzerkorps Tagesmeldung vom 8.3.43 at 1930 hours, frame 3653290.

[28] Vopersal, pg. 204 and NA/T-354, roll 120, 1a KTB SS-Panzerkorps, Darstellung der Ereignisse, 9.3.1943, frame 3753700-3753702.

[29] Weidinger, pg. 92-93.

northwest of Kharkov. Good quality roads ran south and entered Kharkov from the "Leibstandarte" sector. On the following day the division would use these roads to thrust toward the heart of the city.

Hausser Embroiled in Controversy Once Again

While the three divisions of the corps were continuing their attacks around Kharkov, 4. Panzerarmee radioed a query to the SS-Panzerkorps, asking if Kharkov could be seized in a surprise mobile operation on 10 March. Based on the reports it had received from its divisions, up to that moment, the corps replied that in its estimation, such a coup de main could be accomplished. However, seeking some clarification of the precise intent of this communication, Hausser reminded 4. Panzerarmee that such an operation did not lie within the framework of the primary mission that had been assigned to his corps. He asked for a clarification, but the SS-Panzerkorps records do not record that the army issued any further reply during the rest of the day. There are no contradictory orders recorded in the available records of 4. Panzerarmee, so there is no evidence about how Hoth responded, if he did. Apparently Hausser decided that since the issue of seizing Kharkov had been brought up by the army and not contradicted, he had the option of conducting just such an attack if the conditions seemed favorable. This puts the events of the next few days in a very different light from the impression one gains from some accounts describing the actions of the SS-Panzerkorps during its assault upon Kharkov.[30]

Some historians have suggested that Hausser acted without orders and launched costly attacks into the center of the city on 10 March for personal reasons related to the prestige of the SS and the earlier surrender of the city against Hitler's orders. In fact, on 10 March, Heeresgruppe Süd itself radioed an order of the day to 4. Panzerarmee and Armeeabteilung Kempf that again mentioned the possibility of seizing the city in a quick thrust by the SS-Panzerkorps. This communication first stated that Hoth's army was to attack and destroy the remaining Russian forces in Kharkov. The SS-Panzerkorps was to attack through the sector north of Kharkov with the mass of its forces and cut the Soviet lines of communication between the city and Chugujev. These directions are clearly written but there are additional instructions. The last sentence of the order states that in the case of weakening Soviet resistance Kharkov is to be occupied by a quick thrust.[31]

At 1530 hours 9 March, the SS-Panzerkorps issued orders for a general assault upon Kharkov on 10 March, acting on the basis of the communication from 4. Panzerarmee regarding the possibility of seizing the city. Hausser's intentions were reported to 4. Panzerarmee and Hoth was informed that the orders had already been given. There was no contradictory communication received from the army and there is no 4. Panzerarmee order stating that Hausser should not carry out the planned assault. Luftwaffe support was requested and Regiment "Der Führer" was ordered to solidify its control of Korotisch, in order to secure assembly areas for an attack on the western edge of Kharkov by "Das Reich." These preparations were reported to 4. Panzerarmee and at 1730 hours Korpsbefehl Nr. 8, the order to attack Kharkov, was issued and recorded. After all necessary orders had been issued to the divisions and supporting corps troops, XXXXVIII. Panzerkorps was informed about the mission at 2140 hours on 9 March.

Vahl's "Das Reich" was to concentrate in the Korotisch sector, with the mission of attacking the town from the west. However, the division had only a dozen operational tanks and "Totenkopf" was ordered to put together a Panzer Kampfgruppe and send it to reinforce the division's attack on the next day. The Kampfgruppe consisted of II./SS-Pz.Rgt. 3, led by Eugen Kunstmann and Schulze's II./Regiment "Totenkopf." The overall command of the battle group was given to Kunstmann. During the night, the Kampfgruppe assembled and began its move to the "Das Reich" sector. Baum's reinforced regiment was to continue its operations to protect the flank of "Leibstandarte's" attack groups by securing the area north of line Dergatschi-Zirkuny-Tscherkaskoje.[32]

Armeeabteilung Kempf drives toward Kharkov

While 4. Panzerarmee pushed the 3rd Tank Army out of the Msha sector and Hausser prepared to attack Kharkov, Armeeabteilung Kempf steadily gained ground southwest and west of the city, driving deeper into the boundary area between Rybalko's army and the 69th Army. "Grossdeutschland" attack groups and Regiment "Thule" pushed into the area south of the Merchik River, driving the Russians away from the Poltava-Ljubotin-Kharkov railroad line. The 167. and 168. Infanterie-Divisions made steady progress on 8-9 March and 320. Infanterie-Division, with two battle groups, was able to advance in the sector between Kolomak and Valki.

---

[30] NA/T-354, roll 120, 1a KTB SS-Panzerkorps, Darstellung der Ereignisse, 9.3.1943, frame 3753704 and Vopersal, pg. 210-215. The SS-Panzerkorps records read as follows:
   Um 12.15 Funkspruch von der Armee: "Möglichst Charkow durch Handstreich zu nehmen ausnutzen."
   Antwort: Handstreich höchstens 10.3 möglich.
   The SS-Panzerkorps radioed to the army the following query. 'Da die Wegnahme von Charkow nicht im Rahmen der bisherigen Aufträge liegt, wird bei Armee angefragt, ob bisheriger Auftrag bestehen bleibt.' It appears that the army did not issue any contradictory orders, as the record states that 'Antwort darauf erfolgt den ganzen Tag nicht.'
[31] *Befehl des Gewissens*, Aufgabe der 4. Pz. Armee (mission of 4th Panzer Army) pg. 255.
[32] NA/T-354, roll 120, 1a KTB SS-Panzerkorps, Darstellung der Ereignisse, 9.3.1943, frame 3753704.

In XXXXVIII. Panzerkorps' sector, the fighting was heavy, but both divisions were able to make some progress on 9 March. The road conditions remained very poor in most areas. The 11. Panzer-Division's Panzer group which had crossed the Msha River over the Regiment "Deutschland" bridges, finally was able to attack Rakitnoje from the north, assaulting the town at 1130 hours. The Panzergrenadiers of the division were attacking the Russian defenses on the southern edge of the town, when the tank group suddenly assaulted the northwest corner of Rakitnoje. The appearance of German armor from an unexpected direction unnerved the defenders and the intensity of Russian heavy weapons fire coming from the southern sector diminished. This allowed the Panzergrenadiers to breach the town perimeter.

Shortly afterwards, Russian resistance crumbled and the Germans were able to occupy most of Rakitnoje by 1445 hours. One T-34 was disabled in the fighting for the town and several infantry guns were captured or destroyed. The division estimated that it had smashed most of the Russian infantry regiment holding the town. After the fighting wound down in the southern section of the town, Pioniere and bridge building units of 6. Panzer-Division, quickly threw a light pontoon bridge across the river, although it was too light to support tanks. Almost immediately the Panzergrenadiers continued their attack toward Merefa, reaching the villages of Utkovka and Oserjanka. The town of Merefa lay across the shallow river, on the opposite bank. However, the Grenadiers were temporarily without the support of their armor, due to the weight limitations of the light bridge. While 11. Panzer-Division was clearing the remaining Soviet troops out of Rakitnoje, 6. Panzer-Division tried to eliminate the Russian armor that had been operating out of Taranovka.[33]

A 6. Panzer-Division Kampfgruppe attacked Taranovka from the north, in support of a reinforced Panzergrenadier battalion of the division which assaulted the southern sector of Taranovka. With the help of the Panzers, the Grenadiers occupied the southern part of the town and several hours later were able to drive the Russians out of the main part of the town. Only one T-34 was reported destroyed in the town itself and it soon became evident where the rest of the Soviet armor was located. While mopping up operations were still in progress, the division was attacked by a Russian armored group, numbering about twenty tanks. Although twelve of the Russian tanks were knocked out or disabled, the rest found concealed positions around the town. The fighting took on a pattern. Groups of T-34s tried to work their way into the town perimeter repeatedly and German tanks were kept busy counterattacking each attempt.

Using documents taken from some of the knocked out T-34s, German intelligence identified these tanks as belonging to the 2nd Guards Tank Corps.[34]

The LVII. Panzerkorps came under increasingly strong Soviet pressure during 9 March, although 15. Infanterie-Division had some initial success during the early morning. An attack group, strengthened by the division's Sturmgeschütze Abteilung, captured several small towns and took another Soviet position located on a hill north of the town of Galinovka. However, the Russians responded with a series of counterattacks by tanks and infantry that halted the attack. The division's right flank, at Tschepel, encountered stubborn resistance from Soviet troops dug in on a number of nearby hills. Late in the afternoon, elements of the 2nd Tank Corps launched an attack which struck the division near Bairak. A company of German troops occupying Bairak was completely cut off by the Russian thrust.

East of Bairak, elements of the 1st Guards Cavalry Division attacked forward detachments of 17. Panzer-Division. The Germans knocked out nine Russian tanks, after which the attack collapsed. The division remained involved in operations to drive the remaining Soviet infantry out of Kobanka. A few German tanks were able to penetrate into the village and supported the Grenadiers. However, the Russians had emplaced several T-34s in well organized defenses which were supported by machine gun nests and mortars. The T-34s could not be dislodged and Kobanka still remained partially in Soviet hands at nightfall.[35]

The 1. Panzerarmee sector became relatively quiet. There was no large scale Russian offensive action along the entire army front, but there was heavy patrol and infiltration activity. German reconnaissance reported long columns of Russian infantry and motor vehicles continually arriving in the sector east of the Donets, between Izyum and Voroshilovgrad. The Russians were digging in and obviously preparing to repel a German attack across the river. Operations in the 1. Panzerarmee sector entered an essentially static period at that time, with one exception.

The XXXX. Panzerkorps was confronted by a divisional strength attack south of Izyum. Using the cover of night and fog, the Russians had moved amazing amounts of men across the river and inserted these forces into a large swamp on the German side of the river. At night, makeshift roads were built with rocks, sand and timbers. All evidence of these roads was concealed by piles of brush during the daylight hours. The Russians had even brought heavy

---

[33] NA/T-315, roll 598, 1a KTB der 11. Panzer-Division, 9.3.1943, frame 00038.

[34] NA/T-313, roll 367, 1a KTB Tagesmeldung XXXXVIII. Pz Korps vom 9.3.43, frame 3653300.
[35] NA/T-313, roll 367, 1a KTB Tagesmeldung XXXXVIII. Pz Korps vom 9.3.43, frame 3653300.

weapons into this difficult terrain without German detection. In this manner a strong bridgehead position had been established along the bank of the Northern Donets. Because of the nature of the terrain, the Germans had not expected even the Russians to be able to utilize the swamp and the attack came as a complete surprise.

Supported by strong artillery fire and numerous fighter-bombers, the Russian attack burst out of their concealed assembly areas under cover of an early morning fog. The unexpected attack shocked the Germans and the attacking forces were able to occupy several villages south of the river. By late morning, however, the fog burnt off and further Soviet advance was blocked by German assault guns and a battery of 88s, which directed a devastating fire on the spearhead troops. After the attack was halted, the penetration was cleaned up by a counterattack of a Kampfgruppe of 7. Panzer-Division and all lost ground was recovered. The Russians pulled back into the swamp and evaded German pursuit.

Subsequently, 1. Panzerarmee ordered the evacuation of much of the Russian civilian population from the rear areas of the corps, having decided that the populace was providing valuable intelligence and support to the Russian Army. Instead of trying to clean out the extensive swamps, it was decided to wait until the breakup of the ice on the Donets before trying to destroy the Russian troops in the swamp. After this action, the entire 1. Panzerarmee front quieted down to a large extent for the remainder of the month. The only action along the entire front of the Army consisted of artillery fire and incessant patrol and reconnaissance actions. After the second week of March, events in the 1. Panzerarmee sector exerted little influence on the battles for Kharkov.

14

"LEIBSTANDARTE" LEADS THE ASSAULT

The Soviets tried to stem the relentless drive of 4. Panzerarmee toward Kharkov on 9 March. Rybalko's army repelled the attacks of XXXXVIII. Panzerkorps but could not stop the SS divisions from encircling Kharkov. The weak counterattack by the 69th Army failed to halt "Grossdeutschland" and SS Regiment "Thule" from penetrating the front at the boundary between the 40th and 69th Armies. "Grossdeutschland" did not realize it had been counterattacked at all because of the weakness of the Soviet rifle divisions and shortage of tanks. Rybalko's operation was not a counterattack at all. In reality the army conducted a series of holding or rear guard actions. At nightfall on 9 March Rybalko's 3rd Tank Army still held a section of the defensive line along the Msha River between Zmiev and Merefa, southwest of Kharkov. The line was occupied by four weak rifle divisions, their fronts stiffened by a few remaining tanks.

However "Das Reich" and "Leibstandarte" had crossed the river north of Merefa and shattered the 3rd Tank Army front. The SS division's assault destroyed the Soviet 48th Guards Rifle Division. Rybalko had hoped that the remnants of the 6th Guards Cavalry Corps could be used to block "Leibstandarte's" advance but the corps was not able to mount a counterattack. The now exhausted cavalry divisions retreated to the north of Dergatschi, completely avoiding the advance of the division. The 19th Rifle Division was shoved back to the west by "Das Reich's" onslaught and tried to block the advance of the division toward the western perimeter of Kharkov.

While Rybalko tried to organize a new line of defense on 9-10 March, Kempf and Hoth flew to Zaporozsche to speak with Hitler who was once again visiting Manstein's HQ. Each commander gave the Führer a orientation on the situation currently facing their respective army and described the action that had taken place during the last few days. Hitler listened attentively, satisfied now that the German Panzer divisions were once again on the attack. He could see victory in the near future and the recapture of Kharkov, which still was very important to him. Hitler was always cognizant of prestige or politically important victories. The fact that this obsession was sometimes to the detriment of the military was lost on the dictator.

The 4. Panzerarmee continued its concentric attacks on the morning of 10 March, amid speculation that the Russians intended to give up the city. Russian forces were observed moving out of the western and central sectors of the city, marching eastward. Everything appeared to be going in favor of the Germans, except the weather. The roads were still a concern because the unpaved roads could be an impassable ribbons of mud and slush or frozen into rock hard ruts. The added stress on machines due to the failure of drive trains, motors or running gear added to vehicle losses which had greatly reduced the number of vehicles and tanks available to the SS divisions. The three divisions had only 105 operational tanks between them as they gathered for the final assault on Kharkov.

"Totenkopf" had five "Tigers," fourteen Panzer IVs and thirty Panzer IIIs, for a total of forty-nine operational tanks. "Leibstandarte" had thirty main battle tanks and approximately ten light Panzer IIs, while "Das Reich" was able to field only twenty-six tanks. All of Vahl's armored and wheeled vehicles needed extensive maintenance work. The division's trucks and other vehicles were in such bad shape that on 8 March, Vahl notified Hausser that the mechanical condition of the vehicles of his division was critical. He stated that they had been in action for a distance of a thousand kilometers without proper maintenance and specified oil changes. His fear was that the strains placed on the vehicles during the past month would result in the breakdown of many of the remaining tanks if repair and servicing could not be done immediately. The corps replied that the division could not be pulled out of the line and service work could only be done on vehicles that were already in repair at the time.[1]

Panzer divisions always had a number of tanks in various stages of repair. The above numbers were the total of combat ready tanks each division possessed at the time. For example, on 4 March, the SS-Panzerkorps had a total of 112 operational Panzers, not including light tanks and Befehlpanzers. At that date, there were an additional forty tanks in repair shops, with repairable battle damage or mechanical breakdowns. There were forty-one others with damage that required more extensive repairs. Thus, while the corps actually possessed approximately 193 main battle tanks, only about 60% were fit for battle.[2] Repaired tanks were constantly rotating back to the front line formations, just as damaged tanks were steadily being taken to the divisional tank repair formations.

The Army Panzer divisions of 1. and 4. Panzerarmee were also short of tanks, although 11. Panzer-Division had a few more tanks than "Das Reich," reporting that it had twenty-nine operational tanks. In contrast, 17. Panzer-Division had only seven and 6. Panzer-Division had just six Panzers still running of 10 March. Due to this situation, a significant proportion of the available Luftwaffe support was allocated to XXXXVIII. Panzerkorps. The single SS Panzer division operating in the area of 1. Panzerarmee, 5.SS-Panzer-Division "Wiking," suffered from the same shortages of armor as the army units and had less than a dozen tanks. Shortages of tanks were common to all German Panzer divisions by the second year of the war in Russia, not Army divisions exclusively. The enormous losses suffered on the Eastern Front could not be made up by German industry, although production continued to increase until the last months of 1945. It is interesting to note that in spite of the Allied bombing campaign, German factories produced more tanks in 1944 than in any other year of the war.

The SS Divisions assault Kharkov

On 10 March, the SS divisions closed in on Kharkov. "Leibstandarte" continued its drive to swing north of the city, while "Das Reich" attacked the western and southern edges of Kharkov. Regiment "Totenkopf," reinforced with armor and heavy weapons, continued to protect "Leibstandarte" from the threat of attack from the north or northeast. Baum's reinforced regiment left blocking detachments on all the main roads leading into Kharkov, while

SS-Obersturmbannführer Otto Baum. While "Leibstandarte" and "Das Reich" attacked the perimeter of Kharkov, the reinforced Regiment "Totenkopf" blocked the main roads leading into the city from the north. Under command of Baum, the regiment performed a vital service by protecting the communications lines of the three "Leibstandarte" battle groups that pushed toward the northern section of Kharkov. (Credit National Archives)

Becker's Regiment "Eicke" secured the Olshanny sector, blocking any Russian thrust that would threaten SS lines of communication in the sector.

The SS divisions intended to complete regrouping operations before midnight, but the road conditions delayed the columns and the movements to their assigned areas took all night. This deprived the troops of any sleep, but at dawn the attacks began as scheduled. "Das Reich's" Aufklärungsabteilung 2 and elements of Regiment "Der Führer" took over the defense of the Ljubotin area, replacing both SS-PzG.-Rgt. 1 "LAH" and Meyer's Aufklärungsabteilung, freeing them for the swing into the area north of Kharkov. It was intended that "Leibstandarte" battle groups would assemble north of the city on the three main roads that passed through the sector and then drive south toward Kharkov.

---

[1] Weidinger, pg. 92.
[2] NA/T-313, roll 367, Panzerlagemeldung SS-Panzerkorps an 4. Panzerarmee am 4.3.43. frame 8633250.

Columns of Russians were pulling out of the western half of Kharkov. They were moving back across the Udy River, which passed through the western 1/3 of the city from north to south, before exiting the city's southern edge. Hausser planned to destroy these forces before they could pull back across the river and move into the center of the city. He knew the skill and determination with which Russian infantry could defend urban areas if allowed time to dig in and organize their defenses. Brick and stone buildings easily became fortified strong points and furnished snipers ideal firing positions. Once Russian infantry and tanks were entrenched, it took hard fighting to dislodge them. The process was costly in human life as well. Hausser apparently hoped to avoid this situation by capturing the Udy bridges and cutting off the Russian forces in the western part of the city.

"Das Reich" was to attack the western perimeter and force the Russians to turn and defend this area. Kampfgruppe Harmel, made up of Regiment "Deutschland" (minus II./battalion), III./Regiment "Der Führer" and the remaining tanks of the division were to attack the western perimeter. Additional reinforcements to the regiment consisted of a battery of assault guns and attached artillery and Flak guns. Harmel's Kampfgruppe included the tanks of II./SS-Pz.-Rgt. 3, commanded by Kunstmann and Schulze's battalion of Panzergrenadiers. Harmel's attack would allow "Leibstandarte" to drive through Kharkov along the Udy, cut all routes of escape and trap the Soviet forces in the western half of the city.

Regiment "Der Führer" was ordered to swing south of Kharkov and drive to the east, with the objective of reaching the road leading from Kharkov to Merefa. Kampfgruppe Kumm consisted of II./and III./Regiment "Der Führer," II./Regiment "Deutschland" and supporting heavy weapons. This thrust would cut the supply lines running from Kharkov to the 3rd Army divisions still facing XXXXVIII. Panzerkorps. Faced with potential encirclement, Rybalko would then be forced to give up his defenses on the Msha River line. The Luftwaffe was in operation over the entire western half of Kharkov throughout the day, bombing and strafing the Soviet troop columns.[3]

"Das Reich's" attack was delayed when it found that it had to drive Russian troops out of the eastern edge of Korotisch. During the night, Soviet troops had infiltrated into the town under cover of darkness. These troops had to be cleared out by Regiment "Deutschland" before the attack could begin. At 1000 hours Vahl sent a radio report to SS-Panzerkorps HQ, informing the corps that he would attempt to get the attack started by 1200 hours. However, the division was not ready to attack when that deadline arrived. The

Panzergrenadiers of I./Regiment "Totenkopf," the battalion of the division that was equipped with half tracks, are shown climbing into an SdKfz 251. (Credit National Archives)

SS-Obersturmführer Franz Grohmann, a platoon commander in Regiment "Deutschland." Grohmann won the German Cross in Gold for his bravery and leadership during the Kharkov fighting and earlier accomplishments. Led by Heinz Macher's Pioniere company, Regiment "Deutschland" made a successful attack that penetrated into the western suburbs of the city. (Courtesy Mark C. Yerger)

---

[3] Weidinger, pg. 97.

RIGHT: SS-Sturmbannführer Christian Tychsen, the commander of II./SS-Panzer-Regiment 2. Tychsen commanded the handful of "Das Reich's" tanks still remaining in action on 10-11 March, 1943. (Credit National Archives)

FAR RIGHT: In early March, 1943 "Das Reich" division commander Herbert Vahl complained to Reichsführer-SS Heinrich Himmler about the poor state of the division's vehicles. Vahl was concerned enough to tell Himmler that the division was nearly to the point where it could not carry out its assigned missions because so many vehicles were out of action due to mechanical breakdowns. (Mark C. Yerger)

Russians fought stubbornly and even after they were initially pushed out of Korotisch, mounted several counterattacks. In addition, the main road leading into Kharkov was heavily mined and a highway bridge was destroyed by Russian engineers. Both of these conditions resulted in additional delays.

Hausser decided to postpone the division's attack until the next day and at 1220 hours, Ostendorff notified Vahl regarding the new attack time. This allowed the division the rest of the afternoon to complete its assembly. Hausser's decision avoided unnecessary losses incurred by launching a hastily mounted attack, but it also resulted in less than ideal attack conditions on the next day. Since "Das Reich" was not able to attack and fix the Soviet defenders on the western perimeter of Kharkov, the Russians were able to withdraw significant numbers of troops into the center of the city. The Russians were able to organize stronger defensive positions with the additional time given them. This significantly delayed the advance of the division on the next day.[4]

"Leibstandarte" Thrusts into the City

Road conditions delayed "Leibstandarte's" assembly for the attack planned for 10 March, but did not prevent the attack from beginning. The main objectives of Kampfgruppe Witt (Meyer's Aufklärungsabteilung and Witt's Panzergrenadiers) were Tscherkasskoje and Zirkuny which lay north of Kharkov. Good roads passed through the two towns and led directly into the northern section of Kharkov. In order to reach these objectives, the attack columns had to first pass through the town of Dergatschi. By midnight, Kampfgruppe Witt approached Dergatschi, which had been reported to be occupied by the Russians. After a short conference with his battalion commanders, Witt sent out several reconnaissance patrols to gain information about the terrain and Soviet defenses. When the patrols returned, they reported that the town was strongly fortified with extensive entrenchments and was heavily occupied. Witt decided to attack at the break of dawn. Just to the north of the town, the leading battle groups of "Totenkopf" had also arrived in the area, although Witt did not know that at the time. Meyer's Aufklärungsabteilung remained close at hand, in order to exploit any opportunity that might present itself, while Wisch's SS-PzG.-Rgt. 2 "LAH" followed the leading units.

Kampfgruppe Witt was not in position to attack Dergatschi until late morning on 10 March. In addition to these delays, command indecision also played a part in the postponement of the attack. Before the beginning of the battle, the commander of II./SS-PzG.-Rgt. 1, Max Hansen, argued with Panzer battalion commander Martin Gross about how the attack should proceed, evidently in regard to the use of the tanks and their support with infantry. This disagreement resulted in a significant delay before the attack was begun. The heated discussion evidently was not satisfactorily resolved, because Gross abruptly stalked away from Hansen and ordered that the Panzers should begin their attack. The assault on Dergatschi was made by the SS tanks, unsupported by the SS Grenadiers, an unwise choice that could have resulted in unnecessary loss

---

[4] NA/T-354, roll 120, 1a KTB Darstellung der Ereignisse, frame 3753712 and Weidinger, pg. 96.

of armor. In fact, the tank of the commander 7. Kompanie, Obersturmführer Rudolf von Ribbentrop, was nearly knocked out during the following battle.

Ribbentrop was a bystander during the argument between Witt and Hansen that is described above, an event he recounted after the war. After Gross turned away from Hansen, he found Ribbentrop and ordered him to drive straight through the village. Ribbentrop was not happy with this decision and his fears were justified. When the tanks attempted to move down the narrow streets, a Russian jumped on Ribbentrop's tank, with a hand grenade or Molotov cocktail in his hand. The commander of the following tank, SS-Untersturmführer Stollmeier, ordered his gunner to load a high explosive shell and blast the Russian off Ribbentrop's tank. Understandably, the tremendous impact of the high explosive shell stunned and terrified Ribbentrop and his crew, although the tank itself was not damaged.[5]

Stollmeier told Ribbentrop what he had done over the radio. Ribbentrop, who was naturally somewhat disturbed by the drastic nature of this expedient, strongly suggested that Stollmeier could have used his machine gun for that task. However, Stollmeier's machine guns were jammed and the quick thinking tank commander had decided upon an alternate strategy for removing the Russian from the tank. It was effective, although providing a violent and frightening shock for Ribbentrop and his crew.

Taking advantage of the disruptive effect of the tanks moving through the town, the Panzergrenadiers deployed and attacked. Shortly afterward, at 1300 hours, Kraas' I./SS-PzG.-Rgt. 2 "LAH" arrived at Dergatschi. The rest of the regiment was strung out behind it, still struggling through the traffic congestion northwest of Kharkov. Elements of three SS divisions and "Grossdeutschland" were rolling along the main roads and this resulted in massive traffic snarls of regimental columns, supply unit trucks and artillery batteries. Traffic control was a logistical nightmare, made worse by the lack of paved roads in most areas.

In the distance, the crump of mortars and rattle of machine gun fire to the north signaled that "Totenkopf" had already begun its assault on the opposite side of Dergatschi. The I./Regiment "Totenkopf," strengthened by the "Tiger" company of the division, commanded by SS-Hauptsturmführer Wilfried Richter, was already in action, having begun its attack before Kampfgruppe Witt attacked the town. Russian troops concentrated against the "Totenkopf" attack and were forced to redeploy, first against Ribbentrop's tanks and then the attack of Hansen's battalion.[6] Meanwhile fighting continued in the center of the town.

Both Meyer and Witt had decided to bypass the town and push on immediately, driving farther eastward. The Kampfgruppe arrived

"Leibstandarte" half tracks and Marders in the March mud. Only tracked vehicles were able to move through the deep mud of the early spring thaw. Because of the poor road conditions Peiper's half track battalion and Meyer's Aufklärungsabteilung were often called upon to spearhead the division's advance. (Credit National Archives)

at Tscherkasskoje later in the afternoon and Witt's Grenadiers, with support from "Leibstandarte" Panzers, assaulted the town. There was no heavy combat, as the Russians abandoned the town and withdrew to the south, toward Kharkov. After the fall of Tscherkasskoje, Witt turned south, heading toward the northern edge of Kharkov, led by 7. Kompanie of the Panzer Regiment.

Von Ribbentrop's Panzers destroyed two Soviet tanks that were trying to reach the city, leaving them burning and abandoned on the road side. The column made good progress until it reached a large airfield on the northern edge of Kharkov. Around the airport, the Russians had constructed formidable earthen fortifications and a fire fight broke out when the lead elements of Witt's regiment reached that point. It was apparent that the Russian position was a good one and that the Russians intended to fight. Meyer became restless to continue the attack and decided to try to find a way through to the Bolshaja Danilovka-Kharkov road, which was still farther to the east. However, a large forest was between him and the road. Making a decision that was typical of his style of leadership, Meyer decided to go straight through the forest.

By that time darkness was only a few hours away and Witt decided to wait for the rest of the tanks and artillery to assemble. The Grenadiers fell into an exhausted sleep, ringed by tanks whose crews spent a long cold night in their vehicles. During the night, an unknown number of Russian tanks suddenly materialized and raced through the darkness, firing machine guns and cannons. Confusion reigned for a time, as the 76mm guns of T-34s barked, lighting up

[5] Tiemann, Ralf, *Chronicle of the 7. Kompanie: 1.SS-Panzer-Division "Leibstandarte,"* (Atglen) 1998) pg. 43-44.

[6] NA/T-354, roll 118, 1a KTB: SS-Panzerkorps, Tagesmeldung "L-SS-AH" on 10.3.43, frame 3752276.

290

the night. The Russian tanks plunged through the German positions and the SS tank crews could not fire back for fear of hitting their own men or tanks. However, just as suddenly as they appeared, the Russians were gone, vanishing back into the pitch-black night.

Meyer and Wünsche pushed on after Witt halted because they wanted to find a way into the city. Leaving the main road, Meyer ordered his men into the forested terrain southeast of Tscherkasskoje. A forward detachment of his battalion pushed into the woods, which were passable for Schwimmwagen and half tracks. Wünsche immediately decided to accompany Meyer and ordered a number of his tanks to make their way through the woods. The Panzers and a few assault guns turned off the main road and entered the forest, moving down a narrow path through the woods. Meyer's vehicles were able to negotiate the forest lanes, but the assault guns and tanks had a more difficult time making their way past icy spots on frozen hillsides or muddy slopes on the narrow forest track. Some of the tanks and assault guns slid off the path completely and became mired in mud, but the rest of the vehicles slithered and slid forward.[7]

While the heavy vehicles struggled to keep up, a forward detachment of the reconnaissance battalion, consisting primarily of Gerd Bremer's 1./Kompanie, led the advance through the forest to the southeast. Suddenly the lead vehicles came within sight of the Zirkuny-Kharkov road. Along this road a massive Russian column of infantry, tanks and artillery was marching out of Kharkov and heading to the north. These were possibly forces of Kazakov's 69th Army, which by 11 March had been ordered to withdraw through Kharkov and take up defensive positions along the Kharkov-Belgorod road.

Bremer halted about 800 meters from the road, hoping to remain undetected by the Russians. Soon after, Meyer arrived at the front of the column. He was forced to decide if he should withdraw or wait until the rest of the battalion and Wünsche's Panzers arrived. With only a few Schwimmwagen, a Kubelwagen and an eight wheel armored car, there was little that could be done except watch. Even had Meyer had sufficient force to make an attack, deploying in column out of the narrow forest lane was tactical suicide. Meyer realized that under the conditions, he did not dare to attack the greatly superior Russian force. For a time, all that the Germans could do was watch the Russian column pass by and hope that they were not discovered. At that moment however, fate intervened on the side of Meyer's small group. A few half tracks joined the group and the first tanks were rumbling down the path.

Suddenly there was the roar of plane motors and winged shadows flitted quickly over the snow. It was a flight of Stukas that had

SS-Obersturmführer Rudolf von Ribbentrop, commander of 7./Kompanie SS-Panzer-Regiment 1. During the attack upon the town of Dergatschi, Ribbentrop's tank was attacked by a Russian infantryman who climbed onto the tank deck with a Molotov cocktail. The following SS tank, commanded by SS-Untersturmführer Luis Stollmeyer, blew the Russian off Ribbentrop's tank with a high explosive shell. The resulting concussion terrified Ribbentrop and his crew until they found out what had happened from Stollmeyer, who had resorted to the drastic expedient because his machine guns were jammed and inoperable. (The author's collection)

spotted the column and were about to attack. While Meyer and Bremer watched, the gull winged planes gained height and plunged down on the Russians. When bombs and machine gun fire rained down on the column, the attention of the Russians was directed toward the sky. Horses panicked and reared in fright and crews tried to gain control of the frightened animals. Truck drivers drove into the woods, seeking concealment from the planes under cover of trees lining the road.[8]

Immediately seizing his opportunity, Meyer decided to attack in order to take advantage of the confusion and panic caused by the Stuka attacks. Firing red flares to let the German pilots know that

[7] Meyer, Kurt, *Grenadiere*, (Winnipeg: 1994) pg. 109-110.

[8] Ibid. pg. 111.

friendly troops were in the area, the SS vehicles roared forward, heading right at the middle of the Soviet column. The Stukas wagged their wings, signaling that they recognized the German troops and understood the situation. The planes again swept down from the sky, roaring over the length of the column, strafing any group of Russians that attempted to fight back. Several of Wünsche's tanks burst out of the woods and caused further disruption when they blasted the length of the column with cannon fire and machine guns. Then the tanks advanced, reached the road's edge and turned to roll parallel to the column and destroy it. With their anti-tank guns hooked up to horse teams or vehicles, the Russians could not use their 45mm and 76mm guns before the Germans overran the center of the column.

The heavy treads rolled without pause over men, anti-tank guns and wagons, crushing them into twisted piles of scrap. Pandemonium reigned as Stukas roared past at tree top level in strafing runs, machine gunning the Russian infantry and horses. Hundreds of Russians were shocked into surrendering, gathering in tense, apprehensive groups along the side of the road. Surrender, particularly in the first moments after fighting has ended, is always a tension filled moment because those laying down their weapons don't know if their surrender will be accepted. With no time or spare personnel to deal with the prisoners, Meyer and Wünsche pushed on to the south and Kharkov, leaving the presumably much relieved Russians behind. Meyer knew from experience that his only hope was to keep on the move, because to stop was to allow the Russians time to react. When Meyer's SPWs reached the edge of the city, they ran into Soviet tanks and this brought the advance to a halt. Since the Stukas were no longer with them and the element of surprise was lost, Meyer's battalion was forced to withdraw toward the designated assembly area at Bolshaja Danilovka.

During the wild fight, the battalion had become scattered and Meyer anxiously awaited the return of his men during the early evening and the ensuing night. A number of Wünsche's panzers had become stuck in the marshy woodlands and work parties were hauling the tanks out of the muck. Throughout the night, small detachments of the Aufklärungsabteilung and individual tanks of the Panzer battalion found their way to the assembly area. The exhausted Grenadiers and crews threw themselves to the ground and tried to sleep for an hour or two before the next day's action.[9]

While Meyer and Wünsche were engaged in their exploits in the woods south of Bolshaja Danilovka, Sandig's and Kraas' battalions left Dergatschi and thrust to the south from Dergatschi. The column moved on the road and parallel railroad embankment that

SS-Obersturmführer Wilfried Richter (left) the commander of 7. Kompanie of "Totenkopf's" Panzer Regiment. He later led the division's "Tiger" company. Before Richter transferred to the tank regiment he commanded a company of Sturmgeschütz IIIs. (The author's collection)

SS-Obersturmführer Gerd Bremer. Bremer's 1./Kompanie, equipped with Kubelwagen, led the advance of Meyer's battalion into Kharkov. Bremer survived the war and emigrated to Spain, where he died in 1989. (Credit National Archives)

---

[9] Meyer, pg. 112.

entered the northern edge of Kharkov. The two "Leibstandarte" battalions pursued large columns of Russians who were retreating into the city. However, at the edge of Kharkov itself, the Soviets had established solid defensive positions. Supported by heavy Stalinorgel (rocket fire), they stopped the Germans from penetrating farther into the northern sector of Kharkov. Late in the afternoon, Wisch pulled his Grenadiers back and prepared to resume the attack on 11 March. The regiment's attack was to be supported by a battalion of Nebelwerfers, the division's Sturmgeschützabteilung and two battalions of artillery. Baum's reinforced Kampfgruppe was still battling for possession of the town when the "Leibstandarte" battalions continued their assault upon Kharkov.

Elements of "Totenkopf's" Panzer regiment had arrived in the Dergatschi area at 0925 hours. The I./Regiment "Totenkopf" deployed and attacked, supported by the fire power of the division's Panzer IIIs and Richter's "Tiger" company. The heavy tanks ground methodically toward the Soviet positions, as the SS Grenadiers advanced behind them. A storm of anti-tank rifle projectiles and 45mm anti-tank gun shells flew toward the tanks. However, these weapons were absolutely ineffective against the frontal armor of the steel giants and they bounced off the armor plates of the "Tigers," leaving little more than gouges in the steel. With the clanks and bangs of the impacts of anti-tank projectiles resounding in their ears, the tank commanders calmly identified Russian gun positions. They spotted the flashes that pinpointed the presence of a Soviet gun and directed their turret toward the Russian position. While the Russian gun crew watching helplessly, the long barrel swung in their direc-

tion and then fired. The shells from the 88s blasted huts and buildings into ruins. The Russian guns were silenced one after the other.[10]

Baum's Grenadiers of I./Regiment "Totenkopf" fought their way into the town from the north. The familiar pattern of house to house fighting began once again. Later in the morning, to the south, firing could be heard that signaled the attack of Witt's regiment on the town. The Soviet defenses began to collapse when tanks from both divisions careened through the town, shooting up troop columns and destroying gun positions. The Russians were squeezed into the center of the town and the northern half of the town was cleared at 1317 hours. Shortly after noon, caught between the SS attacks from the north and south, the Russians abandoned the town and withdrew to the northeast, harassed by German tanks and artillery. In the afternoon, after wiping out the last pockets of Soviet defenders, Regiment "Totenkopf" informed the SS-Panzerkorps Headquarters that Dergatschi was secured.[11]

Leaving a strong security detachment to block the northern entrance into Dergatschi, Baum resumed the attack to the east, his forward elements arriving at the Tscherkasskoje-Kharkov road at 1500 hours. German maps show it to be paved. For this reason, given the conditions of nearly all secondary roads in the area, it was of vital importance to block this main highway. After gaining access to the road, Baum pressed on, making good time on the paved roadway, until it arrived at the village of Russkoje. The 15./

---

[10] Vopersal, pg. 207-208.
[11] NA/T-354, roll 120, 1a KTB SS-Panzerkorps, Darstellung der Ereignisse, frame 3753712.

ABOVE: The tank of the commander of 1. Kompanie SS-Panzer-Regiment 3. The numbers 101 signify that it is the command tank of the 1st company of the battalion. (Credit National Archives)

RIGHT: An SS Panzer III on one of the main roads leading into Kharkov that was paved. Three different major roads led into the northern 1/3 of Kharkov and met at the large Red Square in the center of the northern section of the city. (Credit National Archives)

Kompanie assaulted the small town and seized it quickly, suffering only light casualties. Baum first organized a strong defensive position at Russkoje, securely blocking the road, then sent out reconnaissance patrols farther to the north.

While Baum secured the village and road, Regiment "Eicke" established defensive positions north and northeast of Olshanny. The town itself was defended by main elements of II./Regiment "Eicke." Other elements of the regiment took over defense of the three Udy River crossings north of Kharkov, over which Baum had launched his initial attack north of Kharkov. Periodically during the day, these troops were engaged in fighting against groups of withdrawing Russians trying to cross the river and reach safety on the eastern bank. Regimental commander Becker sent out two combat groups to the north, in order to secure the roads northwest of Kharkov. One Kampfgruppe reached a railroad station and road intersection at Feski, which was northeast of Olshanny, thus blocking another main route into Kharkov from the north. The other Kampfgruppe struck out due north of Olshanny and occupied the small town of Novaja Kultura, blocking another route toward Kharkov.

That night Dietrich moved his HQ to Dergatschi, in order to be close to the attacking troops on the following day. After arriving in the town Dietrich received a radio communication from Adolf Hitler. During the conversation, Hitler's voiced his regrets about the heavy casualties suffered by the division, but expressed his confidence that the city would soon fall to 'his Leibstandarte.' Hitler ended the conversation with Dietrich by stating that 'if my Leibstandarte attacks with its usual nerve, it cannot fail to tear Kharkov from the enemy's hand.'

With these words Adolf Hitler himself, the supreme military commander of the German armed forces, had endorsed a direct attack upon Kharkov. Sepp Dietrich had always considered that he was under Hitler's direct control since the days when he commanded Hitler's bodyguard detachment and the Führer had given his explicit approval for "Leibstandarte" to attack the city on the next day. That night, the division issued orders for its battle groups to strike into the city.

The XXXXVIII. Panzerkorps stalled on the Msha River

While the SS-Panzerkorps enveloped Kharkov, XXXXVIII. Panzerkorps continued to try to reach the city from the south. The 11. Panzer-Division fought to expand its small bridgeheads on the northern bank of the Msha River, north of Rakitnoje. The corps intended to break free of the Msha sector and swing to the east of Kharkov, in order to make contact with the SS divisions. After linking up with the SS Panzers driving through the area north of the city, Kharkov would be cut off from any contact with other Russian forces. However, the two divisions of the corps were hard pressed to gain any ground during the day. Faced by effective Russian counterattacks and strong artillery fire, the attack stalled quickly. On the western flank, 11. Panzer-Division began its main attack from north of Rakitnoje, but was blocked by Soviet defenses around the village of Oserjanka. The division was counterattacked by a Soviet battle group consisting of several T-34s and a battalion of infantry, but was able to knock out several T-34s and blunt the counterattack. Later in the day, the Panzer regiment drove out Soviet troops holding Utowka and was able to occupy the village by 1500 hours.[12]

The Stavka, in order to stop the German forces driving towards Kharkov, directed Vatutin to counterattack the eastern flank of 4. Panzerarmee. Vatutin struck back with a thrust from the Zmiev area, made by tanks of the relatively fresh 2nd Tank Corps. The apparent aim of the attack was to link up with the Soviet armor in the Taranovka area. The German infantry battalion occupying the southern sector of the town was struck by about forty Russian tanks, supported by strong infantry forces. The Russians attacked from the south and southwest and rolled over the German perimeter defenses. The Russian tanks drove the Panzergrenadiers out of the southern end of Taranovka, destroying a battery of artillery pieces that had been left behind.

In the afternoon, 6. Panzer-Division was forced to stop its offensive operations, in order to regroup and stop the Russian attack. The division launched a counterattack, after receiving the promise of help from the Luftwaffe, which it received. The counterattacking group, with just 6 remaining tanks, supported by Stukas and fighters, drove a part of the Soviet force away from Taranovka, inflicting losses on the Russian armor. The division claimed it destroyed five T-34s and four T-70s, as well as six guns and many infantry weapons and estimated that it had killed 600 Russians during the day's fighting. The 11. Panzer-Division claimed three Russian tanks destroyed and capture of five guns and a heavy mortar. On that day, the corps reached a milestone total of 900 Soviet tanks destroyed from 6 December, 1942 to 10 March, 1943.[13]

The combat in the corps sector remained bitter, with the Russians refusing to give up much ground. Strong Russian elements remained in the area southeast and east of Taranovka, but with the loss of most of its tanks, Vatutin's counterattack had essentially

---

[12] NA/T-313, roll 367,1a KTB, Tagesmeldung der XXXXVIII. Panzerkorps 10.3.1943, frame 8633317.
[13] NA/T-313, roll 367,1a KTB, Tagesmeldung der XXXXVIII. Panzerkorps 10.3.1943, frame 8633321-8633324.

collapsed. However, the remaining Soviet troops constituted a hindrance to the advance of both XXXXVIII. Panzerkorps and LVII. Panzerkorps, occupying a significant proportion of the two weakened division's fire power. The most serious deficiency was lack of infantry strength, because the Panzergrenadier companies were down to forty and fifty men. Some companies were even weaker. The XXXXVIII. Panzerkorps had earlier been notified that it was assigned 106. Infanterie-Division, effective as of 9 March, 1943, however, that division was still arriving and its combat units had not yet begun to reach the combat sector. The division headquarters were not even scheduled to arrive at Ochotschaje until early on 10 March. Total Soviet material losses during the day were reported as twelve tanks, eleven guns, numerous vehicles and many light weapons. The Russian manpower losses for the day were listed as 775 dead and twenty prisoners.[14]

The abnormal ratio of dead to captured is graphic evidence of the bitter nature of the fighting. Whether it reflected that the Russians were fighting to the death or that prisoners could not be secured and were simply shot, is unknown. One of the harsh tragedies of war is that prisoners sometimes present a serious problem to an attacking force far behind enemy lines or heavily engaged in combat. If they can not be guarded adequately and can not be left behind, the choice was grim but inevitable. No combat commander could choose to leave prisoners behind that could pick up their weapons and kill his men or compromise the accomplishment of his mission.

In addition, there were other factors at work in these situations on the Eastern Front. In the murderous heat of battle, sometimes the killing does not automatically stop when an opponent lays down his weapons, particularly if that opponent had moments before inflicted casualties upon the victor. This was particularly true in Russia, where the ideological conditioning that took place on both sides added a sinister and deadly element to surrender. Both sides were guilty of killing men trying to surrender as well as in other circumstances. Men brutalized by years of combat and killing are capable of shocking harshness.

Nor was the killing of prisoners unique to the Russian theater of war. Anyone who believes otherwise is naive about these distinctly uncomfortable and age old realities of war. Allied soldiers shot unarmed German prisoners at times, according to many frank accounts told by American and British veterans and this occurred with greater frequency than it is comfortable to admit.[15] However, the savagery of the war in Russia surpassed anything ever experienced in the West and untold thousands of prisoners were slaughtered by both sides. Certain German troops were more likely to be shot out of hand than others. This was often true with the SS troops,

Russian prisoners, some wounded, limp past German soldiers well equipped for winter weather. The Germans captured millions of Russian soldiers, particularly in the first years of the war. Many prisoners were sent back to Germany and Poland for use as slave labor. They were generally poorly fed and in the winter thousands died of exposure and starvation. Many thousands of the Soviet soldiers captured by the Germans, in particular those of Ukrainian or Cossack origins, decided to work for the Wehrmacht. These men were called "Hiwis" and served in a variety of positions, some even fighting side by side with the Germans, although this was supposedly prohibited. (Credit National Archives)

whose uniform often marked them for death when they surrendered.

As XXXXVIII. Panzerkorps battled to reach the Kharkov area in the Msha sector, LVII. Panzerkorps faced equally determined Soviet forces south of the Northern Donets on 10 March. While 15. Infanterie-Division fought to reach the southern bank of the river, 17. Panzer-Division assaulted Glinischtsche, which was a long narrow town whose northern edge lay on the opposite bank. The southern approaches to the town were bordered by two low hills, each of which was occupied by a Soviet rifle battalion.

In a quick, stunning attack, two battle groups of the Panzer division attacked the flanks of the Russian defenses on both hills. One group consisted of the division's tanks and a regiment of Panzergrenadiers, while the other Kampfgruppe was made up of Panzergrenadiers supported by Flak detachments and assault guns. The two attacks smashed into the Russian positions and rolled right over the two hills. Many of the Russian troops abandoned their trenches and escaped into a nearby wooded area. Others fled across a bridge to the other bank, leaving 300 dead behind. In the confusion, the bridge was not destroyed by the retreating Russian troops.

---

[14] NA/T-313, Nachmeldung zur Tagesmeldung XXXXVIII. Panzerkorps vom 10.3.43, frame 8633317.

[15] See the following sources: Ambrose, Stephen, *Citizen Soldiers: The U.S. Army from the Normandy Beaches to the Bulge to the Surrender of Germany*. pg. 351-356. Foster, Tony, *Meeting of Generals*, pg. 489. Fussell, Paul, *Doing Battle: The Making of a Skeptic*, pg. 124. These sources are not meant as a criticism or justification of such acts by soldiers of any nation. It is intended rather as an illustration of one of the horrors of war and the brutalization of combat soldiers as a result of exposure to these horrors.

When the German Panzergrenadiers reached the southern bank of the river, they could see the town of Tschernyj Bischkin, which lay just across the river from Glinischtsche. It was not possible to cross the bridge however, as the Russians laid down a heavy volume of artillery and machine gun fire on the approaches to the bridge. Within hours both the southern part of the bridge and Glinischtsche were solidly in the hands of the Germans. Although the division was not able to cross to the other side of the river, the forward detachments had the northern approaches to the bridge under observation and fire.

While the division's forward elements fought to secure a river crossing at Glinischtsche, other elements of the division were in action in the rear areas, fighting pockets of bypassed Russian troops. Troops of the division wiped out an isolated Soviet detachment that had been left behind near the town of Ljubizkije, while other small combat groups cleaned up other pockets of Russians on the right flank of the division. Fighting remained heavy in the 15. Infanterie-Division sector also. The Russians were able to prevent the infantry division from reaching the river in that sector. For the day, 15. Infanterie-Division reported the capture of eight guns or anti-tank guns, several vehicles, hundreds of small arms and 233 Soviet prisoners, including three officers.[16]

The operations on 11 March were a modest success for LVII. Panzerkorps, due to the capture of the intact bridge at Glinischtsche, but it remained to be seen if a crossing of the Donets could be accomplished and a bridgehead established on the northern bank. Once Tschernjy Bischkin was captured, 17. Panzer-Division was in striking distance of the Andrejevka-Zmiev-Kharkov railroad, which entered Kharkov on the southeastern corner of the city. The capture of this railroad would cut a main supply line entering the city from the southeast. However, the slow progress of the two Panzer divisions allowed the Russians to continue to supply troops and equipment to Kharkov utilizing this route.

Armeeabteilung Kempf in Action West of Kharkov

While 4. Panzerarmee fought to encircle the city with attacks from the north and south, Armeeabteilung Kempf continued to push the 40th and 69th Armies away from Kharkov. The main attack, made by Regiment "Thule" and "Grossdeutschland" had quickly gained ground, but the weak infantry divisions, particularly, 168. Infanterie-Division, were in no shape to conduct effective offensive operations. The 168. Infanterie-Division, by that date was reduced to a combat troop strength of about 1000 men. It made little offensive

progress on 8 March. During February, the division had lost 178 dead, 478 wounded and 263 missing. There were also 293 men too sick to fight and another forty-eight lost to miscellaneous causes. This was a total loss of 1260 men, which would certainly not have been crippling to a full strength unit, but the division had begun February with a strength of a reinforced regiment. It had received just 107 replacements or recovered wounded during the same period of time. The division had long ago reached the end of its rope.

Bad weather largely grounded the Luftwaffe in the early morning hours, which hindered the progress of the ground operations, although German reconnaissance planes were able to take to the air. Reports from these pilots indicated that the Russians were pulling back out of Achtyrka. Long columns were marching eastward, passing through Bogodukhov and streaming out of the town towards the Kharkov area. The impression was of an opponent who was in full retreat from the Vorskla River-Achtyrka sector. However, all the Russian troops were not in retreat.

The 167. Infanterie-Division was faced with very active Soviet patrolling on its front. The division had a combat strength of 3500 men, which was significantly stronger than 168. Infanterie-Division, but its losses had been heavy during February and its Grenadier regiments were far below establishment strength. However, it made a strong thrust with reinforced I./Grenadier-Regiment 339 east of Sinkiw. The division attacked a number of occupied villages along it front and was able to capture a number of these villages. The division had arrived in the East after a long rest and was not exhausted by months of fighting as was 168. Infanterie-Division.

On the right or eastern flank, the situation with 320. Infanterie-Division was similar. Postel's division had also endured its share of suffering during February, particularly during the division's epic retreat. The fighting from 1-28 February had cost the division 803 dead, 2241 wounded, 1336 missing and nearly a 1000 lost to sickness and other causes. This was a total of 5380 casualties for the month and as a result, it could field only about 2500 combat effectives. Most of these had been in combat for months on end and were very tired and worn down mentally and physically. However, the division had received a total of 1108 replacements or recovered wounded soldiers. It also benefited by the support of Regiment "Thule" and had the tanks of Panzerzug 62 attached to it. While the decimated infantry divisions struggled to gain ground northwest of Bogodukhov and in the Vorskla River valley, "Grossdeutschland" and Regiment "Thule" continued to advance against diminishing Soviet resistance.[17]

---

[16] NA/T-313, roll 367, Tagesmeldung LVII. Panzerkorps vom 11.3.43, frame 8633328.

[17] NA/T-314, roll 490, 1a KTB Tagesmeldung 320. Infanterie-Division an Korps Raus am 8.3.1943, frame 000364.

After several days of bitter fighting, by early morning, 8 March, Soviet will to fight had begun fading away in the woods near Iskrovka. Regiment "Thule" Grenadiers had counted hundreds of Russian dead and had taken nearly 100 prisoners as well as capturing a great deal of weapons and equipment. After the Russians were observed to be withdrawing from the Iskrovka area, the SS regiment renewed its advance. The I./Regiment "Thule" regrouped in the area north of Kolomak during the early afternoon. By 1400 hours, the battalion had moved from Iskrovka to Vysokopol'ye, where it established contact with the reinforced Aufklärungsabteilung "GD" (Gruppe Wätjen). The SS troops took over defense of the town and allowed Gruppe Wätjen to renew its advance to the north, toward the Merchik-Merla Rivers.

One company of I./"Thule" was sent to reinforce II./Regiment "Thule." This company was equipped with amphibious Schwimmwagen as well as Kubelwagen and had good mobility even given the road conditions. Even if these light vehicles became stuck, a few Grenadiers could put shoulders to a fender and get them moving again. The company was used to spearhead another attack upon Schelestovo, made by II./Regiment "Thule" and Grenadier Rgt. 586. Although the town had been cleared out once, it had been reported that the Russians had occupied the town again.

When the company reached Schelestovo, supply troops and stragglers were the only Russian personnel who remained in the town and these were put to flight quickly. After the SS battalion regrouped in the shattered town, reconnaissance detachments were immediately dispatched to the north. The patrols returned and reported that the town of Trudoljubovka was lightly held by the Russians. However, darkness was quickly approaching by this time and the battalion remained in Schelestovo for the night. Meanwhile, I./ "Thule" occupied Vysokopol'ye and II./"Thule" occupied positions in and around Schelestovo.[18]

The "Grossdeutschland" attack groups continued their thrusts to the north on 8 March. The division's objective was to cut the road and rail line leading from Bogodukhov towards Olshanny, thereby preventing the Russians from evacuating Bogodukhov and reinforcing Kharkov with those troops. All three divisional groups made gains during the day, but the division's Panzer group was not able to reach the railroad at Maximovka on 8 March. Road conditions were poor again, because of high wind and a heavy snowfall. The wind blew the snow into meter high drifts which nearly closed most of the roads.

Initially, Strachwitz pushed due east from Kovjagi, moving along the Poltava-Kovjagi-Kharkov rail line and roadway. The col-

umn met little resistance during the early morning hours, but shortly before noon, collided with a weak Soviet defensive position that straddled the rail line near a small rail station. Russian infantry were dug into positions strengthened by a few anti-tank guns. The German column smashed through the Russians, evidently without any great delay. The first tanks of Gruppe Strachwitz arrived at Stary Merchik at 1300 hours, but the Grenadier Regiment remained nearly three hours behind the tanks, having great difficulties moving along the snow covered roads.

After reaching Stary Merchik, on the southern fork of the Merchik River, Gruppe Strachwitz crossed the small river and pushed toward the Bogodukhov area. About two kilometers north of the river, the column was halted by another Russian blocking position. This position was more strongly defended and the column deployed to attack while its self propelled artillery got into position. The half frozen Grenadiers dismounted, climbing down off the tanks, with frozen toes and fingers numbed and weakened by the cold. The SS tanks maneuvered into positions from which they were out of the line of sight of the Russian anti-tank guns and moved forward in cautious bounds, with the Grenadiers trudging through the snow behind them. German artillery shells screamed out of the quickly darkening sky and began to find the range, impacting amongst the village huts with dull thumps. One by one Russian gun positions were silenced and the volume of machine gun fire markedly decreased.

When the level of fire from the villages lessened, the tanks and Grenadiers assaulted the shattered defensive line and broke through the perimeter. The resistance was broken just before dark. "Grossdeutschland" Grenadiers cleared the surviving Russians out the area, escorting a few dazed prisoners to the rear. By nightfall, surviving Soviet troops had withdrawn northwards or dispersed into the wooded hills in the area and Strachwitz decided to occupy secure defensive positions for the rest of the night.

In the center, Gruppe Beuermann left the Kovjagi area and moved to Perekop, where supporting artillery and the tanks of I./ Pz.-Rgt. "GD," under Major Pössel, were assembled. Beuermann's Kampfgruppe was also reinforced by the "Grossdeutschland" Panzerjäger battalion. Meanwhile, I./Füsilier Rgt. "GD" waited at Vysokopol'ye until I./"Thule" completely took over defense of the town in order to secure the supply lines of the attack group. While Gruppe Beuermann awaited the SS troops, mobile recon detachments were sent to scout northward to the Merchik River. On the following day, the Kampfgruppe planned to attack Alexandrovka, which was located on the northern fork of the river, about ten kilometers south of Bogodukhov.

---

[18] Vopersal, pg. 201-202.

The western attack group, Wätjen's reinforced Aufklärungs-abteilung "GD," was in the area north of Schelestovo throughout the morning of 8 March. Its mission was to march north to the Merchik and cross the river at the crossings at Alexandrovka. From there it was to advance to the northeast and cut the Bogodukhov-Olshany road further to the west of Gruppe Strachwitz's advance. By late morning, the Kampfgruppe began assembling at Kovjagi. However, due to the snow covered roads and the heavy divisional traffic along the main road leading out of Kovjagi, the column became fragmented and strung out along the road between Vysokopol'ye and Kovjagi. The majority of the battalion did not arrive until late in the afternoon and as a result, Kampfgruppe Wätjen remained in the town. It was decided to get an early start on the following morning, rather than to try to use the frozen roads after dark. While awaiting the assembly of his Kampfgruppe, Wätjen sent out a number of patrols during the afternoon and these detachments reached the Merchik near the town of Novy Merchik, which was found to be occupied by a Russian battalion.[19]

Primarily due to the weather, the attacks by Korps Raus did not gain much ground and at the end of the day, most of "Grossdeutschland" remained south of the Merchik River. Although the center and left wings of "Grossdeutschland's" attack had not been able to cross the river on 8 March, Strachwitz's tanks were able to reach the southern fork of the Merchik near a crossing site located close to the town of Alexandrovka. After crossing the river, Gruppe Strachwitz's II./Pz. Rgt. "GD," accompanied by the battalion of Panzergrenadiers, arrived at the Bogodukhov-Ljubotin railroad line northwest of Ljubotin. The main railroad exited Bogodukhov's southeast corner, and ran generally eastward until reaching the town of Maximovka. At that point a lateral line branched off the south and intersected with the Poltava-Ljubotin-Kharkov railroad. The main rail line continued east from Maximovka, passed through Ljubotin, then ran directly east into Kharkov. Gruppe Strachwitz intended to push north on this lateral rail line and reach Maximovka on the following day.

The Russians were not able to offer any significant resistance to the Panzer spearhead, beyond weak delaying operations. It seemed that the 69th Army was giving up the territory west of Olshany-Kharkov without a fight, although in reality, Armeeabteilung Kempf had simply not recognized the Russian efforts as a counterattack. This was understandable, given the weakness of the Russian forces and the lack of strong supporting artillery or air support. The 'counterattack' consisted of a few small groups of Russian tanks, inadequately supported by infantry, which were perceived to be rear

guard actions covering the withdrawal of Soviet forces through Bogodukhov. The roads between Bogodukhov and the Kharkov area were filled with columns of marching Russian infantry and large numbers of sleds carrying wounded. In order to cut these roads, on the following day, "Grossdeutschland" was ordered to drive north and seize Maximovka, blocking the primary road east of Bogodukhov.

Gruppe Strachwitz was on the move by dawn. Again, the weather conditions were very bad and many roads were once again covered by deep drifts of wind blown snow. The tanks and half tracks were able to move but the wheeled vehicles of the columns were severely handicapped by the snow and often had to be towed. The tracked vehicles of Gruppe Strachwitz steadily crunched through snow drifts and skidded over icy roads, heading north along a road that paralleled the course of the railroad tracks. The column encountered no significant Russian resistance in the early morning, but it became strung out along the road from Stary Merchik to Maximovka when the wheeled elements of the column fell behind. Strachwitz' tanks, accompanied by the half tracks of I./Gren. Rgt. "GD," pushed on.[20]

By 1025 hours, Gruppe Strachwitz arrived at Bahnhof Maximovka, which was just south of the town of Maximovka. Bogodukhov was just five kilometers to the northwest, primarily on the north bank of the Merla River. A battle group was to attack and seize the village of Popowka, which was located on the Merla, 15 kilometers east of Bogodukhov. A company of tanks left the rail station and moved along the road to the north, toward the town of Maximovka, while the main body of the Kampfgruppe pushed further northward, toward a village named Klenowaje.

Just before reaching Maximovka, the company of "Grossdeutschland" tanks was fired on by Russian tanks, and a brief, but sharp tank battle flared up. The Soviet armored group pulled back to the west, leaving several T-34s immobilized or burning. After routing the Soviet tanks, Gruppe Strachwitz seized Maximovka and secured it by 1700 hours. After all of the Kampfgruppe assembled in the village, the 1./Kompanie of the Gren. Rgt. "GD" mounted the decks of "Tiger" company and pushed farther north. By nightfall the "Tiger" group reached a crossing site of the Merla River, at the village of Popovka. Popovka was on the northern bank of the river, about ten kilometers east of Bogodukhov.[21]

The rest of I./Grenadier Rgt. "GD" deployed in a defensive arc around Maximovka. The battalion moved its headquarters to the

---

[19] *Befehl des Gewissens*, pg. 229-234.

[20] NA/T-314, roll 490, 1a KTB Tagesmeldung Korps Raus, frame 000329-000338.
[21] NA/T-314, roll 490, 1a Korps Raus KTB, and *Befehl des Gewissens*, pgs. 232 to 242.

town of Klenowaje, where two companies took up defensive positions in the village itself. Behind Gruppe Strachwitz, the remaining two battalions of the Grenadier Regiment laboriously attempted to catch up to the armored group. However, they were some distance behind the column, and the leading units of II./Grenadier Rgt. "GD" did not approach Maximovka until 1500 hours. By nightfall, III./ Gren. Rgt. "GD" straggled into the village of Kryssino, which was seven kilometers west of Maximovka. Kryssino lay astride another east-west road leading toward the Bogodukhov area. Kampfgruppe Strachwitz estimated that it had killed 2000 Soviet soldiers during its actions on 9 March.

About twenty kilometers southwest of Maximovka, Kampfgruppe Wätjen went into action at 0515 hours on 9 March, attacking toward the southern branch of the Merchik River. Wätjen made his attack in three columns, each consisting of reinforced companies of the Aufklärungsabteilung. Advancing south of the river, several villages were attacked and cleared of Russians in the morning. However, when the first vehicles reached the river, they found that all of the bridges had been destroyed. There was some delay until a suitable crossing site was found. Once across the Merchik, the Kampfgruppe turned northwest, toward the main river crossing at Alexandrovka. Just as they approached Alexandrovka, the Germans sighted a Russian troop column marching to the east. Assault guns and mobile Flak guns fired on the Russian troops, inflicting heavy losses in men and equipment, before continuing to the Kampfgruppe objective.

When the leading company of the battalion neared Alexandrovka, accurate Russian artillery fire forced it to disperse and take cover. A second column of the Kampfgruppe drove northward, towards a position from which it could block any retreat out of Alexandrovka to the east. While the Germans cleared Russian infantry from houses in the southern section of Alexandrovka, Russian troop columns, consisting of horse drawn sledges, marching infantry and vehicles, fled the town's northern edge. The Russians disappeared into a dense, forested area to the north, covered by a rear guard detachment. In the afternoon, Wätjen received notification that the Füsilier Regiment was to relieve his Kampfgruppe on the following day.[22]

While "Grossdeutschland" fought to establish blocking positions east of Bogodukhov on 9 March, Regiment "Thule" advanced out of the Schelestovo area. It advanced on a broad front, meeting little significant resistance. By late afternoon, one detachment reached the town of Katschalovka, which was about ten kilometers west of Alexandrovka, the point where "Grossdeutschland" crossed

the Merchik. However, there was no contact between the two units and Armeeabteilung Kempf became concerned that the Russians would mount an attack into the gap between them. At 1130 hours, Lammerding was ordered to conduct an aggressive sweep eastwards, in order to close the gap between Regiment "Thule's" right wing and Gruppe Wätjen in the Alexandrovka sector. Lammerding directed the commander of II./Regiment "Thule," Georg Bochmann, to accomplish this mission. The recon patrols arrived at Alexandrovka several hours later, having encountered only small, isolated groups of Russians along the way. The remainder of II./ Rgt. "Thule" cleared Russians from a number of villages in the area west of Alexandrovka.[23]

The concerns of Armeeabteilung Kempf regarding a Russian counterattack were justified. However, the Russians did not attack the boundary area between "Grossdeutschland" and Rgt. "Thule." During the night of 9-10 March, Kazakov's 69th Army ordered the 107th, 340th and 183rd Rifle divisions to counterattack "Grossdeutschland" spearheads east and south of Bogodukhov on the next day. On the afternoon of 10 March, the 69th Army attacked elements of Gruppe Strachwitz at Maximovka. A dozen Russian tanks emerged from Bogodukhov's southeast corner and tried to open the roads from Bogodukhov to the Klenowoje-Bahnhof Maximovka area. The Soviet armored force deployed to attack, but was counterattacked by the Germans upon their flank and during the ensuing tank battle, lost several tanks. The remaining T-34s withdrew from the fighting and returned to Bogodukhov. After the collapse of the Soviet attack, Gruppe Strachwitz waited for resupply trucks to arrive with fuel and ammunition. However, the supply detachment did not arrive until after dark and Strachwitz was forced to remain in the Kryssino area. Elements of the Grenadier Regiment pushed closer to Bogodukhov, occupying two small villages near the southern edge of Bogodukhov. On the following day, the Grenadier Regiment planned to attack the southern sector of the city, while Gruppe Strachwitz crossed the Merla at Popovka and assaulted Bogodukhov from the east. Group Wätjen formed the western pincer of the division's attack. Its left flank was to be secured by Regiment "Thule."[24]

After the failure of the counterattack east of Bogodukhov, on 10 March, Golikov ordered Kazakov's 69th Army to withdraw from the Merchik River area and pull back to positions between Bogodukhov and Kharkov. Kazakov's mission was to defend the important Kharkov-Belgorod road, as well as Bogodukhov. Kazakov, however, feared that his depleted army could not carry out both of these missions and requested that Moskalenko's 40th

---

[22] *Befehl des Gewissens*, pgs 232 to 242, and Vopersal, pg. 206.

[23] *Befehl des Gewissens*, pg. 239 and Vopersal, pg. 206.
[24] NA/T-314, roll 490, 1a KTB Korps Raus, frame 000335-000343.

Army take over the responsibility for defending Bogodukhov. He proposed that he give up two divisions and an infantry brigade to Moskalenko. Golikov agreed to this request, which allowed Kazakov to move his weary divisions into a shorter line between Bogodukhov and Kharkov.

The defense of Bogodukhov was turned over to the 40th Army, which began to reorient itself to take over the defense of the town. However, for a time, Moskalenko had more pressing matters on his mind, primarily due to the Luftwaffe. His headquarters group had been under such heavy attacks by German planes that he was forced to move under cover of darkness to a new location on the night of 10-11 March. While Moskalenko was moving his headquarters detachments, the Germans were preparing to attack the southern flank of his army.

On 11 March, the 40th Army, under pressure from Korps Raus and 2. Armee divisions, began to slowly withdraw eastward. The 167. and 168. Infanterie-Divisions, supported by four divisions of LII. Armee-Korps, followed the withdrawing Russian troops. The 167. Infanterie-Division seized several bridges across the Merla River and occupied the towns of Kolontajev and Kotel'va. The roads east of the towns were full of columns of retreating Soviet troops, marching eastward. Elements of 167. Infanterie-Division conducted reconnaissance probes north of Kotel'va, meeting Soviet rear guard detachments.

Regiment "Thule" received new orders from Korps Raus at 0230 hours 11 March. It was to occupy and block the Merchik River crossings west of Bogodukhov and cover the left or western flank of the advance of 320. Infanterie-Division. It would also help secure "Grossdeutschland's" attack on Alexandrovka and Bogodukhov. The SS detachments were to be replaced later in the day by elements of 167. Infanterie-Division.[25] The point of main effort of the Armeeabteilung Kempf area remained in the attack zone of "Grossdeutschland" and Regiment "Thule," however, when Kazakov's 69th Army began to withdraw even the German infantry divisions were able to make substantial progress.

On the night of 10 March, Manstein radioed Armeeabteilung Kempf, explaining 4. Panzerarmee objectives and detailing Kempf's mission for the next few days. While 4. Panzerarmee destroyed the remaining Soviet forces at Kharkov, Armeeabteilung Kempf was to seize Bogodukhov, in order to protect the SS-Panzerkorps from any attacks upon its northern flank originating from the Graivoron-Borisovka area. Kempf was instructed to break the Russian resistance in the Merla River valley and arrive at a general line of Bogodukhov-Achtyrka. On the following day, "Grossdeutschland" attacked Bogodukhov and the SS-Panzerkorps began the battle for possession of the city of Kharkov.

---

[25] NA/T-314, roll 490, message from Gen.Kdo. Raus on 1220 hours, 10.3.1943, frame 413.

15

THE FALL OF KHARKOV

Korps Raus

The night of 10-11 March and the following morning saw a gradual increase in activity throughout the Korps Raus sector. Troops of 167. Infanterie-Division crossed the Merla River, west of Bogodukhov and marched toward Krasnokutsk. The 320. Infanterie-Division swept through the Merchik River valley, while "Grossdeutschland" prepared to begin its attack on Bogodukhov. German air reconnaissance reported that Russian troop columns were streaming out of the town to the north. The Armeeabteilung 1c (intelligence staff officer) reported that 4000 to 5000 troops and 2000 vehicles had left the town's northeast corner during the night and early morning. While the German infantry divisions pursued the withdrawing Russian troops, "Grossdeutschland" and Regiment "Thule" launched early morning attacks.[1]

Several hours before first light, led by Lammerding, elements of II./Regiment "Thule" advanced under cover of darkness and assaulted Krasnokutsk. After a short battle, the Russian garrison was driven from the town. Meanwhile, a second Regiment "Thule" Kampfgruppe had arrived at Murafa late on 10 March, and found that it was strongly defended. The Soviet troops in Murafa were part of the rear guard detachments hoping to prevent the Germans from crossing the Merchik and blocking the withdrawal of the 40th Army. Evidently these troops abandoned the town during the night, because at 0615 hours a second Kampfgruppe of II./Regiment "Thule" assaulted Murafa and found no Russians in the town. The rest of the regiment began a relocation to the east, towards the Merchik crossings at Alexandrovka.[2]

The 167. Infanterie-Division expanded its bridgeheads to the north and east. At Achtyrka, infantry of the division captured a bridge

over the Vorskla. The Soviet rear guard troops occupying Achtyrka delayed the German infantry most of the morning, before abandoning the town. Mopping up operations continued throughout the rest of the day. Meanwhile, a battalion of the division arrived at Krasnokutsk at 1525 hours. A security detachment relieved the SS troops in the town, while the battalion continued from there toward Murafa, where Regiment "Thule" held the bridge site it seized earlier in the day. The Russians continued to withdraw during the night. By the next morning, most of the rear guards detachments had pulled back from the area west of Bogodukhov and Alexandrovka. German patrols found that they were able to cross the Merchik at many places, without finding any Russians defending bridges or fords. The tail ends of the Soviet columns were still west of Bogodukhov by daylight on 11 March.

At first light, "Grossdeutschland" artillery began shelling Russian positions in Bogodukhov and strong points in the surrounding area. Flights of Stukas appeared over the city in the early morning, dropped their bombs and then harassed Soviet troops with strafing attacks. The long, slow moving columns furnished plenty of easy targets. Since "Grossdeutschland" had cut the roads leading out of the city to the east, the Russians were leaving the town's northern edge. While the Stukas and artillery softened up Bogodukhov, the "Tiger" company left Popovka and moved to the crest of a range of hills northeast of the city. From this high ground, the tanks could fire on the Russian columns, as well as cover the advance of the Grenadier and Füsilier Regiments.

At Alexandrovka, Füsilier Rgt. "Grossdeutschland" began its attack at 1100 hours, led by III./Füsilier Regiment. Alexandrovka was approximately twenty kilometers south of Bogodukhov. The battalion crossed the Merchik at Alexandrovka, then swung to the northwest towards a larger town named Nikitovka in order to se-

---

[1] Vopersal, pg. 213 and *Befehl des Gewissens*, page 260-265.
[2] NA/T-314, roll 490, Korps Raus Tagesmeldung vom 11. 3.1943, frame 431.

cure the left flank of the attack upon Bogodukhov. The remaining two battalions assembled north of Alexandrovka and deployed in dispersed formation, advancing across the flat terrain between Bogodukhov and Alexandrovka. The regiment encountered no strong resistance and passed easily through a large collective farm and reached the southern sector of Bogodukhov with light losses. When the first patrols began to move cautiously into the streets of the town, they found that the Russians had largely evacuated the southern half of the city. The Grenadier Regiment had moved into the city from the east and pushed toward the center of the town, followed by long columns of support troops and reserves.

By late afternoon, the last Soviet columns had escaped to the north and northeast, all the while under fire by the "Grossdeutschland" tanks north of the town. German fighter planes and Stukas made bombing and strafing attacks which forced the marching men to scatter into the open ground on either side of the road. When the German planes left, the survivors packed up their wounded, rejoined the column and marched on. The crunch of bombs and crack of tank guns echoed in the distance when the last Russian troops vanished from sight. The III./Grenadier Rgt. "GD" exited the northern edge of Bogodukhov and occupied two villages about ten kilometers north of the town.

The Aufklärungsabteilung "Grossdeutschland" took up defensive positions in the northeastern section.

The SS-Panzerkorps fights its way into Kharkov

While Korps Raus swept through the Merchik River valley and into Bogodukhov, Hausser's SS divisions began concentric attacks from the west, north and east. Fulfilling Hitler's wishes, three attack groups of "Leibstandarte" moved toward the outskirts of the city on the morning of 11 March. In "Leibstandarte's" zone of attack, furious Russian defensive efforts held up Wisch's SS-PzGren.-Rgt. 2 "LAH." The regiment advanced with two battalions leading and Peiper's battalion in reserve. Krass's battalion moved down the Dergatschi-Kharkov highway until it reached the outskirts of the town of Alexejevka. When the battalion attacked the town, it was halted by heavy Russian machine gun and mortar fire. A Russian infantry counterattack, supported by tanks, drove one company out of the town and the other companies were then forced to

Hugo Kraas, the commander of I./SS-Panzergrenadier-Regiment 2 "LAH," is pictured here as an SS-Standartenführer. He received the Knight's Cross for his role in "Leibstandarte's" recapture of Kharkov and later commanded the regiment. By the end of the war, Kraas had been promoted to SS-Brigadeführer und Generalmajor der Waffen-SS and commanded 12.SS-Panzer-Division "Hitler Jugend." His brother Boris Kraas was an outstanding commander in the Panzerjäger Abteilung of "Totenkopf." Boris did not survive the war and died after receiving his 16th wound in February of 1945. (Courtesy Mark C. Yerger)

RIGHT: SS troops prepare to load a Nebelwerfer with rockets. The six barreled NbW 41 pictured was the most common model of rocket launcher used by the Germans. This model fired 15cm rockets that contained either smoke charges or high explosive. The rockets had a significant effect on the morale of those soldiers on the receiving end of the barrage because of the eerie sound the rocket motors made while in the air. An Army unit, Werferregiment 55, was detailed to support SS-Panzer-Korps operations in Kharkov and remained with the corps throughout the summer of 1943. (Credit National Archives)

withdraw when the Russians attacked their open flank. By noon, the regiment's attack upon Alexejevka had collapsed.

Stuka support was requested and a battery of assault guns were brought up to furnish direct fire support. At 1325 hours, the Stukas arrived and began their attack, while the Sturmgeschütze IIIs and Flak guns blasted Soviet strong points and gun positions. Under cover of this fire, a company under command of SS-Hauptsturmführer Hans Becker attacked a key Russian position on a hilltop on the outskirts of Alexejevka. An assault gun and a Flak gun were knocked out and Becker's company sustained heavy casualties. The attack collapsed and the Grenadiers pulled back.[3]

After the attack stalled a second time, Becker reconnoitered the area and found a small ravine at the base of the hill that provided cover. By using this ravine, a platoon was able to infiltrate behind the hilltop position without being detected by the Soviet infantry. Becker personally led an attack which penetrated the rear of the Russian defenses. This diversion resulted in a lessening of the volume of fire to the front and the rest of the company assaulted the Russian position again. Several buildings on the hill were stormed and cleared of Russians. Immediately the Russians launched a counterattack supported by three tanks, but it failed to dislodge the SS Grenadiers. Although the hill was taken, the Russians remained in control of the town. For his audacity and determination, Becker was awarded the Knight's Cross. Battalion losses for the day were one officer and twenty-five other ranks killed, while five officers and eighty-eight Grenadiers were wounded.

On the right of the highway, Sandig's battalion fought its way forward, in spite of receiving heavy defensive fire from high ground in the Alexejevka area. After reaching the outskirts of the village of Ssewerny, the battalion was able to penetrate into the town and captured a nearby rail road station. The fighting continued at the edge of Alexejevka and Sandig's bloodied men bitterly fought to drive the Russians out of the town. Peiper's half tracks and light armored vehicles moved up, ready to exploit any situation that demanded quick movement and mobile firepower.[4]

Witt's SS-PzG.-Rgt. 1 "LAH" began its attack at 0400 hours, pushing toward the northern airport. The Soviet were solidly entrenched around the perimeter of the landing strips and the regiment tried to outflank the strong point and attack Soviet positions to the west. The Russians mounted a ferocious, but tactically unwise counterattack across the open ground of the airstrips. German machine guns and automatic Flak guns cut down the attackers in droves and the counterattack disintegrated in a hail of fire.

Exploiting the confusion and change of momentum, the SS Grenadiers attacked again, moving behind assault guns. The attack was supported by the automatic 2cm guns and a battalion of Werferregiment 55, a Nebelwerfer unit assigned to the SS-Panzerkorps. Flights of rockets impacted on the designated point of main effort, shattering Soviet resistance and knocking many of the anti-tank guns. SS Grenadiers assaulted the trenches and routed the stunned Soviet infantry. Shortly afterward, the regiment entered the northern edge of Kharkov. An enormous city plaza, the Red Square of Kharkov, lay in the center of the northern quarter of the city.[5]

The first of Witt's Grenadiers entered the Red Plaza at 1230 hours. This thrust, approximately 1 1/2 kilometers deep into the city, threatened the roads that radiated from the Plaza to the west. Witt's advance endangered the lines of communication of those Soviet troops that defended the western half of Kharkov. In response to this threat, General E.E. Belov, the commander of the Soviet forces in Kharkov, pulled more troops out of the western sector and moved them into position to block "Leibstandarte's" advance. The 86th Tank Brigade counterattacked the SS Grenadiers but lost most of its tanks to SS assault guns and anti-tank guns.[6]

The seriousness of the situation forced Belov to commit his last uncommitted armored reserve, the 179th Tank Brigade. During the night of 11-12 March, the brigade launched a fierce counterattack on Witt's Grenadiers. The T-34s knocked out a 8.8cm gun and forced the SS troops to withdraw from the Red Square. The SS Grenadiers pulled back to positions just north of the square. During the hours after midnight, the regiment regrouped and Witt ordered III./SS-PzG.-Rgt 1 to reconnoiter the roads leading into the massive square, believing that Wisch's regiment had reached the square.[7] On that date, the battalion was commanded by SS-Sturmbannführer Wilhelm Weidenhaupt. The former commander, Hubert Meyer, had been wounded on the previous day and was temporarily disabled. The patrol moved cautiously into Red Square late on the night of 11-12 March, under the impression that German Panzergrenadiers were occupying the vast plaza.

Under a moonlit night sky, the company entered the square from a side street and spotted a few infantrymen bundled up and sound asleep on the ground. They asked whether they had reached the positions of SS-PzG.-Rgt. 2 "LAH." One of the sleeping soldiers mumbled a somewhat startled reply in Russian! Other Russians jumped up from and opened fire upon the Germans, who fled

---

[3] Vopersal, pg. 211-212.
[4] Lehmann, pg. 164-165 and T-354, roll 118, 1a KTB SS-Panzerkorps, Tagesmeldung vom 11.3.43, 1700 hours, frame 2293.

[5] T-354, roll 118, 1a KTB SS-Panzerkorps, Tagesmeldung vom 11.3.43, 1700 hours, frame 3572293.
[6] Op cit.
[7] Glantz, pg. 201 and Lehmann, pg. 165.

into the darkness. The men found a hiding place in a cellar, a short distance from the square. When daylight arrived and the men peered out from their shelter, they could not believe their eyes. The entire plaza was full of hundreds of Russian soldiers and a number of tanks. They had no choice but to remain hidden in their cellar until the square was cleared of Russian troops.[8]

Meyer's Aufklärungsabteilung was also on the attack in the cold hours just before dawn of 11 March. At first light, supported by nine of Wünsche's tanks and two self-propelled anti-tank guns, the battalion pushed southwards along the Bolshaya Danilovka-Kharkov road. To the west, Meyer could make out Witt's regiment advancing near the airport and clearly observed the Russians counterattacking the Panzergrenadiers.

Meyer's battalion drove south until two hidden T-34s opened fire on the spearhead of the battalion and destroyed one of the German tanks and Meyer's command vehicle. Several SS tanks maneuvered into firing positions on the flank and knocked out the Soviet tanks, which allowed the battalion to push past the brick works. Meyer's Kampfgruppe reached the eastern edge of Kharkov at 0740 hours.[9] However, due to a shortage of fuel, the battalion couldn't continue its advance. Meyer ordered his men to occupy a graveyard, forming an all round defensive position that commanded the Kharkov-Chuguyev road, the last main artery of communication to the east.

By mid-afternoon, Meyer was under attack by Russian troops seeking to break out of the city before they were cut off. Meyer sent out his 2. Kompanie on a reconnaissance mission to locate a bridge over the Kharkov river, which lay to the west. Meyer hoped to find a safe route that would allow his battalion to receive fuel and ammunition. However, Weiser's company was cut off by the Russians and could not get back to the graveyard. When night fell, Meyer and his men remained trapped. After darkness fell, two trucks reached Meyer's position in the graveyard, bringing a small amount of fuel and ammunition. However, by that time it was too dangerous to attempt to make an escape at night. Meyer and his men remained in an extremely serious position during the entire night and were under constant pressure from Russian infantry and tanks.[10]

While "Leibstandarte" spearheads fought their way into the city, "Das Reich" attempted to break into Kharkov from the west, but they encountered what division reports described as "bitter" Soviet resistance. Kampfgruppe "Harmel" encountered strong Soviet positions between Korotisch and the western edge of Kharkov.

Another of the outstanding soldiers of "Leibstandarte's" Aufklärungsabteilung. SS-Hauptsturmführer Hermann Weiser was the commander of the 2. Kompanie of the battalion, which was equipped with Kubelwagen. After penetrating into the center of Kharkov, Weiser's company was surrounded by Russian infantry, cut off and forced to take shelter in a school. The company defended itself against continuous attacks until Max Wünsche organized a relief attack that dispersed the Russians besieging the school. (Courtesy Mark C. Yerger)

The battle group consisted of Rgt. "Deutschland," III./Rgt. "Der Führer" and Panzergruppe Kunstmann. The handful of "Das Reich" Panzers remaining in action, were commanded by battalion commander Christian Tychsen. Other support troops consisted of a battery of Sturmgeschütze IIIs, the division Pioniere Battalion, and Flak guns.

Harmel's Grenadiers approached the edge of Kharkov at 1600 hours. Shortly afterward, Ehrath's I./Regiment "Deutschland" approached a railroad station along the main railroad line. The Russians occupied the fortified the station and opened up with machine

[8] Lehmann, pg. 166.
[9] T-354, roll 118, 1a KTB SS-Panzerkorps, Tagesmeldung vom 11.3.43, 1700 hours, frame 3752293-3752294.
[10] Meyer, pg. 112.

guns and anti-tank rifles. The battalion attempted to fight its way around the station before it came to a halt under heavy anti-tank gun and artillery fire. A short distance to the east lay the first houses and buildings of Kharkov.[11]

Wisliceny's Grenadiers, supported by four "Totenkopf" Panzer IVs, attempted to capture a bridge on the eastern side of the town but the Russians blew it up just before the first men reached it. After advancing further along the highway, the battalion reached a well placed Russian position that blocked the road. In front of two heavily wooded and fortified hills, the Russians had constructed a deep tank ditch. Behind the ditch were camouflaged infantry positions, anti-tank gun positions and entrenched tanks. Soviet artillery

pieces had the road under direct fire. Heavy 122mm and 152mm high explosive shells blasted the approaches to the tank ditch. Because of the open ground east of the two hills, the Germans could not bring up their own heavy weapons. Without the direct fire support of assault guns and tanks, the Grenadiers had no chance of surviving a frontal attack on the Soviet position and so Harmel called a halt to the attack.[12] At 1600 hours, Harmel and Heinz Macher conducted a careful reconnaissance of the approaches to the Soviet defensive position. The terrain in front of Ehrath's battalion offered better concealment and Harmel decided to attack the tank ditch under cover of darkness from that point. The attack was to be led by Macher's Pioniere company and troops of the Pioniere Abteilung.

---

[11] Weidinger, pg. 98.

[12] Ibid. 99-100.

On 11 March, Regiment "Deutschland" penetrated the western edge of Kharkov in an early morning attack across a well defended tank ditch on the outskirts of the city. Heinz Macher's Pioniere Abteilung, then numbering less than forty men, led the assault and played a key role in the success of the attack. Macher stands on the left, with III./Regiment "Deutschland" commander Günther Wisliceny on the right. (Courtesy Mark C. Yerger)

Walter Pitsch served as a NCO in "Leibstandarte's" Flak Abteilung during the Kharkov fighting. Flak detachments of the division were stationed at several intact bridges in the city in order to protect them from Russian air attacks. A bridge captured by Peiper's battalion was attacked repeatedly by Russian bombers but the SS Flak guns threw up such a storm of shells that the Russian planes were unable to destroy it. (Courtesy Mark C. Yerger)

Shortly before dark, Macher assembled his assault detachment and issued his attack orders. One of the assault platoons was equipped with four flamethrowers.[13] At 0240 hours the attack began, with an assault group of I./Regiment "Deutschland" standing ready to immediately reinforce any breakthrough made by Macher's Pioniere. The lead assault platoon, led by Macher, crept into the night. The German assault guns and heavy weapons held their fire, hoping that the attack group could approach without being detected. Suddenly, when the platoon was only a few meters from the ditch, machine gun and mortar fire erupted from the Russian defensive positions. With their attack discovered, the SS Pioniere made a last quick lunge and tumbled into the shelter of the tank ditch, as mortar shells impacted behind them and a curtain of machine gun fire swept the ground over their heads.

The Germans quickly spotted the muzzle blasts of the Russian heavy weapons. Well directed fire from assault guns and tanks suppressed the Russian defensive fire sufficiently for Macher's group to make an assault over the open ground between the ditch and the first Russian position. Macher organized an assault team to attack the nearest Russian house, while fire groups furnished covering fire on the right and left flank of the assault team. A second assault group prepared to reinforce the first group once a breakthrough had been made.

At 0253, Macher radioed that he was about to launch his attack on the first line of houses. Minutes later, the assault group leapt forward, hurling hand grenades before them and firing machine pistols. Satchel charges were placed against houses and detonated. The explosions collapsed walls and buried Russian machine gun teams in wreckage. Before the dust settled, the assault team leapt through the shattered walls and wiped out the surviving Russian infantry. The second assault team charged forward and seized the nearest adjacent houses, creating a gap in the Russian defenses. Immediately, a company of Regiment "Deutschland" Grenadiers flung themselves across the ditch and into the breach created by Macher's company. By 0315, a penetration three hundreds meters in width was established.[14]

The Russians reacted quickly, launching a counterattack at 0400 hours. Groups of Soviet soldiers leapt from one rubble strewn street to the next, firing submachine guns. Fierce, close range fighting broke out when the Russian attack struck the left flank of Macher's penetration. Russian and German soldiers fought for possession of ruined buildings. Macher organized a counterattack and threw the Russians back temporarily, but it was clear that Macher's attack needed armored support.

A battery of assault guns moved up to the edge of the tank ditch and blazed away at the Russians. Several captured Russian anti-tank guns were turned around and fired at point blank range in support of the Pioniere counterattack. Under cover of this supporting fire, the Pioniere detachment of the Panzer regiment began to fill in a section of the tank ditch. By 0445 hours, half tracks of Kaiser's III./"Der Führer" moved into the bridgehead, in spite of heavy sniper fire and Soviet air attacks. Russian fighter bombers attacked the small bridgehead after daylight. "Das Reich" Flak detachments shot down an attacking Russian IL-2 Sturmovik and kept the Russian aircraft from blunting the attack. At 0515, the first SS tanks crossed over the earthen bridge and cautiously worked their way down the streets between the rows of destroyed houses. Once the tanks crossed the ditch the bridgehead into the city was secured. A number of ferocious Soviet counterattacks were beaten back, with heavy losses inflicted upon the Russian infantry. Enemy losses were twenty-eight prisoners and thirty dead. In comparison, the losses to Macher's company were surprisingly light, considering their role in the attack, because the Pioniere company suffered only 6 wounded and none killed. A large number of Russian light weapons, anti-tank guns and mortars were captured. For his outstanding leadership in this action, as well as previous engagements, Macher was awarded the Knight's Cross on 3 April 1943.[15]

While Regiment "Deutschland" assaulted the western edge of the city on 11 March, Kampfgruppe Kumm pushed into the southern edge of Kharkov. The battle group consisted of reinforced Regiment "Der Führer" and II./Rgt. "D" under Sturmbannführer Hans Bissinger. It's mission was to secure the southeastern flank of Kampfgruppe Harmel, protecting it from counterattacks out of the XXXXVIII. Panzerkorps sector.

XXXXVIII. Panzerkorps

The two Panzer divisions of XXXXVIII. Panzerkorps were able to gain some ground on 11 March, aided by the removal of Soviet armor from its attack sector when Belov brought armor into Kharkov. However, Russian rear guard units fought stubbornly and skillfully from defensive positions along the northern and southern banks of the Msha River and the advance of the corps was slow. The 6. Panzer-Division assaulted the Msha River line in two attack columns, advancing toward Zmiev and its river crossings. The armored group, with the division's few remaining tanks and a company of Panzergrenadiers, was on the left or western flank of the division. Once it reached the river, it was to attack Zmiev's western edge, while a second Kampfgruppe attacked the town from the south.

---

[13] Privately held KTB, information courtesy of Mark C. Yerger.
[14] Op cit.

[15] Yerger Weidinger, pg. 102.

However, the Panzer group had a difficult time after it reached the town of Proletarskoje, which lay about one kilometer south of the Msha. It encountered obstinate resistance from Russian infantry, supported by a few tanks. After a sharp fight, the Germans took the town, destroying nine Soviet tanks. Afterwards, the Kampfgruppe turned toward the east and moved down the southern bank of the river, towards Zmiev. Meanwhile, the second Kampfgruppe had already begun its assault upon Zmiev. However, four kilometers directly south of the town a Soviet rear guard detachment blocked its advance. At 1800 hours, the Panzer Kampfgruppe approached Zmiev from the west, but the southern Kampfgruppe remained stuck in fighting near the town of Gajdary. The decision was made to attack Zmiev with the armored group alone. At nightfall the Panzergrenadier company of the tank group broke into the center of Zmiev.

At dawn, the Russian troops abruptly abandoned the town and withdrew to the north. The Germans found that the Russian force had occupied new defensive positions south of the road and railroads running between Kharkov and Chugujev. These were the last remaining routes of supply running into the city from the east. The failure of XXXXVIII. Panzerkorps to seal off these lines of communication allowed the Russians to funnel supplies and troops into the city and eventually provided an escape route for Soviet troops who would otherwise have been trapped.

Throughout the day, 11. Panzer-Division tried to break through the Russian defenses south of Merefa. It succeeded in crossing the Msha and made some small gains during the day, although losing a half dozen tanks. The division cleared the area southeast of Merefa and occupied the southeast edge of the nearby village of Oserjanka, which was about a kilometer west of Merefa. However, the division made little further progress after it encountered strong anti-tank defenses. The division was struck by repeated counterattacks by Soviet armor. The division's lack of success was reflected by the meager amount of Soviet weapons that were reported captured or destroyed by the division. The days booty included one T-34, seven anti-tank guns and a few mortars and anti-tank rifles. Soviet casualties included a total of 190 dead.[16]

Controversy once again: Hoth and Hausser

During the afternoon a dispute arose between the commander of 4. Panzerarmee, Herman Hoth and Paul Hausser, regarding the employment of the SS- Panzerkorps. The 10 March order received

A good picture of a Russian 7.62 gun that has been abandoned in a village street and taken over by a number of chickens. The gun fired a high velocity anti-tank shell that could penetrate the frontal armor of the Panzer III and Panzer IV at ranges out to 800 to 1000 meters. It was designed as a light artillery piece and fired a high explosive shell also. (Credit National Archives)

from Manstein, stated that Kharkov was to be taken by 'Handstreich' (quick raid) if slackening Russian resistance promised success. Given the circumstances surrounding the SS-Panzerkorps earlier withdrawal from the city, this sentence was a clear invitation to take the city by storm if such an opportunity presented itself. Since Hausser had received many reports that Russian troops were withdrawing from the western edge of the city, it is probable that he thought his divisions could take Kharkov quickly.

The sentence suggesting that the city was to be taken if the opportunity arose, clearly invited just such an aggressive response. German officers were trained to make quick decisions on their own initiative, according to battlefield situations. In addition, Manstein's earlier order had specifically opened the possibility of mounting a quick raid. Hitler himself emphatically fostered just such a course of action when he talked with Dietrich and spoke of "his Leibstandarte" wrenching the city from the Soviets. After the war Hoth said that due to the determined defensive fighting of the Russians in Merefa and Zmiev, against XXXXVIII.-Panzerkorps, it was 'unthinkable that the enemy would give up Kharkov without a fight,' meaning that a quick raid would have had little chance of securing the city. He almost certainly wanted to avoid difficult and costly house to house fighting that could have caused additional heavy losses to the SS divisions because his army would be called upon to play a major role in the German plans for the summer.

However, Hoth bears some responsibility for allowing events to proceed to the point where the intractable momentum of war took over. When Hausser reported that the Russians appeared to be abandoning the western edge of the city, Hoth did not disagree with

---

[16] NA/T-313, roll 367, Tagesmeldung XXXXVIII. Pz. Korps vom 11.3.43, 1940 hours, frame 8633329.

Hausser's estimation of the situation. Nor did he make any attempt to rein in the SS divisions on 10 March, when 1a Ostenforff reported to the army that "Das Reich" was assembling on the western edge of the city and "Leibstandarte" was attacking from the north in three columns. Hoth did not issue any order contradicting Hausser's actions throughout the morning or early afternoon of 11 March. Not until late on 11 March did he issue orders affecting the direction of commitment of the two SS divisions. What circumstances brought about Hoth's reactions? Why did Hoth not issue specific orders to Hausser after he was informed of the SS-Panzerkorps plans until after the SS divisions were already committed to their attacks?

It is possible that the explanation lies in the performance of XXXXVIII. Panzerkorps. By afternoon on 11 March, it became apparent that XXXXVIII. Panzerkorps could not close the encirclement forming east of Kharkov by driving through the Zmiev-Chugujev area and cutting the roads leading out of the eastern edge of Kharkov. Hoth had ordered the two Panzer divisions to accomplish this objective and was faced with a dilemma when it became clear that they could not. Hoth saw that his last chance to trap major elements of the Soviet 3rd Tank Army and the Kharkov garrison was slipping through his fingers. It was only after the failure of XXXXVIII. Panzerkorps to seal off the city's eastern edge that he decided to rein in the SS Panzer Divisions.

Hoth gave new orders that resulted in the regrouping of nearly the entire SS-Panzerkorps. This order issued instructions for the elimination of the Russian forces in the Zmiev-Kharkov-Merefa area and blocking the last remaining exits from the eastern edge of the city. The XXXXVIII. Panzerkorps was directed to regroup and attack towards the Udy River south of Kharkov. The newly arrived 106. Infanterie-Division was to be placed under the corps and committed to an attack on the corps left flank, west of Merefa. "Das Reich" was to replace "Totenkopf" north of Kharkov and take over its mission of blocking the northern approaches to the city. "Totenkopf" was join "Leibstandarte" in an attack that swung entirely around the outskirts of the city and cut the last remaining lines of communication leading out of the city to the east. "Totenkopf" was to assemble northeast of Kharkov and then attack toward the southeast, with the objective of blocking the last escape route from Kharkov, the main road which led to Chugujev, one the Northern Donets.[17]

Post war accounts by both Hoth and Manstein accuse Hausser of attacking Kharkov in violation of directives from 4. Panzerarmee.

A photo of Paul Hausser (center with eye patch) talking with officers of "Totenkopf." This particular picture was taken some months after the recapture of Kharkov, probably during the battle of Kursk. On the far right, in camo smock is Otto Baum. The man wearing the service hat between Hausser and Baum is Hermann Priess, who at the time of the photo was the commander of "Totenkopf." (Courtesy Mark C. Yerger)

However, it is not clear why Hoth allowed the SS divisions to attack into the city on 10 and 11 March if they were in violation of his orders. Hausser's intention was clearly reported to 4. Panzerarmee and the daily reports for 10 March state the position of each of the SS divisions. In *Lost Victories,* Manstein does not specifically mention this incident in detail, but made the comment that 'The SS-Panzerkorps, wishing to lay the recaptured city at "its Führer's feet" as a symbol of victory, was eager to take the shortest route there, so that the Army Group had to intervene vigorously on more than one occasion to ensure that the corps did not launch a frontal assault of Kharkov and become tied down there while enemy elements still fighting to the west of the city were able to make good their escape.'

This statement may be somewhat disingenuous because it is not entirely consistent with the available written records of the formations involved. It also ignores the communications to Hausser from Manstein and by 4. Panzerarmee, in which the possibility of seizing the city by coup de main was first brought. Manstein does not mention this communication in his account of the incident. He probably was not aware of Hitler's comment to Dietrich, in regard to "Leibstandarte" wresting the city from the Russians. However, it is likely that he would have understood the import of Hitler's words, given the circumstances of the previous loss of the city and Sepp Dietrich's personal relationship with Hitler. At least in the pre-war period, Dietrich considered himself ultimately responsible only to Adolf Hitler, above even Himmler and it can be certain that Hitler's comment regarding "Leibstandarte" retaking the city carried a great deal of weight with the former commander of the Führer's personal bodyguard.

---

[17] NA/T-313, roll 367, 4. Panzerarmee radio message to Heeresgruppe Süd. Absicht für 12.3.43 on 11.3.43, frame 8633330 and Funkspruche vom 4. Panzerarmee an SS-Panzerkorps, 11.3.43, 1505 hours, T-354, roll 118, 1a KTB SS-Panzerkorps, Darstellung der Ereignisse, frame 3752292.

It was not until 1505 hours on 11 March that Hausser received the directive from 4. Panzerarmee ordering him to regroup and change the direction of attack of "Das Reich" and "Totenkopf." He immediately protested the order, reminding Hoth of the breakthrough on the western edge of Kharkov by Kampfgruppe Harmel, as well as the involvement of "Leibstandarte" in heavy combat with the Russian forces in the city. At 2100 hours, a SS-Panzerkorps communication to 4. Panzerarmee stated that the road conditions north of the city were poor and it would take "Das Reich" at least a day and a half to pull out of the city and take over the "Totenkopf" positions north of Kharkov. Hausser sent a message to Hoth stating that his intention was to continue the attack by the divisions as planned and after the capture of Kharkov, his corps would regroup for the attack upon the sector east of the city.

At 0115 hours 12 March, Hoth responded with a rejection of Hausser's plan of action and demanded that "Das Reich" and "Totenkopf" regroup according to his orders. Hausser restated his objections to this order and voiced his opinion that for the two divisions to comply with this directive meant that they were to simultaneously carry out a defensive and pursuit mission. In his opinion, that would endanger the successful completion of any of the objectives of 4. Panzerarmee's order because it would furnish additional time for the Soviets to withdraw. At 1150 hours, Hoth replied forcefully. He issued a directive to Hausser demanding once again that he comply with his order. The directive stated that Hausser was personally responsible for carrying out the order to withdraw "Das Reich" from Kharkov and move it to the north. Hoth also demanded a complete report on the realignment of the SS-Panzerkorps, in detail. The wording of the communication left little doubt that Hoth was determined to change the direction of attack and that he was not about to have any more discussion of the matter.

After receiving such a forceful reply from Hoth, Hausser had little choice but to comply with the orders of 4. Panzerarmee or offer to resign. Accordingly, later in the morning, the proper orders were issued to the three SS divisions. While Hausser and Hoth were exchanging messages, "Das Reich" had carried out its assault operations on the western edge of Kharkov. The soldiers of "Das Reich" were fighting and shedding blood for gains that were to be abandoned, possibly for no more compelling reason than Hoth's desire to impose his will upon Hausser.

"Leibstandarte" Reaches Kharkov's Red Square

"Leibstandarte" remained involved in heavy fighting in the central, northern and northeast sectors of the city. The fighting had been intense and costly. By the night of 11-12 March, the division had only seventeen Panzer IVs and six Panzer IIIs still in operation. All of its "Tigers" were out of action, with damage varying from moderate to severe. Two of the heavy tanks were completely destroyed and beyond recovery, due to massive internal explosions. North of Kharkov I./SS-Pz.Gren.-Rgt 2 again assaulted Soviet defensive positions at the edge of the town. The SS Grenadiers penetrated Russian defensive positions after intense, close range fighting. Over the rattle of machine pistols and the ripping blasts from the MG-42s, the heavier explosions of 10cm and 15cm shells could be heard. German casualties mounted, due to murderous fire from numerous snipers and heavy 12.7mm machine guns, some of which had been hauled into the upper stories of buildings. The combat settled into a merciless routine, with no quarter asked or given by either side.

The Russians had hauled 7.62cm anti-tank guns into basements and fired them through narrow slits cut in the walls of houses and buildings. These gun positions were extremely hard to detect until the crew fired the gun and once located were difficult to knock out. The SS Grenadiers rolled their howitzers up close to Soviet strong points and fired over open sights until the Russian anti-tank guns were knocked out and machine gun nests were silenced. Then SS assault teams charged over the rubble strewn streets. Stick grenades flew through windows or doorways and were followed by Grenadiers firing machine pistols or hacking with sharpened spades. Room by room and floor by floor the SS Grenadiers rooted out the Russian infantry. While the brutal fighting raged, barrages of Nebelwerfer rockets screamed overhead, to land in deafening blasts in the distance, shattering streets and buildings.

By mid-morning, the battalion blasted a bloody path into the center of Alexejevka annihilating two Russian rifle battalions. The survivors withdrew, leaving behind nearly a hundred shaken prisoners, including five officers. By 1600 hours the town was firmly in the hands of Krass's battalion and the Grenadiers prepared to move into Kharkov itself. Sandig's battalion then moved forward and reached the edge of Kharkov at 0915 hours. Within an hour, the battalion gained control of a portion of the railroad line entering the city from the northwest. The main rail station was still held by Russian infantry, who defended it well into the later afternoon hours. By nightfall, after hours of bitter fighting, the station taken by the Germans.[18]

At first light I./and III./SS-PzG.-Rgt. 1 "LAH" moved down the streets leading into Red Square. The battalions organized assault teams, each supported by a tank and the heavy weapons of the regiment, the 7.5cm and 15cm infantry guns. The tanks moved cautiously down the city streets. The Grenadiers followed them closely,

---

[18] Lehmann, pg. 168-170.

weapons ready, in order to protect them from Russian infantry with anti-tank weapons and Molotov cocktails. Methodically, the SS assault teams cleared each city block, eliminating any Russian resistance with point blank howitzer and tank gun fire. By 1000 hours, the two battalions had fought their way through the northern section of Kharkov and approached Red Square. Behind them lay shattered buildings, smoking tanks and dead or dying Russian infantry.[19]

Meanwhile, Hansen's battalion had somehow managed to reach the area adjacent to the square without major difficulties. Hansen's men had encountered only Russian snipers, who had killed a number of SS soldiers, including two company commanders. The battalion got into position in the rear of the Russian troops who were fighting the I./ and III./battalions. Threatened with encirclement, the Soviet infantry slipped away, vanishing like wraiths through the ruined streets and buildings. Toward late afternoon, von Ribbentrop was ordered to move his tank company up and protect the infantry from counterattacks by Russian tanks. The SS Panzers set off through the debris strewn, smoke filled streets and headed toward Hansen's battalion.

Just as they approached the square, a knocked out Russian tank blocked the road and Ribbentrop dismounted in order to attach cables to the vehicle and haul it out of the road. As soon as Ribbentrop's Panzer IV moved the Russian tank to the side, the next SS tank, commanded by SS-Untersturmführer Stollmeier, moved past Ribbentrop. Stollmeier's tank disappeared down the street. A short time later, a T-34 spotted the Panzer IV and fired, hitting the front of the tank's turret. The shell penetrated the turret armor and killed Stollmeier, his gunner and the loader. Only the driver and radio operator escaped the stricken Panzer, which burned out in the square.[20]

Peiper's SPW battalion seized an intact bridge over the Kharkov River and reached the Square, where he made contact with Witt. Peiper made an attempt to break through to rescue Meyer, whose battalion was still surrounded in the cemetery. Two half tracks were loaded with supplies and tins of fuel. Escorted by a squad of Grenadiers and accompanied by a tank, the small group headed toward the embattled graveyard perimeter. Although the tank was knocked out by a hit from an anti-tank gun, the half tracks succeeded in fighting their way to the cemetery position. For a time, Weiser's company remained surrounded and isolated in a school building, where it had taken up defensive positions on the previous afternoon. Just as it seemed the SS men would inevitably be overwhelmed, Wünsche led several tanks to the building and drove the Russians away, freeing Weiser and his men.[21]

SS-Sturmbannführer Max Hansen, commander of II./SS-Panzergrenadier-Regiment 2 "LAH." Elements of Hansen's battalion were the first German troops to reach Kharkov's Red Square, which served as an assembly point for "Leibstandarte's" Panzergrenadier regiments and the division's tanks. The fighting for the Square and the surrounding sections of the city was extremely bitter. The SS troops found themselves in combat with hardened Russian infantry and tough NKVD troops, supported by T-34s and artillery. Hansen was one of the most decorated soldiers of his division, having already won the Knight's Cross, Iron Cross and German Cross in Gold and other decorations. (Courtesy Mark C. Yerger)

While "Leibstandarte" pushed into the city, "Das Reich" had been deepening its penetration into the western edge of the city. At 1000 hours, the division reported that Wisliceny's III./Regiment "Deutschland" had deepened its breakthrough to a distance of one kilometer. SS tanks and assault guns were rolling toward the center of the city. At 1210 hours, Harmel received orders to pull his men out of the penetration, in preparation for the division's move north. It must have been incomprehensible to Harmel that he was to abandon his hard won gains. However, he obeyed his orders and received his new mission.

---

[19] Lehmann, pg. 168-170.
[20] Kurowski, Franz, *Panzer Aces*, (Winnipeg: 1992), pg. 115.
[21] Lehmann, pg. 170-172.

RIGHT: SS-Oberscharführer Kurt Sametreiter served in SS-Panzerjäger-Abteilung 1 during the recapture of Kharkov. The self-propelled guns of the division were used to secure the flanks of the Panzergrenadier battalions while they fought down the streets of Kharkov. (Credit National Archives)

FAR RIGHT: Werner Wolff, an SS-Untersturmführer in Peiper's half track battalion. Peiper led his unit into the city and stormed across a bridge in the center of the city, capturing it intact. Wolff led a platoon of the battalion during the thrust toward the Red Square. (Credit National Archives)

The regiment was to pass through the northern perimeter of Kharkov and move into the area due east of Kharkov. The objective was the enormous Tractor Works at Lossevo, located on the Kharkov-Chugujev road. This highway was the main thoroughfare leading into the city's southeast corner and the Lossevo Tractor Works straddled the road, less than a kilometer from the edge of the city. Harmel was to attack the factory complex from the north, while Regiment "Der Führer" was to drive through the southern perimeter of Kharkov and attack the huge factory complex from the west. By afternoon, Wisliceny battalion began to pull out of the penetration.[22] However, some of the units of the Kampfgruppe remained tied up in fighting and all of them could not be withdrawn at once. It was not until after nightfall that Harmel finally got all elements of his attack group disengaged from combat. He decided to wait until dawn to begin the move toward Dergatschi.

The Operations of Kampfgruppe Baum

In the meantime, "Totenkopf" began to regroup according to its new orders. On the morning of 12 March, I./SS-Pz.Rgt. 3 was replaced by SS-Pz. Aufklärungs-abteilung 3 and ordered to join Kampfgruppe Baum at Zirkuny. Baum's attack group prepared to thrust from Zirkuny to the southeast, in order to reach the bridges over the Northern Donets at Chugujev. However, before this mis-

sion could be carried out, a Luftwaffe reconnaissance report informed Baum that an elongated column of 60 Russian tanks had been spotted leaving Chugujev and moving north. The Russians had brought up new forces from the east, crossed the Northern Donets and were throwing them against the Germans as they arrived. Hausser decided to send IV./SS Artillerie-Rgt. 3, which was assembled in Olshanny, to reinforce Baum.

By late afternoon, the lead Soviet tanks were spotted near the village of Bolschaja Babka, which was about ten kilometers east of Zirkuny. Later in the day, the Soviet armor turned toward elements of Baum's Kampfgruppe located near the town of Bolshaja Danilovka. The Soviet armor, with dozens of Russian infantrymen clinging to the tank decks, broke through forward detachments of Kampfgruppe Baum and advanced upon Bolshaja Danilovka. At that time, a flight of Stukas pounced on the T-34s and destroyed a number of the Soviet tanks. Most of the surviving tanks scattered and took shelter in a nearby forest, close to the village of Bairak. They were accompanied by a column of horse drawn artillery which took shelter under the trees. The Stukas dropped their remaining bombs on the woods, inflicting little further damage upon the Russian tanks, but the tree bursts slaughtered the horses and artillery crews.

After the Soviet tanks pulled back into the forest, Kampfgruppe Baum occupied Bairak and organized a defensive perimeter. Soon afterwards the Russians left the shelter of the woods and attacked the eastern edge of the town with tanks and infantry. The attack was thrown back after the loss of several Soviet light tanks. Just

---

[22] NA/T-354, roll 118, Tagesmeldung von SS-Pz. Gren. Div. "Das Reich" vom 11.3.1943, frame 3752292 and Weidinger, pg. 98-100.

after dark, IV./SS Artillerie-Rgt. 3 arrived east of Bairak and took up positions in a sheltering woods, not knowing that it was the same forest where the Stukas had attacked the Russian column earlier in the day. With the coming of first light, the cannoneers saw evidence of the grisly work done by the Stukas and German artillery. Pieces of horses and men were hanging from tree limbs all around their positions. Daylight also revealed III./SS-Artillierie-Rgt. 3 taking up positions near them.[23]

During the night of 12-13 March, Baum prepared to launch his attack toward Chugujev and the nearby bridge over the Northern Donets River. Baum planned to drive south, reach the Chugujev-Kharkov highway and then follow it eastward until arriving at Chugujev. However, there were several villages in the regiment's path that were defended by Russian infantry. Soviet armor had been sighted approaching from the east, near the village of Ssorokovka. In order to protect the division's flank, the III./Regiment "Totenkopf" assembled near Bairak and prepared to attack the Russian forces in the Ssorokovka area. The battalion was to provide flank security for the attack of Kampfgruppe Baum, whose primary objective remained the Chugujev-Kharkov road.[24]

While the SS divisions continued their operations in and around the city of Kharkov, XXXXVIII. Panzerkorps was also regrouping. Hoth obviously had hoped that with the SS Panzer divisions thrusting into the rear areas of the Soviet forces south and east of Kharkov, the Russian combat strength in the Msha-Udy River area would be weakened. A dwindling of Soviet combat strength was expected to allow the two Army Panzer divisions to drive northward from Zmiev and link up with the SS units east of Kharkov. However, in spite of the supporting attacks of the SS divisions, XXXXVIII. Panzerkorps was not able to make a decisive breakthrough in the sector of either division. Although Zmiev was solidly in the hands of 6. Panzer-Division, the bridge over the river was destroyed on the night of 11-12. The division's attempts to continue its advance to the north were frustrated by the Russians, who occupied strong defensive positions which were well supported by artillery and studded with formidable anti-tank gun positions. Even though the Luftwaffe conducted effective supporting operations, the division was thrown back by the Russians and was not able to establish a firm bridgehead across the river.

The advance of 11. Panzer-Division did not gain much ground either, due to a strong counterattack by the Russians, which originated from Merefa. Soviet infantry, supported by tanks of the 170th

An extensively damaged tank belonging to "Totenkopf's" SS-Panzer-Regiment 3, which was knocked out during the division's operations on 12-13 March, 1943. A Soviet shell apparently struck the front drive wheel, shattering it and peeling off the sheet steel covering the track. The road wheels are missing also, but this may have been due to initial repair operations. (Credit National Archives)

Tank Brigade, stopped the division in its tracks. The counterattack was turned back, with the loss of one T-34. However, the divisions columns were not able to regroup and get moving again. Units of 106. Infanterie-Division began arriving on the afternoon of 12 March, the first regimental Kampfgruppe assembling at Rakitnoje.[25]

The LVII. Panzerkorps continued to try to establish firm bridgeheads over the Donets, on the right (eastern) flank of XXXXVIII. Panzerkorps. The 15. Infanterie-Division, reinforced with tanks and assault guns of 17. Panzer-Division, took several small towns which lay in the marshy southern bank of the Donets, only five kilometers southeast of Andrejevka. The Russians still held defensive positions protecting the river, which prevented the infantry division from bridgeheads across the Donets.

On the left flank of the corps, 17. Panzer-Division established firm control of the town of Glinischtsche, which also lay on the Donets. It must have been obvious to the Russians that the two divisions did not have the strength to force the river and did not seriously threaten the lines of communication running through the area between Andrejevka. Reconnaissance units of 17. Panzer-Division spotted a long Soviet column moving north, toward Kharkov. The column consisted of infantry and all types of heavy weapons, including artillery and armor. However the division could do nothing to prevent the Russians from moving troops and supplies through Chugujev and on to Kharkov.[26]

[23] Vopersal, pg. 222.
[24] NA/T-354, roll 118, Tagesmeldung der SS-"Totenkopf" Division an SS-Panzerkorps am 12.3.1943.

[25] NA/ T-313, roll 367, Tagesmeldung LVII. Panzerkorps, vom 12.3.43, 1915 hours, frame 8633340.
[26] Op cit.

Korps Raus and Regiment "Thule"

The divisions of Korps Raus pursued withdrawing Russian troops along its entire front on 12 March, as intermingled troops of Kazakov's 69th Army and 40th Army slowly pulled back eastward. The right flank unit of the corps, 320. Infanterie-Division, moved forward into the Bogodukhov-Maximovka sector. On the left or western flank, 167. Infanterie-Division advanced in a northeast direction, through the sector west of Bogodukhov. The division's objective was to clean up groups of Russian stragglers, throw out reconnaissance patrols past the Achtyrka-Gubarovka road and probe for enemy presence in the Vorskla River valley. Korps Raus instructed the division to establish contact with 2. Armee's 332. Infanterie-Division on its western flank and with Regiment "Thule" on its right or eastern flank. The division was also assigned the task of protecting the important bridge across the Vorskla located at Achtyrka. Postel's 320. Infanterie-Division was ordered to establish contact with elements of "Totenkopf" northwest of Olshanny. A strong battle group of at least regimental size was to be left in the area of Bairak, which was the boundary between the division and "Totenkopf." The division's left flank, reinforced by Regiment "Thule," was to block the area northwest of Bogodukhov and conduct reconnaissance sweeps north of the city. Good roads led to the Bogodukhov area from the Vorskla River valley, thus offering the Russians a potential route of attack upon "Grossdeutschland's" left flank. Regiment "Thule" advanced into the area west of Kharkov, but later in the day, the regiment received orders directing it to leave 320. Infanterie-Division and proceed to Olshanny. This move was to begin as soon as the regiment was replaced by units of 167. Infanterie-Division. After having been detached from the "Totenkopf" Division since its arrival in Russia, the regiment was to rejoin its parent formation.[27]

Meanwhile, "Grossdeutschland" thrust to the northeast from Bogodukhov, towards the town of Graivoron, which lay in center of the Vorskla River Valley. In the darkness of 11-12 March, Aufklärungsabteilung "GD" moved up to spearhead the attack. The battalion was reinforced with the division's Sturmgeschütze battalion and a battery of heavy Flak guns. Following behind the forward detachment was Grenadier Regiment "GD" and Gruppe Strachwitz. Bringing up the rear were the columns of the Füsilier Regiment "GD."

After being delayed due to traffic jams in the Bogodukhov area, the reinforced Aufklärungsabteilung finally left the town at 0530 hours. A lead detachment of wheeled armored cars and Sturmgeschütze ran into a Russian position located in a village about

Josef Swientek, another "Totenkopf" officer who was decorated for bravery during the 11 months of fighting in the Demyansk pocket. He was awarded the German Cross in Gold on 22 July, 1942. Swientek, as an SS-Sturmbannführer, commanded II./SS-Artillerie-Regiment 3 and later won the Knight's Cross as commander of the regiment. (Courtesy Mark C. Yerger)

eight kilometers north of Bogodukhov. A camouflaged 7.62cm anti-tank gun fired on the column and forced it to halt. The assault gun battery commander moved his vehicle forward, trying to spot the gun's muzzle blast. Before he could locate the firing position, shells from the anti-tank gun struck the Sturmgeschütz, killing the battery commander and members of the crew. The death of the battery commander seemed to have shocked the men and the battalion remained in the village without moving for some time. At that time the division commander, Generalleutnant Hörnlein, landed in a Fieseler Storch and gathered the unit commanders beside the road. After the commanding general reminded his men of the importance of their mission, the advance resumed again at 0900 hours. A Flak detachment was left behind to secure the village.[28]

---

[27] NA/T-314, roll 490, Korps Raus: Aufträge für 12.3.43, Korpsbefehl nr. 20, frame 000427 and Vopersal, pg. 222-223.

[28] Spaeter, pg. 66.

An hour later, the lead detachments reached the outskirts of the town of Pissarevka. Russian infantry occupied trenches and houses on the edge of the town. Russian artillery shelled the column from a hill to the east. Immediately a squadron of the reconnaissance battalion and a few assault guns were sent out to attack the artillery position from the flank. At 1400 hours, the Panzers of II./Pz.-Rgt. "GD" rolled over the flat, slush flooded terrain around Pissarevka. At the same time, the Füsilier battalion began its attack. In a short time the Russian artillery position was overrun and the Füsilier Regiment entered Pissarevka. The Russians abandoned many of their positions, making no effort to save their artillery. Russian gun crews in trucks and sledges withdrew to the north, while many of Russian infantry fled toward the nearby town of Graivoron.

From Pissarevka, the Kampfgruppe turned east, driving to the northeast over the Pissarevka-Graivoron road, which roughly paralleled the course of the Vorskla River. Just before the column began an attack upon Graivoron, the "Tiger" company and I./Pz.-Rgt.

"GD" arrived from the south. The heavy tanks rumbled up to the edge of the town and knocked out many of the anti-tank gun positions. With most of the Soviet fire suppressed, the Grenadiers dismounted from their half tracks and assaulted the defensive perimeter.

By this time, darkness had fallen and the village streets were lit by the flames of burning houses and vehicles. While the Germans cleared the last Russians out of the western and southern sections of the town, the sounds of Russian tanks and other vehicles could be heard east of Graivoron. The "Grossdeutschland" tanks and SPWs were extremely low on fuel at that point and could not pursue the Russians. Fuel could not be brought up until the following day and so the Kampfgruppe dug in and occupied defensive positions for the night. Shortly after midnight on 13 March, Armeeabteilung Kempf was informed was mopping up the last Russian stragglers in the town.[29]

---

[29] Spaeter, pg. 66.

SS assault guns and tanks with Panzergrenadiers aboard move into the western outskirts of Kharkov after Regiment "Deutschland" breached the tank ditch and penetrated Russian defenses. The Sturmgeschütz III in the foreground has a "Das Reich" marking on its rear armor. The tanks belonged either to Kampfgruppe Kunstmann or to Tychsen's battalion. (Courtesy Mark C. Yerger)

The SS-Panzerkorps Clears Kharkov

On the morning of 13 March the normal fog was absent and temperatures rose quickly after sunrise. All movements by the SS-Panzerkorps outside of Kharkov were hindered due to the soft ground which was promptly churned into deep mud. Inside of the city, elements of the 48th Rifle Division, 62nd Guards Rifle Division and the 195th Tank Brigade fought bitterly, forcing the SS divisions to clear the southern and eastern sections of the city block by block. Troops of the 17th NKVD Brigade, the 19th Rifle Division, the 25th Guards Rifle Division and assorted fragments of other Soviet formations tried to organize a defense. Rybalko's 3rd Tank Army still held a strong defensive line along the Msha, south of the city, but the army's rear was potentially threatened by Kampfgruppe Baum's swing around Kharkov. Regiment "Der Führer" blasted a path through the southern sector of the city, moving toward the southeastern corner of the city. These attacks threatened to sever the army's lines of communication to Kharkov.[30]

Nevertheless, the Russians had defended many of their strong points with near suicidal determination. There were still avenues of retreat out of the southern edge and the southeastern corner of Kharkov, since XXXXVIII. Panzerkorps remained south of the Msha River. The paved road leading out of the southeast corner of Kharkov, which passed through Rogan and continued on to Chugujev, was the main highway exiting the city. Another road and parallel railroad left the southern edge of the city, passed through Ossnova and ran due south to Zmiev. Smaller roads radiated from the eastern edge of the city, but these were already blocked by Kampfgruppe Baum in the Bolshaja Danilovka-Bairak area.[31]

Inside of Kharkov, "Leibstandarte" continued operations to seize the center of the city and clear out the remaining Soviet troops. The division had only seventeen Panzer IVs and five Panzer IIIs still in operation. Dietrich brought his Panzergrenadier regiments on line and began to squeeze the Russians out of the city, pushing them into the path of Kampfgruppe Harmel and SS "Totenkopf." Meyer's battalion held its positions astride the Kharkov-Rogan-Chugujev road in the center of the city. On the morning of 13 March, "Leibstandarte's" Panzergrenadiers assaulted the Russian positions in the center of the city. The Kharkov River wound through Kharkov, dividing it roughly into western and eastern halves. Many of the bridges over the river remained intact, presumably to allow those Russian units still west of the river to cross over. In order to hold the bridges open for their comrades, the Soviet soldiers fought for every square inch of their position. Each building or house had to

Street fighting in Kharkov. An SS machine gun team stands behind a road block thrown up to obstruct a Kharkov street. The Russians bitterly resisted the SS and in many sectors of the city the defenders fought to the last man. Often it was necessary to blast the Russian infantry out of basements and fortified buildings using howitzers or assault guns. (Courtesy Mark C. Yerger)

A group of SS Grenadiers rests after fighting their way into the city, while in the background a building burns. The two story building behind the men shows the affects of the ferocious fighting that characterized the combat in Kharkov. Most of the glass in its windows has been blown out and wreckage clogs the street. (Courtesy Mark C. Yerger)

be completely cleared and all its defenders killed or wounded, before resistance stopped. If there were gaps between the attacking German battalions, Russian infantry or NKVD troops infiltrated down alleys or through basements and reoccupied buildings that had once been cleared. For this reason, the regiments closed ranks and methodically swept the city clean.[32]

Wisch's SS-PzG.-Rgt. 2, on the right flank of the division, was given the task of crossing the Kharkov River at the Wassiljewskij Bridge and forming a bridgehead to allow Peiper's battalion to clear

---

[30] Glantz, pg. 203.
[31] NA/T-313, Tagesmeldung 4. Panzerarmee vom 13.3.43, an Heeresgruppe Süd, 2100 hours 13.3.1943.

[32] Lehmann, pg. 173-174.

the length of Petinska Street. Petinska Street was a main thorough-fare which ran through the center of Kharkov and until it inter-sected a second main city thoroughfare, Staro-Moskowska Street. These two broad avenues merged to form the road which ran from Kharkov to Chugujev. Meyer's battalion held the intersection where the two streets met and thus it was extremely important to retain possession of his position. However, Meyer was still short of am-munition and fuel and was under heavy pressure by Soviet infantry and tanks. Peiper was ordered to cross the Wassiljewski Bridge and clear Staro-Moskowka Street block by block until he reached Meyer's battalion.

Peiper's attack began during the morning of 13 March after seizing the Wassiljewski bridge. The crossing site was not secure and remained under fire from Russian artillery and anti-tank gun fire constantly. Russian snipers fired from rooftops and windows along the route of the battalion. The Soviet soldiers occupied base-ments and cut firing slits at ground level or crawled into the rubble of destroyed buildings and found nearly undetectable firing positions. However, Peiper had experienced street fighting with Russians be-fore and organized his Kampfgruppe accordingly.

SS tanks and assault guns accompanied the battalion and the companies were assigned 15cm infantry guns or 10cm howitzers. When the battalion met heavy fire from a fortified strong point the howitzers were unlimbered and wheeled into position, protected by assault guns and Marder. Firing at point blank range, the howit-zers blasted Soviet positions until their shells collapsed entire walls, burying snipers, anti-tank guns and their crews. Flame throwers squirted streams of flaming oil into sniper's dens and burned out machine gun nests. Then the SS Grenadiers stormed forward, leap-ing into shattered buildings, hurling hand grenades before them. Once having cleared the building's bottom level, each floor had to be cleared out systematically. Peiper's men slowly fought their way through the debris choked streets, leaving behind a trail of smoking ruins and Russian dead.

By 1300 hours, Peiper was able to establish contact with Meyer at the Voltschansk crossroads. The rest of the regiment crossed the river pushed down a side street to the south, toward the main rail station in the southern section of the city, known as Bahnhof Nord Don. Kraas' battalion led the attack, following in Peiper's wake of death and destruction.[33]

While Peiper cleared a bloody path through the center of Kharkov, Witt's regiment began its assault to the north of Staro-Moskowsk Street. The Panzergrenadiers crossed the river without difficulty and then regrouped near an industrial area known as

Plechaniwski Rayon, just to the east of the huge southern rail sta-tion. A regiment of NKVD troops had erected heavily defended road blocks and positioned tanks at key spots along the streets. Building by building, the NKVD troops were rooted out of their positions and forced to pull back or be killed. By days end, although exhausted by the ferocious fighting, "Leibstandarte" assault groups had nearly reached the eastern edge of the city. The NKVD regi-ment left scores of dead in the smoking rubble and withdrew into the enormous brick buildings of the Tractor Factory.

The few remaining Soviet troops defending the Kharkov River line began to withdraw, protected by rear guard detachments. The threat of encirclement posed by Kampfgruppe Baum doomed any effort to hold the city and the bloody swath torn through the center of Kharkov by "Leibstandarte" had forced even the fanatical NKVD troops to abandon the city. Kumm's Regiment "Der Führer" and II./"Deutschland," (Bissinger) were able to advance quickly due to the fading Soviet resistance and approached the Chugujev road near the Tractor Factory.[34]

Meanwhile, Kampfgruppe Harmel began its move through the northern edge of the city, passing through Red Square, where the forlorn wreckage of German and Russian tanks, burnt and black-ened, still remained. Whole blocks of the city were destroyed and streets were nearly blocked by the debris and wreckage of the fight-ing. At 1200 hours, the Kampfgruppe rolled onto Staro-Moskowska Street. From there, the battle group moved down the road toward the Tractor Works. The forward detachments reached the area north of the vast factory complex by late afternoon, in spite of several attacks by Soviet fighter-bombers along the way.

Regiment "Eicke" made its way eastward, but its columns be-came spread out over several kilometers of roads crowded with combat elements of three divisions. When the leading battalion, III./Regiment "Eicke" reached Bolshaja Danilovka, northeast of Kharkov, II./"Eicke" had just arrived at Zirkuny and I./"Eicke" still had not passed through Dergatschi. Bringing up the rear was Regi-ment "Thule," which was still northwest of the city on 13 March.[35] Straggling elements of II./SS-Panzer-Rgt. 3 had just entered Zirkuny when the town was unexpectedly attacked by Soviet infantry and twenty T-34s. The Russians attack struck the north edge of the town of Zirkuny, where defensive fire from the German tanks and SS Panzer-Pioniere-Kompanie 3 put ten Soviet tanks out of action.[36]

The main element of Baum's battle group, with its eastern flank secured from attack by III./Regiment "Totenkopf" at Ssorokovka,

---

[33] Lehmann, pg. 173 and NA/ T-354, roll 118, Stadtplan Charkov, frame 3752328.

[34] NA/T-354, roll 118, Tagesmeldung SS-Division "Das Reich" an SS-Panzerkorps, 13.3.43, frame 3752329.

[35] NA/T-354, roll 118, Tagesmeldung SS-Pz. Gren. Division "Totenkopf" an SS-Panzerkorps, 13.3.43, frame 3752333.

[36] Vopersal, pg. 223.

approached the Rogan area from the north. The IV./SS-Artillerie-Rgt. 3 was ordered to support Baum's advance and left its encampment in the macabre forest near the Soviet collective farm. The battalion had gone only about three kilometers when the cry arose that there were Russian tanks visible in a nearby woods. Swiftly the cannoneers prepared to defend themselves from attack, unlimbering their guns and breaking out ammunition. However, after they had nervously waited for nearly a half hour, the message was given that the tanks had probably belonged to "Das Reich."

The veteran artillerymen of the battalion did not believe this report and were skeptical. Their suspicions soon proved correct, because just as the column was about to get underway once again, Soviet tanks opened fire from concealed positions in a wooded area to the left of the road. The first shot landed a hundred meters short of the Germans, exploding harmlessly. Several other T-34s took the column under fire and killed or wounded a number of the artillerymen. The SS gunners quickly wheeled their guns around to face the Russian tanks, which were not accompanied by infantry. The tanks remained in the trees, choosing to fire from concealed positions, instead of assaulting the German column and using fire and movement to destroy the battalion. Several Russian tanks were struck by German shells and black columns of oily smoke climbed into the sky. High explosive shells blanketed the woods and when SS tanks became visible in the distance, the T-34s withdrew to the east, leaving three of their number behind.[37]

The tanks belonged to SS-Hauptsturmführer Erwin Meierdress's I./SS-Panzer-Rgt. 3. The battalion had been delayed because the roads were still covered with snow in places and the morning was very foggy. Because of the poor weather, it took the column a long time to close up and move just a few kilometers closer to Rogan. The column did not arrive in the Rogan area until 1500 hours. Just after arriving at the crest of a hill north of the town's railway station, a poorly executed Soviet counterattack struck the lead elements of the column. At a distance of two kilometers, a line of T-34s rolled toward the Germans, the small figures of trotting infantrymen visible between each tank. The Russians had made the mistake of revealing their attack while still too far away to direct effective fire on the German armor.

Meierdress's tanks quickly deployed and began to fire at the approaching Soviet tanks, while the Panzergrenadiers hurriedly took shelter from the Soviet fire. The superiority of German optics became immediately apparent when long range fire from the SS gunners knocked out ten T-34s. The surviving tanks abandoned their attack and scurried for cover in a nearby ravine. However, the Rus-

sian tanks soon advanced again and Baum's column remained occupied by a series of attacks and counterattacks that lasted the entire day. Meierdress' tanks knocked out an additional seven Soviet tanks but in spite of inflicting substantial losses upon the Russians, Baum's Kampfgruppe was sufficiently delayed by the fighting to prevent it from occupying Rogan.

XXXXVIII. Panzerkorps

In the XXXXVIII. Panzerkorps sector,11. Panzer and 6. Panzer halted combat operations with only ten kilometers separating them from Rogan. The 106. Infanterie-Division took over the Panzer division's positions along the Msha River between Zmiev and Merefa, allowing them to pull back their armor. Infantry from the newly arrived division moved into place on the southern river bank at several points west of Merefa, replacing elements of 6. Panzer-Division. The two Panzer divisions realigned their combat units in accordance with their change in direction of attack. The 6. Panzer-Division assembled in and around Novaja Vodolaga, while 11. Panzer-Division moved further to the northwest, in order to concentrate near Ljubotin. A few elements of the division's Flak and reconnaissance battalion remained behind in order to support the operations of 106. Infanterie-Division. The 6. Panzer-Division had only fifteen operational Panzer IIIs and Panzer IVs, while 11. Panzer-Division was slightly stronger, with twenty-eight Panzer IIIs and IVs.

In the clarity of hindsight, the two divisions would probably have played a more significant part in subsequent events had they stayed in their former positions, particularly since so little ground lay between them and Baum's regiment. Just as Hoth decided to redirect the corps direction of attack due to its failure to cross the Msha, Soviet resistance began to melt away in the sector south of Kharkov, between Merefa and Zmiev. Sensing the diminishing Russian strength, the remaining elements of 11. Panzer-Division joined 106. Infanterie-Division and occupied Zmiev. By the afternoon, even the Russian artillery fire began to fade away, as more and more guns were withdrawn. While Soviet artillery faded away, Russian planes became more active over the area beginning at daylight. Luftwaffe fighters had to accompany Stukas and other ground attack aircraft in order to protect them from Russian interference. In spite of the evidence that the Russians were pulling back from large sections of the Msha River line, most of the tanks and mobile artillery of the two Panzer divisions continued to move westward according to Hoth's orders.[38]

[37] Vopersal, pg. 224.

[38] NA/T-313, roll 367, Tagesmeldung 4. Panzerarmee, 13.3.1943, frames 8633351, 8633353-54 and 8633358.

Kharkov Falls to the SS-Panzerkorps

At the close of 13 March, it was apparent to the SS commanders that Kharkov would fall in to their hands again very soon, barring some unlikely reversal. The last elements of the Soviet 19th Rifle Division and parts of the 350th Rifle Division had already pulled back to the southern sector of the city. They were pursued by Kumm's Regiment "Der Führer." "Leibstandarte" cleared the area around Red Square and had pushed the remnants of the 17th NKVD Brigade and fragments of several other rifle divisions out of the center of Kharkov. The remaining tanks of the 86th and 179th Tank Brigades and parts of the 19th Rifle Division held the Tractor Factory. Dispersed elements of the 62nd Guards Rifle Division, the 25th Guards Rifle Division and the 195th Tank Brigade were shoved into an area southeast of Kharkov. This salient was bordered on the west by the sector of 11. Panzer-Division and on the east by 6. Panzer-Divison's thrust toward Chugujev. The 106. Infanterie-Division and elements of the two Panzer divisions immediately began to comb the Russians out of the salient.[39]

In an effort to restore solid communications with Kharkov, Vatutin committed a regiment of the 6th Army's 113th Rifle Division against Baum's Kampfgruppe at Rogan, in an attempt to protect the vital bridges over the Northern Donets located at Chugujev. Vatutin also brought up the 2nd Guards and 1st Guards Cavalry Divisions of the 1st Guards Cavalry Corps to support the rifle regiment's counterattacks on "Totenkopf." The Soviet tanks that attacked the SS columns in Bolshaja Danilovka and around Rogan belonged to these divisions.[40] Although the cavalry divisions successfully delayed the advance of the SS battle group, Baum was able to renew his attack on 14 March and Kampfgruppe Harmel's arrival at the western edge of the Tractor Factory further strengthened the German ring around the eastern edge of Kharkov.

The 3rd Tank Army front was rapidly disintegrating on 13 March. Rybalko had little food or fuel and his supplies of ammunition were dangerously low. The last major remaining line of supply available to the army was severed when Baum cut the Kharkov-Rogan-Chugujev road. There were still gaps in the German front through which small amounts of supplies could reach Rybalko's divisions. However, the Luftwaffe was in control of the air throughout the sector and attacked Soviet troops with little effective interference from the Russian air force. Vatutin brought up new forces from the east and these troops crossed the Northern Donets at Chugujev. There was still a slim hope that the cavalry divisions and the 113th Rifle Division would be able to fight through the SS battle groups and reestablish a supply route. However, this last tenuous hope was dashed by Baum and Harmel on the following day.

The situation was much the same in the north. Russian mobile formations were brought up from the east and committed against the thrusts of Korps Raus north of Kharkov. From the area west of Bogodukhov, "Grossdeutschland" marched down the length of the Vorskla River valley in a northeastern direction. The 3rd Guards Tank Corps was approaching from the east and its tanks launched attacks upon the division as soon as they arrived. The southern tip of the 40th Army was split off from the main body of the army by "Grossdeutschland's" drive toward the town of Borisovka. Meanwhile, the 167. and 320. Infanterie-Divisions had concentrated in the Bogodukhov area on 13 March. As these divisions came on line they began to rapidly approach the roads and rail lines that ran out of Kharkov's northern edge and extended to Belgorod. Soviet forces in position to block the SS-Panzerkorps, which rolled toward them from the south, were then threatened on their western flank by the approach of Armeeabteilung Kempf's infantry divisions.

The Fall of Kharkov

Just after dawn on 13 March, Regiment "Der Führer" made its way through the debris strewn streets of Kharkov. To the north, the sound of machine gun fire could sometimes be heard, in between the faint crump of mortar shells and the distant rumblings of artillery fire. To the east, the noise of distant battle was discernible, evidence of the attack by Baum and Harmel on the Tractor Factory. Sylvester Stadler's II./"Der Führer" led the advance of the regiment. His battalion crossed the Udy River where it exited the southern edge of Kharkov at 1200 hours and left the southeast edge of Kharkov a short time later. Kumm sent out reconnaissance patrols to the north and south, along the river. The patrols reported that groups of Russian troops of all types were withdrawing from the Udy-Msha River area southeast of Kharkov, destroying many of the remaining bridges over the river.[41]

Kampfgruppe Baum had pulled back north of Rogan, into more secure defensive positions after the end of the fighting on the previous day. The Kampfgruppe resumed its attack before daybreak on 13 March. The first elements of the Kampfgruppe arrived at a point northwest of Rogan by 1130 hours. By early afternoon, SS tanks and half tracks full of Grenadiers moved into position near a hill north of the Rogan rail station. The column of IV. SS-Artillerie-Rgt. 3 followed in their wake. Shortly after passing the hill, the column was attacked by a large force of Russian tanks, which could be seen advancing from the east. The tanks of I./SS-Pz.Rgt. 3, under command of Meierdress, wheeled to face the charging T-34s. The Panzergrenadiers scurried to find cover and took up defensive

[39] Glantz, pg. 203.
[40] Ibid. pg. 204-206.

[41] NA/T-354, roll 120, 1a KTB SS -Panzerkorps, frame 3753742 and 3753744.

positions behind a screen of assault guns and Panzerjäger batteries. Seven T-34s were knocked out and the first attack was turned back. The Russians regrouped and continued to attack the flanks of the column with small groups of tanks. However, the Kampfgruppe pushed through these attacks and at 1800 hours Baum reported by radio that he had captured Rogan and blocked the Kharkov-Chugujev highway. Elements of the Kampfgruppe reconnoitered toward the Tractor Works and made contact with troops of Harmel's regiment. Russian tanks continued to probe positions around Rogan throughout the hours after midnight but the highway remained in possession of the Germans.[42]

Kampfgruppe Harmel deployed for its attack upon the Tractor Works at 1500 hours. Immediately the first units to enter the factory complex became involved in heavy fighting. Russian infantry had burrowed into the basements of the huge brick buildings. T-34s were concealed in piles of rubble, serving as steel pill boxes to buttress their defenses. A steady rain of Soviet artillery shells fell over the entire area but the fire was not observed fire and proved to be more of a nuisance than an effective defensive deterrent. The sprawling factory complex, with its solid brick buildings and industrial towers, made fire direction difficult for both sides because observers could not see where the shells were falling.

However, the SS artillery battalions supporting the attack on the factory devised a fire plan to systematically advance the shelling along specified attack zones and thereby support the advance of their infantry even without fire adjustments. Using this fire plan, the Grenadiers began to methodically blast the Russians out of the factory buildings. The surrounding alleys and streets had to be sealed off, in order to prevent the Russians from bringing reinforcements up while the structure was under attack or infiltrating troops out of the building once it fell.

As the main body of his Kampfgruppe fought its way into the Tractor Works, Harmel led a company strength reconnaissance group to check the situation on his eastern flank. He was accompanied by Heinz Macher, who during the night had assumed the position of regimental adjutant. It was this detachment which made contact with a "Totenkopf" reconnaissance detachment near Bahnhof Rogan. The railroad station was occupied by Harmel's tanks. At that time the tanks were very low on fuel. Due to the previously mentioned poor road conditions and the impossible congestion on the roads around the northern edge of Kharkov, a limited number of supply trucks were able to catch up with the rapidly moving SS battle groups. Harmel's tanks remained immobile for the rest of the day, while the irate commander fumed at the delay. Fuel resupply

A T-34 model 1943 knocked out in the streets of a Russian village. The Russian troops defending the southern section of Kharkov were forced out of the city by "Leibstandarte." Some of them, including the bulk of the NKVD troops and a number of T-34s, withdrew to the enormous Tractor Factory at Lossevo, which was located east of Kharkov. "Totenkopf" knocked out a number of these tanks before they could take up positions in the factory. Note that although the turret is larger than earlier models, the tank does not have a commander's cupola or a radio antenna. (Credit National Archives)

was finally accomplished by air drops late on the following morning.

While Harmel tanks sat idle at Rogan's railroad station, Kampfgruppe Baum, led by the Panzer group, pushed due south. The tanks reached a work station on a rail spur extending from the main Kharkov-Chugujev railroad about two hours later. Shortly afterward, the armored group reached the main railroad line which ran eastward another ten kilometers before entering Chugujev's western edge. Three T-34s and three T-70s were knocked out by "Totenkopf" tanks during the drive to the railroad.[43]

With the capture of Rogan and its railway station, the last remaining main lines of communication into Kharkov were cut and the 3rd Tank Army was isolated. Immediately the Russians reacted to the situation with counterattacks designed to reestablish control of the railroad line. A small group of tanks belonging to the 1st Guards Cavalry Corps attacked a battalion of Grenadiers Baum had left at Rogan, but were not able to dislodge the Germans from the town. After this attack was repulsed, a stronger attack struck Baum's tanks at the head of the column and forced it to halt and fight. Continued aggressive attacks by Russian tanks forced Baum to pull back toward Rogan.

After inflicting additional losses upon the T-34s, Baum again struck out toward Chugujev. At 1100 hours, the column approached a hill about seven kilometers southeast of Rogan which was occu-

---

[42] Vopersal, pg. 222-225.

[43] Weidinger, pg .111.

pied by the Russians. At this point, the "Totenkopf" tanks were also dangerously low on fuel. For three hours Baum's vehicles remained motionless until a Luftwaffe airdrop could be arranged. While the tanks waited to be resupplied, two companies of I./Rgt. "Totenkopf" assaulted the Russian hilltop position. After brief fighting, the hill was taken by the Germans and the Russian infantry withdrew to the east, but quickly rallied. The Soviet troops launched a ferocious counterattack which stormed up the eastern side of the hill before the SS troops could establish an organized defense. This time the fighting was ferocious and took place at close quarters.

Once again the Russian infantry attack was repulsed and the survivors withdrew to the east, leaving many dead lying on the hill side. As they pulled back, a Russian column appeared on the road to the southeast and tried to join the retreating Soviet infantry that had just withdrawn from the hill. However, the relief attempt was turned back by artillery fire and at 1400 hours, planes carrying fuel canisters appeared and dropped their precious cargo to the waiting SS tanks via parachute. Once refueled, the entire attack column resumed its march. Just before entering the small town of Kamennaja Jaruga, which was only a few kilometers west of Chugujev, a flight of Stukas appeared and circled lazily overhead, in anticipation of supporting the advance of Baum's Kampfgruppe.[44]

Led by Reder's half track battalion the column reached the outskirts of Kamennaja Jaruga. A small, marshy river flowed through the town and was the last natural obstacle between Kampfgruppe Baum and Chugujev. Reconnaissance revealed that the village was held by Soviet infantry and reinforced by anti-tank guns. A half dozen tanks could be seen moving through the center of the town. A forward artillery observer radioed their locations to the waiting Stukas. The dive bombers screamed down, placing their bombs with pinpoint accuracy and were able to destroy several Russian tanks.

While the smoke from the last bombs still hung in the air, Reder's battalion dismounted assaulted the village. The SS Grenadiers took the southern half of the village, supported by heavy machine gun fire and German armor. The 250lb bombs of the Stukas had torn gaps in the Russian perimeter, obliterating huts that sheltered the defenders, although here and there a Russian machine gun began to fire. The stuttering, slower rate of fire contrasted with the buzzsaw rip of the German MG-42s. A battery of 2cm and 3.7cm Flak guns shelled Soviet firing positions on the edge of Kamennaja Jaruga. Explosive shells from the Flak guns blasted holes through walls and riddled doorways with shell fragments. The curtain of fire smothered Russian gun positions that had survived the Stuka attacks and flame thrower teams were quickly able to get close enough to burn out Russian strong points.

The first houses were quickly cleared of Russian troops, who were no doubt stunned by the ferocity of the assault upon the village. After savage fighting on both sides of the road leading to the approaches of a bridge over the river, the Grenadiers moved into the southern sector of the town. Russian infantry continued to fight back and house to house combat continued until after dark. The SS Grenadiers steadily pushed to the eastern edge of Kamennaja Jaruga and by midnight the devastated town was secured. Soviet dead, wrecked trucks, abandoned guns and destroyed tanks were left strewn about the village. Baum's Kampfgruppe resumed its thrust toward Chugujev and by 0145 hours, Meierdress' tank battalion, with Grenadiers perched upon the tank decks, approached the town. In the distance lay the Northern Donets and the key bridges.[45]

When Baum thrust towards the river, other elements of "Totenkopf" moved eastward through the road net north of Kharkov. The Soviet air force was very active in that sector because most of the German planes were in other areas. Russian ground attack planes bombed and strafed a column of Regiment "Eicke," but the main Soviet effort was directed against III./Regiment "Eicke" in Bolshaja Danilovka. Regiment "Thule" was delayed by road congestion and did not pass through Dergatschi until 14 March, its progress also hindered by the mud of the Russian spring thaw and Russian air attacks.[46]

During 12-14 March, elements of Becker's Regiment "Eicke" completely took over the "Totenkopf" blocking positions north and northeast of Kharkov. North of the city, the regiment secured the rail lines and roads leading into Kharkov from the northeast. Sturmbannführer Max Kuhn's III./"Eicke" occupied Bolshaja Danilovka, while II./"Eicke," defended Zirkuny. SS-Sturmbannführer Kurt Launer's Grenadiers repulsed several Russian attacks during the morning, all of which were supported by tanks. The regiment was reinforced by SS-Aufklärungsabteilung 3 and attached artillery.

Becker sent out company strength patrols to explore the area northeast of Bolshaja Danilovka. One of these patrols reached the village of Lipzy and reported that the Russians had pulled back northward on a broad front, leaving Lipzy undefended. The SS-Aufklärungsabteilung 3 quickly occupied the village and established a defensive position. Meanwhile, a company of I./Regiment "Eicke," reinforced by the Pioniere of 16./Kompanie took the nearby town of Wesseloje with little resistance from the Russians. The occupation of Wesseloje blocked the main road leading south from the Northern Donets crossing at the large town of Voltschansk.[47]

---

[44] Vopersal, pg. 226.

[45] Ibid. pg. 227.

[46] NA/T-354, roll 118, KTB 1a SS-Panzerkorps, Tagesmeldung von SS-PzGren. Division "Totenkopf" 13.3.43, frame 3752333.

[47] Vopersal, pg. 227-228.

In Kharkov itself, while "Das Reich" and "Totenkopf" encircled the city to the southeast and east, "Leibstandarte" fought to drive Soviet troops out of their few remaining defensive positions. By 1755 hours, the SS-Panzerkorps reported that only isolated pockets of Russians were still fighting in Kharkov itself. A large pocket containing dispersed elements of the 3rd Tank Army was beginning to take shape southeast of the city, formed between the SS battle groups east of Kharkov and the XXXXVIII. Panzerkorps, which was still on the Msha and Udy river lines. Baum's Kampfgruppe blocked the mouth of the northern edge of the salient. An open corridor extended eastward to Zmiev and a bridge over the Northern Donets which was about ten kilometers south of Chugujev. German air reconnaissance reported that the Russians were busily constructing entrenchments on the west bank of the river. It was evident they intended to defend the corridor because reinforcements were crossing the Northern Donets at Zmiev and westward.

The XXXXVIII. Panzerkorps pursued retreating Soviet troops which withdrew toward Zmiev. Tanks of the 6. Panzer-Division returned to the Msha sector and supported infantry combat groups of 106. Infanterie-Division in a belated thrust toward the Chugujev road. After mopping up weak resistance at several villages on the north bank of the river, mobile spearheads turned to the east where the Udy River joined the course of the Northern Donets just south of Chugujev. A 6. Panzer-Division Kampfgruppe followed the course of the small river, intending to rendezvous with Baum at Chugujev. Farther to the west, tanks and Panzergrenadiers of 11. Panzer-Division arrived at Korotisch and moved eastward, on the southern flank of Kumm's Regiment "Der Führer." The division drove past the southern edge of Kharkov, reaching the Udy River at the town of Karatschewka, where they found the bridge over the river had been destroyed. However, the division succeeded in establishing two bridgeheads over the river from where it planned to thrust east and reach the town of Besljudowka, which was only about five kilometers south of the Tractor Factory.[48]

The LVII. Panzerkorps moved slowly northward, on a line of attack east of the XXXXVIII. Panzerkorps sector. A battalion of 15. Infanterie-Division took the village of Pervomaiskoje, driving out weak Russian forces, which withdrew over the river to positions on the opposite bank. Shortly after taking the town, a battalion strength Russian counterattack struck the German infantry. Fighting for possession of the village continued until late in the afternoon. The 17. Panzer-Division continued to hold a small bridge over the Donets at Tscherwonji Donez, in spite of an attempt by a Russian assault troop to destroy it. Northwest of the town of Glinischtsche contact was established with a reconnaissance detachment of 106. Infanterie-Division.[49]

On the night of 14-15 March, Rybalko radioed Golikov and asked for permission to withdraw from his remaining positions southeast of Kharkov. Golikov granted his request, as there was no realistic alternative. Rybalko had few tanks or heavy weapons and no fuel to move them if he had wanted to. His only hope was to save the surviving men, in order to build up a new tank army with the survivors. Tanks were more plentiful than trained tank crewmen.

While Rybalko and the remaining fragments of his army planned their escape, Heeresgruppe Süd radioed Sepp Dietrich in order to inform him that he had been awarded the Swords to his Knight's Cross for carrying out Hitler's wish for the division to recapture Kharkov. An OKW communiqué to Manstein congratulated the army group for the victory at Kharkov. Manstein relayed his thanks and appreciation to the men and officers of the three SS divisions. The SS-Panzerkorps noted that "Totenkopf" reported taking prisoners from seven different Russian brigades or divisions on 14 March.[50]

Armeeabteilung Kempf

During 14 March, Armeeabteilung Kempf had some difficulties rearranging the regiments of Postel's 320. Infanterie-Division for its planned operations against the 69th Army line between Dergatschi and Tomarovka. Once again Postel seemed to have difficulty understanding his responsibilities on the flanks of the division and some discussion ensued over the alignment of his division's combat units. At that time, Kempf, responding to reports of the division from the previous day, ordered Postel to regroup his division so that its main strength was on the right flank, which was exposed by the departure of "Totenkopf." The 1a of the division responded that the division's alignment was according to the orders received from Korps Raus. Apparently, the main strength of the division was in the Bogodukhov area, on the western flank, where a reinforced regiment occupied positions in and north of the town. The division was reinforced by several units, including Panzerjäger-Kompanie 106, Sturm-Bataillon 393 and three additional artillery battalions. Also attached to the division was a company of heavy anti-tank guns and Flak-Abteilung 81. Kempf emphatically made it clear that the division was to align most of its strength on its right flank because of

[48] NA/T-313, roll 367, Tagesmeldung an 4. Panzerarmee vom XXXXVIII. Pz -Korps,14.3.43. frame 8633367.

[49] NA/T-313, roll 367, Tagesmeldung an 4. Panzerarmee vom LVII. Pz -Korps,14.3.43. frame 8633366.
[50] Glantz, pg. 205.

the realignment of "Totenkopf" and the arrival of strong elements of the 2nd Guards Tank Corps near Belgorod. The Soviet tank corps had been sent to reinforce Kazakov's 69th Army and was gradually moving its 175 tanks westward.

Kempf wanted the additional mobile units and anti-tank gun strength of the division posted on its eastern flank, in order to protect the boundary between the right flank of his Armeeabteilung and the northern flank of the SS-Panzerkorps. A poorly defended right flank left a possible weak spot through which the Russians might strike with the newly arrived 2nd Guards Tank Corps. It is evident that Postel's previous difficulties with defending the flanks of his division concerned Kempf.[51]

Later in the morning, the 1a of Armeeabteilung Kempf spoke with Generalleutnant Raus regarding the situation with 320. Infanterie-Division. Raus apparently found no intentional fault with Postel and offered an explanation for the placement of the units of the division. Raus stated that the alignment of the division reflected the requirements of the prior mission of the corps and the alignment that the corps had felt required to accomplish that mission. Furthermore, Raus explained, Postel had not been adequately informed about the changing situation on his eastern flank. Raus did admit that the division was not correctly concentrated in regard to the situation at that time however, although he offered no explanation for Postel's delay. He assured Kempf that the division would regroup according to his instructions, indicating that he had already issued the necessary orders to set this realignment into motion. One can probably safely assume that Postel received an earful from Raus over the embarrassing situation.

The regrouping of 320. Infanterie-Division limited any forward progress it may otherwise have made on 14 March. Both Postel's division and 167. Infanterie-Division lacked sufficient mobility to keep up with the "Grossdeutschland" spearheads. While the two infantry divisions slowly moved through the area on both sides of Bogodukhov, "Grossdeutschland" mobile spearheads attacked northeast, through the Vorskla Valley. The route of "Grossdeutschland's" advance generally followed the boundary between the 69th Army's northern flank and the southern flank of the 40th Army. Reconnaissance patrols motoring north of the boundary found that the Russians had abandoned the sector north of the Vorskla River.

During its advance on 13 March, the division had smashed through elements of the Soviet 100th and 309th Rifle Divisions and the few tanks of the 5th Guards Tank Corps. Golikov was concerned about the progress of "Grossdeutschland" because it threat-

Sturmgeschütz IIIs provide overwatch protection for a German column of half tracks and other vehicles moving along a road in the background. This is another photo that illustrates the emptiness of the Russian steppe. (Credit National Archives)

ened to collapse the flank of the 69th Army. As a result, on 13 March, Moskalenko ordered the 3rd Tank Corps to move to Tomarovka, intending to throw it into the path of the German division before it reached Tomarovka. Belgorod lay only fifteen kilometers to the east. The 5th Guards Tank Corps was to attack from the north, supported by the 100th Rifle Division and attempt to cut the lines of communication of "Grossdeutschland" at Graivoron. The 3rd Guards Tank Corps moved into a position that put it astride the advance of "Grossdeutschland" on 14 March.[52]

"Grossdeutschland's" initial objective was the town of Borisovka, which was only ten kilometers from Tomarovka. Near the southern entrance of Borisovka a tank battle flared up when Soviet tanks attacked the head of the division's column. After losing several T-34s, the Russians withdrew from the village and Borisovka was occupied by the German troops without difficulty. A battalion of the Grenadier Regiment "GD" occupied a perimeter around the village and prepared to defend the town. Strachwitz's Panzer regiment took up positions in the eastern end of Borisovka, awaiting the expected counterattack by Soviet armor.

On 14 March, "Grossdeutschland" reconnaissance patrols spotted Soviet armor advancing towards Borisovka from the east and north. A German reconnaissance plane reported that a group of over thirty T-34s from the 2nd Guards Tank Corps was moving toward the town from the east. A 3rd Tank Corps battle group, consisting of ten tanks and eighty other vehicles, was approaching from Tomarovka. Additional tank columns were approaching from Belgorod. Reconnaissance patrols had reported a total of more than sixty tanks which were on a collision course with "Grossdeutschland."[53]

---

[51] Glantz, pg. 205 and *Befehl des Gewissens*, pg. 287.

[52] Spaeter, pg. 68-69 and *Befehl des Gewissens*, pg. 289.
[53] *Befehl des Gewissens*, pg. 289-290.

The always aggressive Strachwitz decided to strike first. He launched a spoiling attack upon the Russian tank force approaching from the east, in order to disrupt the timing of the attack. The assault guns of Sturmgeschütze Abteilung "GD" and the Aufklärungsabteilung "GD" concentrated at Borisovka. The assault guns carried two companies of Grenadiers piled on to the vehicle decks. At 0900 hours the battle group left Borisovka and had traveled east for about thirty minutes when a forward detachment spotted two T-34s on a distant hilltop. The Russians did not see the German column.

A flanking attack by a Sturmgeschütz battery caught the Russians off guard and fourteen tanks were knocked out. However, after the remaining T-34s had raced away, a large Soviet column was spotted in the distance. A light German recon plane dropped a note that stated there were at least 100 or more Russian tanks approaching from the east. This must have been the 2nd Guards Tank Corps, because no other Soviet armored force in the area had that many tanks. After receiving this information, Strachwitz deployed his tanks in a screen north of Borisovka, while the assault guns prepared an ambush for the Russians. Battalion commander, Hauptmann Magold, placed his Sturmgeschütze in concealed positions on several small wooded hills. Magold positioned one battery of assault guns in reserve, echeloned to the rear of his eastern flank.

Shortly afterwards the first wave of T-34s rolled over the crest of a broad, low ridge to the east. Under orders not to fire until the Russians were within 500 meters, the German gunners squinted through their sights and waited. A second wave of Russian armor crested the ridge and turned north, toward Borisovka. More and more T-34s spilled into the gentle valley, moving across the front of the assault guns. The first volley ripped through the air and shells struck five or six of the leading tanks. Soon the familiar black columns of smoke rose into the air from a half dozen burning Russian tanks. Only when Magold had seen that he was not being outflanked himself, did he commit the reserve battery. He ordered the battery to strike the Russians from the rear. Due to the iron fire discipline and the deadly accurate fire from the 7.5cm assault guns, the Russians lost approximately twenty-five tanks.[54]

The Russian tank group that veered northward suddenly swept into range of the "Grossdeutschland" tanks in position near Borisovka. An intense tank battle raged for the entire afternoon, with thrusts and counter thrusts by both sides. "Grossdeutschland" reported that it knocked out a total of forty-four Soviet tanks for the day. However, there were many T-34s still in action, and more arriving from the east. When darkness fell, a group of ten T-34s approached an earthen bridge on the north edge of the town. Soviet infantry infiltrated German positions without being detected and suddenly launched attacks at several points on the perimeter.[55]

The night was broken by the sounds of explosions and shattering bursts of machine gun fire. Confusion reigned in the darkened streets and houses and buildings began to burn, illuminating the darkness with their flames. Banks of smoke drifted in dense clouds between buildings, making it difficult to recognize friend or foe. The confusion provided an opportunity for the Russian tanks to break into the town, but "Grossdeutschland" tanks were waiting for them. Three times groups of T-34s tried to get across the bridge, but each time they were turned back. Eight disabled T-34s were left scattered around the elevated road leading across the bridge. After the collapse of the third attack, the Russians halted their tank assaults for the night, although fighting between Russian infantry and the Grenadiers of "Grossdeutschland" continued until morning.

"Grossdeutschland's" thrust northward through the length of the Vorskla River valley to Borisovka had deepened the penetration on the southern flank of Moskalenko's 40th Army. Elements of two Soviet tank corps had counterattacked the German division, but were not able to stop its attack. In spite of holding a significant numerical superiority, Russian armor took a beating, as the two Russian tank corps lost a total of about forty-five tanks for the day. Although "Grossdeutschland" was outnumbered by more than two to one, it lost just six tanks on 14 March. In the defensive fighting, the division's "Tigers" had proved especially valuable and were praised by "Grossdeutschland's" Ia in his report to Armeeabteilung Kempf.

The day of 14 March was an important date throughout the Kharkov sector and was marked by significant events in the areas of the SS-Panzerkorps, XXXXVIII. Panzerkorps and Armeeabteilung Kempf. The center of Kharkov had all but been cleared by "Leibstandarte," while "Totenkopf" and "Das Reich" had encircled the city. The 3rd Tank Army had ceased to exist as an armored force on that date, consisting only of several battered rifle divisions and tanks crews without T-34s. The 6th Army had committed mobile reserves across the Donets in an attempt to establish contact with Rybalko's army, but Kampfgruppe Baum and Regiment "Eicke" repeatedly blunted the 6th Army thrusts, throwing back the 1st Guards Cavalry Corps in the Bolshaja Danilovka-Chugujev area. The main elements of the remaining effective Soviet units, including the survivors of the 17th NKVD Brigade, 19th Rifle Division and the 86th and 179th Tank Brigades remained encircled in the Tractor Factory, while others slipped through German lines and escaped to the east.[56]

South of Kharkov, XXXXVIII. Panzerkorps finally had pushed across the Msha and Udy Rivers and was on the verge of joining

[54] *Befehl des Gewissens,* pg. 289 and Spaeter, pg. 70-71.
[55] Op cit.
[56] *Befehl des Gewissens,* pg. 291 and Spaeter, pg. 72.

hands with SS tankers southeast of the city. At 1910 hours, Hoth radioed Kempf with an optimistic appraisal for the following day. He stated that within the hour Kharkov would be completely in German hands and that 4. Panzerarmee attacks were all proceeding well. It was Hoth's expectation that on the morning of 15 March, his spearheads would reach the Donets southeast of Chugujev but that mopping up operations south and east of Kharkov would continue for some days yet.[57]

After the capture of Kharkov, Heeresgruppe Süd hoped to take Belgorod and destroy the Soviet forces still southeast of the city. Manstein also hoped to eliminate the large Kursk salient, north of Kharkov and Belgorod. There are substantial doubts whether such an operation could have been successfully orchestrated because the spring muddy season was beginning. Manstein had no fresh Panzer reserves to commit to a continuation of a major offensive north of Belgorod. The divisions which had carried the burden of the offensive operations were worn down from many weeks of combat. None of the SS divisions had more than thirty to forty tanks by 15 March. The Panzer divisions of XXXXVIII. and LVII. Panzerkorps had even fewer tanks. All tanks were badly in need of repair and overhauls. The mechanical condition of many of the trucks, half tracks and other vehicles was deteriorating because proper maintenance could not be carried out. The German repair detachments were forced to do makeshift repairs and return vehicles to action without proper preventive maintenance. This was due to the chronic shortage of all types of vehicles which prevented a suitable rotation of vehicles for scheduled maintenance. This unavoidable situation led to a more rapid loss of mechanized equipment than should have occurred. However, the most serious losses were in manpower, which was even harder to replace than the machines and vehicles of the division. The Panzergrenadier companies of the Army and SS divisions often numbered less than fifty men. Sometimes significantly less. In fact, German infantry losses, although they paled in contrast to the scale of Soviet casualties, could not be replaced by early 1943. Casualties in other combat arms were also high, particularly in the assault gun and Panzer battalions.

Whether the Panzer divisions of 4. Panzerarmee could have carried out another major offensive given these conditions is open to question but appears unlikely. It is almost certain that if they had been committed to a subsequent operation without rest, they would have not been able to muster the tank and troop strength required for the summer operations. By the end of March, Hitler's mind was already turning to his plans for offensive operations slated for the summer of 1943. However, the Kharkov counteroffensive was not quite over and there remained more fighting to be done. In the week after the recapture of Kharkov, 4. Panzerarmee and Armeeabteilung Kempf continued their attacks, with the brunt of the fighting again born by the SS divisions and "Grossdeutschland."

---

[57] Glantz, pg. 206.

16

ON TO BELGOROD

Hoth ordered the SS-Panzerkorps to make assault detachments available as soon as possible and ready them for the advance on Belgorod. In co-operation with Armeeabteilung Kempf, the SS divisions were to advance to Belgorod and block the crossings of the Northern Donets in order to prevent the Soviets from bringing reserves across the river. On 15 March, "Leibstandarte" concluded its mopping up operations in Kharkov and in the Rogan area. "Das Reich" was ordered to clean out the Udy valley to the outskirts of Chugujev and then assemble for an advance to the north, along the Northern Donets River toward Voltschansk. Kampfgruppe Harmel continued to fight near the Tractor Works. The division had thirty-five operational tanks and only six assault guns. This total included the Panzers of Kampfgruppe Kunstmann. By this time, "Totenkopf" was also significantly poor in armor and had only twenty-five tanks and eight assault guns on 15 March. Its missions were to conduct reconnaissance operations in force toward Voltschansk with Regiment "Eicke," and defend the northern approaches to Kharkov with Regiment "Thule." Meanwhile Kampfgruppe Baum was to take Chugujev, assisted by 6. Panzer-Division.

Baum's Kampfgruppe assembled for the attack upon Chugujev before dawn on 15 March. At 0148 hours, III./Regiment "Totenkopf" led the attack on the town, moving down the Kamennaja Jaruga-Chugujev road. At the same time, I./Regiment "Totenkopf" assaulted the town, advancing along the rail road line that entered the southern edge of Chugujev. By 0948 hours, the town was reported captured, although the main bridge over the Donets was blown up before the Germans could prevent its destruction. The capture of Chugujev was an important accomplishment, for it meant that the Russians could not easily bring additional forces over the river at that point. Kampfgruppe Baum prepared to hold the town and also

block the withdrawal of Soviet forces from the Udy valley. Meanwhile, north of the town, the 1st Guards Cavalry Corps assembled tanks and infantry forces in preparation for attacking Baum. During the next few days, the cavalry divisions launched a series of violent attacks against Baum's Kampfgruppe in an attempt to retake Chugujev.[1]

Regiments "Eicke" and "Thule" continued to push farther east and north along the main roads radiating from the city. Their mission was to clear any remaining Russians out of the villages and towns that lay astride these roads. A company of I./Regiment "Eicke" marched north from Dergatschi until reaching the village of Prudjanka, fifteen kilometers north of Kharkov. The company found that the village was abandoned. From Lipzy, the rest of I./Regiment "Eicke," led by the Pioniere of 16./Kompanie, moved toward the Soviet held village of Bolshaja Prochody. The battalion's march was delayed by mine fields south of the town. The Pioniere company cleared paths through the mines and the battalion slowly fought its way into the town, finally driving the Russians out by midnight. Northeast of Zirkuny, III./"Eicke" occupied Rogan, Ssorokovka and Zirkuny itself. Elements of II./"Eicke" and SS Aufklärungsabteilung 3 held Lipzy, while I./Regiment "Thule" took over possession of Kamennaja Jaruga, replacing security elements of Regiment "Totenkopf."[2]

Kampfgruppe Kumm, with II./"Deutschland" still attached in place of III./"Der Führer," began its march to the Tractor Works at Lossewo at 0600 hours, crossing the Udy River south of Kharkov. Kumm's battle group was reinforced by SS-Kradschützeabteilung

---

[1] Vopersal, pg. 230 and NA/T-354, roll 118, Tagesmeldung SS Pz.Gren. "Totenkopf" an SS-Panzerkorps am 15.3.1943.
[2] NA/T-354, roll 120, 1a KTB SS-Panzerkorps, Darstellung der Ereignisse, frame 3753754 and Vopersal, pg. 231-235.

2 and a few patched up Sturmgeschütze IIIs. Supported by divisional artillery, the Kampfgruppe crossed the river and assaulted weak Russian positions on the outskirts of Ossnova, which was a short distance southwest of the Tractor Works. An estimated battalion of Soviet infantry put up token resistance for a short time before fading away. The SS Grenadiers encountered little other significant resistance until they reached the edge of the Tractor Works where the Russians still held major portions of the factory complex. At that time, the Grenadiers were involved once again in typically tough and brutal street fighting. Soviet forces were estimated to be about two regiments of infantry and a half dozen tanks. Each side street and factory building was defended tenaciously by the NKVD troops and Russian infantry.[3]

The deadly routine of street fighting was always a particularly nasty type of fighting. Opponents are engaged at close range, often separated only by a wall or hallway. Attackers could only gain possession of a stubbornly defended room or floor of a building by closing with the defenders and killing them. There is no room for maneuver or grand strategy, it is kill or be killed, with grenade, machine gun or hand to hand fighting. The Germans had developed specific tactics from their bitter experience in fighting Russian troops in towns and cities. Assault guns and howitzers were put in position to fire upon Soviet positions at point blank range, while assault groups with grenades and automatic weapons crouched in readiness. First the Sturmgeschütz or howitzers blasted the target building with high explosive shells, killing the defenders or stunning them temporarily. Then the assault troops rushed the building, covered by sheets of machine gun fire which plastered windows and side streets. While the streets still echoed from the explosions of grenades and demolition charges, the SS Grenadiers leaped into the building. A favorite weapon utilized by German infantry for clearing buildings were captured Russian PPSH-41 submachine guns.

While the German and Russian infantry were locked in their lethal contest, tanks and assault guns engaged in a deadly cat and mouse game. Soviet tanks lurked in hidden positions in the shadows of destroyed buildings or concealed under piles of debris. German armor had to move cautiously, for a hit from a T-34's gun at the close ranges normally encountered in street fighting resulted in death or mutilation for the crew. Even the armor of a "Tiger" could be penetrated at point blank range. The thinner side or rear armor was particularly vulnerable. The SS Panzergrenadiers and Panzers worked together, with the infantry protecting the tanks from close range infantry anti-tank weapons. By late morning, Kampfgruppe

Kumm had penetrated the western edge of the Tractor Works, but ground was gained slowly.

"Leibstandarte" cleaned out the area southeast of Kharkov, mopping up the last groups of Russian stragglers. These operations continued for the entire day. By this time, most of the Russian troops except for those in the Tractor Works were hoping to slip between the SS columns east of the city and reach the Donets. Other groups took refuge in the forests south of the city or north of Chugujev. Meyer's Aufklärungsabteilung attacked down the Kharkov-Chugujev road in the afternoon, linking up with Kampfgruppe Kumm at the Tractor Works. Peiper's battalion relocated to the northern sector of the city, where it prepared to lead the attack upon Belgorod.

While the SS-Panzerkorps mopped up in Kharkov and the area east of the city, XXXXVIII. Panzerkorps continued its thrust north. Both divisions encountered company or battalion sized Soviet forces trying to escape to the east. South of Ossnova, the 11. Panzer-Division's tank group stumbled into Soviet infantry trying to escape the trap closing around them. The division's twenty-four tanks assaulted the Russian force and overran it, scattering the Russians. Those who escaped fled into nearby wooded areas. After completing mopping up operations, the division's Kradschützen-Bataillon motored north, reaching the rail station north of the town of Besljudowka. The town itself was found to be occupied by a strong Soviet force, including armor. A careful reconnaissance revealed at least nine tanks, strong anti-tank gun positions and a large number of infantry. After receiving these reports, the division regrouped and established defensive positions for the night, in preparation for assaulting Besljudowka in the morning.[4]

Hemmed in by the advance of the German Panzer divisions, a large pocket of Soviet troops was forming south of Chugujev and east of Zmiev. The 106. Infanterie-Division began operations to squeeze the Russians troops out of the southern portion of this pocket. The 6. Panzer-Division also became involved in fighting numerous Soviet groups trying to reach safety. On the southern bank of the Udy River, near the bridgeheads west of Chugujev, the division blocked the escape of two such groups who tried to cross the river and escape. The Russians pulled back into the forested swampy areas in that area and disappeared. Several Russian artillery pieces, a number of anti-tank guns and other heavy weapons were captured and a large number of prisoners were taken. The remaining tanks of 6. Panzer-Division turned in the direction of Chugujev, where Baum waited their arrival, unaware that the division had only six tanks still operational.

[3] Weidinger, pgs. 114-116.

[4] T-313, roll 367, 4. Panzerarmee Tagesmeldung an Heeresgruppe Süd and Tagesmeldung SS-Panzerkorps vom 15.31943, frame 8633371 and 8633377.

However, when the forward detachments reached the town of Tscheremuschnaja, they ran into a Soviet rifle battalion which had taken up defensive positions around the town. This solidly entrenched force stopped the German advance in its tracks. The infantry in the town belonged to the 25th Guards Rifle Division. Elements of the 62nd Guards Rifle Division and the Czechoslovakian Battalion reinforced the division, helping it hold the sector around the town. Although light contact had been made with SS troops at Besljudowka and Ossnowa, the corps had not broken free south of Kharkov and was not able to free the SS-Panzerkorps for other operations. The two divisions did destroy small groups of Soviet forces that crossed their path but both had very few tanks left and their Panzergrenadier battalions were worn down to the strength of companies.[5]

"Grossdeutschland" at Borisovka

On 15 March, "Grossdeutschland" battled converging forces of three tank corps around Borisovka, which was about sixty kilometers north of Kharkov. Elements of the 5th Tank Corps, 2nd Guards Tank Corps and the 3rd Tank Corps were identified by German intelligence. The 3rd Tank Corps was estimated to possess fifty tanks and the 2nd Guards Tank Corps had approximately 125-150 tanks still running. Between the three corps, the amount of armor concentrated against "Grossdeutschland" exceeded two hundred tanks. Early morning air reconnaissance reported a new group of about forty-five Russian tanks approaching from east of the town. Numerous Russian fighters provided air cover for the advance. For the first time in weeks, the Germans had to provide a fighter escort for Stuka attacks against the Soviet armor. It was necessary to occupy the Russian fighters or force them away from the Stukas. The Stuka was an excellent dive bomber, but was extremely vulnerable to faster, more agile and heavily armed fighter planes.

In Borisovka, shortly before dawn, the noise of approaching tank motors alerted the Panzer crews that the Russians were about to attack the bridge embankment on the northern edge of the town again. The sound of tracks and motors grew louder. Suddenly, twenty or more T-34s charged across the embankment. Their dark outlines could just be seen in the early dawn light and German anti-tank guns began to fire, striking several of the Soviet tanks. Eight to ten T-34s lurched to the side, slid down the embankment and somehow kept moving, roaring away down nearby side streets. Most of these tanks were able to escape from the town and return to their own lines, although several were knocked out by "Grossdeutschland"

Grenadiers. A number of T-34s were hit and knocked out before they could cross. Their hulks blocked the road that ran along the top of the embankment.[6]

The Füsilier-Rgt. "GD" was ordered to move to Borisovka. A battalion of the regiment arrived and took up positions west of the town. By noon, a battalion of the Füsilier-Rgt. was halfway between Graivoron and Borisovka and the third battalion was moving up also. By the end of the day, much of "Grossdeutschland's" strength was concentrated around Borisovka, awaiting the next move by the Russians. However, the Füsilier Rgt. had secured the division's extended and fragile line of supply, which was then unprotected. Patrols motored up and down the Vorskla River valley between Borisovka and Graivoron in order to spot any Soviet threat.[7]

As feared, the Russians soon attacked the division's supply line. From north of the Vorskla River Valley, a battalion of Soviet infantry attacked Graivoron. A battalion of Füsiliers and divisional artillery crushed the Russian assault, which was made over open ground without tanks or effective artillery support. "Grossdeutschland" was not able to advance beyond Borisovka on 15 March. The 3rd Tank Corps made repeated assaults on the town perimeter although anti-tank guns and Marders knocked out many of the T-34s. However, the Russian tank attacks tied up all of the division's armor and mobile formations. Further offensive progress was not possible until the Soviet pressure upon the division was relieved. The increased presence of Russian fighters and ground attack aircraft was noted by "Grossdeutschland" reports to Armeeabteilung Kempf. The division requested increased air reconnaissance and fighter protection from Russian bomber attacks and noted that it had knocked out more than twenty Russian tanks in the morning fighting.

In the afternoon, reconnaissance patrols found that the Russians were gathering north and east of Borisovka in significant strength, with infantry occupying several nearby villages in great numbers. However, patrols found that the Russians had withdrawn from the area to the southwest, abandoning positions along a rail line which ran south from Borisovka, along the Udy River. The Aufklärungsabteilung provided the only screen of the division's eastern flank. This situation did not present a danger because 320. and 167. Infanterie-Divisions steadily closed up ranks on either flank of "Grossdeutschland" on 15 March, although they remained echeloned behind the more mobile formation. Deployed in regimental battle groups, the two divisions methodically pursued withdrawing rifle divisions of the 69th and 40th Armies as they fell back to the east. By the following day, the two divisions were to

---

[5] Glantz, pg. 206 and Tagesmeldung der XXXXVIII. Panzerkorps vom 15.3.1943, frame 863375.

[6] Spaeter, pg. 73.
[7] *Befehl des Gewissens*, pg. 295-297.

move up to a line on either side of Graivoron, straddling the supply line of "Grossdeutschland."

"Leibstandarte" pushes North

Carrying out the orders of 4. Panzerarmee, the SS-Panzerkorps struck northward on 16 March, in an operation designed to relieve the Soviet pressure against "Grossdeutschland" by attacking the Russian forces east of Borisovka. "Leibstandarte" assembled Wisch's regiment in Kharkov's Red Square, which the Germans had renamed Platz der "Leibstandarte." The division had only twenty-nine operational tanks, including just two "Tigers." At 0630 hours, Wisch's SS-PzG.-Rgt. 2 "LAH" set out from the square along the main road exiting Kharkov to the north. The regiment was reinforced by the tanks of 5./Kompanie of the Panzer regiment and I./ Werferregiment 55. Wisch's objective was to gain control of the main road leading north toward Belgorod at a point where it passed near the town of Dementejewka. It was known that the Russians had occupied defensive positions east of Dementejewka, but their strength was still undetermined.[8]

During the night of 15-16 March, the column passed through the positions of I./Regiment "Eicke" west of Lipzy, moving north toward Dementejevka. Reconnaissance detachments spotted Russian tanks and evidence of fortified positions south of Dementejewka and near the neighboring village of Prochody. Sandig's battalion attacked from the march and assaulted forward Russian positions south of Prochody. The battalion drove the Russian defenders to the north, however, after pushing through Prochody, it struck the main defensive line north of the town. The Russians had constructed formidable earthworks and trench systems along the southern perimeter of a small forest. When the battalion came up against the primary Soviet positions along the wood line, it was stopped cold by dense machine gun fire and shelling from heavy mortars. A number of Soviet tanks emerged from the wooded area and shelled the battalion, which withdrew hurriedly to cover.

The stout defenses and the vigor with which they were defended evidently surprised the Germans, because previously the Russians were in retreat everywhere. After Wisch reported the unexpectedly strong Russian position to HQs, the divisional Ia, Sturmbannführer Rudolf Lehmann decided to make his own evaluation of the situation. Within the hour Lehmann arrived, conferred with Sandig and Wisch, and then conducted a personal reconnaissance of the area. At 1100 hours, he relayed to the SS-Panzerkorps HQs his estimation of the situation and the strength of the position.

"Leibstandarte" 1a Rudolf Lehmann personally directed the advance of the division north of Kharkov after the leading troops came upon an unexpectedly strong Soviet defensive position near the town of Dementejevka on 16 March. (Courtesy Mark C. Yerger)

The Russians had emplaced at least twenty guns in support of their infantry positions and an unknown number of tanks were in the area.[9]

Lehmann noted the strong defensive positions in the woods and decided to probe for a weak spot in the Soviet defenses on the flank of the forest position. He directed Peiper's battalion to swing to the right, around Prochody and attack through the forest against the rear and eastern flank of the Soviet defenses. Sandig was to begin a frontal attack upon Dementejewka itself, while Kraas was to swing to the left of the town and attack the western flank. Lehmann organized Stuka attacks, fire missions from the Nebelwerfer battal-

[8] NA/T-354, roll 118, Tagesmeldung Pz.Gren. Division "Leibstandarte-SS-Adolf Hitler" vom 16.3.1943. frame 3752392.

[9] NA/T-354, roll 120, 1a KTB SS-Panzerkorps, Darstellung der Ereignisse, frame 3753762 and Lehmann, pg. 117.

ion and artillery support by I./and III./Artillerie-Regiment "LAH." The most important objective of the attack, which was assigned to Peiper, was a range of forested hills east of Dementejevka. From these positions, the Grenadiers could attack the forest area from the rear. The battalion quickly swung its SPWs to the northeast, in preparation for a quick thrust into the rear of the Soviet defenses or to seize the initiative due to any unexpected development.[10]

The regiment moved its heavy infantry howitzers and mortars into position to furnish fire support for the Grenadiers. The Panzers of 5./Kompanie deployed to the front and at 1530 hours, rockets from I./Werferregiment 55 screamed overhead, trailing plumes of white smoke. The barrage of artillery shells and Nebelwerfer rockets struck the hills in front of Sandig's battalion. Sprays of ice fragments and mud flew into the air as the enormous volume of fire smothered sections of the Soviet positions. The Stukas supported Peiper's battalion, which arrived without difficulty at its objective. Sandig's battalion broke through the main Russian defenses at 1800 hours, arriving at Prochody shortly afterward. Soviet resistance from the defensive system on the edge of the forest was lighter than expected. The Russians may have withdrawn after Peiper had taken up positions in their rear. After dark, the battalions organized their defenses and mopped up the entrenchments on the hills.

The Tractor Works Falls

While "Leibstandarte" began the thrust north toward Belgorod, in order to reduce pressure upon "Grossdeutschland," the fighting went on east of Kharkov. Kampfgruppe Kumm had fought its way into the Tractor Factory on the previous day and during the night prepared to resume the fighting for the factory complex on 16 March. At daylight, the SS Grenadiers, assisted by Panzers and the last six assault guns of the division, launched attacks on Soviet positions in the factory complex. The attack was supported by Nebelwerfers of II./Werferregiment 55 and divisional artillery. Resistance was surprisingly light and it soon became evident that the Russians were withdrawing from the factory. By 0830 hours, most of the Tractor Works was in German hands.[11]

About 2000 Army and NKVD troops slipped away toward the north, probably surprising the Germans with a breakout attempt in that direction. Rear guard detachments skillfully covered the retreat of the main body and it moved cross country to the northeast, until it ran into positions of III./Regiment "Eicke" a kilometer southeast of Bairak, at the town of Prelestnyj. The SS Grenadiers ener-

Theodore Wisch, commander of SS-Panzergrenadier-Regiment 2 "LAH" (left) and Jochen Peiper (right) the commander of the half track battalion of the division. On 16 March, Peiper's battalion stood poised to plunge north and take the important town of Belgorod. (Credit National Archives)

getically counterattacked the Russian group, which regrouped and bypassed Prelestnyj. At 1130 hours, Fick's Kradschützen Bataillon attacked and dispersed a smaller group of NKVD troops at the town of Novo Alexandrovka. This was probably the rear guard detachment making its way toward safety. The main body of the NKVD regiment, along with its attached Army troops, reached the lines of the 1st Guards Cavalry Corps later in the day.

Other groups of Russian infantry, tanks or detachments of mixed personnel, fought their way out of areas east or southeast of Kharkov, trying to pass between the German battle groups. Most of these troops reached safety, as there were large gaps between the SS attack columns, which were forced to remain on roads in most in-

---

[10] Op cit.
[11] Weidinger, pg. 125 and NA/T- 354, roll 120, 1a KTB der SS-Panzerkorps, Darstellung der Ereignisse, 16.31943. frame 3753760.

stances. The Soviets avoided the roads and German troops. Even some Russian armor reached safety in this manner, in spite of the deep mud and flooded countryside. A few tanks of the 195th Tank Brigade and infantry from the 48th Guards Rifle Division reached the lines of 113th Rifle Division on the eastern bank of the Northern Donets.[12]

However, not all of the Soviet troops escaped without incident. Numerous battalion sized contingents collided with German troops throughout the area east of Kharkov, setting off vicious fire fights. Kampfgruppe Harmel was kept busy during 16 March, reacting to several of these desperate attacks. East of the Kharkov-Zirkuny road, one of the larger of these groups was encircled by the Germans and destroyed. Losses included one hundred dead, three T-34s destroyed and the capture of several prisoners. Russian planes were operating over the area and gave support to these escaping Russians by attacking German columns in the area east of Kharkov.

While the two main battle groups of "Das Reich" were occu-

pied cleaning up the last Soviet troops southeast of Kharkov, Fick's Kradschützen-Bataillon 2 motored along a secondary road that led out of Kharkov to the northeast. The battalion reached a point that was only about ten kilometers west of the Northern Donets, where it attacked a lightly defended village and took it by 1800 hours. Patrols reported strong Russian forces moving along roads just to the north, which were probably elements of the 1st Guards Cavalry Corps.

At the same time, Hans Weiss' SS-Aufklärungsabteilung 2 also moved to the north after leaving Kharkov. Hours later the battalion arrived at the edge of Lipzy, its progress having been slowed considerably by poor road conditions. Lipzy was defended by II./Regiment "Eicke." Earlier in the day, several Soviet tanks had tested the battalion's perimeter. After losing a T-34 to an anti-tank gun, the Russians withdrew, but soon returned in strength just as Weiss' battalion arrived.

A force of thirty Soviet tanks attacked from the northeast, attempting to overrun the "Totenkopf" battalion. Immediately Weiss directed his battalion to support the "Totenkopf" Panzergrenadiers

---

[12] Vopersal, pg. 234 and Glantz, pg. 206-208.

SS Grenadiers after the end of the fighting in the Russian Tractor Works at Lossevo. The plant was converted to make T-34s by the Russians during the war and had been put back into operation after they recaptured it. The Germans appropriated a number of complete or nearly complete T-34s, which were used by the SS, particularly "Das Reich." (Courtesy Mark C. Yerger)

and it soon became heavily involved in the fighting. The Russian tanks tried to establish concealed firing positions from which to cover attacks on the perimeter. The Germans reacted to these attempts by moving a mobile group of self-propelled anti-tank guns and tank-killer detachments into position to counter each Russian breakthrough attempt. The Russian attacks and counter thrusts by the SS Panzerjäger went on throughout the day, without decisive results.

During the fighting, a small combat group of Russians left the main group, bypassed German defenses at Lipzy and proceeded to the south until it contacted forward positions of I./Regiment "Eicke" at the village of Russkoje Tischki. The Soviet combat group ran into SS blocking positions on the road leading into the village and deployed to attack the village. However, the Russians were unable to break through the SS positions and broke off the fight. When the small Russian force attempted to pull back, it was counterattacked by Weiss' reconnaissance battalion and driven off.[13]

Kampfgruppe Baum defends Chugujev

While Regiment "Eicke" fought off Russian attacks in the Lipzy area, Kampfgruppe Baum came under attack at Chugujev. The Soviet 113th Rifle Division, supported by armor of the 1st Guards Cavalry Division, attacked "Totenkopf" positions in the northern section of Chugujev during the night. Russian tanks and infantry broke through SS defenses, driving the SS Grenadiers out of several rows of houses. A few Soviet tanks rumbled into the town and cautiously worked down the narrow streets, accompanied by groups of Russian infantry. German tanks and assault guns launched at counterattack just after midnight. The attack halted the Soviet progress and began to drive the attackers back to the edge of town. At dawn, most of the town remained in German hands, although the Russians held on to a strip of houses on the perimeter. The fighting had been fierce and casualties on both sides were substantial.[14]

Just as the fighting died down in the northern sector, it picked up in intensity on the southwestern edge of Chugujev. Russian artillery on the eastern bank of the Donets supported the attack, dropping heavy concentrations of artillery fire on German positions in the town. Hundreds of Russian infantry burst out of wooded areas near the town and charged the perimeter. The German forward po-

---

[13] Vopersal, pg. 233.
[14] Vopersal, pg. 234-235.

RIGHT: On 16-17 March, SS-Sturmbannführer Jakob Fick's motorcycle battalion pursued and dispersed retreating Soviet Army and NKVD troops who broke out of the Tractor Works and attempted to escape over the Northern Donets across bridges located at the town of Chugujev. (Courtesy Mark C. Yerger)

SS-Sturmbannführer Christian Hansen, the commander of "Leibstandarte's" SS-Pioniere-Abteilung 1. The Pioniere battalion of "Leibstandarte" was not as active in the fighting compared to "Totenkopf's" battalion, commanded by Max Seela, but provided valuable combat support when the division fought in urban areas. Hansen's battalion was equipped with satchel charges and other high explosives which were useful in breaching walls of defended buildings. (Courtesy Mark C. Yerger)

sitions were overrun or eliminated and the massed infantry attack was on the verge of breaking into the town. At that time, tank company commander SS-Hauptsturmführer Waldemar Riefkogel took matters into his own hands. With the three other tanks of his company, Riefkogel charged into the battle and struck the flank of the Soviet advance. The sudden appearance of German armor startled the Russian infantry and broke the momentum of the attack. Two T-34s were damaged and the rest began to withdraw. Without tank support, the Russian infantry pulled back into the forest. One German tank was hit and put out of action.[15]

At 1330 hours, a second Russian attack struck the northern corner of the town. The assault once more threatened to break through the German lines until Riefkogel and his tanks again appeared on the scene. Riefkogel and his two remaining tanks knocked out the last two T-34s supporting the attack, although another of the SS Panzers was disabled by Russian return fire. Riefkogel directed his tanks to charge into the midst of the Russian infantry and attack them with machine gun fire. Once more Reifkogel's quick actions broke up the attack and the Russians fell back into the shelter of the woods north of Chugujev.

Later in the afternoon, at 1700 hours, large numbers of Russian planes flew in at low level to bomb and strafe German positions along the town perimeter. Soviet artillery and rocket fire also crashed into the smoking, half destroyed town. A line of T-34s emerged from the woods beyond the southwestern edge of Chugujev, followed by masses of brown uniformed Russians. Many of the Soviet infantry fell to machine gun fire or were knocked down by German mortar fire. Hundreds more charged forward, shouting hoarsely and raced toward the German line with long bayonets fixed. The first wave of brown uniformed Russians stormed over the German positions on the perimeter. Groups of SS riflemen in foxholes and MG-42 machine gun positions disappeared under a wave of brown. The German defensive perimeter cracked and then gave way.[16]

Soviet infantry forced the SS Grenadiers out of the first houses, followed by T-34s which pushed down the narrow streets and fired from between destroyed buildings and houses. The tanks blasted German positions from close range with cannon fire, routing the SS Grenadiers before they could stop the Russian advance. The momentum of battle was with the Russians, who seized one row of houses after the other. There was no time to organize another defensive position before Russian assault troops stormed forward again. With most of Baum's available reserves fighting in the still threatened northwest perimeter, the situation quickly became critical.

By 16 March, SS-Hauptsturmführer Walter Kniep's assault gun battalion had only six vehicles still in operation, due to combat losses and mechanical problems. Kniep stands with arms folded on the left. (Courtesy Mark C. Yerger)

At that moment, for the third time in the day and in spite of several wounds, Riefkogel charged into the battle, this time with only a single accompanying tank. Under Riefkogel's leadership, the two tanks counterattacked the advancing Russians, one furnishing covering fire while the other advanced. The two tanks knocked out the T-34s supporting the Russian infantry and once again charged through the Russians, cutting many down with machine gun fire. With the two German tanks creating havoc in their midst, the Soviet infantry attack lost its momentum and they pulled back.

Given a breathing space by Riefkogel, the SS Grenadiers rallied and counterattacked, driving the Russians out of most of the southern section of the town. However, large numbers of Soviet infantry remained in the northwestern sector, where they occupied houses and hastily dug foxholes. Nine Russian tanks were disabled or destroyed during the attacks on 16 March, most of which were put out of action by Riefkogel and his tanks. The situation remained critical, as the Russians still held portions of the town in both the northern and southern sectors. Late that night it became apparent that the Russian attacks from outside of the town had halted, at least temporarily, but fighting inside Chugujev itself continued.[17]

[15] National Archives, Personnel file of Waldemar Riefkogel, *Vorschlag für die Verleihung des Ritter-kreuzes des Eisernen Kreuzes* and Vopersal, pg. 236-237.

[16] Vopersal, pg. 237.

[17] Riefkogel, *Vorschlag für die Verleihung des Ritterkreuzes* and Vopersal, pg. 236.

The XXXXVIII. Panzerkorps

While the divisions of the SS-Panzerkorps fought off counterattacks at Chugujev and regrouped for the thrust toward Belgorod, XXXXVIII. Panzerkorps fought its way slowly east. The 106. Infanterie-Division took Tscheremuschnaja, located about a kilometer northeast of Zmiev, at 0900 hours. From there, the Grenadiers pushed due north and were approaching the west bank of the Northern Donets by the end of the day. A Kampfgruppe of 6. Panzer-Division blocked the Udy crossings along a sector whose eastern boundary lay about 15 miles west of Chugujev, while its Panzer group scattered a group of Russian troops that had taken up positions in a wooded area north of Wodjanoje. The survivors of this Soviet force filtered out of the area to the north, while the division's tanks moved along the river bank toward Chugujev.

At first light, 11. Panzer-Division attacked the town of Besljudowka, which lay about five kilometers southwest of the Tractor Factory, close enough to hear the sounds of fighting as Kampfgruppe Kumm conducted its attacks on the factory complex. Besljudowka was abandoned by the Russians without a fight and the tank group of the division passed through the town and thrust east along the north bank of the Udy River. After passing Lisogubowka, the battle group ran into the survivors of the Soviet force dispersed by 6. Panzer-Division north of Wodjanoje and deployed to attack them. The Panzers overran the unfortunate Russian column and forced the scattered remnants to flee eastward. The division's lead elements turned north and approached Rogan by the end of the day.

By this time, both of the army Panzer divisions were nearly exhausted, having been in combat almost continuously since the previous summer. Between them the two divisions had only forty-three operational tanks and about a dozen assault guns. The material and equipment losses of the two divisions were also serious. An example of the shortages of equipment can be seen by contrasting anti-tank gun strength of the newly arrived infantry division and the two Panzers divisions. The 106. Infanterie-Division had twenty-eight heavy anti-tank guns (7.5cm Pak 40s) while by 16 March, 11. Panzer-Division had only one 7.5cm gun and 6. Panzer-Division had thirteen guns of various calibers, including six captured Russian 7.62cm guns.[18]

Two other seriously depleted formations, the infantry divisions of Korps Raus, also made limited progress on 16 March. Fortunately for the Germans, Soviet attention was focused primarily upon "Grossdeutschland's" attack through the Vorskla River valley. Neither infantry division reported any significant enemy pressure along

[18] NA/T-313, roll 367, Tagesmeldung XXXXVIII. Panzerkorps an 4. Panzerarmee, frame 8633405.

SS-Hauptsturmführer Waldemar Reifkogel repeatedly counterattacked Russian infantry and tank forces assaulting Kampfgruppe Baum in the town of Chugujev. With only two other tanks, Reifkogel broke up three attacks and destroyed several T-34s. He continued the fight even though wounded during the fighting and outnumbered by Russian tanks by a three to one margin. Reifkogel played a significant role in preventing the Russians from retaking the town. (Courtesy Mark C. Yerger)

its front during the day. The 320. Infanterie-Division cleared an estimated two companies of Russian stragglers out of Zolochev. By the end of the day, the two divisions arrived at a line on Mironowka-Zolochev-Graivoron, slowly closing up on either flank of the "Grossdeutschland."

Although the situation was largely quiet in the rest of the Korps Raus sector, heavy fighting continued in and around Borisovka, where "Grossdeutschland" fought to hold its gains. Although the three Soviet tank corps had more tanks than the division possessed, German accounts reveal that the Russians never concentrated their armor for one decisive attack. Instead of mounting simultaneous, concentric attacks with two to three combined arms groups, each built around a basis of forty to fifty tanks, the Russians never mounted an effort that seriously threatened to overwhelm the division.

The German advantage in tactical command flexibility and quick response to the events of battle combined with superior training, was often the decisive factor in German successes against greatly numerically superior Russian formations. Due primarily to the critical shortcomings of Russian armored units and T-34 design, as discussed earlier, Soviet armor normally had to have an overwhelming numerical superiority in offensive actions to provide a reasonable chance of success against first rate German Panzer troops. Even facing a substantial superiority in numbers, in most cases, the Germans defeated Russian tank troops by using their inherent advantages to the maximum. German tactical superiority is demonstrated by the events of 16 March. On that day approximately thirty-five "Grossdeutschland" tanks defeated over 100 Soviet tanks in a series of battles and suffered relatively light losses.

At 0430 hours the Russians attacked from southeast of Borisovka with tanks and infantry. While this attack was in full swing, German air reconnaissance reported another twenty Russian tanks advancing on the town from Tomarovka, a medium sized town seven kilometers northeast of Borisovka. The Russian tanks attacked the division's defensive perimeter on the northern section at 0800 hours, but recoiled after losing seven T-34s. The attack from the southeast was also thrown back after a brief fight. The Russians did not press this attack with their normal aggressiveness and when they withdrew, the Germans evidently thought that it would be possible to exploit the situation.[19]

The II./Panzer-Rgt. "GD" followed the withdrawing force of T-34s, hoping to ambush them while they fell back to their assembly areas. However, the Germans were unpleasantly surprised when they unexpectedly ran into a second group of Russian tanks. The German tanks also came under fire from anti-tank guns entrenched in a strong infantry position near the village of Striguny. The German tanks were not able to maneuver freely due to heavy flanking fire from the anti-tank guns and this put them at a serious disadvantage. Several "Grossdeutschland" Panzers were hit and disabled in short order when the Russian tanks swarmed around them. The battalion was immediately forced onto the defensive and had to beat a hasty retreat.

Meanwhile, I./Panzer Rgt. "GD" moved toward the village of Stanovoje, which was located three kilometers east of Borisovka. In this attack, the Germans came up against a Soviet tank force that was not as alert as those who bloodied II./Panzer Rgt. "GD." The battalion discovered that the Russians had provided inadequate security for their assembly area. The Panzer battalion was able to surprise the Russian tankers in a two pronged attack. A number of Russian tanks were knocked out or disabled and the attack forced the others to disperse. By the end of the engagement, more than twenty Soviet tanks were destroyed.[20]

While these tank battles were raging east of Borisovka, the Füsilier-Rgt. "GD" defended the divisional supply lines running the length of the Vorskla River Valley and the division's Aufklärungsabteilung screened the area southeast of the road net. The battalion attempted to move to the Olshanny-Zolochev area in order to block an intersection on the Kharkov-Belgorod road southeast of Borisovka. However, it was hampered by poor road conditions and struggled to move through melting snow, mud and slush. It eventually became completely bogged down and reported that it could not reach the intersection which lay east of the small town of Ssossnowka. Ssossnowka was only five kilometers from Dementejevka, where "Leibstandarte" had encountered stiff opposition. Even the battalion's half tracks could make little headway and contact was not established with the SS troops.[21] A company of the Aufklärungsabteilung was ordered to patrol a secondary road, where earlier in the day, Soviet infantry had been reported to be in the area. The patrol did not locate any Soviet troops and returned.

By evening, the division estimated that it destroyed a total of forty-six Russian tanks at a cost of only four of its own. Although the Russians had lost a large number of tanks, they halted the division's advance. "Grossdeutschland" could not continue with its attack upon Belgorod due to the constant Soviet pressure directed at its flanks and the main forward positions at Borisovka. The division had hoped to push on to the town of Tomarovka, which was seven kilometers northeast of Borisovka. There were good highways leading from Tomarovka into Belgorod, which was only twenty kilometers to the southeast. The Soviet counterattacks, however costly they may have been to the Russian command, succeeded in stopping "Grossdeutschland" from establishing a bridgehead for an assault upon Belgorod.

Armeeabteilung Kempf directed the division to renew its advance toward Belgorod on 17 March. Division commander Hörnlein was instructed to block the railroad and main highways entering the southern section of Belgorod from Kharkov and if possible, capture the city by a quick strike with a mobile group. Hörnlein intended to capture Tomarovka in order to secure access to the good roads leading to Belgorod. While "Grossdeutschland" thrust toward Belgorod, the advance by the SS-Panzerkorps was designed to attack the southern flank of the 2nd Guards Tank Corps and force the Russians to turn away from "Grossdeutschland." While the main elements of the division assaulted Tomarovka, the reinforced Füsilier Rgt. "GD" was to move up and seize the town of Chotlmyshsk. This operation was designed to cut the lines of communications of Soviet forces threatening the main road at a point between Borisovka and Graivoron.[22]

The SS Divisions Regroup

"Leibstandarte" resumed its attacks northward, moving into Prochody on the morning of 17 March. Cautious SS Grenadiers entered the silent, seemingly deserted village soon after dawn. The village had been abandoned by the Russians during the night. Only long distance machine gun fire and a few mortar shells greeted the attack. The thrusts against the flank of the wooded defensive position had rendered it untenable and by 0930 the entrenchments were

---

[19] *Befehl des Gewissens*, pg. 305.
[20] Spaeter, pg. 75 and *Befehl des Gewissens*, pg. 306.
[21] *Befehl des Gewissens*, pg. 307.
[22] Op cit. pg. 307.

reported clear of any Russian troops. The half tracks of Peiper's battalion slithered and slid over the road leading into Prochody, making excruciatingly slow progress. Although at night the temperatures still often dropped below freezing and froze the muddy roads, by mid-morning temperatures regularly grew warmer and vehicular traffic turned each quickly softening road into a morass. Peiper's SPWs passed through the village and turned northward while the roads were still somewhat passable. Soon however, the sun came out and the mud reduced the speed of the battalion to a snail's pace.[23]

About five kilometers north of Prochody, Peiper's lead detachment, which included the tanks, came under fire from a Russian anti-tank gun and heavy infantry weapons. One tank was knocked out by an anti-tank gun shell and the remainder of the group pulled back quickly into cover. After the column halted, the Grenadiers dismounted and deployed, while the self-propelled guns got into position to give supporting fire. A platoon of Peiper's Grenadiers assaulted the Soviet position, working forward under cover of cannon fire, automatic Flak guns and machine guns. The road block was cleared just before dark, after which Peiper called a halt to operations for the day, allowing his exhausted men time to get a few hours rest.

During the time Peiper and von Ribbentrop's 7./Kompanie were fighting in the Prochody area, II./SS-PzG.-Rgt. 2 moved up to a position west of the village. The battalion had advanced along a railroad track that ran parallel to the main road leading north, while Kraas's battalion remained in Dementejevka, as regimental reserve. Reconnaissance patrols reported a strong Russian defensive position further to the north, which lay on the regiment's proposed route of advance. During the night, plans were made to assault the Russian position on the following morning, with support from a Stuka attack.[24]

While "Leibstandarte" thrust north toward Belgorod, "Das Reich" and "Totenkopf" occupied and cleared the areas east and northeast of Kharkov. Several of the columns were delayed by repeated Soviet air attacks and in general, it appears the Russian air force was increasingly active in the area. Russian ground attack planes and fighters strafed and bombed moving units and supply troops of the corps and generally proved to be a nuisance. However, unlike Western air power of 1944-45, which often completely smothered any large scale movements of German armor in France, the Russian air attacks did not seriously hinder any of the columns.

Ernst Barkmann, a tank commander in "Das Reich," who won the Knight's Cross later in the war. Barkmann initially served as a Panzergrenadier, before he was wounded in action. He transferred to SS-Panzer-Regiment 2 in April, 1942 and was with 4. Kompanie when the division returned to Russia. (Courtesy Mark C. Yerger)

While it is likely that the Russian air force inflicted casualties and vehicle losses upon the Germans, they did not result in the total disruption of movement and attacks like those often related by veterans of operations in the west. German records of Western operations clearly describe the difficulties or even the impossibility of operating with American or British planes in control of the air.

There is not a great deal of information about the Soviet air force's operations against the Germans. Unfortunately, this aspect of the war is rarely described by either German or Russian sources. The failure of Russian air attacks to halt German attack columns with any consistency may have been due to the presence of numerous mobile 2cm or 3.7cm automatic Flak guns. German fighter cover may also have played a part, at least in the first years of the war in Russia. Other dynamics might also have been at work, but the Flak guns were definitely present in many German columns and could have disrupted Russian air attacks. The 2cm automatic guns, particularly in the Flakvierling configuration (four guns in a synchronized mounting) could throw up an impressive amount of explosive shells. The automatic 3.7 Flak gun did not have a similar large

_____
[23] Tiemann, pg. 45.
[24] NA/T-354, roll 118, Tagesmeldung vom 17.3.1943 von "Leibstandarte.-SS-A.H." frame 3752431 and Lehmann, pg. 178.

volume of fire, but had a longer effective range and its larger projectile guaranteed significant damage if it struck its intended target.

"Das Reich" division commander Herbert Vahl ordered Harmel to finish resupply operations during the night and set out for Lipzy at dawn. By noon, the leading detachments of the regiment reached the outskirts of the town, where Weiss's Aufklärungsabteilung was still fighting alongside of "Totenkopf" Grenadiers against Russian tanks.

Meanwhile, Regiment "Der Führer," reinforced by the Kradschützen-Bataillon and Tychsen's II./SS-Pz.-Rgt. 2, left assembly areas east of the Tractor Works, advancing in a parallel attack. Its immediate objective was the town of Nepokrytoje, which was about ten kilometers southeast of Lipzy. Led by Fick's motorcycle troops and II./Regiment "Der Führer" (Stadler), the column swiftly passed through several small villages before arriving at Nepokrytoje and finding it occupied by the Russians. A company of Grenadiers assaulted the town, which was defended by a Soviet rifle platoon. Supported by tanks and assault guns, the Grenadiers pushed the Russian troops into a small perimeter on the northern end of the village. At that point, the fighting settled down into the familiar, bitter house to house combat. The Germans were forced to take each fiercely defended strong point and house by close assault. During the fighting for Nepokrytoje, the Kradschützen-Bataillon bypassed the village and continued on to the north. By 1700 hours, Fick's battalion reported that it had reached the village of Petrovskoje, about five kilometers further to the north.[25]

In contrast to the offensive operations of the other two SS divisions, "Totenkopf" was primarily engaged in defensive fighting. Kampfgruppe Baum continued to defend Chugujev, while Regiment "Thule" and Regiment "Eicke" clashed with attacking Russian forces north and northeast of Kharkov. During the morning hours of 17 March, the tank group of 6. Panzer-Division, designated as Kampfgruppe Oppeln, finally arrived at Chugujev. The battle group was named for Oberst von Oppeln-Bronikowski, the commander of Panzer-Regiment 11.

However, von Oppeln did not have enough tanks or heavy weapons to assume the entire defense of Chugujev. He was able to lend valuable support to Baum's attempts to clear the stubborn Russian infantry out of the southern and northwestern sections of Chugujev. The additional tanks and assault guns first reinforced Regiment "Totenkopf" Grenadiers in attacks against Soviet infantry entrenched along the elevated railroad embankment running through the south end of Chugujev. The SS Grenadiers and Army

SS-Hauptsturmführer Ernst Tetsch also served in "Das Reich's" Panzer Regiment during the Kharkov fighting. He commanded the "Tiger" company and later in the war became the regimental adjutant. In 1944, he was the commander of I./SS-Panzer-Regiment 2 and ended the war in command of the Panzer regiment of 10. SS-Panzer-Division "Frundsberg." (Courtesy Mark C. Yerger)

tanks cooperated in attacks that drove the Russians out of their fighting holes and entrenchments dug into the embankment.

After driving the Russian out of the southern sector of Chugujev, Baum turned his attention to the Russians in the northern part of the town. There were a number of tanks in that sector, most of which were concealed in ruined buildings. The Army tanks and the SS Grenadiers rooted out the Soviets and destroyed twenty-one entrenched T-34s and T-70s during the fighting. The commander of III./"Totenkopf," SS-Sturmbannführer Schubach, was wounded in the fighting and the command of the battalion was taken over by SS-Sturmbannführer Karl Ullrich, the commander of the SS-Panzerkorps Pioniere troops. By the afternoon, the town was generally cleared of any remaining Russian forces. It was assumed that Kampfgruppe Oppeln would be able to retain possession of the town, since the Russians occupying the town had been eliminated. Regi-

[25] NA/T-354, roll 118, Tagesmeldung vom 17.3.1943 von SS-Division "Das Reich," frame 3752430 and Weidinger, pgs. 127-128.

ments "Eicke" and "Thule" were ordered to sweep the Russians out of the wooded area north of Chugujev. "Totenkopf" was to form the right or eastern flank of the SS-Panzerkorps attack toward the Belgorod sector. It was responsible for clearing the west bank of the Northern Donets River and blocking the crossing at Voltschansk.

During the night of 16-17 March, Regiment "Thule" assembled north of the Tractor Factory, in preparation for launching its operation north of Chugujev. The regiment's first objective was the town of Saroshnoje, which was five kilometers northwest of Chugujev and lay on the border of the forest occupied by the Russians. The I./Regiment "Thule" assembled at Kamennaja Jaruga, a town between Chugujev and Saroshnoje, while II./Regiment "Thule" was stationed a few kilometers to the northwest. Near the village of Ssorokovka, major elements of Regiment "Eicke" were in position to advance to the town of Bolshaja Babka, which was on the west bank of the Donets.

Before I./Regiment "Thule" completely assembled for the attacks scheduled to begin at 0545 hours, the regiment's outposts at Kamennaja Jaruga were attacked. The perimeter security posts occupied by the battalion's 1./Kompanie were overrun by Russian armor and infantry which suddenly charged out of the night. Racing T-34s careened around corners and sped down the town streets, with packs of Russian infantry clinging to the tank decks and firing rifles and submachine guns wildly. Half dazed Germans grabbed machine pistols and grenades and stumbled into the fight. Machine gun fire and the explosions of grenades echoed throughout the town.[26]

Two German anti-tank guns were lost when Russian tanks rolled right over the guns and several others could not be reached. The tide began to turn when Regiment "Thule's" 2./Kompanie quickly organized and launched a ferocious counterattack against the Russians. Machine gun fire from MG-42s swept Soviet infantry from the tank decks and forced them to seek cover in the nearest house or building. When the T-34s lost their infantry support SS Grenadiers were able to attack the tanks with close quarter anti-tank weapons. Two T-34s were disabled with magnetic anti-tank grenades. Taking advantage of the counterattack of 2./Kompanie, three 7.5cm anti-tank guns were manned and went into action. The gun crews knocked out two other T-34s.

The battalion commander, SS-Hauptsturmführer Ernst Häussler, led his headquarters staff into the fight and concentrated on attacking the supporting Russian infantry, which had gone to ground. The counterattacks by Häussler and 2./Kompanie regained the initiative and the rest of the battalion rallied. A total of nine Soviet tanks

were knocked out during the fighting. The SS battalion closely followed the withdrawing Russians in order to prevent the Soviets from regrouping and attacking again. However, the Russians made no attempt to repeat their attack and the town grew quiet once again. Häussler attempted to reorganize his battalion quickly but could not launch his attack at the designated time.[27]

SS-Hauptsturmführer Deege's II./Regiment "Thule" launched its attack on time and advanced toward Saroshnoje. After the battalion reached the village, Deege halted and waited for Häussler's Grenadiers to arrive. As a result his battalion sat idle for over two hours. At 1000 hours, Häussler moved up on the right flank of Deege's battalion and the attack began. The regiment was supported by the tanks of SS-Hauptsturmführer Richter's 7./Kompanie, which slithered and slid across the marshy terrain. Even gentle slopes were sometimes treacherous, even for tracked vehicles. Tank motors roared and spinning tracks threw up great gouts of earth behind them as they plowed through the deep mud. Behind the tanks, widely dispersed lines of Grenadiers trudged through the slush, rifles ready and MG-42 teams prepared for action.

A half dozen Panzer IIIs and IVs, their white camouflage now a dirty gray, moved slowly forward, grinding toward the Russian positions. The first Soviet defensive strong point was located on a hill a short distance east of Saroshnoje. As the Grenadiers and tanks moved forward, German planes swooped down to join the action. While fighters roared high overhead, providing cover, Stukas made their plunging dives, their 250lb bombs throwing up great clouds of black smoke and earth. At a distance of 500 meters, Russian machine gun fire began to rattle and the battalion suffered its first casualties. At that critical point, a more dangerous enemy appeared in the distance.

Russian tanks were detected gathering southwest of Saroshnoje. Groups of three to five tanks arrived until a total of twenty T-34s were visible. Suddenly gun flashes could be seen, followed by the whirring sound of shells passing over head. Some of the German tanks wheeled around and began to fire back, while others remained with the SS Grenadiers. In the distance, a column of black smoke marked the spot where a German shell found its intended target. Then the SS Panzers and Grenadiers reached the edge of the woods, where they were temporarily shielded from the view of the Soviet tanks.

After approaching the edge of the forest without encountering resistance, the I./"Thule" Grenadiers swung left and attacked the hill where the machine gun fire originated. Behind them Richter's tanks spread out in battle formation, as the battalion's Schwimmwagen company closed up with the Grenadiers. When the Germans

[26] NA/T-354, roll 118, Tagesmeldung vom 17.3.1943 von SS-Division "Totenkopf," frame 3752429 and Vopersal, pgs. 240-241.

[27] Op cit.

left the forest, they were spotted by the T-34s. Quickly the Russian gunners found the range. first one, then a second German tank was hit and began to burn. After a third tank was hit and disabled, Richter pulled his company into cover. Without the tanks, the attack collapsed and the SS Grenadiers withdrew to the shelter of the woods. Meanwhile, II./Regiment "Thule" had broken into the western edge of Saroshnoje, but was subsequently forced to pull back by Soviet counterattacks. Regiment commander Lammerding met with the two battalion commanders while artillery support was organized for the next attack. A battery of assault guns arrived and were moved up to support the next attack.[28]

While the two battalions regrouped, a forward observer from the artillery regiment arrived and set up an observation post and radio. He directed the fire of the howitzers of IV./SS-Artillerie-Rgt. 3 upon the concealed Soviet tanks. The guns began to find the range and fired for effect on the Soviet positions. When the high explosive shells blanketed the Russian defensive positions, Grenadiers of I./Regiment "Thule" assembled for the next assault. The battalion was supported by the battery of assault guns.

The explosions of the howitzers tore holes in the Soviet perimeter as the forward observer walked shells back and forth over the crest of the hill. At 1410 hours, two companies of the battalion attacked again while machine gun fire and mortar shells raked the Grenadiers as they advanced by leaps and bounds. Columns of mud and ice were thrown into the air by the Soviet mortar shells but the machine gun fire diminished markedly when the assault guns roared up the gentle slope of the hill and reached the crest of the hill. The Grenadiers found that most of the Russians had abandoned the hill and fled into the town.

In the meantime, II./"Thule" attacked Saroshnoje and became involved in house to house fighting. A veteran of the division called the night battle a 'cat and mouse' game. It was a game the Germans won on that day, because the SS assault troops forced the Russian infantry out of the town. Without the support of their infantry, the Russian tanks became vulnerable to attacks by German infantry. One T-34 after the other was set afire or immobilized, their crews forced to abandon their blazing vehicles. There were few survivors as most were shot down when they tried to run for cover. The award document for Häussler's German Cross in Gold states that there were eight Russian tanks knocked out in the fighting.[29]

By nightfall, Saroshnoje was in German hands, its streets cluttered with destroyed Soviet tanks, Russian dead and abandoned heavy weapons. Buildings and shattered houses in the ruined village burned while the Grenadiers loaded their wounded on assault guns for evacuation. After II./Regiment "Thule" established a defensive perimeter around Saroshnoje, I./Regiment "Thule," was

SS-Sturmbannführer Karl Ullrich (center with binoculars) took over command of Joachim Schubach's battalion of Panzergrenadiers on 17 March, 1943 after Schubach was wounded. Ullrich later commanded Regiment "Totenkopf" and was the last commander of 5. SS-Panzer-Division "Wiking." Otto Baum considered Ullrich to be the finest soldier he had come into contact with during the war. Ullrich was awarded the Knight's Cross while serving with the division in the Demyansk salient and subsequently won the Oakleaves. (The authors collection)

ordered to return to Kamennaja Jaruga for the night. The line of weary soldiers marched wearily into the darkness, passing the tanks of the "Tiger" company which arrived at Saroshnoje, accompanied by a platoon of Pioniere.

In the distance, the sounds of combat were suddenly heard coming from the direction of Kamennaja Jaruga, which was only occupied by "Totenkopf" artillery batteries. A marauding group of T-34s emerged from between two houses and passed between the positions of two batteries of howitzers, throwing the artillerymen into an uproar. Several SS cannoneers grabbed magnetic grenades or grenade bundles and attempted to attack the Russian tanks careening around the town. After killing and wounding a number of the SS guns crews, the Soviet tanks abruptly vanished back into the night. By the time that I./Regiment "Thule" arrived, the fighting was over.

Regiment "Eicke" had been in combat for the whole day, fighting in the sector north of Saroshnoje and Kamennaja Jaruga. At 0545 hours, II./Regiment "Eicke" attacked and occupied Ssorokowa, about five kilometers north of Regiment "Thule's" zone of attack. After clearing the village, the battalion moved into a wooded area to the east, while III./Regiment "Eicke" bypassed Ssorokowa and stormed into the next village. The battalion then formed up again and advanced to the southeast, arriving at a position on the northern flank of II./"Eicke," astride the road leading to Bolshaja Babka. After reaching this point, both battle groups halted for the day and established defensive positions blocking the roads leading into the area from crossings sites over the Northern Donets.[30]

[28] Vopersal, pgs. 240-241.
[29] Op cit.

[30] Vopersal, pg. 243.

The Panzer divisions of XXXXVIII. Panzerkorps remained unable to break out of the area southeast of Kharkov. With the exception of Kampfgruppe Oppeln of 6. Panzer-Division in Chugujev, most of the two divisions were still engaged in combat against encircled Russian forces in wooded areas near the towns of Lisogubowka or Besljudowka.[31] East of Chugujev 106. Infanterie-Division battle groups still fought to clear Russians from the southern bank of the Udy. A 6. Panzer-Division Kampfgruppe, consisting of Panzergrenadiers, Pioniere troops and Flak guns, cooperated with elements of 11. Panzer-Division armor to reduce three separate pockets of Russian troops entrenched in field fortifications along the Udy River. The Russians conducted a stubborn, well led defense in these battles. The 4. Panzerarmee records mention that Soviet officers were active and conspicuous in leading their troops during the fighting.[32]

The first attacks on the encircled Soviets failed to break into the main pocket of resistance and the German infantry pulled back to regroup and await the arrival of heavy weapons. After bringing up artillery, a second assault began at 1615 hours and remained in progress at nightfall. Meanwhile, the Panzer group of 11. Panzer-Division, with most of its few remaining tanks, thrust northeastward from the Besljudowka area, with the intention of replacing Kampfgruppe Harmel at the Tractor Works. It eliminated several small groups of Russian stragglers between Rogan and the huge factory complex but was not able to reach the factory complex.

"Grossdeutschland" Attacked

In the Graivoron-Borisovka area, the night of 16-17 March passed with little activity in "Grossdeutschland's" area. The Russian 69th Army continued to strengthen its defensive positions along the Udy River which ran roughly parallel to "Grossdeutschland's" advance. The Soviet 161st Rifle Division held well prepared defensive lines forming a salient around the town of Udy. Tanks of the 5th Guards Tank Corps were stationed at strong points along the perimeter. In most cases, the T-34s were dug in, serving as steel fortifications rather than as a mobile attack force. The 167. Infanterie-Division planned to attack, a task that did not promise to be easy, due to the Russian tanks in the town. At 1640 hours, 167. Infanterie-Division reported that it had taken the town of Oleiniki, which was only four kilometers west of the town of Udy. The Werfer Abteilung of the division replaced "Grossdeutschland's" Füsilier battalion in

Golowtschino, allowing these troops to be utilized in the attack upon Belgorod.

By first light, the Füsilier Regiment began its attack on Chotmyshsk, which was two kilometers north of the Graivoron-Borisovka road. The regiment's mission was to destroy Russian forces in the town and build up defensive strong points that would protect the road leading from Graivoron into Borisovka. "Grossdeutschland" had to accomplish this task, because 2. Armee's 332. Infanterie-Division was not able to secure the road. The division had replaced the 320. Infanterie-Division and allowed Armeeabteilung Kempf to move Postel's division into the area southwest of the Graivoron-Borisovka road. The Soviet 100th Rifle Division, reinforced by elements of the 206th Rifle Division, had delayed the progress of 332. Infanterie-Division, fighting from well prepared defensive positions. The result of this delay was to weaken "Grossdeutschland's" attack upon Tomarovka because it could not utilize the entire Füsilier Regiment.

At first the sector remained quiet and there were no attacks upon the division during the early morning hours. However, at 1110 hours, "Grossdeutschland" was informed by Armeeabteilung Kempf that air reconnaissance had detected a long Russian column on the move south of Tomarovka. The Soviet force included at least fifteen tanks and was only four to five kilometers from "Grossdeutschland" positions at Borisovka when the report was received.[33] Immediately Hörnlein, the division commander, requested a Stuka attack on the armored group advancing upon Borisovka, however, he was informed that the attack could not be made because the Stukas were engaged in operations supporting 320. and 167. Infanterie-Division's advance west of the Borisovka-Graivoron road. Since it could get no help from the Luftwaffe, the division decided to engage the Soviet column with long range artillery interdiction fire north of Borisovka. Reconnaissance patrols were sent out, but the reported Russian armor could not be located.[34]

The mystery of the missing tank column was answered at midmorning when fifteen T-34s raced toward Borisovka from the northeast. The surprised "Grossdeutschland" troops managed to destroy or damage five of the Soviet tanks, but the rest took up positions among houses in the northern section of the town. The Soviet infantry quickly dismounted and dug in, burrowing under houses and chopping firing holes through cellar walls. In a short time, this force established a solid defensive position inside the town. The Russians repelled the first counterattacks and refused to be dislodged. This situation resulted in the further draining of divisional strength, due to the necessity of eliminating or at least containing the Soviet

[31] The 6. Panzer-Division had 22 tanks, including 3 Flamm-Panzer (flame throwing tanks) 11 Panzer IIIs and 8 Panzer IVs. The division also had 9 Sturmgeschütze and 10 heavy anti-tank guns.
[32] NA/T-354, roll 367, Tagesmeldung XXXXVIII. Panzerkorps vom 16.31943, frame 8633389.
[33] *Befehl des Gewissens*, pg. 314.
[34] *Befehl des Gewissens*. pg 315-316.

battle group. The division could not spare any armor, as all of its tanks remained in close contact with the Soviet forces pressing in from all directions. The battalion of Füsiliers on the march from Golowtschino was ordered to reinforce the detachments encircling the Russian tanks in Borisovka.

The Attack Upon Tomarovka

"Grossdeutschland" planned to thrust north on 19 March and take Tomarovka. Elements of the Soviet 3rd and 5th Tank Corps, supported by the 305th, 309th and 340th Rifle Divisions, defended the approaches to Tomarovka and the area east of the Borisovka-Tomarovka road. The three rifle divisions were mere shells of their former strength by this time, however, and it is likely that each was approximately at regimental strength. The two tank corps had been decimated in the fighting against "Grossdeutschland" over the course of the last three days and were not at full strength either. Many of the 2nd Guards Tank Corps tanks had been knocked out in fighting against "Grossdeutschland."[35]

A successful German assault on Tomarovka, coupled with the capture of Belgorod by the SS divisions, threatened to encircle a pocket of Russian forces between the Vorskla River Valley and the Udy River. Roughly centered on the town of Udy, the western edge of the salient was created when "Grossdeutschland" thrust into the Vorskla River valley. When Wisch's regiment pushed beyond the blocking positions at Dementejewka and Mal. Prochody, the eastern border of the salient was formed.

Inside the rapidly forming Udy pocket were at least five weak rifle divisions and much of the remaining armor of the 2nd and 5th Guards Tank Corps. However, "Grossdeutschland" had not yet taken Tomarovka and fifteen kilometers still separated the SS spearheads from Belgorod. The mouth of the pocket, which lay between Tomarovka and Belgorod, was still wide open. On 18 March, the Germans attempted to close this exit route and encircle the Soviet forces in the Udy River-Vorskla River sector.

The SS-Panzerkorps advance on Belgorod

The SS-Panzerkorps resumed its attacks towards Belgorod on 18 March, led by Peiper's reinforced battalion. Kampfgruppe Harmel also thrust north from the area east of Kharkov, pushing toward Belgorod. "Totenkopf" slowly moved along western bank of the Donets, clearing the Russian forces out of the swampy, forested marshland. "Das Reich" began its attack at 0400 hours, with Regi-

Half tracks of Peiper's battalion lined up in the middle of a Russian village. Dietrich was determined that his division would be the first to reach Belgorod and he chose Peiper to make the thrust north. He could not have made a better choice because although Peiper had only a reinforced battalion he executed a text book mobile operation and seized the town on 18 March, 1943. (Credit National Archives)

ment "Der Führer" on the right and Regiment "Deutschland," still supported by Kuntsmann's tanks, on the left. Kumm's regiment had assembled during the night in the village of Nepokrytoje and began its advance before dawn, moving while the roads were still frozen. The handful of tanks remaining to Tychsen's tank battalion led the advance, with Grenadiers huddling on the tank decks, warming themselves by the heat coming up through the motor grills. Along the roads and in the small villages, large amounts of Russian vehicles, guns and other war material laid abandoned or destroyed. Burned out trucks, corpses and horse carcasses testified to the action of Stukas and Messerschmitts. By 0645 hours, Regiment "Der Führer" reached the villages of Wesseloje and Wyssokij, where the Russians put up token resistance and then disappeared to the east and north.[36] After leaving Wyssokij, the regiment swung northeast, in order to clear any remaining Russian forces from an extensive range of wooded terrain that lay along the west bank of the Donets, south of Belgorod. By the afternoon, the sun was up and the roads were in horrible condition, as melting snow had swollen the river and its tributaries. Depressions and low spots in the roads were completely flooded, with up to a meter of swift flowing water. Some of the deeper depressions had to be forded like rivers.

Regiment "Deutschland" encountered no Soviet resistance and quickly outdistanced Kumm's battle group. At 1100 hours, with II./ "Deutschland" in the lead, detachments of the battalion reached the town of Brodok which was expected to be heavily defended. The tanks of Kampfgruppe Kunstmann, loaded with "Das Reich"

---

[35] Glantz, pg. 208.

[36] NA/T-354, roll118, Tagesmeldung vom 17.3.1943 von SS-Division "Das Reich," frame 3753770 and Weidinger, pg. 128.

Panzergrenadiers and supported by several Flak guns, cautiously approached the town. The Grenadiers clutched their machine guns and grenades, while tank commanders tensely scanned the terrain, searching for concealed T-34s. After patrols entered Brodok, they found it empty of Russian troops, and shortly afterwards, Wisliceny's III./"Deutschland" joined II./Regiment "Deutschland." At that point, Kampfgruppe Harmel was less than ten kilometers south of Belgorod and it appeared that Harmel's regiment would win the race to the town.[37]

Wisliceny's battalion took over the lead and did not encounter any significant opposition until it came within five kilometers of the southern edge of Belgorod, where the forward detachments ran into a Soviet blocking position. The roadblock was manned by a small detachment of Russian infantry and ten to fifteen T-34s which were unsupported by artillery or anti-tank guns. The flanks of the Soviet battle group were open and the Germans quickly discovered this fact. SS tanks swept around the road block and attacked the position from the rear while the assault guns of the Sturmgeschütze-Bataillon, directed by its commander, Hauptsturmführer Walter Kniep attacked from the front. Stukas swooped down to bomb the Soviet position, even while the German tanks maneuvered into firing positions.

With the Flak guns firing streams of 2cm explosive shells and Stukas dropping bombs upon the Russian positions, the Grenadiers launched their assault upon the entrenchments and routed the Russian infantry. The Russian tanks were dug-in and proved easy victims for assault guns and SS tank killer teams. The T-34 crews remained in their tanks, firing their guns until the tanks were knocked out. Kampfgruppe Harmel estimated that it destroyed a total of four-

Loaded with Panzergrenadiers, "Leibstandarte" half tracks move out of a Russian village. Kampfgruppe Peiper raced through Russian lines, the lead elements leaving behind the main body, which was reinforced with tanks and Flak guns. (Credit National Archives)

teen Russian tanks during the morning. By 1525 hours, III./Regiment "Deutschland" reported that it was approaching the southern outskirts of Belgorod. Russian heavy machine guns began to fire and mortar shells impacted along the road, forcing the lead detachments of Grenadiers to dismount. Assault guns and self-propelled Flak guns moved up, found suitable firing locations and blasted Russian strong points. Under cover of this effective fire support, the Grenadiers were able to reach the southern perimeter of Belgorod by late afternoon.[38]

---

[37] NA/T-354, roll120, 1a KTB: Darstellung der Ereignisse, frame 3753770 and Weidinger, pg. 129.

[38] NA/T-354, roll 120, 1a KTB: Darstellung der Ereignisse, frame 3753774 and Weidinger, pg. 131-134.

A column of "Leibstandarte" half tracks and Sturmgeschütze III move through a village. This picture was probably taken in early March, because the deep snow covering road has obviously started to melt and become slush. (Credit National Archives)

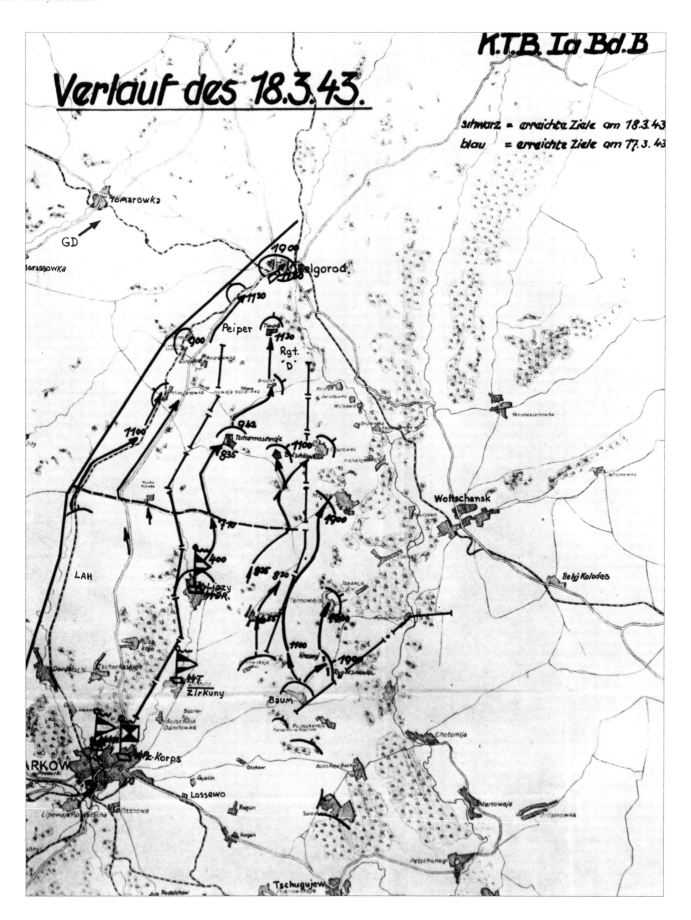

During the early morning hours of 18 March, "Totenkopf" remained tied up fighting with elements of the 1st Guards Cavalry Corps and the 113th Rifle Division in the area north of Chugujev and Kamennaja Jaruga. The division had thirty-two tanks ready for action, including twenty-two of the dependable Panzer IIIs, all of which were equipped with the long barreled 5cm gun. Of the division's "Tigers," only three were still running by that date. In a report to the SS-Panzerkorps the division reported that during the period from 8 to 17 March, it had destroyed or disabled seventy-one Russian tanks, seventy-six guns and captured fifty-one horses. It had taken a total of 337 prisoners, including five officers and had counted 878 Russian dead. Large amounts of small arms, vehicles and ammunition had been destroyed or captured, as well as hundreds of machine guns and mortars. German troops often used certain captured Russian weapons to supplement their firepower. Among the weapons they most commonly appropriated were the extremely effective 12cm mortars, 7.6cm anti-tank guns and the PPSH-41 submachine gun.[39]

By afternoon, additional elements of 6. Panzer-Division arrived at Chugujev, which allowed Kampfgruppe Baum to begin to turn over control of the town to the army division. Although the heavy fighting of the past few days seemed to be over, the situation in the town had not completely settled down. In the early morning hours just before daylight, a Soviet infantry attack broke through the defensive line manned by III./Regiment "Totenkopf." Eventually a counterattack by two flame throwing tanks of Kampfgruppe Oppeln helped throw the Russians out of the town. The change over took place without incident and Baum began to pull his regiment out of the town and assemble it northwest of Chugujev.[40]

Max Kühn's III./Regiment "Eicke" remained heavily involved with fighting at Bolshaja Babka, but the other two battalions of the regiment assembled for an attack to the northeast, parallel to the course of the river. The division's mission was to protect the eastern flank of the other two divisions of the SS-Panzerkorps. In contrast to the weakening Soviet resistance south of Belgorod, the "Totenkopf" battalions faced more determined Soviet troops, who fought hard to keep their bridgeheads on the west bank of the Donets. SS-Sturmbannführer Fritz Knochlein's I./Regiment "Eicke" became embroiled in a bitter battle for possession of the village of Peremoga.

The fierce fighting cost the battalion a company commander, SS-Untersturmführer Friedrich Erdmann and numerous other casualties. At 1700 hours, the costly fighting continued to rage and was particularly difficult in the northern section of Peremoga. The Russians fought back bitterly and resisted all attempts by the battalion to clear the village.

At 1100 hours, II./"Eicke" rolled northward from the Lipzy area. Accompanied by I./SS-Pz.-Rgt. 3, the column made very slow progress, due to the deep mud and extreme flooding. Time and again the column had to halt while a half track or truck had to be pulled out of the mud. At nightfall, the battalion arrived at the southern edge of the village of Ternovaja. Battalion commander Launer called a halt to the advance, in order for his exhausted men to rest.[41]

Meanwhile, Kampfgruppe Baum left its assembly areas at Nepokrytoje in the morning and motored north. The road conditions were extremely bad in this sector also, however by 1900 hours, the half track battalion was only five kilometers from the western edge of Voltschansk. They were fired upon by Russians from a nearby hill near the town of Murom. The rest of the column, including IV./SS-Artillerie-Rgt. 3, was strung out to the south, mired in the black sticky soup, nearly impassable for anything other than tracked vehicles. Baum could not be certain when the rest of his Kampfgruppe would arrive and decided to wait until the arrival of his artillery before trying to assault Murom.

At nightfall, the division's three Grenadier regiments were spread out along a fifteen kilometer wide front between Zirkuny and the Northern Donets River. Regiment "Thule" remained in the Saroshnoje sector and was designated as corps reserve. The progress in the division's area was limited throughout the day by extremely bad road conditions. The terrain was completely flooded in many areas and low spots in roads often were completely washed out. Ditches became streams and streams became rushing torrents of water that were difficult to bridge. The flooding made movement nearly impossible and caused severe strains on men and machines.

Kampfgruppe Peiper Captures Belgorod

"Leibstandarte" won the race to take Belgorod, after "Grossdeutschland" remained embattled in the Borisovka area and "Das Reich" was delayed south of the town. After advancing within striking distance of the southern edge of Belgorod on the previous day, Dietrich was aware that he nearly had the town in his grasp. Rudolf

OPPOSITE: After the fall of Kharkov, the SS-Panzerkorps raced toward the town of Belgorod. Mobile groups of both "Leibstandarte" and "Das Reich" led the way while "Totenkopf" moved slowly northward along the west bank of the Northern Donets River after turning over Chugujev to 6. Panzer-Division. The division experienced extremely difficult road conditions due to flooding. Peiper's III./SS-PzGren. Rgt. 2 "LAH" won the race to Belgorod, seizing the town before Rgt. "Deutschland" fought its way into the city. Harmel's column was delayed when its forward detachment was attacked by German planes, causing a number of casualties and loss of vehicles.

[39] NA/T-354, roll 118, Tagesmeldung SS-Division "Totenkopf" vom 18.31943, frame 3752451.
[40] Vopersal, pg. 244.
[41] NA/T-354, roll 118, Tagesmeldung SS-Division "Totenkopf" vom 18.31943, frame 3752451 and Vopersal, page 244.

The picture shows a typical stretch of road encountered by Kampfgruppe Peiper during its thrust toward Belgorod. Peiper defended upon speed to protect the flanks of his battalion. He encountered and avoided Russian troops several times during the attack, including a tank repair unit that his lead detachment shot up as it raced through a small Russian town. The Russian tanks regrouped and made life more difficult for the main body of Peiper's column when it arrived at the same village. (Credit National Archives)

Lehmann and Peiper conferred during the night of 17-18 March, regarding the possibility of reaching Belgorod by a daring thrust from the division's forward position. Von Ribbentrop's 7./Kompanie was ordered to reinforce Peiper's SPWs and two of the division's "Tigers" were also assigned to the battalion. At first light, Peiper gathered his company commanders and briefed them about the attack upon Belgorod. He likely stressed that the column had to keep moving, using its speed and mobility as a weapon. If the battalion allowed itself to be delayed, the Soviets could react and block their advance, which would allow Russian forces to attack their flank.

At 0645 hours, after conducting a reconnaissance along the initial route of advance, Peiper's half tracks sped northward. The battalion's advance was accompanied by flights of Stukas and Me-110 twin engine bombers. A weak road block held up the battalion's advance for a brief time until Stukas lined up overhead and dove upon the Russian position. Peiper ordered his battalion forward, taking advantage of the confusion resulting from the air attacks. The lead vehicles of the column raced past the shattered road block before the stunned Russians could react. Assault guns and tanks fired on the move, while Flak guns, mounted on half tracks, poured out a steady stream of shells at any visible target. By 0710 hours, Peiper radioed that his battalion had broken through the first Soviet position and was on its way north.

At 1000 hours, Peiper radioed that his lead units had reached the village of Krassnoje, which was only about a kilometer southwest of Belgorod. Two Soviet tanks had been knocked out during the advance, but the column had encountered very little other resistance. Retreating Russian columns could be seen to the east and west. Krassnoje was found to be abandoned by the Russians. Without pausing, the tanks and half tracks raced through the town, plowing through icy mud and slush.[42]

The speeding German vehicles reached a village where a Russian tank repair crew had set up shop. Several disabled T-34s lay about, in various stages of repair and the Russians were just stirring about, preparing to begin their morning routine. Suddenly the German column rolled through the village and the Soviet mechanics were startled when speeding German tanks raced past them, followed by a company of Grenadiers in armored half tracks. The Grenadiers cut loose with a barrage of small arms fire as they sped through the center of the village. The company's half tracks were able to pass through the village before the stunned Soviet soldiers could fire back. A number of Soviet tanks were manned by their crew or mechanics and were able to escape, fleeing into the countryside. These tanks, after noting that the lead elements of the German column had continued to advance to the north, soon returned to their shop. They opened fire on the following German units when they reached the village. Pandemonium broke out in the narrow streets of the village when the Russian tanks suddenly fired on half tracks full of SS Grenadiers. The crews threw out smoke grenades and raced down side streets to avoid the cannon shells that whistled after them.

By that time, the forward elements of Kampfgruppe Peiper had arrived at the southwestern edge of Belgorod. The Russians had

---

[42] NA/T-354, roll 120, 1a KTB: Darstellung der Ereignisse, frame 3753774 and Lehmann, pg. 178.

apparently nearly abandoned the city by that time. The lead vehicles entered a small ravine at the southern edge of the town and when they came out at the other end, rolled over a bridge. After the tanks passed across the bridge, Belgorod lay before them. At 1135 hours, Peiper radioed division HQs, stating simply that, 'Belgorod taken in surprise attack. Eight enemy tanks destroyed. Commander of the III./2.' Peiper had won the race to reach Belgorod. Almost immediately, he had to defend his newly won prize.[43]

At 1210 hours, a group of T-34s, which probably belonged to the 2nd Guards Tank Corps, counterattacked Peiper's group from the northwest. Fortunately for Peiper's small Kampfgruppe, the two "Tigers" had been able to arrive by that time. The 88s took a heavy toll on the attacking Russian tanks, firing on them at long range. Peiper's report to division headquarters stated that the two heavy tanks hit seventeen tanks, disabling or destroying all of them. While Peiper was consolidating his position, Kampfgruppe Harmel entered the town a short distance to the east. This column had entered the southern outskirts of the city just as a flight of German bombers appeared over the town. The SS spearheads had advanced so quickly that the Luftwaffe had not yet been informed of the presence of German troops in Belgorod. The German planes conducted what Weidinger described as "a text book bombing run" on the Regiment "Deutschland" Grenadiers, causing substantial casualties.

Peiper's attack was a classic example of a successful mobile thrust that depended on speed, combined arms fire power and timely air support. In such an operation, the essential weapons were speed and coordination of armor, infantry and air support. A lightning thrust through the tactical depth of a much more numerous defender depends on the ability of the attacking force to avoid delays and keep moving. Once the thrust stalls and becomes stationary, the defender is allowed time to locate the mobile group and react defensively.

One must also take into account the likely state of morale of the Soviet forces defending the sector. The first Soviet position that Peiper broke through to begin his speedy attack was little more than a weakly defended roadblock. Once past it, there was little between Peiper and Belgorod. It is to his credit that he recognized the realities of the situation as well as the opportunities presented to him and took full advantage of the capabilities of his combat group, primarily its mobility and firepower. His skillful and daring tactics paid off in reduced casualties, as his losses for the day consisted of one dead and 16 wounded. Peiper was awarded the Knight's Cross for his capture of Belgorod, in addition to previous accomplishments.

A "Leibstandarte" Panzer III on the outskirts of Belgorod after Peiper's Kampfgruppe took the town. The Russian church in the background was a well known landmark on the southern edge of Belgorod. (Credit National Archives)

After Peiper reported the capture of Belgorod, Dietrich quickly moved to shove other troops toward the town. The II./SS-PzG.-Rgt. 2 "LAH" (Sandig) followed in Peiper's wake, passing through numerous towns and villages which were unoccupied by Russian troops. At 1000 hours, while pushing along a railroad line that roughly paralleled Peiper's route of advance, Sandig's battalion ran into a number of T-34s, possibly from the tank repair detachment that had been disrupted by Peiper's attack. By 1515 hours, the Russian tanks withdrew and shortly afterward, the battalion made contact with elements of "Grossdeutschland" approximately four kilometers west of the march route taken by Peiper. The battalion established defensive positions southwest and west of Belgorod. Remaining in Dementejewka, Kraas's I./SS-PzG.-Rgt. 2 was in reserve throughout the morning. Kraas was ordered to leave Dementejewka on the next day and to secure the section of road leading to Belgorod.

The XXXXVIII. Panzerkorps took over the defense of Kharkov on 18 March, as most of the units of its three divisions remained in combat along both banks of the Udy southeast of the city. The reinforced Panzer group of 6. Panzer-Division held its positions in Chugujev and the Panzer group of 11. Panzer-Division was in action north of Rogan. The main forces of both 6. and 11. Panzer-Divisions conducted systematic artillery attacks on the remaining Soviet forces in the forests west of Lisogubowka. A second group of Russians, trapped in a wooded area west of Chugujev, was eliminated by concentric attacks on the pocket by Panzergrenadiers, assault guns and Flak units. While the two divisions mopped up in these sectors, 106. Infanterie-Division was in action along the banks of the Udy also, fighting off a desperate attack by a Russian battle

---

[43] NA/T-354, roll 120, 1a KTB: Darstellung der Ereignisse, frame 3753774 and Lehmann, pg. 178.

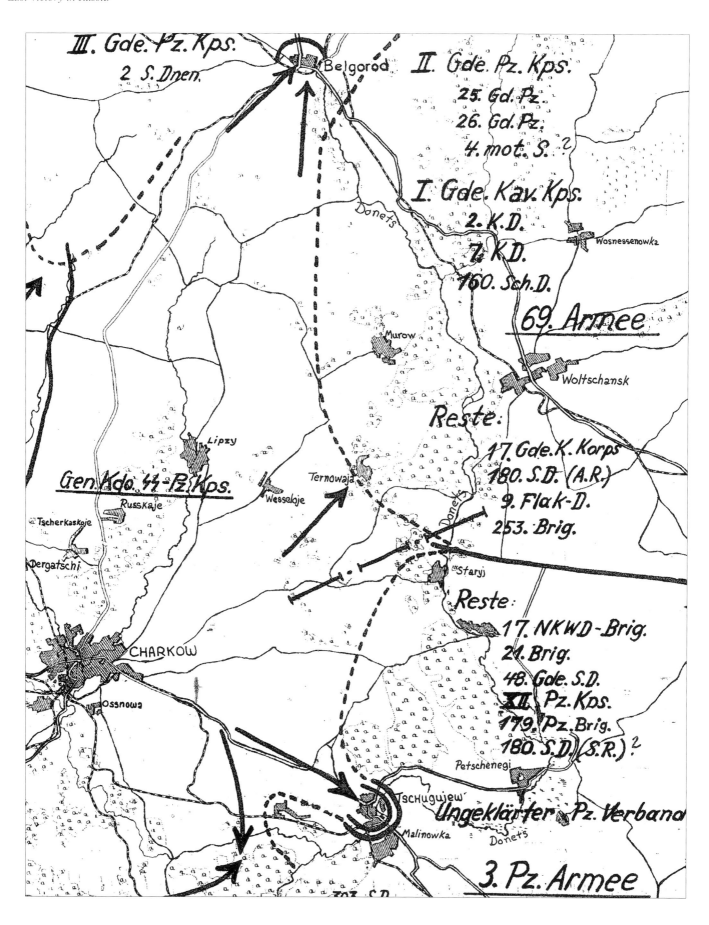

group trying to escape destruction. Near Mochnatschi Station, which lay along the rail line running from Kharkov into Chugujev, survivors of a Russian rifle division attempted to break through the lines of the division and escape to the east. The doomed Russians were counterattacked, most killed or captured, while the rest scattered into the countryside.

Kampfgruppe Oppeln remained in Chugujev and received some additional infantry reinforcements. At 0400 hours, tanks of 11. Panzer-Division departed from the Rogan area and pushed toward the western bank of the Northern Donets. By mid-morning, the Panzers approached the villages of Fedorowka and Panfilowka, which lay astride the road west of the river. At that point, the forward elements of the column were fired upon by Soviet troops holding the two villages. These Russian troops were in solidly constructed defensive field positions and strong points inside the villages. The volume of fire from Russian heavy weapons halted the advance of the weak battle group. Several batteries of the division's artillery was brought up and the guns pounded Soviet positions through out the night, softening them up for a continuation of the attack on 19 March.

"Grossdeutschland"

At Borisovka, 18 March began with a resumption of attacks by "Grossdeutschland" Grenadiers and assault guns on the encircled Russian tanks in the center of the town. The Soviets defended themselves with great tenacity and although they lost another three tanks by 0630 hours, still held their ground. However, their perimeter steadily shrunk and early in the morning, the Ia of the division informed Armeeabteilung Kempf that he expected the situation to be cleared up by the end of the day. At 0900 hours, the Ia subsequently informed Kempf that eight Russian tanks remained encircled in Borissowka, where they had taken up positions in a small depression and resisted all attempts to destroy them. The division requested a Stuka attack on the Russian tanks, hoping to knock them out from the air. In the meantime, the Panzerjäger-Abteilung "GD" arrived to reconnoiter the situation and find ways to eliminate the Soviet tanks.[44]

---

[44] Spaeter, pg. 76.

OPPOSITE: The map shows the positions of the surviving elements of the 3rd Tank Army and the NKVD units that defended Kharkov after they were pushed out of the city a month earlier. The Germans drove most of the Soviet forces back over the Northern Donets and controlled the west bank of the river from Kharkov to Belgorod by the beginning of the spring rainy season. The area north of Belgorod formed the southern flank of the Kursk bulge and was the sector from which Heeresgruppe Süd launched Operation "Citadel" in the summer of 1943.

In spite of the situation in Borisovka, the division planned to proceed with its attack on Tomarovka. The divisional Panzerjäger-Abteilung "GD" and a detachment of Pioniere were to keep the surrounded T-34s bottled up in Borisovka so that they could not harm the offensive operations by breaking out at an inopportune moment. It was not absolutely necessary to eliminate all of the Russian tanks, as long as they were contained in the town.

Gruppe Strachwitz, supported by I./Gren. Rgt. "GD," left Borisovka at 1030 hours, accompanied by Stukas and twin engine Me-110s. The "Grossdeutschland" assault gun battalion was to secure the march route of the attack group by occupying the area north of Besonovka, the first objective. About four kilometers east of Borisovka, a small force of Russian tanks attacked the column from the north, forcing it to turn and fight. After one of the Russian tanks was hit and destroyed, the rest pulled back and the column resumed its advance. The surviving Russian tanks remained in the area after they regrouped and they promptly caused trouble for the next elements of the column that passed their way. The Panzer spearhead, with Grenadiers riding on the tank decks, had traveled about three kilometers farther east when it heard tank gun fire behind it.

The Füsilier Regiment was fired on by the Russian tanks and several vehicles were disabled. The Füsiliers suffered a number of casualties but the column continued to move. Shortly afterward, approximately twenty to twenty-five Russian tanks attacked the "Grossdeutschland" tank group from the north. The two tank groups maneuvered into position and the fighting gradually became heavier after a group of T-34s made a slashing attack upon the flank of Gruppe Strachwitz. The German tanks counterattacked and the Russians pretended to withdraw. When the Germans followed the retreating Russian tanks, they were ambushed by a concealed Pakfront of anti-tank guns. Four German tanks were disabled or destroyed before the others realized that they had been drawn into a trap and made their escape. Strachwitz regrouped his tanks and launched a counterthrust which succeeded in knocking out six T-34s. "Grossdeutschland" claimed that it damaged or destroyed fifteen Russian tanks during the fighting. However, the division did not advance any further that day. After nightfall, the fighting gradually diminished and the division called a halt to offensive operations. Reconnaissance patrols pushed further east and made contact with SS security troops along the "Leibstandarte" march route, south of Belgorod.[45]

The 320. Infanterie-Division slowly moved into the Udy River Valley, which extended northward from Kharkov, nearly parallel to the advance of Kampfgruppe Peiper's attack route to Belgorod. At 0815 hours, elements of the division made contact with SS security

---

[45] *Befehl des Gewissens*, pg. 319 and Spaeter, pg. 77.

detachments guarding the march route that Peiper had taken on the previous day. Korps Raus had closed ranks with the west flank of the SS-Panzerkorps advance, protecting it from attack out of the Udy River Valley.

Meanwhile, further to the west, 167. Infanterie-Division moved up the Vorskla River Valley, taking over defense of "Grossdeutschland's" supply route. Its right or eastern flank was adjacent to 320. Infanterie-Division's left flank. Grenadiers of the division assaulted Udy and cleared the northwest section of Russian infantry by 1150 hours. The Russians abandoned the rest of the town and the Germans occupied the eastern section by late in the afternoon. The two divisions had secured "Grossdeutschland's" western flank.

The 332. Infanterie-Division of Heeresgruppe Mitte's 2. Armee was to have reached the Graivoron area and secured the eastern flank of the division. However, it made very little progress and the division claimed that it was too weak to accomplish that task. This was not a critical failure at that time, because the Russians were pulling back along the entire front north of the Vorskla River and were no longer a threat to "Grossdeutschland's" supply lines.[46]

On 19 March, Armeeabteilung Kempf received new mission orders. Over the next few days, the army was to replace the divisions of 4. Panzerarmee in the Belgorod area. Heeresgruppe Süd informed Kempf that he was to take over most of the sector in order to allow Hoth's Panzer divisions to withdraw. Kempf was notified that he was to receive the 106. and 39. Infanterie-Divisions in April. The 4. Panzerarmee divisions were to be withdrawn in order to be rebuilt for the coming summer offensive operations.[47]

"Grossdeutschland" continued its attacks upon Tomarovka on 19 March, after regrouping during the night. Gruppe Strachwitz drove north in the early morning hours of the day, advancing in two attack groups. At 0700 hours, the right Kampfgruppe, consisting of the Panzer Regiment "GD" and Grenadier Regiment "GD," reported that it was only three kilometers from Tomarovka, however, the other group was held up by an attack of Russian tanks. It appeared that an unexpectedly large tank battle was in the making at Tomarovka, because German air reconnaissance reported that another Soviet armored column was heading toward Tomarovka. This battle group consisted of ten to fifteen T-34s and sixty other vehicles.

Shortly before noon, Gruppe Strachwitz reached Tomarovka, which was declared to be solidly in the hands of the division by 1255 hours. The left Kampfgruppe, consisting of the Aufklärungs-abteilung and two batteries of assault guns, did not reach Tomarovka until 1620 hours. Reports for the day indicated that the Panzer Regiment alone destroyed thirty-one Soviet tanks, twenty-nine anti-tank guns and two artillery pieces. Another fifteen Soviet tanks were destroyed in the fighting south of Tomarovka. The Sturmgeschütze Bataillon destroyed six additional tanks and the Grenadiers knocked out another. This was a total of fifty Soviet tanks destroyed or put out of action by the division during the day. The Panzer Regiment was credited with the destruction of most of the Soviet armor.[48]

For his leadership of the Panzer Regiment in March, Oberst von Strachwitz was recommended for the Oak Leaves to his Knight's Cross. Heeresgruppe Süd agreed with the recommendation, noting that during the period from 7 to 19 March, the division was credited with the destruction of 233 Russian tanks, eight armored cars, 308 guns and anti-tank guns and assorted other heavy weapons. On 21 March, Strachwitz took over command of the division, after Generalleutnant Hörnlein fell sick and had to be evacuated.

During the next several days, the fighting gradually became less intense in the Tomarovka-Belgorod area. On the morning of 21 March, the entire front of Korps Raus remained quiet except for patrol activity and numerous Russian air attacks. The Soviet air force conducted a series of air attacks upon German troops in Tomarovka and a few T-34s raided the road between Graivoron and Tomarovka. The Russians attempted to damage or destroy rail centers through out the sector. Poltava was also attacked by groups of Soviet fighter bombers which dropped high explosive and fire bombs. The Russians made intensive efforts to disable rail bridges and a nearby Luftwaffe airfield. A number of German planes were hit and destroyed on the ground during the raids.

In the 4. Panzerarmee area, the spring weather conditions were growing worse every day, limiting the combat effectiveness of the Panzer divisions. Even the infantry and horses were having extreme difficulties slogging through the ever deepening mud. The tanks and wheeled vehicles needed maintenance and repair and the men were also worn down and in need of rest after the weeks of combat. By the third week of March, the offensive operations of the army gradually diminished due to the weather and exhaustion of the men. Armeeabteilung Kempf stabilized its front north of Belgorod and the Panzer divisions of Hoth's army and "Grossdeutschland" were withdrawn from the fighting. By the end of the month, Manstein's Kharkov counteroffensive had come to a halt.

[46] *Befehl des Gewissens*, pg. 320.
[47] NA/T-312, roll 48, 1a KTB Armeeabteilung Kempf, Tagesmeldungen an 19.3.1943, frame 7560766.

[48] Spaeter, pg. 77 and NA/T-312, roll 48, 1a KTB of Armeeabteilung Kempf on 19.3.1943, frame 7560769-0772.

CONCLUSIONS

17

The recapture of Belgorod and the clearing of much of the western bank of the Northern Donets were the final accomplishments of the Kharkov counteroffensive conducted by Heeresgruppe Süd. Although he had achieved success beyond any reasonable expectations, the counteroffensive had not accomplished as much as Manstein had hoped. In particular, he wanted to pinch off the Kursk salient, in cooperation with Heeresgruppe Mitte. This would have shortened the front considerably and freed up a significant amount of reserves. If Manstein had been able to eliminate the Kursk bulge, the events of the summer of 1943 would probably have been altered to some extent. At the least, Hitler's plans for the Kursk bulge would have been changed because the salient figured prominently in German operational preparations during the spring months.

In any event, after Heeresgruppe Mitte decided that it was not able to conduct further offensive operations, Manstein had little choice but to accept what had been accomplished. Even if Heeresgruppe Mitte had been able to support a continuation of the offensive, Manstein's own troops may not have been capable of additional sustained offensive actions, due to vehicle and tank attrition and heavy manpower losses. This was particularly true of the Army divisions, but the three SS divisions were also worn down. "Leibstandarte" reported a total of 167 officers and 4373 men killed, wounded and missing during the Kharkov fighting, while "Das Reich" lost 102 officers and 4396 men. "Totenkopf" was in slightly better condition, having been spared the bitter defensive fighting for Kharkov but it sustained losses of 94 officers and 2170 men. The total combat losses of the SS-Panzerkorps, including corps troops, were 365 officers and 11,154 men killed, wounded or missing by 20 March, 1943. Tank and vehicles losses were also heavy.

None of the SS divisions had more than thirty-five operational tanks.

During the coming months, the three SS divisions received substantial numbers of replacements, many of which were mediocre to average quality replacements. The SS could no longer replace its losses with the same quality of men that made up the divisions of January, 1943. None of the three premier SS divisions would ever again be made up entirely of the superbly conditioned, well trained men and officers that had rolled into Russia in early 1943. Luftwaffe troops were used to replace many of the three division's losses, particularly those of "Leibstandarte" These men were fine human material but had not been trained for ground combat and were not schooled in the SS traditions and command style.

For the first time, large numbers of men came to the divisions who were not volunteers. In fact, many were not even German nationals. Himmler had scoured Europe to find human material for his divisions and he first cast his eye upon Rumanian, Hungarian or even French nationals of German ancestry. These 'Volksdeutsche' were conscripted into SS service by the thousands in 1943, but they did not equal the superb quality of the SS volunteers of the first years of the war.

In "Leibstandarte's" case there were additional losses of key officers and experienced men. Soon after the Kharkov fighting was over, the division had to supply cadre and officers to staff a new SS division which was to be built from Hitler Youth boys. This division was known as 12. SS-Panzerdivision "Hitlerjugend" and was commanded by Fritz Witt. The division even lost its commander, Sepp Dietrich, who turned over command of "Leibstandarte" to Theodore Wisch. Max Wünsche, Kurt Meyer, Walter Staudinger and the Flakabteilung commander, Bernhard Krause, all left "Leibstandarte" to serve under Witt in the new division. The

Panzerjägerabteilung and I./SS-Panzerregiment 1 were also detached from the division and sent to France to become part of "Hitlerjugend."

Of course, in spite of the losses suffered by the Army and SS divisions, Manstein and his commanders could look back with justifiable satisfaction upon the events of late February and March. During the counteroffensive, 4. Panzerarmee calculated that it had destroyed a total of 567 Russian tanks, 1072 guns and over a thousand anti-tank guns. It counted 40,130 Russian dead and captured a total of 12,430 Soviet soldiers. A substantial number of partially completed T-34s were captured when the Tractor Works was seized by the SS divisions.[1]

More important than Soviet losses was the fact that the Russians had been prevented from accomplishing the objective of their 1943 winter offensives, which was to inflict a fatal defeat on the German armies in southern Russia. The series of Soviet offensives that unfolded one after the other in the weeks after the fall of Stalingrad weakened the German armies in southern Russia and brought them to the edge of a complete collapse. However, the understandable optimism of the Soviet High Command, which spread to Stalin and even Zhukov, led to decisions that overextended their armies, pushing them beyond their capabilities. The mistakes of the Soviet command, coupled with the resistance of the German 6. Armee, gave Manstein the opportunity he needed.

A great deal of the available Soviet divisions were sucked into the fight against the German 6. Armee in the Stalingrad pocket. These resources remained tied up at Stalingrad until February, when it was too late to use them in what could have been a decisive defeat to the German forces in southern Russia. As a result, the armies carrying out Operations "Gallop" and "Star" were handicapped by a lack of sufficient artillery, tank strength and supplies. The enormous amount of Soviet manpower and equipment which was consumed by the Stalingrad cauldron was not available on the Northern Donets at the critical time. The strategic importance of these reserves, if they had been used to strengthen the Voronezh and Southwest Fronts, cannot be overestimated.

In *Lost Victories*, Manstein wrote at length in regard to the disposition of Soviet forces and the failure of the Stavka to concentrate sufficient forces at the decisive point, which in his mind, was the drive to the Sea of Azov. He remarked first on the decision by the Soviet command to assemble the heavy concentration of forces arrayed against 6. Armee.

Himmler and Dietrich tour the Tractor Factory which was put back into operation by the SS divisions. The Germans completed a number of T-34s that had been left unfinished by the Russians. Some were sent back to Germany for training purposes, while others were used to supplement the division's tanks. Himmler is in the center of the picture, while Dietrich has his back to the camera. Georg Schönberger is in the black Panzer uniform to Dietrich's right. (Courtesy Mark C. Yerger)

In the first phase of the winter campaign it undoubtedly tied down unnecessarily large forces against Sixth Army in order to make doubly sure of its prize. In doing so, it let slip the chance to cut off the German southern wing's supply lines on the lower Don.[2]

Manstein clearly stated his belief that the Soviet command failed to pursue a decisive victory with enough single minded intensity of purpose. He believed that the Russians should have 'staked everything on quickly crossing the Donets and reaching Rostov,' regardless of potential operational risks, which he acknowledged.

[2] Manstein, pg. 440.

Schönberger and Himmler examining a damaged T-34 turret outside the Tractor Works. The turret was removed from a T-34 that was knocked out by the Germans. It was struck by a shell that punched through the gun's mantlet and penetrated the interior of the turret. (Courtesy Mark C. Yerger)

[1] Many of these tanks were sent back to training areas or to Germany. About thirty were put into service as part of "Das Reich's" Panzer regiment and were used in combat until the end of the summer of 1943. In fact, the first tank commanded by Emil Seibold, the leading tank ace of the division, was one of these T-34s.

But anyone who is not prepared to take such risks will never achieve decisive and – as was essential in this case – speedy results . . . Even after the successful breakthrough against the Hungarian Army, which tore open the German front from the Donets to Voronezh, the Soviet command still failed to press on with sufficient speed and strength in the decisive direction . . . Instead of putting all its eggs in one basket and simply leaving a strong, concentrated shock group to provide offensive protection to the west, it squandered its forces in a series of far-ranging, uncoordinated thrusts at Akhtyrka and Poltava by way of Kursk.[3]

Manstein described Paulus' 6. Armee as snatching 'the palm of an annihilating victory against the German southern wing from the enemy's hand.' He supported Hitler decision in early January of refusing to allow the army to surrender by pointing out that the army still had a decisive role to play. Manstein also noted that had the army given up the battle shortly after it had been surrounded, 'the Russians could have thrown in such an extra weight of forces at the crucial spots that their aim to encircle the whole southern wing of the German front would most probably been achieved.'

Colonel David Glantz, in his invaluable study of Donbas operations, *From the Don to the Dnepr*, also believed that the death struggles of the Axis troops defending Stalingrad affected the course of Operations "Gallop" and "Star," because the Soviet forces committed to the battle for Stalingrad were tied up too long to exert a possibly decisive influence upon the course of the two subsequent Soviet offensives. When the armies of the Voronezh and Southwestern Front began to run out steam in February, the Soviet armies which had been fighting at Stalingrad were just beginning to relocate toward the west. Stalin allowed too much of his military strength to remain tied up on the Don, while the tank corps of Mobile Group Popov and the 3rd Tank Army withered away at the end of overextended supply lines. Manstein correctly understood the situation and gambled that he could survive the weakening Soviet advance until it was possible to assemble his meager Panzer reserves and then turn and strike a decisive blow. The 6. Armee thus played a major role in the events of February and March of 1943. The sacrifices of the Stalingrad garrison allowed Manstein to gather his reserves for his masterful counterstroke against the Soviet armies advancing toward the Dnepr and through the area west of Kharkov.

The most important of the reserves available to 4. Panzerarmee was the SS-Panzerkorps, whose divisions returned to the Eastern Front beginning in late January. The SS Panzer divisions formed

"Das Reich" took possession of about twenty of these tanks and painted them in German colors with a large cross painted on the side of the turret. In the weeks following the capture of Kharkov, one tank battalion from each of the SS Panzer Divisions was sent back to Germany to be equipped with the new "Panther tanks." "Das Reich" had eighteen captured T-34s that were used until they broke down or were knocked out. The battalions equipped with "Panthers" did not return to the divisions until late summer of 1943, after Operation "Citadel." (Credit National Archives)

The leading tank ace of "Das Reich" was Emil Seibold, who won the Knight's Cross in the last days of the war. The first tank that Seibold commanded was one of the captured T-34s from the Tractor Factory. Shown here as an SS-Obersharführer, he became a tank platoon commander by the end of World War II. (Courtesy Mark C. Yerger)

---

[3] Op cit.

Several German soldiers sit upon the wall of a building that borders the Red Square of Kharkov. The picture shows only one small section of the huge square. This picture was apparently taken some time after the fighting because the debris has been cleaned up and the buildings repaired. (Credit National Archives)

After the fighting was over the SS divisions counted their dead and wounded and rewarded the living with decorations. Here "Das Reich" division commander Walter Krüger has just given Knight's Crosses and other awards to officers from his division. From the left are Otto Kumm, Christian Tychsen, Karl Worthmann, Silvester Stadler, Vincenz Kaiser and Hans Weiss. (Courtesy Mark C. Yerger)

the main attack group of Hoth's army, as they were the strongest Panzer divisions available to Heeresgruppe Süd. Of course, it was fortunate for the Germans that they were available at all. Decisions made by Hitler nearly resulted in the destruction of the SS-Panzerkorps in February. Only Paul Hausser's defiance of Hitler's orders and his subsequent refusal to oversee the annihilation of the SS-Panzerkorps, enabled the SS divisions to escape a Soviet noose tightening around Kharkov. This controversial decision, although militarily correct, was against his superior officers specific orders to the contrary. Had an Army general committed this act he would have undoubtedly been removed from command or worse. It is clear however, that if Hausser had not issued the withdrawal order, major portions of "Das Reich" and probably "Leibstandarte" would have been cut off and possibly destroyed. Both divisions had already sustained heavy losses in tanks and men and if they had remained in the city, could have sustained severe additional losses of men and equipment. In that event, Manstein would not have had the only divisions which were strong and fresh enough to conduct the counteroffensive.

Fortunately for Manstein and Heeresgruppe Süd, "Leibstandarte" and "Das Reich" survived relatively intact, although "Das Reich" suffered substantial tank losses during the withdrawal. As a result, both divisions were available for the counterattack launched by 4. Panzerarmee on 19 February. By that time, "Totenkopf" had arrived, with its full complement of tanks. Although it initially suffered from command and combat inexperience in the Panzer regiment, the division played a significant role in the counteroffensive. The determined and aggressive young Panzer battalion commanders of Eicke's division grew into their

command roles quickly and proved able to lead their battalions in very effective operations after the early stages of the counteroffensive. The division provided a vital infusion of mobility, armor and fresh manpower to both 4. Panzerarmee and Armeeabteilung Kempf. In fact, without "Totenkopf" and the other two SS divisions, Manstein would not have been able to launch his stunning counteroffensive at all. The Army Panzer divisions were all too weak and most were engaged in heavy fighting and could not be withdrawn from the front.

I believe that the Kharkov counteroffensive was the crowning achievement of the Waffen-SS divisions during World War II. Anyone who doubts the fighting ability of the three divisions need only study the events of February and March of 1943. It is obvious from the German records and personal accounts of the fighting, that the SS divisions had to pass through a learning period in regard to the use of its new armor. Command inexperience played a role in this period of adjustment, which was very brief, because the aggressive nature and arrogant confidence of the young SS commanders proved ideal for leading armor and mobile operations. Although the three Panzer regiments were commanded by officers of varying ability, most of the battalion and company commanders were excellent officers, well suited to the command of mobile and armored troops.

Dietrich was well served by Georg Schönberger, his Panzer regiment commander. Max Wünsche and Martin Gross were two energetic and inspiring battalion leaders. Wünsche in particular seemed to possess the gift of making quick decisions in the heat of battle. He and Kurt Meyer formed a dynamic team on many occasions during "Leibstandarte's" difficult defensive operations in February, 1943. Another member of the regiment, Michael Wittmann, became the most successful tank commander of World War II, before his death in France in the summer of 1944.

"Totenkopf's" Panzer regiment commander, Karl Leiner, did not show great aptitude for leading armored operations. He did not properly concentrate his armor and was responsible for several tactical mistakes in the commitment of his regiment. However, the battalion commanders, Erwin Meierdress and Eugen Kunstmann, were excellent officers. Waldemar Riefkogel was an outstanding example of a brave and skillful tank company commander. It must be remembered that the division did not have time to conduct adequate training with its tanks, particularly with its "Tiger's" This lack of training certainly affected the division's performance to some extent.

The first commander of "Das Reich's" Panzer regiment, Herbert Vahl, was a competent officer who transferred to the SS from the Army. He took command of the entire division on 10 February and was replaced by Hans-Albin von Reitzenstein, who was a dynamic leader. He commanded the Panzer regiment during some of its greatest triumphs. Christian Tychsen and Herbert Kuhlmann were effective tank battalion commanders. Tychsen was a bold and aggressive tank commander with an instinctive understanding of tank operations and the proper use of armor.

To a large part, it was the efforts of these divisions which enabled Manstein's brilliant counterstroke to snatch the initiative from the Russians in early 1943. The German riposte at Kharkov resulted in a stinging defeat for the Russians and prolonged the war on the Eastern Front. Using the SS Panzergrenadier divisions, Manstein stopped the westward march of the Soviet armies before they crossed the Dnepr and subsequently bloodied the Voronezh and Southwestern Fronts. By the end of March, 1943, after the completion of the counteroffensive, the Russians had lost much of the territory which they had regained during the period from November of 1942 to February of 1943. They also had suffered such heavy losses that the Soviet high command needed months to repair their shattered armies in southern Russia.

By the end of March 1943, the front stabilized into the configuration that governed the plans of both sides during the months before the fateful summer of 1943. When the rains of spring brought an end to mobile operations in the sector, Hitler attention was drawn to the large Kursk salient. His generals were already preparing for the last major German offensive of the war by mid-April. The Kursk bulge was the strategic legacy of the Kharkov counterattack.

The summer offensive was code named Operation "Citadel" and again the SS Panzer divisions played a major role. In July of 1943, the three premier divisions of the Waffen-SS fought together for the last time. Paul Hausser led "Leibstandarte," "Das Reich" and "Totenkopf" into the massive conflagration known as the battle of Kursk. Operation "Citadel" failed, in spite of enormous sacrifices made by the soldiers of the Waffen-SS and Army. After the defeat at Kursk, the tide of war on the Eastern Front, the decisive front of World War II, turned against the Germans for the last time.

However, in the spring of 1943, the SS Panzer Divisions and the German Army had swept the Russian armies back to the east in disarray. Manstein's counteroffensive of February and March of 1943 changed the strategic tide of World War II. Manstein's masterful counterattack gave the initiative back to the Germans and wrested what appeared to be a sure victory from the grasp of the Russians. The SS divisions played the decisive role in this counteroffensive, providing the major impetus to the counterattack which gave Germany its last major victory of the war, the recapture of Kharkov in March of 1943.

APPENDIX

SS Divisional Structure and Commanders

1.SS-Panzergrenadier-Division "Leibstandarte-SS-Adolf Hitler"

Division commander: SS-Obergruppenführer Josef "Sepp" Dietrich

1a- SS-Sturmbannführer Rudolf Lehmann

1.SS-Panzergrenadier-Regiment "Leibstandarte-SS-Adolf Hitler": commander – SS-Standartenführer Fritz Witt
  I./SS-Sturmbannführer Albert Frey
  II./SS-Sturmbannführer Max Hansen
  III./SS-Hauptsturmführer Hubert Meyer until February 9, 1943 then SS-Obersturmbannführer Wilhelm Weidenhaupt

2.SS-Panzergrenadier-Regiment "Leibstandarte-SS-Adolf Hitler": commander – SS-Standartenführer Theodor Wisch
  I./SS-Sturmbannführer Hugo Kraas
  II./SS-Sturmbannführer Rudolf Sandig
  III./(halftrack battalion) SS-Sturmbannführer Jochen Peiper

SS-Panzer-Regiment 1: commander – SS-Obersturmbannführer Georg Schönberger
  I./SS-Sturmbannführer Max Wünsche
  II./SS-Sturmbannführer Martin Gross

SS-Panzer-Artillerie-Regiment 1: commander – Standartenführer Walter Staudinger
  I./SS-Hauptsturmführer Franz Steineck
  II./(self-propelled) SS-Sturmbannführer Ernst Luhmann
  III./SS-Sturmbannführer Fritz Schröder
  IV./SS-Sturmbannführer Leopold Sedleczek

SS Aufklärungsabteilung 1: SS-Sturmbannführer Kurt Meyer

SS Sturmgeschütze Abteilung 1: SS-Sturmbannführer Heinz von Westernhagen

SS Panzerjäger Abteilung 1: SS-Sturmbannführer Jakob Hanreich

SS Flak Bataillon 1: SS-Sturmbannführer Bernhard Krause

SS Pioniere Abteilung 1: SS-Sturmbannführer Christian Hansen

2.SS-Panzergrenadier-Division "Das Reich"

Division commander: SS-Gruppenführer Georg Keppler until 10 February, 1943 when SS-Oberführer Herbert Vahl took command

1a- SS-Sturmbannführer Max Schültz

SS-Panzergrenadier-Regiment 3 "Deutschland" – commander SS-Standartenführer Heinz Harmel
    I./SS-Sturmbannführer Fritz Ehrath
    II./SS-Sturmbannführer Hans Bissinger
    III./SS-Sturmbannführer Günther Wisliceny

SS-Panzergrenadier-Regiment 4 "Der Führer": commander – SS-Obersturmbannführer Otto Kumm
    I./SS-Hauptsturmführer Hans Opificius (battalion detached)
    II./SS-Obersturmbannführer Sylvester Stadler
    III./(halftrack battalion) SS-Hauptsturmführer Vincenz Kaiser

SS-Panzer-Regiment 2: commander – SS-Standartenführer Herbert Vahl until 10 February, when SS-Obersturmbannführer Hans-Albin von Reitzenstein took command
    I./SS-Obersturmbannführer Hans-Albin von Reitzenstein until 10 February, then SS-Sturmbannführer Herbert Kuhlmann
    II./SS-Sturmbannführer Christian Tychsen

SS-Panzer-Artillerie-Regiment 2: commander – SS-Oberführer Kurt Brasack
    I./SS-Sturmbannführer Heinz Lorenz
    II./SS-Sturmbannführer Oskar Drexler
    III./(self-propelled) SS-Hauptsturmführer Friedrich Eichberger
    IV./SS-Hauptsturmführer Karl Kreutz

SS Aufklärungsabteilung 1: SS-Hauptsturmführer Hans Weiss

SS Sturmgeschütze Abteilung 1: SS-Hauptsturmführer Walter Kniep

SS Panzerjäger Abteilung 2: SS-Hauptsturmführer Erhard Asbahr

SS Flak Bataillon 2: SS-Hauptsturmführer Hans Blume

SS Pioniere Abteilung 1: SS-Obersturmführer Josef Kuhlmann

SS Kradschütze Bataillon: SS-Sturmbannführer Jakob Fick

3. SS-Panzergrenadier-Division "Totenkopf"

Division commander: SS-Obergruppenführer Theodor Eicke until 26 February, then SS-Brigadeführer Max Simon

1a- SS-Sturmbannführer Rudolf Schneider

SS-Panzergrenadier-Regiment 1 "Totenkopf": commander – SS- Standartenführer Max Simon until 26 February, then SS-Obersturmbannführer Otto Baum
    I./(halftrack battalion) Baum until 26 February, then SS-Hauptsturmführer Walter Reder
    II./SS-Sturmbannführer Wilhelm Schulze
    III./SS-Sturmbannführer Ernst Häussler until 22 February, then SS-Sturmbannführer Joachim Schubach until 17 March,
    when SS-Sturmbannführer Karl Ullrich took command of the battalion

SS-Panzergrenadier-Regiment 3 "Theodor Eicke": commander – SS-Standartenführer Hellmuth Becker
    I./SS-Sturmbannführer Fritz Knochlein
    II./SS-Sturmbannführer Kurt Launer
    III./SS-Sturmbannführer Max Kühn

SS-Schützen-Regiment "Thule": commander – SS-Obersturmbannführer Heinz Lammerding
    I./SS-Sturmbannführer Franz Kleffner until 22 February, then Sturmbannführer Ernst Häussler
    II./SS-Sturmbannführer Georg Bochmann until 19 February, then SS-Hauptsturmführer Werner Deege

SS-Panzer-Regiment 3: commander – SS-Sturmbannführer Karl Leiner
    I./SS-Hauptsturmführer Erwin Meierdress
    II./SS-Hauptsturmführer Eugen Kunstmann

SS-Panzer-Artillerie-Regiment 3: commander – SS-Standartenführer Hermann Priess
    I./SS-Hauptsturmführer Alfred Schützenhofer
    II./SS-Sturmbannführer Josef Swientek
    III./SS-Sturmbannführer Franz Jakob
    IV./SS-Obersturmbannführer Hans Sander

SS Aufklärungsabteilung 3: SS-Sturmbannführer Walter Bestmann

SS Sturmgeschütze Abteilung 3: SS-Hauptsturmführer Werner Korff

SS Panzerjäger Abteilung 3: SS-Hauptsturmführer Armin Grunert

SS Flak Bataillon 3: SS-Obersturmbannführer Otto Kron

SS Pioniere Abteilung 3: SS-Sturmbannführer Max Seela

SOURCES

I. Micro-filmed captured German records from the National Archives of the United States (Archives II, at College Park, Maryland) primarily 1a KTB or Kriegstagebuch of the following formations:

<u>Record Group T-312</u>, Records of German Field Commands, Armies

Armeeabteilung Lanz/Kempf as transcribed in *Befehl des Gewissens - Charkow Winter 1943*: Osnabrück: Munin Verlag, 1976.

Armeeabteilung Fretter-Pico (formerly XXX. Armeekorps) roll 1613

<u>Record Group T-313</u>, Records of German Field Commands, Panzer Armies

Panzerarmeeoberkommando 1 - roll 46

Panzerarmeeoberkommando 4 - roll 367

<u>Record Group T-314,</u> Records of German Field Commands Army Corps

Generalkommando z.b.V. Cramer, later Raus- roll 489, 490

Generalkommando XXXX. Panzerkorps - roll 967

Generalkommando XXXXVIII. Panzerkorps - roll

<u>Record Group T-315,</u> Records of German Field Commands, divisions

1a KTB Darstellung der Ereignisse 19. Panzer-Division - roll 723

1a KTB Darstellung der Ereignisse 11. Panzer-Division - roll 598

<u>Record Group T- 354,</u> Miscellaneous SS Records: Einwandererzentralstelle, Waffen-SS and SS Oberabschnitte

Generalkommando II. SS Panzerkorps - rolls 118, 120

II. Memoirs and books by former German Army, 3rd Reich or Waffen-SS veterans

Lehmann, Rudolf, 1.SS Panzer *Division - "Leibstandarte Adolf Hitler.* vol. III, Winnipeg: J.J. Fedorowicz Publishing, 1993.

The Goebbel's Diaries, edited by Lochner, Louis P. (London: 1948) pg. 265.

Manstein, Erich von, *Lost Victories*. Novato: Presidio Press, 1982.

Mellenthin, Generalmajor F.W., *The 48th Panzercorps: November 1942 to July 1944.* Germantown. Ostfront Publishing, 1994. *Panzer Battles: A Study of the Employment of Armor in the Second World War. New* York: Ballantine Books, 1960.

Steiner, Felix, *Die Freiwilligen: Idee und Opfergang.* Göttingen: Plesse Verlag, 1958.

Ullrich, Karl. *Wie ein Fels im Meer - Kriegsgeschichte der 3. SS Panzerdivision, "Totenkopf":* vol. 1 and 2, Osnabrück: Munin-Verlag. 1987.

Vopersal, Wolfgang, *Soldaten-Kämpfer-Kameraden - Marsch und Kämpfe der SS-Totenkopfdivision :* vol. III, Osnabrück: Truppenkameradschaft der 3. SS Panzer Division.

Weidinger, Otto, *Division Das Reich - Der Weg der 2. SS Panzer Division "Das Reich."* vol. 4, Osnabrück: Munin Verlag.

Kameraden bis zum Ende - Das SS Panzergrenadier Regiment 4, "Der Führer" 1938 bis 1945. vol. IV, Göttingen: Verlag K.W. Schütz. 1987.

Others

Das Regiment "Deutschland" 1934-1945. "Deutschland" Regiment kameradschaft, 1987.

Die Geheimen Tagesberichte der Deutschen Wehrmachtführung im Zweiten Weltkrieg, 1939-1945. vol. 7, 1993.

III. Books

Ambrose, Stephen, *Citizen Soldiers: The U.S. Army from the Normandy Beaches to the Bulge to the Surrender of Germany.* New York: Simon and Schuster, 1997.

Armstrong, Col. Richard N., *Red Army Tank Commanders - The Armored Guards.* Atglen: Schiffer Military History, 1994. *Red Army Legacies: Essays on Forces, Capabilities and Personalities.* Atglen: Schiffer Military History, 1995.

Bender, Roger James and Taylor, Hugh Page, *Uniforms, Organization and History of the Waffen-SS.* 5 volumes. San Jose: R. James Bender Publishing, 1986.

Carell, Paul, Scor*ched Earth: The Russian-German War, 1943-1944.* Atglen, Schiffer Military History, 1994.

Clark, Alan, *Barbarossa: The Russian-German Conflict - 1941-45,* New York: William Morrow and Company.

Corti, Eugenio, *Few Returned: Twenty-eight Days on the Russian Front Winter 1942-1943.* Columbia and London: Universtiy of Missouri Press, 1997

Erickson, John, *The Road to Berlin.* Boulder: Westview Press, 1983.

Foster, Tony, *Meeting of Generals,* Ontario: Methuen Publications, 1986.

Fussell, Paul, *Doing Battle: The Making of a Skeptic,* New York: Little, Brown and Company, 1996.

Gilbert, Felix, *Hitler Directs His War.* London: Tandem Books, 1950.

Glantz, Col. David M., *Soviet Military Deception in the Second World War.* London: Frank Cass and Co. Ltd, 1989.

From the Don to the Dnepr: Soviet Offensive Operations, December 1942 - August 1943. London: Frank Cass and Co. Ltd, 1991.

Glantz, David, Jukes Geoffrey, Erickson, John et al. *Stalin's Generals ,* New York: The Grove Press, 1993.

Hinze, Rolf., *Die 19. Infanterie und Panzer-Division,* Düsseldorf: Verlag Dr. Rolf Hinze, 1997.

Koehl, Robert L. *The Black Corps: The Structure and Power Struggles of the Nazi SS.* Madison: University of Wisconsin Press, 1983.

Krausnick, Helmut et al, *Anatomy of the SS State.* New York: Walker and Co.

Kurowski, Franz, *Panzer Aces,* Winnipeg: J.J. Fedorowicz Publishing, 1993.

Lucas, James, *"Das Reich" - The Military Role of the 2nd SS Division.* London: Arms and Armour Press, 1991.

Manteuffel, General Hasso von, *Die 7. Panzer - Division im Zweiten Weltkrieg, 1939-1945,* Freidberg: Podzun-Pallas-Verlag, 1986.

Mitcham, Samuel W., *Hitler's Legions - The German Army Order of Battle, World War II.* Briar Cliff Manor, Stein and Day, 1985.

Newton, Steven H., *German Battle Tactics on the Russian Front, 1941-1945.* Atglen: Schiffer Military Publishing, 1994.

Niehorster, Dr. Leo W.G., *German World War II Organizational Series. Vol. 3/II:* Hannover: Germany, 1992.

Paul, Wolfgang, *Brennpunkte - Die Geschichte der 6. Panzer-Division.* Osnabrück: Biblio Verlag, 1993.

Raus, Erhard, German Defense Tactics against Russian Break-throughs, *The Anvil of War: German Generalship in Defense on the Eastern Front.* edited by Peter G. Tsouras. London: Greenhill Books, 1994.

Reinhardt, Klaus, *Moscow-The Turning Point: The Failure of Hitler's Strategy in the Winter of 1941-42.* Oxford: Berg Publishers Ltd.

Reitlinger, Gerald, *The SS: Alibi of a Nation.* London: Arms and Armour Press, 1981.

Sadarananda, Dana V., *Beyond Stalingrad: Manstein and the Operations of Army Group Don.* New York: Praeger, 1990.

Schneider, Jost W., *Their Honor was Loyalty! An illustrated and documentary history of the Knight's Cross holders of the Waffen-SS and Police - 1940-1945. Sa*n Jose: R. James Bender Publishing.

Seaton, Albert, *The Russo-German War: 1941-45.* New York: Praeger Publishers, 1971.

Sharp, Charles C., *Soviet Order of Battle: "School of Battle" - Soviet Tank Corps and Tank Brigades: January 1942 to 1945,* Vol. 2: West Chester, George F. Nafziger-publisher, 1995.

Shtemenko, General of the Army S.M., *The Soviet General Staff at War 1941-1945*. Moscow, Progress Publishers. 1970.

Spaeter, Helmuth, *Die Geschichte der Panzer-Korps "Grossdeutschland."* Bielefeld: Biblio Verlag,1958.

Stein, George H., *The Waffen-SS-Hitler's Elite Guard at War - 1939-1945*. London: Cornell University Press, 1966.

Sydnor, Charles W. *Soldiers of Destruction: The SS Death's Head Division, 1933-1945*. Princeton: Princeton University Press, 1977.

Tiemann, Ralf, *Chronicle of the 7. Panzer-Kompanie - 1. SS-Panzer-Division "Leibstandarte"* Atglen: Schiffer Military History, 1998.

Tsouras, Peter G. (editor) *The Anvil of War: German Generalship in Defense on the Eastern Front*. London: Greenhill Books, 1994.

Van Creveld, Martin, *Fighting Power: German and U.S. Army Performance, 1939-1945.*

Wegner, Bernd, *The Waffen-SS - Organization, Ideology and Function*. Oxford: Basil Blackwell Inc. 1990.

Wray, Major Timothy A., *Standing Fast: German Defensive Doctrine on the Russian Front During World War II*. Combat Studies

Institute:U.S. Army Command and General Staff College, 1986.

Yerger, Mark C. *Knights of Steel: The Structure, Developement and Personalities of the 2.SS-Panzer-Division "Das Reich."* Vol. I, Hershey: Horetsky Publishing, 1989. *Knights of Steel,* Vol. II, Lancaster: Mark C. Yerger Publisher, 1994.

Waffen-SS Commanders : The Army, Corps and Divisional Leaders of a Legend. vol. I and II, Atglen: Schiffer Military History.

SS-Sturmbannführer Ernst August Krag - Träger des Ritterkreuzes mit Eichenlaub und Kommandeur SS-Sturmgeschütze-abteilung 2. Atglen: Schiffer Military History 1996.

Zhukov, Marshal Georgi K., *Marshal Zhukov's Greatest Battles*. New York and Evanston: Harper and Row, Publishers.

Ziemke, Earl F. and Bauer, Magda, *Stalingrad to Berlin: The German Defeat in the East*. Army Historical Series: Center of Military History, U.S.Army, Washington, 1968.

Interviews of German officers conducted by the United States Army after the Second World War.

C-058, Experience Gained in Combat with Russian Infantry.

D-154, Experience with Russian Methods of Warfare and Their Utilization at the Waffen-SS Panzergrenadier School.

D-253, Anti-Tank Defense in the East.

INDEX